# THIS BUSINESS OF TELEVISION™

## Revised and Updated Third Edition

HOWARD J. BLUMENTHAL AND OLIVER R. GOODENOUGH

BILLBOARD BOOKS
An imprint of Watson-Guptill Publications/New York

Executive Editor: Bob Nirkind
Project Editor: Amy Dorta
Production Manager: Hector Campbell
Interior design: Cheryl Viker
Cover design: Spencer Drate & Judith Salavetz

Copyright © 2006 Howard Blumenthal & Oliver Goodenough
First published in 2006 by Billboard Books,
An imprint of Watson-Guptill Publications,
A division of VNU Business Media, Inc.,
770 Broadway, New York, NY 10003
www.wgpub.com

ISBN-13: 978-08230-7763-2
ISBN-10: 0-8230-7763-2

Library of Congress Cataloging-in-Publication Data
The CIP data for this title is on file with the Library of Congress
Library of Congress Control Number: 2005932890

Every effort has been made to obtain permission for the material in this book.
The author, editors, and publisher sincerely apologize for any inadvertent errors
or omissions and will be happy to correct them in future editions.

Printed in the United States
First printing, 2006
1 2 3 4 5 6 7 8 9 / 14 13 12 11 10 09 08 07 06

# PREFACE TO
# THE THIRD EDITION

*This Business of Television* has two purposes.

First, the book is a desktop reference covering all facets of television and its related businesses. A marketer seeking insight into network strategy will find useful information here. A producer will find useful advice about developing, pitching, producing, and deal-making. A writer considering membership in the Writers Guild of America will find a summary of WGA activities, including areas of jurisdiction, an explanation of key agreements and their terms, and membership information. An advertising sales executive making the move from traditional broadcast to a regional sports network will learn the structure of that business. The growth of big media companies and the role of small ones; the terms of a contract for rights or with a performer; the convergence of technology, government, marketing, and global corporations; what to discuss when hiring an agent—these are among the many topics covered in this new third edition of *This Business of Television.*

The book's second purpose is to provide a legal overview of the television business. Lengthy sections on intellectual property, personal rights, financing, and regulation should function as indispensable reference material. While a book like this cannot possibly detail all the nuances of, for example, copyright law, it does discuss in plain language the legal underpinnings of television and other media businesses. Excerpts from some of the most important legal sources and an extensive collection of useful boilerplate agreements for common business deals fill the Appendices.

We sincerely hope that you find *This Business of Television* to be a useful work. If you have comments, kindly send them to: authors@thisbusinessoftelevision.com.

Howard J. Blumenthal and Oliver R. Goodenough
October 2005

# BEFORE USING THE INFORMATION IN THIS BOOK

The information and forms provided in *This Business of Television* are intended for background use only. This book should *not* serve as a substitute for the expertise that can be provided only by an experienced specialist, such as an attorney or accountant. It is not our intention to transform an untrained individual into an "instant expert." Instead, our goal is to create an informed television or video professional who will be prepared to make optimum use of an attorney, accountant, or other qualified advisor. The reader is encouraged to hire a lawyer to review final versions of forms and contracts, to secure an accountant for tax and accounting matters, and to retain the services of an expert financial advisor.

This book was originally written in 1990 and revised through 2005. We have attempted to keep our facts and figures accurate through 2004. In some cases, legal contracts and agreements may be out of synchronization with this date. We encourage readers to continue their research by consulting industry trade magazines and other professionals working in the business for updated information.

# TABLE OF CONTENTS

# ACKNOWLEDGMENTS

Before we get into the many individuals and companies who helped us put together this third edition, a most sincere thank-you to our executive editor at Billboard Books, Bob Nirkind, whose professional enthusiasm for this project will now be measured in decades. Bob, your confidence and your ongoing support are deeply appreciated. We also thank Amy Dorta, whose editing skills and perseverance have improved many a page.

The world of television has become quite diverse, and so has our thank-you list. On the government side of things, our thanks to Nai Tam at the FCC's Video Services Division for helping to explain digital television in the U.S.

In advertising, thank you to Mike Shaw, who runs ABC's sales and media operation, and to Joanne Harmelin, whose Harmelin Media sets a standard for media firms. For information about Nielsen's ratings service, Jo LaVerde could not have been more helpful.

On the convention and trade show side, thank you to Victor Harwood, whose spectacular Digital Hollywood conferences are the very best way to understand what's happening in the U.S. television industry. Thank you also to the staff of NCTA's National Show and to MIPTV, the essential international marketplace for anyone who wants to do business outside the U.S.

For television history, we rely upon David Schwartz.

When discussing production, Jonathan Meath of MeathMedia and Diane Vilagi of Scholastic Productions have been consistently helpful through more than one edition of *This Business of Television*. Carol Sato helped us to sort through the AFM material in the music section. AFTRA's Chris DeHaan, SAG's Ilyanne Kichaven, and the DGA's Allison Holmes devoted special attention to this project, and for this we are grateful.

From the stations' angle, thanks to Todd Lopes, who explained LPTV from his perspective at Cocola Broadcasting. For the chapter on satellite television, we relied upon the good advice of DIRECTV's Robert Mercer and EchoStar's Steve Caulk.

Trade publication and Web site editors were enormously helpful. Thank you to Michael Kokernak at Backchannelmedia, and to cable television expert Simon Applebaum, currently of *CableWorld* magazine, who has also been helpful in the preparation of previous editions. On the public television side, *Current* editor Steve Behrens made all the difference.

We relied upon the kindness of new friends for the international section. For this edition, we thank the CFTPA's Jane Thompson, Fremantle Media's Debra Johnson, Televisa's Manuel Gilardi, Canal+'s Laurence Gallot, the Australian Film Commission's Rosemary Curtis, RTE's Edel Edwards, Flanders 1 Image's Christian De Schutter, and a very nice fellow from China's CCTV who asked not to be identified in print. We also thank NHK's Fumina Koike and the BBC's Nigel Paine, as well as ARTE's Françoise Landesque, SVT's Susana Thunell, and independent Brazilian producer Adriano Civita. Also helpful were ARD Degeto's Erna Heinrich and Venevisión's Mario Castro.

Other executives who helped us include Norman Barnum, Charles Nordlander, Julian Dickens, Steve Goldmintz, The Outdoor Channel's Jake Hartwick, Rainbow's Ellen Kroner, FOX's Lou D'Ermilio, and Turner's Shirley Powell. A surprising number of executives asked to be left off this list so that they could provide inside stories without fear of job loss (!). To all of you, thank you.

Special personal thanks to Ariel Schwartz, Howard's partner at New Century Television, who graciously allowed time off to complete this project at times when the young company probably needed more attention.

We're certain that we've forgotten to thank a few hundred people who, over the course of a million phone calls and brief meetings at trade shows, provided small and large bits of information. To all of you, our apologies for omitting you from this list, and our thanks for your help as well.

# INTRODUCTION: DEFINING TELEVISION

Earlier editions of this book began with a lengthy history of American and global broadcasting. During the 15 years that this book has been published in its various editions, the television business has changed dramatically. While academically interesting, stories of inventor Alexander Graham Bell, media pioneer David Sarnoff, and the early years of RCA, NBC, and CBS are no longer as relevant as they were when we wrote our first edition in 1990. Readers who are interested in this extended history are encouraged to read *Watching TV: Six Decades of American Television* (Second Edition), by Harry Castleman and Walter J. Podrazik, and *Tube of Plenty: The Evolution of American Television*, by Erik Barnouw. Our book begins with a cursory overview of the first century of television and picks up in the 1970s, as the preliminary outline of television's modern shape starts to become clear.

## EARLY TECHNOLOGY AND REGULATION

The development of contemporary media is rooted in the era just after World War I, as returning soliders began to experiment with the radio technology they had seen during military service. Back at home, they purchased parts and built radio transmitters and receivers. Mostly, they spoke to one another, sometimes telling stories, sometimes playing music. The technology was rudimentary, but its popularity increased rapidly, and by the early 1920s, thousands of households owned a radio set.

At this time, AT&T believed radio to be an extension of its telephone service and looked to control broadcasting. At the same time, General Electric and Westinghouse pursued the potential of radio receivers for the home. General Electric already owned the assets of American Marconi, the result of a British Marconi divestiture orchestrated by the U.S. Navy, which then controlled all wireless communications (wireless had traditionally been associated with ship-to-shore transmissions). These assets were held in its new company called Radio Corporation of America, or RCA. By the early 1920s, the government was issuing hundreds of radio licenses to corporations like AT&T, Westinghouse, and General Electric; to newspapers like the *Chicago Tribune*; and to entrepreneurs of every sort.

Within five years, radio stations in most major cities were connected via telephone cables which enabled stations in different cities to share programs. These telephone cables were controlled by AT&T, which denied access to its competitors who could not, therefore, build or operate permanent radio networks. After the government intervened, a settlement was negotiated: AT&T would provide the connecting lines but would sell its radio stations and related technology to General Electric's RCA subsidiary. Westinghouse added its stations to RCA, and a new entity was born in 1927: the National Broadcasting Company, or NBC.

By this time, radio's business model was clear: accumulate audiences with entertainment programming and require sponsors to pay a fee to be associated with these programs. Some companies paid for exclusive sponsorship; others paid for commercial time within the program or between programs. With minor variations, this model has remained unchanged for over 75 years.

By 1927, NBC was operating the nation's two largest and most popular radio networks: NBC Red and NBC Blue. A year later, William Paley bought the fledgling United Independent Broadcasters, renamed it the Columbia Broadcasting System (CBS), and began aggressively seeking affiliates in major cities. Smaller radio networks captured some listeners, but for about 15 years, network radio was dominated by NBC. When the FCC required NBC to sell one of its radio networks in 1943, the spin-off became the American Broadcasting Company, or ABC.

The technical development of television dates back to the 1880s, but image clarity was a more daunting limitation than capturing sound for radio until 1939, when RCA engineers managed fully 441 lines of resolution. In 1941, the National Television System Committee (NTSC), representing 15 leading electronic manufacturers, approved the 525-line system still in use today (although new high-definition [HD] standards can now double the resolution). The advent of World War II delayed the development of commercial television broadcasting, but the radio networks were busily experimenting with new television program formats (often based upon popular radio programs).

## THE EVOLUTION OF NETWORK PROGRAMMING

Contemporary television began in 1948, when ABC, CBS, and NBC began broadcasting for four hours each night. Programs were modest, consisting of talk shows, sports coverage, public affairs, and the occasional variety show. There were, however, glimmers of hope for television as an entertainment medium. In 1948, Sid Caesar, Ed Sullivan, and Milton Berle hosted early versions of their popular series. By the early 1950s, situation comedies were beginning to replace the low-cost filler, and more stars hosted variety series. Costly dramatic series emerged first as live drama, then found a more viable commercial model by replacing high-quality New York theater with programs featuring cowboys, cops, and other American icons as leading characters—this format had proven very popular on radio, and it remains popular today. Inexpensive game shows were also popular prime-time entertainment.

As tastes changed, network programming executives learned to adjust the mix. In the fall of 1958, there were a dozen game shows on the prime-time schedules; in 1962, there were four; and by 1967, game shows were found only on daytime schedules. In 1999, game shows were again popular for an instant due to the success of *Who Wants to Be a Millionaire*. Similarly, variety shows featuring big stars were among the 1950s' and 1960s' most popular shows; schedules were filled with hour-long programs featuring Jackie Gleason, Perry Como, Danny Kaye, Sid Caesar, Red Skelton, and others. By the 1970s, only Carol Burnett remained, and now decades have passed since we've seen a successful weekly variety show. Some years, it's all about cop shows; others, it's about single-parent families. In the early 2000s, the trend has been reality shows, which cost less than network comedies and dramas, and tend to attract a desirable younger audience more likely to develop lifelong patterns as consumers (older consumers are less likely to switch or try new brands). Despite decades of creative development, nearly all of these formats can be traced back to similar radio programs. The same is true of daytime programs: Talk shows and soap operas have occupied homemakers since the early 1930s.

## REINVENTING THE TELEVISION INDUSTRY

From the start, network television has been dominated by a handful of companies. DuMont was a fourth network until 1956, and for several years in the 1960s and 1970s station groups shared programs in quasi networks (Metromedia, for example). A true fourth network emerged in mid-1986, when Rupert Murdoch's News Corporation purchased several major market stations and created the FOX network. In 1995, UPN was formed by Paramount and Chris-Craft Industries, and a network of stations owned by Tribune Broadcasting and other station groups became The WB Network.

From the 1950s until the 1980s, most local television stations were owned by a combination of large corporations, regional media companies, and local businesses, such as newspapers or radio stations. By the mid-1980s, investment banks and Wall Street favored the buying, selling, and consolidation of local radio and television stations into larger and more powerful corporate station groups. The Federal Communications Commission (FCC) and other government agencies have generally supported this movement toward media consolidation.

One reason for government approval of broadcast television ownership consolidation has been the widespread growth of new networks distributed via cable television and satellites. This process began in the mid-1970s when the fledgling HBO and WTCG/Atlanta (now TBS) rented satellite time to distribute their signals nationwide. By the mid-1980s, many of today's popular cable television networks were already operating, but their distribution was limited; a decade later, cable networks were seriously eroding broadcast network ratings. The widespread availability of movies on tapes, discs, and, most recently, through digital on-demand systems has further eroded viewership. The popularity of video games and the Internet has also affected television viewing.

Like local television broadcasters, local cable television systems were originally small operations, locally owned or affiliated with regional owners of multiple systems (MSOs). As MSOs have acquired cable systems—and one another—consolidation has become commonplace. In addition, many MSOs own substantial stakes in the programming networks they carry.

In some cities, educational television stations were broadcasting in the early 1950s. The present-day system of public television broadcasting did not take shape until 1967, when the Carnegie Commission on Educational Television recommended that Congress establish a corporation for public television. Later that year, Congress established the Corporation for Public Broadcasting (CPB) as both a funding source for public television stations and a buffer between Congress and the new public network. What began as a noncommercial network financed by the government and foundation grants has since become a confederation of independently owned nonprofit stations that have become indispensable to certain audience segments. Public television is especially popular with viewers who enjoy high-quality documentaries, opera, classical music, news, nature shows, drama, and British comedy, but its sometimes conflicting purpose is to serve a far broader audience.

## TELEVISION IN THE NEW MILLENNIUM

Completing the story is an increasing number of alternative uses for the television medium. Large corporations have long used video to communicate with employees, train the sales force, present and sell products and services, and more. Coursework on video has been popular since the 1970s, albeit within a relatively small market. Exercise tapes have been commonplace for 20 years; cooking shows have a longer history. Art and music instruction, preschool education, travelogues, and other specialties have proven especially well suited to the video medium and to video publishing. With the widespread acceptance of broadband Internet service, video has become a part of many Web sites. Promotional CDs and DVDs are now routinely used by colleges and universities to promote their institutions. Several companies have developed subscription and promotion businesses based upon Internet distribution of video programming. For many families, video has supplemented or even replaced family snapshots. High school students now create "films" using small, relatively inexpensive camcorders and editing their work on surprisingly sophisticated desktop computer systems. Many of these alternative forms of television are evolving rapidly, often in fits and starts.

So what, exactly, is *television*? In this book, we're careful not to define the term too narrowly. Certainly, television is NBC, CBS, ABC, and the other broadcast networks. Television is also the many program networks accessed by subscription to cable or satellite services. Television is an international business and, increasingly, a global enterprise. It is also a conglomeration of new technologies that distort and expand traditional program delivery: VHS, DVD, TiVo, portable video players, and screens that play movies in cars and on planes. Television these days includes the video files that play on your computer and the ones that play on supersized screens in Times Square. It is the video that your preteenager makes when she dreams of becoming a filmmaker, but it's also the nightly news, the Super Bowl, and the thousands of commercials we watch each month. Television is a medium in evolution, the basis of a related group of industries that have been steadily mutating for more than half a century.

If you are a part of "the industry"—or if you want to be—you must be prepared to embrace change. And you must understand that television is rarely about fine art. Television has always been a commercial endeavor. With few exceptions, television is about the money.

# PART 1

# DISTRIBUTION

Although the general public may view television as an entertainment or news medium, the *business* of television is all about the distribution of television programs, motion pictures, brand messages, and advertisements. This is, of course, an oversimplification. Each of the above disciplines is itself an industry: television program and motion picture production; brand management; and advertising. At the heart of the largest television companies, you will find a well-tuned distribution machine.

# CHAPTER 1
# BROADCAST TELEVISION

In the United States, a broadcast network is a branded collection of 100 to 200 local television (or radio) stations that promote and exhibit the same program schedule all day and much of the night. This system permits a television network to build national audiences for programs and performers. The primary revenue stream for these programs is the sale of audience access in the form of commercial time. Secondary revenue streams include DVD sales of the most popular programs, as well as ancillary distribution of these programs on cable networks, to airlines, and to broadcast and cable television networks outside the U.S. The principal operating costs associated with operating a network include personnel in a wide range of specialized departments, including program development and production. The principal capital costs include network operations and engineering, particularly the costs associated with the constant updating of studio facilities, and master control.

Los Angeles is generally the headquarters for network programming, but news, marketing, advertising sales, and executive management are all based in New York City. Senior corporate management is typically bicoastal. Notable exceptions include Telemundo, which is based in Miami, Florida, as well as UPN, WB, and FOX, all based in Los Angeles.

## NETWORK STRUCTURE AND PROGRAMMING

Acknowledging specific variations in organizational structure from one network to the next, most broadcast networks are similar in their operations. The *entertainment division* is the most powerful group, as it controls daytime and prime-time programming. A *news division* is responsible for evening newscasts, prime-time magazine shows, the occasional special, the Sunday morning schedule, and, in some cases, the weekday morning show. The *sports division* is responsible for much of the weekend daytime schedule, and for special sporting events such as the Kentucky Derby and the World Series. An *advertising sales group* is responsible for all network ad sales. *Marketing* is often a separate group, frequently allied with promotion, and sometimes tied into *research* (whose functions also serve both programming and advertising sales). In some cases, *operations* is a part of this division as well. All *technology and engineering* is part of a single division. *Services groups* such as finance, law, and human resources are either at the corporate level or are provided by the larger corporation that owns the network.

Typically, a senior network executive supervises relationships with the network's affiliated local stations; this group may be called, simply, *the network*. Often, a broadcast network has other interests (such as ownership and management of cable television networks), and these ventures may also be represented at the senior management level. Most networks also own a production company.

Each network relies mainly upon the entertainment division for its success. The division is usually organized in specialized groups. One group is responsible for the development and production of prime-time comedy series. A parallel group handles dramatic series and, often, made-for-television movies. A group devoted to alternative programs develops and supervises the production of these formats, most often reality series. Most network specials are awards shows and the occasional concert; these may be managed by one of the other groups or by a small group of executives and coordinators assigned mostly to annual productions, such as the Oscars or the Macy's Thanksgiving Day Parade. Typically, the prime-time departments are headed by an entertainment division president, with various vice presidents responsible for development and current productions, and for support in scheduling, casting, and contract negotiation. Most programs are produced by the network's own personnel (all news, sports), or by production companies in a kind of joint venture with a network division (most prime-time), or, in some cases, by production companies who operate independently of the network (some prime-time, some daytime, most or all children's). The boundaries are made more complicated by corporate ownership of multiple entities. For example, CBS fills its Saturday morning schedule with programs from Nickelodeon; both are owned by Viacom.

## COSTS, REVENUES, AND MARKETS

In the most general terms, a half-hour prime-time episode is licensed to a broadcast network for $500,000 to $1 million, while an hour costs the network between $1 million and $5 million. To pay for this programming, most network programs include about 20 commercial slots (each 30 seconds long) per hour, plus promotional spots for the network's other programming. As the fall 2004 season opened, the trade magazine *TV Week* reported sales per 30-second advertising spot in the range of $70,000 (for CBS's *JAG*) to $138,000 (for NBC's *Fear Factor*) to $315,000 (for CBS's *Everybody Loves Raymond*). The highest rate, for certain episodes of FOX's *American Idol*, topped $600,000 per 30-second spot. In general—assuming all 20 spots (or 10 minutes) of advertising time are sold at a modest average of $125,000 per 30-second spot—a network earns roughly

$5 million per hour (the figure is higher during certain types of programs, lower for others). These revenues fund not only program production, but all aspects of network operations. Networks do not, however, control the entire day's schedule. Instead, the networks typically run about half the day (two to three hours in the morning, two to three hours in daytime, a half-hour of evening news, three hours of prime, and two to three hours of late-night). The rest of the day is programmed by affiliates with local news and syndicated programming.

Since the networks do not broadcast directly to viewers, their relationship with roughly 200 local broadcast affiliates is key to their success. The most important affiliates for each network are located in the largest markets (see page 6).

## BROADCAST STATIONS

The business of local broadcasting is wholly different from the business of the networks. A local broadcaster is licensed by the FCC to transmit a television signal within a specific Dominant Market Area (DMA), a geographic region that typically includes a city, its nearby suburbs, and some outlying areas. Nearly all local television stations have exclusive relationships with television networks; for example, only WBAL/Channel 11 may broadcast NBC programs in Baltimore. When an FCC license is granted, the station promises to manage its affairs in the public interest and to serve its local community in an unbiased manner. On occasion, a station's operations may be questioned by local community groups, and from time to time, a station's practices are reviewed by the FCC. Rarely does this process result in anything more than a warning or a small fine; licenses are almost never revoked.

There are 1,243 commercial television stations in the U.S., including 585 VHF channels (2–13) and 767 UHF stations (14–59), plus over 2,100 low-power (LPTV) stations. (The spectrum allotment was 14–83 until the 1970s, reduced to 14–69 in 1999, and recently reduced to 14–59. With the introduction of digital television, it will be further reduced to 14–51.) Nearly all stations broadcast in the top 225 largest American cities or metropolitan areas. Nearly all of these "metros" are served by at least five stations, each affiliated with a major broadcast network: ABC, CBS, NBC, FOX, and PBS. According to the FCC, the average TV household in the U.S. can receive 13 over-the-air television stations.

Over the next few years, this configuration will change as the U.S. moves from an analog (NTSC) television system to a digital (DTV) system. Current VHF and UHF broadcasters, for example, will likely operate multiple television channels and offer additional data services. Many broadcasters will change their channel numbers—this is due in part to new interference patterns with digital broadcast antennas, and in part to the FCC's change in channels available for television broadcasting (channels 52–59 will no longer be used for broadcasting).

## Station Ownership

Local broadcast stations are most often owned by either a large media company or a regional station group. In Philadelphia, for example, KYW/3 is a CBS station, owned by Viacom (which owns CBS); WPVI/Channel 6 is an ABC station, owned by Disney (which owns ABC); and WCAU/Channel 10 is an NBC station, owned by NBC. The WB affiliate, WPHL/Channel 17, is owned by Tribune (which also owns about 20 percent of The WB Network); WTXF/Channel 29 is the FOX station, owned by News Corp. (which owns FOX); and the UPN affiliate is WPSG/Channel 57, also owned by Viacom. Several other UHF signals also reach the area; these are used for religious programming or home shopping. In addition, Philadelphia is served by two public television stations: WHYY is the PBS affiliate, and in a somewhat unusual situation, WYBE is one of the few public television stations that do not fill their schedules with PBS programming.

Although the names of the owners may differ, the overall situation is mirrored in both the U.S.'s large and midsized metropolitan areas. For example, in Rochester, New York, WHEC, or NBC/10, is owned by Hubbard Broadcasting; WOKR/13, the ABC station, is owned by Clear Channel; and WROC/8, the CBS station, is owned by Nexstar, and is one of that station group's 42 television stations in the U.S. While WUHF, or FOX/31, is owned by another large group, (Sinclair Broadcast Group, with 62 stations), WBGT, the UPN station, is a low-power (LPTV) broadcaster owned by a smaller operator that also owns another station in nearby Ithaca, New York. The WB station is a cable-only affiliate, part of Rochester Television Ventures, whose ownership is shared by Time Warner Cable (which serves over 70 percent of the market) and The WB. From a local viewer's or advertiser's perspective, both the UPN and WB affiliates are on par with their traditional full-power broadcast counterparts (though they may charge slightly less for commercial time because their coverage area is slightly smaller). There is one PBS member station, WXXI/Channel 21.

## Station Groups

Group ownership has become the dominant form of station ownership in the U.S.—and most stations are owned by companies with holdings in other media. The rules regarding media ownership have changed several times since the 1940s, and recent decisions, related to the 1996 Telecommunications Act, strongly favor group ownership. (This is a topic of some controversy; one side believes that larger corporations are more likely to serve the public, and the other believes that diverse media ownership is a better idea.) The current rules set no limit on the number of stations that can be owned by a single entity. However, a single company cannot own two stations within a single market (i.e., no two stations whose "grade B contours"—the outer extent of their transmission areas—overlap). The only significant limitation in the current rules is the overall reach of the station group—no more than 35 percent of the U.S. population.

There are nuances, however. A UHF station is assessed at half the value of VHF stations for the percentage limit, so a single company could theoretically own UHF stations reaching 50 percent of the U.S. and still comply with the rules. Rules are also relaxed for companies that are more than half-owned by minority groups.

The largest station groups are owned by NBC, CBS, ABC, and FOX (or by their subsidiaries). Among the station groups that do not directly own a network, Hearst-Argyle Television is one of the larger operators, with about two dozen stations covering just under 20 percent of the U.S. A half-dozen stations, including major market stations in Detroit, Houston, and Miami, are owned by Post-Newsweek. In addition to the station groups operated by large media companies (many of them detailed in Chapter 20), there are dozens of smaller operators, most often regional owners of smaller stations. The Smith Broadcasting Group, for example, operates stations in Santa Barbara, California; Utica, New York; Burlington, Vermont; and three Alaskan cities.

## Television Markets

Markets are ranked by the total number of households with television sets that can generally receive broadcasts from a particular city's principal broadcasters—a notion whose utility is fading as the majority of television households now define themselves primarily as cable households.

In today's rapidly changing media marketplace, the relative size of local markets is no longer of broad importance; most of the industry is concerned with national and global activity. Instead, this data is mainly of interest to media buyers, program syndicators, and companies that buy and sell stations. New York City remains the largest television market with over seven million television households in five boroughs and nearby counties; it represents 6.7 percent of all U.S. households. When combined with Los Angeles (5 percent), Chicago (3.2 percent), Philadelphia (2.6 percent), and Boston (2.2 percent), these top five markets represent just short of 20 percent of U.S. viewers. According to Nielsen Media (www.nielsenmedia.com), add the next five markets—San Francisco/Oakland/San Jose; Dallas/Fort Worth; Washington, DC; Atlanta; and Detroit—and the total coverage is just short of 30 percent. The top 26 markets (number 26 is San Diego, with slightly over 1 million households) represent half of U.S. television households.

Just about half of the country's television households are located in or near the top 25 markets. The relative significance of, say, the 900,000 households in Kansas City or the 500,000 in Tulsa is limited to additional revenues from a syndicated program or regional ad buys. For local news personnel, a jump from Spokane (market number 80) to Nashville (market number 30) may also be significant in terms of salary and career opportunity. As television audiences become more fragmented, however, the market sizes may prove misleading—particularly for advertisers seeking particular ethnic or demographic groups, as gross market size may be a misleading indicator of actual population composition within a specific region.

## Structure of a Local Television Station

Most television stations are organized along similar lines.

The *general manager (GM)*, frequently a vice president of the company that owns the station, oversees day-to-day operations. The most important aspect of the job is ensuring revenue growth while protecting the station's valuable FCC license (although, as stated before, this is almost never revoked). Responsibility for revenue growth is related primarily to the success of the news operation, and to the savvy scheduling of syndicated programs that fill gaps in the daytime schedule. In recent years, the choice of programs has been made at the group level, leaving the local manager with a decision only about when the programs will be scheduled. Responsibility for the license is bolstered by positive relationships with community institutions and civic groups, and by judicious supervision of the station's news and other local programming. The GM also works closely with the sales department (many GMs came up through sales) to set rates for commercials, time periods, and specific contracts.

The *sales department* manages the station's commercial inventory, sells local spots, and works with the station's rep firm (see page 79) to sell national spots. Sales is often responsible for the *traffic department*, which prepares the commercial log; the log indicates to master control which commercials and programs to play and when to play them, and tells the billing department how to invoice advertisers. *Research* (audience measurement) and *special events* are often part of the sales department as well.

The *creative services department*, often guided by the station group's agenda, shapes and promotes the station as a consumer brand. The creative services department typically handles on-air promotion, advertisements for the station's programming in other media (newspaper ads, sides of buses), public relations, and special promotional tie-ins. At some stations, these functions are segregated into on-air and off-air departments.

At most local stations, the *programming department* is no longer a powerful force. The big deals are typically negotiated at the group level; individual stations no longer buy important shows on their own. Few stations produce their own programming (outside of news and, perhaps, public affairs), so the programming department's functions are largely related to scheduling some selection of syndicated programs to fill time slots and the occasional special, such as a parade.

The *engineering* or *operations department* supervises the station's technical and maintenance staff; runs the studios, control rooms, master control, and transmission facilities; and acquires new equipment. With the transition to digital television, this group has gained importance.

The *public affairs* or *community affairs department* encourages interaction between station personnel and the community; this may take the form of locally produced talk or magazine programs and/or public appearances by the stations' on-air news personnel and certain executives.

The *production department*—sometimes part of the programming department—which may employ producers and directors, produces commercials for local advertisers, and schedules the non-news use of studio and editing facilities.

The *business* or *finance department* is responsible not only for traditional accounting functions but also for the overall financial operation of the station.

Each of these departments has its own manager, director, or vice president—titles are determined by the policies of the station group or by local tradition.

The following describes, in general terms, typical network affiliate expenditures (similar theory may be applied to other, non-network stations):

News is the biggest cost item, and also the largest revenue producer. In many of the top 50 markets, the average cost of news is approximately 20 to 25 percent of the total operating budget. In "news hungry" cities such as New York and Washington, DC, the figure approaches 30 percent; in smaller markets, about 15 percent of the budget is spent on news.

In larger markets, an equivalent amount is spent on programming. Once again, the amount will be higher (25 percent or more) in the largest markets, and lower (roughly 15 percent) in smaller ones. Stations can lower the cost of programming by bartering their airtime. Many stations also sell full half-hours or hours to religious broadcasters and infomercial promoters, thereby both reducing the need to buy programming and generating revenue for time periods with minimal viewership.

For every local station, advertising sales is the primary source of revenue. The salespeople who generate this revenue are paid a base salary, and earn a 15 to 20 percent commission on sales (a newer or more aggressive station may pay slightly more). This commission is a relatively large part of the station's operating budget.

The general and administrative (G&A) budget pays for the physical studio, office, and transmitter facilities, and for the station's general manager and business staff. This often accounts for 30 to 35 percent of the operating budget.

Capital costs run approximately 5 percent of the annual budget. These costs include technical equipment and the inevitable upgrades, plus office equipment, cars for the sales staff, etc. Conversion to digital television has increased this expenditure in recent years.

Major network affiliates in the largest markets typically achieve 30 percent profitability, year in and year out. In a rough year, the number may drop to the high 20s. The most successful affiliates approach 40 percent. Often, this is an NBC affiliate benefiting from an even-numbered year, when Olympic coverage or elections—or both—allow extraordinary revenues without commensurate expenses. A large network affiliate earns over $500 million in revenues per year. The economics are considerably different for smaller stations, where profitability in the $10 million to $20 million range is common.

## Network Affiliation

In today's marketplace, nearly every commercial television station is affiliated with a network: ABC, CBS, NBC, FOX, The WB, UPN, Telemundo, Univision, TeleFutura, or a religious network (such as Trinity Broadcasting) or a home shopping network.

The affiliate relationship between the networks and local television stations is based upon compatible needs. The networks' program schedules must reach as many households as possible, which is best accomplished through affiliated stations in every television market. The local stations need programming to fill their schedules, which the networks supply without a requirement for direct cash payment.

The *quid pro quo* between the network and its affiliate works as follows: The network provides a schedule of programs, with national or regional commercials included, as well as financial compensation for the airtime. The programs are offered to the affiliate, but if the affiliate chooses not to clear the time to run every program, then another station in the market may secure a clearance for that program (the transaction is often instigated by a competitive station; the network is obligated to do business with the station requesting the program). Affiliates may choose to schedule programs as they deem appropriate, though the network's affiliate relations department usually encourages stations to run programs in accordance with the network schedule.

The networks theoretically buy airtime from their affiliates, but the formulas used to determine the rates are arcane and sometimes blatantly unfair. In larger markets, the network provides only a fraction of an affiliate's overall revenues, while in smaller markets, network compensation contributes as much as 25 to 30 percent of revenues. In general, the smaller the market, the greater the percentage of its revenues is network compensation ("netcomp"). For ABC, CBS, and NBC, a typical netcomp formula is based upon: the number of commercial minutes in the hour, and the ratio of those sold nationally versus those sold locally; the "daypart" (programming time of day), which takes into account the size and demographic profile of the audience; the size of the market; the relative strength of the station versus that of others in the market; and the amount of time that the program occupies. In the ten largest television markets, the total annual netcomp to each affiliate is likely to be less than $2 million. In smaller markets, the figure will be several hundreds of thousands of dollars a year, or even less. NBC and CBS each pay approximately $200 million per year in netcomp; ABC pays approximately $170 million.

FOX does not compensate its affiliates. Instead, stations pay FOX when programs exceed ratings expectations. The WB uses a similar plan (it is, in fact, based on the FOX plan). UPN was designed as a program source by and for station groups, so strictly speaking, UPN is not a network.

The relationship between affiliates and the network is subject to FCC regulations (see page 45). Networks may not control the rates, nor may they represent their affiliates, for the sale of non-network time; of course, this provision excludes network O&Os (stations owned and operated by the network or its affiliated companies).

However, network affiliation dictates an overall programming strategy for local stations. News is a large part of just about every network affiliate operation. Affiliates of ABC, CBS, and NBC depend upon their networks for a national news feed, or national material used in local newscasts (see page 222). Typically, the network feed is one of several sources, such as CONUS and other news-feed services.

Besides news, most network affiliates program only a limited number of local hours per day: a few hours on weekday mornings, several more in the late afternoons. These slots are typically filled by syndicated programs. Outside of news programs, locally produced programs, once a mainstay, are now almost nonexistent on U.S. television.

ABC, CBS, and NBC maintain approximately 200 affiliated stations. FOX covers about 95 percent of the country with approximately 170 affiliates, and UPN has 180 affiliates. The WB distributes via 98 broadcast affiliates plus their 100+ Station Group, which consists of about 125 cable affiliates where the signal is available only to cable subscribers because The WB has no broadcast affiliate in that market. Univision operates in a similar manner, with 17 full-power and 7 low-power broadcast-owned stations, plus 18 full-power and 13 low-power affiliates, and nearly 1,800 cable affiliates. The same corporation owns TeleFutura, with 18 full-power and 13 low-power O&Os, plus 30 broadcast and 98 cable affiliates. Telemundo has 15 O&Os plus 36 broadcast affiliates, as well as carriage on over 650 cable and wireless systems. In all, Telemundo reaches 92 percent of Hispanics in 118 markets.

## LPTV

To date, the FCC has licensed approximately 2,000 low-power television (LPTV) stations—half of them since 1991. An LPTV station serves a very narrow geographic area—typically 20 to 40 miles—so by definition, these operations are small in scale, with start-up costs of around $250,000 and annual operating costs of $500,000 to $750,000, with a half-dozen people on staff. The smartest owners manage multiple LPTV stations, centralizing operations for maximum efficiency and profit. LPTV is nontraditional broadcasting, so the stations and station groups do not typically buy individual programs, but instead carry specific network feeds. In the most extreme cases, no staff is required—just someone to check on the transmitter from time to time. Most LPTV stations feed low-cost satellite networks to subscribers; programming consists mostly of religious shows, home shopping, MTV2, and Spanish-language services. Local programs, if offered at all, are usually on the order of cable's public-access channels. More importantly, the network feeds typically contain "local avails" (available time slots for advertising) that can be sold by the LPTV operator. Some colleges and universities operate LPTV channels, in part to serve local communities and in part to provide an educational experience for students.

Interestingly, there is no limit to the number of LPTV stations that can be operated by a single entity. Cocola Broadcasting, for example, owns two dozen stations in various western states. In the Fresno, California, area alone, the company operates KVHF/4 with Jewelry Television; KFAZ/8 with Aztec America, a Spanish-language channel; KCWB/13 with a Hispanic music video service called HTV; KJKZ/27 for Shop At Home TV; KJEO/32 with a combination of Urban America TV and America One; KSDI/33 with MTV2; KHSC/38 with HSN, the Home Shopping Network; KMCF with America's Store, another home shopping network; KGMC/43, with a variety of programming including America's Store, an HSN network; KVVG/54 with Almavision, another Hispanic network; and KMSG/55, which runs Aztec America. Fresno is arguably the most active LPTV market in the nation, and provides a good example of the varied uses of this unique form of broadcast television.

LPTV stations typically do not benefit from the "must-carry" rights associated with full-power broadcast stations, so local cable operators tend not to carry their signals. Therefore, the most effective LPTV markets are those where cable penetration is lower than the national average—where viewers benefit from additional over-the-air channels.

# CHAPTER 2
# CABLE TELEVISION

Nearly 75 million U.S. households (just under 70 percent of total U.S. television households) subscribe to cable television. The majority of cable networks also serve additional subscribers via satellite services. In total, each of the top 20 "cable" networks serves nearly 90 million U.S. households.

## CABLE NETWORKS

### Revenue Model

Cable networks improve upon the advertising-based broadcast network model by adding a subscription revenue stream. Each network's monthly service is sold to a cable system operator at a wholesale price. The operator then marks up the monthly price, but sells the channel as part of a bundle of services for a flat monthly subscription fee. (The exception is a pay television service, such as HBO, which is sold outside of the bundle as a premium service.) Some cable networks also benefit from additional revenues derived from domestic or foreign television program sales, plus merchandising and license fees, and, increasingly, from the sale of programs or series on DVD direct to consumers. Web site advertising revenues add to the top line.

For the cable operator, the good news here is the ongoing subscription revenue: Imagine 80 million households paying a monthly fee of 5¢—that's $4 million per month, or $48 million per year.

In addition, there are advertising revenues. A cable television network of moderate size would likely sell about $10 million in national advertising per month, or about $120 million per year. Given a commercial load of approximately 30 available slots per hour, and about 15 hours per day of valuable time, that's almost 500 spots to sell per day, or about 15,000 units per month. Prices on cable networks are considerably lower than prices on national broadcast networks, with an average rate per 30-second unit of less than $700—sometimes far less.

This average-sized cable network, therefore, grosses approximately $150 million per year in subscription fees and advertising revenues. Top networks take in far more, both in subscription fees (for ESPN, approximately $2.50 per month) and advertising revenues.

Rates paid by cable operators to the networks are about 3¢ to 5¢ for the smallest or newest networks (some charge nothing at all to encourage a larger base for advertising). Established but smaller or less significant networks charge up to a dollar or more. The most powerful networks charge $2 or more per subscriber. These deals are made more complicated by many other factors, including the relative power of the multiple-system operator (MSO; see page 15), the number of networks being carried, the need for the network supplier to launch a new network, and so on. This is all negotiable, but the networks try to keep their basic rates in place to secure improved negotiating positions nationwide.

## Operations

The costs associated with operating a cable network vary widely, depending upon the program content. CNN requires a worldwide news-gathering operation and constant studio activity; ESPN covers events throughout the U.S. and the world, and also produces a healthy number of studio-based and location-based programs only tangentially related to event coverage; nearly all of the programming seen on Nickelodeon is original children's product, much of it made by or for the network. Some programming can be reused in other countries or in the home video market; some cannot. Some programming has shelf life (*Sex and the City*), while much of it does not (*Baseball Tonight*).

A second variable that dramatically affects cable network cost structures is the way the corporation is set up. Corporations that operate multiple cable networks—i.e., MTV Networks, NBC, Discovery, and Turner—often combine operations of several networks in a single operations center. Cable networks with a broadcast parent, such as ABC Family (ABC), or CNBC and Bravo (NBC), may not carry certain costs in their own budgets. Advertising sales, business and legal affairs, accounting, senior corporate management, technology and engineering resources, and Web site operations are among the resources commonly shared by cable networks under common ownership. Stand-alone cable networks, such as The Weather Channel, are essentially unrelated to other entities and must pay all their own costs.

In general, a cable network is led by a *president* or *CEO*. This role typically involves interaction with corporate management and coordination of the network's varied departments. Many cable network presidents came up the ranks through the programming side of the business, a situation generally unlike the career paths for broadcast leadership (where executives' backgrounds, more often than not, are in advertising sales). Programming is the single most important aspect of a cable network's operation: the brand differentiator, the reason why advertisers choose to spend their money with one network instead of the dozens of other available choices.

Early on in a network's evolution, the *affiliate relations group* is charged with signing up cable systems to carry the network. This is usually a top priority for senior management. Once accomplished, the affiliate relations group is transformed into a *promotional marketing group*, responsible for maintaining high visibility for the network at a local level. The group also encourages cable operators to place the network in an advantageous channel location, preferably at a low number.

An *advertising sales group* sells national advertising; local advertising is left to the local cable operator, sold by an interconnect set up by operators in a given market, or handled by a third party. National Cable Communications and Comcast Spotlight are examples of nationwide companies that sell local time on cable systems, but these companies are managed on a regional basis. A marketing group is responsible also for promotion, outbound advertising, and public relations.

Some networks support substantial studio complexes (CNN in Atlanta, Georgia, and ESPN in Bristol, Connecticut, for example); others require no studios at all (except, perhaps, for "wraparounds"—short segments before and after films—as in the case of Turner Classic Movies, or video clips, as on some VH1 specials). All cable networks require a video library (both on analog tapes and in digital storage formats), a master control facility, editing rooms, and access to one or more satellite uplinks; the signal is then received by each individual cable operator's downlink. The technology involved in this operation is typically less complex and robust than one would find in a broadcast network facility.

Other cable network departments are modest in comparison with those at broadcast networks: a small law department, a finance group that typically relies upon the mother corporation, a few employees to staff IT (information technology), human resources, and other support services.

In terms of costs, annual commitment varies widely, depending mostly upon programming. It might be fair to estimate the annual programming budget for a midsized cable network to be $100 million to $125 million, which is perhaps half of the annual operating cost for the network. Economics related to start-up channels differ. A smaller start-up, with distribution primarily via satellite and digital cable, may spend $25 million (plus programming costs) to reach the end of its first year; a larger start-up, owned by a major media company, spends several times that amount, about $50 million to $100 million from launch through the end of the first year.

Looking to the future, some cable networks earn ancillary revenues through nascent "video-on-demand" (VOD) operations (see Chapter 4), through the sales of DVD versions of their popular programs, or through other merchandising or licensing opportunities. Nickelodeon has been especially successful in licensing its logo and various program assets to a wide range of licensees, as evidenced by the abundance of *SpongeBob SquarePants*, *Blue's Clues*, and *Rugrats* merchandise found in toy stores and in children's departments of soft-goods retailers. Unlike most cable networks thus far, Nickelodeon has developed a multi-billion-dollar business based upon licensing. For their part, CNN, ESPN, and The Weather Channel have been aggressive in new media, offering branded versions of their service on the Web and on handheld devices. To date, new media has been about information dissemination, but the potential for entertainment to become a stronger advertising environment has been discussed for more than a decade.

Historically, the growth of cable networks has been constrained by available channel capacity at the local level. With current technology, digital cable can support many hundreds of channels, but the road is difficult for smaller networks because of the costs of programming, technology, and operations, and because of the limited revenue streams available from advertising (smaller cable networks receive little, if any, revenue from cable systems). One solution for a smaller network is satellite distribution—the cost structure is often more favorable to the small network. Another is Internet distribution, which provides a more direct connection between network and viewer. VOD has also become a nursery for small cable networks; cable VOD does not require a 24/7 operation, so the cost and revenue structures are substantially different from typical cable network operations.

Over 300 cable networks are currently available in the U.S.

## CABLE SYSTEM OPERATORS

A cable operator is a company with a contract to provide a local municipality with cable television service. This agreement is typically exclusive, or it might as well be; building new cable television access to households via coaxial cables is rarely attempted. Most local cable operators are owned by large multiple-system operators, or MSOs. Each MSO operates in the same manner, negotiating a carriage agreement with each network and generally providing a small fee per subscriber per month in exchange for use of the channel. The MSO may sell commercial spots during or adjacent to the network's programming. The agreement may include a promise to promote the cable network locally or to participate in a number of promotions per year.

As of 2005, Comcast was by far the largest MSO in the U.S. with over 21 million subscribers—nearly one in three U.S. cable households. Time Warner Cable was second with about half as many subscribers. Cox and Charter were next on the list, each with about 6 million subscribers (the same size as Adelphia, which may be sold in the near future). Together, these companies served about 50 million households, or two in three U.S. cable households. Several other operators boasted over 1 million subscribers: Cablevision, Brighthouse, Mediacom, and Insight Communications. The remaining one-third of the country was served by small operators, often with fewer than 250,000 subscribers. With under 200,000 subscribers in Georgia and Florida, Knology (number 22 on the MSO list) reported about $200 million in 2004 revenues through a combination of cable, broadband, and related services. (This brief example suggests that each U.S. cable household is worth, on average, $1,000 per year in revenues—a fair rule of thumb.)

The activities of MSOs typically occur at the local level. The largest single expense is the maintenance and upgrading of technology: set-top boxes, master control (the "head end"), satellite downlink facilities, the rental or lease of these services. Broadband Internet access via cable modem has become a meaningful aspect of the local cable operator's business; roughly one in two cable households also becomes a cable broadband customer. Beyond infrastructure, there is ongoing customer service—not much of an issue unless weather or other events interrupt service. A finance department issues monthly bills, collects payments, and pays cable networks for the use of their services. For cable television service, sales is usually a nonissue; three in four households routinely buy cable service, and the remaining one in four does not. After trying to change their behavior for more than 25 years, the cable industry no longer markets to the non-buyers in any substantive manner. The greater potential lies in selling ancillary services, such as broadband Internet connections, to existing customers. Money is to be made as well in conversion to the digital cable platform (more channels for a higher monthly fee) and in cable VOD, which essentially competes with video rental stores and related services. Digital video recorders (DVRs) are also part of cable service, essentially offering a set-top box with a smarter version of a built-in VCR.

There are about 9,000 local cable systems in the U.S. (see Chapter 7 for a discussion on cable regulation). Approximately 95 percent of U.S. television households are "passed" by cable—that is, capable of receiving a signal because a cable passes near their homes—and about 68 percent of U.S. television households choose to subscribe. Roughly 25 million households use cable modems to access the Internet, a number likely to rise over the next few years.

## REGIONAL CABLE NETWORKS

Regional cable networks are an old idea, dating back to the Madison Square Garden Network's founding in 1969. The concept began to take shape in other cities in the 1980s, mainly as a way to distribute sports programming within limited geographic areas. Today, there are over 80 regional cable networks. The largest ones are sports networks: FOX Sports Net South, in Atlanta, has over 9 million subscribers, followed by MSG in the New York metropolitan area with 8.6 million. As a rule, news networks are far smaller: ChicagoLand Television Network, for example, has fewer than 2 million subscribers. Other local news networks in San Diego, central Florida, Long Island, Washington, DC, and elsewhere have fewer than 1 million subscribers, and often count their subscribers in the hundreds of thousands.

## PAY CABLE

According to Walter Troy Spencer, "The concept of pay TV is almost as old as the practical technology of television itself. As early as 1938, viewers in England could watch prizefights telecast in theaters." Of course, all cable and satellite television is "pay television" in that consumers pay to watch. Still, the older term for premium services—sold separately from the bundle of basic channels—remains in use. By "pay cable," old-timers are referring to HBO, Showtime, and several movie channels available to cable subscribers who pay a premium monthly fee. In today's world, the many motion pictures available via cable VOD are also a form of premium programming.

Regardless of the terms used, the model is the same: Premium services are sold separately, offered at a wholesale price to cable operators who mark up the price when they retail the service to subscribers. Similarly, a local cable operator may buy the VOD rights to a film (typically as part of a package of many films) for $2.50 per subscriber and resell it for $3.50, for a profit of $1.00 per film.

Fewer than half of cable subscribers also subscribe to a pay cable network.

## SET-TOP BOXES AND VOD

For over two decades, a cable franchise has been a license to print money: The retransmission of cable networks has proven to be one of the most profitable niches within the television industry. Many operators have enjoyed a near monopoly in providing the likes of ESPN, Nickelodeon, CNN, and MTV to tens of millions of U.S. households. For much of this period, direct-to-home satellites have offered similar services for a comparable monthly fee, but a combination of an entrenched cable industry and scattershot marketing by the satellite industry have protected the cable operators' unique position.

One of the peculiar aspects of cable television operation is the ubiquitous "cable box," now a small computer capable of doing far more than switching channels. The latest generations of cable boxes—or, in more contemporary lingo, "set-top boxes"—contain digital storage, include upgradeable chipsets (to make the old box do new tricks, such as delivering high-definition television), deliver some Internet services, and operate as a digital video recorder (DVR) for services similar to TiVo.

Cable set-top boxes will eventually compete with Internet-based delivery systems (or incorporate Internet technology) capable of delivering digital versions of cable program networks without the use of the cable system's coaxial cable infrastructure. Fiber optics, for example, will deliver images of superior quality on more channels, on the same line as household Internet service. Microsoft's IPTV is one such platform likely to be marketed by telephone companies (for decades, cable operators have wanted a piece of the telephone market, and telephone companies have wanted a piece of the cable market).

At the same time, convergence devices continue to emerge. For several years, consumer electronics manufacturers have promised various forms of wireless television. With wireless home networks now commonplace, television is unlikely to remain an experience fixed in any one place. Instead, truly portable television screens are likely to be viewed anywhere in or near the house. The screens are likely to offer computing and Internet services as well.

# CHAPTER 3
# SATELLITE TELEVISION

The history of the consumer satellite business dates back to 1976, not long after the first cable networks were distributed via satellite. By 1979, some 5,000 home satellite systems were in use, each costing an average of $10,000. By 1985, the price was $5,000, and more than a half-million dishes were shipped. By 1990, dishes cost about $2,000, and about three million were in use in the U.S. Still, satellite reception required a somewhat specialized customer. With the introduction of new, smaller satellite dishes (made possible through the use of a different frequency spectrum; see page 38), along with consumer-friendly tuning equipment, 1994 and 1995 saw the national launch of Primestar, DIRECTV, and USSB; 1996 brought EchoStar's DISH Network.

A decade later, the marketplace has sorted itself out with two remaining competitors: DIRECTV, with about 14 million subscribers, and DISH Network, with more than 11 million (see page 61). Both are owned by public companies. Both offer hundreds of channels, including many special-interest networks not typically found on most cable systems. In recent years, both organizations have negotiated carriage agreements with nearly all of the major cable networks. In theory, the networks compete with one another and against cable television on the basis of technical innovation, and for some consumers this is an appealing differentiator. Most consumers, however, make their choices on the basis of available programming and price.

## TECHNOLOGY AND OPERATIONS

Operationally, satellite distribution is less complicated than cable distribution. The technology is newer, so there is no physical infrastructure to manage (other than monitoring the satellites and operating the uplink centers). A series of frequencies known as "Ku" is allotted by the FCC for direct broadcast satellite (DBS) transmission. EchoStar currently utilizes and operates nine Ku-band satellites, which generally reach the 48 contiguous states, plus Alaska, Hawaii, and Puerto Rico. The newest of these satellites operates on the "Ka" band, allowing for future growth in broadband services. DIRECTV operates seven Ku-band satellites and is planning to launch four Ka-band satellites in the next three years to expand its capacity. Programming is uplinked (sent via large satellite dish to each individual satellite) from various terrestrial locations, then retransmitted digitally via direct broadcast satellite platforms to 20-inch satellite dishes pointed at a specific angle to receive the signals.

Unlike cable television, each of the satellite companies operates nationally, offering program packages to television households via the Internet or a toll-free telephone number. In addition, DISH Network is sold through about 10,000 retailers. The physical devices are available via the Internet or directly from the companies, but are more often purchased and installed by a dealer network composed of consumer electronics stores and local shops. A marketing department works on dealer promotions and direct-to-consumer promotions, while a program department makes carriage deals with cable networks. Both DIRECTV and DISH Network offer a similar assortment of general interest, sports, and movie channels seen on cable television, but both companies add international channels and interactive channels generally unavailable on cable. The U.S. satellite business employs no affiliates, so there is no affiliate relations function.

## BUSINESS MODEL

The launch of a satellite distribution business requires multiple satellites and the control of a large number of *transponders* (the part of the satellite that receives and subsequently retransmits the signals), along with associated terrestrial uplink facilities. In addition, each consumer must either buy or rent the satellite equivalent of a television tuner (usually called a "receiver" or a "set-top box") to select channels, as well as a 20-inch dish, which must be positioned carefully in order to receive signals. As with cable television, the tuner and dish are provided to consumers at no charge (typically with free installation) because the monthly fees cover these costs. (Initially, these services attempted to recoup investment by charging consumers for this special equipment; this approach appealed to early adopters, but it rarely succeeds as the company encounters a mass market.) Consumers do, however, pay a premium or fee for the inclusion of a DVR and for high-definition service. Consumers are allowed to select from several tiers of programming service (each tier offering more channels for a higher monthly fee) and are encouraged to buy into an up-sell for movies, sports, and/ or adult programming.

As with any media subscription business, multiple years are required in order to recoup the initial investment in technology, marketing, and setup, but over time, customer loyalty provides a reliable ongoing revenue stream. The principal costs connected with the satellite business, apart from the ongoing costs of technology, are the wholesale costs associated with the carriage of specific program networks. When signing a channel for carriage, the satellite companies often seek a combination of exclusivity—largely to keep the new channels away from one another and from the cable distributors—plus several minutes of commercial slots per hour and guaranteed monthly fees to cover costs. In return, the new channel receives a percentage of subscription revenues and, of course, national distribution. In addition, the satellite companies typically try to negotiate for some sort of marketing commitment specific to their distribution.

The model is similar in the U.K. and in other countries. Programming rules vary (there is no adult programming on the U.K.'s Sky TV, for example), and the specific program services are intended for local audiences (as with cricket and British football [soccer], plus NFL football from the U.S., on the U.K.'s Sky sports service). In many countries, a higher percentage of television viewers subscribe to satellite than cable television—the reverse of the situation in the U.S. In some cases, cable television's infrastructure was not built in a meaningful way nationwide; in others, satellite operators offered an appealing combination of technology, programming, and pricing, so consumers signed up for satellite service before cable was able to gain a foothold.

# CHAPTER 4
# HOME VIDEO AND NEW FORMS OF DISTRIBUTION

Although television was first envisioned in the late 1800s, a combination of world wars and the Depression delayed its national debut until the late 1940s. The initial decade of television was monochromatic, but by 1954, RCA was already selling its first color television set. The next 20 years were relatively stable, with progressive improvements in image quality and general adoption of color television. By the mid-1970s, cable television offered improved picture quality, particularly for viewers who lived far from the stations' transmitters or behind a mountain. Arcade video games were adapted for use on home screens, and the video game industry was born. Five years later, everyone was talking about the new VHS and Betamax home video recorders, while simultaneously wondering whether it was time to start a cable subscription in order to watch CNN, MTV, and other new cable networks. Then, in the 1980s, came another period of relative stability: a decade of promise, with little substantial change in cable or home video. By the time the long-promised home satellite dishes arrived in the 1990s, most households were already cable subscribers and unwilling to change. By the mid-1990s, everything started changing again with the DVD, new generations of computers with the power to edit video, and, of course, the Internet.

## DVD

Videodiscs were first attempted seriously as commercial products in the opening half of the 1980s, and for the next 20 years, LaserVision satisfied a relatively small number of videophiles with high-quality audio and video presentations. Since the 1997 launch of the digital videodisc (DVD) format, over 80 million DVD players have been sold in the U.S. It would be fair to say that well over half of U.S. television households currently own at least one DVD player.

The DVD industry has invigorated the home video rental and direct-sale business ("sell-through"). For its first two decades, video software was often priced beyond the reach of consumers, whose behavior primarily involved rental from video stores. Motion picture studios were still somewhat insecure about consumers owning their products, so many home videos were made available with retail prices well above $50. With the arrival of DVDs, motion pictures have become popular consumer products, typically priced below $30, and often below $20. The result has been an extremely robust sell-through marketplace in which DVD revenues often exceed box office revenues for individual pictures. What's more, the consumer marketplace has created a second chance for many pictures and an alternative releasing system for others. Certainly, the growth of the DVD business has been encouraged by the popularity of home theaters, as high-quality sound and images now provide consumers with an additional reason to purchase and own specific motion pictures. Special features, such as interviews with the director, further encourage the sale.

As with any consumer product, the difference between *gross revenue* (the price paid by the consumer) and *net revenue* (the amount received by the content rights holder) is substantial. Given a $30 retail product, for example, roughly half is retail markup (which covers store operations and profit), leaving roughly $15. Mastering and authoring costs deduct about $2, leaving $13. The DVD and its packaging cost about $2, leaving $11. The costs associated with warehousing, inventory, and shipping deduct another $1, leaving $10. Finally, few DVDs succeed without a marketing budget, and although this budget varies depending upon the title, it would be fair to deduct an additional $2 for marketing costs, leaving $8 in net revenue. These calculations vary widely depending upon the way the product reaches the consumer—if it's sold directly by the producer via a Web site, then there is no deduction for retail markup—and so on. Still, as a rule, it's fair to assume that a DVD sold at retail will eventually return approximately 10 to 25 percent of its retail price to the rights holder.

The selection of programs and marketing strategies for DVDs has become quite sophisticated. Often, DVDs are sold in boxed sets, assuring a higher unit price. Many popular and vintage television series are now marketed as DVDs, often as boxed sets, providing new direct-to-consumer revenue for distributors who previously collected all of their revenues from sales to television networks or stations.

## VIDEO-ON-DEMAND (VOD)

With digital cable comes video-on-demand, a system that allows individual viewers to directly access video files for playback through their enhanced set-top cable boxes. For the most part, VOD's success is related to available movie and sports programming, although some television shows more recently have also proven successful as VOD entries. Comcast's VOD service provides over 100 million movies per month, usually for about $3 per unit. Mag Rack, owned by Cablevision, presents an interesting variation on the cable VOD theme. Launched before most people had heard the term "VOD," Mag Rack provides small special-interest channels to niche audiences. Each of these channels is called a "video magazine," hence the name Mag Rack. In 2004, Mag Rack offered 30 such channels.

Each cable operator allots 40 hours of server space for Mag Rack programming, so about 25 percent of Mag Rack's programs are refreshed monthly. The question, of course, is whether anybody is watching. Current television technology does not provide answers. Still, the concept of video files played from servers is catching on. The average cable operator runs about 1,000 hours of server space (circa 2004), but this number will increase as the cost of these digital storage devices continues to drop, and as cable operators more completely understand the requirements of a successful VOD business.

The number of VOD movies on cable television systems is likely to increase for several years. Rights are inexpensive, movie packages are widely available to cable operators, and consumers are beginning to appreciate the convenience of accessing movies from an on-screen menu. The question here concerns the future role of cable television as the supplier. As Internet capabilities increase with additional bandwidth, it seems likely that consumers will bypass their cable operators for VOD movies, instead accessing a somewhat larger video and movie library from VOD Internet services that specialize in this form of distribution. Most likely, these services will be owned by the motion picture studios which, by eliminating the cable system as middleman, will develop a direct relationship with consumers and retain a greater percentage of revenues.

## DIGITAL VIDEO RECORDING, EDITING, AND PLAYBACK

By the early 2000s, computer processing power and storage had reached a point at which video files could be successfully stored and retrieved at the consumer level. This technological milestone made TiVo possible—the first significant broad-based play in the field of computerized recording and playback in the home. TiVo is now categorized as a digital video recorder (DVR): a service that typically allows consumers to select specific programs from an on-screen menu, and record them for later viewing. While this capability has been available—without the on-screen menu—for 25 years via the VHS recorder now found in just about every U.S. household, TiVo was a breakthrough because its system is smarter, easier to use, and more versatile. Consumers customarily purchase a box (a combination tuner and hard disc) from TiVo, and then pay a monthly fee for use of the TiVo service.

Cable and satellite providers are now offering a similar service, with one critical difference: they are adding the hard disc to their existing consumer boxes. In addition, they are bundling the DVR service fees with their regular monthly subscription charges. In time, DVRs are likely to become as commonplace as VCRs, and easy-to-use on-screen schedule interfaces are likely to become common as well. In other words, this service is likely to become commoditized—not an up-sell or a stand-alone service, but a standard aspect of cable and satellite service.

Digital video recordings have applications beyond DVRs; video-on-demand services are also enabled by digital video. In this distribution scheme, a consumer with an enhanced ("digital") cable box or satellite box can select a digital recording of a television program or motion picture. The system is smart enough to match the account of the viewer with the specific program being viewed—and to charge the viewer's account accordingly. Programs and movies are typically purchased in various-sized lots by the VOD provider, then offered at a retail markup to individual consumers. VOD providers and rights owners are paid on the basis of performance: If the program is purchased by a large number of viewers, then a larger amount of royalties will be collected. If the program is not widely viewed, then the payments will be smaller.

Digital video is also the basis for the latest generations of video camcorders, currently in the MiniDV format. This digital format allows consumers as well as professionals to record at or near broadcast quality using camcorders costing $1,000 to $5,000 (although certainly, superior lenses, proper lighting, special audio equipment, and other professional characteristics are required for truly professional-level work). Digital video, also available in the DVCAM format (similar to MiniDV but more robust), is well suited to desktop editing systems. For more professional work, Avid systems are often used, but many producers have become adept in the use of Apple's Final Cut Pro and similar products retailing for $1,000 or less. A competent recording and editing setup can be assembled for under $10,000. This allows many producers to work at home or in small offices, shunning the older-style post-production facilities in favor of controlling the end product more completely and at a considerably lower cost. Of course, one person is now doing the work of many; this eliminates jobs and job opportunities, and also increases (rather dramatically) the number of hours required of the producer on any given project.

Another unique aspect of digital video is its range of playback options. Much of the television programming seen today on cable and broadcast networks is the result of a digital production process: After shooting and editing digitally, the resulting digital master is still good old-fashioned videotape. In time, however, these digital tape formats are likely to be replaced by digital discs, and then disappear altogether as finished program masters become master digital files, not master tapes.

Analog television signals tend to travel in one of three ways: broadcast (through the air), cablecast (through coaxial cables), or distributed on videotape. Digital signals can be transmitted and distributed in a similar manner, but one additional possibility is also available: the broadband Internet. Video playback is now a standard feature on many Web sites. In addition, new businesses have been developed with an eye toward the special features available when television programming is distributed via the Internet. For one, this approach makes good use of existing Internet features, including buttons, links to Web sites, simultaneous chat, and, perhaps most important, data collection and analysis. When a video file is viewed by an Internet consumer, viewing behavior can be recorded, analyzed, and used as market intelligence. One such system, New Century Television (developed by one of this book's authors), operates video-on-demand channels on a variety of special-interest topics. Some such channels are available for viewing at no charge because they are funded for marketing purposes by one of the company's clients. Other channels are available only via subscription. This approach provides content suppliers with a royalty based not upon ratings, but upon actual minute-by-minute viewership. Internet distribution provides yet another benefit: a system that operates on a global basis. New Century Television's channels are viewed in over 50 countries, typically apart from the watchful eye of each country's television regulatory agencies. Several similar systems are in use for the distribution of motion pictures via the Internet.

## DIGITAL BROADCASTING (DTV)

When this book is revised for its fourth edition, probably around the year 2010, our current system of analog television will be but a memory. The FCC and Congress have provided a second channel to every station, and they have mandated that every station vacate one of its two current frequencies to make VHF and UHF available for advanced wireless and public safety uses. The new DTV channels will offer either high-definition programming (which requires more bandwidth than the current allotments allow) or multiple channels with programming in standard resolution. The new frequency allotment for television will be channels 2–51.

One possible impediment to this futuristic mandate is the consumer's willingness to change. In order to receive DTV signals, a consumer must purchase (or otherwise acquire) a new DTV-equipped television set or a converter box that will permit DTV programming to be seen on an existing television set. It is possible, and quite likely, that these converter boxes will be integrated into a version of our current cable and satellite boxes. Congress has optimistically set December 31, 2006, as the date when the transition to DTV must be complete. Most likely, this date will be extended due to a second provision in the mandate: at least 85 percent of homes within an area must be able to watch DTV programming. It is unclear whether this 85 percent figure refers to the transmission or the reception of the DTV signals—the FCC is currently reviewing this question—but the existing deadline may come too soon to enforce this provision.

# PART 2

# REGULATION OF DISTRIBUTION

# CHAPTER 5

# FCC BASICS

The Federal Communications Commission (FCC) is the principal government agency regulating the television business. Its jurisdiction covers the means of mass television distribution: traditional broadcast, cable, and satellite, as well as most emerging television technologies at the intersection of telephone, Internet, computing, and digital signals. Only home and business videos that do not use radio, wire, fiber, or other means of instantaneous mass distribution currently escape FCC control. The FCC also regulates interstate telephone and related communication services.

## ORIGINS OF THE FCC

Television broadcasting involves sending signals on specific frequencies of radio waves. Radio waves are like light: There is a continuous spectrum of different waves, like the colors of the rainbow in the visible spectrum. Each small "color" gradation of the radio waves provides a different frequency, or *broadcast channel.* The spectrum of useful radio waves is broad, but not limitless. Some portions of the spectrum, like the FM band, travel limited distances, and can be reused in other parts of the country. Other frequencies, like the AM and shortwave bands, can travel great distances—particularly at night, when the reflective effect of the ionosphere is greater. If there are two stations broadcasting on the same frequency within range of each other, the signals will cross and interfere with each other, resulting in poor reception.

The first attempt at broadcast regulation in the U.S. was the Radio Act of 1912, which provided for the licensing of radio broadcasters by the Secretary of Commerce. Basically, this law allowed anyone who applied to get a license. Transmission was largely in Morse code; as long as the airwaves were plentiful and the broadcasters few, there was no need to police who used what band. With the widespread introduction in the 1920s of sound reproduction via radio, however, the commercial potential of radio became clear, and the number of stations skyrocketed.

Faced with the need to bring some order to the use of a now-crowded spectrum, Congress passed the 1927 Radio Act, which set up the Federal Radio

Commission. The Commission was empowered to pick and choose among potential broadcasters, assigning specific frequencies to particular licensees. The 1927 Act mandated that the standard for deciding who would qualify for a license was to be one of "public interest, convenience, and necessity." This phrase, the basis for regulating monopolies, had come into use in connection with the licensing of "natural monopolies": public utilities (such as water, gas, phone, and electric companies) and common carriers (such as railroads). When the 1927 Radio Act was drawn up, Congress thought that a "public interest, convenience, and necessity" approach should be used in dividing up the radio spectrum—even though the radio spectrum at that time provided enough diversity to prevent a true monopoly in most locations.

The 1927 Act was in effect until Congress adopted the Communications Act of 1934, which has remained the basis of communications law ever since. Although closely modeled on its 1927 predecessor, the 1934 Act created a new agency, the FCC, which took over the functions of the Radio Commission. The FCC also assumed, from the Interstate Commerce Commission, jurisdiction over interstate telephone and telegraph communications.

The FCC is a quasi-autonomous commission that has elements of each of the legislative, judicial, and executive branches of government. It is one of a group of independent regulatory agencies that provide expert oversight in various areas of commercial activity. Others include the Federal Aviation Agency (FAA), the Federal Trade Commission (FTC), and the Securities and Exchange Commission (SEC). Each agency was established by an act of Congress, which set an overall framework of law and delegate the elaboration and implementation of that law to the agency.

## ORGANIZATION OF THE FCC

The FCC consists of five commissioners, one of whom serves as chairman. These commissioners are nominated by the president for staggered five-year terms; the president cannot appoint more than three of the five from one political party, and all appointments are subject to Senate approval. The commissioners oversee a staff of about 2,000, and the chairman serves as the executive officer, whose actions are subject to the approval of the majority of the commission. Notwithstanding the president's role in naming the commissioners, Congress has traditionally held great power to influence the FCC. The proposed 2006 budget for the FCC topped $304 million, of which a target of $280 million was set for the FCC to raise through fees and other generated income.

As of 2005, the FCC included the Commission itself and 16 major staff units, six of which are the major operational bureaus: Wireline Competition, Enforcement and International. The other principal units are the Office of Engineering and Technology, the Office of General Counsel, the Office of Managing Director, the Office of Media Relations, the Office of Administrative Law Judges, the Office of Plans and Policy, the Office of Communications Business Opportunities, the Office of Workplace Diversity, and the Office of Legislative Affairs. Many of these branches report to the managing director; the more independent Office of Inspector General reports directly to the Commission. The Media Bureau oversees many aspects of broadcast and cable television, as well as radio stations and new mass-media video technologies. The International Bureau handles some satellite issues. These organizational lines are periodically reviewed and adjusted.

The Commissioners set overall approaches; policy specifics are generally articulated at the staff level, then reviewed by the Commission before being adopted as official actions. The staff handles applications for licensing and renewal, again with the Commission approving significant actions before they become official.

## FUNCTIONING OF THE FCC

In its control of television, the FCC performs several distinct functions: rulemaking, licensing and registration, adjudication, enforcement, and informal influence. Contacts with industry and public representatives during some activities must be "on the record," i.e., documented to provide a public record and a fair opportunity for all sides to be heard. Other types of contacts, such as informal lobbying, go undocumented.

*Rulemaking* is just what it sounds like: the process of issuing new rules and regulations, and amending or deleting existing ones. Rulemaking is governed by both internal FCC procedures and federal laws, including the Administrative Procedure Act and related regulations. Proposals for change may come from the public or regulated industries, or they may percolate within the FCC itself, often in response to less formal pressures from public and industry representatives, members of Congress, or the administration. The formal procedure can begin with a notice of inquiry, which designates general interest in making a change. Once discussion has moved to the point where a specific change is contemplated, the FCC announces a notice of proposed rulemaking and invites comments. If the proposed change is of sufficient importance or controversy, an oral hearing in front of the Commission may be scheduled, though this is unusual. Once all the comments have been considered, the staff prepares—and the Commission reviews and issues—a report and order. This document sets out the final rule or regulation, describing the rationale behind it. As with most FCC actions, the final report and order can be appealed to the U.S. Court of Appeals for the District of Columbia for judicial review.

*Licensing* is the method by which the broadcast spectrum allocations controlled by the FCC are made and reviewed; it is described in detail starting on page 34. Cable systems go through the simpler process of *registration* (see page 49).

*Adjudication* refers to the process by which the FCC settles disputes, either between private parties (as in a license challenge or the awarding of a new channel) or between the FCC and a private party (as in a disputed disciplinary action). In a formal adjudication, there will be a hearing, conducted in accordance with the Administrative Procedure Act and the general requirements of due process. The first hearing is usually before an administrative law judge—a specially designated staff attorney. These hearings are modeled on traditional trials, with sworn testimony, opposing lawyers, and the like. The decisions of the administrative law judges are subject to appeal within the FCC, first to the Review Board, then to the full Commission. As usual with such administrative determinations, further appeals—to the Court of Appeals, and thereafter the Supreme Court—are possible. If all appeals are pursued, adjudication can be time-consuming and expensive.

*Enforcement* involves action by the FCC to correct what it sees as lapses or wrongdoing by entities subject to its jurisdiction. Most commonly, this involves a broadcast licensee violating required practices. The worst penalty that can be imposed is the loss of a license, either through a failure to renew (which is rare) or an outright revocation (rarer still). This extreme penalty is usually imposed only if the licensee has a history of flagrant mismanagement, deception bordering on fraud, or gross negligence. For less serious transgressions, short-term or conditional renewals may be given, or fines assessed. The announced cause is seldom related to program content, since both the First Amendment and Section 326 of the 1934 Act prohibit censorship. As notorious cases like the 2004 Janet Jackson Super Bowl halftime incident sometimes demonstrate, however, programming considered indecent or obscene is an exception to this principle, and is treated differently under both the Constitution and the 1934 Act (see page 350). License renewal protests are even less likely to be brought since changes were made under the 1996 Telecommunications Act preventing competitive challenge.

*Informal influence* describes the FCC's ability—and willingness—to affect the television world without going through formal action. A concerned telephone call or letter from the FCC, for example, will certainly get the attention of a station manager. Public statements, articles, and congressional testimony by Commission members and senior staff are also followed closely by the industry.

## FCC PHILOSOPHY

Since its birth in 1934, the FCC has undergone an unusual number of changes in both its underlying philosophy and its rules and administrative actions. Some of this is inevitable in industries that have evolved over the years as much as television and other communications businesses have. Historically speaking, when faced with a change in the television business, the FCC has reacted in a predictable fashion. First, the agency ignores the change; then, it tries to protect the status quo; and finally, with a certain degree of public and congressional prodding, it incorporates the changes into a new status quo.

There is some justification, under the 1934 Act, for the FCC's protective tendency. The 1934 Act called on the FCC to regulate in the public interest, and from the beginning, the FCC has viewed this to mean strong, free broadcast service at the local level. This interpretation has made the health of the local broadcast station of particular concern to the FCC. Much of its conservatism has been motivated by this principle, rather than simply by knee-jerk protection of the establishment.

The FCC gave recognition to the new medium of television in 1941, approving the first attempts at commercial broadcasting. From 1948 to 1952, the licensing of television stations was suspended in order to allow the FCC to study potential interference problems and develop an orderly system of assigning portions of the broadcast spectrum to particular stations. In 1952, when licensing recommenced, the UHF channels were allocated as well. With the promulgation of color standards in 1953, a basic framework for broadcast television appeared complete.

The history of cable regulation, discussed more fully in Chapter 7, was marked by the FCC (in typical form) first ignoring the phenomenon of cable television, then trying to suppress it, and finally encouraging it within the FCC's sphere of control. The resulting Cable Communications Policy Act of 1984 clearly put cable operations under FCC authority—and clearly limited that authority in several respects.

The 1980s saw a sizable deregulation of the communications industry, sparked by the deregulatory spirit which climaxed during the Reagan presidency. But deregulation also gained impetus from a weakening in the argument that had led to the creation of the FCC in the first place. With cable, low-power broadcasting, and home video, many new programming sources became available to most Americans; expanding satellite, digital, and Internet television continue this trend. The rationale behind the FCC's regulation of broadcasting, in contrast, was that since there were only so many channels in the broadcast spectrum, television had to be treated as a natural monopoly. Since viewers now have a wider range of options, the FCC has returned on many issues to the accepted verities of a free-market, *laissez-faire* approach.

With a few notable exceptions, such as cable rate regulation, this trend toward lessening control continued through the 1990s and into the new millennium. Congressional action in both the 1992 Cable Act and the 1996 Telecommunications Act has spurred some of these changes, as has the march of technological innovation. The FCC itself has become more and more comfortable with competition as a defining ethos, a trend that further accelerated under the chairmanship of Michael Powell, which ended in 2005. Nonetheless, the government remains a player. The biggest current challenge to the traditional structure is driven by a technological change—digital television—and the congressional mandate it entails. The reordering of the radio spectrum involved in making a transition from analog to digital broadcasting is shaking up the old order, as discussed more fully starting on page 39.

The patchwork of FCC control and permissiveness is described in the chapters that follow: Chapter 6 deals with the regulation of broadcast television; Chapter 7, with the regulation of cable; and Chapter 8, with satellite delivery and other new technologies.

# CHAPTER 6
# THE FCC AND BROADCAST REGULATION

The FCC regulates broadcast television at both the local and network levels. The local control is the most pervasive—the very existence of local broadcast stations depends upon obtaining and renewing an FCC license. In the past, the FCC's intervention at the network level had a considerable effect on shaping the structure of the television industry, but these restrictions have been significantly loosened over the past decade.

## LOCAL REGULATION: TRADITIONAL LICENSING

The FCC decides who can use the broadcast airwaves, and exercises this authority by granting broadcast licenses to individuals and companies. Such a license is required for any significant broadcast activity, including all broadcast television. FCC licenses are quite specific as to the type of service permitted, the assigned frequency, the location of the transmitter, the applicable technical standards, and the signal strength. In television, the licensing process begins with the potential station identifying an available frequency and location. Ever since the early 1950s, the FCC has maintained a list of predetermined allocations for television channels, and few standard VHF and UHF frequencies are unassigned. (There are some "low-power" allocations still available; see page 40.) This process, while still applicable for traditional applications, is now taking a back seat to the spectrum upheaval accompanying the changeover to digital television (see page 38).

Sometimes, new allocations are approved or are open for assignment; on rare occasions, an existing license may be revoked or abandoned, creating a new opening. The 1996 Telecommunications Act removed the possibility of a competitive challenge at renewal times. Now, a "disinterested" challenge must be made, and only after the license is revoked will new applications be entertained.

Presuming that a frequency is available, the first step in seeking a license is filing an application for a construction permit. When issued, this permit allows a period of time to build the specified broadcasting facilities and to get them running properly. For television stations, this interval has typically been 18 to 24 months, although the changeover to digital has been disrupting normal operations. Once the facilities are built, the FCC will review the technical and other pertinent performance data and, if satisfied, will issue the actual broadcast license to the station. Television licenses run for eight years, a reflection of the changes made by the 1996 Telecommunications Act,.

In order to obtain a license or, for that matter, a construction permit, the licensee must meet a series of statutory requirements. First, the licensee must be a U.S. citizen or a company owned principally by U.S. citizens. With corporate licenses, direct foreign ownership of more than 20 percent is prohibited; indirect ownership can't exceed 25 percent. For example, when Rupert Murdoch and his News Corporation acquired the stations that would constitute the FOX network, Murdoch changed his citizenship from Australian to American. Second, the applicant must qualify as to character. Stations are supposed to be assigned to promote the public interest, so an owner with a serious criminal record or other major character defects would be undesirable. The third requirement is one of financial resources. This means not only the ability to build the facility, but also the ability to operate without revenues for some months when starting up broadcasting. The fourth requirement is to meet technical standards, such as protecting other stations from interference.

In granting a license, the FCC can consider other qualifications, such as minority involvement or local control. Additional criteria used to be considered if there were competing applications for the same openings, as is often the case with new applications. Since 1999, however, competing requests have been decided by a bidding process, with the resulting money going to the U.S. Treasury. Until then, the significant value granted by a television broadcast license to its holder was strictly a private benefit.

Once a license is granted, the licensee must comply with a wide range of technical and operating requirements, described starting at page 43.

## RESTRICTIONS ON LICENSE-HOLDING

Restrictions on excessive concentration of media ownership, both within particular markets and across the United States, have long been part of communications law. With the increasing reliance on market forces as opposed to regulation, and in light of the perception that cable, satellite, and the Internet are providing new competitive forces, these rules have been under attack in Congress, in the courts, and at the FCC itself. The 1996 Telecommunications Act mandated a reexamination of most traditional approaches to regulation. Following this directive, the FCC has proposed changes, but free market–oriented federal courts have overturned many of the proposals, and the process has been slow to resolve. Indeed, given the degree of flux, the clearest rule at any given moment is that the current rules are likely to change. We suggest that those needing to follow the latest developments consult the FCC Web page (www.fcc.gov), which regularly posts updates on these matters.

## LOCAL OWNERSHIP

The history, at least, is clear. In order to promote diversity of media ownership on the local level, the FCC adopted rules in 1975 that prohibited ownership of both broadcasting properties and newspapers in the same market. For instance, when a subsidiary of Murdoch's News Corporation acquired Channel 5 in New York City, the parent company had to sell the *New York Post*. Most newspaper/television ownership combinations that existed before the rule went into effect, however, did not require divestiture. Furthermore, under this "duopoly" rule, no entity was permitted to hold more than one license for television service in a given market, absent a highly unusual waiver. There were also limitations on combining ownership of radio service with television service in a given market, although some pre-1970 combinations including AM, FM, and television were "grandfathered," or permitted because they existed before the rule took effect.

The 1996 Telecommunications Act specifically directed the FCC to examine loosening these ownership restrictions. Since then, the FCC has tried to promulgate revised rules, and various parties have successfully challenged many of the revisions in court. On the whole, the results have required even greater market freedom, and not a return to stricter control. The 2003 version of the FCC rules (still on the table but subject to court-mandated revision when this book was written) would allow multiple-station ownership in a single market under the following circumstances:

- In markets with five or more stations, single ownership of two stations would be permitted, provided that only one of these stations is in the top four in ratings.

- In markets with 18 or more stations, single ownership of 3 stations, but only one in the top four in ratings.

- Both commercial and noncommercial stations would be counted in determining the number of stations in a market.

- Case-by-case waivers would be possible for further concentration.

Cross-media limits have also been modified in these pending rules. In smaller markets of three or fewer full-power stations, newspaper/broadcast or radio/ television cross-ownership would now be allowed. In markets with four to eight stations, a daily newspaper could be owned in combination with either (i) one television station and up to 50 percent of the normal radio limit or (ii) the full radio limit without any television station. In markets with more than eight stations, the limits would be abolished completely.

## NATIONAL OWNERSHIP

To ensure diversity at the national level, the FCC for a long time maintained rules limiting the total number of broadcast stations that could be subject to common ownership. The 1996 Telecommunications Act significantly reduced this restriction. It did away with many of the limits applicable to commercial radio—a step that has led to a tremendous increase in concentration and a decrease in format diversity in that media segment. A vibrant market in stations does not necessarily equate to a vibrant market in formats and points of view.

With respect to television, the current proposed rules would drop all numerical limits on station ownership, but would retain limits on unified control of stations to a maximum share of 45 percent of the aggregate national audience. (UHF stations only count half of their market households in determining the controlled percentage.) In 2004, Congress stepped in and legislated a cap of 39 percent. Given the uncertainty and change that have characterized this question, this is unlikely to be the last word on the subject.

## EQUAL EMPLOYMENT OPPORTUNITY

For many years, the FCC required any licensee with five or more employees to establish and maintain an equal employment opportunity (EEO) program, which contained targets for actual percentages of minority and women employees. The goal was to increase the employment of women and minorities in the broadcast industry. These rules were not significantly modified in the 1996 Telecommunications Act, but in 1998 they were thrown out as unconstitutional violations of the Fifth Amendment's Equal Protection Clause. The case involved a Lutheran-owned station specializing in classical music, which argued that its format and denominational affiliation raised particular problems for minority recruitment.

In response to this court action, the FCC revised its rules. The new approach retains the goal of establishing equal opportunity, the affirmative prohibition against discrimination, and the requirement for maintaining an active equal-opportunity program. While a number of steps are mandated—including consciousness-raising and -monitoring within the company, outreach into minority communities, and the posting of reports in the station's public file and their filing with the FCC—no longer is there any specific goal for a result of these efforts. The FCC will consider a licensee's EEO compliance at license renewal time, at midterm review for larger broadcasters, and through random audits.

Cable operators are also required to maintain an EEO plan. Unlike broadcasters, however, cable operators do not have to file the EEO plan with the FCC as part of a certification request. Instead, they must file annual reports on their actual employment personnel practices; these reports, as well as the EEO plan, are reviewed both at the time of filing and during the recertification process. Cable companies have been fined for noncompliance—and in some cases, they have lost their certification to operate (see page 51).

## REGULATION OF HIGH-DEFINITION TELEVISION (HDTV) AND DIGITAL TELEVISION (DTV)

Conversion to digital is the challenge for U.S. broadcast television in the first decade of the twenty-first century, and the FCC is right in the thick of the process, adopting a standard for digital broadcasting, creating a DTV Table of Allotments, awarding DTV licenses, establishing operating rules for the new service, and overseeing the physical build-out of digital broadcast stations. As the FCC itself puts it, "The transition to digital television is a massive and complex undertaking, affecting virtually every segment of the television industry and every American who watches television."

The U.S. was a historical leader in the introduction of television service. There have been drawbacks to this leadership: For many years, the U.S. was stuck using a relatively primitive technical standard—the National Television System Committee, or NTSC—developed in the 1940s. The limited number of "lines" and the restricted aspect ratio (the ratio of screen width to height) of the American standard have resulted in poor detail resolution to the broadcast image and a constricted view. For years, much of the rest of the world enjoyed a somewhat better system (the British PAL system and the French system offer 625 lines, for roughly 20 percent more image clarity than the 525-line NTSC system developed by the U.S.). All of this is changing with the introduction of digital television.

The catalyst for the changeover is high-definition television (HDTV). There is no technical law that says pictures can't be bigger, wider, and clearer, and indeed better standards were developed in the 1990s. There is, however, a technical law that says that bigger, more detailed pictures require greater bandwidth in order to deliver all that information. The existing frequency allocations, premised on the needs of the NTSC, simply couldn't do the job using traditional analog technology. The answer provided by the FCC was to switch the whole system over to digital delivery. When the digital format is combined with sophisticated compression techniques under the MPEG2 standard, suddenly a terrific HDTV image can be accommodated by the portion of the spectrum traditionally licensed to an old-fashioned NTSC station.

Congress and the FCC seized on this, devising a plan to make the transition from the old world of VHF and UHF frequency allocations to a new world of digital stations. The basic idea is to have a transition period, where both the old and the new coexist awhile for each station, after which analog will be fully phased out and the old frequencies surrendered. In the meantime, starting from scratch once again to determine the new allocation of the spectrum, a new, more efficient map of frequency distributions around the nation should be the final result. A happy by-product of all this efficiency is the freeing up of the top end of the old television spectrum: The 24 megahertz of spectrum currently used for television broadcast channels 63, 64, 68, and 69 will be returned and given over for emergency service use. The remaining 84 MHz in the 700-MHz band (currently television broadcast channels 59–62 and 65–66) will be auctioned off for cell phone and other communications uses.

Although HDTV was the catalyst, it is not the necessary end product of the changeover for any given station. The FCC has recognized not just one digital broadcast standard but several, including ATSC, DVB, digital cable, telco TV, ARIB, and other alternatives such as DIRECTV for DBS. The standards provide a varying level of improvement in definition and aspect ratios. Some are "interlaced" in the fashion of the old NTSC standard, and some are not, more resembling computer screens. This set of choices allows market forces to help sort out the preferable result. It also allows broadcasters using a standard-definition television (SDTV) version of DTV to elect to run multiple channels (or channels plus data streaming) in the newly allocated bandwidth.

The goals of making better, more diverse service possible, with greater market choice and a more efficient use of the spectrum, are excellent. However, with all the choices, interests, and players, the implementation is complicated, expensive, and subject to midcourse corrections and time extensions.

A major step forward has been to work out manufacturing standards that will allow digital televisions (and the set-top boxes that will be used with older, analog televisions) to interpret and display the different possibilities that a station might elect. In 2002, the FCC adopted the DTV Tuner Order, requiring that all television receivers manufactured or shipped in the U.S. with screen sizes of 13 inches and above be capable of receiving DTV signals over the air no later than July 1, 2007. Cable compatibility has also been addressed: Using specifications developed by the cable and consumer electronics industries, the FCC adopted its 2003 Plug and Play Order, allowing consumers to plug their cable directly into their new digital TV sets without the need of a set-top box.

The general guiding framework for this changeover involves the grant of new frequencies; the election of existing stations to fill them up (made complicated by the ability of stations to make swaps and deals on the new allocations); a variety of adjustments to reflect interference and other technical concerns that may appear as the implementation progresses; and then a rolling-out phase of the old analog licenses. As of August 2004, the FCC reported 1,411 DTV stations on the air in some fashion, in markets that serve over 99 percent of U.S. television households. Full duplication of service was expected in 2005, and a final switchover by the end of 2006 for commercial stations. Choices regarding formats and the number and quality of services provided may take even longer to settle out, as the chicken-and-egg process of consumers buying HDTV equipment and of broadcasters providing HDTV service goes forward.

Protection against unauthorized copying is an additional concern in the DTV changeover that merits mention. Until recently, television broadcasts were not a significant source for widely distributed "pirate" copies of programs, films, etc. Analog TV and VHS videotape had problems with signal degradation and were effectively incompatible with Internet file-sharing. Digital television, by contrast, like digital music, is a much friendlier medium for unauthorized capture and redistribution. To combat this, the FCC has adopted a redistribution control system, also known as the "broadcast flag," for digital broadcast television. By providing reasonable protection for digital broadcast television, the FCC hopes to ensure the continued availability of high-value content on broadcast television. In a 2005 court decision, however, the broadcast flag approach was held to be beyond the FCC's authority, putting the whole issue into play again.

## REGULATION OF LOW-POWER TELEVISION (LPTV)

When the original spectrum allocation structure was set up in 1952, the goal was to permit every community in the U.S. to receive at least one television station, and to offer at least two channels to as many communities as possible. To prevent signal interference between broadcasters on the same channel in certain adjacent areas, a patchwork of assignments was made, particularly on the VHF band. This setup left a number of frequency gaps too small to be filled by normal full-power stations.

In 1982, as part of the move to broaden viewer options, the FCC made licenses available for a new kind of television station that, because it would operate at considerably reduced power, could be slotted into such a gap. LPTV stations and translator stations (extending the reach of existing stations), limited to an effective radiated power of 3 kilowatts (VHF) and 150 kilowatts (UHF), fit the bill. To help the FCC deal with the rush of applications that accompanied this change, Congress amended the 1934 Communications Act, allowing the FCC to hold an initial lottery among the potential applicants for each low-power opening. This arrangement took the place of an FCC evaluation of each applicant according to the "public interest, convenience, or necessity" standard. Once the lottery produced a winner, the winner's application was still studied on its own merits to ensure that it met the necessary standards described on page 35.

Currently, the FCC opens periodic filing windows for LPTV applications rather than running a continuous process. If there are multiple applications for a frequency, the FCC holds an auction procedure to decide who gets the allocation. Because of the fragmented nature of LPTV, many rules applicable to standard stations do not apply. For instance, there is no upper limit on the number of low-power stations that can be owned by a single group, and LPTV stations don't have to maintain public files. According to the FCC, in 2005 there were more than 2,000 licensed and operational LPTV stations, 250 of which were part of a statewide network in Alaska. In the lower 48 states, approximately 1,500 stations were operated by 700 licensees in nearly 750 towns and cities, with approximately two-thirds of the stations serving rural communities. In addition, there were approximately 5,000 translator stations, mostly in the western mountainous states. While many low-power stations have been licensed and are locally important, they have had only limited economic impact on the television industry as a whole.

## REGULATION OF MULTIPOINT DELIVERY SYSTEM

Another hybrid class of broadcast service is multipoint delivery (MDS, or MDTV), sometimes called "wireless cable." A pair of UHF band segments has been set aside by the FCC for mid-range and local transmissions on a line-of-sight basis. A special converter receives the signals and feeds them to the television on an otherwise unused normal broadcast channel. Many of these small transmitters (the "multipoints") may be scattered around a service area, similar to mobile phone cells. Because of the need for a converter and other technical limitations, the multipoint systems have been slow to catch on, particularly in areas already wired for cable, although systems offering a greater selection of channels have had some success. The potential to use MDTV interactively, and to provide data transmission and even telephone service, has produced renewed interest in this service.

## LICENSE RENEWALS

The 1934 Communications Act sets television licenses to a term of eight years, at which time they come up for review and renewal. Up until 1981, this was a time-consuming ordeal, requiring reams of supporting material on how the station was serving the public interest, convenience, and necessity. As part of deregulation, the renewal application was shortened to "postcard" size, although certain attachments relating to broadcast violence complaints may still be necessary.

An application is due four months before the license expires. A "public-interest" review is still carried out, but it largely consists, at least at the FCC level, of looking into any complaints from the public or any record of non-compliance with FCC rules and procedures. If the record is clean, renewal is customarily granted at the staff level unless it is contested by some third party. The 1996 Act created a level of "renewal expectancy" as to the substance of the review. Since the broadcaster must give notice of the upcoming renewal on its own airwaves, this action alone can occasionally spark disgruntled viewers to complain. Any parties who wish to contest the renewal can search the station's public inspection file (see below) for evidence of lapses and failures. Prior to enactment of the 1996 Act, a competing applicant could mount a combination challenge and replacement application. This direct incentive to bringing a challenge has now been dropped, leading to a decrease in the already small number of challenges.

If the station has problems with its record, or if there is a contest from a concerned third party, there may be a further FCC review on the matter, sometimes before an administrative law judge. That judge's decision is subject to appeal to the Commission and the courts. A contested renewal is a rarity, however, and a successful challenge to a license renewal is even more unusual. Even so, challengers have sometimes prevailed—and because a failure to renew is, in effect, a commercial death sentence, even the slim possibility that renewal might not happen encourages broadcasters to comply with the FCC's requirements.

## PUBLIC INSPECTION FILE

Under FCC regulations, every television station has to maintain a public inspection file. This file must contain a wide variety of information, including (1) copies of the license renewal application, Ownership Report forms, and Annual Employment forms; (2) information on station ownership, network affiliation, management agreements, political broadcasts, and children's programming; (3) the FCC publication *The Public and Broadcasting—A Procedure Manual*; and (4) letters and other communications from the public and from citizen groups.

Certification that the public information file is complete is a necessary part of the renewal process. While the file must be kept available for public inspection (electronic availability is a possibility), the public seldom looks at it, though potential challengers to a station's license renewal will.

## LICENSE TRANSFERS

The FCC regulates the transfer of station licenses—not only when occasioned by the outright sale of the business or of the company holding the license, but also as part of any material change of ownership. Even the conversion of the owning company from corporate to partnership form, without any change of ultimate control, would have to be cleared with the FCC. As one would expect, minor adjustments in company structure or in the makeup of minority ownership could be reported on abbreviated forms and would receive little, if any, scrutiny.

The transfer of control of a station, however, is a more serious matter. In theory, a television broadcast license cannot be sold. Either the company holding the license is sold, or the facilities and goodwill of the station are sold to an entity that asks the FCC to reassign it the license. In either event, the FCC reviews the change to ensure that it is consistent with the public-interest standard. Prior to deregulation, this review process was rigorous, and the possibility of challenge was an ever-present threat; more recently, however, this degree of scrutiny has been relaxed. The FCC has also eliminated the "anti-trafficking" rules that had previously prevented the sale of a station within three years of a prior transfer.

The FCC's relaxations of these rules, the increased maximum number of stations that can be owned by any one group, and the easy availability of mergers-and-acquisitions financing in the 1980s led to a major boom in station sales during the 1980s. The early 1990s saw less activity, but station sales picked up again in the aftermath of the 1996 Telecommunications Act, although the uncertainty surrounding the relaxation of multiple-ownership rules has cooled things off a bit. If the rules settle out in a permissive fashion, further transfer activity is likely.

## STATION OPERATIONS

In addition to overseeing the birth, life, and death of television stations, the FCC controls many of the operating procedures of a station. Keeping on top of the wide range of technical, management, and content-related requirements is an important element in managing a television station.

First of all, there are a number of technical and housekeeping rules for television broadcasters. Station identification messages (either visual or aural) must be televised hourly (as close to on-the-hour as is reasonably possible) and also at the beginning and end of each broadcast day. Certain logs must be kept, although the number of logs has been greatly reduced since deregulation, and such logs need cover only certain technical matters. Every station must also maintain the Emergency Broadcast System. Closed captioning or other means of making audio content available to the hearing impaired is required in some cases.

Some FCC rules govern advertising (see Chapter 14), particularly during children's programming. Federal law also requires a station to disclose commercial support of programming, and prohibits a station from receiving undisclosed compensation for the inclusion of material in a broadcast. These restrictions have their origin in the "payola" scandals of popular music on radio in the 1950s, when disc jockeys took bribes to play certain songs. Section 507 of the Communications Act prohibits a station, or any other entity connected with the production or broadcasting of a television program, from accepting or paying "valuable consideration" (which need not be cash) for the broadcast of any matter without disclosing the fact of that payment to the viewers. Section 507 is the reason for the "promotional consideration" announcements familiar to game show viewers. It is typical for television employment contracts to contain a provision requiring the employee to obey Section 507.

## POLITICAL BROADCASTING

Until it was dropped by the FCC in 1987, the "fairness doctrine" required that stations offer a reasonable opportunity for groups or individuals to express opposing points of view on controversial subjects of public importance. This requirement was a corollary to the "natural monopoly" view of television broadcasting; as that philosophy faded in the 1980s, so did support for the fairness doctrine. One related prohibition, the "personal attack rule," continues to provide a right to respond on the air to "personal attacks" broadcast against specific individuals or groups.

There is another vestige of the fairness doctrine concept in the limited field of political broadcasts: Under Section 315 of the Communications Act, a television broadcaster that gives or sells airtime to one candidate for a particular political office must provide an "equal opportunity" to other legally qualified candidates for the same office. There are exceptions, though, for coverage of a candidate in bona fide newscasts, interviews, and documentaries. Thus, the appearance on *Meet the Press* or a local news program of a candidate who is legitimately in the news does not mean that other candidates are entitled to an equal amount of airtime. Since televised debates are generally viewed as part of news coverage, they also fall outside Section 315. On the other hand, if a station does sell television advertising to one candidate, it must be willing to sell it on the same terms to competitors for the same office.

Broadcasters are limited in the rates that they can charge candidates for political ads. At no time may a station charge more for a political ad than for "comparable use." During the 45 days before a primary and the 60 days before a general or special election, the charges cannot exceed those offered to the station's most-favored commercial advertisers, including any applicable discounts.

The final aspect of these politically related rules is the "reasonable access" provision. This applies only to candidates for federal elective office: the president, the vice president, and congressmen. In short, broadcasters must sell, or give (a less likely option), reasonable amounts of advertising time for candidates for these offices to get their messages across.

In each of these situations, there is a definition of the kind of legally qualified candidate for public office who is entitled to benefit from these rules. In practice, most stations are happy to comply with these rules, as they provide an excuse to charge political candidates full rates for the periodic barrage of ads. With the increasing pressure for campaign finance reform and for getting some public value back from the essentially free spectrum allocation to broadcasters, there are periodic proposals to give free advertising access to federal candidates. The future of these proposals is questionable.

## CHILDREN'S BROADCASTING

The FCC's rules on broadcasting aimed at children are discussed in Chapter 14.

# NETWORK ISSUES

There are four principal areas in which the FCC traditionally governed the operations of network television: (1) affiliation agreements, (2) multiple-station ownership, (3) prime-time access, and (4) the financial interest and syndication ("fin-syn") rules. In the deregulatory atmosphere of the past decades, all but the first have been repealed or extensively modified.

## Affiliation Agreements

The FCC protects the local affiliates in their relationships with the broadcast networks, most importantly by preventing the network from forcing affiliates to take their programming. The affiliates may decline to take any given network offering for a host of reasons. In addition, the affiliation cannot be exclusive: The affiliate is allowed to take programs from any other source with which it can reach agreement, including another network. Other regulations prevent the network from controlling the affiliate's own advertising inventory, either by setting rates or by acting as a national sales representative for the station. The rules now permit affiliation with companies operating two or more networks, unless such combination includes more than one of the current "big four"—ABC, CBS, NBC, and FOX—or a combination of one of the big four with The WB or UPN. The old rule that set a two-year maximum for the length of an affiliation agreement was dropped in 1989.

## Multiple-Station Ownership

The FCC rules about multiple-station ownership in effect before the 1996 Telecommunications Act had the result over the years of keeping most network affiliates under separate ownership from the networks themselves. Nonetheless, each of the networks—including FOX—assembled a formidable group of network-owned and -operated stations (O&Os) in most of the key markets. The independent stations in these markets also tend to be owned by major station groups. Since these markets are critical to the success of syndicated program offerings, the networks (through their O&Os) and the major station groups are big players in the syndication scene. To this extent, the FCC's ownership restrictions never achieved their objectives. In the aftermath of the 1996 Act, these rules have been substantially reworked (see page 37).

## Prime-Time Access

For many years, the FCC helped independent program suppliers, which faced a small number of broadcasters in the major markets, by imposing the prime-time access rules. In 1995, the rules were rescinded, effective August 30, 1996.

## The Financial Interest and Syndication Rules

The most important of the FCC's former network restrictions were the financial interest and syndication (fin-syn) rules. In their classic form, these rules completely barred the networks from acquiring any financial interest in the broadcast of outside-produced programs (those not solely produced by the network), other than the right to exhibit the programs on the network.

With the growing power of satellite, cable, and other broadcast networks, the potential for network domination was seen to be receding, and the need for additional network resources was seen to be increasing. This perception led to the full repeal of fin-syn rules by the FCC in 1995. The model for program ownership has since changed, with networks, both broadcast and cable, seeking to lock up as many territories and distribution streams as possible. The losers in this repeal have been independent producers, who have been converted in most instances to hired hands rather than asset owners in the television marketplace.

# CHAPTER 7
# CABLE REGULATION

Cable television is subject to a regulatory structure that works on three levels: federal, state, and local.

## FEDERAL CABLE REGULATION

At the federal level, the FCC has clear authority, granted by the Cable Communications Policy Act of 1984, to regulate the operation of cable systems. This was not always the case. In the 1950s, when cable television was launching, the FCC took a hands-off position. Cable operations tended to be small, and to the extent that they had any impact on broadcasting, they merely expanded the reach of established stations into areas where the stations would not otherwise have been received.

The FCC's *laissez-faire* attitude changed in the early 1960s, as more and more cable operators began to "import" signals from beyond the local area. These distant signals were picked up in an operator's local broadcast area, then transmitted (usually by microwave relay) to a distant cable company, which in turn "cable-cast" them as supplemental channels. This action provided both the grounds and the means for regulation by the FCC. For the first time, local stations started viewing cable as a competitor to their operations rather than as merely an extension of those operations. The FCC shared this concern, and sought to protect established broadcasters. The microwave or other telecommunications link that usually brought the distant signal to the cable company was a common carrier or a radio transmission—and those forms were clearly subject to FCC jurisdiction.

In 1966, the FCC issued a series of rules on cable. The first was the "must-carry" rule, which required a cable system to carry the signals of all the local stations. A second rule called for blacking out distant signals when they duplicated programs offered by a local broadcaster. A third rule flatly prohibited the importation of distant signals into the biggest 100 markets, although cable systems could file with the FCC requesting permission and giving justification for why such service was necessary (permission was seldom granted). At about the same time, FCC regulations made it impractical for telephone companies to be involved as cable-service providers—thus barring one of the strongest potential cable operators from the business.

The FCC's right to maintain these and other restrictions was challenged both in the courts and in Congress. In 1968, the Supreme Court affirmed the FCC's jurisdiction over cable to an extent "reasonably ancillary to the effective performance of the Commission's various responsibilities for the regulation of broadcasting." In 1970, the FCC imposed the "anti-siphoning" rule, which greatly restricted the showing of movies and sports events on cable services. In 1972, a compromise was worked out between the cable industry, the FCC, and the broadcasting interests; this agreement settled the issue of FCC control over cable and relaxed the distant-signal rules so that wiring the top 100 television markets for cable could continue.

Two further developments spurred cable growth in the mid-1970s—one technical, the other legal. On the technical level, modern communications satellites suddenly made national signal transmission much less expensive; until then, the major broadcast networks had used much more costly cable and microwave networks to distribute their services around the country. In 1975, HBO used a satellite link to become the first cable programming service available nationwide, followed by Ted Turner's WTCG, an independent station licensed to operate in Atlanta and later renamed WTBS (and subsequently, TBS Superstation). On the legal end, the FCC's anti-siphoning rules were struck down in the courts in 1977 for violating the First Amendment. In the deregulatory climate of the Reagan years, the FCC further loosened its distant-signal rules. In 1984, Congress adopted the Cable Communications Policy Act as an amendment to the Communications Act of 1934. This, together with the 1992 Cable Television Consumer Protection and Competition Act, forms the statutory basis for FCC regulation of cable television.

## The 1984 and 1992 Cable Acts

The 1984 Cable Act (which became Title VI of the Communications Act of 1934) granted the FCC the express power to regulate cable television. In many instances, this power totally preempts the authority of state and local governments. Even in those areas where state and local action is permitted, the 1984 Act provided guidelines and parameters. The 1984 Act also made clear the fact that cable services, like broadcast television, are not common carriers, and therefore do not have to provide general access to all comers. The 1992 Cable Act both added to and subtracted from the regulatory mantle, and the 1996 Telecommunications Act further changed aspects of the overall picture.

### Definition of a Cable System

The 1984 Cable Act provided a definition of a "cable system" covered by its provisions: If the cables utilize public rights-of-way of any kind, the installation is likely to be a cable system, and thus subject to regulation. Small cable systems with fewer than 1,000 subscribers, however, are exempt from many of the general rules. If the lines stay within one continuous property, such as common antennae for an apartment complex, the system may not be covered by the FCC jurisdiction.

## Registration
All cable systems that carry any broadcast signals must be registered with the FCC. Registration takes the form of a filing that discloses information about the system—who its owners are, for example, and which services are to be carried on the system. In addition to FCC registration, the 1984 Cable Act requires that all cable systems be franchised by state or local authorities (see page 53).

## Local Station Carriage
One of the perennial battlegrounds in cable regulation is the relationship between cable systems and local broadcasters. One aspect of this struggle is the "must-carry" rule, requiring cable systems to carry all local broadcast signals. The rule has had a checkered history. It survived the enactment of the 1984 Cable Act but was thrown out in 1985 by court order as a violation of the First Amendment. A subsequent effort by the FCC to redraft the must-carry rule to meet First Amendment scrutiny also failed. Congress entered the picture with the 1992 Cable Act, by way of a somewhat different approach. A local station was given the choice between opting for the grant of a free "retransmission consent" coupled with must-carry, on the one hand, or negotiating an arm's-length retransmission agreement with the cable provider on the other. As implemented by FCC rules, this version of must-carry divides up the cable universe into three tiers: systems with 12 or fewer channels, systems with 13 to 36 channels, and systems with more than 36 channels. The first group must carry at least three local commercial stations and one "public" station. The second and third groups must carry "all" local commercial stations and at least one-third of the total available cable channels, plus all the non-duplicative local "public" stations (at least one and up to three for the second group; at least three for the third). Low-power stations (see page 11), with some exceptions, do not qualify for must-carry status.

As with many other areas, the conversion to digital complicates the must-carry rules. During the transition period, a station that broadcasts in both digital and analog modes can only require cable transmission of its analog signal. As soon as a station converts to digital and releases its analog signals, it can require carriage of the digital standard.

These rules also give the broadcast channels limited rights to designate channel allocation in the cable system, and require the cable system to maintain minimum signal-quality standards. If the broadcast station does not opt for the forced free-consent/must-carry deal, then it can either forbid carriage or seek compensation to permit it. These choices were initially made in 1993, and they are revisited by each station every three years. Many stations opt for the free-consent/must-carry option. As it has turned out, the initial negotiations delivered little cost compensation, although some powerful station owners were able to squeeze out additional channel space from the cable owners for other projects, often in a six-year deal. The contentiousness of each cycle varies, with arguments in 2000 between Time Warner Cable and Disney/ABC among the most notable. Whatever the rules, cable systems have generally carried most local broadcast channels, perhaps because subscribers expect it.

## Distant Signal Rules

It is permissible for a cable system to import signals broadcast from other communities, subject to the specific blackout provisions discussed below and to payment of the mandated copyright fees. Importation is generally done via microwave or satellite, using common carriers. Broadcast stations, by contrast, have no right to rebroadcast material from other stations without consent.

FCC rules still restrict importing material from distant channels that duplicates local transmissions. For instance, the law allows a local station to prevent a cable system from carrying network programming that originates from a distant source and duplicates network programming carried by the local station. In addition, there is a blackout provision that can apply to syndicated programming duplicated from a distant station. In order to avail itself of this protection, the local station running the syndicated programming must have an agreement with the syndicator that provides for local exclusivity, and must give notice of the request for this protection to both the FCC and the local cable company.

## Sports Blackouts

Cable companies cannot import a distant signal in order to circumvent the blackout of a sports event on a local channel. These blackouts are negotiated by teams so that a local broadcast of a game will not undercut fan interest in attending the game itself.

## Original Programming and Technical Standards

The FCC does not require that a cable system carry any non-broadcast channels. If, however, the system produces its own programming, many generally applicable FCC rules apply. These rules include those pertaining to equal-opportunity advertising for political candidates (page 52); lotteries and gambling-related cablecasting (page 97); and sponsorship identification, sponsor lists, and payola prevention (page 43). Original cable programming has also been covered by anti-obscenity rules (page 289), although not by the indecency standards applicable to broadcast television. Congressional pressure is rising to extend the indecency standards to cable television as well, although this raises significant issues under the First Amendment.

The FCC also has jurisdiction over technical standards for cable television. Under the 1984 Act, most of these requirements were softened to become simply guidelines that help promote standardization within the industry. The 1992 Act introduced some additional standards, particularly relating to signal noise and color signals. Other technical requirements relate to testing and signal leakage. The conversion to digital has had an impact here as well. The FCC has either mandated or recognized industry agreement on a number of technical issues, including technical operating standards and the "plug and play" compatibility of television sets sold in the U.S. with digital cable signals.

## Equal Employment Opportunity

Cable systems are subject to the equal employment opportunity requirements of the Communications Act and the FCC. Successful court challenges in the 1990s led to the scrapping of the FCC's former approach, which looked to actual results in hiring. The new rules, promulgated in 2002, focus on recruitment efforts rather than particular results. For the most part, the FCC guidelines and policies that apply to cable systems resemble those applicable to broadcasters, which are described in detail in Chapter 6. The variations include somewhat different reporting requirements.

## Cross-Ownership

Prior to 1996, there were a number of cross-ownership restrictions on cable. For instance, cross-ownership between broadcasting stations and cable operations was prohibited; national broadcast networks could not own any cable *systems*, and local broadcasters could not own cable systems within their broadcast area. It is worth noting that these restrictions applied to ownership of cable systems, and not to program services or networks. The broadcast networks indeed have had financial interests in cable *networks* for some time (see Chapter 19). The 1996 Act eliminated the broadcast network ownership ban, although it allowed the FCC certain rulemaking authority to ensure fair treatment of other, nonaffiliated services and stations.

Under the pre-1996 rules, telephone companies were prohibited from owning cable systems within the areas for which they provided local telephone service; these restrictions were also repealed by the 1996 Act. Restrictions on cross-ownership between cable systems and multipoint delivery systems (see page 41) have largely survived the 1996 Act, although exemptions can now exist where a cable operator faces effective competition from other sources.

The 1996 Act also removed the statutory prohibition against cross-ownership between local broadcast stations and local cable services, but retained the FCC's authority to maintain a regulatory ban. These rules were in turn thrown out by a 2002 court decision, and cross-ownership is now permitted in this context as well.

## Anti-piracy and Theft of Services

The 1984 Cable Act made it expressly illegal to take signals from a cable system without authorization. This sets up punishment for the use of private taps and "black box" decoders, ranging from a relatively small fine and jail sentence for private users, to up to $50,000 and two years in jail for first-time offenders engaging in signal theft for profit, and up to $100,000 and five years for repeaters. The affected cable system can sue for damages. State laws may also apply.

With the advent of a digital standard, the possibilities for piracy from a cable signal have added a new concern to cable operators and content providers. The higher-quality digital signal greatly increases the possibility that a subscriber could copy a program and then traffic in it, whether through physical copies or through Internet file-sharing. Federal response to this concern has included rules on encoding programming and on the availability of output connectors from digital devices. The "broadcast flag" (discussed on page 40) would also supply protection in the cable context, provided it survives its legal challenges.

## Rate Regulation

The regulation of cable rates has had a varied history, with the pendulum swinging back and forth on whether regulation is a good idea or not. The most recent congressional action on this issue, the Telecommunications Act of 1996, largely did away with rate regulation in favor of free-market practices. Only systems that do not face "effective competition" are subject to regulation, and those only face regulation on the basic service tier pricing. Effective competition exists for systems with either (i) low penetration (less than 30 percent); (ii) "overbuild" with the availability of more than one multi-channel service (which can include satellite), and with the second most popular service going to at least 15 percent of the local households; (iii) municipal ownership; or (iv) telephone system competition. The combined result of these tests has been to remove much of the country from cable rate regulation.

## Political Broadcast Rules

Some of the rules governing political access that apply to broadcast television (see page 43) have cable equivalents. These apply mainly to cable operators who have "cablecasting" channels over which they have programming control. Public-access channels are not generally included. For instance, the equal-access rule applies: If time is made available for purchase to one candidate, it must be made available to all those running for the same office. Personal attack and political editorial rules also apply, requiring notice to the affected party and a reasonable opportunity to respond.

# COPYRIGHT ASPECTS OF CABLE TELEVISION

All material carried by cable television—including programs, commercials, and music—must be cleared for copyright permission. In the case of original cable programming, such as that provided by Showtime, MTV, and other basic and pay cable services, the cablecast itself is a public performance and requires a license from the copyright proprietor (page 264). Under the old 1909 Copyright Act, the retransmission by cable of material broadcast on an over-the-air station was not considered a new performance or duplication. Therefore, the license obtained by the original broadcaster extended to subsequent cable distribution.

This was changed by the 1976 Copyright Act, which set up a compulsory license structure for cable companies retransmitting broadcast signals. Under this arrangement, the cable system can transmit nonlocal broadcast signals, provided it pays the broadcaster an appropriate fee (which is collected and administered by the Copyright Royalty Tribunal; see discussion on page 268). The basis on which these fees are calculated depends on the cable system's level of revenues and on the form that they file. *Short-form systems* (those with less than $379,600 in semian-nual gross receipts in 2005) pay a relatively small amount for transmitting an unlimited number of imported signals: 0.5 percent of gross receipts up to $189,800 and 1 percent of gross receipts thereafter. *Long-form systems*, with more than $379,600 in annual gross receipts, pay a larger amount determined by a complicated formula based on the kind and number of stations the cable system carries, and on whether the system is in a top-100 market or not. For a cable system in a top-50 market, these formulas can make the first imported signal—if it is from an independent station—cost royalties totaling almost 1.5 percent of gross receipts, with fees for additional signals trailing off from there. There is also a charge of 3.75 percent of gross receipts for carrying each distant signal in excess of the number that would have been permitted under the FCC's pre-1980 rules.

Once received, the royalties are divided by the Tribunal among the copyright owners of the programs carried, who must each file a claim to share in the pot. Among the major beneficiaries have been the copyright owners of movies and sports programs.

# STATE AND LOCAL CABLE REGULATION

At the state and local level, a patchwork of regulatory systems has evolved. Some states have set up quite active statewide regulatory boards for cable; other states leave regulation largely to the local communities. State and local control arises not only from the general legislative power, but also from the ability to govern the access of the cable company to the public rights-of-way. This access is neces-sary for maintaining and operating a system of any size, since cable can run throughout a community only if it follows the public roads, either aboveground on poles or belowground in conduits.

Access to these roads is in the hands of the state government or the municipalities.

State and local regulation is restricted, however, to those areas where the FCC has not asserted exclusive jurisdiction. While the states and localities can govern franchising and utility-pole attachments, subject to the requirements of the 1984 Act, they are largely prohibited from otherwise interfering in the operations of cable systems. The major addition to state and local authority under the 1992 Act was the administration of rate regulation for the basic tier.

## Franchising

The most important means by which states and local communities control cable is the franchising of cable systems. The power to franchise comes from control of the public rights-of-way. The 1984 Act set only sketchy parameters for franchising, but it also made holding a franchise a requirement for FCC registration. In most states, the franchising power has been delegated to the local level, where it is normally exercised by the city or town council.

The typical franchising process goes as follows. First, the local government may seek knowledgeable advisors to help it through the technical and legal considerations in awarding a cable franchise. The next step is usually a request for proposals, which announces to the cable television industry that the locality would like to award a franchise. Then comes the response from the interested cable companies, which submit proposals (often of great length) suggesting what they will offer and why each is the best candidate to provide the service requested. For better or worse, local political connections and concerns can sometimes influence this process, providing work for well-connected lawyers, lobbyists, and other local consultants with clout. The selection process continues with a review of the competing proposals. This review usually involves an investigation by the local council and its advisors of the applicants and their proposals—an inspection of their finances, their operating experience, and the feasibility of the various promises they make. In the process of this review, there should be a public hearing on the merits of each proposal, at which community members and other interested parties can air their views.

Once a potential franchise has been chosen, the town council or other franchising authority negotiates an agreement with the company, based on the proposal and setting forth the terms of the franchise. The financial deal is subject to a Cable Act limitation: No more than 5 percent of gross revenues from the franchised service can be taken as the franchise fee. The agreement also includes the franchise term; technical and construction specifications; and requirements for certain levels of service, including the number of channels set aside for community access, local educational use, and other public-interest uses. Most franchises are awarded on a nonexclusive basis; in theory, another company can approach the municipality and propose the wiring of a further system within the service area.

As a practical matter, given the high costs of entry, it is relatively rare for another service to come in and bid on a territory that has already been franchised. Nonetheless, franchise agreements are often challenged in court by disappointed claimants, who cite alleged flaws in the way the franchise was awarded.

When a franchise comes up for renewal, the Cable Act provides certain safeguards to protect the interests of the existing franchisee. As modified by the 1992 Act, the process now has two stages: a relatively informal first-stage proceeding under section 626(a), and a more formal proposal and response under section 626(c). The 626(a) proceeding comes either at the franchisee's request—which must be given within a six-month period starting three years before the renewal date—or at the initiative of the franchising authority. There are two principal themes in the process: (1) the needs of the community, and (2) the record of the cable operator. This initial procedure helps to get the various agendas on the table. It is followed by the preparation of a formal proposal for renewal by the operator. Once this is received, the franchising authority must either renew relatively automatically without a hearing based on the proposal, or it must hold a formal hearing and review under section 626(c). The hearing evaluates the level of service according to the following criteria, as specified in the Cable Act:

(A) The cable operator has substantially complied with the material terms of the existing franchise and with applicable law;

(B) The quality of the operator's service, including signal quality, response to consumer complaints, and billing practices, but without regard to the mix or the level of cable services or other services provided over the system, has been reasonable in light of community needs;

(C) The operator has the financial, legal, and technical ability to provide the services, facilities, and equipment as set forth in the operator's proposal; and

(D) The operator's proposal is reasonable to meet the future cable-related community needs and interests, taking into account the cost of meeting such needs and interests.

Although the franchising authority can theoretically deny a renewal to the existing operator, it can do so only if the franchisee has a documented record of poor performance or inability to meet one of these four criteria. The franchise authority may not consider a competing offer, except perhaps to help provide background for evaluating these criteria. This process acts to cut down the leverage of the municipality at renewal time, and helps protect the status quo. By now, the most desirable franchises in the country have been awarded, and franchises coming up for renewal are the main arena for competition between cable operators.

## Utility-pole Attachments

The states are permitted to control the attachment of cable lines to existing telephone and electric utility poles and conduits. In most circumstances, it is more sensible (and cheaper) for a cable company to add its cable lines to these poles and conduits than to set up new poles or dig new underground channels. This puts the cable company at the mercy of the owner of existing poles and conduits. In order to prevent extortionate requests and to encourage the installation of cable, most states and localities have adopted roles capping the rates that can be charged for such pole attachments. To the extent that states and localities had not adopted appropriate rules to govern this, the FCC retained jurisdiction, and the 1996 Act gave more power to the FCC, further strengthening the rights of cable operators and other telecommunication carriers to utility-pole access.

## Rate Regulation

Federal rate control has been a field of hotly contested action, as described on page 52. At this writing, state and local governments can be involved in regulating the rates charged by cable companies for their basic-tier service in those instances where regulation is permitted in accordance with the federal rules.

## Other Rules and Preemption

The issue of cross-ownership of cable stations and other media outlets has largely been preempted by the Cable Act and the FCC, as have all aspects of satellite television. However, states and localities do retain their normal power to enact rules for reasons of public benefit and general safety.

# CHAPTER 8
# REGULATION OF SATELLITE BROADCASTING AND NEW TECHNOLOGIES

With the beginning of the twenty-first century, technology is overturning the relatively settled broadcast/cable duality that covered electronic television distribution during the last part of the 1900s. Satellite and multipoint delivery systems (MDS) have become well established in the marketplace, making significant inroads. Video via phone lines and phone via cable are coming into the mix. Access to video through Internet connections—both legal and illegal—is blossoming as transmission speeds increase and as digital compression and other techniques reduce the data required for computer-generated pictures. DVD has proved a hugely popular format for home-stored product. Successive generations of cell phones are becoming more and more video capable.

Against this background of change, however, there are familiar themes in the possible regulatory interventions. Notwithstanding the variety of channels on offer on each of these systems, the opportunity to provide a bundle of channels, i.e., to be a system, remains limited. In cable, the cost of entry is high: stringing wire across poles through the service area. As described in the previous chapter, this has tended to produce and sustain a monopoly in most areas. Satellite services are limited to a relative handful per country by the international allocation of orbital slots for direct broadcast satellite (DBS) operators. Multipoint services face frequency-allocation limits that in turn constrain the possibility for unlimited entry. Furthermore, the economies of these systems are such that regional, national, or even international services are favored over local providers.

The upshot is that there may be significant choices of channels within a particular service, and some choice between the mediums of distribution, but the number of services available to each consumer within a particular medium of delivery—whether broadcast, cable, or satellite—has remained relatively few. Given this set of dynamics, most of the multi-channel distribution systems have come to look like the video equivalent of competing shopping malls: "competitors" offering nearly identical selections of national-chain retailers with similar, rather bland product lines. There is little room for the vibrancy and diversity of an urban shopping street.

The big potential exception to this is the Web. Electronic access and cheap production techniques may lead to a plethora of outlets, from highly professional services to home computer video-bloggers. The Web can now be added to local terrestrial broadcasters and public-access cable as an outlet for local and offbeat programs. The Web is also a highly accessible medium for putting viewers in touch with suppliers of specialty home video product, helping to drive specialty DVD distribution (see Chapter 26). Somewhat ironically, the leader in keeping video opportunities varied has been the adult programming industry, where the combination of social marginalization with high profitability has stimulated considerable ingenuity.

The wild card is in some ways the FCC: What kind of competition will its regulatory policies promote? The FCC's regulation of television has carried over into satellite, telephone, Internet, and the other new distribution technologies; the only areas in which the FCC is not somehow involved are home and business video, which do not use any form of mass electronic distribution. By and large, the FCC has promoted competition between these different sources of multi-channel systems, removing the walls to entry that had stood between the providers of what used to be technically different services. At least there now can be a number of "video shopping malls" in the same town. How much FCC regulation preserves the possibility of access to a wide range of specialty services will also be a measure of how much real competition exists.

## REGULATION OF SATELLITE TELEVISION

From the beginning of the "space age," the FCC has regulated the services of communication satellites under its authority over radio transmissions and common carriers in the communications business. This gives a baseline for government intervention, both in the U.S. and in other countries. On the issues of satellite location and frequency allocation and on most aspects of direct broadcast satellites, the UN-affiliated International Telecommunications Union (ITU) plays a role as well. The roles governing domestic and international services have grown differently over time, and each needs to be looked at in its historical and technical context. The origin of this regulation, both domestic and international, was in the role of satellites as common-carrier communication links, one of whose uses was carrying television signals to local stations and cable systems. Direct broadcast satellite delivery to the *home* (DBS) is a relative newcomer. Its regulation grows out of the old communications regulatory structure, but presents its own new challenges as well.

### U.S. Network Feeds via Satellite

The launching of satellites for communications use dates back to the 1960s and 1970s. At the time, the principal envisioned uses were phone, telex, and other data transmission functions. While from early on the FCC has controlled rates and technical aspects for communications satellites, since 1972 it has maintained an "open skies" policy with respect to domestic communication satellite services, allowing almost any technically competent and financially qualified company to launch and operate a domestic communications satellite. The result of the open skies policy has been an abundance of satellite communications channels that could be used to transmit television programming as well as voice and data. On the reception front, the FCC dropped its regulation of receive-only satellite antennae in 1979, and the Telecommunications Act of 1996 gives the FCC the affirmative power to preempt most local regulation in the area. These developments helped make satellite the carrier of choice for the national feeds of broadcast and cable networks alike—replacing the land lines and microwave systems of earlier eras.

Since there were stringent cross-ownership restrictions between common carriers on the one hand and broadcasters/cable systems on the other, the television companies have not owned or leased their own satellite facilities for this kind of use. Instead, they contract with common-carrier satellite companies to carry the signals. The technical nature of the satellites handling these feeds has required relatively large antennae for reception. The intention of these transmissions was to deliver broadcast, and later cable, network services to licensed users such as local affiliates and cable lead-ends, where large, industrial-sized receivers would be little impediment.

In the early days of satellite-transmitted television feeds, most signals were open and unscrambled. Consequently, the business of supplying these large receiving dishes to private individuals became viable. While the initial investment was significant, many people, particularly in remote areas with no cable service, installed dishes and settled back to enjoy shows plucked out of the air, ostensibly free of charge. This led to two steps to prevent what the cable services (and especially the pay services) saw as a threat to their revenues: scrambling and legal restrictions.

Scrambling significantly decreases one's ability to intercept a viewable signal, although bootleg "black boxes" to descramble signals do exist. Such unauthorized intercepts were rendered illegal, however. By a balancing legal mandate, the scrambled channels had to be licensed by their providers in areas where these signals are not otherwise available via cable and/or broadcast stations. A legitimate business evolved in issuing such licenses and their implementing decoders. Since the offerings available without paying for decoders then grew less interesting, the sale of dishes for picking up common-carrier satellite television feeds stagnated. In recent years, it has been essentially replaced by a much more interesting technology—direct broadcast television—and the big dishes of this early stage of satellite television are now largely abandoned relics in rural backyards.

## International Communications Satellites

While the domestic communications satellite business has burgeoned in a relatively unregulated environment, international service was initially confined to two authorized vehicles. In 1962, an act of Congress established the Communication Satellite Corporation (COMSAT). It was given broad powers to work internationally to promote and run space-based communications, and was for a time the principal owner of satellites providing such service.

Another outgrowth of this 1962 legislation was the eventual formation of the International Telecommunications Satellite Organization (INTELSAT), an international body whose powers derived from the interlocking set of agreements between its participating member countries. INTELSAT owns and operates a global satellite system aimed particularly at international telecommunications traffic. Together, COMSAT and INTELSAT for some time effectively monopolized U.S.-based, transborder satellite communications, including transoceanic feeds of television programming such as international news reports. There are other national and regional satellite unions, such as ARABSAT, EUTELSAT (the European Telecommunications Satellite Organization), and INTERSPUTNIK, which serves the former Soviet bloc.

With respect to the U.S., this monopoly started to crack in the 1980s, when legislation permitted competition. The U.S. has authorized progressively wider international penetration of satellite service under FCC control, and the ORBIT Act of 2000 laid out a plan for an increasingly free market approach to international satellite ownership. In response, INTELSAT has privatized itself. In 1998, it authorized the creation of New Skies Satellite, N.V., a privately held company based in the Netherlands, which picked up a portion of INTELSAT's network. In 2001, INTELSAT itself become a Bermudan private company, INTELSAT Ltd., which has been in the process of transitioning to public ownership.

## International Regulation of Frequencies and Orbital Positions

In one sense, the room for satellites to orbit the earth is vast. Nonetheless, certain kinds of usable locations are surprisingly limited. This is particularly true of the coveted "geosynchronous" locations, a band around the equator at a very precise altitude (around 23,000 miles) where the orbiting satellite keeps perfect time with the rotation of the earth, thereby appearing, from the standpoint of a ground observer, to stay dependably in the same spot in the sky. The alternative for continuous service is a sizable fleet of "nonstationary" satellites, which hand communications links off to one another like stations in a cellular phone network. While such a revolving service is practicable for many communications devices, it is less useful for television delivery, where a fixed antenna aimed at a particular location in the sky has been the rule.

The slots for geosynchronous placement are constrained by the potential for signal interference from satellites operating with similar frequencies in nearby spots in the sky. Since the frequencies suitable and reserved for satellite transmissions, both up and down, are also limited by technical factors, the potential for chaos in a free-for-all satellite world became apparent early on.

The ITU had long mediated ground-based broadcast frequency overlaps between nations. In 1963, it took on the coordination of satellite frequencies, and in 1973 added the assignment of orbital positions. In the early days, the ITU made its allocations on a "first come, first served" basis. This gave the two major space-exploring nations, the U.S. and the U.S.S.R., a head start in snapping up orbital placement resources. In 1985, the developing countries managed to get the issue of equitable access onto the ITU agenda, and a compromise was reached that reserved enough orbital slots and frequencies to allow each ITU member country to meet its communication needs while letting most other services continue to be assigned "first come, first served." Because the frequencies suitable for DBS service are further limited, and because access for this kind of service is seen as a matter of national security in many countries, specific DBS orbital and frequency assignments were suggested by the ITU in this process.

In recent years, however, the ITU system has been breaking down. The ITU is essentially a voluntary coordination service; it has little means of enforcement. With the increasing value of satellite coverage, aggressive entrepreneurs, often working with small countries, have registered prime orbital "real estate" well beyond any domestic needs. Registration requests are all too literally skyrocketing, and in at least one instance a wholly unauthorized satellite was launched. Calls have been made for reorganizing the ITU system, but so far little action has been taken.

## Direct Broadcast Satellite Service

Satellites have moved from being a means of transmitting programs for delivery to the home via another technology (broadcast or cable) to providing a primary mode of home delivery. The provider list has shaken out into a duopoly: DIRECTV (owned by News Corp.) and EchoStar. Compression technology and increasing numbers of satellites have allowed a burgeoning of channel offerings—approaching 1,000 on DIRECTV in 2005.

The regulation of U.S. DBS service is somewhat schizophrenic: The FCC approach is relatively hands-off against a background of internationally mandated scarcity. The key to a commercially successful DBS service has been the use of medium- and high-power satellites (100 to 400 watts per transponder), which have allowed the use of receiver dish antennas as small as 18 inches. The signals are sent in digital code to increase capacity and prevent piracy. Unauthorized descrambling is against federal law.

Domestically, the FCC regulates every direct broadcast satellite originally under its general authority over the radio broadcast spectrum. This authority was specifically confirmed by the 1996 Act. The first request for a DBS license came in 1980; by 1982, the FCC had established procedures and rules for granting licenses. These "interim" rules—still in effect—have some provisions similar to those for broadcast stations. For instance, there are equal employment opportunity requirements, including one for filing an EEO plan as part of the application for initiating a DBS service if the operator exercises programming control. The rules mandate a modest level of noncommercial, educational program content—4 percent. Foreign ownership and control of a DBS service was originally restricted, but this element was repealed in 2002, and ownership is now largely left to market forces. The FCC did block a proposed merger of EchoStar and DIRECTV in 2002, citing the need to keep competition going in this technology. In allocating new DBS satellite availability, the FCC has also adopted rules designed to encourage new entries into the market.

As with cable, carriage of local broadcast stations has been a battleground. In 1999, Congress passed the Satellite Home Viewer Improvement Act (SHVIA), which provided rules similar to those applicable to cable for local station and network carriage. This approach was extended until 2009 by the Satellite Home Viewer Extension and Reauthorization Act of 2004 (SHVERA). There are a number of conflicting interests here. Local broadcasters don't want viewers substituting distant signals of network programming for the local version, thus cutting down on the local advertising revenue. On the other hand, they also have concerns about the free use of their signals and letting others sell access to programs for which the local stations have to pay. DBS providers want to devote precious transponder space to channels of their choosing. Copyright licensing is a further concern.

The SHVIA/SHVERA approach has provided a compromise on these issues. First of all, copyright questions can be resolved either by a privately negotiated copyright clearance or by a statutory copyright license. DBS providers can supply distant signals of broadcast services to subscribers whose reception of terrestrial signals from local broadcasters falls below a specified standard. For subscribers who could get good reception over the air, more complicated rules apply. If the DBS carrier decides to offer any local terrestrial channel in a given market on the statutory license approach, then it must make the opportunity available to all other local broadcasters in that market. The local stations then get to elect whether to require/permit that to go forward. The coverage can then be provided on a must-carry basis (essentially free to the DBS service) or on a consensual basis (on negotiated terms).

The interface of must-carry with the transition to digital has created further issues. For the moment, must-carry does not fully apply to digital channels, and DBS providers can require the subscriber to get a second dish to receive terrestrial digital services that are carried—a requirement not allowed for analog signals. As the digital revolution moves forward, further changes in these rules can be anticipated.

The FCC grants construction permits and DBS licenses—technically, interim licenses—to applicants once a public comment period and a staff review determine that the proposed system is in the public interest. The review is done on a case-by-case basis.

Once granted, the normal license term is currently ten years. An unusually long (six-year) construction period is allowed. The technical specifications of a

DBS service must agree with international standards. Licensing under these standards is not the real hurdle for most would-be DBS providers; getting access to enough transponders at one of the internationally designated U.S. DBS orbital slots is the greater challenge.

The last variable in the allocation of slots and the delivery of service involves transboundary delivery. The "footprint" of the DBS satellite, i.e., the area on Earth where its signal can be received, does not respect national boundaries. Signals for U.S. services overlap into Mexico and Canada, and their satellites will cover some or all of the U.S. There are even small island nations in the Pacific whose service footprint hits portions of the U.S. Looking outward, the FCC has declared information access a human right, and will not limit the spillover of U.S. services abroad. Looking inward, it has approved an application by DIRECTV to offer services into the U.S. via Canadian slot locations. Canada, for its part, has implemented rules blocking the reception of U.S. DBS north of the border, although Canadian courts have challenged these rules. There is further discussion of media distribution in a globalizing world in Chapter 50.

## REGULATION OF MULTIPOINT SYSTEMS

Multipoint systems rely on microwave transmission to create a number of video services, including what is sometimes called "wireless cable" (see page 41). Multipoint service can be viewed as a kind of cellular television: Instead of multiple nodes of telephone services, there are multiple nodes in a given territory for short-range microwave transmission of video signals. Under its general oversight of the radio spectrum, the FCC has regulated these systems as well. As in many areas of FCC supervision, history is important. This mode of transmission was originally viewed as a means to deliver instructional television, and this is still provided for. Some services deliver video to commercial users and redistributors such as hotels, sometimes on a common carrier basis. Others are set up to deliver traditional cable/satellite channels to subscribers—MDS service.

The regulatory model is familiar: FCC licensing is required. Much of the framework comes from the 1992 Cable Act. There are ownership restrictions, which keep cable operators out but allow telephone providers in. Spectrum allocation is now controlled, for the most part, by FCC auctions. Providers are subject to cable-style equal employment opportunity requirements, emergency alert compliance, and carriage regulation for broadcast signals. Although MDS is popular in some areas, it has not taken off as much as once expected.

## REGULATION OF VIDEO-ON-DEMAND

Broadcast, cable, and satellite all share a common pattern: However many channels may be offered, each channel is essentially a set stream of programming, determined by the provider. The viewer can decide whether or not to dip into a particular stream, but must take, at any given time, what is in the stream at that moment. Viewers hunger for the opportunity to assert more control, picking and choosing both the content and the time to view it. This "video-on-demand" (VOD) requirement can be supplied by owning a home video device, such as a DVD or VHS player, and possessing a copy of the program—a good solution, but one that requires trips to the store or to a rental outlet, or Internet shopping, to get a copy, all of which are barriers to instant gratification. Time-shifting devices, such as TiVO (see page 273) give some flexibility. Web streaming and the delivery of video via Internet files are increasingly helpful, although still limited by most viewers' Internet access speed. True VOD—the directed remote delivery of programs in high-quality formats as and when called for—has been a unfulfilled consumer desire. Technical and regulatory requirements have stood in its way.

Optical fiber is still viewed by many as the video-on-demand delivery system of the future. It has a huge capacity for data transmission, and could carry an unprecedented number of program options in the regular channel format. In addition, it is a fully two-way medium, permitting instant pay-per-view ordering, video-on-demand delivery, and other interactive services. With some exceptions, fiber-optic installation has been the province of the telephone companies, which had originally been shut out of ownership of broadcasting and cable facilities in those areas where they provide phone service. The seemingly natural combination of audio and video systems under one network required a change in this basic restriction, and so the 1996 Act dropped the prohibition, with only a few caveats.

## IMPACT OF THE 1996 TELECOMMUNICATIONS ACT

The 1996 Act lowered most of the barriers keeping telephone companies out of the television business. It specifically repealed the prohibition of telephone company ownership of cable systems in geographic areas where the telephone company also provides *local exchange service (LEC)*. As a bow to preserving competition, the local exchange provider cannot purchase an existing cable system unless there is significant competition from other sources (see page 51). Nor is this the only way for LECs to get into the video programming business. They may also provide multipoint services (see page 41), common-carrier businesses for other providers, and "switched video," i.e., an interactive pay-per-view service giving video-on-demand but without providing a scheduled service.

Another available option is the idea of an *open video system* (OVS). This is a kind of hybrid between a common-carrier and a cable service, which in theory will offer a call-up, on-demand access for scheduled services. OVS operation still does require certification by the FCC. The process sets rules requiring relatively open access to interested programming service providers on reasonable and nondiscriminatory terms. It also protects providers of sports, network, and syndicated programs against exclusivity and non-duplication. For instance, an OVS cannot favor its own offerings in operating the system. Certification also frees up the OVS provider for many—although by no means all—of the regulations that apply to cable services. Among those that remain are public, education, and governmental access rules and must-carry rules on local public and commercial broadcast services.

The ability to deliver high-quality video via existing phone lines, even in an age of high compression, remains a source of concern. Optical fiber is excellent, but expensive to bring all the way to the home. In many places, the last connection for a phone is still old-fashioned, thin, low-capacity, copper wire. The coaxial lines of cable companies remain attractive vehicles for high-capacity, two-way switched services—the same as phones provide, only better. And in an interesting turnabout, under the 1996 Act cable systems can also offer local exchange access, i.e., traditional phone service.

The 1996 Act envisioned a variety of delivery systems—switched and unswitched, via traditional broadcast, multipoint send-and-receive broadcast, satellite and interactive satellite, telephone and cable connections using wire and fiber and transmitting scheduled services and pay-per-view, on-demand access— all going head-to-head. Republican control of the presidency, Congress, and, increasingly, the federal courts has further removed regulatory barriers. The FCC nonetheless is keeping its hand in most of these areas, and increasing regulation is always possible. There are huge amounts of money at stake, and neither political party is immune to lobbying by the powerful and entrenched. The remaining wild card, yet to come to its full potential and yet to be integrated into the regulatory structure, is the Internet.

## VIDEO VIA THE INTERNET

The Internet is already a powerful, if still somewhat crude, source of video. For users with the right technology (a powerful computer and a high-speed Internet connection), literally hundreds of television and radio signals can be accessed in real time from the home pages of broadcasters around the world. A computer in California can access Brazilian, Mexican, or even Croatian television feeds. The picture has low fidelity, but the sound is decent, and as connection speeds increase and compression gets better, viewing quality will go up. In addition, the number of dedicated Internet program sources is burgeoning, with a mixture including do-it-yourself video-bloggers, high-quality specialty providers, and erotica. And then there is the illegal side, particularly file-sharing of pirated copies of films. This variety is beginning to establish a truly open, on-demand video system, where any Web site can become a programming source.

The legal challenges inherent in this environment are many and varied, from copyright questions to access charges to censorship. On one level, the FCC is a recognized regulator of the building blocks of the Internet, setting standards and regulating the telecommunications access points such as telephone connections via DSL and dialup, and cable and satellite delivery. So far, the approach in the U.S. has been relatively *laissez-faire*. Government has yet to involve itself in the video aspects of the Web. The one significant content initiative to date, an anti-indecency law, was declared unconstitutional. Other initiatives are likely to follow. In other countries, notably China, the government is trying hard to monitor and censor Internet content. The only certainties are that the regulatory system will change significantly once again over the next few years to meet the challenge of the Net, and that new challenges will loom on the horizon from unforeseen sources before we even expect them.

# PART 3

# AUDIENCE MEASUREMENT AND ADVERTISING

In the United States and throughout most of the world, television and consumer advertising are closely allied. Broadcast networks and stations derive nearly all of their revenue from the sale of commercial time. Advertising revenues for television broadcasting exceed $40 billion per year; this figure represents the bulk of U.S. television broadcasting revenues. For cable, $20 billion in advertising revenues represents about 40 percent of total revenues; the remainder of cable's $50 billion take is collected in monthly subscriber fees.

Television advertising is based upon a business model established in the 1920s by radio broadcasters. Networks fill most of their airtime with programs of interest to audiences, and allow sponsors to purchase airtime within or adjacent to these programs in order to reach these audiences. If a program is especially popular, then the airtime sold to sponsors is considered more valuable, and sold at a higher price. As the system evolved, it became clear that different programs appealed to different audiences; sponsors whose products were intended for housewives, for example, purchased airtime on programs whose audiences were, primarily, housewives.

In order to assure fair pricing, it became necessary to measure the size and characteristics of the audience listening to—and later, watching—each program.

# CHAPTER 9

# AUDIENCE MEASUREMENT AND RATINGS

The place where television and advertising meet is audience measurement. A program may generate buzz, but the actual number of audience members who watched the program (and its commercials) is what matters to the advertiser. Lacking a system for accurate measurement of every individual viewer's habits, advertisers have long relied upon statistical sampling as a reasonable measure of viewership.

In the 1930s and 1940s, Hooperatings simply phoned random households and asked what radio station they were listening to. Another company, The Pulse, asked people on the street what radio stations and programs they had heard recently. As television evolved, so did the systems for collecting data. Several thousand households were provided with diaries, in which they were instructed to note every program watched (and paid a nominal fee for their effort). The diary system was roundly criticized for its many imperfections—families forgot to write things down or wrote incorrect information or noted programs they thought they "should" be watching—but it was the best available system for decades.

A far better system, implemented in the 1990s, is the People Meter, an electronic device attached to the television set. The People Meter notes what was watched, then reports the results to a central database. However, the People Meter is not entirely automatic: from time to time, a red light flashes, requiring the current viewer to press his or her personal button on the People Meter's box. These tell the system who is watching television at that moment (there is also a button for guests, who are encouraged to provide age and gender by pressing other buttons). Of course, the selection of households for People Meter measurement is critical, because each household's viewing patterns theoretically represent the viewing patterns of tens of thousands of American households. Currently, 5,100 sample households represent nearly 100 million actual households. Whether a rotating sample of 800 Los Angeles households truly represents the viewing patterns of 5.4 million households in that market has always been questionable, even after logical proof is provided.

The Nielsen Television Index (NTI) is Nielsen Media Resource's national system for measuring broadcast network audiences. Households are paid $50 for the People Meter installation; they remain in the sample for two years, and for their participation receive token gifts from a merchandise catalog (most gift items are worth less than $20).

Nielsen is currently rolling out Local People Meters (LPMs) for the measurement of hundreds of households in just about every key metropolitan area in the U.S., providing an increasingly rapid means of relaying viewership statistics to advertising agencies and television programmers.

Nielsen collects data via written diary in over 200 U.S. television markets, and via some form of electronic surveying in over 50 markets. No other company provides comparable services (Arbitron no longer measures television, focusing instead on radio). All of the electronic data is collected daily, processed overnight, and made available to Nielsen clients the next morning. Despite the inevitable imperfections, the data available from Nielsen is the only data available, so it is used to make over $60 billion annually in purchase decisions.

The ratings data is distributed in several ways. The most traditional approach is the monstrously complicated ratings book (known as Viewers in Profile, or VIP), which is published quarterly and contains only local data. VIP is generally divided into three large sections listing every station, every program, every time slot, every key demographic within a market. One section is devoted to a profile of the market and the specific research sample, indicating the total number of television sets, the percentage of households with cable service, the demographic breakdown of the sample, and more. The Program Averages section details performance of individual programs. The third section, Time Period, lists viewership by each 15- or 30-minute slot. A fourth section breaks down viewership by demographic group (Men 18–49, Children 6–11, Persons 12–24, etc.).

The massive amounts of information provided in these quarterly books should not be used casually; some training is necessary in order to extract accurate information. For salespeople on the road and busy executives, the national Pocketpiece report provides summary information that's easier to navigate. For general office use, Nielsen clients are provided with database access via computer; this approach allows users to query, for example, the number of women 18–24 who watched a particular program on Tuesdays from 8:00 P.M. until 8:15 P.M., and then compare this data to the viewing habits of other groups or within other time slots. Both means of reviewing information are useful, albeit for different purposes.

Local stations and other Nielsen clients receive three basic types of information from Nielsen: a program's rating, its share, and the gross number of viewers watching the station during each quarter hour.

## AUDIENCE SHARE

A program's *share* is the percentage of total *viewing* households whose sets were tuned to that program, a calculation based not upon the total number of U.S.

households, but upon the number of households actually watching television while that program is on the air.

To calculate the audience share, one must know the total number of viewing households, or the *HUT* (*homes/households using television*) *level*. During prime time, for example, HUT levels are frequently over 50 percent. For many years, the number of television households has hovered just over 100 million, so the industry more or less drops the "percent" and simply considers the HUT level to be 50. With roughly 110 million television households now in the U.S., HUT level of 50 would equal 55 million households.

If the HUT level at 8:00 P.M. on a Thursday is 50 and a program achieves a 20 share, then 20 percent of the 55 million households, or 11 million households, are watching the program. It is also possible to compute in reverse. During the week of November 29 to December 5, 2004, NBC's *Law & Order* was the number 15 show in the U.S. with a 15 share and a gross audience of just over 11 million households. Given this information, it's easy enough to compute the HUT level: if 15 percent equals 11 million households, then the HUT level for *Law & Order*'s time slot (Wednesday 10:00 P.M.–11:00 P.M.) would be just over 73. By comparison, during the same week, CBS's *Everybody Loves Raymond* scored an 18 share with 13.5 million households; during that time period (Monday 9:00 P.M.–9:30 P.M.), the HUT level was 75, so each share point is worth slightly more in terms of gross viewership.

Why does any of this matter? In fact, share points are not used to calculate the cost of advertising. Instead, they provide television programmers with the audience measurement statistics necessary to make decisions about scheduling.

## AUDIENCE RATINGS

A program's *rating* is the percentage of *total television households* in the sample area whose sets were tuned to that program. Unlike audience share, which compares one program's appeal to viewers with others in the time slot, audience ratings compare all programs in a more or less equal-handed manner. The presumption, which is reasonable, goes like this: If a program is likely to draw a large audience, then the programmer will be smart enough to place it in an appropriate slot. Reruns of *The Brady Bunch*, for example, draw a far smaller audience than new episodes of *CSI: Miami*.

The *Law & Order* episode mentioned above achieved a 10.2 rating—in raw numbers, 10.2 percent of the 110 million U.S. television households, or 11 million households. *Everybody Loves Raymond*'s rating was a 12.3, worth about 13.5 million households.

### Demographics

The rating itself provides the national advertiser with only partial information. For many (if not most) products, the question is not only "How many households?" but also "Who are they?" More specifically, the "who" question is answered in terms of geographic distribution, age, and income level. On NBC, CBS, and ABC networks, most prime-time programs appeal equally to men and to women (with the occasional exception, such as a figure skating competition, which attracts more female viewers). But the demographic mix for a particular cable program—or cable network—is often heavy skewed toward one particular demographic group. Lifetime, for example, attracts a predominantly female audience.

## Rating Points and GRPs

When a media buyer compares possible buys in prime-time television, he or she consider rating points based upon specific demographic groups. For example, women comprise approximately 60 million of the 180 million available television viewers in the U.S. (110 million households x 2.2 people per household). If the audience for a particular program was comprised of an equal number of men, women, and children, and its national rating was a 15, then 5 rating points would be associated with women. If the product being advertised was a hair color formula specifically for women, then the only viewers who mattered to that advertiser would be represented by those 5 rating points.

For an advertiser with a national budget, a single commercial would hardly be effective. In television advertising, a commercial must be seen many times in order for a viewer to take notice, and more times in order for him or her to take action. Rather than buying just one commercial worth 5 rating points, the advertiser would more likely buy 500 rating points associated with the target audience. To put this another way, the media buyer is purchasing 500 gross rating points, or a GRP of 500.

How much should the media buyer pay for those points? Should the price per point be the same for each commercial placement? When a program is successful, its cost per spot is typically high, and when a program's audience is smaller, the cost per spot is typically lower. During the 2004 season of *Law & Order*, the price per 30-second spot was about $225,000. Given its 10.2 rating, the cost per rating point was $22,000. By comparison, the 30-second spots on *Everybody Loves Raymond* went for $315,000; divide by its 12.3 rating, and the cost per ratings point was nearly $26,000. The costs per spot and per rating point are generally lower during the daytime hours, as well as on many cable networks. With 500 GRPs to buy, this $10 million negotiation would likely level out at about $20,000 per point, in part because of the number of points purchased, and probably because some lower-priced shows would be negotiated into the mix.

Reach and frequency are the key to successful media buying. *Reach* captures the concept of a message finding its way to an appropriate audience. *Frequency* is the number of times that each household within the target is likely to see the commercial. Television advertising is most effective with relatively high frequency levels (sometimes to a point of diminishing returns, sometimes not).

## Cable Ratings

In the 1985–1986 season, total cable rating points for prime time rarely exceeded 5 points—at a time when ABC, CBS, and NBC each scored a rough average of 15 points. Today, the total cable rating is about 30 points, and each of the network's ratings is around 6 points. The steady growth of cable viewership has accompanied a comparable decline in viewership of ABC, CBS, and NBC—although certainly, FOX, UPN, The WB, the Internet, video games, and DVDs have also impacted the broadcast networks' ratings. In terms of audience share, cable now claims about 45 percent of the audience, and the larger networks claim about the same amount (the remainder is either watching public television, pay television networks, or prerecorded media).

Significant cable audience measurement occurs only on the national level; local markets are meaningful only for the local cable advertising market (see page 80), which is not yet a significant force in the industry. Data on cable viewing is gathered through the same diaries, electronic meters, and People Meters used to collect information on national broadcast television viewing.

The most successful cable series typically score a national rating of about 3. One clear difference between cable and broadcast ratings is that many of the highest rated shows are not schedule in prime time. Instead, Nickelodeon routinely dominates the list of top shows with Saturday and Sunday morning programming watched by an average of 3 million households. A week before our sample week in late November 2004, the Saturday morning airing of *SpongeBob SquarePants* on Nickelodeon was the highest-rated regularly scheduled show with a 2.9 rating, watched by 3.2 million households. The Saturday evening airing of *Law & Order: SVU* on USA Network got a 2.8 rating and was watched by 3.1 million homes.

## Syndicated Program Ratings

Nielsen's syndication service (previously called Cassandra) provides data on individual syndicated programs. In addition to household and demographic data, this service reports comparative information regarding lead-ins (programs that precede another program, presumably bringing some of their viewers to the subsequent show), as well as competitive history. These statistics are developed on a market-by-market basis, but their cumulative nationwide results are frequently used to compare the relative ratings success of syndicated programs. At the end of every sweeps period, Nielsen provides rankings of syndicated shows.

# CHAPTER 10
# NETWORK TELEVISION ADVERTISING

In the early days of television, advertisers often bought *full sponsorships*. For example, Revlon was the sole or principal sponsor of *The $64,000 Question*, and even into the 1960s, it was not uncommon to see the name of the sponsor in the title of the series: *Kraft Music Hall*, *The Bell Telephone Hour*, and so on. The tradition continues with the Hallmark Hall of Fame movie series and with the occasional high-profile motion picture presented, often without commercial interruption, by a car company. Some sponsors have long associations with public television programs as well.

Somewhat more common in today's marketplace is the *participating sponsorship*, in which a small group of advertisers will buy most or all of the available advertising within a particular program or series (Major League Baseball's World Series, for example). Often, the advertisers receive more than commercial time; they also receive "billboards" at the top of the show, alongside the program's introduction.

The most common type of advertising in today's television, however, is based upon campaigns that place an advertiser's commercials throughout the schedule and on many networks.

## THE UPFRONT MARKET

When buying broadcast and cable network programming, media buyers seek a cumulative audience offering the desired demographics, psychographics (see page 159), and geographic skew.

### Network Prime Time

Immediately after each network's program department announces the prime-time schedule for the fall season, the network sales departments begin selling commercial time "up front" on those programs. They offer advertisers approximately 65 to 75 percent of prime-time available spots ("avails") at a 15 percent discount. This prime-time upfront buying season generally begins in May (or as early as March for Saturday morning children's programming and for other day-parts) and goes through early July.

The advertising agency's media planning department, in conjunction with the account group and media buyers, works closely with each client, and eventually makes recommendations on the best way to reach the target audience. The advertising agency then registers the client's budget with the network, along with a request for a package of shows that reach the client's target audience. The network sales department responds with a proposal detailing the number of spots available, the programs, and their air dates. Based on estimates of how the package will perform, the network and the agency negotiate a cost per thousand viewers (CPM), which may actually be cost per thousand households if only one viewer in each household is in the proper demographic category. The network and advertiser also work out the details: the list of shows, the dates on which the spots will appear, and the probable rating.

Negotiations are staged on several fronts. For instance, the advertiser can commit to the length of the campaign, but the degree of commitment can vary. If the client commits to 52 weeks, the deal is likely to be more flexible than a deal for a smaller commitment. A deal might include the option to cancel up to 25 percent of the order for first quarter, for example. Rates are likely to be lower if the advertiser buys more time overall, or more time in less desirable shows. Or, the agency may want more units within specific programs—"Can you give me one more *Without a Trace* and take out a *JAG*?"—or may require a lower CPM to compensate for potentially low ratings (which translate into a missed opportunity to reach some viewers). When a provisional deal is made, the time is reserved, and the network will not sell that inventory within a specified number of days. In the interim, the agency presents the package to the client for approval. The client usually approves, but only after discussing problems with the deal: the cost is higher than it should be, the program mix is not right, and such. As a rule, a hold on network time is a commitment; held time is rarely released.

When negotiating in the upfront market, the cost per rating point is useful information as the basis for deal-making; deals, often in the hundreds of millions of dollars, are made on the basis of guaranteed gross rating points (GRPs) within specific demographics, and within certain programs on the schedule. There is risk on both sides, particularly with regard to placement of commercials in new programs. Working from the estimated ratings, the network guarantees to deliver a minimum number of GRPs within a specific demographic, and if a new or existing program fails to deliver, then the network makes good on its commitment, adding rating points by placing additional commercials in other programs ("make-goods") to make up the difference. The new shows and dates, however, may not be desirable ones, or may not otherwise meet the client's needs. A successful agency avoids make-goods by accurately estimating and buying time in programs for which the anticipated ratings and the actual ratings are most likely to be similar.

If a program delivers a *greater* number of rating points than anticipated, then one of three things happens: (1) The advertiser walks away happy (this is the most common scenario, as the networks tend to avoid annoying their best customers), or (2) the over-performance becomes a negotiating chit, to be employed as needed, or, most often in today's more aggressive business environment, (3) the network commits to a specific number of GRPs for the season, and when the commitment is satisfied, the remaining commercial time is sold to other advertisers. This places enormous pressure on programming departments and producers, since higher ratings immediately translate into additional rating points, and with enough rating points, commitments can be more rapidly satisfied, allowing more inventory units to be sold.

A client with a $10 million network prime-time budget might assign $3 million to $4 million to each network. The average cost of a spot works out to about $125,000, so the client's budget would probably buy 80 prime-time spots. A spot on a top-rated show costs roughly $300,000 to $400,000; a spot on a lower-rated show with comparatively weak performance, about $75,000.

For the networks, the upfront market provides an opportunity to sell the majority of its available inventory in a highly competitive environment. The benefit of the upfront buy is that the revenue is booked; the downsides are the 15 percent discount offered and the need to make good on programs that did not perform as hoped or planned. For the client, the upfront buy assures the best possible commercial positions, and saves money, but the prospect of make-goods can put the client in the position of having commercials run on the wrong shows.

It is not unusual for a major network to sell as much as 80 percent of its inventory during the upfront season. Overall, the upfront market is worth about $8 billion. The major networks take in about $1 billion to $2 billion each.

## Daytime, News, and Sports

In fact, the upfront concept has worked so well for prime time that it has been expanded into daytime and network news and extended to include cable advertising. (Cable's 2003 upfront sales were worth $6 billion. The syndication upfront market is worth about $2 billion.)

Compared with the cost of prime time, advertising on daytime is inexpensive. The CPM for women under 50 years of age during daytime (about $5, on average) is roughly 25 percent of the CPM for the same group during prime time (about $20). Daytime television still delivers a relatively "pure" audience of women under 50. While maintaining traditional ties with household, food, and other longtime daypart advertisers, networks have been wooing new types of sponsors (e.g., automotive companies) into daytime, with only limited success.

The upfront buying season for network news also takes place during the summer. Most advertisers buy time on the news because it is the best way to reach the 25–54 and 55-plus groups.

The key concept for sports programs, from the perspective of large national advertisers, is exclusivity. Spots in major national events are sold on an exclusive basis within product categories. In automotive, one of the larger categories for sports advertising, the general rule is one domestic and one foreign automotive sponsor. Beer, soft drinks, and fast food may also be subject to exclusive buys. Many exclusivity agreements are negotiated well in advance, often for more than one year. Because of the pervasiveness of exclusivity, the idea of an upfront buying season is not as strict here as in other parts of network television. The sales department gets to work selling time shortly after rights to sports events are purchased. Many sports programs are sold on a series basis: some or all of the baseball or football season, for example. A sponsor with one or more spots in each game is called a "strip sponsor." A spot participant can also buy time in individual events, although most spots are not sold individually, but instead as part of a package.

Among network events, the weekly NFL broadcasts are the best performers; the cost of a spot on a regular telecast is over $500,000 per 30-second spot (a 30-second spot on the Super Bowl costs over $1 million dollars. The cost of an average prime-time spot, by comparison, is approximately $170,000. A spot during a sports event with somewhat less appeal, such as a weekend bowling match, would cost about $20,000. Much of this is dependent upon the competitive market environment; in a very soft market, these rates drop by as much as 50 percent.

## The Scatter Market and Spot Sales

Of course, the upfront market is not the only opportunity for advertisers to purchase time. The "scatter" market opens several days before the start of the new quarter, offering negotiated packages of sold inventory. Although the available inventory may vary in terms of quality, this market is often more effective than the third and least desirable means of purchasing, the "spot" market, in which individual commercial slots are sold as available. In theory, an attentive media buyer can snatch good deals in the scatter and spot markets because the inventory is perishable: Once the time passes, if the slot is not filled with a commercial, the network makes no money at all. In practice, the network uses these spots to fulfill GRP commitments from the upfront market, and also offers its best customers the best opportunities. Still, a skillful media buyer can play the market with good results.

When a media buyer is ready to negotiate price, the time of year may be as significant as the rating. A media buyer planning for a political campaign, for example, would find spots to be far less valuable in July than in late October. Similarly, for many consumer products, time in mid-December is far more valuable than time in February.

Makers of automotive products are, by a large margin, the largest buyers of spot TV. The next two categories (foods and consumer services such as telephone companies) are about one-third as large. Advertising categories worth $1 billion or more to network television include automotive (mostly automobile manufacturers), proprietary medicines (aspirins, cold and flu remedies, etc.), food and food products, toiletries and toilet goods, restaurants (mostly fast food), and consumer services (mostly telephone, some online).

## TRENDS

There are a lot of ways of taking a snapshot of a television audience. One day's worth of data makes interesting newspaper copy and *USA Today* charts, but researchers tend not to look at data in that way. It's far more important to analyze audience trends over time. Trend analysis provides networks with a clear picture of a program's performance within a specific demographic, often with other factors—competition, lead-in, overall performance of the night's programming, amount of promotion, related news stories—reported in alignment with the trend's peaks and valleys. This information is then used to renew or cancel programs, and to make long-term media buying decisions.

# CHAPTER 11

# LOCAL TELEVISION ADVERTISING

The rating and share information detailed in Chapter 9 relates to the national television audience. For many advertisers, the purchase of time on local stations can provide a higher concentration of desirable viewers.

Four times each year—in November, February, May, and July—Nielsen measures local station viewership. Stations and networks are well aware of these measurement periods, so they pack schedules with programming that's likely to score higher-than-normal ratings. Why? Because the ratings information collected during these "sweeps" periods sets advertisement pricing for the remaining months of the year. (As People Meters become commomnplace, this situation may eventually change.)

## MANAGING INVENTORY

Two types of advertising buys ("inventory") are available on local stations: (1) time slots that the network leaves open for affiliates during and between its own programs, and (2) slots that are available on syndicated and local shows.

The cost of these commercial spots is tied, in a general way, to ratings. The most popular shows usually command the highest prices, but this is not always the case. Local sales managers exercise considerable flexibility over their inventory. They can price each spot according to market conditions, and they routinely change their prices. It's a game—sell the inventory at the highest possible price before it expires—but a game that must be played carefully. If prices are reduced at the last minute because a sales manager needs to close a month with additional revenues, then advertisers will learn to wait until the end of the month before they buy time. The objective is not simply to sell the current inventory, but to develop long-term client relationships with advertisers whose sales improve as a result of television exposure.

ABC, CBS, and NBC affiliates have less time available for sale locally than affiliates to UPN or WB (FOX is somewhere in between). Most of the affiliates' avails are in news or syndicated programs. A network affiliate's weekday inventory of 30-second spots totals about 200 units (somewhat higher during political campaigns). A station's inventory is further reduced by barter transactions: in essence, a syndicator provides a program at no charge to the station but trades for, or "holds back," some ad slots—say, four-and-a-half of perhaps six or six-and-a-half minutes of commercial time (the actual ratio varies by program and by deal).

Approximately 30 percent of FOX, WB, or UPN stations' commercial revenues typically pay for barter programming; for network affiliates, the number is lower, usually about 20 percent. It is common for a station to trade airtime for goods; if, for example, a station needs cars, it might trade $50,000 of airtime for a like amount in automobiles from a local dealer. This practice is also common for office furniture and in deals with restaurants and hotels, and is not limited to trades within the station's local area. Complicated barter transactions involving multiple stations have become common; some stations like them, others do not. Of course, stations generally prefer to receive cash for their commercial time, since local sale of commercial time accounts for 30 to 40 percent of a station's revenues, depending upon market size.

## SALES MANAGERS AND REP FIRMS

The station's local sales manager handles sales to local clients, taking orders from established customers and presenting new packages based on well-known advertiser needs. In the largest markets, a very high percentage of sales is made through advertising agencies.

Regional or national advertisers who want to buy time in a local market work with each station's national sales representative, or "rep firm," to negotiate prices and time slots. Reps work exclusively for one station in each market, and operate as extensions of the station's sales staff. The station's rep firm receives a call from an advertising agency whose client needs to buy time on a certain station. The rep firm then meets with the station's national sales manager to assemble a competitive package based on the dates, the cost of reaching the target audience, and the dayparts that the agency wants to buy on its client's behalf. The agency and the rep firm negotiate, and the station receives an order.

Rep firms often account for more than 50 percent of the station's sales. These sales are often commissioned at 6 to 10 percent—less than the amount that would be paid to the station's internal sales staff. In addition, nearly all of the sales made by rep firms are associated with advertising agencies or media buyers, who typically extract a 15 percent commission. This is less often true of local sales, where deals are more often made directly with local businesses—and without an advertising agency commission.

Rep firms do more than sell advertising time; they also advise their clients as to which syndicated programs are the most promising. Many station groups are now selling their own local spots, effectively replacing a rep firm by doing the work in-house. This situation has allowed rep firms to work with more than one station in each market—a clear break with a long-standing tradition.

## COMMERCIAL RATES

Even within a single market, there is considerable variation in the cost of commercial spots. As a starting point, the cost is based on the number of people who see the show—or, more accurately, on Nielsen's estimate of viewership. The price also depends upon the available inventory; how anxious the sales manager is to sell off the time; the prices charged by the competition; the size of the overall package and its component parts; the anticipated ratings; and the skill of the sales staff. In prime time, the networks typically provide about two minutes per hour for local sale. In New York City and Los Angeles, the nation's largest markets, the average local spot during major network prime time costs about $10,000 to $15,000. On a hit series, where demand is high, the cost per spot can be as much as $100,000. Spots on the 6:00 P.M. news cost about $3,000, and on the 11:00 P.M. news, about twice as much. A large network affiliate is likely to gross more than $300 million in annual advertising sales. In a top-20 market, the gross is more likely in the $400 million to $800 million range. The primary determinant of annual earnings is not ratings performance, but the number of available viewers within any given market.

The prices for commercial spots are based upon each program's ratings. When an advertising media planner determines how best to market a product, he or she orders the purchase of a certain number of gross rating points in a particular market. The media buyer then purchases programs whose ratings equate to the GRP formula (see page 74), and generally spreads the buy so that it favors stations whose programs suit the demographic requirements of the media plan. A product seeking a younger audience, for example, might be best served by purchasing time on a cable network such as FOX.

## FROM THE ADVERTISER'S PERSPECTIVE

The process of placing national advertising on local stations begins with a media plan—a strategic breakout for the entire year. The client determines the plan's broad requirements; the advertising agency refines the strategy, produces the commercials, and buys the time.

Once the list of target markets is determined by agency and client, the agency contacts some or all of the stations in each market (often through a rep firm) and makes an avail request. Specifically, this might be a buy for the first quarter, favoring men 18–49, requiring 700 GRPs per week, distributed 30 percent in prime time, 15 percent in early fringe (before evening news), 15 percent in late fringe (after late news), and 40 percent in daytime. The avail request might also specify the amount of money that the advertiser is willing to pay: $200 per rating point in early fringe and $350 in prime time, for example.

In trying to reach all of the viewers in a given market, the agency purchases time on most or all of the stations. Each station responds to the avail request, and then the negotiations begin, often with the involvement of a national rep firm. Stations agree to sell some spots, but hold back others in anticipation of higher rates from other advertisers. For example, an advertiser who needs to reach teenagers may be willing to pay a premium for a spot in *The Simpsons*, while an advertiser with more general needs might also buy *The Simpsons* but not at a premium price. The station's sales manager makes decisions not only on price, however. Since advertising time is perishable, it may be wiser to sell for 75 percent of the desired rate than to wait and have the time unsold. There is no highest or lowest available rate; rates are based entirely on supply and demand.

Although some stations publish rate cards, the consensus is that rates are generally negotiable. Rates in published directories are based on polls of media buyers nationwide, and they can be a useful starting point for negotiations. This marketplace changes rapidly, however, so rates are likely to be out-of-date soon after publication.

Stations are expected to report or "post" results. If the station sold commercial time based on an average 4 rating, and the program gets only a 2 rating, then the station arranges a make-good for the advertiser in the form of additional advertising time. Stations do not refund money paid for advertising, and a good sales manager ensures important clients' success on his or her station by filling open commercial slots with additional client spots, at no charge. This is generally preferable to using the commercial time for per-inquiry advertising (see page 184) or for direct-response advertising (see page 82).

Unlike broadcast and cable network television, there is no upfront buying season associated with local television. Spots are sold as little as 24 hours in advance, but most are sold weeks, months, or quarters in advance of scheduled airing. Annual deals between key stations and key advertisers are common.

In most local markets, automotive advertising is the largest category, representing perhaps one-third of sales. In the largest markets, buying is done by the brand (area Ford dealers, for example) because the cost of effective advertising is too large for an individual dealer. In smaller markets, and on smaller stations in larger markets, individual dealers are significant accounts. In the largest markets, retail (usually department stores) are also very large advertisers, as are lottery, movies, and other entertainment clients. Local banks, credit cards, and insurance companies also advertise heavily on local television. Pharmaceutical advertising, on the other hand, tends to be national because their direct-to-consumer spots require more detailed information in national print magazines. .

In many markets, the concept of *value-added selling* is popular. Stations sell not only airtime, but involvement in station promotions as well. This approach is often used to encourage advertisers who do not typically advertise on television. A Christmas tree-lighting ceremony, a prostate cancer awareness campaign, or a marathon race can all provide unique marketing opportunities as part of many stations' strategies.

## DIRECT-RESPONSE ADVERTISING

Direct-response advertising, used mainly for the sale of magazine subscriptions, books, and records, allows stations to fill unsold time. Direct-response advertisers pay reduced rates for standby positions within a "wide rotator"—a large chunk of the schedule. If the station is sold out, the spots don't run.

Many stations do not run direct-response or per-inquiry advertising. Instead, they fill open time with promos, encouraging viewers to watch other shows on the schedule, or with public-service announcements that fulfill FCC public-service mandates.

# CHAPTER 12

# NEW APPROACHES TO TELEVISION ADVERTISING

The popularity of cable television and home video has complicated the audience measurement process. Many viewers, armed with remote controls, bounce back and forth between numerous broadcast and cable channels within limited periods. In just one minute, a viewer armed with a remote control can easily sample a dozen channels. Were this easily measured and reported, the value of the information would be dubious at best. For example, a viewer who is more or less simultaneously viewing three or four programs would be difficult to count for advertising purposes; indeed, it is often the ads that are skipped.

Home video also presents a special challenge for audience measurement. Normally, broadcast and cable viewing data is collected by noting the channel number, either from the viewer's diary entries or by connecting a meter to the television's tuner. As for *time-shifting* (recording broadcast or cable programs for viewing at a later date), People Meter systems can measure a program as it is being recorded, but cannot determine whether it is actually watched, or how many times. In order to collect data on other aspects of home video, it is necessary to know the name of the software being played—be it a video game, a video-cassette, or a DVD—and how it is being used. Manual identification of video is relatively simple (a viewer need only write down a title), but this information cannot be verified. More reliable electronic identification requires an embedded code on every piece of software and a reading mechanism connected to the video game or VCR.

## NIELSEN'S A/P METERING SYSTEM

In 2004, Nielsen slowly began a national rollout of just such an identification system: the Active/Passive Metering System (A/P Metering). The A/P Meter employs one sensor located near each TV set in the household. Each sensor reads codes embedded in the audio and video signals. To make this work, every program or commercial (and even every video game) must be tagged with a unique embedded code. If there is no code, the A/P Meter records part of the audio and video track, then sends this digital sample back to Nielsen for matching against a catalog. Future versions are expected to measure DVR (digital video recorder) usage and other new technologies.

Identification is only part of the issue, though. If a videocassette contains a commercial, a sponsor needs to know if the commercial was viewed, how many times, and whether it was viewed at standard speed or at a faster speed.

As television changes, audience measurement must change as well. Dozens of channels are becoming hundreds. VCRs and DVRs make possible time-shift viewing and scanning through commercials. Digital communications will enable more viewership options, in terms of not only the program watched but also the format (widescreen, high-definition, standard resolution, and so forth). Convergence with computers and telephones will allow interactive television. Audience measurement in this rapidly changing environment, where even the definition of the term "program" is questionable, will change all of the rules. This is not a wild-eyed future; in some form, it is a future that is emerging today.

## PRODUCT PLACEMENTS

When television was young, advertisers often required more than just commercials to market their products. On some situation comedies, for example, the characters were seen using the sponsor's products. During variety shows, it was not unusual for the star performer to appear in a live commercial, pitching floor wax or a soft drink. On game shows, contestants' podiums were often decorated with sponsor logos. In short, the advertisers' messages were a part of the show.

This approach was reborn in the late 1990s with a conception called *product placement*. On older programs, boxes of cereal or other products are digitally inserted into certain scenes. On new programs, the sponsor pays a product placement fee to the producer and to the network in exchange for integration in the content of the program. Nielsen, only one of several services offering tracking services, now measures product placement by asking viewers a number of questions—Who is the sponsor? What is being advertised or promoted? When and where are the placements seen?—and reporting on the answers

For advertisers, producers, and networks, there is not yet a meaningful, ratings-like measurement tool for the pricing of product placement. Nor is there a standard unit to be bought or sold, like a 30-second spot. Instead, every deal is a negotiation with many gray areas. For example, consider the inclusion of a Coca-Cola product within a sitcom: Does the price differ if the container is a can or a bottle or a large cup with an easily seen logo? What is the relative difference in price if the Coca-Cola is held versus being enjoyed by a lead character? What if a secondary character takes a swig instead, or in addition? What is the price if the product is mentioned by name? And so on.

To date, most deals for inclusion in network series have been in the range of hundreds of thousands of dollars, with some in the $1 million to $5 million range. A relatively small number of advertisers currently participate, but many more are either experimenting or anticipating some placement in the near future. This type of advertising has a lot of buzz behind it, and it is growing rapidly. In the statistics-bound advertising industry, it seems likely that a meaningful measurement system will evolve as product placement becomes a more commonplace media buy.

# CHAPTER 13
# ADVERTISING AGENCIES

A full-service advertising agency provides its clients with consumer and market research, as well as the development, implementation, and evaluation of advertising strategies and campaigns. Agencies typically provide a higher level of creative services and media-buying skills than their clients maintain in-house.

The largest clients tend to work with the largest advertising agencies. As is the case with media companies, advertising agencies have become quite sizable and powerful through consolidation; many now operate as global enterprises. Smaller agency offices in key cities serve client needs, but each client also has access to the media-buying clout associated with the larger agency. Many large agencies also own smaller, boutique-style agencies that specialize in specific market segments, such as the youth or college market, or the Hispanic audience. Some boutiques focus exclusively upon creative campaigns; others specialize only in media buying. Many agencies also own one or more public relations firms and, often, a promotional marketing company to develop sweepstakes, street team campaigns, tie-ins, and other unconventional approaches.

The largest agencies bill over $1 billion per year, mainly as a result of buying expensive network television time for their clients and producing costly television commercials to play in these time slots—for example, Johnson & Johnson and PepsiCo are both half-billion-dollar accounts. Some large companies work primarily with one agency, while others work with several—each agency handles one or more of the company's brands. The latter approach allows each brand to be served by the agency best suited to its needs.

Network television, including ABC, CBS, NBC, FOX, UPN, WB, and PAX, sold $47 billion in advertising for 2004. In addition, syndicated television sold nearly $4 billion in advertising, and local broadcast television generated sales revenues of over $18 million in the top 100 markets. Cable television accounts for about $20 billion in ad revenues per year.

In 2002, GM was television's top advertiser, spending nearly $1.5 billion for commercials in network, spot, cable, and syndicated programs. Procter & Gamble spent about $1 billion, followed by DaimlerChrysler and AOL Time Warner in the $900 million range, Philip Morris (now Altria, which owns Kraft) at about $800 million, Ford at about $700 million, and Disney at just over $600 million. Johnson & Johnson, Pfizer, McDonald's, PepsiCo, and General Mills were roughly in the same league. Far more advertisers spend between $100 million and $200 million; 50 of the top 100 television advertisers spent in this range that year.

Network television remains the champ in terms of large expenditures. The top 25 network television advertisers each spent between $175 million and $660 million in 2002. The amounts in cable television were about half as much, and the amounts spent for syndicated programs were a quarter the size of network expenditures.

A closer look at Ford, consistently one of television's top advertisers, reveals 2003 spending for network television at $449 million, spot TV at $277 million, syndicated TV at $12 million, cable TV networks at $105 million, and Spanish-language TV at $26 million for a total of $869 million in television spending—roughly one-third of Ford's total U.S. advertising budget of $2.2 billion. Magazine and newspaper advertising combined represented $478 million, just under half as much as Ford spent on television. Other expenditures were spread over outdoor/billboard ($10 million); radio ($32 million), Internet ($26 million), Yellow Pages ($22 million); and business publications ($7 million). All that advertising paid off: In 2003, Ford's worldwide sales were $164 billion.

## BUSINESS MODEL

An advertising agency makes money in three ways.

First, the agency receives a commission on every media buy. In today's world, large clients negotiate long-term deals with their agencies based loosely on a commission of 15 percent (or less). For example, the agency would actually buy a 30-second spot for $850, bill the client for $1,000, and retain $150 as a commission. If client billings total $1 million for a year, the agency retains $150,000 in commissions. The agency's commission or fee structure can be negotiated as part of the client-agency agreement.

Using the Ford example, Zubi Advertising Services provided both media-buying and advertising services for the Hispanic markets. On Spanish-language television alone, where Ford's 2003 ad spending was $26 million, it would be reasonable to assume a 15 percent commission (or nearly $4 million) for Zubi. Ford is one of many companies that now buy their own media (through advertising division Ford Motor Media), but the deal between Ford and its national agency, Ogilvy & Mather Worldwide, is confidential. Every account has its own particular structure, with some functions in-house, others out-of-house, and some with peculiar arrangements. Still, the standard-percentage commission for a media-buying deal is the key to the financial stability of the advertising agency world.

Second, the agency may receive a fee for its services, often a monthly retainer that the client will pay in addition to, in lieu of, or in combination with the agency's commissions. The monthly retainer generally reflects the number of hours spent by members of the account and creative teams working on the assignment. For example, a designer earning $1,000 per week might spend half of her time on a certain account, or 20 hours per week. This time is billed at approximately three times the labor cost; the markup covers taxes, benefits, operations, overhead, supervisory management, and other related expenses, as well as profit. So the client is billed $1,500 for the artist's 20 hours of work per week. Unlike legal charges, this billing is based not on the time logged by any one or two persons, but upon a reasonable estimate of the hours spent by the team assembled for and assigned to a given project.

Third, the agency receives a percentage of production costs. When the agency arranges for the production of a commercial or series of commercials, it bills the client for the cost of production. In addition, the agency often receives a markup on production costs, typically about 10 percent.

## AGENCY ORGANIZATION

An advertising agency is typically organized in three basic groups.

*Creative services* develops the advertising concepts, refines them as required by the account team and the client, then produces the commercials and other materials. A creative director is the senior person on the creative team; one creative director may be responsible for several accounts. The team also consists of an art director, designers, and a copywriter.

*Account services* is responsible for client relations. This group's account executives work with the writers, designers, creative directors, copy directors, and art directors in creative services to assure that the client's needs are met, the storyboards and commercials are consistent with the marketing strategy, and production is proceeding in accordance with the client's requirements and budget limitations. The account executive is the senior person on the account team; one account supervisor usually manages several accounts.

*Media services* negotiates for airtime and other media buys on the client's behalf. Media services is also the source of detailed market and audience research. The data and the accompanying analysis are used to plan creative strategies and campaigns, and to intelligently buy media that will reach the optimum demographic and psychographic audience.

An advertising agency's senior executives are typically concerned with maintaining good relationships with existing clients and bringing new clients into the agency. Agency executives have historically been former account executives and creative directors. As media buying has become critical to agency revenue and success, former media buyers are also becoming agency executives.

Other agency departments are comparable to those found in any sort of company: accounting, human resources, information technology, facilities management, and so on.

## MEDIA-BUYING DECISIONS

For a media buyer planning a national campaign, television is often part of the mix. The environment has been changing and continues to change, and in general, the media buyer must keep a close eye on audience fragmentation, alternative forms of advertising and marketing, and new technologies. Still, if you're charged with selling Tide or Coca-Cola or a new Toyota, or a major motion picture, television is almost certainly going to be a part of the media-buying plan.

There are several reasons why television may be an appropriate buying decision. The first, and perhaps the most obvious, is that television commercials allow images to move and make whatever noises are necessary to sell the product. Television is simply a better way to sell products than radio (no images), magazines (no noise or movement), outdoor billboard advertising (no noise or movement), or motion pictures (less reliable audience measurement, unpredictable demographic mix). Television time can be purchased on a national, regional, local, or extra-local basis. What's more, television reaches viewers in their own homes, with advertisements appearing either within or adjacent to programs that people choose to watch with focused attention.

Television advertising has its drawbacks as well. The cost of producing a television commercial is routinely higher than the cost of producing advertising materials for radio, print, billboards, or other media. Clutter is an issue, too. There are just too many commercials, so it's difficult to be noticed, even if the "flight" includes many plays of the same commercial. Ultimately, the success of the media buys will be measured by other market research. Specifically, a market research firm specializing in the retail sector will determine whether sales increased or shifted, or whether market share improved, as a result of the television advertising campaign (and other factors that may have supported the campaign).

### Media Planning

The process begins by identifying a target audience, and then determining the most effective media to reach this audience. Television competes with radio, newspapers, outdoor advertising, and promotional opportunities. The first consideration is *reach*—the statistics related to finding the target audience within a defined geographic area. The second consideration is *frequency*—the number of messages that this audience will receive over a specific period of time.

The key to successful media buying is effectiveness within the target demographic. For example, assume a campaign whose target is 100 percent men, ages 18–24. If a media buyer purchases commercial time on a program watched by

100 percent men ages 18–24, then the buy is "optimal." More likely, the best available program will offer 80 percent men 18–24, with the remaining 20 percent of viewers scattered among younger and older men, and some women—then the buy is "efficient," but not optimal. If the buy is only 50 percent effective, then it might be said that the buyer is paying twice the CPM in order to reach that same target audience.

These calculations provide only a glimpse into the complexity associated with contemporary media buying. Algorithms are useful, but their utility is always swamped by the marketplace realities of negotiated pricing. In other words, a network or local advertising salesperson, hoping to bring in or build on a client relationship, or make a month's quota, may offer deals that simply do not fit easily into the somewhat rigid world of data analysis. It's an interesting balance: extremely detailed data manipulation meets the high-flying world of advertising sales.

## PRODUCING TELEVISION COMMERICALS

Although most viewers are numbed by the sheer volume of messages coming from their television each day, a great deal of research, strategy, discussion, creative activity, and money goes into the production of every campaign in order to cause consumers to buy the product or service, or to remember the product the very next time they go shopping.

Typically, the campaign comes about as the result of a specific marketing initiative. The initiative may involve the introduction of a new product or a product based upon an existing brand name. If the product is backed by enough money to buy television time, it has likely come about as a result of substantial market research, focus groups, consumer testing, and so on. The person in command is a brand manager, charged with either launching a new product or improving the sales or market share of an existing product. In each of these situations, the brand manager will be clear on some essential information necessary for a successful campaign, such as the intended target market, the pricing, and the distribution avenues. If the product is new, it may not yet have a name, a logo, or a package design.

The advertising agency may be new or may have a history with the client. In either situation, the first step is to review all that is known about the product, the customer, the market, the competition, the distribution, and the strategy. The agency begins its work by uncovering questions or issues that may have seemed unimportant or obscured from the client's point of view. Then the agency does some market research of its own to learn more about the open issues. In time, as a result of numerous internal meetings at the agency, one or more creative directions emerge. These concepts are then explained to the client, usually with the help of a storyboard and other media materials. This "pitch" meeting typically results in the selection of one idea from a set of three possible directions. Budgets for production and media buying may be discussed in a general way; specifics are worked out after the creative direction becomes clear.

The agency and the client work out the tactical aspects of the campaign: Will the commercial run nationally or in specific markets? Will there be one commercial or several? What are the budget trade-offs and the creative trade-offs? Over the course of several weeks, the storyboards are finalized and readied to send out for various directors and production companies to bid on.

Some commercials are produced directly by the advertising agency, but many are outsourced to production companies led by directors who specialize in commercial production. The approved storyboard is often submitted to three such companies, each of whom offers wisdom and creative ideas in hopes of getting hired. Only one is hired, but the ideas are freely used if they make sense, typically without compensation of the companies who did not get the job. The choice of director and production company is often based upon reputation, previous experience with the client and/or with similar work, the quality of the director or company's "reel" (past work, now more often distributed via DVD), and whether the director can work within the available budget range. Budgets vary depending upon the campaign and the client's needs; the average is in the low $200,000 range.

The director works with the agency on casting, scripting, and the choice of crew and locations. A national spot generally requires several weeks of pre-production: designing and building sets; choosing locations; composing, arranging, and recording music; and attending to the many small details that are part of any video production. The shoot itself usually lasts between one and three days for one or more commercials. Some spots require more time if the commercial is more elaborate. The client often attends the shoot, delicately balancing his or her role as company representative with a supportive role that encourages the creative and production teams to do their best work—sometimes, these two goals conflict.

Production is completed in the editing room (where scenes are assembled and graphics are added) and in the sound-editing room (where the voice-over, sound effects, and music are added, and where the soundtrack is mixed and equalized).

## Testing Commercials

For most campaigns, several different commercials are produced and then tested by being shown to various groups of people who buy similar products. Commercials are analyzed on the basis of their appeal to specific demographic, psychographic, and geographic groups. While a network spot must appeal to the widest possible audience within a specific target category (such as children), many spots are produced with narrower national audiences in mind—urban black viewers, for example. Other spots are produced for specific regions where certain product preferences are already strong or need strengthening. A commercial should test successfully before it is placed on the air. While remakes can be quite expensive, the long-term cost of the commercial time—and the potential effect of a successful campaign on a product's market penetration and market share—can more than justify the additional expenditure.

# CHAPTER 14
# REGULATION OF ADVERTISING

American television advertising is subject to rules and regulations at a number of different levels. Content can be scrutinized and controlled, principally by the Federal Trade Commission at the federal level and by a variety of governmental authorities at the state and local levels. There are also a limited number of rules, enforced by the FCC, regarding the amounts and types of advertising carried on broadcast stations, cable, and other FCC-regulated media. Finally, there is regulation by the industry itself: Stations, networks, and cable companies all have their own standards on what they will accept. In addition, there are industry groups, made up of advertising agencies and their clients, which suggest certain codes of practice.

## THE FTC AND CONTROL OF ADVERTISING

The Federal Trade Commission (FTC) is the government's principal overseer of the content and methods of advertising; in fact, it regulates advertising across all fields of publication—not just television. The FTC is an independent agency, like the FCC (see Chapter 5), with five commissioners nominated by the president and confirmed by Congress.

When the FTC was set up in 1912, its principal intended purpose was to regulate in the area of antitrust law, an area in which it remains involved. The legislation that established the FTC, however, included the power to regulate unfair business practices, and from the beginning, this jurisdiction was held to cover false advertising. The FTC's power to control false advertising has been confirmed and expanded by congressional action in the years since, most importantly by the Wheeler-Lea Act in 1938. Section 5(a)(1) of the Federal Trade Commission Act now prohibits both "unfair methods of competition in commerce" and "unfair or deceptive acts or practices in commerce," and the Act gives the FTC the power to intervene and prevent both. These phrases have been interpreted to include false, misleading, or deceptive advertising. The "commerce" referred to in the Act is interstate commerce or international commerce; a finding of interstate commerce will generally be made in the case of an advertisement delivered via a television station, a cable or satellite service, or the Internet.

The Federal Trade Commission Improvement Act of 1975 gave the FTC authorization to establish industry-wide trade rules over and above the prevention of deceptive advertising. One consequence of the 1975 Act was the FTC's proposal of extensive restrictions on children's advertising on television. The proposal was not only controversial at the time, but also became an oft-cited example of burdensome overregulation. Continuing concern about children's television led Congress to enact, in 1990, a set of laws governing many aspects of children's television (see page 293). There are a number of other laws administered by the FTC with application to the advertising of specific kinds of products and services, such as consumer lending and cigarettes.

The backlash against regulation that started in the 1980s and has continued into the twenty-first century has affected the FTC as well, and the Commission's power to set industry-wide trade rules on advertising fairness is now more restricted. The FTC is still empowered, however, to investigate and resolve individual cases of advertising deception. Complaints can be filed with the FTC by a consumer; a competitor; Congress; or any local, state, or federal agency.

## "DECEPTIVE": THE STANDARD

"Deceptive" advertising was defined in 1983 by a three-member majority of the Commission as a "representation, omission or practice that is likely to mislead the consumer acting reasonably in the circumstances to the consumer's detriment." The more traditional formulation, reaffirmed by the other members of the Commission, states that an act is deceptive if it has a tendency or capacity to mislead a substantial number of consumers in a material way. Is there a difference between these definitions? Some interpretations say *yes*. The first approach might require proof of *actual* injury, while the second requires only that the advertising have the *capacity* to mislead. In practice, it has been held that regardless of which standard is applied, no actual injury need take place for the FTC to step in.

In determining whether or not an advertisement is deceptive, the FTC asks whether the *average* purchaser—not necessarily the least sophisticated or least intelligent possible buyer—would be deceived. Specially targeted ads, however, are examined in light of the target audiences. Advertising directed at children, for instance, may be judged by a standard reflecting the lesser sophistication of a younger audience. The context of the entire ad is considered in deciding whether or not the advertisement is deceptive. Thus, the "Joe Isuzu" ads that ran some years ago, combining blatant lies about Isuzu cars with the statement that lies are being told, would not be deemed deceptive. Endorsements by celebrities and other pitchmen in television ads are a source of concern in FTC review, and infomercials need to be properly disclosed as sponsored broadcasts.

False information can be visual as well as verbal or written. A depiction of a product can be touched up in such a way as to make the picture itself a misleading item. In one commercial that caused difficulty, a knife was shown cutting through a nail, which it could indeed do. When the cutting edge was shown later in the commercial, however, a different knife was substituted, which looked fresh and perfect. This was deemed a deceptive practice. Similarly, in one demonstration comparing shaving creams, the advertiser added foreign substances to the competitors' creams to make its own cream look superior. Time-compression photographs can be deceptive in that they present a distorted picture of a product's characteristics; some disclosure of the elapsed time must be made to avoid deceptive practice. The use of an actor in a white doctor's coat can give the false impression that the product is endorsed by doctors. As much care should be taken in avoiding misrepresentation through images as through words.

Whether written, verbal, or visual, the misrepresentation need not be an affirmative one. Leaving out important details can be as much a source of deception as putting in affirmative lies.

For advertisers seeking to avoid false or misleading ads, the first line of defense should be common sense: Be truthful in fact and in spirit. In making statements about a product, the advertiser and the creative people at the advertising agency should stick closely to substantiated facts. From the FTC standpoint, the key element is to have adequate backup—gathered in advance—for product claims. If the advertiser does not have proof that the product will do what is claimed, the statement simply should not be made.

As any observer of American advertising will surely understand, however, advertising statements are not limited to dry facts. A certain level of exaggeration and hyperbole is par for the course in the advertising world, and is permitted as "puffing." Generalizations like "it's great," "amazing," or "wonderful" make no specific claim that can deceive or mislead, and the average buyer will know to discount them. Claims that a brand of toothpaste will "Beautify the smile" or that a sewing machine is "Almost human" have also been permitted under this standard. Unfortunately, the line between permitted puffing and punishable deception is not always clear.

Most large advertising agencies have in-house legal counsel who review all advertising copy with an eye toward avoiding deceptive claims; smaller firms frequently retain outside counsel to examine the material. It is strongly recommended that any advertising campaign involving claims of performance or superiority over other brands should be vetted by an attorney.

## Guides

The FTC has issued a series of guides (available at www.ftc.gov) concerning particular products and practices, which are part of the FTC's regulations at 16 CFR, Subchapter B. Some of the guides focus on specific methods of advertising, including bait advertising, debt collection, endorsements and testimonials, the use of the word "free," guarantees, and statements about prices. Others guides are directed at specific products, claims, or industries, including those concerning automobile fuel economy, beauty schools, pet foods, film and film processing, vocational schools, and so on.

## Consumer Protection Trade Rules

In addition to the guides that concern deceptive advertising, the FTC has issued rules on a variety of commercial practices. Most of these rules focus on consumer protection issues that do not affect the television industry (for example, telemarketing and Internet spam). One rule, though, concerns advertising about the size of television picture tubes. There are also rules on advertising consumer-credit and leasing arrangements.

The most important of the FTC's consumer protection rules related to television—those governing advertising aimed at children—were never adopted. In 1980, bowing to industry concerns, Congress intervened to suspend consideration of the rules. In 1990, however, Congress took steps to rectify its prior FTC interference through a mandate to the FCC (see page 98). The FTC does, as a matter of policy, pay particular attention to ads directed at children when applying generally applicable standards. The 1998 Children's Online Privacy Protection Act gave the FTC authority over using the Web to collect personal information from children—a jurisdiction that could apply to some interactive Web television services.

## The FTC and Complaints Against Advertisers

Complaints against advertisers can come from competitors, consumers, or the FTC's own internal monitoring staff. After investigating, the FTC takes one of several courses of action. Most often, it looks for voluntary compliance, requesting that the advertiser change the offending commercial or remove it from the air, and the advertiser complies or works out a compromise with the FTC. If that doesn't work, the FTC may issue an administrative complaint, which can lead to a cease-and-desist order insisting that the offending ad be removed. The advertiser may also agree to sign a consent decree in which the company does not admit guilt, but agrees to stop running the commercials and to refrain from similar practices in future advertisements.

In the case of knowing violations, the FTC can impose civil penalties ranging from thousands to millions of dollars, depending on the nature of the violation. Sometimes advertisers are ordered to give full or partial refunds to all consumers who bought the product. Fines of up to $11,000 per day can be assessed for failure to obey an FTC order. In severe situations involving food, drugs, medical devices, and cosmetics—where the FTC has broader authority—the Commission may ask the Department of Justice to try the advertiser on a misdemeanor charge.

Advertisers are given 20 days to respond to FTC requests; this period can sometimes be extended. Advertisers may appeal decisions to the full Commission, and final FTC decisions can eventually be appealed in the federal court system.

## THE FCC AND ADVERTISING CONTENT

The FCC has largely given up its role as a regulator of material content in advertising. The 1934 Communications Act does allow the FCC to suspend the license of any broadcaster transmitting false or deceptive signals or communications. Nonetheless, as early as the 1970s, the FCC recognized the greater expertise of the FTC on these matters, and by 1985, the FCC had dropped most of its specific policies on false and misleading advertising. However, the FCC still makes broadcasters generally responsible for controlling any false, misleading, or deceptive matter over the air, by virtue of the public-interest standard.

### FCC Prohibitions on Television Advertising

The FCC has a policy against subliminal advertising (messages that are so brief or so inconspicuous that they work only at a subconscious level), holding this technique to be against the public interest. When Republican ads in the 2000 presidential campaign were accused of containing a subliminal message, an inquiry was made but no further action was taken. Specific federal legislation also bars advertising cigarettes, small cigars, and smokeless tobacco on the electronic media under the jurisdiction of the FCC, including cable television and satellite transmissions. The mention of a cigarette producer that sponsors a sports contest or other reported event is acceptable, however, provided that the references are not so exaggerated that they become, in effect, commercial messages.

There are also long-standing statutory and FCC prohibitions against television advertising of certain kinds of lotteries and gambling activities. In a commercial context, a prohibited lottery has (1) a prize, which is (2) awarded by chance, and (3) involves entrants who have paid money or supplied some other valuable consideration (which can include the purchase of a product). A "contest" that lacks one of these elements is exempt, and can be advertised on television. For instance, if "no purchase is necessary to enter and win," the element of consideration is missing. If the prizes are awarded on the basis of some bona fide measure of skill, the element of chance is not there. However, since the interpretation of these rules can get quite technical, consulting with legal counsel is advisable before advertising a contest on television.

In the past, these rules prohibited the advertisement of gambling activities in general. With the spread of state lotteries and other legal gambling activities, Congress amended the law in 1990 to permit the advertising via broadcast of Indian tribe casinos and most legitimate lottery and gambling activities (including other casinos) that are legal in the state in which they are conducted. Because of the skill involved in picking a winner and because you can attend without betting, the advertising of horse racing did not come under the old bans.

Telemarketing, from infomercials to cable shopping channels, is regulated under a mix of FCC and FTC rules. The FTC requires that infomercial-style programming make periodic disclosure that the program is a paid-for commercial and not a regular consumer program, and there are further restrictions on infomercials aimed at children under age 12 (see page 293). Both the FTC and the FCC have targeted telemarketers who charge for phone conversations, such as psychics and adult-oriented services. The 1992 Telephone Disclosure and Dispute Resolution Act mandated a series of protections, including clear disclosure of costs in all telemarketing ads (including television commercials), avoiding ads targeted at children, and avoiding the use of "800" or other usually toll-free numbers to initiate the call. These restrictions have been imposed on the telemarketers by FTC rules and on the phone companies by FCC rules.

The FCC has dropped many of its old rules banning particular kinds of advertising. These discarded prohibitions include rules on ads for alcoholic beverages and astrology. Minor limitations on beer ads (for example, advertisers cannot list the alcohol content of beers in most states) and states' control over liquor commercials have both persisted but have been thrown into question by a 1996 Supreme Court ruling.

## Children's Television

After many false starts at the regulatory level, Congress enacted the Children's Television Act of 1990. This law mandated that the FCC impose limits on the amount of advertising allowed during children's programs. It also directed the FCC to review compliance with these restrictions in connection with license renewals, as well as to evaluate the licensee's attention to the educational and informational needs of children in its programming. Finally, the Act calls on the FCC to tackle the issues of program-length commercials and the general commercialization of children's television. As described on page 293, FCC rules limit advertising time during children's programs to no more than 10.5 minutes per hour on weekends and 12 minutes on weekdays. The FCC has also defined program-length commercials as programs linked to a product in which commercials for that product are aired.

## LIMITS ON ADVERTISING TIME

As a general matter, television stations and cable operators are not obligated to accept commercials at all. Those that do accept commercials may turn down particular ones they do not wish to run, provided the reason doesn't invoke some other general principle of the law. Stations and cable operators are not "common carriers" in this respect, and there are no minimums. The main exceptions to this principle are the equal opportunity and reasonable-access rules for political advertising (see page 43).

The broadcast networks, most cable companies, and most individual broadcast stations do set limits on the number of ads that they carry on their programs. These amounts vary, depending on the time period and the particular medium involved. For instance, the major networks have generally restricted advertising on prime-time programs to 8 to 10 minutes per hour; for their daytime programming, the maximum has typically been 12 to 15 minutes. Ad time on cable and local stations may run in the range of 12 to 15 minutes per hour, or even more in daytime segments. Special events like the Olympics can attract more than the usual number of ads. As television advertising revenue has been squeezed by competition from other media, the temptation to increase the number of minutes per hour has been felt by some.

Until 1984, the FCC set its own limits on the total amount of commercial time that could be included in television programming. Ad time was generally restricted to 16 commercial minutes per programming hour. In June 1984, however, these rules were repealed in keeping with the general deregulation of television broadcasting. The policy now is to allow the balance between ads and programming to be set by the marketplace and factors of public acceptance. The private sector used to have its own rules on the maximum number of commercials, and the National Association of Broadcasters suggested time limits in its Television Code. The Code and its limits, however, were effectively abolished in 1982 in connection with the settlement of antitrust litigation. As described previously, the FCC does continue to set limits on the amount of advertising on children's television.

Public broadcast stations are supposedly prohibited from airing advertisements to promote any for-profit product or service, and from carrying ads for or against any political candidates. Public television generally avoids any resemblance to commercial television, although contemporary underwriting spots occasionally resemble television ads (see page 181).

## UNFAIR COMPETITION AND THE LANHAM ACT

Certain federal and state laws permit companies and individuals to take private legal action to prevent certain kinds of false advertising, under the theory that it constitutes unfair competition to misdescribe one's own product or to lie about a competitor's. The most important of these laws is Section 43(a) of the Federal Lanham Act § 1125, available through the FTC Web site, www.ftc.gov.

In the context of advertising, Section 43(a) allows damaged parties to sue over misrepresentations about the nature, characteristics, qualities, or geographic origin of goods, services, or commercial activities. The Lanham Act applies to direct trademark violations—for instance, the use of the word "Coca-Cola" on a product not manufactured by the Coca-Cola company. It also forbids advertising a product as if it were made by a certain company or endorsed by an individual when that simply is not the case. The claims need not be made explicitly; false involvement or endorsement can also be implied. The Lanham Act can affect certain kinds of comparative ads if there is the implication that the manufacturer of the other product is in some way endorsing the advertisement or the statements in it.

The Lanham Act does not provide for private action against all false advertising, however. Most courts have held that false claims which have nothing to do with the origin or quality of the goods are simply not covered; a few courts and certain commentators have construed the Lanham Act a bit more broadly. In addition, the right to sue is limited to competitors or to the person or company whose involvement is being impermissibly suggested. The Lanham Act does not give the general public a right to sue for these misrepresentations.

## STATE LAWS

Many states have adopted unfair competition laws that provide protections similar to those given under the Lanham Act. As a general matter, it must be proved that the advertising confuses the buying public as to the origin of the goods and services being advertised. Some states allow claims for other kinds of deceptions, not necessarily limited to those about origin.

The states frequently have their own laws prohibiting false advertising in general. One form of these is generically called "Printer's Ink" laws; another, less common model is the Uniform Deceptive Trade Practice Act. Whatever the approach, enforcement will vary widely, depending on the priority given by the state regulatory and prosecuting authorities to deceptive advertising. The Association of Attorneys General has from time to time encouraged its members to actively pursue false advertising claims. There are even some local rules, administered by bodies such as a municipal consumer-protection commission or bureau, which concern local advertising practices.

## CONSUMER CLAIMS

It is possible for consumers to bring claims against false advertising, either singly or as part of a class action. The legal theories for such actions include fraud, misrepresentation, breach of contract, and breach of warranties, express and implied. Since, in many cases of misleading advertising, the harm to any one individual is likely to be small in comparison to the legal costs, almost every such suit is brought on a class-action basis, and the rules on class actions can be fairly restrictive. Although they have been successfully maintained in some instances, and at times have produced significant monetary recoveries, consumer suits for false advertising are uncommon.

## INDUSTRY REVIEW OF ADVERTISING CONTENT

The first step in checking the content of a commercial occurs between the client and the advertising agency. As the ad is scripted and storyboarded, it is often reviewed by the ad agency's counsel and, in many instances, the client's counsel as well; advertising that makes affirmative claims will be subject to particular scrutiny. Substantiating backup is assembled for any claims made, and general attention is given to the legal issues not only pertaining to advertising itself, but also to matters of copyright clearance, privacy and publicity, and those content restrictions that apply to all television programs.

The broadcast networks can be quite active in reviewing the content of the advertisements they run, sometimes insisting that they be allowed some input at the storyboard level. A network's review involves not only the substantive questions of legal compliance, but also the advertisement's adherence to network standards and practices. The fallout from the controversial 2004 Super Bowl broadcast, which also included a number of vulgar ads, has included greater scrutiny of ads for indecency. Areas of particular sensitivity at the network level include beer and wine, toys, over-the-counter drugs, contraceptives, and astrology. The networks have also declined to run advertising for distilled alcoholic beverages. All in all, such standards are fairly predictable when the reader recalls that networks are mass-market outlets concerned with their image and accustomed to avoiding controversy.

Cable is, by and large, much more permissive about advertising than broadcast is (with the exception of the ABC Family Channel and other consciously wholesome companies), and local stations vary greatly in terms of tolerance. As a result, cable companies are more lenient in their internal review of commercials.

Various trade groups of advertising agencies and their clients have issued guidelines for their members to follow in making ads. These relatively platitudinous and commonsensical codes have helped shape the attitudes of the industry for the better, in turn influencing the types of ads that appear on television. One such guide covers children's advertising. Some groups have even set up review committees with the power to recommend (but not force) the change or withdrawal of potentially offensive ads. The American Association of Advertising Agencies (AAAA) has been active both in promoting a creative code (adopted in 1962) and in setting up a review system. In 1971, the AAAA joined with the Council of Better Business Bureaus, the Association of National Advertisers, and the American Advertising Federation to establish the National Advertising Division (NAD; information available at www.nadreview.org), which reviews ads for misleading or deceptive content; the National Advertising Review Board

(NARB), which hears appeals; and the National Advertising Review Council, which sets policies. Children's advertising is monitored by the Children's Advertising Review Unit of the Council of Better Business Bureaus (www.caru.org).

Compliance with NAD and NARB rulings is voluntary but remarkably uniform, at least among reputable companies. Noncompliance would bring adverse publicity to an advertiser and can be reported to the appropriate governmental agency for action.

# PART 4

# THE PROGRAMMING BUSINESS

# CHAPTER 15

# PROGRAMMING TO MARKET SEGMENTS

As television in the United States has evolved, its principal purpose has become the distribution of commercials. That is, television networks in the U.S. exist primarily to deliver audiences composed of specific demographics to advertisers. This relationship between advertising and television is nothing new, but the widespread use of television as an advertising medium is more extreme than it has been in the past.

A brief historical view may be helpful. From the very start of radio broadcasting, advertisers provided the funds to produce programming in exchange for associations with those programs. As television evolved, it followed radio's model: Some programs were fully sponsored by a single company, and others were periodically interrupted for commercials. As with radio, certain dayparts were more likely to deliver certain audiences. Evenings, for example, delivered family audiences, while the daytime schedule was primarily for women, who stayed at home in large numbers until the 1970s. By the 1980s, it was clear that this audience segmentation strategy could be applied not only to dayparts but to whole networks. Children could be reached through a network especially for them: Nickelodeon. Women could be reached both day and night with appropriate programming on Lifetime. Through the 1990s, the connection between cable networks and advertisers became stronger, ratifying the audience segmentation strategy and making it the rule for the management of existing cable networks and the launch of new ones. Along the way, Nickelodeon and MTV taught the television industry about the value and importance of network branding: Television networks began to be marketed as consumer products and services.

The result is an impressive, nearly perfect ladder of audience wrangling for the benefit of advertisers.

## AGE GROUPS

### Children Age 2–5

The longtime CBS morning entry *Captain Kangaroo* established the roots of preschool television. From these roots grew *Sesame Street*, a franchise whose original strategy was to use the imagery and style of commercial television to teach reading and math fundamentals, as well as social skills. Nickelodeon grew from the same family tree, first as a noncommercial network whose longer-form programs often resembled segments seen on *Sesame Street* or other Children's Television Workshop (now Sesame Workshop) programs. With older children away in school, the Nick Jr. network has become the television solution for preschool children. Popular programs include *Blues Clues, Dora the Explorer,* and *Little Bill.*

On Nickelodeon's networks, the business model for this particular daypart is not advertising. Instead, the model is commercial-free programming with a merchandising and licensing revenue stream. These young viewers are easily converted to mainstream Nickelodeon viewers, especially if an older sibling watches the channel. Cartoon Network and Disney Channel also run a morning preschool block with a similar business model and goals.

Public television has retained a foothold in its preschool television roots so effectively established with *Sesame Street* and *Mister Rogers' Neighborhood.* Today *Bob the Builder, Jay Jay the Jet Plane, Teletubbies,* and *Boobah* are all supported, to varying degrees, by licensing revenues (and by CPB and other program funds, by foundations and corporations, and by "Viewers Like You."

Although this specific category, children 2–5, is not reported in the Nielsen books, it is possible to derive its viewership because children 2–11 and children 6–11 are regularly reported.

A total of 19.5 million people in the U.S. are age 2–6 years.

## Boys Age 6–11, Girls Age 6–11

Nickelodeon is the clear choice for both boys and girls in this age group, not only as a television network but also as a brand. On digital cable, Nickelodeon offers several brand extensions: Noggin (a somewhat brainier version of Nickelodeon, once co-owned with Sesame Workshop); Nickelodeon GaS (Games and Sports); and NickToons, an all-cartoon network. Cartoon Network is a popular alternative. Boys in this age group tend to watch some sports (particularly in the older range of the demographic), while girls tend to watch celebrity and fashion programming.

The broadcast networks, once dominant in this demographic with their Saturday morning children's blocks, have ceded much of this audience to Nickelodeon. In fact, CBS's Saturday morning schedule is programmed by Nickelodeon. ABC also provides a Saturday morning children's block. Local FOX and WB affiliates continue to program weekday cartoons in the late afternoon, a practice that goes back 40 years to their own origins as independent local stations counterprogramming against strong ABC, CBS, and NBC affiliates.

Public television stations also offer late-afternoon programs for children, partly to serve a specific audience (which is no longer as underserved as it once was) and partly because it's difficult to imagine a reasonably priced alternative for a late-afternoon PBS schedule. Programs in the 2004–2005 season included three animated series: *Cyberchase*, *Arthur*, and *Maya & Miguel*.

Despite various attempts to equalize boys and girls, advertisers know that these groups are very different types of consumers. While both genders pester their parents to buy fast food, soft drinks, candy, and cereal, most toy companies, for example, are organized in two groups: boys' toys and girls' toys.

Some 25 million people in the U.S. are age 6–11 years.

## Preteen Boys, Preteen Girls

When studying children and media, developmental psychologists have noted an aging-up trend. Over time, particularly through the 1990s, children's media habits have matured more and more rapidly. The tastes and interests of the 13-year-old in the 1970s are now more comparable to those of an 11-year-old today, and perhaps even a 10-year-old. This is the age when a child becomes a preteen, or a "tween" or "tweenager."

Most tweens combine childhood viewing habits with those of a teenager. This is the age when some people begin watching MTV, but continue to watch Nickelodeon and Cartoon Network. The WB Network has done well with this audience, as have FOX and, from time to time, ABC. Beware, however, of broad generalizations, as the only truly meaningful statistics are found at the level of the individual show. For example, *Friends* was extremely popular with tween girls on NBC, and continues to deliver this audience in syndication. Noggin has recently repositioned part of its schedule to serve this demographic, following the pattern of success established by the Nickelodeon network several years before.

Certain sports do an especially good job delivering boys in this audience. Wrestling and basketball are very popular, but not across the entire population. There is no precise parallel for girls. Some watch reality shows on the broadcast networks, others favor MTV; some are fascinated by E! Entertainment Television and smaller networks like Style, others watch network sitcoms or soaps. Certainly, UPN has been successful in its play for this audience, with sitcoms featuring young, attractive, black casts.

Tweens are not broken out separately in Nielsen's books, and their statistics are not easily extrapolated—Nielsen can provide special breakdowns upon request. If the reader includes ages 11 and 12 in the tween population, then the size of the audience is about 8 million U.S. citizens.

## Boys Age 12–17

Teenage boys represent a very specific, defined demographic with real consumer purchasing power. In general, this audience is delivered by MTV and ESPN, with Comedy Central gaining popularity, and some fragmented viewership of Nickelodeon and Cartoon Network based upon childhood patterns. This is also a significant movie audience, both in the theaters and on television (action adventures and certain comedies are strong draws). In this demographic, the Internet and video games are eroding overall television viewership; music also distracts the audience from television, but this is nothing new.

There are about 12.5 million boys age 12–17 living in the U.S.

## Girls Age 12–17

While an increasing number of girls watch sports, their predominant viewing habits are related to music, comedy, and stories. MTV and sitcoms are the best way to reach this audience, but again, the childhood viewing habits remain part of the pattern through the mid-teens. Like boys, girls in this age group are strongly attracted to movies and to the Internet. Girls may watch the occasional sitcom or reality show, but by and large, it's music and comedy for this demographic.

There are about 12.5 million girls age 12–17 living in the U.S.

## Men Age 18–24

Interest in sports remains strong at this age and is likely to broaden and deepen, so while ESPN viewership remains high, other sports may also occupy an increasing percentage of viewing hours. Interest in MTV begins to fade, while Spike and G4 (a video game network) pick up viewers in this band. There's not much on broadcast network television for this age group except on FOX, where *The Simpsons* finds the heart of its increasingly broad audience. Reality shows also deliver this audience, as do action movies. The combination of video games and the Internet is often a more powerful draw than television programming.

Note that Nielsen reports viewership for the overlapping 12–24 and 18–34 segments. Network programmers tend to focus their target markets somewhat more precisely.

There are nearly 14 million men age 18–24 in the U.S.

## Women Age 18–24

As with the men, interest in MTV fades, but here VH1 picks up the viewers. E! and Style networks find the heart of their audience in this demographic, and Lifetime just begins to pick up the older part of this segment. For some parts of this audience, network sitcoms and soaps deliver meaningful numbers. There's also interest in the various makeover and design shows on TLC and HGTV that touch the upper range of this demo.

There are over 13 million women age 18–24 in the U.S.

## Men Age 25–34

They're almost done with MTV, may still watch Spike for a few years, and never stopped watching lots of sports, both on the broadcast networks and on ESPN. Now, however, men are likely to add CNN and MSNBC, and a healthy amount of straight news, business news, sports news, and political programming. They also watch cop shows and action series on the broadcast networks. Most have lost or are gradually losing their interest in video games, but they remain steady Internet users. The more upscale members of this demographic tend to watch less television, and so, the cost of reaching them may be comparatively high.

There are about 20 million men in this age group in the U.S.

## Women Age 25–34

The most valuable audience segment because of both time spent viewing and purchase power, women age 25–34 are both homemakers and businesspeople. These women are Mom, but they may also be the boss at the office. They may not be married at all, and they may not have children. Overall, they are the key target market for broadcast network sitcoms and dramas, and the largest audience for soaps. They watch the network or local news at least once a night, remaining extremely loyal to favorite newscasters, often for decades. Lifetime programs exclusively for this demographic and a slightly older one; VH1 also delivers this audience in substantial numbers. They are the primary audience for Food Network, HGTV, Style, Oxygen, and TLC. They are the target for America's largest advertisers—the steady consumers who make the American economy work.

There are about 20 million women in this age group in the U.S.

## Men Age 35–49

Although these men may watch Comedy Central or VH1 for the fun of it, their television viewing tends to be filled with various types of news and sports programming, with the occasional favorite broadcast network drama added to fill the evenings. They have enormous purchasing power, both at home and in business, and a television program or network that consistently delivers this audience can be quite valuable to the likes of IBM, Merrill Lynch, or a national accounting firm. Many such commercials are seen on Sunday mornings, when the smartest, most affluent members of this segment watch political news programming.

There are about 32 million men in this age group in the U.S.

## Women Age 35–49

A traditional core of the broadcast network audience, an increasing number of these women are now watching movies and series on cable networks. They watch some news but not much music, sports, or business programming. Mostly, this audience watches television for light entertainment and regular daily news. They are the heart of the PBS audience, both daytime and nighttime, and an important segment within the audience for lifestyle programming (i.e., TLC and HGTV).

There are about 32 million women in this age group in the U.S.

## Men Age 50–64

Apart from news, sports, movies, and the occasional network drama, this audience finds itself somewhat underserved by cable networks. The History Channel delivers some of this audience, as does its sister network, A&E, but both are fairly specific in their program types. The same might be said of Discovery and its various digital spin-off networks. Although men in this segment share viewing habits with those of slightly younger men, they are more affluent and more selective in their viewing habits.

Note that Nielsen reports for 25–54, 35–64, and 50-plus. Once again, programmers tend to focus somewhat more precisely.

There are about 20 million men in this age category in the U.S.

## Women Age 50–64

Still an important component in the broadcast prime-time and daytime audiences, this audience tends to drift into special interests, such as A&E and, quite significantly, QVC. Women in this demographic are also likely to seek out particular programs of interest on particular networks: PBS's *Antiques Roadshow*, for example, is popular with this group.

There are nearly 22 million women in this age category in the U.S.

## Men Age 65-plus

Remarkably, given their spending power and the size of the audience (one in eight men is over 65 years old), this is a rather uninteresting audience to television advertisers—except, perhaps, clients in the personal finance and brokerage business. Generally, the way to reach men 65-plus is as a small segment of the network news or sports audience, but neither is efficient: The majority of these audiences are not men 65-plus. In fact, there are about 14 million men over age 65 in the U.S, and by comparison nearly 22 million men ages 30–39. Men are living longer, but the demographic change is not yet significant in television programming or marketing terms.

Nielsen does not report any specific viewership group over 64 years; their 50-plus category is probably an old-fashioned way to look at the world.

## Women Age 65-plus

In general, this audience is treated as an extension of the women age 50–64 audience. Despite the fact that these women have more spending power, more leisure time, and less direct family responsibility, the television industry does not program specifically for this age group.

In fact, there are about 50 percent more women age 65-plus (about 22 million women) than there are men in the same category.

## OTHER CATEGORIES

### Young Parents

This is a desirable audience because young mothers are already strong consumers, quite reliant upon brands that they will purchase for decades. Fathers don't really figure into this equation, except with regard to real estate and automobile purchases. Mothers make the buying decisions. They are reached by several cable networks—notably Lifetime, TLC, Oxygen, and VH1—and by the broadcast networks through soaps and sitcoms, as well as by the syndicated talk shows on local television stations.

## Spanish-Speaking

This audience has only recently captured the interest of big media. NBC now owns Telemundo, a large Spanish-language broadcast network, which competes with Univision and several smaller broadcast and cable networks to serve the Hispanic population in the U.S. This effort is supported by consumer goods companies that now maintain internal divisions devoted exclusively to products for the Hispanic market, and by advertisers who sell products to all markets, including Hispanic consumers.

According to the U.S. Census Bureau, 12.5 percent of Americans claim Hispanic or Latino heritage—more than 35 million people. Approximately 28 million people speak Spanish at home.

## Upscale vs. Lower Income

As a rule, television is not an ideal medium to reach upscale audiences. Public television tends to "sell" this audience to its underwriters, and several "nonfiction" networks, including Discovery Channel, CNN, and CNBC, skew more upscale in terms of income and education levels. For the most part, however, upscale audiences are better reached through print media.

Lower-income audiences tend to watch more television (an inexpensive entertainment option). Their viewing habits are somewhat more diverse, but tend to "heavy up" on daytime talk shows, certain sports programs, courtroom shows, and situation comedies.

If upscale is defined as having a household income of $100,000 or more, then only 10 percent of the population is upscale. (A similar number earn less than $10,000 per year.) If the definition is widened to $75,000 or more, then 20 percent of the population falls in this category (22 percent earns less than $20,000).

## GENERAL AUDIENCES

Although cable television tends toward segmentation, the big money comes from advertisers for television shows that are watched by many different demographic groups. Certainly, this is the strategy for most of the prime-time schedule on CBS, NBC, and ABC (the strategies employed by FOX, UPN, and The WB tend to be somewhat more specific). Some cable networks may skew toward men or women 25–49 years old, but some of the largest cable networks program for general audiences—TBS, USA, and TNT are examples.

## REACHING SMALLER AUDIENCES

Until recently, cable and satellite networks focused on relatively large niche audiences. Turner Classic Movies, Country Music Television, Food Network, and The Golf Channel are examples. As the emergence of digital cable and the growing popularity of satellite television added new channel capacity to a previously constrained universe, smaller niche networks were developed. Some serve very specific ethnic groups; AZN, for example, serves Asian audiences, and Univision serves Hispanics. Others satisfy very specific lifestyle needs; WISDOM TV and Oasis TV serve people who are especially aware of the connection between mind, body, and spirit, while Discovery Wings features only programs for flying enthusiasts. Cable VOD (video-on-demand) is sometimes used to test consumer interest with a smaller number of programs (requiring a smaller investment) prior to the launch of a 24/7 channel with a limited audience. Comcast's Anime Channel is one such example.

## DAYPART STRATEGIES

Although there is brand value in a consistent 24/7 schedule serving just one broad demographic, some channels follow the old broadcast television tradition of "dayparting." In this strategy, the programs change as the audience changes through the day. For example, NBC begins its program day with *Today*, whose first hour is strongly oriented toward news, and whose second and third hours are lighter fare. Most NBC affiliates then program talk shows and local news until the NBC network soap schedule begins. Then it's afternoon talk shows, whose audience is primarily women, followed by local and network news, whose audience begins strongly female but becomes more of a mix as afternoon becomes evening. The prime-time schedule is for general audiences. Late-night (*The Tonight Show with Jay Leno*) assumes an adult audience (no children), and later, a younger adult audience (*Late Night with Conan O'Brien*). Some cable networks follow a similar strategy, showing afternoon cartoons when the kids are home from school, and others simply sell off parts of their schedule when a meaningful audience is unavailable for their content (hence, paid programming for infomercials).

# CHAPTER 16

# THE ECONOMICS OF PROGRAMMING AND PRODUCTION

From the perspective of the audience, television shows are simply entertainment. Audiences don't think much about budgets or the economics of production, but a low-cost production may lack the standard necessary to attract or retain an audience. In today's media-savvy society, audiences easily recognize the differences in budget levels between, say, a major motion picture with world-class special effects and big name performers; a prime-time television series shot in a limited number of rooms with a small ensemble cost; and a cable series hosted by an unknown and featuring, for example, the makeover of a suburban living room.

Audiences tend to watch productions that feature stars and storylines—but not always. The reality shows popular in the early 2000s broke the rules: No stars, limited scripting, simple locations. Most hour-long reality shows simply cost less than hour-long dramatic series. If the network can sell commercial time on the reality show for the same price that it charged advertisers for the spots on a drama, the series is more profitable. Basically, that's the theory behind production economics: As a rule, the network will pay as little as possible for the highest possible rating. Of course, this is an oversimplification, as programmers are not motivated by ratings alone.

## RETURN ON INVESTMENT

Television shows cost tens or hundreds of thousands of dollars to produce. An inexpensive cable series rarely costs less than $30,000 per episode, so an order of 13 weekly episodes is nearly $400,000. The result is 13 shows, each 30 minutes long. Of course, the network requires far more programming for that 13-week period: If this particular half-hour series ran twice daily, the network would still require 23 hours per day, 7 days per week, for 13 weeks. If the network produced a similar original series to fill all of that time, and ran each half-hour twice, the investment would be 23 x 7 x 13 x $30,000, or a total of over $62 million. On this basis, the annual investment would be nearly a quarter-billion dollars.

If each of these half hours ran not twice but four times, then the annual programming investment would be reduced to about $125 million. If each episode ran eight times—not unusual for a cable network over the course of a year—then the programming investment would be just over $62 million. Often, this investment is further reduced by acquiring programs that were previously produced for other networks; often, these episodes can be acquired for $5,000 each, and sometimes for less.

Different networks employ different programming investment strategies. Some invest heavily in series that play in prime-time, and simply acquire the remainder of their schedule from programs. Others invest in programs that cost considerably more than $30,000 per episode, and easily justify the additional investment through higher advertising revenues. Some cable networks, including The Weather Channel and CNBC, are heavily formatted, and focus almost entirely upon programs produced in their own studios (internal productions often cost less than those produced by outside companies).

## ANTICIPATED REVENUES AND PRODUCTION BUDGETS

If a television commercial within a given half-hour show can be sold for $10,000, and the half hour contains a dozen available commercial slots, then the value of that half hour totals $120,000. If the half-hour show airs a second time, the spots may be worth the same amount, but may also be discounted for a total of, say, $100,000. If each of six additional airings of the show was worth an average of $50,000, then a total of $520,000 would have been earned by the episode.

How much should the network invest in the production of that episode? The answer is probably in the $75,000 to $100,000 range. The other $400,000 is a contribution to network operating costs, salaries, marketing efforts, maintaining and upgrading equipment, and, of course, the profit that the network is expected to earn annually.

Advertising has never been the only source of revenue for a television program. Often, programs are sold to other networks, both in the U.S. and throughout the world. Some programs are suitable for multiple networks: HBO's *Sex and the City*, for example, has also been successful for TBS. Other programs, such as CNN's *Larry King Live*, are less likely to be sold to other networks. Still, CNN is able to re-purpose its own programming for its many networks—the CNN Airport Network, for example. Some programs earn substantial revenues in syndication: *Seinfeld* has been successful on both TBS and FOX stations. Certain programs are suitable for export to English-speaking countries and also to non-English-speaking countries, where new voices are typically dubbed in local languages. Some television properties find new markets as DVDs; the boxed sets of *The Sopranos*, for example, have been strong sellers. But the majority of programs produced for television see none, or almost none, of these revenues. They are purpose-built for a particular network, and they must sustain themselves on their own ratings and advertising revenues.

## THE REAL COSTS OF PRODUCTION

Even the smallest of television production companies handles a fair amount of cash. The relatively modest $30,000 production of 13 half hours provides the production company with $390,000 in working capital. A well-managed production company would target approximately 20 or 25 percent of this revenue for overhead—a term that covers the hard costs of operating a business as well as (hopefully) a profit. Those hard costs are often ignored by the network, but they are real just the same. The costs associated with an office, an accountant, an attorney, travel, project development, sales, building relationships, computers, telephones, support staff—all of these make it possible for the production company to operate, and to provide the services necessary for the projects to be made.

On any production, the largest budget line item is staff. Television production is enormously labor-intensive. Every production requires at least one senior-level producer, and a staff of several producers is often required. Assuming an average of $1,500 per producer, and perhaps three producers for the $30,000 series, that's a $4,500 weekly investment. In order to develop, produce, edit, and deliver 13 episodes, these producers are likely to be employed for at least ten weeks. At minimum, that's $45,000, more than 10 percent of the overall budget. Support staff would require an additional 10 percent. Four performers, each paid $500 per episode, would cost $26,000, and by the time they're clothed, housed, made up, rehearsed, and so on, they, too, require one-tenth of the budget. Bear in mind that 20 percent is being held back for overhead, and now half the budget is gone. The other half must pay for crew, equipment, locations, travel, meals, post-production, and more. Add it all up, and the 20 percent margin may prove optimistic.

The real costs of prime-time network television programs operate at a somewhat higher scale, but the basic concepts are similar. An episode of *The West Wing*, for example, costs well over $2 million, and sometimes as much as $4 million. When the show was at its ratings peak, the return on such an investment was possible through high advertising rates.

The real costs of prime-time pilots also add more risk to the process. In the case of *The West Wing*, the pilot episode apparently cost about $5 million (this would be one of the more costly pilots in network television history). If a series becomes a success, this investment can be recouped. If the series never goes on the air—and this happens more often than anyone would like to admit—then the cost is absorbed by the network and/or the studio's development budget and, in theory, a lesson is learned for "next time."

## THE INEVITABLE NEGOTIATIONS

Every new project's production is something of a new adventure. If the program is based upon an existing format, then the budgeting and planning exercise can be done with the benefit of experience. If the program is a new idea, or one that benefits from a creative team charged with instigating change, then the initial budget estimate may prove unreliable. What's more, every production is subject to "the production gods"—those unseen forces that cause the lead performer to break a leg or the digital editing system to crash and destroy weeks of work. Sometimes, the producer or director is not as competent as his or her résumé suggests. Sometimes, the network changes its requirements or its creative direction while the project is in production. Often, the cause is not the individual budget line items, but the amount of time actually required to complete the production—the number of days actually required to shoot with a full crew, or the number of weeks required to edit. And sometimes, the production company takes the assignment knowing that its costs will not be covered—hoping that somehow things will turn out all right.

Although the network executives are loathe to admit it, additional budget money is always available. A network simply will not invest $390,000 in a television series and then refuse to pay an additional $50,000 to assure its successful completion. There may be angry words, somebody might get fired, and there may be accountants studying the production company's budget "actuals," but the network never (okay, almost never) walks away from a project.

Of course, production companies are cautious about requesting additional money. To do so, unless the situation is dire, suggests bad management and may jeopardize future opportunities. Then again, a production company that delivers an inferior project because it did not ask for the additional money may be in an even worse position.

## PROFIT IMPLICATIONS

Each network's senior management requires the programming and production investment to end up in line with budget projections. The program department attempts to work generally within that budget, but its goal is ratings success, a step or two removed from the actual revenue numbers generated by each program. Few programmers become deeply involved with the sales group—and fewer take the time to look at a Profit and Loss (P/L) statement that might be prepared by the accounting department. In fact, few television productions are scrutinized by the analysis that a P/L report would provide.

In some situations, key creative people or production companies have every reason to care about the project's P/L. The reason: profit participation. That is, as part of an employee package, they personally benefit from the profits earned by the project. In most situations, production overages are added to the cost side, and so, profits are reduced. Sometimes, these overages give the network or program owner license to add even more deductions.

If the creative or production team does not participate in profits—and this situation is the more common by far—then its goal is simple: it is hired to make the best possible television show. If the project goes over budget, then the network (or the production company) pays the difference. The production team may find itself working in a stressful environment and may benefit from the overage, as it is paid for additional days or weeks of work.

# CHAPTER 17

# PROGRAM SALES

In today's programming marketplace, there are three principal markets: domestic broadcast, domestic cable, and foreign broadcast/cable.

## THE DOMESTIC BROADCAST MARKET

This market breaks, somewhat unevenly, into programs produced by and for the broadcast networks (*Without a Trace, Good Morning America*), programs produced for syndication to individual local television stations (*The Tony Danza Show, Jeopardy!*), and programs produced by local television stations (*Channel 6 Action News, Eyewitness News*).

### Programs Produced by/for Broadcast Networks

There are, in essence, six program buyers in this category: CBS, NBC, ABC, FOX, UPN, and The WB. To a somewhat lesser extent, i (formerly PAX) and PBS also buy programs.

The four largest networks (ABC, CBS, NBC, FOX) produce an abundance of news and sports programming. Although there is some buying and selling with regard to sports (see Chapter 30), news programs are produced, by and large, for the network's own consumption. In some cases, they are licensed to networks outside the U.S. for daily broadcast.

For all of these broadcast networks, programs seen during prime time are acquired from production companies. In most cases, the production company is affiliated with the television division of a motion picture studio (e.g., Twentieth Television, part of Twentieth Century FOX). The production company earns fees for its production work, serves as employer for the staff, and acts as a bank for monies not yet available to the production. The studio typically retains control of the distribution rights—the right to sell the program after it is shown twice on broadcast network prime time. The studio may release DVDs, sell the series to a cable network, place the series in broadcast syndication, and/or sell the rights to networks outside of the U.S. This program sales effort is an essential component in program production financing—the network's license fees, which allow the two airings in prime time, are rarely sufficient to cover the production costs.

More than half of each network's prime-time schedule is produced by production companies working in association with the network's own internal production company. That is, the network's production division is a partner in the production—it may provide funding, and it may control distribution. When the CBS Productions logo appears at the end of a program shown on CBS, the program has been produced in association with the network's own production company.

## Programs Produced for Local Market Syndication

The syndication model has been intact for about 75 years. In today's marketplace, for example, WPVI in Philadelphia programs the ABC feed every morning and through many of the daytime, evening, and prime-time hours. WPVI's active local news operation fills many of the non-network hours, but the station fills certain daily time slots with syndicated programming. These include 9:00 A.M. to 10:00 A.M. (*Live with Regis and Kelly*), 4:00 P.M. to 5:00 P.M. (*Oprah*), 7:00 P.M. to 7:30 P.M. (*Jeopardy!*), and 7:30 P.M. to 8:00 P.M. (*Wheel of Fortune*). Station groups tend to negotiate for their owned stations; this combination of syndicated programs is often found on ABC-owned and -operated stations. In fact, one syndication company, King World, supplies three of the four programs; *Live with Regis and Kelly* is syndicated by Buena Vista, which, like WPVI, is owed by Disney. On network affiliates, most of the big money in syndication comes from the late-afternoon and early evening slots.

Most of the programs seen on network affiliates in the mid-morning, late afternoon, and early evening are well-established properties subject to long-term (five years or more) agreements between station groups and distributors. It is difficult for a new program to establish itself in any of these key franchise slots. Most attempts to build new programs based upon popular television performers fail after a year or two. Wayne Brady, Jane Pauley, Dr. Joy Browne, and Martin Short are among the many whom daytime audiences have rejected. A smaller number succeed, and when they do, they tend to remain on daytime schedules for years: Dr. Phil, Ellen DeGeneres, Rosie O'Donnell, and Tony Danza among them. Why does Wayne Brady fail when Ellen DeGeneres succeeds? Syndication executives can theorize, do market research, hire and fire producers, change formats, and add guest hosts, but the truth is, nobody really understands what makes a hit series. The best one can do is to avoid the most obvious mistakes.

Entertainment news programs seem to work best in the spot before and after the evening news. The same is true for the few traditional game shows on the daily schedule. *Entertainment Tonight* and the somewhat newer *Access Hollywood* are long-term franchises that successfully move audiences from the afternoon schedule to the local news, or from the network news into the network's prime-time schedule. *Jeopardy!*, *Wheel of Fortune*, and *Hollywood Squares* are among the few traditional game shows that have proven successful as franchises, almost always programmed in the 7:00 P.M.–8:00 P.M. time slot. All three are based upon programs that have been on television for more than 25 years. Syndicators rarely attempt to launch new entertainment magazines or game shows.

## Syndicated Programs on FOX, UPN, and WB Affiliates

Most markets have six or fewer commercial television stations broadcasting traditional entertainment programming. Other licensees may exist, but these are most often affiliated with, owned by, or purchase the majority of their programming from a religious organization (see page 192), a home shopping network (see page 184), or a Spanish-language network. Some stations also offer a few hours of "paid programming"—airtime sold in full half hours or hours for use as infomercials.

As of 2004, The WB programmed six nights per week, mostly one or two hours per night, but provided no daytime network programming. Similarly, UPN programmed only on Monday through Friday from 8:00 P.M. until 10:00 P.M., with Thursday nights devoted entirely to one program, *WWE Smackdown!*. FOX programs from 8:00 P.M. until 10:00 P.M. on every night of the week (except Sundays, when it begins at 7:00 P.M.). In addition, FOX programs on Sunday mornings, plus weekend sports programming.

FOX stations typically fill their schedules with first-run syndicated programs. Many FOX stations are heavy on courtroom shows and on the few well-known talk shows that have not been picked up by the larger network affiliates. For example, in Rochester, New York, local FOX affiliate WUHF runs both *The Jerry Springer Show* and *Maury*. Many FOX stations also run *Seinfeld* and *The Simpsons* in the slot prior to prime time. The strategy makes sense: These comedy series set up the stations' prime-time schedule with younger viewers who watch a more contemporary form of comedy.

UPN affiliates tend to buy off-network reruns, often with appeal to either a younger female audience or to African-American viewers. The WB affiliates follow a similar strategy but tend to run a cartoon block on weekday afternoons.

In fact, the size of the audience available to most UPN and WB affiliates is too small to profitably sell the airtime in syndicated programs for the entire day. Instead, many affiliates run a shopping service, such as Jewelry Television, which requires less effort, produces a reasonable if modest return, and fills the overnight hours.

## Programs Produced by Local Television Stations

In general, local television stations produce news programs that are valuable only in their local markets. From time to time, an enterprising news director or station manager will develop a news segment that can be shown in other markets— perhaps a health segment for stations lacking their own health reporter—but these are the exception. As a rule, program sales are not an activity relevant to locally produced television programs in the U.S.

## PROGRAMS DISTRIBUTED TO DOMESTIC CABLE NETWORKS

The television distributor, or syndicator, is not limited to the broadcast market. The role of a distributor is to find the most profitable market for its program wares and to make the best possible deals. For many off-network programs, the key market is no longer the broadcast station; instead, cable networks have become the most active marketplace. A look at the 2004–2005 daytime schedule finds a great many off-network programs on several cable networks: *Saved by the Bell*, *Mama's Family*, *Dawson's Creek*, *Rockford Files*, *Magnum P.I.*, and *The Cosby Show* on TBS; *Charmed*, *ER*, *Judging Amy*, *NYPD Blue*, *Touched by an Angel*, and *Law & Order* on TNT; *Murder She Wrote* and *Third Watch* on A&E; and *The West Wing* and *Columbo* on Bravo. Many of these programs are surprisingly old, and nearly all are used to fill either daytime hours or, in the case of a series with some heat, like *The West Wing*, in the 11:00 P.M. slot for viewers who have not yet tired of prime time and do not watch the local news.

As audiences and advertising dollars have migrated from broadcast to cable networks, most of the larger networks have dramatically reduced their reliance upon off-network programs. Many of these networks now have libraries of their own programs, produced for their own prime time. Several others, notably TNT, TBS, and TV Land, have evolved a strategy in which off-network programming becomes an asset. TBS, for example, has successfully built a comedy block with strong appeal to ages 18–34 around *Seinfeld*, *Friends*, and *Sex and the City*.

With fewer hour-long dramas produced by the broadcast networks (due in part to the popularity of reality shows), and relatively few comedy series with a sufficient number of weekly episodes to fill a daily slot (a five-day strip), the off-network market for cable series is not likely to experience dramatic growth in the near future. A&E, once a big buyer of off-network hours, has been producing more original programming to attract a younger audience, and with series like *Growing Up Gotti*, the strategy is proving successful. With the success of *Queer Eye for the Straight Guy*, NBC is learning how to use Bravo as more than just an ancillary network for its older product. USA Network now produces a healthy amount of programming, so it, too, is less of a market for syndicated product. The two general-interest Turner networks, TBS and TNT, are among the few consistent buyers of large amounts of off-network product. Newer cable networks tend toward very specific interests—such as professional tennis or NFL or video games or anime—and tend not to buy off-network programming.

## PROGRAMS DISTRIBUTED TO FOREIGN MARKETS

Although few programs produced outside the U.S. are shown on U.S. broadcast or cable networks, many U.S. programs are seen throughout the world. Some are shown with their American soundtracks intact, some are shown with subtitles, and some are dubbed by actors speaking the local language.

In the 1990s, the international marketplace for all programming expanded with the introduction of new privately owned broadcast channels, new satellite channels and new cable networks, particularly in Europe, Asia, and Latin America (see Part 11). Old rules were broken; no longer were dramatic programs (like the 1980s hit *Dallas*) the principal U.S. exports. Now, popular U.S. series like *Friends*, *Seinfeld*, and *The Simpsons* were as likely to gain high ratings. At the same time, many U.S. cable networks established themselves as local networks in specific countries. MTV, for example, now operates cable networks under its own brand name in dozens of countries.

As U.S. product has become commonplace, however, many countries have limited the number of hours of imported programming that may be shown with a kind of quota system.

As with broadcast and cable buyers in the U.S., deals are made for international sales on the basis of an exclusive or semi-exclusive territorial buy for a limited term—the larger the territory, the higher the price per episode. Programs are sold to local broadcasters and to cable networks.

One useful resource for prices paid in the international marketplace can be found on the Web by visiting www.worldscreen.com/priceindex.php. This page is part of the World Screen News Web site, an industry trade publication that covers the buying and selling of programs in the international marketplace.

## International Format Rights

Some programs, such as game shows and reality shows, are not easily imported because local audiences prefer to see hosts and contestants from their own countries. It is sometimes possible, however, to sell the rights to produce a program locally rather than selling the original version of the program itself. In television game shows, there is a long tradition of format rights sales. *The Price Is Right* and *Wheel of Fortune*, for example, are seen in many other countries. The format for these programs is similar or identical to the format seen in the U.S., as are the special features associated with each format (pricing games, a large wheel and letter board), but the hosts, program names, logos, music, and contestants are clearly produced to encourage local viewership. On the flip side, some series seen in the U.S. are format imports from other countries. These include *Who Wants to Be A Millionaire*, which was originally produced in England, and several reality series from the European producer Endemol, notably *Big Brother* and *The Amazing Race*.

In fact, it is difficult to protect any game show or reality show concept under current U.S. intellectual property laws, and the situation becomes somewhat more complicated because intellectual property rules differ by country. Often, when a program is licensed, the network's decision to acquire the program is based in part upon the format itself, and in part upon the success that the program's name, style, and presentation have achieved in other countries.

Format rights are common in game and reality shows, but uncommon in other types of programming. Prices paid for these rights vary widely. If the series is an enormous prime-time hit, and both the buyer and seller are major players, the cost will be far higher than for a game show series intended simply to fill a daytime slot.

## ORIGINAL PROGRAMMING FOR DOMESTIC SYNDICATION

There are essentially three types of original programming produced for syndication: talk shows, game shows, and entertainment magazines. The odds of developing and producing a new talk show with an interesting host are tough, but each season, one or two newcomers emerge. Typically, these programs are produced by a very experienced "show runner"—a producer whose past credentials are likely to include key production roles on successful talk shows, such as *The Sally Jesse Raphael Show* or *The Rosie O'Donnell Show*. There is no rule for what type of personality or background makes a great talk show host, but most successful hosts have years as either entertainers or broadcasters. Rosie O'Donnell was an actress and comedian; Ellen DeGeneres was a comedian; Tony Danza was an actor and sometime singer; Montel Williams was a marine; Dr. Phil was a medical doctor; Regis Philbin was a broadcaster; Maury Povich was a news anchor and longtime local talk show host; Jerry Springer was a mayor; and Sally Jesse Raphael was a radio talk show host.

A successful talk show must have a host whose audience appeal is strong, but this is only part of the formula. The show runner must place the host in a comfortable situation with the right types of guests. Both Ellen DeGeneres and Tony Danza are best with celebrity guests, with the occasional "regular person" in the mix for human interest. Montel Williams is generally best with regular people and strong story lines. With a poor assortment of celebrity guests (often the result of poor ratings), too much pressure is placed upon the host and the comedy routines concocted with a limited writing staff and limited production resources.

Successful series make it look easy with a friendly, comfortable, often humorous flow of guests who are fun, with situations that are surprising, and with an undeniable (often magical) connection between host and audience. Make no mistake, however: A daily talk show is an enormous amount of work requiring an extremely skilled, experienced staff. In addition to the booking requirements for a five-day week (at least a few guests per day) and the preparation of each segment so that it's fun to watch, or at least interesting, there's the constant threat of last-minute guest cancellations or schedule changes.

The most successful syndicated shows measure their longevity in decades. The longest-running syndicated series, with 33 years of production, is *Soul Train*. The second longest-running slot is shared by *Entertainment Tonight* (24 years) and Roger Ebert's movie review show (first with Gene Siskel, now with Richard

Roeper). Many of the most successful syndicated series are approaching 20 years of service: *Oprah*, *Wheel of Fortune*, *Jeopardy!*, *Inside Edition*, and *Live with Regis and Kelly* (previously, Kathy Lee). These remarkable success stories leave little room for new syndicated properties.

New game shows are the exception, not the rule. During the past decade, only two new game shows have emerged as syndication successes. One is *Hollywood Squares*, a series with nine celebrities of varying levels of fame, based upon a very successful 1960s hit series; the other is *Who Wants to Be a Millionaire*, based upon a recent prime-time juggernaut. The fact is, there are almost no available slots and little interest from station groups for new game shows.

Entertainment magazine shows require enormous resources, so only large media companies can afford to launch these types of projects. With four current series—Paramount's *Entertainment Tonight* and *The Insider*, NBC's *Access Hollywood*, and Warner Bros.' *Extra*—well positioned in the best time slots (typically 7:00 P.M.–8:00 P.M. weekdays, competing against *Jeopardy!* and *Wheel of Fortune*), there is little opportunity for a new series of this type.

## SYNDICATION ECONOMICS

Traditionally, syndicated programs have been sold in one of three ways: for *cash*, for *barter*, or for a combination of *cash plus barter*. In today's marketplace, off-network episodes may be sold to television station groups, but they are more often sold to cable networks.

A *cash* deal is straightforward. Most often, the rights to a network series are owned or controlled by the studio that produced it for the network. When the series is renewed for a third or fourth season, it is shopped to several cable networks to determine the level of interest. If a deal can be made at this stage, then the series does not go into broadcast syndication, at least not in the short term. One of the largest such deals was A&E's acquisition of HBO's *The Sopranos*—78 episodes (seasons one through six) for $2.5 million per episode, for four years beginning in 2006. For the distributor (in this case, HBO—not a syndicator, but serving a similar purpose here), this process is straightforward and simple: no need to service 50 or 100 individual stations, no need to sell advertising, no need to do anything except make the deal and collect the payment. Compare this deal to the previous record from 2002, in which TNT paid an estimated $700,000 for new *Law & Order* episodes and $250,000 for series episodes that had previously run on A&E.

Most cable networks are reluctant to invest $100 million in any series. The premium cost is ultimately passed on to advertisers, who may or may not see comparative value for the higher prices charged. Often, a deal involves a *barter* arrangement in which the syndicator is provided with a number of commercial minutes per hour that it may sell as an additional source of revenue. This allows the cable network to still make the deal without spending the cash.

A deal may also be made with individual broadcast stations or, more often, with a number of station groups. This situation typically involves several dozen deals, each individually negotiated. A successful series will earn over $200,000 per episode in the largest markets, far less in the smaller ones. Here, a cash deal is often *blended* with a barter deal. Cash plus barter deals are more complicated, but they are relatively common, particularly among programs in the daytime and early evening schedule. Barter deals are the least desirable for syndicators, as they contain the most risk, and tend to be offered for less desirable programming.

As a rule, the initial license fee paid to the studio or production company by the network or syndicator should be sufficient to cover production costs and overhead. Network dramas are sometimes produced at a deficit; the production company or studio relies upon syndication revenues both to break even and to make a profit. Original programming for syndication is typically shown just once, or in some cases twice (most often to allow for a summer hiatus), and because additional revenues are not available from future plays, the onetime fee per episode typically covers both production costs and profits.

Budgets for syndicated series are generally in the range of $250,000 to $750,000 per week of five hour-long episodes, or about $50,000 to $150,000 per episode. Half-hour shows cost about 25 percent to 30 percent less. A premium may be paid for a well-known host, long-term success, an irreplaceable game show format, or an entertainment news magazine whose production requirements are complex and expensive. It's safe to assume at least 40 weeks of new production per year, so the total investment in a year's series is likely to be 40 x $500,000, or about $20 million, or perhaps more accurately, $15 million to $30 million per year for an hour-long show.

With 20 commercial slots, each 30 seconds long, per hour-long episode, a $125,000 daily investment would break even on its production commitment at $6,250 per spot. Add the typical 35 percent sales commission charged by the syndicator, plus 15 percent more for the syndicator's sales expenses, and the total is about $12,000. Although prices vary, successful daytime or evening series bring in about $50,000 per spot. Most off-network series seen on cable networks are not as profitable, more likely to bring in about $10,000 per 30-second spot— often much less if the series airs in daytime. Still, the series generally becomes profitable because cable networks typically schedule each episode many times throughout the life of the acquisition agreement.

Rather than relying upon outside vendors, each syndication company maintains a related company whose sole purpose is the sale of commercial time garnered in barter deals. Camelot, for example, is the barter advertising arm of King World.

# PART 5
# BIG MEDIA

# CHAPTER 18

# THE RISE OF BIG MEDIA

In previous editions of this book, the history of television (and radio) was told as a story of technological development, social change, government interaction, politics, and the growth of local and national businesses. These paths have led to a media industry dominated by enormous companies whose assets include most of the nation's leading television and radio stations, all of the largest broadcast and cable networks, and many of the largest studios and production companies, as well as magazines, outdoor advertising (billboards), and most of the media distribution systems. Some of these big media companies have grown from authentic broadcast roots; all have grown and prospered as a result of acquisitions. Many are significant participants in the international media business as well.

## ADVERTISING, CORPORATE INTERESTS, AND BIG MEDIA

As a rule, the primary revenue stream for these large media companies is *advertising*. Big media companies provide access to target customers for the nation's largest consumer products companies, including GM ($3.5 billion per year), Procter & Gamble ($3.2 billion), Ford ($2.2 billion), and McDonalds ($1.3 billion). (Each year, *Advertising Age*, a trade magazine, publishes a special issue listing top advertisers and their spending breakdowns by media: amount spent on magazines, newspapers, outdoor/billboards, radio, and various types of television-network TV, spot TV, syndicated TV, and cable TV. The issue is typically published in late June.)

The close relationship between big media and large advertisers has caused many government leaders and consumer groups to question the objectivity of big media news operations. As a rule, big media news operations tend to steer clear of all but the biggest stories about their advertisers or the advertisers' parent companies. In fact, several big media companies are owned by even larger corporations whose interests and activities involve international geopolitics, environmental issues, and more—General Electric, for example, owns NBC Universal. In general, big media in the U.S. interprets news as something other than investigative journalism related to corporate practices. News is about ratings, and at the local level, that usually means coverage of local violence. At the national level, coverage tends more toward politics, natural disasters, popular culture, and human interest.

## BIG MEDIA'S PRIORITIES

Big media companies typically own and operate many smaller companies. Each of these companies is independently managed, and is required to generate an annual profit, generally as a percentage of revenues. Of course, some companies in the portfolio generate more profits than others. Companies that do not perform are likely to be perceived as internal problems and allowed to adjust strategy for a period of up to a few years. After several years of underperformance, the company's senior management is changed or the company is sold.

The performance of individual companies is rarely made public, except within a category of related companies. For example, revenues and expenses associated with specific cable networks are rarely reported; instead, the "cable networks group" is more likely to be included on documents filed with the SEC, such as the corporation's 10-K Annual Report.

Ultimately, the performance of individual divisions matters for three reasons. First, short-term (quarterly) corporate results are posted for Wall Street and for investors. These results affect the corporation's stock price. The stock price often affects investor confidence in corporate management and the effectiveness of the corporation's board of directors, which often affects the overall direction of the corporation. Second, performance matters because the numbers determine the ability of the corporation to arrange for credit at the most favorable rates. Third, in a marketplace where nearly every asset is ultimately available for acquisition, performance affects the value of the asset.

Admittedly, the first two of these big media priorities are rarely shared by the individual manager working at a local television station, or by employees of a midsized cable network. Rarely are these people significant investors, and they are likewise generally unaffected by the corporation's ability to borrow money at favorable rates. The third priority is the one that matters most to employees: The possibility of acquisition due to poor performance is often associated with job loss.

## OWNERSHIP AND CONTROL

As the competitive environment has evolved, it has become necessary for the largest media companies to own a major asset associated with every aspect of the media business—or so the big media company executives believe. A fully integrated media conglomerate would likely include one or more companies for motion picture and television development and production; one or more cable or broadcast networks (for distribution); a strategic combination of print and Web assets (for promotion); and a range of local media, including television stations, radio stations, newspapers, outdoor media companies, and other related assets.

Media companies routinely do business with one another: Twentieth Television supplies NBC, Paramount sells programs to ABC, and so on. Still, senior corporate management encourages a high level of interaction divisions, in part to encourage synergies, but mostly to collect the higher profits associated with ownership of revenue streams from as many productive markets as possible. When a CBS series is produced by Paramount Television, then syndicated by Viacom, with a spin-off book series from Simon & Schuster and a children's version produced for Nickelodeon—this is considered a major win for the senior management of Viacom. To encourage this type of synergy, each of the networks has established its own productions unit (CBS Productions, for example), which often serves as coproducer for programs seen on its sister network.

## RULES GOVERNING BIG MEDIA

Large media companies are generally controlled by the same laws governing other U.S. corporations. They are required to disclose financial information, and they are required to comply with specific laws and regulations. One such FCC regulation limits the number of television stations and/or the percentage of the U.S. television audience that can be reached by a single company's broadcast television assets. Details regarding this regulation are found on page 6.

In addition, all media are limited with regard to content and advertising. Some of these regulations are based upon law (see pages 93 and 97) and others are based upon general guidelines self-imposed by each media industry.

# CHAPTER 19
# THE LARGEST MEDIA COMPANIES

This chapter covers the large media companies whose assets include the U.S. broadcast networks: NBC Universal (NBC), Disney (ABC), Viacom (CBS, UPN), Time Warner (The WB), and FOX. Other large media companies, including those who do not own U.S. broadcast networks, are covered in the next chapter.

## NBC UNIVERSAL

### Principal Assets and Power Base

As the corporate name makes clear, NBC Universal's principal power base is a combination of one of the U.S.'s most successful broadcast television networks and one of the most successful movie studios. Each of these major assets unfolds into a long list of powerful properties. NBC operates not only the U.S. broadcast network, but also several cable networks, including Telemundo, which serves the increasingly profitable Hispanic audience. NBC also operates several cable networks, and maintains investment positions in others. NBC was an early player in European satellite channels, so its principal programming properties, such as *The Tonight Show with Jay Leno*, are well established outside the U.S. NBC no longer owns radio stations but continues to operate television stations in just about every major U.S. market. The network's news leadership has been expanded with two cable networks: MSNBC and CNBC. With the addition of Universal Pictures, NBC and one of its most prolific, long-term suppliers have become one. NBC Universal's power in Washington, DC, and in governments throughout the world is enhanced by its ownership by GE, a major global military and infrastructure supplier. No other U.S. media company is built on such a solid foundation.

NBC Universal's annual revenues are in the range of $15 billion. The NBC Television Network's sales are about $7 billion per year.

### History: How NBC Universal Came Together

Founded in 1926 to resolve disputes between radio pioneers General Electric, RCA, and Westinghouse, NBC was formed to acquire these companies' fledgling radio stations and consolidate them into what became known as a "network." NBC rapidly expanded its network to include more and more radio stations, and by the early 1930s, NBC was successfully operating the two most successful radio networks in the U.S.—NBC Red and NBC Blue. By combining national distribution with a program schedule filled with celebrities (Jack Benny, Burns & Allen, Bob Hope, and many more), the NBC networks easily attracted national advertisers. The mastermind behind this plan was David Sarnoff, who consistently placed NBC in the role of innovator: first coast-to-coast radio broadcast (1927's Rose Bowl), first license for a commercial television station (in 1941—now WNBC/New York), first color television broadcast (1953), and so on. For most of the twentieth century, NBC was a leader in network television, local television, network radio, and local radio. It was the very model of a mid-twentieth century media company. Most NBC-owned and -operated stations have been so for a half-century or more: WNBC/New York, KNBC/Los Angeles, and WMAQ/Chicago are the largest. (WCAU/Philadelphia is a newer affiliate, the result of a swap with CBS for longtime NBC affiliate KYW.)

For much of its history, NBC was owned by RCA, the sole owner from 1932 until RCA was acquired by General Electric in 1986. (GE divested RCA's consumer electronics business, which was sold to the French company Thompson, but retained NBC.)

Although NBC and RCA demonstrated their conception of television at the 1939 New York World's Fair, the introduction was delayed until after the end of World War II. With a stronger affiliate network than either CBS or the far newer ABC (see pages 00, 00), NBC was a programming innovator from the start. The network established a morning show (*Today*) and a late-night program (eventually known as *Tonight*), plus groundbreaking news and sports coverage. NBC's early remote broadcasts were made possible by the company's close relationship with RCA's engineering staff, allowing, for example, the first color coverage of Major League Baseball's World Series as early as 1955.

From the 1950s until the 1970s, NBC executives were primarily concerned with the transition to color television and the increasingly competitive programming environment in a reasonably stable broadcast industry. From time to time, a local station changed its affiliation to or from NBC, but most of the business activity was related to the popularity of *The Dean Martin Show* or *Bonanza*, or the gradual replacement of older series from the 1960s with a more contemporary program mix for the emerging audiences of the 1970s. By the mid-1980s, it was clear that cable television and international expansion were essential. NBC did some investing, then launched its own consumer news and business channel ("CNBC" abbreviates that original mission, and also conveniently translates as "cable NBC"). A joint venture with Microsoft launched NBC into both the Internet space and a second news network, MSNBC.

Several years before the young NBC was formed, the entrepreneurial team at the fledgling Universal Pictures was building what would become one of the most successful motion picture studios. The company began in 1909 under Carl Laemmle as the Independent Moving Picture Company of America (IMP), then merged in 1912 with five other companies to provide end-to-end movie production, distribution, and exhibition as Universal Film Manufacturing. By 1915, the company was producing films at its own Universal City. For the next three decades, Universal was a leader in horror films, but generally operated in the lower echelons of the movie business. The studio was acquired by Decca Records in 1951. A short time later, MCA's Revue Studios became one of the busiest television program suppliers in Hollywood; renamed Universal Television, the company became a leader in crime drama and action/adventure, producing many series for NBC (including, in recent years, the various *Law & Order* series).

To make sense of the next series of events, it is necessary to go back to 1924 and the formation of Music Corporation of America, which became a leading talent agency known as MCA. By 1962, MCA—led by Lew Wasserman, the model of a contemporary studio boss—owned not only Decca Records but Universal Pictures as well. In the early 1990s, MCA partnered with the Japanese company Matsushita (owner of the Panasonic brand in the U.S., along with many other businesses). By 1995, MCA was controlled by Seagram. By 1998, as a result of many mergers, the Dutch corporation Philips owned a large number of record labels—notably Verve, London, Decca, Deutsche Grammophon, A&M, Motown, Island, and Def Jam—which it sold to Seagram. The resulting organization became known as the Universal Music Group.

In a rather convoluted series of events related to media entrepreneur Barry Diller, generally in the 2001–2004 period, Universal sold and subsequently reacquired interest in Universal Television, USA Network, and Sci-Fi Network; all are now part of the NBC Universal family of companies. In addition to its U.S. television operations, NBC Universal operates CNBC Europe and CNBC Asia Pacific in a venture with Dow Jones. NBC Universal also operates Sci-Fi, 13th Street (action and adventure), Studio Universal (movies), and USA Network in Europe and in Latin America.

NBC Universal is 80 percent owned by General Electric; Vivendi Universal owns the remaining 20 percent.

## Other Significant (Non-TV) Media Assets

NBC has always been a broadcasting company. As a rule, the company has not invested in nor started businesses unrelated to either television or radio broadcasting, or new forms of distribution for television. The company's corporate focus on programming, marketing, and distribution has sometimes seemed limiting, particularly when other media companies were buying book publishers or outdoor advertising/billboard companies.

The merger with Universal changes this strategy, but only to a limited extent. Universal's principal businesses are television program production (with a large number of program hours for NBC) and motion picture production and distribution. Many of Universal's investments have been in production companies (Brillstein-Grey, October Films) and in cable or pay networks throughout the world. Universal has some investments in publishing, mostly outside the U.S., and in theme parks both here and in Japan, but its largest non-television asset is its music business. The Universal Music Group is one of the world's largest, a massive conglomerate whose many acquisitions include the former Polygram classical music labels (Philips, Deutsche Grammophon, London), plus many pop labels (Motown) and a significant music publishing operation. Many of Universal's investments in interactive media have been related to the music industry.

## DISNEY ABC

### Principal Assets and Power Base

Disney's power base is built on a foundation of successful animated films and one of the world's most successful licensing and merchandising operations. ABC's power base is a half-century of broadcast television and radio network operations, and its national system of affiliated stations. The company's successful cable ventures include ESPN, a leader in sports television and an ideal companion for ABC Sports. Over time, Disney has expanded from its animation and family entertainment base by forming new companies without a Disney name: Touchstone Pictures is a mainstream Hollywood motion picture studio, and Buena Vista is a traditional television program distributor (*Regis & Kelly Live*, *The Tony Danza Show*, etc.).

Disney is a $31 billion company, with about $12 billion in annual revenues coming from ABC, Inc. Of those revenues, $4.6 billion is provided by ESPN—a very substantial contributor, but Disney owns only 80 percent (the other 20 percent is owned by Hearst).

### History: How Disney ABC Came Together

Of Disney and ABC, Disney is by far the older company. Disney's story begins in the 1920s, when young Walt Disney formed a company to produce and ultimately distribute animated motion pictures. Until the 1940s, the Disney studio regularly experienced financial troubles. High-stakes gambles, such as the building of Disneyland, provide interesting reading for popular culture historians. With television, Disney became a household name, and with *The Mickey Mouse Club* (which aired on ABC), Disney's merchandising became a national phenomenon. After founder Walt Disney's death, the company seemed to lose some of its magic, and in the 1970s, Disney's future was unclear. By the 1980s, however, a new charismatic chairman emerged in former ABC executive Michael Eisner.

ABC was formed as a result of a Justice Department ruling that required NBC to divest itself of one of its two radio networks (NBC Red or NBC Blue). Since NBC Blue was the weaker network, it was sold in 1943. The buyer was Life Savers magnate Edward J. Noble, who came into broadcasting at a time when his competitors were diverting radio profits to build expensive television stations. Lacking stars, programs, and cash, Noble carefully managed his resources and focused on building television stations in five major markets: New York City, Los Angeles, Chicago, San Francisco, and Detroit (which was a more significant market in the 1940s than it is today). Building the stations was financially draining, and building an entire network was beyond Noble's capability. In 1951, after being romanced by CBS (which wanted ABC's stations but planned to disband the budding network), Noble sold ABC to United Paramount Theatres (which was also formed as a result of antitrust divestiture). Paramount executive Leonard Goldenson took charge. Like NBC's Sarnoff and CBS's William S. Paley, Goldenson possessed the combination of entrepreneurial guts, business savvy, sensitivity to audience needs, and vision to build a national television network. Still, ABC struggled until the 1970s. It had fewer affiliates than NBC or CBS, so its audiences were always smaller and its advertising revenues were thinner. Within these limitations, ABC became an innovator: It was, for example, the first network to look to the Hollywood studios for programming. (This may seem like an obvious idea now, but at the time, it was radical thinking.) ABC leaned on gimmicky exploitation (*Batman, Charlie's Angels*) and on new forms, like the miniseries. The resulting successes were used as leverage to build the affiliate network.

In an effort to build additional revenue streams, ABC invested in magazine publishing, record labels, and new media ventures, including cable networks. As the network's financial situation stabilized, corporate attention shifted to the organization's future: finding a successor to Leonard Goldenson. At the time, few executives were perceived to be sufficiently talented, experienced, or worthy of such a role. But in 1985, this issue was resolved as ABC merged with Capital Cities Communications, a company that owned ABC affiliates as well as publishing and radio assets similar to ABC's own portfolio. ABC was sold to Capital Cities for $3.5 billion, the first time a broadcast network had been sold in the U.S. since 1951. The sale transformed the way the U.S. broadcast industry thought of itself: The new owners were businesspeople, not larger-than-life media legends. This recasting would set the stage for more than 20 years of business deals in which networks were bought and sold, and new networks were created.

By the time of the merger, ABC was already an active player in new media. In 1984, the network had acquired ESPN from Getty, and soon after, it sold 20 percent of the network to Nabisco (which then sold its share to Hearst). ABC was, and remains, a significant owner in the cable networks A&E and Lifetime.

As these networks grew stronger—they have been among the U.S.'s top cable networks for decades—ABC's value increased. In 1995, Disney made history with an offer to purchase ABC. The event was historically significant for several reasons. First, it was the second largest deal ever offered for the purchase of a U.S. company—$19 billion. Second, here was a movie studio buying a television network—nothing in the history of U.S. broadcasting suggested that such a thing was possible, or even conceivable. Third, this was the largest U.S. media deal of all time.

ABC, Disney, and ESPN are active in the international television marketplace. A Disney Channel operates in each of about a dozen countries. ESPN operates sports networks or offers sports programming on 30 networks reaching nearly 200 countries. In addition, Disney and its various entities have also invested in various international production companies.

## Other Significant (Non-TV) Media Assets

In recent years, Disney has owned several sports teams, including baseball's Los Angeles Dodgers and California Angels, and hockey's Anaheim Mighty Ducks. Disney operates theme parks in southern California, Florida, Japan, and France. In addition, Disney operates a variety of leisure properties, a cruise line, and a book publisher (Hyperion Books). Disney has also become a very significant producer of Broadway shows, such as *The Lion King* and *Beauty and the Beast*; the success of these shows and the elaborate restoration of aged Broadway theaters has helped to reinvigorate New York City's Times Square and 42nd Street. The company also owns over 50 radio stations, many of them in major markets, and programs a variety of radio formats (Radio Disney, ESPN Radio) and a variety of music formats, plus sports, business, talk, and other programs. Disney's licensing operation is among the largest in the world; licensing assets include Mickey Mouse and other longtime Disney animation favorites, plus a large portfolio of newer characters from *The Lion King* and other animated films produced since the 1990s.

## VIACOM

### Principal Assets and Power Base

The symmetry associated with contemporary media ownership is sometimes startling. ABC was acquired by one of its earliest producing partners, Disney. NBC was first spun out of a negotiation involving GE, RCA, and Westinghouse, and was later acquired by GE; NBC later acquired its largest producing supplier, Universal. Likewise, Viacom was formed when the U.S. government required CBS to leave the program syndication business; decades later, Viacom acquired CBS. Of course, these are not accidents. They are the results of longtime business relationships between executives associated with each of these companies.

Viacom's power base is built on broadcast and cable television networks, distribution of television programming, and significant assets in radio and retail distribution. Viacom owns CBS and, since 2000, UPN. Viacom also owns MTV Networks, whose domestic assets include MTV, Nickelodeon, VH1, Spike, and many smaller networks. In addition, this media kingdom includes several powerful television syndicators (CBS Enterprises, Paramount, and King World); Paramount (motion pictures and television); the Showtime pay cable network; Blockbuster Video; movie theaters; a major outdoor advertising company; and a very large number of radio stations known as Infinity Broadcasting. Many of these assets are companies that have developed over the past 25 years: MTV, for example, debuted in 1981, and Blockbuster Video opened its first retail storefront in 1985. Viacom has been especially successful in exporting its U.S. properties, more or less intact, into markets outside the U.S., often retaining control of creative, marketing, and distribution in the process. Advertising is a principal source of revenues; few large media companies rival Viacom in terms of sheer mass-market research and target audience marketing.

Viacom's 2003 sales were over $26 billion. The cable networks contributed over $5 billion, with just over $1 billion coming from Showtime Networks; the remaining $4 billion came from MTV Networks. BET is roughly a half-billion-dollar business. The CBS network business is worth over $4 billion, and UPN adds another quarter billion. In addition, Viacom television station groups (CBS stations, Paramount stations) add nearly $2 billion per year.

## History: How Viacom Came Together

Although Viacom is arguably the most contemporary of the major players, its roots precede the 1920s. The story begins in 1912—several years earlier than other media companies—when Adolph Zukor founded the Famous Players Film Corp., which soon merged to become an early version of Paramount Pictures. The company remained independent until 1966, when it was sold to Gulf + Western, a conglomeration of essentially unrelated investments. By 1989, Gulf + Western was known as Paramount Communications, and in 1994, Viacom bought Paramount Pictures for $10 billion.

CBS Radio went on the air in 1927 as the Columbia Phonograph Broadcasting System. In 1928, William S. Paley, whose father's cigar company had been advertising on the network, bought CBS. In the next several decades, CBS became NBC's strongest competitor. Thanks to Edward R. Murrow, Walter Cronkite, and other newsmen, CBS emerged from World War II as the model of American radio broadcast journalism. When it came to television, CBS fell behind, then gained a significant advantage as CBS lawyers developed a clever tax loophole. Armed with this tactic, Paley and his program department lured some of NBC Radio's biggest stars. In time, CBS became home to many of television's most popular variety shows starring Jack Benny, Red Skelton, Burns and Allen, Danny

Kaye, Jackie Gleason—the list goes on. CBS also became home to the immensely popular (and later harshly criticized) situation comedy *Amos n' Andy*, as well as the evergreen smash hit *I Love Lucy*. While NBC built its power base from a combination of technology, a strong and powerful distribution system, and stars, CBS depended primarily on the power of television's most important differentiator: programming.

For many years, CBS tried to parallel NBC in the area of technology development. CBS engineers developed a color television system, for example, but it was not adopted. CBS also devised some promising early versions of a home video recording device but never yielded a successful consumer product. CBS engineers did develop the long-playing record album, or LP, which remained the standard for two decades (and has recently enjoyed a small comeback).

In 1986, CBS made a notable change when investor Laurence Tisch took control of the company—a move that blocked a potential acquisition by Ted Turner. Tisch then sold off CBS's non-broadcast assets, including Columbia Records (whose catalog includes Billie Holiday, Bob Dylan, Leonard Bernstein, and many Broadway treasures) and a large magazine publishing group. In 1995, CBS was sold to Westinghouse for just over $5 billion. Within a year or so, Westinghouse shed its other businesses to concentrate on broadcasting; during this period, the corporation acquired Infinity Broadcasting, a large radio station group whose outdoor advertising business formed the base for today's larger Viacom outdoor advertising enterprise. In 1999, CBS acquired King World, the large syndicator behind *Jeopardy!*, *Oprah*, and *Wheel of Fortune*. Later that year, CBS was sold to Viacom for $37 billion.

Back in 1970, the FCC required ABC, CBS, and NBC to get out of the program distribution business. Specifically, the networks were no longer allowed to sell programs to local stations—a seemingly minor change from today's perspective, but a substantial change at the time. ABC spun off rights to programs such as *The Love Boat* and *Dark Shadows* to a new, independent company called Worldvision (acquired by Taft Broadcasting in 1979). NBC's *Bonanza*, *You Bet Your Life*, *Concentration*, and some sitcoms were sold to Republic Television. The company that spun off from CBS was endowed with the strongest library—*The Andy Griffith Show*, *The Dick Van Dyke Show*, *I Love Lucy*, and *The Honeymooners* are among the most consistent off-network properties in terms of long-term syndication success. More than 30 years later, these programs remain popular on yet another Viacom property, the TV Land cable network. Through the 1970s and 1980s, Viacom emerged as a strong force with assets beyond syndication.

Nickelodeon and MTV were developed not by Viacom, but by Warner Communications (now Time Warner). At the time, that corporation's Warner Cable was aggressively establishing exclusive local franchise deals to build local cable television operations. One tactic used to encourage local governments—and ultimately, local consumers—to sign with Warner Cable was programming for underserved family members. By offering a channel for teenagers (MTV) and another for children (then commercial-free Nickelodeon), Warner Cable presented a perceived advantage. Unfortunately, the cost of actually building the cable systems proved far higher than anticipated; in the end, Warner sold the networks to Viacom in 1986 for $685 million. Nickelodeon's annual revenues now exceed $1.2 billion, and MTV's revenues are comparable.

Today's Viacom emerged as Sumner Redstone, an operator of movie theaters under the National Amusements Inc. (NAI) name, made a large investment and essentially took over the company in 1987. That same year, Wayne Huizenga, whose fortune was made with trash service provider Waste Management, acquired the Blockbuster home video retail stores. In 1994, Viacom bought Blockbuster for about $8 billion.

In the television industry, Viacom is unique because it owns two of the six broadcast networks: CBS and UPN. UPN, the United Paramount Network, debuted on January 16, 1995. The network took shape about a year before, as station groups United Television and Chris-Craft Industries joined forces with Paramount, a leading studio. The current structure, called Viacom Television Stations, includes 20 CBS stations, 18 Paramount stations (UPN affiliates), and 1 independent station.

Viacom's 2004 revenues totaled $22.5 billion.

## Other Significant (Non-TV) Media Assets

Viacom has been among the most acquisitive media corporations. Its entrepreneurial culture has built MTV and Nickelodeon into worldwide brands with considerable reach beyond television (motion pictures, product licensing, etc.). Blockbuster provides reach and power in movie and video game distribution, and provides Viacom with about $6 billion in annual revenues. Viacom's outdoor advertising venture is one of the nation's largest, a roughly $2 billion business. Viacom's radio business, Infinity Broadcasting, operates 185 radio stations—plus the CBS Radio Network, now mainly a source of hourly newscasts for business news and talk radio stations—and is also a $2 billion business.

# TIME WARNER

## Principal Assets and Power Base

As the two parts of its corporate name suggest, Time Warner draws its strength from the magazines of the former Time, Inc. and from the popularity of television programs and movies made and distributed by Warner Bros. For a brief period, Time Warner was positioned as the media company of the future when it merged with AOL and briefly traded as AOL Time Warner, but the company has since returned to its core businesses as priorities. Time Warner owns 70 percent of The WB Television Network. The HBO unit operates HBO and Cinemax. The Turner Broadcasting System operates CNN, TBS, TNT, Turner Classic Movies, and Cartoon Network. Today's Time Warner also owns some of the publishing industry's best magazines in *Time, Entertainment Weekly, People, Sports Illustrated,* and *Fortune.* Other well-established Warner Bros. properties include the movie studio and television production/distribution operation, numerous record labels, book publishing and distribution, and AOL, which remains one of the largest companies on the Internet.

Time Warner's 2004 sales were about $42 billion. Nearly 10 percent of these revenues came from HBO and its related properties. The WB provided $700 million, while the Turner Broadcasting System networks contributed about $9 billion. Time Warner Cable generates about $8 billion per year in sales—a very significant corporate contributor, about the size of the entire Warner Bros. entertainment division (movie studio, television studio, etc.) and about 50 percent larger than Time, Inc.

## History: How Time Warner Came Together

The Warner Bros. story begins as the four Warner brothers relocate to southern California to make movies. After a few fledgling years, they incorporated as Warner Brothers Pictures in 1923, and made history with the first talking picture—featuring superstar Al Jolson—in 1927. The next decades established Warner Bros. as a movie studio with a distinct, streetwise style. Even their animations (Bugs Bunny debuted in 1940) displayed attitude. In 1944, Leon Schlesinger sold his animation studio—Looney Tunes—to Warner Bros. Pictures. In 1948, Warner sold its library to MGM and, like all motion picture studios, was also forced to sell the motion picture theaters that were the foundation of the highly controlled "studio system." When this system collapsed, the studios faltered. Eventually, the assets of Warner Bros. Pictures were acquired by Seven Arts, Ltd. in 1967 for $84 million.

That same year, Kinney National Company—an operator of funeral parlors, parking lots, and limousine services—bought DC Comics, All-American Comics, and the Ashley Famous talent agency (similar to today's William Morris Agency). The effort was led by entrepreneur Steve Ross, and when Kinney bought Warner Bros.-Seven Arts in 1969, Ross became the architect of a new Warner Communications, renamed in 1972.

Before the change in ownership, Seven Arts had acquired Atlantic Records. The Warner Bros. studio owned Warner Bros. Records as well as Frank Sinatra's Reprise records, which it had acquired from the singer in 1963. Entrepreneur Jac Holzman sold his successful folk music label, Elektra, in 1970. These record labels remain the core of the Warner Music Group.

Since the 1970s, Warner has maintained an interest in technology. The company acquired Atari, an early video game and home computer leader, in 1978 (and later sold it when market changes caused Atari to lose considerable sums). Warner also led the way for a more modern approach to cable television, moving the industry from retransmission of existing channels into the distribution of new channels made expressly for cable television subscribers. In 2000, Warner (by then Time Warner) management was wooed by the promise of the Internet and the success assured by an enormous merger (over $180 billion) with AOL. After AOL lost over $50 billion in one quarter, the corporate name was changed from AOL Time Warner back to Time Warner. Rumors about an AOL sale have persisted ever since.

The history of Time, Inc. (formerly Time-Life) also brings together multiple paths of media development. In 1923, two Baltimore news reporters concocted *Time* magazine, and by 1930, Henry Luce (whose partner died early) had launched a second magazine, *Fortune*. *Life* magazine followed in 1936. *Sports Illustrated* came later, in 1954, but it was more than 20 years before the next major Time, Inc. magazine: *People*. The final giant in this publishing empire, *Entertainment Weekly*, was established in 1990. On the book publishing side, Time-Life Books began in 1963, and Little, Brown was acquired in 1968. Time, Inc. entered the television business in 1972 with the acquisition of a very early version of Home Box Office (HBO). Time, Inc. merged with Warner Communications in 1989.

The final strand of the story comes from Atlanta entrepreneur Ted Turner, who built on the weak foundation of his father's failing billboard business to buy a small television station, which he renamed WTCG (later WTBS, now simply TBS). Like HBO's founders, Turner was among the first to realize the potential of satellite distribution to cable systems: With just one deal, and amidst all sorts of negative reactions from the industry, Turner placed his signal on "the bird" and transformed an insignificant Atlanta UHF station into a national network. Turner then bought another station, sold it, and used the money to fund another start-up that the traditional television industry hoped would go away: CNN, the Cable News Network. Turner bought the Atlanta Braves in 1976, turning them into a winning team and a national phenomenon. In 1986, Turner bought MGM, gaining access to MGM, UA, and old Warner Bros. libraries; this was the basis for Turner Classic Movies. In 1991, Turner acquired Hanna-Barbera, the foundation for Cartoon Network, launched in 1992.

After a failed attempt to acquire CBS, Turner attempted several other acquisitions. Unable to build the scale that he felt was required to successfully operate a contemporary media company, he sold out to Time Warner in 1996.

By this time, AOL was a major success story in the media business. Having grown from 1 million subscribers in 1994, AOL subsequently acquired its largest competitor, CompuServe, as well as the promising Web browser, Netscape. The acquisitions continued as AOL positioned itself to be the most powerful of online companies. At the time, longtime Time Warner chief Gerry Levin was considering the company's future leadership and came upon the idea of Steve

Case, who became the chairman of the merged AOL Time Warner.

Meanwhile, AOL Time Warner bolstered its publishing assets. Already a successful book publisher (Warner Books), the company acquired Times Mirror magazines (*Golf, Skiing, Field & Stream*, etc.) and the U.K.'s largest magazine publisher, IPC Group (80 magazines, including *Woman's Weekly, Horse & Hound, Marie Claire*, and *What's On TV*).

On the television side, Time Warner has long been among the largest operators of cable systems in the U.S.; both of its pre-merger companies, Time, Inc. and Warner Cable, were large cable operators. The current Time Warner Cable, built on this foundation and upon many smaller acquisitions, is the nation's second largest MSO with over 10 million cable subscribers (number one Comcast has over 22 million). Warner Bros. launched The WB Network in 1995. As the newest broadcast network, The WB's affiliates are not all traditional VHF or UHF stations; some affiliates, particularly in the smallest markets, are LPTV operators, and in some markets, The WB has no broadcast affiliate, only cable outlets. Despite Time, Inc.'s and CNN's traditions of news coverage, The WB does not maintain a national news operation.

Most of The WB Network's larger affiliates belong to the Tribune station group: WPIX in New York, KTLA in Los Angeles, WGN in Chicago, WPHL in Philadelphia, WLVI in Boston, and WBDN in Washington, DC (which is managed, but not owned, by Tribune). With few exceptions (notably in New York, Los Angeles, and Chicago), all of The WB Network's affiliates are UHF stations. Still, the network has affiliates in all major markets, and in most (but not all) medium-sized markets.

## Other Significant (Non-TV) Media Assets

Time Warner owns Book-of-the-Month Club; Little, Brown; Warner Books; and Sunset Books; but it no longer owns Time-Life Inc., the direct-marketing company for books and music (sold to Zelnick Media in 2004). It is no surprise that Time, Inc. owns a lot of magazines, including *Money, Business 2.0, Teen People, In Style, Southern Living, Cooking Light, Parenting, Real Simple*, and dozens more— plus DC Comics and *MAD* magazine.

Time Warner also owns the largest of the music publishers (Warner Chappell) and a great many record labels, including Rhino, Giant, Maverick, Revolution, and more.

## FOX (NEWS CORPORATION)

### Principal Assets and Power Base

Under Rupert Murdoch's leadership, FOX has been able to transform a group of also-ran television stations into not one but several significant national television networks. FOX's principal assets are the Twentieth Century FOX motion picture and television operations, a robust sports outfit, broadcast television affiliates, and solid international operations, particularly in the Pacific Rim, where the company was started. FOX also benefits from News Corp.'s extensive holdings in print media, primarily as a newspaper publisher but also as the owner of HarperCollins and the former Hearst publishing arm, which includes William Morrow and Avon Books.

News Corp. is a major satellite operator in the U.K. with its BSkyB service (the equivalent of our DIRECTV, but far more popular). FOXTEL operates cable and satellite services in Australia. Star TV reaches 300 million viewers in over 50 Asian countries and is watched by 100 million viewers daily.

As of 2004, FOX was a $12 billion company, part of the $24 billion News Corp. empire.

## History: How FOX and News Corporation Came Together

In the 1950s, there were four networks: CBS, NBC, a fairly scrappy ABC, and a very scrappy DuMont Network. Due to the success of several major market stations in its network, DuMont survived until 1955. When DuMont folded, John Kluge bought New York's WNBD (renamed WNEW) and a handful of other major market stations. He called the company Metromedia, and built a mid-sized conglomeration of television and radio stations. The stations aired alternative programming—children's cartoons in the afternoons, and a popular children's variety show on Sunday mornings called *Wonderama*. In 1985, the Metromedia stations were sold to Rupert Murdoch's News Corporation and became the FOX station group (WNEW became WNYW). This group reached approximately 20 percent of television households, and became the basis for the new FOX network.

Previously, Murdoch had purchased Twentieth Century FOX. News Corporation was already a successful operator of television and film operations in Australia and publishing operations in the U.K., but in 1985, no company outside the U.S was allowed to own broadcast stations here, and certainly no such company would be allowed to build a television network. The situation was further complicated by the media ownership rules then in effect: Murdoch already owned the *New York Post*, so he was unable to simultaneously own a television station in New York City. Ultimately, these problems were negotiated toward solutions. FOX Broadcasting is a U.S. company, though News Corporation remained based in Australia. Its global connections are discussed further in Chapter 22.

Unlike many large media companies, FOX has been facile in both acquiring and developing new properties. Its most recent acquisitions include a controlling stake in DIRECTV, the U.S. satellite alternative to cable television. FOX Sports has been built through innovative deals with what had been Rainbow Media's (Cablevision) local pay cable sports operations, and by aggressive rights negotiations for NFL Football, Major League Baseball's World Series, and other high-profile events. FOX News was built not so much as an extension of the FOX broadcast network to compete with ABC, CBS, and NBC, but instead as a cable network to compete with CNN and MSNBC—a forward-thinking approach.

The FOX broadcast network provides the company with daily access into nearly all U.S. television households. A small number of popular series quickly built the network into a real competitor: *America's Most Wanted, Beverly Hills 90210, The X-Files*, sports coverage, and of course, *The Simpsons*, one of television's most consistently popular series for almost two decades. Each program was, and is, groundbreaking in its own way, a real alternative when compared with the output of ABC, CBS, and NBC.

## Other Significant (Non-TV) Media Assets

Living in the U.S., it is difficult to understand the reach and impact of News Corporation. In the U.K., News Corp. owns several popular national newspapers: *News of the World* and *The Sun* (both tabloids, revealing a cornerstone of News Corporation's newspaper publishing strategy), and *The Times/Sunday Times*. In Australia, News Corp. owns *The Daily Telegraph* and many smaller papers in the region, including the *Sunday Tasmanian* and the *Fiji Times*.

## LIBERTY MEDIA

### Principal Assets and Power Base

Liberty is a holding company, not a hands-on operator, that currently owns QVC, plus half of Discovery Communications, Court TV, and GSN (formerly Game Show Network). Liberty also owns cable and telephone systems in Latin America and other regions. In addition, Liberty owns a stake in Time Warner, Viacom, News Corporation, and Motorola—permitting an unusually clear view of the competitive landscape and an advantageous position for potential acquisitions.

Liberty Media's 2004 revenues were just under $8 billion. QVC is the largest contributor to revenues.

### History: How Liberty Media Came Together

Formed in the early 1990s, Liberty grew out of cable network assets owned by TCI, which was then a large MSO. From an asset acquisition perspective, Liberty Media is, ultimately, a shareholder in a variety of corporations. From a financial perspective, however, the complexities of high-finance transactions between various Liberty and TCI entities is an impressive exercise in tracking stocks, mergers, spin-offs, and more.

## Other Significant (Non-TV) Media Assets

Liberty Media is primarily concerned with investments in cable television networks and large media companies. Investments in telecommunications companies fill out the portfolio.

# CHAPTER 20

# THE NEXT LEVEL DOWN

As a rule, there are two forces at work in the media business. One is *acquisition*; examples include Viacom and Time Warner, and Comcast (see below). The other is the *entrepreneurial start-up*; several of the companies in this chapter, notably Discovery Networks, are examples. In recent years, the largest media companies have become so much larger than the smaller ones that new ventures have been discouraged. Comcast will certainly grow larger, most likely with a major acquisition (it has already attempted to acquire Disney). Some of the midsized companies will merge with one another to gain scale and clout. Others will be acquired by larger U.S. media companies, and by media companies in Europe and Asia with a taste for a U.S. presence. Still others will be sold to entrepreneurs who envision a different future for these companies' assets. Even the longtime traditional media companies are likely to be "in play" in the coming years—particularly the midsized companies with cable networks seen in more than 80 million households.

## COMCAST

### Principal Assets and Power Base
Comcast's power base comes from its near monopoly on cable service to nearly a third of all U.S. cable households (twice the number of its nearest competitor) and from the monthly fees collected in over 22 million households. Assuming a very conservative $40 per month charge, that's $820 million collected per month, or about $10 billion per year. What is remarkable about this? Comcast does not produce nor does it market these services in any meaningful manner. Comcast essentially provides a utility-style service that two out of three U.S. households simply will not live without.

As suggested by a $54 billion bid (albeit unsuccessful) for Disney in 2004, Comcast is poised to become one of the largest U.S. media companies.

### History: How Comcast Came Together
Comcast's story begins with the acquisition in 1963 of a single Mississippi cable system with just 1,200 subscribers. A decade later, Comcast was a public company,

a promising enterprise with a few hundred thousand cable subscribers. By the mid-1980s, Comcast crossed the million subscriber threshold, and shortly afterward, it invested in the new QVC network. By 1988, with just 2 million subscribers, Comcast was the nation's fifth largest MSO. To date, the growth was primarily through acquisitions and upgrades of existing cable systems. By 1994, Comcast was the third largest MSO, again via acquisitions, with about 3.5 million subscribers. A year later, the subscriber count was up to 4.3 million.

During the late 1980s and early 1990s, Comcast was also building a cellular telephone business, which was ultimately sold in 1999 to SBC.

The modern version of Comcast began to take shape in 1995, as the company took control of QVC; a year or so later, Comcast Spectacor was put together to operate sports teams, sports facilities, and a regional sports network. In 1997, Microsoft invested $1 million in Comcast, and Comcast acquired a 40 percent interest in E! Entertainment Television. Meanwhile, the company continued to acquire cable systems and other MSOs; by 2002, with the completion of AT&T's cable systems, Comcast served over 20 million U.S. cable households. On the programming side, Comcast invested in The Golf Channel and Outdoor Life in 2001, when it also launched its first video-on-demand service. A year later, the video game network G4 was added to the portfolio, and TV One, geared toward African American viewers, soon became another Comcast venture. A regional sports network in Chicago launched in 2004.

## Other Significant (Non-TV) Media Assets

Comcast has been remarkably focused, investing in cable systems, cable networks, and sports teams (and facilities). All of these assets are directly related to television.

# DISCOVERY COMMUNICATIONS (DCI)

## Principal Assets and Power Base

Like MTV and Nickelodeon, Discovery builds brands based upon cable television viewership. First came Discovery Channel in 1985, filled with interesting alternative programming (nature and travel documentaries, for example); then The Learning Channel, which found its way by inventing cable lifestyle programming (series about home makeovers and personal stories); and then the launch of a series of digital channels in an era when many competitors were still just considering the idea. Discovery has expanded its brand into classroom education (with the acquisition of United Learning) and into the retail space with Discovery stores. The company has also been a solid, reliable player outside the U.S. All of these activities point to an extremely clear corporate mission that has been managed with remarkable consistency for two decades. Discovery Communications' focus on health, science, travel, nature, animals, and lifestyle has earned it a place in the viewing habits of many consumers.

DCI is owned by three companies: Liberty Media owns about 49 percent, and Cox Communications and Advance/Newhouse Communications each own about 25 percent. With around 5,000 employees, DCI's sales were about $1.7 billion in 2004.

## History: How Discovery Communications Came Together

Discovery Communications was built through a combination of homegrown networks and acquisition of underdeveloped networks. Discovery and Animal Planet were internally developed. The Learning Channel was acquired in 1991. Travel Channel began as a project when the defunct airline TWA was acquired in 1997. Discovery Health was put together as a result of a merger with a FOX health network project. The retail stores were once known as The Nature Company, prior to Discovery's acquisition in 1996. Joint ventures with the BBC and with the *New York Times* have each resulted in new cable channels (BBC America and Discovery Times, respectively).

## Other Significant (Non-TV) Media Assets

Discovery has been successful in developing television properties that can be exploited in other industries. A successful licensing program is now associated with *Trading Spaces*, *Monster Garage*, and the Animal Planet network, for example.

Discovery has also become a meaningful brand in book publishing (through licenses and deals, generally not its own publishing) and in educational products and services.


# E. W. SCRIPPS

## Principal Assets and Power Base

Scripps owns several major market network affiliates, plus large newspapers in Tennessee and Colorado, but the company's national impact is felt mostly through its ownership of the popular Food Network and HGTV cable program services.

Scripps annual sales exceed $2 billion. The fastest-growing division, responsible for about one-third of revenues, is the Scripps Networks group, which also includes the Fine Living and DIY networks. Still, more than one-third of revenues comes from local newspaper operations. The remaining one-third comes from television stations, plus the Shop At Home network and United Media.

## History: How E. W. Scripps Came Together

Through the years, Scripps has been an active buyer and seller of local newspaper, radio, television, and cable properties. The company has also participated in a variety of new media ventures, for use by both newspapers and consumers.

This story begins in 1878, when Edward Scripps borrowed $10,000 to start a newspaper for the urban worker, the *Cleveland Penny Press*. By 1900, he had founded papers in San Diego, Los Angeles, Seattle, Kansas City, Cincinnati, and Akron (all very small cities at the time). Within the course of 50 years, Scripps founded and acquired dozens of newspapers. United Feature Syndicate was added in 1922 to supply newspapers with syndicated feature articles and comics. As more newspapers were bought, merged, and occasionally sold, Scripps entered the radio station business in the 1930s and the television station business in the 1940s, mostly in and around Ohio. In the 1980s, Scripps owned cable systems, since sold to Comcast. In 1993, Scripps launched HGTV, a successful cable network, and in 1997, Scripps bought out partner AH Belo to control Food Network.

## Other Significant (Non-TV) Media Assets

Since the 1920s, Scripps has owned United Feature Syndicate, responsible for *Peanuts*, *Garfield*, *Dilbert*, and many other popular comic features.

# THE HEARST CORPORATION

## Principal Assets and Power Base

Today's Hearst is less about newspapers (they own just 13, but three are large papers in Houston, San Francisco, and Seattle) than about magazines and television. Well-known Hearst magazines include *Cosmopolitan*, *Esquire*, *Good Housekeeping*, *Harper's BAZAAR*, *Marie Claire*, *O: The Oprah Magazine*, *Redbook*, and *Seventeen*. More significant are Hearst's television businesses and investments, which include significant positions in A&E, The History Channel, Lifetime, and ESPN. Hearst-Argyle Television, a public company in which Hearst is a majority shareholder, owns 27 local television stations, including major network affiliates in Boston (WCVB), Pittsburgh (WTAE), Tampa (WMOR), and Baltimore (WBAL). Hearst-Argyle is the second largest station group in the U.S. that is not controlled by a network. Hearst Entertainment produces made-for-television movies and several cable series; it also distributes various animated series based mostly upon King Features properties (see following page).

Hearst-Argyle Television's 2004 sales were just short of $800 million. Overall, Hearst's annual sales for 2003 were an estimated $4.1 billion.

## History: How the Hearst Corporation Came Together

The Hearst empire was begun by a wealthy California rancher, George Hearst, who became a U.S. Senator in 1886. At the time, his son William Randolph Hearst was 23 years old. And that's where the story begins. The younger Hearst first took control of the *San Francisco Examiner*, then acquired the *New York Journal* in 1895. By 1920, Hearst controlled newspapers across the country. The magazine business got started in 1903, when Hearst concocted an idea for a publication for automobile enthusiasts; it was called, simply, *Motor*. Two years later, Hearst acquired *Cosmopolitan*, which was, at the time, a popular fiction magazine. In 1911, *Good Housekeeping* was acquired. Over the decades, more magazines were added, notably *Esquire, Popular Mechanics,* and *Redbook*. In the 1920s, Hearst became known as a producer and distributor of newsreels (these later became a foundation for cable's History Channel). Radio and television stations followed. Along the way, Hearst has been an investor and active partner in cable network development. The company was a founding partner in both A&E and Lifetime, and in the early 1990s became a part owner of ESPN. Investments in new media have encouraged the success of iVillage, XM Satellite Radio, and other ventures.

## Other Significant (Non-TV) Media Assets

One outgrowth of Hearst's aggressive newspaper business has been King Features Syndicate, the leading distributor of comics. The syndicate controls such well-known characters as Popeye, Blondie, and Dennis the Menace, and also builds newer properties, such as Zippy the Pinhead and Bizarro. King Features also distributes newspaper columns and editorial cartoons. Hearst is also a significant publisher of business-to-business magazines, particularly in the automotive industry.

## BELO

### Principal Assets and Power Base

Belo's roots are in the Texas newspaper business, but the company now exerts roughly equal power in newspaper publishing and television broadcasting. The *Dallas Morning News* is its largest daily newspaper, and its list of other papers is brief: just three. On the television side, Belo owns 19 stations including properties in Dallas/Fort Worth, Houston, Seattle/Tacoma, and Phoenix. In addition, Belo owns two regional cable news networks and operates four more in partnership with Cox.

Belo is a $1.5 billion media company.

### History: How Belo Came Together

In 1842, the *Daily News* was founded in Galveston; it became the most powerful newspaper in Texas. Forty years later, the company founded the *Dallas Morning News* to cover northern Texas. In 1922, the company started WFAA radio, the first large Texas radio station, and in 1950, Belo acquired a Dallas television station, which became WFAA-TV. Today's Belo came together as a result of various acquisitions and trades in the 1980s and 1990s: first the purchase of KHOU in

Houston, then WWL in New Orleans. The big deal was 1997's acquisition of Rhode Island's *Providence Journal*, a newspaper acquisition that included the Seattle television station KING-TV and other stations, plus NWCN (NorthWest Cable News). Additional television station acquisitions followed.

## Other Significant (Non-TV) Media Assets

Belo's investments in new interactive businesses have been generally focused on Web sites related to their television stations and newspapers.

# BERTELSMANN MEDIA WORLDWIDE

## Principal Assets and Power Base

With over 70,000 employees and annual revenues exceeding $20 billion, Bertelsmann is one of the world's largest media conglomerates. The corporation is not especially well known in the U.S. because it owns no television networks or movie studios here. Still, roughly one-quarter of Bertelsmann's revenues come from the U.S., largely the result of the company's U.S.–based Random House book publishing and distribution operation, and a collection of record labels now operated jointly with Sony. In Germany and throughout Europe, Bertelsmann is well known as the owner of RTL—a major player in the television industry—as a large music label operation, and as a multifaceted book publisher, distributor, and book club operator.

The corporation's annual sales exceed $20 billion.

## History: How Bertelsmann Came Together

The company started in the same small German town where it is currently head-quartered: Gütersloh. In 1835, Carl Bertelsmann started printing and publishing hymnbooks; this activity expanded into a religious publishing house. By the 1840s, Bertelsmann was also publishing the Brothers Grimm and other popular authors. The company continued as a German book publisher through World War II. In the 1950s, Bertelsmann began to expand from printing and publishing into book clubs, then, in 1958, into its first record label, Ariola, and into duplication of audiovisual media with a new company, Sonopress. In 1964, Bertelsmann acquired Ufa, a film and television production company. By 1969, the corporation was a 25 percent owner of Gruner + Jahr, the magazine publisher responsible for *Der Stern* and other titles; today, Bertelsmann owns 75 percent of G + J.

Bertelsmann's modern era began in 1979 with the acquisition of the mid-sized U.S. record label Arista. Next, in 1980, came Bantam Books (then the largest paperback publisher in the world), and in 1984, through Ufa, Bertelsmann became 40 percent owner of Germany's first privately owned television station, RTL. In 1986, Doubleday books and RCA Records were added. This era brought a consolidated U.S. book operation known as Bantam Doubleday Dell, and a consolidated global music operation, Bertelsmann Music Group. The acquisition of Random House in 1998 consolidated the corporation's position as a leader in U.S. book publishing. By 2000, RTL had become a major force in European broadcasting with 18 television stations and 22 radio stations, plus the merged entities once known as CFA-Ufa and Pearson Television. Bertelsmann now owns 90 percent of RTL. Bertelsmann's music group added the large independent Zomba in 2002. By that time, the book and music clubs, known collectively as Direct Group Bertelsmann, counted nearly 30 million members in two dozen countries.

## Other Significant (Non-TV) Media Assets

Bertelsmann's book publishing, music publishing, and record labels allow the company considerable reach into many phases of the entertainment industry. For example, Bertelsmann has been deeply involved in the Elvis Presley estate and in the careers of Britney Spears, Dr. Seuss, John Grisham, author Richard North Patterson—the list is very long. Through its television acquisitions, Bertelsmann's assets also include the old Goodson-Todman library throughout the world (*The Price Is Right*, for example), as well as *American Idol*. A 2004 combination resulted in a 50/50 joint venture in the record label enterprise, so the former Sony Music Entertainment and BMG Entertainment are now one company with annual sales in the $8 billion range. In 2005, Bertelsmann sold its Gruner + Jahr U.S. magazine publishing subsidiary.

# CABLEVISION

## Principal Assets and Power Base

Cablevision's stronghold has been its cable television systems in and around New York City. From this foundation, Cablevision has built a variety of cable networks, including Bravo (since acquired by NBC), American Movie Classics, and a large number of regional sports services. In addition, Cablevision has acquired entertainment and sports venues in the metropolitan area, as well as sports teams.

Cablevision's annual revenues are roughly $5 billion. The majority of this revenue is generated by consumer services, such as cable television and cable modems for high-speed Internet access.

## History: How Cablevision Came Together

Cablevision's story begins in 1965, when Charles Dolan and Time, Inc. won the cable franchise to serve Manhattan. By 1973, Dolan had sold his interest in the Manhattan system and acquired Time's Long Island cable operation. In 1976, Cablevision launched its first regional sports channel in the New York metropolitan area (a pioneering effort), and in 1981 established a similar channel in New England. Other regional sports networks followed. In the early 1980s, Cablevision developed Bravo, then a performing arts network, and American Movie Classics, filled with vintage Hollywood films; the early 1990s added Much Music and the Independent Film Channel. During the past few years, Romance Classics has relaunched as WE!, a women's channel, and MuchMusic (acquired from Canada's CHUM) has been very successfully relaunched as fuse, a music channel. Nearly all of this activity has been home-grown, with minimal acquisition. Cablevision's IFC (Independent Film Channel) now produces and finances films for theatrical release, too.

Cablevision is one of the few media companies with sufficient development activity to justify a corporate group devoted only to emerging networks—these include fuse, IFC, a video-on-demand service called Mag Rack (see page 23), and local channels.

Cablevision's longtime partnership with FOX Sports was restructured in 2005. Cablevision owns FSN New York, FSN Chicago, and half of FSN New England, plus 60 percent of FSN Bay Area, while FOX owns the national FOX Sports Net, plus FSN Ohio and FSN Florida.

## Other Significant (Non-TV) Media Assets

Cablevision's acquisitions have essentially been in three categories: cable systems (such as TCI on Long Island, with over 800,000 subscribers), sports venues (Madison Square Garden), and entertainment venues (Radio City Entertainment, with a 25-year lease on Radio City Music Hall). Cablevision has also bought and sold a consumer electronics retailer (The Wiz) and a movie theater chain (Clearview). Cablevision owns basketball's New York Knicks, and hockey's New York Rangers.


# COX ENTERPRISES

## Principal Assets and Power Base

With over 6.5 million customers, Cox is the fourth largest cable operator in the U.S. Cox Radio is the third largest radio station owner in the U.S.; it either owns or operates over 70 stations in 18 markets. Cox also operates television stations, newspapers, and specialized Web sites. A 25 percent ownership stake in DCI (Discovery Communications) also adds ongoing revenues.

Cox's annual sales exceed $10 billion.

## History: How Cox Enterprises Came Together

The Cox story begins in 1898, when James Cox purchased a Dayton newspaper. In 1934, Cox added a radio station in Dayton, and in 1939 followed a similar strategy by acquiring the *Atlanta Journal* and WSB. By 1948, Cox's Atlanta operation had grown to include WSB-TV and WSB-FM radio. Over time, more radio stations, television stations, and newspapers were launched and acquired, along with cable systems. In 1995, Cox merged with Times Mirror's cable systems, creating the current large cable operator Cox Communications. The company went private in 2004 and is now part of Cox Enterprises.

## Other Significant (Non-TV) Media Assets

Cox is a player in automotive auctions and automotive communications. Manheim Auctions is the largest automobile auction company in the world, operating over 100 facilities with over 35,000 employees. The company's successful *Auto Trader* business, including www.autotrader.com, leads the industry.

# CLEAR CHANNEL COMMUNICATIONS

## Principal Assets and Power Base

Clear Channel owns about 40 television stations, significant among station groups but minor in comparison with the company's ownership of over 1,000 local radio stations. The corporation also owns Katz Media Group, a rep firm that sells local radio and television spot advertising.

Today's Clear Channel is a $10 billion company primarily engaged in radio (about $4 billion), live entertainment (about $3 billion), and outdoor advertising (about $2.5 billion). Ownership or management of roughly 40 television stations generates less than $1 billion.

## History: How Clear Channel Came Together

Clear Channel's history begins with outdoor advertising in 1901, eventually resulting in a 1995 company known as Eller Media, which was acquired by Clear Channel Outdoor in 1997. Additional acquisitions include the Ackerley Group, previously a large competitor.

In fact, Clear Channel started in 1972 with the formation of San Antonio Broadcasting and the acquisition of an FM radio station. With 12 radio stations in seven markets, the company went public in 1984. The television station group started in 1988 with the acquisition of a Mobile, Alabama/Pensacola, Florida station. For the next decade or so, Clear Channel continued to acquire radio and television stations, often benefiting from changes in media ownership rules. Still, by 1997 Clear Channel owned or operated 170 radio stations—about one-eighth of the current total. A year later, Clear Channel started building on the outdoor advertising business through acquisitions. With the 1999 acquisition of Jacor, the total radio station count was 625. More acquisitions followed in 2000, including SFX Entertainment (live concert promotion) and Ackerley.

## Other Significant (Non-TV) Media Assets

Clear Channel's outdoor advertising business encompasses far more than road-side billboards. Through Clear Channel Outdoor, it is possible to advertise on street furniture, mall displays, mass transit displays, and much more.

# GANNETT

## Principal Assets and Power Base

On a national level, Gannett's principal asset is *USA Today*, a national daily newspaper with a circulation over two million. Among large media companies, Gannett's television exposure has been generally limited to the ownership of a station group (22 stations covering about 18 percent of the U.S.).

Gannett's 2004 sales totaled $7.4 billion.

## History: How Gannett Came Together

Gannett traces its roots to the 1906 purchase of a half-interest in an Elmira, New York, newspaper by Frank Gannett. Several more papers in upstate New York followed, and by 1947, the company operated 21 newspapers and seven radio stations. By 1979, mostly as a result of mergers and acquisitions, Gannett boasted 78 daily newspapers, 14 radio stations, and 7 television stations. *USA Today* debuted in 1982—the first major effort at a daily national newspaper. Today, Gannett is the largest U.S. newspaper publisher.

## Other Significant (Non-TV) Media Assets

Until 1996, Gannett was a major player in outdoor advertising (in that year, the company also sold the market research organization, Louis Harris, in an attempt to focus on core activities). Gannett also owns Newsquest, a large regional newspaper publisher in the U.K.

# LANDMARK

## Principal Assets and Power Base

Landmark is a newspaper publisher with daily and weekly papers in and around Virginia. The company also owns The Weather Channel, as well as a television station in Las Vegas, Nevada, and another in Nashville, Tennessee.

Based in Norfolk, Virginia, the company's 2003 revenues totaled $743 million.

## History: How Landmark Came Together

As with many regional success stories, Landmark began and flourished as a result of the persistence and vision of one entrepreneur. In this case, the visionary was

Samuel Slover, a New Yorker who established himself in Virginia by buying and building newspapers. In 1954, Slover's nephew Frank Batten took over as publisher of the *Virginian-Pilot*. A decade later, Batten started to expand the company into radio and television station ownership and into cable television systems. During Batten's tenure, Landmark built and launched The Weather Channel in less than a year. Simple but effective, this remarkable concept—one of cable's most successful brands—has expanded into a successful Internet operation as well.

## Other Significant (Non-TV) Media Assets

With Cox, Landmark owns Trader Publishing, a specialty publisher of classified advertising magazines (*Auto Trader*, for example).

# THE TRIBUNE COMPANY

## Principal Assets and Power Base

The Tribune Company's traditional source of power has been the *Chicago Tribune* newspaper. In today's marketplace, dominated as it is by television, the company's 26 television stations (many in top markets) and its partial ownership of The WB Network sometimes overshadows the importance of the print division of the business. Tribune's stations in New York City, Los Angeles, Chicago, Philadelphia, Boston, Dallas, Atlanta, Houston, St. Louis, and other cities provide an extremely strong broadcasting base. Tribune's print assets are equally powerful: *Newsday* (suburban New York City), the *Los Angeles Times*, and the *Chicago Tribune* are among the nation's largest daily newspapers.

Tribune's 2004 sales were $5.7 billion. Part of this is attributed to the company's 22 percent ownership of The WB, whose annual sales were $700 million in 2004.

## History: How the Tribune Company Came Together

The Tribune Company started, appropriately, with the founding of the *Chicago Tribune* in 1847. The newspaper was followed, in 1924, by a sister radio station, WGN (whose call letters abbreviated "World's Greatest Newspaper"). WGN-TV was launched in 1948; WPIX/New York followed shortly afterward, and then KTLA/Los Angeles was added. While acquiring additional newspapers and television stations, the company also moved into sports in 1981 with the purchase of the Chicago Cubs. The baseball games provided popular programming for WGN-TV, now a superstation seen throughout the U.S. Tribune Entertainment began in 1975 as the distributor of the *U.S. Farm Report* and now produces and/or distributes roughly a dozen programs for cable and broadcast syndication.

## Other Significant (Non-TV) Media Assets

Besides the Cubs, Tribune owns *Chicago* magazine.

## THE WASHINGTON POST COMPANY

### Principal Assets and Power Base

The Washington Post Company's longtime ownership of its namesake paper and *Newsweek* magazine has been its traditional base.

The company's 2004 sales totaled over $3.3 billion.

### History: How the Washington Post Company Came Together

Founded as a Democratic paper in the nation's capital in 1877, the *Post* soon bought out its closest (Republican) competitor. In 1916, a Warren Harding crony pushed the *Post* into Republican territory; it was in receivership a short time later and was then purchased and operated by a nonpartisan, modern publisher in 1918. In 1947, the *Post* bought WTOP, a Washington radio station, and three years later bought a Washington television station and renamed it WTOP-TV. *Newsweek* was acquired in 1961. Katherine Graham, wife of the publisher, took charge of the *Post* after his death in 1963 and proved a strong, savvy manager, an extremely influential force. More newspapers and television stations followed.

### Other Significant (Non-TV) Media Assets

In addition to *Newsweek*, the Washington Post Company owns Kaplan, an educational services company.

## PAXSON COMMUNICATIONS

### Principal Assets and Power Base

Formerly known as PAX TV, i: Independent Television is the seventh largest broadcast television network, and the newest (started in 1998). By combining broadcast, cable, and satellite distribution, Paxson reaches 95 million U.S. households. The network's branding and programming policies are appropriate to early 2000s conservatism: the network emphasizes "family values." Rather than programming the full schedule, i sells parts of its schedule to infomercial providers.

### History: How Paxson Communications Came Together

The company started in 1991 and soon became one of Florida's largest radio station groups. In 1997, the radio stations were sold to concentrate only on television. In 1998, PAX TV was started as a television network, and a year later, NBC invested $415 million in the new venture. NBC sells i's spot advertising and handles other sales and market research functions. In addition, local NBC stations sell local time for the i affiliates in their markets. The company's founder, Lloyd Paxson, was the creator and president of Home Shopping Network and the creator and cofounder of the Christian Network (a nonprofit entity that broadcasts the Worship television service to more than 70 percent of U.S. homes). This past history helps to explain some of i's programming strategy. The network continues to innovate; it will be interesting to see how Paxson operates in the new digital era.

Reported sales for 2003 were $270 million. Paxson does not hold any substantial non-television media assets.

# CHAPTER 21

# BRANDING IN THE TELEVISION INDUSTRY

## HISTORY AND EVOLUTION OF TELEVISION BRANDS

When there were just three commercial networks, marketing was uncomplicated. Each network had its own logo and its particular identity. CBS had "the eye," rural sitcoms (*The Beverly Hillbillies*), star-studded variety shows (Jackie Gleason, Red Skelton), and evening news (Walter Cronkite). NBC used several different logos (the NBC chimes and other corporate identifiers plus the famous peacock, originally associated with its color television programs), and featured popular dramas (*Bonanza, Dragnet, The Man from U.N.C.L.E.*) and game shows (*Concentration, Jeopardy!* ), plus the *Today* show in the morning and Johnny Carson late-night. ABC took longer to build an identity, but the combination of Roone Arledge's sports, upgraded news, stronger leadership, and the success of its 1970s sitcoms (*Happy Days*) defined ABC's brand.

There was no compelling reason to develop a sophisticated system of branding. Still, as a sign of its own uniqueness, CBS helped to establish the concept of a rigid guide to corporate branding by carefully designing a unified system that graphically connected all presentations of the corporation's identity. This system is now common in most large corporations. Until the 1980s, discussions about television branding were generally limited to network identities, some local station identities, names of shows, and names of the stars appearing in those shows.

MTV changed everything. This upstart network changed the rules by introducing a logo that was fun. A giant three-dimensional M filled with goldfish? A logo built from cartoon bricks? A logo with personality was just part of the story: MTV was all about attitude and identity. It was more than a cable service that played music videos. MTV sold tour jackets, sweatshirts, t-shirts—anything that would get its logo into the lives of its viewers. MTV was a brand.

A few years later, Nickelodeon began to play the same game, eventually with more flair and greater impact than MTV. Nick's logo was no logo at all. Instead, it was the word "Nickelodeon" in simple white letters played against a vivid orange background. The background could take any shape: a dinosaur, an airship, a fish. It could be two- or three-dimensional. Bright orange became Nickelodeon's color (actually, slime green became associated with Nick as well).

These two networks were among the first to understand the changing television environment. In a world with dozens and eventually hundreds of television channels, those with the most clearly differentiated brands would be the ones most likely to succeed. A relatively small group of networks soon established brands with equally clear identities: Cartoon Network, CNN, ESPN, The History Channel, The Golf Channel, The Tennis Channel, TV Land, and The Weather Channel. General interest networks, such as TBS, A&E, and USA Network, have never established clear brand identities (they have, however, succeeded as a result of excellent distribution and smart programming choices).

## The Branding of Local Television

For television's first few decades, local television stations were, quite literally, "the only game in town." Each had its own logo, typically a number and four call letters. Sometimes, there was a slogan used on air: "Best in View, Channel 2" was used by WCBS in New York. Sometimes, there was a unified visual, such as the number 7 in a circle, used by ABC's owned and operated stations. Most stations were simply identified by their channel number and their call letters.

As the cable networks demonstrated the power of brand development in the 1980s, the broadcast television networks transformed their local brand strategy in the 1990s. For example, WCAU in Philadelphia is known as NBC10. In a market where WCAU has been a part of life since broadcasting began—it was a cornerstone of the original CBS radio network—many Philadelphians would struggle if asked for the station's call letters today. In Philadelphia, as in cities throughout the country, the NBC logo is the dominant graphic theme in the branding materials. The Channel 10's call letters, once the primary brand, are now secondary. Many stations do not use the call letters at all, except as required by the FCC or in business documents.

A brand is defined as more than a logo. As branding experts dug deeper into the world of local television marketing, it became clear that news was the primary differentiator at the local level. The result: Most local network affiliates now tie their local tagline into local news. Examples include "5 On Your Side" (WEWS/Cleveland) and "Where News Comes First" (WESH/Orlando). Web sites associated with television stations support the orientation toward local news; most station sites are, in fact, local news sources that contain secondary links to network television programs.

## BRAND DEVELOPMENT

Among the lessons taught by MTV: the brand must be consistent, it must be ubiquitous, and, if the brand is going to become popular, it must be fun. NBC has taken this lesson seriously. On one corner of New York City's Rockefeller Center is the *Today* show headquarters, often with happy crowds outside holding up signs. On the opposite corner is the large NBC Experience, a multimedia retail store with elaborate special effects, a small museum, and, of course, endless NBC merchandise—including the ubiquitous peacock. The combination has proven one of midtown's more popular tourist attractions. Of course, many people also visit New York City and leave with a *Saturday Night Live* (an NBC program for three decades) t-shirt or an NBC Sports coffee mug.

There is equity in brands—real long-term value in a logo and an identity that paint a clear picture in the minds of customers. Today's marketing students are taught about the importance of developing and managing brands.

This process begins with a complete understanding of the target customer—an understanding that starts with demographics (age, income, etc.) but extends deeply into "psychographics" (why people behave as they do, who they believe they are, groups with whom they identify).

The market research and corporate adoption of audience understanding is essential, but it's only the starting place. The corporation must also deliver a product that matches the audience's wants, needs, desires, aspirations, and sensibilities. MTV has set the standard here, but networks like The Weather Channel have done an excellent job (with somewhat more modest ambitions).

Once these pieces are in place (not much can be done until they are firmly established), then the merchandising begins in earnest. Merchandise must be based upon the network's greatest successes; nobody except a contrarian would buy a t-shirt celebrating the network's lowest-rated series. With success in merchandising, it is possible to produce motion pictures (*Dora the Explorer*, *Rugrats*), create toys (*South Park*), put on touring shows (*Blue's Clues*), sell home video product lines (*Saturday Night Live*, *Seinfeld*, *The Sopranos*), and develop a broad range of other merchandise.

## Brand Value and Brand Equity

Although the merchandise becomes the most conspicuous, most visual implementation of the brand—and sometimes the most profitable—a good brand contains even more value. The term "brand equity" is used to describe the total present and future value of a particular brand. Some aspects of this value are easy to calculate—the value of a given contract, for example—but others are more difficult to set up in pure dollar terms. In fact, brand valuation has become a discipline of its own, with firms specializing in such valuations for corporate mergers and acquisitions, and for tax purposes.

How much is a brand worth? Interbrands, a consulting firm specializing in brand marketing, characterizes the value of the world's top brands in tens of billions of dollars. While this list may be self-serving—the company is routinely hired to build top brands—Interbrands's calculations are routinely published by top business publications, and so they are perceived both as credible and as reasonable as any other measure. On their 2004 list, published in *BusinessWeek*,

McDonald's brand value was over $25 billion, and the Marlboro brand was worth nearly as much. MTV's brand—not the network, not the people, not the tangible assets, just the brand—was worth over $6 billion.

As a brand becomes popular, and remains popular, it develops an iconic value of its own. People who are, or were, associated with the television property become more valuable in the television and motion picture marketplace. Agents take an interest. New projects are sold on the basis of the person's contribution to the previous project's brand equity.

In the case of a brand based upon a specific television series, the value of the property (sometimes called a "franchise") is usually highest while the show is on the air—but this is not always true. *Star Trek* is an example of a brand based upon a television series that is not necessarily current. *The Flintstones* is another—think Flintstones vitamins, taken every day by millions of children. Sometimes, a television property's brand value is sufficiently high to justify a motion picture, such as *Charlie's Angels*, decades after the series has left the network schedule. Many performers understand their television personas to be brands as well, and they've learned to exploit these properties for the brands they are. Barbara Eden's five seasons on *I Dream of Jeannie* ended in 1970, but she has remained active, almost exclusively on the basis of this role, for more than 30 years. TV Land, a cable network which merrily exploits aged television brands, has helped to keep performers like Eden in the public eye.

Brands associated with television series and performers tend to maintain some form of brand equity for decades. A small fan base, personal appearances, Web sites, the occasional popular culture book (Barry Williams's *Growing Up Brady*), and reunion specials all help to extend the brand. Brands associated with television networks, on the other hand, require constant attention. The marketplace is fiercely competitive, and even a quarter of a rating point means additional advertising revenues. In this regard, a network with a clearly defined brand identity operates at an advantage over a comparable network with an identity that is not as well articulated. For example, it's not unusual to check in on The Weather Channel or Cartoon Network or Bloomberg several times each day, but the same behavior does not apply (in most households) to PBS or to A&E.

Often, program strategies are closely linked to branding. The Weather Channel is perceived as a kind of utility—people don't tune in for a specific television show so much as to check a local forecast. Comedy Central is built from individual shows, but for a particular demographic (younger men, notably), it's a reliable place to find something funny. A network whose schedule is filled with a variety of program types cannot rely upon the brand alone to build and maintain an audience. Instead, the branding must be focused upon specific series within the network's schedule. For example, the spring 2005 USA Network schedule was filled with movies, plus reruns of *Coach*, *Law & Order: SVU*, and the NBC series *The Biggest Loser*—not much branding opportunity for these series because they are not generally associated with USA. Instead, USA's focus is on its popular series, particularly *Monk*. A&E has followed a similar strategy, first with *Biography* (subsequently known as *A&E's Biography* to connect the network's brand with its most successful program), later with *Growing Up Gotti* and other popular A&E series.

## Brand Architecture

With a major corporation, it is necessary to consider an overall brand architecture, a unified scheme and strategy that allows each brand to flourish. Viacom has succeeded by keeping its name somewhat in the background. Most people don't realize that MTV, Nickelodeon, the Paramount studio, King World, and CBS are all Viacom companies. On the other hand, FOX has employed its brand name to great advantage, first by separating and simplifying the brand for television: No longer is it called Twentieth Century FOX, except when used for motion pictures. The simple, snappy FOX name is now used to identify program services associated with news (FOX News), sports (FOX Sports), and various entertainment networks. NBC Universal's brand architecture is less even-handed; there is a well-known brand called NBC, lesser known brands called MSNBC and CNBC, and a shopping service called ShopNBC. In addition, there's USA Network, which NBC currently uses for secondary play of some of its programming, and Bravo, which has its own identity to some degree but sometimes serves a similar purpose. Is there a single NBC Universal brand architecture? Not quite in the sense of FOX or Viacom. ABC suffers from an even deeper identity crisis; its owner, Disney, is clearly the stronger brand.

## BRAND MANAGEMENT

The first rule of brand management, just as the medical profession requires, is "Do no harm." A brand manager must never place the brand in a situation or alliance that may damage its long-term value. The second rule often conflicts with the first: "Risks are often required to grow the brand."

Through the 1980s and early 1990s, the actor Kelsey Grammer established himself as a particular type of comedy character on the successful sitcom *Cheers*. He then started appearing as Sideshow Bob on *The Simpsons*—not a big stretch. He was lucky enough to continue playing his *Cheers* character, Dr. Frasier Crane, as star of another successful series, *Frasier*. Working from this base, Grammer expanded his career; serving as executive producer on *Frasier* and then on other (lesser-known) series (including *In-Laws* and *Gary the Rat*). In 2005, after *Frasier* left the air, he became an executive producer on a new NBC series, *Medium*. As an actor, he has appeared in many television specials, movies, and in New York theater, particularly as Cassio in a Broadway production of Shakespeare's *Othello*. His career has survived cocaine addiction and other mishaps.

Woody Harrelson, another *Cheers* regular more or less ignored his *Cheers* brand identity and, playing against type, redefined his career as an actor with *White Man Can't Jump*, *Natural Born Killers*, and other well-received dramatic films. Kirstie Alley has worked steadily since *Cheers*, but has struggled to find another character with a clear identity. In time, she used her weight increase and the stories surrounding it to define a new character featured in the Showtime series *Fat Actress*. Is this a risky re-branding strategy or a funny, self-deprecating idea that could lead to other opportunities? That's a question performers face year after year, especially when their best-known roles are fading from syndication and B-level cable time slots.

Brand management for an ongoing television franchise, such as *Jeopardy!* or *NBC Nightly News*, must be handled in a more gradual and generally more conservative manner. Apart from its stage setting and graphics, *Jeopardy!* doesn't change much from year to year—viewers like it just the way it is. *NBC Nightly News* helped Tom Brokaw become an icon, then gracefully introduced the designated newcomer, Brian Williams, over a period of years. The transition seemed natural, honorable, and apparently acceptable to longtime viewers. The *Today* show introduced both Al Roker and Matt Lauer over time, first as a replacement weatherman and a newsreader, respectively, then as lead performers. The key concept: If the brand franchise is a longtime favorite, make changes gradually.

If the brand is not well established, then it's more reasonable to take a risk. For the broadcast networks, this risk often occurs in the edgier after-midnight period, where Conan O'Brien, David Letterman, and others have matured while preparing for better time slots. In the interim, each established a unique brand identity—a unique personality for himself and his style of comedy.

## Aging Brands

Brands do not last forever. A list of popular brands from radio days would be largely unfamiliar today. Black-and-white television series are almost never seen on contemporary television; just about anything produced prior to 1965 (except *I Love Lucy*) is ancient history, and for most viewers, anything that's more than a decade old really isn't worth watching.

Sometimes, it makes sense for an aging brand to gracefully say "goodbye," as the popular late-night talk show host Johnny Carson did. Sometimes, television networks stick with a long-running series for longer than advisable, hoping to benefit from any remaining brand equity for just one more season.

Some brands never quite connect with their potential, and age very rapidly. One example is the former Game Show Network, which found that viewers didn't much care about old or new game shows in sufficient numbers. The network was merged with a technology network that was also underperforming. The new GSN is still finding its way, but its new, younger, tech-savvy positioning is promising. Other brands simply lose their traction with key target demographics and attract a progressively older audience. For example, PBS is attempting to confront the fact that many of its viewers are well over age 50.

## New Brands

Most often, television show launches are more closely associated with encouraging viewership than with brand building. This is typically accomplished through a combination of on-air promotion, print advertising, public relations encouraging press mentions and positive reviews, and a variety of special promotions. Once people are watching, then the brand development and brand management processes may be activated, initially through promotions, publicity, and tie-ins with other popular brands, and then through activities in which the new brand is the draw.

Cable network launches are more systematized, anxious to develop a recognizable and desirable brand from the start. Firms specializing in launching new cable networks can provide entrepreneurs and company executives with appropriate marketing, promotion, public relations, and distribution strategies.

# CHAPTER 22
# REGULATION OF GLOBAL MEDIA COMPANIES

Globalization may be a bit of a cliché, but it is having considerable impact on the television business. In the not-so-distant "old days," the largest units in the television business were essentially national. Dissemination of television—whether by broadcast, cable, or even satellite—was subject to national regulation, through the FCC in the U.S. and through equivalent bodies in many other jurisdictions. In many countries, radio and television were delivered by government monopolies, such as the BBC. Even where private broadcasting was the rule, as in the U.S., national ownership requirements and other barriers to entry helped to make each country its own separate television domain. Of course, television companies often licensed productions to each other, but even this was (and in some cases, still is) subject to national content limitations.

As described in Chapters 19 and 20, the largest media companies, like News Corporation, Time Warner, and Bertelsmann, have outgrown the model of national companies and now play a direct role in the delivery of television around the world. While restrictions remain, today's largest companies have gone beyond being licensors and distributors and have become true global players.

News Corporation—the parent of the FOX television companies—serves as a good example. By 2004, it had at least partial ownership of direct broadcast television services and cable systems reaching the U.S. (DIRECTV), Britain (Sky), Italy (Sky Italia), Mexico (Innova), Brazil (Sky Brazil), Australia (FOXTEL), China (Phoenix Satellite Television and 18 affiliated cable systems), and India (Hathway Cable and Datacom). Its terrestrial broadcasting stations (principally in the U.S., but including bTV in Bulgaria) and multiple programming networks around the world complete its television holdings. And television isn't its only business. News Corp. also owns important newspapers (including *The Times* of London, the *New York Post*, and a number of Australian papers), the FOX film studio, HarperCollins Publishers, and a variety of other enterprises in and around the news and entertainment businesses, including Russia's leading billboard advertising company.

Several of the biggest media companies have this kind of global scope, a situation that has made life more complicated for their lawyers and executives. These companies must deal with the regulatory systems of each of the jurisdictions where they are players in television delivery. Instead of satisfying just one set of rules, now companies must comply with several sets of legal—and political— requirements. These rules include financial regulations, telecommunications laws, and content regulation. Pleasing many masters in many countries is not always easy, even when all of them are playing by neutral, free speech–inspired rules. Sadly, even the most democratic governments are not immune to using regulatory schemes to meddle with content, rewarding sympathetic treatment on television programs with business opportunities. And the wider the global reach of a company, the more governments, democratic and otherwise, it will need to keep happy.

## FINANCIAL REGULATION

Large companies, particularly those with public shareholders, are subject to a range of financial regulations. In the United States, those range from the requirements of the state of incorporation to the relatively stringent oversight of the Securities and Exchange Commission (SEC). In an effort to promote fair and transparent markets, a wide range of reporting requirements make a significant amount of information about public companies readily available. Indeed, filings available from the Web site www.sec.gov and from the investor relations pages of individual company sites have been important references in the writing of this book. In addition to direct financial regulation by the government, listing on U.S. stock exchanges makes the company subject to rules of the exchange, adding a further layer of compliance.

Returning to our example, News Corporation was founded in Australia and remained incorporated in Australia for many years. In 2004, however, shareholders approved transferring the corporate domicile to the United States, a move that would make it a more attractive investment in the critical U.S. financial markets. With a primary listing on the New York Stock Exchange, it would also be eligible for inclusion in U.S. stock indices and for investment in related index funds. Rupert Murdoch, chairman and chief executive, made it clear that News Corp. would keep an Australian Stock Exchange listing as well—good news for tradition, but one more complication for his lawyers. As mentioned on page 35, Mr. Murdoch himself had already made a similar transition, from Australian to U.S. citizenship, in connection with acquiring the FOX television stations.

In addition to securities law regulation, some countries impose special requirements for foreign investment and control of local business. These rules range from mere registration, through requirements for local investment partners, to outright prohibition. Even countries such as the U.S., which are generally hands-off on foreign investment, may place restrictions on foreign broadcast ownership.

## COMMUNICATIONS LAW

Most countries impose significant layers of regulation on the ownership and conduct of businesses delivering television to viewers. The U.S. regimes, overseen by the FCC, are described in Chapters 5 through 8, and do not need to be recapitulated here. It is sobering to recall that just about every jurisdiction where a global company is engaged in such a business will have its own version of these rules and procedures. You don't just rent some equipment and set up shop.

Although in the U.S. there are occasional allegations of politically inspired interference with broadcasters by the FCC, the protections of the First Amendment are taken seriously by most players. This is not necessarily the case in other countries. Even in Italy, an established democracy and member of the EU, the direct control of Mediaset (one of the country's two terrestrial television giants) has been a key element in the election of Silvio Berlusconi as prime minister. There have been a number of allegations that, once in office, Berlusconi's government heavily influenced government broadcaster RAI (the other giant in the market) to provide favorable coverage. This dominance helped prolong his government notwithstanding significant political ups and downs. The challenges are significant for a Canal+ or a News Corporation entering Italy as a DBS provider in such a politically charged atmosphere.

## CENSORSHIP

Even more challenging is dealing with a government that explicitly condones censorship, such as China. In its controlled liberalization of society and the economy, the emphasis by the government is decidedly on the control. The Chinese government actively monitors incoming programming feeds and has been known to shut off distribution, even to hotels and licensed foreigners, of programs it deems excessively critical. For instance, in 2002 CNN and BBC coverage of the Communist Party's Congress was blacked out.

There have been allegations that China has used both threats of direct censorship and its ability to favor or terminate the reception by its populace of satellite signals to influence how international television companies depict China in their news and entertainment offerings. In 2001, for instance, there were allegations of an understanding between News Corporation and the Chinese leadership over the penetration by News Corp.'s Star of the Asian satellite and cable market. A Beijing-based spokesman for News Corp., quoted by the BBC, confirmed, "We won't do programs that are offensive in China." He continued, "If you call this self-censorship, then of course we're doing a kind of self-censorship." Programming would focus on game shows and other noncontroversial formats. The BBC had its own stake in this report: In 1994, Star dropped the BBC's international news from its service because it presented a program critical of Mao that offended the authorities.

Even more concerning, China has exerted its influence over News Corp.'s behavior outside China as well. In 1995, for instance, Basic Books, a HarperCollins division, brought out an English-language version of Deng Maomao's book *My Father Deng Xiaping*, a flattering biography of the Chinese leader. Rupert Murdoch oversaw a number of high-profile launch events for the book. By contrast, Chris Patten, a former British governor of Hong Kong and no fan of the Chinese regime, had a publishing deal with HarperCollins UK for a book about his experiences in Asia. When it became clear that the book would offend the Chinese authorities, the deal was canceled at Murdoch's instructions. Some have even suggested that news coverage on China in News Corp.'s newspapers and in the FOX news service has been tempered as well.

News Corp. is not the only global media company accused of using self-censorship to win favor with China. In 1998, Gary Bauer, a prominent conservative and proponent of human rights in China, wanted Time Warner's CNN to run an advertisement highly critical of China's repression of dissent. CNN declined the ad, citing a network policy against airing advocacy ads. Bauer explained CNN's action by citing a January 1998 meeting of Time Warner's chairman and CEO with then–Chinese President Jiang Zemin.

Whatever the merit of any particular allegation, the potential for difficulty is clear; the more global a television company becomes and the more governments it must keep happy, the greater the pressure for it to keep its programming mild and inoffensive. Picking fights with powerful interests may be good journalism, but in the regulated world of television it can be bad business. On his decision to drop the BBC in China, Murdoch is quoted in a 1995 *New Yorker* profile as saying, "We're not proud of that decision. It was the only way."

# PART 6

# A BROADER DEFINITION OF TELEVISION

# CHAPTER 23

# PUBLIC TELEVISION

Public television differs from commercial television in many ways. Perhaps the most important is the purpose of public television: it is, in the truest and perhaps purest sense, a public service. Public television exists in the United States to provide education, information, culture, and enlightenment. Each public television entity is a nonprofit corporation whose principal—and often sole—purpose is to serve the community. Each public television station is operated locally, with a local board of directors, a local staff, and a local community advisory board. There is no national ownership, only membership organizations to which individual public television stations may belong.

The largest of these membership organizations is known as the Public Broadcasting Service (PBS)—a programming network. Unlike the commercial networks, which own many of their largest local broadcasters and manage the other affiliates with a very tight business relationship, PBS's member stations may or may not play any given program at any given time, and may choose not to run the program at all. Unlike the commercial networks, which pay their local stations to run programming (with commercials included), member stations pay annual fees to PBS for the use of their programs, providing nearly half of the PBS budget. The stations also produce and find funding for many of the programs seen on the PBS schedule. And, again unlike the commercial networks, PBS cannot and does not produce any of its own programs. PBS also receives government money for its operation, but not directly. Instead, PBS receives an annual grant from CPB (Corporation for Public Broadcasting), which receives an annual congressional appropriation (see next page).

## HISTORY OF PUBLIC TELEVISION

Noncommercial television began in 1953 when KUHT went on the air in Houston, Texas. Over the next 15 years, noncommercial stations started up in most large markets. Educational programming was presented along with some programming for younger children, and some cultural and arts programming. Financial support was elusive. There was no uniform system for financing noncommercial broadcasting, so individual stations devised their own schemes for raising money.

Through the early 1960s, the idea of a viable alternative to commercial television became a political agenda item. The BBC, in the U.K., was often held up as a model: a national broadcasting system for the public good, funded by a tax on every television set in use. In the U.S., various organizations attempted to put together a public network with some combination of local, national, educational, cultural, social, or political focus. Although the efforts were well intentioned, not much happened until 1967, when the Carnegie Commission on Educational Television (CCET) completed a two-year study recommending that Congress establish a noncommercial television system with a broader view than the old educational concept—a service that would be called "public television." The new service would not be educational (in the report, the word "educational" was deemed somber and static). Public television would include an improved form of instructional or classroom television during the day and high-quality general interest programs in the evening. CCET also recommended that existing noncommercial stations be joined in a network that would be supported by federal funds.

Many of the Carnegie Commission's suggestions were made a part of the Public Broadcasting Act of 1967, which structured ongoing federal support for the new public broadcasting system.

## CORPORATION FOR PUBLIC BROADCASTING (CPB)

The Public Broadcasting Act of 1967, an act of Congress, also created the Corporation for Public Broadcasting; CPB, in turn, created the Public Broadcasting Service (PBS) in 1969 and National Public Radio (NPR) in 1970. Proposed by CCET, the new CPB was intended to serve as a buffer between the government and the new public broadcasters (see below).

In fact, CPB has served that purpose. However, the original CCET concept—a board of directors composed of government appointees and private citizens—was changed to a board composed entirely of government appointees. The result has been a closer relationship between the federal government and public television than was originally intended. CPB's principal role is the distribution of an annual congressional appropriation to public television stations and producers. In addition, according to the Public Broadcasting Act of 1967, CPB is responsible for (1) encouraging the development of a wide range of program suppliers, maintaining high-quality program standards, and assuring balanced reporting on controversial topics; (2) interconnecting stations in a network that allows stations to program and schedule in accordance with local desires; (3) nurturing new station development and conducting research and training; and (4) operating a program archive.

CPB's total annual budget is a congressional appropriation of approximately $400 million (as of 2005), which provides approximately 15 percent of the aggregate U.S. public television revenues. In general, Congress grants this money without a specific agenda; CPB is managed (by political appointees) to serve the public interest as it sees fit. Any possible agenda may be filtered by the individual station, which may or may not decide to run a particular program.

In its day-to-day operations, CPB's principal activities are the partial or full funding of programs heard on public radio and seen on public television stations; partial funding for radio and television station operations and growth; the promotion of digital television within the public television system; and various activities related to educational television. CPB is the largest single source of funding for public television programming, concentrating generally on arts, culture, children, diversity, documentary, drama, history, and science.

CPB works closely with PBS to determine which programs are to be funded and how much money will be apportioned for each project. An annual report (available at www.cpb.org) lists the projects that were funded by CPB each year. In 2003, for example, some grants were over $1 million: *Wide Angle*, a series produced by WNET, received $1.2 million for its second season, and Capitol Concerts, Inc., received $799,000 for a pair of patriotic concerts that air annually on Memorial Day and Independence Day. A *Reading Rainbow* Web site project was given $149,500. In addition, CPB and PBS each pay $7 million into the Program Challenge Fund. Among the projects funded, or partially funded by the Fund are a documentary about Madison Square Garden (for $100,000) and a four-part series from National Geographic Television about environmental issues. One CPB initiative—called "Where Fun and Learning Click!"—provided $9.2 million to Scholastic for *Maya & Miguel*, a new children's series. Another fund, in association with the U.K.'s Carlton Television, partially funded the six-part WNET project *Broadway*.

The largest single program-funding activity is related to the NPS, or National Program Service (known to general viewers as the PBS schedule), supplied by PBS to member stations, mainly for their prime-time and children's lineups. This fund is established at $22.5 million per year. From WNET, *American Experience* (season 16) received $3.8 million, *Great Performances* (season 30) was given $2 million, and *American Masters* (season 16) received $1.2 million. *Arthur*, a children's series from WGBH, received $825,000 for its seventh season, and the same station's revised *ZOOM* was funded with $1 million for its fifth season. Produced by Scholastic, *Clifford the Big Red Dog* received $1 million. Sesame Workshop was given $1.3 million for *Sesame Street*'s thirty-fourth season. *News Hour* was funded at an even higher level: $5.7 million. *NOVA*'s thirtieth season received $3.7 million.

It is important to note that few, if any, of these grants paid the entire costs of production and promotion for a program or series. The federal money channeled through CPB remains only one leg of the stool that supports production budgets. In most cases, additional funding was sought and received from corporate underwriting, foundation grants, stations' support of PBS, and other sources.

## PUBLIC BROADCASTING SERVICE (PBS)

The Public Broadcasting Act also required that CPB create a public television network—the Public Broadcasting Service. PBS debuted in 1970, with 12 hours of programming per week provided by National Educational Television (NET).

The network concept did not last long. The Nixon administration, dismayed by a perceived liberal bias in news and information programs on public television, stymied the network's growth by vetoing a significant funding measure. What happened next is open to interpretation. Some say that, to further limit the power of a potentially unfriendly network, the administration forced PBS to reorganize in 1973, decentralizing power and strengthening individual stations. Others say that PBS's own leaders decided to decentralize as a means to avoid White House or federal government influence. Either way, PBS became a membership organization, funded largely by dues paid by locally owned and operated member stations. Under the 1973 Partnership Agreement, CPB was required to allocate a specific portion of its budget—roughly 50 percent—to local stations.

For fiscal year 2004, PBS reported operating revenues of $330 million. Of this total, the largest component was $156 million received from member stations, which pay an annual fee to receive PBS programs, distribution, and other services. Grants from CPB and the federal government provided an additional $80 million, and a further $41 million was earned through educational product sales. The remaining $56 million came mostly from royalties and license fees, and from investments. An additional $184 million was invested in program development and production by foundations, corporations, and individual underwriters, but this money was generally collected by producers of these programs or the member stations who presented the project to the system.

On the expense side, the total in 2004 was $316.7 million. Of this figure, 60 percent went to National Program Service content and to promotion and online costs. Costs associated with marketing totaled 18 percent. Interconnection, development, media relations, and related services totaled 9 percent. Pass-through—the money that comes right to the door, such as cable royalties—was 8 percent. Education grants made by PBS that do not go to programming—for initiatives such as Right to Learn, Teacher Line, and Literacy Link—made up 6 percent. Other content, such as SIP (Station Independence Programming, better known as pledge specials) and PLUS (a syndicated service that offers more programming options, including the well-known *Austin City Limits*), made up 4 percent of the total PBS expenditure. Note, however, that the funding of some public television services has become a political football; these allotments may change in the near future, and some funding lines may disappear completely.

Although the ways in which money travels between CPB, PBS, and PBS member stations is somewhat convoluted, member stations ultimately finance PBS by providing more than 85 percent of PBS's annual operating budget. The remaining 15 percent comes from ancillary revenues—including the sale, rental, and licensing of PBS programs to institutions such as schools and hospitals—and from a satellite-based data delivery system. Less than 2 percent of PBS's annual budget comes directly from CPB.

## PBS Organization

The organization of PBS resembles other media organizations. Key functional departments, each led by several executives, include programming, technology and operations, marketing (including promotion, media relations, and brand management), finance, and law. In addition, PBS supports a group devoted to new and emerging businesses related to education, licensing, Web development, datacasting, and e-commerce.

The NPS, or National Program Service, is the main PBS feed, typically containing the programs seen on prime time and children's programs seen during parts of the daytime schedule. Programs on the NPS feed often appear on the same day and at the same time on many PBS stations (making promotion easier). However, individual stations are protective of their own autonomy and retain the ability to air their own productions or other programs at times that they decide are best for their local markets.

The PBS Plus service provides additional programs, but these may or may not appear with any regularity in all markets, and often do not air at any regular time. PBS Plus includes how-to, self-help, news, and informational programs. In addition, PBS acquires and distributes specials for use by stations during pledge campaigns. Often, these are performance-based, and skew older to the demographic more likely to donate (age 40-plus).

PBS Kids is the brand name for the blocks of children's programming seen on PBS, focused entirely on nonviolent, family-friendly programming. Some specific curriculum goals for preschool children are partially supported by Ready to Learn, an initiative funded in part by the U.S. Department of Education to enhance PBS Kids programming with extensive community outreach and Internet activities. Services include workshops for parents, childcare providers, and other early childhood professionals, as well as connections to Head Start, Parent Teacher Associations, and other organizations.

PBS Teacher Source provides lessons and activities to be used in conjunction with public television programs. One example is a set of nine lesson plans related to media literacy from the children's series *Arthur*. Most stations supply schools with support materials provided by program producers and community organizations.

PBS Enterprises develops goods and services, many of which are related to new technologies. Its National Datacast, Inc., subsidiary uses an invisible portion of the broadcast signal to transmit data for clients' businesses. PBS Engineering is a research and development (R&D) group that works on behalf of the system; its accomplishments include the nation's first satellite distribution system and the development of closed captioning.

## PUBLIC TELEVISION PROGRAMMING

With the exception of home shopping channels and religious broadcasters, even the most successful local public television station routinely attracts the smallest audience of any broadcast station in the market. In general, PBS occupies a ratings position that's equal to the most popular cable networks, but only about 10 or 15 percent of the size of the audience attracted by CBS, NBC, or ABC. Programs on PBS usually outperform The History Channel, Food Network, Discovery Channel, and other networks sometimes perceived as similar, often by a 3:1 or 2:1 ratio. (In fact, these networks are not similar to PBS, as even the most cursory programming comparison will demonstrate.)

PBS is the foremost distributor of programming to public television stations (but not the only one; see following page). However, PBS does not produce its own programs. Instead, NPS acquires programs produced by member stations and PBS distributes these programs, also providing partial funding to some projects. The most prolific member stations are WGBH/Boston (*NOVA, American Experience, Antiques Roadshow, Frontline, Arthur, New Yankee Workshop, Victory Garden*); WNET/New York (*Nature, Great Performances, American Masters, Charlie Rose*); and WETA/Washington (*Washington Week*).

Most member stations contribute the occasional special, and some contribute several specials to the national service each year, but most do not. In a few instances, member stations are responsible for a single long-term, national series such as *Austin City Limits*, which is produced by KLRU on the University of Texas campus at Austin. Some member stations produce a considerable amount of original programming for their own schedules. WPBS in Watertown, New York, produces *The Gardener*, a hunting series called *Cabin Country*, three fishing series, *Streamside, Rod & Reel*, and *The New Fly Fisher*, and more. Kentucky Public Television, one of many state public television systems, produces an outdoor series, *Kentucky Afield*, plus a popular bluegrass series called *Jubilee* that is seen on many other stations. Mississippi Public Broadcasting's outdoors series is called, appropriately, *Mississippi Outdoors*. Maryland Public Broadcasting is a very busy producer, responsible for a weekly automotive series, *Motor Week*, as well as sixteen seasons of *Outdoors Maryland* and a range of cooking shows. Many public television stations have also produced specials about local history. For example, *Sin, Fire & Gold* was produced by San Francisco's KQED to tell the story of the Barbary Coast era. In Pittsburgh, WQED was the longtime home to national favorite *Mister Rogers' Neighborhood*, but its pop culture documentaries, such as *Great Old Amusement Parks* and *The Hot Dog Program*, have been successful on other stations as well. Many popular local specials are also made available, usually on a regional level, on home video.

PBS is not the only distributor of programs to public television stations. American Public Television (APT)—based in Boston and previously known as American Program Service (APS)—distributes a large number of the programs seen on public television, including movie packages, series once seen on commercial networks, and popular British situation comedies, known as "Britcoms." The National Educational Telecommunications Association (NETA) distributes a wide range of specialty programming; based in Columbia, South Carolina, it was formerly known as SECA, the Southern Educational Communications Association. BBC Worldwide Americas, through BBC Sales, distributes many Britcoms and other programs directly to stations. Each station to use these services pays an annual membership fee that includes access to the programs. Member stations provide programs for distribution by these services, but do not ordinarily receive compensation for their carriage on other public television stations.

As A&E, The History Channel, Discovery Channel, HGTV, The Learning Channel, Food Network, Nickelodeon, Nick Jr., and other cable networks nibble off pieces of PBS's distinctive programming profile, there are questions about the long-term viability of PBS's program strategies. Additional concerns about the aging of the baby boomer audience deepen the long-term challenges for PBS.

## Program Production

Staff or freelancers working at public television stations are responsible for the production of many series and specials. Others are handled by a production company, either working independently or working closely with a local public television station for fund-raising and other resources. For example, the long-running *Sesame Street* is produced by its own Sesame Workshop, a media company that includes publishing, licensing, home video, and other activities. On the other hand, A La Carte Productions works with WNET/New York on *Daisy Cooks! with Daisy Martinez*, a Hispanic cooking series. Pilot Productions is responsible for *Globe Trekker* and Martha Stewart Television produces *Everyday Food*, both in association with WETA/Washington. *Curious George* is a coproduction of WGBH/Boston and Universal Home Entertainment. Many smaller film companies are put together specifically for one or several projects, and often work with local stations throughout the country. Lion Television makes *History Detectives* and Actual Films produced *Rape of Europa*, each in association with Oregon Public Broadcasting. Indigo Studios put together *Our Finest Hour: The Apollo 8 Story* with WTTW/Chicago's national productions unit. (A list of these projects, along with contact information, is available at www.current.org/pipeline.)

In general, the time span from concept to air is about twice as long in public television as it is in commercial television. It is not unusual for a project to spend more than a year in development, and to appear on a schedule fully two or three years after its initial conception. Part of the reason for this extended period is the need to raise money for each individual project. With a somewhat limited potential for return, public television has not attracted the level of investment associated with commercial television. This is true of the entire public television system as well as for individual programs.

A station may provide a small amount of initial funding for development, but the station (or the producer) must then meet with potential sources of funding. The first stop is typically CPB and/or PBS, two organizations that regularly provide at least partial funding for development and production. Often, this partial funding then requires the station and/or producer to pitch the project to other sources of funding—including nonprofit foundations, national endowments, or corporate underwriters for whom the funding of public television programs is one of many activities. These organizations tend to attach their names and resources to multiple projects, thereby minimizing the risk of providing a high percentage of funds for any one project. In short, putting the financing package together is often time-consuming, regardless of the team's credentials and the quality of the program concept.

Projects produced for public television must meet an extraordinarily high threshold of quality in order to maintain public television's brand identity, particularly in prime time. As a result, production schedules tend to run longer than in the commercial world. In addition, many public television programs require the authority of experts in the field, who review scripts and rough cuts. This process enhances the quality of the project, but also increases expense as scripts are rewritten and additional editing is required. The project budget is likely to include more than the physical cost of production, however. Other costs include closed captioning, outreach marketing to schools or community groups, and promotional marketing. Because PBS is not quite a network, it has no significant network promotion budget, so each program must pay for its own advertising, public relations, and promotion. In order to fund its national program activities, the producing station takes a markup (usually called "station overhead") of approximately 20 percent of the overall project cost (sometimes more). When added together, these additional expenses can add as much as one-third to the program's cost.

All of the above is uniformly true for the programs seen in prime time. The situation for daytime and weekend programming is somewhat different, as cooking or sewing shows are not held to the same type of standard as, say, *American Masters*. Programs are of high quality but require lesser amounts of scripting, rewriting, editing, re-editing, and sound mixing.

Many public television stations and state networks are deeply involved in the production and distribution of educational programs for classroom and adult education. These programs are often less elaborate in terms of production. However, many of these projects are held to very high standards with regard to accountability—the number of students who viewed the program, the tests taken, and the specific results achieved by each student.

## Program Funding

Nearly $400 million is spent on public television programs annually—just over 20 percent of public television's annual income (roughly $2.2 billion).

In 2003, public television stations provided 29 percent of the funds for national productions, or just under $114 million, while corporations provided an additional 22 percent (just over $83 million) and foundations provided 16 percent (an additional $62 million). Producers, mainly through sales of foreign and home video rights, funded over 14 percent, or $55 million. CPB provided 10 percent, for an additional $37 million. Various federal agencies and related organizations (see below) contributed 7 percent, or $26 million. Individuals provided just 2 percent, or $7.7 million. In other words, funding for public television programs comes from a wide array of sources. This is tough on producers, and limits the types of programs produced; it is also, however, an extraordinary model that would be harshly criticized in a business plan but somehow works adequately in practice.

As mentioned above, some public television programs receive funds from federal agencies. The Department of Education, for example, provides funding for the *Ready to Learn* initiative. The National Endowment for the Humanities (NEH) grants production dollars for *American Experience*, and the National Endowment for the Arts (NEA) provides partial funding for *Great Performances*, *American Masters*, and *Live from Lincoln Center*. The National Science Foundation helps to fund *Rough Science*. Some of these grants must be matched by monies from other sources, frequently dollar for dollar.

Private foundations and trusts have been essential to financing such public television staples as *Sesame Street* and *American Experience*, and special series such as Ken Burns's *The Civil War*. Charities and foundations often support local public television stations or local carriage of national programs, as well as other public initiatives. The many foundations supporting public television include the Ford Foundation, the Charles H. Revson Foundation, and the Geraldine R. Dodge Foundation.

Many corporations are provide funding for national and local productions. *Dragon Tales* receives money from Kellogg's. *New Yankee Workshop* is funded in part by Minwax and Porter Cable. A look at the supporters of Sesame Workshop reveals a diverse list that includes McDonald's, Beaches (the resort company), McKinsey & Company, former FOX children's chief Margaret Loesch, Fleet

Bank, the Rockefeller Brothers Fund, Mr. and Mrs. Murray Kushner, the Asia Society, literary agent Lynn Nesbit, and many more.

## PBS Rules Regarding Program Financing

PBS strictly limits the ways in which production financing can be arranged, and the ways that the financing sources may be credited on the air. The philosophy behind these rules encourages public television to maintain its noncommercial image amongst viewers and legislators, and to ensure that editorial control of programming cannot be surrendered in exchange for financial backing. In other words, airtime cannot be traded for any form of sponsorship or financing.

These rules intentionally handicap underwriting credits so that they are not competitive with network television commercials. Many potential underwriters find these rules too restrictive; the result is a far smaller pool of potential underwriters whose intent is, most often, doing good rather than marketing in any sense related to traditional advertising. As costs increase and availability of other monies remains steady or decreases, underwriting rules are often discussed and reassessed. There is great sensitivity here; any step toward commercialism is viewed as a step on a path toward the end of government funding and, possibly, a loss of audience support.

In general, each funding arrangement is filtered by three key questions: Is there a possibility that the underwriter could exercise editorial control over the program's content? Might the public *perceive* that the underwriter has exercised editorial control? After viewing the program, would a reasonable person assume that the purpose of the program was the promotion of the funder's products or services? To this end, there are specific rules regarding length and content of on-screen credits, the number of underwriter credits, acceptance of in-kind goods and services, and more. There are special rules regarding children's and how-to programs. These are all available to producers and to the general public in a comprehensive document, *PBS National Program Funding Standards and Practices*, or by visiting www.pbs.org/producers/guidelines/. There are many nuances and potential inconsistencies, so public television program producers are always wise to check with PBS before making commitments for underwriting credits.

## Licensing Revenues from Children's Programs

A successful children's television program inevitably results in toys, books, CDs, and other products. Often, the annual revenues associated with successful series exceed $500 million per year. Given a 5 percent return to the license holder, the net revenues would be $25 million per year. These dollars are often used to fund operating costs, production costs, outreach, and new project development. As a rule, the individual creator whose work was the basis of the children's series receives a percentage of the net, as does a licensing agent, if any (licensing can be a staff function). While it might be said that some children's programs are program-length commercials for the sale of merchandise, the need for funding of quality children's programs on public television generally outweighs the concerns about the commercial activities of children's television producers.

Two of the most prolific producers of children's programs are Hit Entertainment and Scholastic, both commercial concerns with extensive television, publishing, and licensing operations. Boston's WGBH and Sesame Workshop are equally prolific, but both operate as nonprofit companies.


## PUBLIC TELEVISION STATIONS

There are 356 public television stations in the U.S., operated by about half as many entities. Of these 176 licensees, 89 are community organizations, 59 are colleges or universities, and 28 are local or state educational or municipal authorities. Almost all are PBS members. Some of these entities own a single station, like WXXI in Rochester, New York. Some own a large station and a smaller one, like WNET in New York City and its sister WLIW in nearby Long Island. Some cover whole states: Kentucky Educational Television, for example, is the second largest television network in the world with 16 analog and 16 digital transmitters in its state system. By comparison, the Maine Public Television Network operates five stations, and New Jersey Network operates four.

### Economics of Local Public Television Stations

Generally, public television stations build their budgets from a variety of sources including annual federal (CPB) and, in some cases, state grants; private contributions; foundation grants; corporate gifts; in-kind services; program sales; auctions; underwriting; membership; other fund-raising events; and entrepreneurial ventures such as online sales of DVDs and other merchandise. For example, Twin Cities Public Television in St. Paul, Minnesota, took in $23.5 million in unrestricted revenues for fiscal year 2004. The largest contributor was individual memberships, whose revenue line totaled $8.6 million, or more than one-third of the budget. Earned income from various revenue-producing activities was larger than most public television organizations: $2.4 million. CPB and PBS provided $1.9 million, and the state of Minnesota added about $200,000 in grants. Corporations provided $1.4 million, and foundations another $800,000. Bequests, which are related to major giving initiatives, contributed nearly $800,000 more. The station added $466,000 in donated goods and professional services.

How was the money spent? The biggest chunk—$12.4 million, or half the budget—was spent on programming and production (including fees to PBS, APT, and other program suppliers). Another $2.2 million was spent on broadcasting—the distribution of those programs. Fund-raising generates considerable revenue, but there are associated costs: The budget lines for fund-raising, underwriting, and grant solicitations totaled $4.8 million (to raise over $10 million). The general and administrative (G&A) line was $2.8 million.

In comparison, New Hampshire Public Television, a statewide system serving no large cities, operated in fiscal year 2003 with about $9 million, one-third of which was provided by state and federal grants. Membership accounted for $2.7 million in revenues, and the combination of corporate underwriting and foundation grants provided $1.1 million. The remaining income was generated by a combination of major gifts from individuals ($250,000), auctions ($600,000), magazine advertising ($40,000), events and endowments ($25,000), facilities rentals ($750,000), and other activities ($200,000).

Every station's situation is different. There is no single model that applies across all, or even many, stations. Stations in smaller markets than Minneapolis-St. Paul are likely to have smaller budgets. Some states provide very significant funding for public television; others do not. Some markets are more compatible with public television's notion of individual membership; others have more near-at-hand corporations or foundations. Some stations are in markets with more than one public television station, some are operated as a part of a college or university, and some are combined TV/AM/FM operations.

## GOVERNMENT REGULATION

Government intervention in the conduct of public broadcasting has three principle components: allocating spectrum, regulating sponsorships, and providing financial support.

### Station Allocation

A critical historical step in creating today's public television landscape was the reservation of 10 percent of the allocable broadcast channels for licensing to noncommercial, educational (NCE) broadcast stations, first in 1945 for FM radio and then in 1952 for television. (Since AM radio was licensed prior to that time, no reservation was made there.) In accordance with FCC regulations, NCE licenses are typically held by nonprofits, state and local governments, and colleges and universities (including those with religious affiliations). By FCC regulation, stations that receive NCE licenses are required to furnish "a nonprofit and noncommercial service." Principal among these imposed restrictions are the limits on the nature of sponsorship announcements.

### Sponsorship Restrictions

As described above, PBS has rules governing how its member stations may raise money from businesses and other sponsors. The FCC also regulates this process, and its rules underlie the PBS requirements. Section 399b of the Communications Act provides that "No public broadcast station may make its facilities available to any person for the broadcasting of any advertisement." As interpreted by FCC regulations and policy statements, stations may identify business sponsors but may not promote them. The identification may include (1) logograms or slogans that identify and do not promote, (2) location information, (3) value-neutral descriptions of a product line or service, and (4) brand and trade names and product or service listings. The announcement must not interrupt the program in question.

The FCC sites the following examples of announcements that are not permissible:

- Announcements containing price information, including any announcement of interest rate information or other indication of savings or value associated with the product, such as "7.7 percent interest rate available now."

- Announcements containing a call to action, such as "Stop by our showroom to see a model" or "Try product X next time you buy oil."

- Announcements containing an inducement to buy, sell, rent, or lease, such as "Six months' free service," "A bonus available this week," or "Special gift for the first 50 visitors."

The FCC has recognized that it may be difficult at times to distinguish between announcements that promote and those that identify. Nonetheless public broadcast licensees are expected to review their donor or underwriter acknowledgments and make reasonable good faith judgments. While most national players in the sponsorship game understand the rules and don't push them too hard, many local sponsors with less sophistication make requests that go over the line. Stations can be tempted by the dollars, but they should be careful; those violating the rules are subject to fines and, potentially, to even more drastic remedies.

## Financial Support

At the federal level, government support for public broadcasting was a product of the 1960s and the concerns bubbling up at that time over television quality. In 1962, the Educational Television Facilities Act established a capital grant program for noncommercial broadcast facilities. As the decade progressed, concern over the quality of television increased, and in 1967, Congress passed the Public Broadcasting Act. As described above, this legislation established the Corporation for Public Broadcasting as a nonprofit and nongovernmental body that could serve as a conduit for governmental funding for educational broadcasting, on both television and radio. In setting up a conduit for federal support, care was taken to insulate the end product from political and bureaucratic pressure. CPB would work with stations, but would not carry on any broadcasting of its own.

The Public Broadcasting Act also added Section 396(g)(1)(A) to the Communications Act, which required that CPB-funded activities observe "strict adherence to objectivity and balance in all programs or series of programs of a controversial nature." A 1975 case held that this language provided instructions to the CPB, and a benchmark for congressional review in the appropriations process, but not a mandate for FCC review, which it felt could open the door to political meddling. A further provision had prohibited editorializing by a station receiving CPB funding. This was held unconstitutional by a closely divided U.S. Supreme Court in 1984.

The policy of insulating public broadcasting from political influence was somewhat compromised from the start by the makeup of the CPB Board of Directors, which governs CPB, sets policy, and establishes programming priorities. The president of the United States appoints each Board member, who, after confirmation by the Senate, serves a six-year term. The Board appoints the president and chief executive officer, who in turn names the other corporate officers. When executive appointment is coupled with Congress's power of the purse over appropriations, the opportunities for political influence do exist, and over time, allegations of undue influence have come from both ends of the political spectrum.

# CHAPTER 24

# HOME SHOPPING

In one form or another, home shopping dates back to the 1950s. Today's televised shopping business is worth well over $10 billion per year. Although dominated by QVC, there are several other home shopping networks, plus the older direct-response and paid-programming ("infomercial") formats.

## SHORT-FORM DIRECT RESPONSE: PER INQUIRY

Since the start of television, many local stations have allotted a percentage of their unsold commercial time to direct marketers. The cost of media time for a 30- or 60-second spot is, of course, considerably less than the cost of an entire half-hour. The format has been particularly successful with magazine subscriptions, household "miracles," automotive accessories, and a variety of gadgets.

Direct marketers work with television stations and cable networks in several ways. A large amount of low-value inventory may be purchased at a deeply discounted rate. Typically, this time would fetch a very small dollar amount from traditional clients, or would go unsold, so the station or network is often pleased to release the inventory, even at a low price. Alternatively, the direct marketer may purchase time within specific parts of the schedule, again most often early in the morning, late in the evening, or overnight, when fewer people are watching and the station or network is willing to accept a low rate for the spots. Occasionally, the station or network may partner with the direct marketer, accepting a percentage of sales in lieu of upfront payment. (There are some success stories here, but most often, the direct marketer gets the time for free and the station or network is left with little to show for its investment.) In other cases, stations or networks may be paid on the basis of the number of phone calls received by the marketer.

The most common format for this short-form application of television merchandising is known as *per inquiry* (*PI*) advertising. The deal begins with a supplier, typically a manufacturer or distributor, who identifies a product suitable for this specialized form of direct marketing. The product is typically priced in the $20 to $50 range, and sometimes higher. The product should appear to be special or unique, the sort of merchandise that might not be found in retail stores ("as seen on TV"). The supplier produces the commercial and hires a broker to place it on cable networks and local broadcast stations. The broker typically receives about 15 percent of the product's selling price. The cable network or local station does not receive a cash payment in exchange for the airtime. Instead, the commercial is shown and the network or station receives a percentage of each sale attributable to its activities, usually 25 to 35 percent of the selling price.

The viewer calls the 800 number on the TV screen and reaches a telemarketing clearinghouse—a firm hired by the supplier to take product orders. This firm charges the supplier one fee for each call for information, a higher fee for each call resulting in a sale, and a still higher fee for each call that can be transformed into an "up-sell"—a sale of multiple or additional products. The price per call is typically $1 to $3, though these figures vary depending upon the size of the firm, the time spent per call, the number of orders, and so on.

The supplier receives customer payments and an accounting from the telemarketing firm, then passes the payments and records on to the broker. The broker deducts the agreed-upon percentage, then pays the station or cable network. Stations and networks are dependent upon accurate, honest recordkeeping for their income, so they are likely to require approval of the telemarketing company or, in some cases, to insist upon using a particular company for this purpose. Since the station owns the airtime, it is in a position to force this decision.

PI marketing generally requires testing. Several commercials may be produced before one proves to be successful; several venues may be tried before finding the one or two cable networks most suitable for a particular product. Broadcast television stations, whose audiences are broader and less segmented than cable networks, usually start new PI spots during the overnight period, then schedule the most profitable ones in late-evening and early-morning time slots. Stations are under no obligation to schedule the spots at all, and may program them in any manner that seems reasonable.

## PROGRAM-LENGTH COMMERCIALS: INFOMERCIALS

Several unrelated factors stimulated the growth of the infomercial industry in the 1980s. The first was a change in FCC regulations, allowing broadcasters to air more than 16 minutes of commercial advertising per hour. The second was consumer acceptance of credit cards and toll-free (800) telephone numbers. The third factor was the emergence of new cable television networks that were unable to fill their airtime profitably; entrepreneurs purchased the airtime (as they do today) for relatively low prices, then filled the hours with program-length commercials. In today's marketplace, even the largest network affiliates in major markets sell their overnight hours for use as paid programming, as do CNBC, Discovery, Lifetime, and many other large cable networks. The reasoning is simple enough: More money can be made by selling the less desirable airtime outright than by filling it with regular programming and selling commercials. For many local stations and cable networks, HUT (Households Using Television) levels and resulting ratings are simply too low to follow a traditional programming and advertising strategy.

Of course, the infomercial provider must be able to recoup and profit after the purchase of the airtime. If the infomercial provider purchases a half-hour for $3,500—a reasonable price in the overnight hours—then the provider's net must exceed $3,500. Given a $49.95 retail price with, perhaps, a $35 net (after cost of goods, call center, and other services) to the marketer, break-even would occur when 100 units were sold. If one in 100 viewers made a purchase, then 10,000 viewers would be required to break even on the purchase price of the airtime. More likely, one in several hundred viewers would buy, so the required viewers would be 50,000 or more. Of course, the cost of the television production also must be profitably covered by total sales. If a program costs $50,000 to produce, and the infomercial runs 50 times, then each airing must return the equivalent of $1,000 to cover production.

To be more specific, the cost of goods for any product sold through this channel is typically about 20 percent of the selling price. The product must appeal to the middle of the market and below. Its benefits must be obvious, unique, and easily understood through a television demonstration. The best products clearly demonstrate their potential to save customers substantial amounts of time, effort, or money. As you watch and analyze infomercials, you will inevitably notice the testimonials—real people who have used the product and attest to the results. You'll also notice the importance of a guarantee. It is essential that a company is established with experience in developing and marketing products, producing the programs and commercials, and buying the airtime. In a marketplace where three out of every four products routinely fail, it makes sense for every marketer to learn the business by working with companies that have succeeded—companies that understand the business and its pitfalls.

In order to maximize the return on this risk, infomercial companies have become sophisticated in their understanding of the marketplace. A single infomercial might be tested in several markets, with a slightly different offer in each. At $49.95, the beauty system might be perceived as too costly, but at $59.95 with two free refills, the value proposition might be just right. The cost of airtime is a big expense, but follow-up sales to customers acquired via television are not nearly as expensive. Customers of the same beauty care system might call an 800 number to order refills (this is "inbound telemarketing"). Or, an outbound telemarketing service might call customers who purchased the system with a special offer; outbound telemarketing to the company's own customer list can be very profitable.

Celebrity endorsements are often (but not always) effective selling tools, especially if the celebrity is sincerely committed to the product, as in the case of

Victoria Principal, whose Principal Secret cosmetic and skin care product line has earned hundreds of millions of dollars in sales. Guthy-Renker, an industry leader behind Principal Secret, has also been successful in marketing videotapes of Dean Martin's and Carol Burnett's television variety shows; the same company sells Tony Robbins's videotapes. Another example is an acne care system called Proactiv Solution, which has been represented by actress Judith Light, singer/actress Vanessa Williams, model Elle MacPherson, singer Jessica Simpson, and hip-hop entrepreneur Sean "Diddy" Combs.

Cost of goods and potential profit margin are critical. A low cost of goods and a high retail price are, of course, a good combination. Still, a relatively small margin may be acceptable if the product lends itself to continuity sales (sales to customers who may purchase refills, additional parts or additional episodes of *The Dean Martin Show*, other related products, etc.). Fitness, health, and beauty products have been among the most successful in this retail channel. Self-improvement products related to earning power have also worked. Like the book and movie businesses, the hits more than compensate for the flops. Only one in every four infomercial products earns back its investment in media and production; but when a product succeeds, it can make a tremendous amount of money—hundreds of millions of dollars. In 2003, Guthy-Renker's revenues were over $900 million.

Ultimately, direct response television is a game of numbers. The players are becoming increasingly sophisticated, and service firms have emerged for the purpose of data collection and analysis. One such firm, backchannelmedia, offers extensive information about available paid-programming slots on television stations throughout the U.S., and about the demographics and buying patterns associated with specific Designated Market Areas (DMAs). For more information and a free daily newsletter on industry topics, visit www.backchannelmedia.com.

## SHOPPING NETWORKS

The contemporary home shopping business began in 1977, when the owner of a Florida radio station accepted merchandise (112 electric can openers) in place of cash to settle an advertiser's debt. The station offered the merchandise over the air for sale; listeners called in to order and drove to the station to pick up their purchases. Seeing an opportunity, entrepreneurs leased time on a local cable system and discovered that the idea worked in the local Tampa Bay market. After considering expansion to other Florida markets, the venture instead rented satellite time and, in 1985, went national as the Home Shopping Network (HSN).

Soon, there were 30 television shopping services. QVC (Quality, Value, Convenience) debuted in November 1986. After a late 1980s shakeout, three networks remained. QVC has emerged as the industry leader, followed by HSN, Shop NBC, Shop at Home, and Jewelry Television.

In 2004, QVC's sales were just under $5 billion. Its story is filled with stunning statistics. For example, the company receives approximately 200 million phone calls each year (most sales are by phone rather than Internet). Some 29 million people have shopped at QVC to date, plus approximately 200,000 new customers every month. Nearly one in three QVC programs are related, in some way, to jewelry. QVC reaches just about every cable and satellite household in the U.S., while QVC U.K. reaches over 13 million households in England, Ireland, and Scotland. QVC Deutschland adds 34 million households, and QVC Japan (a joint venture with Matsui) operates 24 hours a day for nearly 12 million homes. QVC is owned by Liberty Media.

HSN is a subsidiary of IAC/Interactive Corp. (in which Liberty Media is a large shareholder), which also owns Match.com, Expedia, Ticketmaster, and other companies mainly involved in electronic transactions. The key player here is Barry Diller, who leads IAC and was previously the CEO of FOX and, subsequently, QVC. In terms of employees, calls received, and units shipped, HSN is about one-third the size of QVC.

ValueVision owns and operates ShopNBC, the third largest shopping network. The network reported 2003 sales of over $600 million, and reaches over 55 million cable and satellite households. Approximately 40 percent of ValueVision is owned by GE Equity and by NBC.

Jewelry Television, launched in 2004, almost immediately became one of the nation's top jewelry retailers. Through a combination of full-power and LPTV broadcasters, cable companies, and satellite distribution, Jewelry Television is available in over 70 million U.S. households. The company does roughly $300 million in sales per year, but it is growing rapidly.

## Doing Business with a Home Shopping Network

With 24 hours to fill each day, the home shopping networks are constantly seeking out new products that solve a problem, lend themselves to presentation on television, and generate audience interest. Networks buy products at a low wholesale price. Rapid inventory turnover and volume sales are central to a successful home shopping operation. It is also possible to contact QVC and other shopping networks via their Web sites, and via special buyer's events that are scheduled from time to time in major markets. In addition, it is possible to submit a product for review by QVC via the company's Web site. Agents who specialize in connecting product providers to shopping networks typically charge 10 to 15 percent of sales; the best agencies are those with a multi-year track record and a reasonable number of recent product placements. (As with any agency relationship, a required up-front payment is almost always a warning sign.)

Networks have become very sophisticated in their product selection process; it is not unusual for a network buyer to ask detailed questions about manufacturing, financing, and other close-to-the-bone issues. There's a good reason: The network's reputation is on the line with every product sold.

The best products demonstrate effectively on television, clearly solve a problem or make life easier, have broad audience appeal, and are somehow unique or unusual. QVC's minimum wholesale order is usually $20,000. The system is quite rigid: QVC must have the merchandise in its warehouse in order to fulfill quickly (four out of every five orders ship within 24 hours). Most products are priced in the $15 to $100 range. A successful product sells several thousand units during and immediately after a five-minute program segment. QVC does not charge for order placement, however the supplier must invest in a sufficient number of finished units to satisfy QVC's purchase order. That said, if QVC does not sell all of the units, they are typically returned to the supplier, who must sell them elsewhere in order to recoup or earn a profit.

The financial relationship between cable operators and shopping networks is unique, unlike the relationship for any other program service. The cable operator receives approximately 5 percent of the gross collected revenues within its service area (calculated by zip code).

## Trust, Customer Service, and Infrastructure

One key to success in any form of television shopping is *trust*. Viewers must trust the people who are selling the products on television. Customers interact directly with the on-camera hosts through telephone conversations, and a relationship is built—not just for the person on the phone, but for other viewers who identify with what's being said. These relationships enhance the trusting relationship between customer and retailer.

Another key to success is *customer service*. Once the relationship is built, it must be maintained and nurtured by an enormous backroom customer service operation. Many products are carefully tested before they are approved for sale by the network. Customer service representatives are available 24 hours a day to answer consumer questions about products, handle credit issues, and follow up on lost merchandise and returns. A small army is employed in order entry (taking orders by phone) and fulfillment (working in the warehouse or shipping)—and this figure increases during the busy fourth quarter of the year.

The staff required to operate a shopping channel is large in comparison with other television channels, but comparable to direct marketing operations of similar size. QVC's 15,000 employees and seven warehouses represent the largest such operation in the industry. More than 100 QVC buyers visit trade shows, factories, and other facilities, identify products appropriate for this distribution channel, and make quantity deals. The merchandise is then shipped to the network's warehouses, and programmers schedule segments to sell the merchandise. If the product is exclusive for a short period, it may go on the air within days. If the product requires the production of a special videotape to explain its unique features or operation, several weeks may pass before it is scheduled. On QVC, approximately ten to twelve products are shown per hour.

Other departments include inventory control, information technology (IT), finance, affiliate relations, merchandising, and broadcasting. At QVC (HSN uses a similar model), the broadcasting department is headed by an executive vice president who also serves as executive producer. A vice president of talent supervises about 20 performers working three- to four-hour shifts each day, three or four days each week. Several managers take care of specific production tasks: control room operations, post-production, and backstage operations (displaying products). Even acknowledging the use of technical and process efficiencies (robotic cameras, for example), a large support staff is required to enable a network that operates 24 hours a day.

## HOME SHOPPING OUTSIDE THE U.S.

Direct-response firms regularly purchase media time and produce commercials throughout the world. In some countries, rules regarding direct marketing require specific disclosures, and may restrict some product categories. Some countries do not permit testimonials, for example. It's very important that local rules are carefully followed in relation to quality control, packaging, shipping, and other specifics. Local tendencies also must be considered, too: Outside of North America, where the physical space available in homes is typically limited, consumers tend not to buy physically large products. Quality matters; consumers do not hesitate to return products that do not fit their needs.

One industry leader, Williams Worldwide Television, works with direct-response distributors in over 70 countries. These distributors buy the local media time, take care of inbound telemarketing, and carry out fulfillment. Distributors pre-purchase the best slots, and are constantly in search of products suitable for their markets. This places Williams in the position of logistical coordinator for a worldwide network of distributors. Sales of products outside the U.S. are beginning to exceed domestic sales; in time, the world market will regularly exceed U.S. sales. When a product is successful, hundreds of thousands of units are sold. Generally, the best markets are Europe, Japan, Korea, and Australia; South and Central America tend to be more price sensitive, but the market is growing there and in China.

Web sales are also a significant contributor to foreign direct-response sales, and becoming more so.

In Europe, home shopping channels are well established. QVC's operations in the U.K. and in Germany are described above. Germany is also the home base for HSE24, which also serves Switzerland and Belgium. In addition, RTL Shop operates in Germany and, via satellite and through time on other networks, throughout Europe.

## GOVERNMENT REGULATION

As discussed above, television shopping became legally possible in 1981, when the FTC dropped regulations that had mandated maximum amounts of advertising that could be broadcast per hour. In the absence of legal limits, 24/7 became the practical "limit," and networks devoted to interactive shopping via television became a permanent part of the electronic landscape.

Another important regulatory step in the expansion of home shopping was the 1993 decision by the FCC that home shopping broadcast channels qualified for cable "must-carry" treatment (see page 49), thus mandating their delivery via cable as well. This issue is being revisited in light of the new digital television rules. Given the possibility that each channel in the new digital broadcast world can potentially split itself into four "low-definition" services, and that some of these may be devoted to data transmission and similar uses that would be unsuitable for cable service inclusion, at this writing there is a battle over whether a home shopping service in such a split channel might be left off "must carry" as well. The stakes over uncompensated carriage by cable of a commercial shopping outlet are relatively high, and the outcome of the battle is hard to predict.

Finally, shopping channels and infomercials are subject to the general FTC and FCC rules governing truthful advertising and sales (see Chapter 14).

## INDUSTRY REGULATION

There is a measure of self-regulation being applied to home shopping, infomercials, and similar uses of television. The Electronic Retailing Association (ERA), which also covers online and radio-based retailing, has set up the Electronic Retailing Self-Regulation Program (ERSP). The ERA has in fact worked to correct abuses, referring particularly egregious cases to the FTC, although its ability to be a major force for discipline in the field is undercut by staffing limits. The ERA can be contacted at www.savvyshopper.org.

# CHAPTER 25
# RELIGIOUS TELEVISION

## HISTORY AND EVOLUTION OF RELIGIOUS TELEVISION

Approximately one in ten commercially licensed television stations in the U.S. is a full-time religious broadcaster. Several of the largest U.S. cable networks are religious television services. Although the economic model and mission differ from traditional television, religious television is a vital part of the landscape in the U.S. and in many other parts of the world. And it is growing.

Televised religion has its roots in traveling shows, typically held in tents and hosted by evangelists (the tradition of tent shows continues to this day). In 1923, the first "radio church" was formed; there was no physical building, only a microphone, a transmitter, and listeners. Still, the religious broadcasters saw the medium as a gift from God to spread The Word of God. And so, an easy alliance came into existence with broadcasters selling airtime to religious organizations. Religious programming has managed to reach a huge audience: *The Lutheran Hour*, for example, reached 700 million listeners worldwide in the 1940s. Host Walter Maier was world-famous—the Billy Graham of his day. There were many others, some locally famous, some nationally known. Some were involved in scandals related to misappropriation of funds, even in those early days.

For most of broadcast history, networks (first on radio, then on television) sometimes allowed religious broadcasters to buy airtime, and sometimes prohibited such purchases. Until the 1960s, the broadcast networks maintained a certain number of hours on their weekly schedules for noncommercial programming; this "sustaining" time was provided free to various organizations, including religious broadcasters. But by and large, broadcasters have not provided free airtime to religious ventures.

Although the image of a television preacher is a common one, religious television also encompasses talk shows, music programs, children's programs, and the occasional dramatic program. In today's television environment, most religious programming appears on the paid-programming portion of local stations and cable networks, on dedicated broadcast or cable networks (such as TBN), and on their satellite equivalents. CBS broadcast *For Our Times* until 1988, but religious programming is almost never found on broadcast network television today.

It's interesting to note that faith-based programming is proving to be a meaningful marketing force in the conversion of the remaining broadcast television households to cable households, and in the conversion of analog cable households to digital households. Faith-based networks are a growth industry, and much of this growth is due to the accurate perception that these networks provide a family-friendly alternative to more aggressive broadcast and cable program fare.

## TELEVISION MINISTRIES

A television ministry is a unique operation. It's a nonprofit corporation whose primary purpose is to spread The Word of God by providing television programs seen throughout the country and, often, throughout the world. A television minister may or may not be a certified religious leader; some are teachers, others are preachers, and some are simply gifted personalities whom people enjoy watching on television.

A ministry earns money by requesting financial support from viewers in exchange for worship-related programming—it's not unlike public television in this regard. No federal or state law restricts these televised requests, provided that there is no fraud involved nor funding of criminal activities. Well over half of the revenues are used to produce television programming and to buy airtime for its broadcast; in this regard, religious television is similar to direct-response television. What percentage of a ministry's revenues should be allotted to television productions? Will a more lavish set, or higher quality cameras, or a dedicated television studio spread The Word of God more effectively? How about a limousine so that the minister can appear relaxed and focused on television? One might argue that these are unfortunate uses of monies provided by faithful viewers; one might also argue that these items are typically associated with first-class prime-time programs, so they are entirely appropriate here. Sometimes, it is difficult to draw the line between a first-class operation and abuse of trust. And sometimes, as in several notorious cases in the 1980s, the exploitation is readily apparent. To limit abuses, the industry has established the Evangelical Council for Financial Accountability (ECFA), but not every ministry is a member.

A substantial percentage of the revenues from religious television is used to purchase airtime. In one distribution scheme, the model is very similar to the direct-response shopping model. Local television stations and most cable television networks allot some overnight and weekend morning hours to paid programming. That is, the station or network sells the entire half-hour to a single entity, typically a ministry or a direct marketer. In both cases, the cost of the airtime should be less than the amount of money raised during the half-hour. In the case of the ministry, additional distribution is always meaningful (to spread The Word of God), so a precise return on investment may not be a priority for each slot purchased. Still, many ministries have become savvy about their media buys: If the money is being invested, why not invest where the highest available return is available?

TBN (Trinity Broadcasting Network) is one of several television networks dedicated entirely to religious programming. In the commercial world, these networks might provide airtime in exchange for a percentage of revenues. In the religious world, this would require a level of transactions and accounting uncommon for ministries. Instead, the network either sells the airtime to the ministry, or the network pays the ministry for the right to air the program.

Benny Hinn is one of television's most popular evangelists. His ministry produces a series entitled *This Is Your Day!*, which airs daily on several networks: INSP (Inspiration Network), TBN, and Daystar. In addition, the program is seen on nearly 100 local television stations, generally in paid-programming slots.

Crystal Cathedral Ministries, featuring Dr. Robert Schuller, has operated for a half-century. Its program, *Hour of Power*, appears on Lifetime, Discovery, TBN, various satellite channels, and an assortment of local television stations.

Bishop T. D. Jakes hosts the daily talk show *The Potter's Touch*, on TBN. *Time* magazine named Jakes "America's Best Preacher" in 1991. His multicultural church, serving a local population in Dallas, Texas, has 28,000 members; it is one of the fastest-growing congregations in the country.

Author and public speaker Kay Arthur is not clergy, but she is enormously popular with religious audiences. Her ministry is called Precept Ministries International (formerly Reach Out), and as a member of the ECFA, she posts financial information on her Web site. Revenues from publishing, radio and television broadcasts, conferences, and workshops totaled over $12.5 million in 2003.

In Touch Ministries, featuring Dr. Charles Stanley, reported to the ECFA total income of over $60 million in 2003, with over $45 million spent on "Program Services," which certainly includes television production and airtime. Dr. Stanley's broadcasts are seen throughout the U.S. and, according to the ministry's Web site, In Touch "now reaches every nation on earth."

Several dozen ministries are widely seen on multiple television networks in the U.S., and maintain a significant presence throughout the world. Some exist principally to spread The Word of God through preaching, talk shows, and other television formats. Often, these ministries also adopt specific projects, such as the building or maintenance of an orphanage in another country. Many ministries engage in "crusades," essentially fund-raising campaigns either for their own benefit or for the benefit of a designated charitable cause.

## RELIGIOUS TELEVISION NETWORKS

Unlike most conventional television networks, religious networks typically operate with a combination of broadcast and cable outlets. Several large networks operate in the U.S., including TBN (Trinity Broadcasting Network), Daystar, EWTN (Eternal Word Television Network), and INSP (Inspiration Network). In addition, there are smaller regional networks, such as the Chicago-based Total Living Network. Another variation on the traditional format is Sky Angel, a satellite service.

Trinity Broadcasting Network is the world's largest religious network. The *Los Angeles Times* reported TBN's 2002 viewer donations as $120 million; an additional $37 million in revenues came from the sale of airtime and rights to programs; dividends and interest added $13 million; and a miscellaneous category added another $1 million. Total revenues: $171 million, with about $110 million in expenses. The surplus, over $60 million for 2002, was questioned by the newspaper. Another report showed cash assets of $583 million. In 2004, TBN purchased a UHF channel in Philadelphia for $47 million; TBN is now a top-ten station group with a lineup rivaling ABC and NBC. With a large domestic and international distribution system, the most desirable programming from well-known ministries, and its share of quality original programs, TBN is also seen throughout the world via satellite.

The second largest network, Daystar, operates 22 local television stations in the U.S. (making it the tenth largest station group in the U.S. in terms of coverage) and covers the world with multiple satellite signals. Daystar's schedule combines traditional religious programming with talk shows (Joni Lamb, known simply as "Joni," is the network's star talk-show host).

i does not promote itself as a religious network. However, the network does broadcast many hours of religious programming every day. Overnight hours are programmed by Worship TV. During the day, the schedule is paid programming. From 5:00 P.M. until midnight, i features family-friendly programming. In the 2004–2005 season, for example, the network featured game shows (*Family Feud*) and drama (*Sue Thomas, F.B.Eye*), plus a reality show (*Cold Turkey*). Paxson Communications is one of the largest television station groups in the U.S.—the fourth-largest in terms of coverage, with 58 stations (i covers more of the U.S. than ABC does).

EWTN, a Global Catholic Network, claims to be the largest religious media network in the world, reaching over 100 million households in over 100 countries. EWTN's media operation includes not only television (both English- and Spanish-language), but also AM and FM radio stations delivered via satellite, a shortwave radio station, and a publishing operation. The network's origins are inspiring: founder Mother Angelica and four other nuns supported themselves by selling fishing lures and peanuts, then built a television studio in a garage— and grew into one of the world's largest media operations.

Among the smaller networks, INSP is distributed to over 20 million cable households; the same organization has launched a growing inspirational lifestyle network that includes children's programming, music, and more. Owned by the

Southern Baptists, FamilyNet is seen in over 30 million households; the network airs approximately 50 hours of programming per week. FE-TV is a Spanish-language Christian network seen primarily in Texas and Oklahoma.

Sky Angel is a subscription television and radio network filled with Christian and family programming. This special service is affiliated with DISH Network, which may also be purchased along with Sky Angel service. For $12 per month plus equipment and installation (tax deductible, as it is a religious contribution), viewers receive three dozen television channels. Sky Angel operates several of its own channels, such as Angel One (filled with programs from over 150 ministries) and a children's channel. Spirit, a Christian music TV service, is also primarily available via Sky Angel.

Pat Robertson is credited with changing the system of television ministries. Along with HBO and Ted Turner's TBS, Robertson's *The 700 Club* was an early purchaser of satellite time. This not only circumvented the awkward system of shipping videocassettes, it also dramatically increased the number of television stations that could receive the program. Early in its history, the Christian Broadcasting Network was a traditional network; it owned about a dozen television stations. The promise of satellite technology changed CBN's approach. In 1997, CBN, then a large U.S. cable network controlled by Robertson, sold to FOX, forming the foundation for the FOX Family Channel, which was subsequently sold for approximately $3 billion to become ABC Family. Programs are still distributed under the CBN brand, but the network no longer exists in its original form. Talk/variety show *The 700 Club*, one of CBN's most consistently popular programs, is now seen on ABC Family, on TBN, and during the paid-programming slots on many local television stations. Another program, *CBN Newswatch*, is also seen on various local television stations, as well as on FamilyNet. *Living the Life* is shown on ABC Family and on various religious networks and local stations. CBN and its related companies reported $239 million in 2003 revenues, most of which was used to operate its ministry. Cash on hand plus investments in 2003 totaled approximately $8 million.

## REGULATION OF RELIGIOUS TELEVISION

Although its transactional foundation is akin to home shopping—because on-screen personalities ask viewers to send money—religious programming is often presented as a variation on educational programming or programming in the public interest. In fact, religious programming is classified as educational programming. Religious television channels operate under the same type of broadcast license as many public television stations.

The Evangelical Council for Financial Accountability is a self-regulatory group that represents a number of religious television organizations, with over $5 billion in combined income. Any organization with 501(c)(3) (nonprofit) status and over $500,000 in either income or expenses is required to submit to an outside audit. The results of that audit are publicly available. There are more standards, all intended to protect the industry from further missteps. For example, the majority of board of directors seats must be occupied by people who are neither family members nor employees.

In 1999 and 2000, the FCC looked like it would review and possibly reverse the broadcast world's classification of religion as education. In the waning days of the Clinton administration, a three-to-two vote of the Commission raised the idea that programming aimed at proselytizing a particular religious view would not constitute general educational programming. This suggestion drew a quick and ferocious congressional counterattack. The response was so effective that a month later, on its own motion, the FCC reversed this portion of its ruling and left fully sectarian religious broadcasting as a part of the educational television landscape. A similar approach has been applied to satellite television, where religious programs and networks have been given channels reserved for public-interest use.

Religious networks have fought suggestions for "unbundling" cable, i.e. proposals that would make cable service available on an "à la carte" basis, allowing individual channels to be purchased. The religious networks fear that they would be affirmatively ordered by a relatively narrow slice of the viewing public, making religious television a self-selecting exercise in "preaching to the choir."

A relaxation of generally applicable rules for religious television has been explicitly granted in the equal employment opportunity regulations (see page 37), where an exemption has been carved out to allow preference in hiring to members of a particular denomination.

Given the political strength of evangelical religious groups in the U.S. at this writing, there is little likelihood that governmental regulation of religious television will become more intrusive any time soon.

# CHAPTER 26
# HOME VIDEO

Until the mid-1970s, television programs were presented to consumers in only one way: through a limited number of over-the-air television channels. These channels presented programs either live or recorded on two-inch videotapes (whose associated machinery was the size of an automobile), or on film. Most consumers were aware of videotape machines, but the idea of having one in your home or apartment was as crazy as, say, owning your own computer.

Everything changed in 1976, when Sony introduced the Betamax, the first practical videocassette recorder (VCR) for the home (this unit replaced a 1975 Betamax TV/VCR combo, which sold poorly). By the early 1980s, VCRs were a product in demand, but Sony's superior Betamax system lost the market to the VHS system favored by most consumer electronics manufacturers. Consumers learned to use their VCRs to record programs for later viewing and began to build libraries. A 1983 Supreme Court case (*Sony Corp v. Universal City Studios*) decided that recording programs for personal in-home viewing was fair use and not a copyright violation. As is so often the case in the entertainment business, lawsuits to prevent one use are paralleled by related business-building activities—often within the same corporation. By the mid-1980s, Universal and other movie studios were providing videotapes of their films to consumers, as both sale and rental items. Through the 1980s, video was primarily a rental business—video stores purchased films on videocassette, but prices were kept high (often above $50) to discourage consumer purchase, particularly on newer film titles.

By the mid-1990s, the studios were moving toward a sell-through model, with prices under $20. The rapid acceptance of the new DVD format further encouraged consumer purchases. In 2004, studios earned about 20 percent more in home video than they did in theaters. Some films are more successful in home video than in theaters: A reasonably successful film earns $50 million or more in its theatrical release, while it is not unusual to see home video revenues for the same film in the $60 million to $100 million range—a figure that combines VHS and DVD sales to consumers and to video stores.

In 2005, it became clear that consumers would begin moving toward a new form of direct distribution: the Internet. Although several systems were in various phases of development and early market acceptance when this edition was published, the efficiency of movie and television program distribution via broadband Internet is clearly far greater than any physical system. What is more, this approach allows the most evolved content owners to control their own distribution—without a middleman. For the motion picture studios, so reluctant to release their movies to television in the 1950s and to home video in the 1980s, the world is a different place. Studios that once maintained relationships only with motion picture theaters (and, until the 1950s, theaters that were owned by the studios themselves) now willingly develop relationships with individual consumers.

## MAINSTREAM PRODUCT

From the start, home video and direct-to-consumer products have been dominated by one product category: movies. Every studio operates its own home video label, and, in general, the label's content is directly tied to the films released by the studio or its affiliated companies. With the rise of DVDs and the widespread popularity of several television programs (notably the HBO series *Sex and the City* and *The Sopranos*), consumers now routinely purchase and rent television shows as well. Boxed sets of multiple full seasons of *Seinfeld* and *The Simpsons* have proven especially popular on DVD. As a rule, these titles are still controlled by the movie studios.

For home video sales, product is sold through multiple channels. Large retail chains, such as Blockbuster and Wal-Mart, tend to purchase product directly from the labels. The majority of video retail accounts are serviced with two-step distribution, which operates as follows: A video distributor, such as Ingram, takes orders from video chains and individual stores, and then preorders quantities of each title before a "pre-book" or "order cut-off" date. The label then ships product to Ingram, which ships to a chain's warehouse(s) or to individual stores. The store decides whether to sell or to rent the product, but the label determines the first date of sale (known as the "street date") for each new title.

## OPERATION OF A HOME VIDEO LABEL

The supply side of the home video business is dominated by labels that operate as sister companies to motion picture studios. Smaller labels generally require a special type of product profile or a unique distribution system in order to survive. Kultur, for example, offers arts programming, such as opera, classical music, and ballet. KINO Video specializes in silent films and other collectibles.

A home video label is organized very much like a book or record company. A senior executive, typically a president, oversees all aspects of the operation. A programming department is responsible for the acquisition of new titles and for original productions, if any. The operations department supervises duplication, packaging, warehousing, shipping, and inventory. The marketing department creates the package design, sales literature, and dealer promotions. The sales department sells certain accounts directly and supervises the work of independent distributors and reps for other accounts. An accounting department takes care of billing and royalties, as well as traditional bookkeeping and reporting functions.

## VIDEO RETAIL

Viacom's Blockbuster subsidiary operates over 8,500 video retail stores in the U.S.; in 2002, these stores generated 80 percent of Blockbuster's $5.5 billion in revenues. Blockbuster also operates 2,600 stores in 27 other countries.

Hollywood Video is the second largest such chain in the world, with over 2,000 stores. Its own estimates place the chain's market share at approximately 11 percent. (Based upon this statistic, it would be fair to set Blockbuster's market share at about 60 percent.) Including the company's Game Crazy video game retail stores, 2003 revenues were $1.5 billion. In 2005, Hollywood Video acquired Movie Gallery, previously the second-largest chain, also with about 2,000 stores. Together, Hollywood Video and Movie Gallery are about one-third the size of Blockbuster.

The retail environment for video has changed dramatically since the previous (1998) edition of this book. As the prices of video products—particularly DVDs—have dropped, the distribution patterns have changed. Blockbuster and Movie Gallery (along with its newly acquired Hollywood Video chain) operate over 12,000 stores in the U.S. Borders, Barnes & Noble, Target, Wal-Mart, and other large retail chains now sell video products in large numbers, too. The Internet has also become a force, both in the rental business (Netflix and its competitors are discussed below), and in sell-through (Amazon for the broadest selection; specialty sites for niche genres). In 1998, some 95 percent of video retailers owned just one store. Many of these stores have not survived.

As smaller specialty video retailers have faded and chain stores have thrived, many consumers have turned to alternative sources for their software. There are various reasons why: hassle of rental returns, too-brief rental periods, and above all, limited selection. In this environment, Netflix, an Internet-based video rental library, has established a new type of consumer rental business.

Netflix offers over 50,000 titles—easily three times more than even the largest neighborhood video store—and allows the consumer to borrow three DVD titles at any time. There is no deadline for the return of these DVDs, but they must be returned in order to borrow other titles. There are no late fees. Instead, Netflix works with a monthly subscription charge, including shipping to and from the consumer's home.

The Netflix model is based upon one key assumption: that the monthly subscription cost ensures profitability each and every month. Netflix works with a fairly narrow margin. It purchases, maintains, and regularly updates a substantial inventory of individual *SKUs* (stock keeping units or, in plain lingo, "titles") and a sufficient number of units within each SKU to keep most of the customers happy most of the time. Costs associated with shipping to and from must be carefully managed; pennies matter. So, too, must the operation be efficient; every minute saved in picking and packing at the warehouse matters. The business makes sense only as a volume play—currently, Netflix has two million members. The subscription fee provides a sufficient amount of cash to develop and implement processes, efficiencies, and very competitive inventory acquisition deals. (In fact, many of the customers signed on to different deals, so the above numbers are not pure, but the basic analysis remains sound.) In the three months ending September 30, 2004, Netflix's subscription revenues were $140 million (roughly double the same period in 2003). The reported cost of revenues was about $70 million, and the operating costs deduct over $50 million more, leaving a $20 million net income for the quarter. Part of the Netflix model is a somewhat unusual relationship with the studios: a revenue-sharing deal which allows Netflix to both purchase inventory at a reduced rate and also return or exchange product at the end of a specified period. Netflix also relies upon an amortization approach to its video library, a unique and clever variation on the usual theme. In short, Netflix has brought a more sophisticated financial discipline to the home video business, which has allowed the company to grow quickly and establish itself as a force in the industry.

## SPECIAL-INTEREST VIDEO

Although the majority of home video products sold and rented are motion pictures (and now, television programs), the industry has long supported a nonfiction sector. Fitness, how-to, documentary, children's, and religious categories are among many special-interest programs distributed mainly on videocassettes and DVDs. Smaller special-interest groups are served by highly specific categories, such as blacksmithing, kayaking, tai chi, kung fu, dog training, and coaching soccer.

Programs produced for home video vary in terms of production quality. The production budget should be based upon the economics of the marketplace. In order to encourage direct sales to consumers, many special-interest videos are now priced around $20. If the product is sold directly by the producer (most often through a Web site), then the entire $20—plus a shipping and handling fee of perhaps $5—provides the producer with revenues of $25 per unit. It would be fair to assume a $3 cost of goods (DVD duplication, packaging) and a $2 cost of shipment (shipping materials plus actual shipment), reducing the net to $20. Unit sales of home videos vary widely, in part due to the level of interest in the subject matter and the success of competitive products, as well as marketing and distribution. If this particular product sold a relatively modest 1,000 units, the producer would break even at $20,000. If the product sold 5,000 units, netting $100,000, it would have been reasonable to spend $50,000 on production plus $25,000 on marketing; in this formula, the profit would be $25,000.

In most cases, the producer sells only a percentage of products directly. Retailers generate additional sales, but they typically buy at 30 to 50 percent off the retail price. Products sold through mail-order catalogs may be purchased at a deeper discount.

There are many possible distribution schemes for special-interest video products. As a general rule, special-interest videos are of limited interest at the retail level, even to retailers who specialize in the category. Therefore, it is essential to spend as much time, money, and energy on marketing as on production; many special-interest video producers have found themselves with award-winning tapes that went unsold because of insufficient or ineffective marketing or distribution. Some categories are better than others; cooking tapes, for example, may be a tough sell, but tapes featuring certain fitness instructors and some extreme sports instructors perform well, even in retail stores. Art instruction tapes are sidelines for art supply stores, and most such stores do not carry any tapes at all. This scenario is very common, not only in the art materials world, but in just about every special-interest category. Extremely targeted direct marketing seems to be the best approach for many special-interest categories. However, rules here are made to be broken. Some independent producers drive to every possible retail outlet in the region, sell a handful of tapes to local merchants, and manage to move more than 30,000 units. Others take the same approach and move fewer than 500. Some producers succeed with a mail-order business. Others flop.

## VIDEO CLUBS

Video clubs are now as common as record and book clubs, and follow the same procedures. A consumer signs up, receives one or more videotapes or DVDs for a very low price (e.g., five DVDs at 49¢ each), and agrees to purchase a specified number of products in the future. Some clubs resemble catalog operations, using positive-option sales—the consumer buys only what he or she wants.

Negative-option clubs are more complicated. The club promotes a title as its monthly selection; club members who want to buy the title do nothing, but members who do not want the title must notify the club within a specified period, otherwise they will receive it and must pay for it. The negative-option format has been successful for Columbia House, BMG Video Club, and Time-Life Video Club.

Continuity or subscription clubs are used to sell certain product lines. Columbia House, for example, offers a variety of popular television series on

DVD. The consumer buys the first one for $4.95 and then receives a new one every four to six weeks, paying $12.49 for each DVD, until he or she decides to cancel. Continuity distribution is best for series programming: examples include *The Carol Burnett Show*, *I Love Lucy*, *Twilight Zone*, *Star Trek*, and many more. Television series, movies on a theme topic, and military histories are among the best-sellers. Once again, the clubs buy at below-wholesale prices.

# CHAPTER 27

# NEW TECHNOLOGIES

## PROGRESS

The story of television has always been closely aligned with the story of technology's progress. The 1930s and 1940s brought the technologies that made television a viable mass medium. In the 1950s and 1960s, color television became a reality. By the 1970s, consumers were expanding the very definition of television by plugging devices into their television sets: cable boxes, satellite receivers, video games, and by the 1980s, VCRs and videodisc players. The 1990s brought the Internet, but it was not until the first decade of the new millennium that the Internet's impact on television could be clearly imagined.

As desktop computers increased in power and capability, it became possible to transform analog files into digital files, and to store and edit these digital files. With the addition of DSL and cable modem connections, it became possible for many households and small offices to send and receive video files. In essence, these technologies provided the necessary infrastructure for a global television station, distributed via the Internet, essentially without direct regulation by the FCC or other government agencies.

A short time later, new wireless devices emerged, first to play short video segments. As internal memory increased and compression schemes improved, the devices could play longer video programs. The interaction between telephones, audio/video players, audio/video recorders, and infrastructure essentially redefines the conception of television. The new definition sheds any notion of viewing at an appointed or scheduled time; programs are always available on demand. Now, programs are whatever the person happens to be watching at the time: a sports event or a business meeting, a music video or a promotional advertisement. Television programs are no longer viewed only at home. With wireless, television or video are watched wherever the person happens to be. Traditional 30-second commercials are associated with conventional cable or broadcast television—an aging idea in a fast-moving world.

Existing distribution technologies tend to be inflexible. Traditional broadcast television requires a large terrestrial antenna, a transmission facility, and at least one television set in every household. Traditional cable television requires an extensive wired infrastructure that must be maintained and upgraded from time to time, as well as a set-top box in every subscribing household, along with a connection to every television set subscribing to the service. Traditional satellite television services involve less infrastructure (no network of cables, for example) but require an 18-inch satellite dish that must be precisely aimed at a point in the sky.

New distribution technologies, on the other hand, tend to be flexible. An Internet-based television system requires only wireless access to an Internet connection, typically within several hundred feet of the viewing device. A wireless television system makes use of alternative transmit/receive technologies, allowing even greater mobility. New technologies tend to be purchased by consumers who are willing to trade a component for the latest version, thus encouraging more widespread acceptance of, for example, progressively faster and more efficient wireless local area networks, or multipurpose handheld devices (phones, viewers, etc.). New technologies also tend to benefit from periodic software upgrades, a notion borrowed from the computing world that allows for improved viewer experiences or additional capabilities.

## THE POTENTIAL POWER OF SMALL-SCALE TELEVISION

Since the 1970s, there has been a small population of community activists and television producers who have encouraged an alternative view of television. As big companies gained power, these producers emphasized the potential of community-based television projects. To varying degrees, some public television stations have participated in these projects. More often, these efforts have found a place on local cable television systems, once called "local origination" or "local O," and currently known as "public access."

Several factors have conspired to improve the plight of these fledgling efforts in three key areas: production, post-production, and distribution.

With the MiniDV and DV videotape formats, it is now possible to record a video signal acceptable to broadcast engineers on a camcorder costing under $5,000, and in some cases under $1,500. Superior cameras deliver superior images, but many cable networks now routinely make use of MiniDV camcorders for their location work. Material recorded on a $10,000 DVCAM camcorder is acceptable, considering even the most demanding of television engineering standards. Raw videotape stock costs about $30 for an hour-long cassette—a very reasonable price. Professional quality MiniDV tapes cost less than $15. Add a lightweight lighting kit, a pair of microphones, a mixer, a good tripod, and a few other accessories, and the total cost for a production package is likely to be as low as $3,000 to $5,000 for a professional MiniDV setup and $15,000 to $30,000 for a professional DVCAM package. It is possible, however, to put together a clever little budget MiniDV package, and a very capable one at that, for as little as $2,000.

An equally significant change has occurred in video post-production. Once requiring a large suite of interconnected video devices, a professional staff editor, and several support engineers, video editing has been reduced to a process akin to word processing or manipulating images in Adobe Photoshop. Apple Computer has been providing video editing software (iMovie) for years, at no charge to those who purchase a new Apple computer. For serious producers, Apple's more sophisticated Final Cut Pro is the standard. Together with a powerful computer, a sufficiently large flat screen, and a modest audio setup, the cost of Apple's desktop editing system is under $5,000. Once again, it is possible to assemble the necessary pieces on a budget of half that amount. It is now common for high school and college students to develop competency using this equipment; relative novices tend to learn it quickly as well.

With the exception of the physical distribution of videocassettes or videodiscs, widespread distribution of television or video product has traditionally required either a transmitter, a cable head end (the master control facility associated with cable distribution), or a satellite transponder. In fact, each of these has been available for rental, lease, or purchase (as in the case of paid programming) for decades. With new technology, the video supplier is no longer reliant upon third-party gatekeepers. A specialized computer known as a video server is, in essence, all that is required to distribute video throughout the world via the Internet. Many video producers and distributors now routinely rent space on video servers and buy bandwidth for the distribution of video to computers. In time, these video servers (and others like them) will also be used to distribute video to properly equipped television sets and to various portable devices.

Some of these new television services are small-scale by design, intended to distribute particular types of programming to audiences within a limited geographic region or with a particular interest. Most often, these activities are operated by a small number of individuals, usually without a particular business ambition in mind. Video blogs are one of several such examples.

Other services make use of the highly targeted capabilities of this new system, and offer business applications to specific groups. Several services specialize in the recording and limited distribution of video depositions for legal proceedings. Others specialize in job training.

Several consumer services have also emerged. New Century Television, developed by one of this book's authors, develops and distributes video-on-demand channels via the Internet. Some channels are built and distributed for clients, principally for marketing communications. In general, the contents of these channels are produced with MiniDV cameras and desktop editing. Others are offered to consumers who subscribe to the service in order to watch special-interest video programming, such as a video-on-demand channel filled with art instruction programs (The Artist's Channel). The company's channels are watched in over 50 countries, a remarkable example of small television's potential to change the entire television distribution marketplace.

# HIGH-DEFINITION TELEVISION (HDTV)

After languishing in the late 1990s, HDTV came into its own through the convergence of an FCC initiative for digital television; a continued consumer interest in home theater; a move by consumer electronics manufacturers to widescreen television sets; and a relentless push by industry groups (producers, engineers, etc.) to encourage production of new programs in the HDTV format.

HDTV is distributed in several ways. The first and most popular way is over the air. As broadcast television stations currently operate two channels in each market (one analog, one digital), network affiliates have begun to operate the second channel as an HDTV outlet (see page 38). By 2005, many network prime-time television programs were produced and distributed in HDTV; equally popular are HDTV channels available on digital cable television systems. The HDTV channels found on broadcast and cable require considerably more bandwidth than traditional channels—there is more information transmitted to compose the higher-resolution image—and, in theory, this approach to using the additional bandwidth will prove more profitable than alternative uses, since a digital channel is also capable of transmitting multiple old-style analog channels. The technology was too new in 2005 to understand consumer acceptance or its impact on the industry.

# PART 7

# PROGRAM DEVELOPMENT AND PROGRAMMING

# CHAPTER 28
# PRIME-TIME ENTERTAINMENT

As a general rule, each broadcast network's schedule is dominated by situation comedies and dramatic series. From time to time, other types of programs become quite common, due to either audience popularity or a comparatively low price of production—or both. In 2005, for example, reality shows and news magazines occupied a substantial number of evening time slots.

Take ABC: The prime-time schedule for a week in February 2005 included seven hours of drama, five hours of reality, four hours of variety shows (mostly *America's Funniest Home Videos*), four hours of sitcoms (eight half-hour series), and two hours of news magazines. The CBS schedule showed a similar ratio, but was heavier on drama, with eight hours (several *CSI* episodes), and lighter on variety, with just one hour. In this particular week, CBS was airing a two-hour *The Amazing Race*, a blend of game and reality show, plus two additional hours of reality series. There were three hours of sitcoms and three hours of news as well.

If you take the time to track network prime-time schedules for a month, you'll find that there's a scheduling game—a competitive race for that additional rating point—a tendency to go heavier on series that are working and to postpone or sideline series that are not. Nearly half the schedule is in a state of flux at any given time; the other half adheres to reliable time slots for popular series. For example, prior to the 2005–2006 season, NBC's *The West Wing* occupied a Wednesday 9:00 P.M. slot for a number of years.

## DRAMATIC SERIES

In the 2004–2005 season, the vast majority of dramatic series were related to criminal investigations: *Law & Order, CSI, Without a Trace, NYPD Blue, Numb3rs, Cold Case, Crossing Jordan, Medium*, and more. The popular *Joan of Arcadia* was one exception: a dramatic series about a family whose daughter regularly talks to God. In the past, the networks have featured a range of dramatic series (medical, Western, family, school, legal, etc.), but most of these themes have proven less popular with contemporary audiences than criminal investigations.

In an effort to differentiate essentially similar series, elements of medicine (*Crossing Jordan*), psychic power (*Medium*), or other genres have been injected into investigative themes. To put this another way, the networks tend to focus on a very limited number of program types, tinkering with elements rather than introducing an entirely new form—except, of course, when a network is small, or needs to reinvent itself.

HBO is the quintessential small network, in only about one-sixth of television households. HBO takes chances, and many of their gambles have paid off with a long list of successful examples in drama, including *The Sopranos* (about contemporary mafia), *Six Feet Under* (a dysfunctional family operating a funeral business), *Oz* (prison drama), and *Deadwood* (a Western).

When ABC needed to do some reinventing, the results were *Lost* and *Desperate Housewives*—both nominated for multiple Emmys. The first combines aspects of a reality show with a drama. The second adds adult female relationships, sex, and loopy storylines to the usual family/neighborhood formula.

FOX tends to work with a small number of dramas. Historically, they have been high-impact, used to build brand in the same way that HBO does with its original series. The impressive list of FOX series in this category includes *24*, *The OC*, *Beverly Hills 90210*, and *The X Files*.

## Development

As a rule, a network prime-time drama is a coproduction between the television arm of a motion picture studio and an experienced producer with strong writing or storytelling credentials. For example, NBC's successful *Law & Order* franchise is a coproduction of Universal Television and Wolf Films. Dick Wolf started as a writer on Steven Bochco's 1981 series *Hill Street Blues*, then wrote and served as executive producer on the popular series *Miami Vice*. In 1990, after a half-dozen other executive producer gigs on dramatic series, he started *Law & Order*.

Every prime-time drama begins in one of three ways. The first and most common is when a writer-producer meets ("does lunch") with an agent or a network executive, and a general theme emerges. The writer then locks himself or herself in a room for a few weeks and writes either a treatment or a script. A second, somewhat less common way is the reverse: first the writing, then the lunch. A third approach is when a notable celebrity and his or her agent decide that the time is right to star in a network prime-time series. When this occurs (and it often does), a writer-producer is assigned to the project, and the process begins with a meeting between the celebrity and his or her representatives, the writer-producer and his or her agent, and several executives from the network and from the studio.

Regardless of how this process starts, the writer ends up in a room for a few weeks writing a script. Then there are meetings, changes in characters, changes in setting, discussions about casting, discussions about directors, and sometimes, changes in writers. Most of the time, the process reaches a dead end after a meeting or two, or after several drafts. If, almost miraculously, the producer, writer, studio, network, and desired cast members all align on the same idea at the same time, then a pilot is planned and produced. Each network produces several dozen pilot episodes per year in hopes of filling just a handful of open slots.

For the 2005–2006 season, ABC committed to eleven pilots for dramatic series. Eight were Touchstone television projects (like ABC, Touchstone is owned by Disney); the other three came from Warner Bros. NBC, with fewer open slots on its prime-time schedule, committed to just six pilots—four from NBC Universal.

The cost of a typical pilot for a dramatic series exceeds $2 million; if there are many changes, the cost can go much higher. Often, pilots are re-shot or re-edited, sometimes with different scenes, different actors, different endings.

## Production

Whether a pilot episode or a series, the production of a network drama resembles the production of a motion picture. It is shot on film, typically with portions on a soundstage and portions on location. The technical crew and stage crew are film people; the job functions are similar, if not identical, to roles on a motion picture crew. There are, however, differences. The cast is typically small, and the pace faster: An hour-long drama is shot in just a few days. Most dramatic series focus on four or five main characters, rather than a movie's larger cast. Much of the activity is based in just a few settings that are used in every episode: a courtroom, an office, a home. For most series, location work is kept to a minimum. Series that do use location work—the *Law & Order* shows, for example—tend to keep the complexity and the number of speaking characters in these scenes to a minimum. Just about every prime-time series is highly formatted; this, too, allows for cost-efficient production. For example, *Without a Trace* routinely begins with a disappearance scene at the top of the show. The lead characters then spend about half of each episode speaking to one another in an office setting. The location scenes typically involve two or three of the lead characters and, usually, one or two "bad guys" along with the victim. This particular series adds some spice with the occasional crowd scene at a nightclub, school, or on the street, but these scenes are few and carefully controlled.

This approach to production—which begins in the writing, as all scripts must adhere to these limitations—permits an hour of television drama (about 35 minutes of original content, after the deduction of 20 or more minutes for commercials, promos, titles, and credits) to be produced and delivered for just over $1 million per episode.

An experienced line producer can successfully plan for, say, 15 or 20 episodes to be produced over the course of 40 weeks. An order of this size allows for considerable efficiencies in hiring staff and crew, securing cast and locations, and so forth. Despite the potential efficiencies, however, plans are often sacked by erratic network commitments. When a network orders just five episodes, these efficiencies are harder to find and costs are more difficult to control; sometimes, the complexity is increased by a second small order of episodes while the first are in the midst of production. This situation is one reason why networks essentially do their business with large studios; one or the other company can absorb the loss, or bankroll any necessary bridge financing. A small production company would quickly become frustrated with the financial tinkering required for many network projects.

In fact, there are multiple management functions associated with every network drama.

The *writers*, who are sometimes called *producers* or *writer-producers*, focus on stories, characters, and changes due to production limitations. One or more writers are assigned to each episode. They might work in the production office, at home, or in their own offices. Stories and scripts are reviewed and revised by working closely with the program's story editor and other writer-producers.

The *director* works directly with the performers, the technical crew, and the wardrobe, scenic, and (if necessary) special effects staff. Later, he or she may also edit the episode. Some series work with only one or two directors; others work with a rotating group of several more. Much of the director's time is spent either in planning meetings, in a rehearsal hall, in the soundstage, or on location.

The *production staff* works behind the scenes, essentially connecting the writers' concepts with the realities of the director's needs while shooting. They arrange for locations, casting, and the many small details, from catering to transportation to teachers for child actors.

*Post-production* is a separate function, now essentially a nonlinear digital process. Still, there is screening required, and rough cuts, approvals, and sound mixing. The process has become easier and more sophisticated, but the steps are essentially unchanged (see page 380).

## COMEDIES

Most network comedies are intended to appeal to a broad audience, often younger and sometimes less educated and with a somewhat lower income than the viewers who watch dramas. Typically aired in the 8:00 P.M. to10:00 P.M. time slots, comedies now routinely compete with reality shows that are often placed in the same time slots by other networks. Comedy series tend to skew younger and, in recent years, also reliably deliver certain segments of African-American viewers via the UPN schedule.

Television comedies are typically produced on videotape, either in television studios or in sound studios equipped for television production. They are, in many ways, a hybrid between traditional studio-based production and dramatic television production.

## Development

As with a drama, a television comedy begins with one or more writers experienced in the form. The creative team behind CBS's *Everybody Loves Raymond*, for example, includes Phil Rosenthal, who came up as a writer and producer on the popular sitcom *Coach*. The writer is typically charged with developing the concept, which is then connected ("attached") to one or more performers, often celebrities or comedians who are either available or already under contract to the network. The concept is scripted, performed in a rehearsal hall, piloted, and developed for production. As with dramas, the majority of concepts are dropped in the early stages, most often because executives have a particular conception in mind for a particular time slot. Comedies are rarely developed simply because they are funny. They are developed because a particular series is fading in popularity and must be replaced, or because a lead-in is required, or because a particular performer has become available. Writers and performers frequently find themselves frustrated by the process because there are so many factors involved in getting on the air—and so few of them are directly related to the show itself.

The broadcast networks commit to more comedy pilots than drama pilots. For the 2005-2006 season, for example, NBC made nineteen comedy pilots compared with just six dramatic pilots. More than half of these were made by, or in association with, NBC Universal's television production unit.

## Production

Nearly all comedies are produced in a soundstage or studio in front of a live audience. Most of the action takes place in just a few rooms (often a living room and/or kitchen, or an office). Exterior scenes are uncommon. From the perspective of the live audience, the sitcom feels like theater—the story is performed from beginning to end, stopping only for commercial breaks. In fact, the performance seen by the live audience is one of two or three such performances (one is usually a dress rehearsal). The best parts of each performance are edited together; some retakes are inevitably added into the mix. These performances are the result of about five days of working together. The first is devoted to a "table reading"—a read-through by the cast with writers, producers, staff, crew, and executives around the perimeter. Next comes a walk-through on the set. Once the director and actors are comfortable with positions, cameras are added, typically on the third day. After rehearsal and fixes of specific scenes, the performances begin. The whole process takes about a week per episode. This routine is followed by about a week of post-production to edit scenes together, cut the episode to time, and add sound effects, music, and (of course) "sweetening," such as audience laughter.

A sitcom is usually licensed to the network for $500,000 to $700,000 per episode, but with a cast of well-paid performers, the costs can be twice that amount or more. The six performers on the popular series *Friends* eventually earned $1 million per episode, and NBC agreed to pay $10 million per episode to producer Warner Bros., making *Friends* the most expensive prime-time series of all time. This was an unusual situation, however, as the series was an extremely valuable asset for NBC with a long history of delivering a desirable demographic, in large numbers, to the network's advertisers. In short, the deal was worth the money—and NBC could scarcely risk losing its most successful series.

## REALITY SHOWS

Four rules generally define reality shows and set them apart from the traditional network fare of comedies and dramas. First, reality shows do not generally involve actors (in the traditional sense). Second, reality shows may be planned, but they are not written in the same sense as a comedy or drama. Third, they are produced on location. Fourth, they have a special gimmick—something that makes the whole idea of the show worth watching. In general, reality shows cost less to produce than hour-long dramas, but they are, in fact, a poor long-term investment. A successful network drama can continue to produce revenues in syndication and on cable for a decade or more; reality shows have far less value in secondary markets. However, reality shows that get ratings can be very profitable in the short-term, both for the producer and for the network, and as such, they are aligned with the current practices associated with most corporations. High ratings equal high advertising rates, and reality shows are also funded by product placement (see page 84).

### Development

At first, producers, performers, writers, and executives believed that reality shows were a gimmick, a passing fad. When the first few series demonstrated signs of real success, more shows were soon added. Some of the gimmicks were quite ridiculous, but others worked well enough to perpetuate the format. And, sure enough, younger viewers were tuning into prime-time television to watch the likes of CBS's *Survivor*. Advertisers liked the ratings and the demographics. More shows were added. Established shows were "rested," then brought back to even higher ratings. By the early 2000s, reality series had become a staple of the network schedules.

While dramas and comedies are bought on the reputation of the writers and performers, reality shows are bought by the networks on the basis of the producer's track record and on the potential of the idea (sometimes, as in the case of NBC's *The Apprentice*, the idea also involves a celebrity). The range of ideas is impressive: *Airline* follows customers and employees of Southwest Airlines; *The Amazing Race* is a multifaceted outdoor competition that travels the world; *The Apprentice* is about making business decisions; *American Idol* is a talent competition; *Average Joe* is one of many choose-your-mate shows. And those are just a smattering of the series that begin with the letter "a."

Mark Burnett is a leading producer of reality shows—the man behind *The Apprentice* and *Survivor*. Burnett's talent is storytelling, of course, but without a traditional script or actors. He also excels in generating buzz, and in promoting his properties alongside sponsors. The Dutch company Endemol produces *Fear Factor* and *Extreme Makeover*, two sturdy formats that have been sold into many national markets, including the U.S. The British company FremantleMedia holds the format rights to *Idol*, which airs in two dozen countries—including in the U.S. on FOX as *American Idol*.

Reality shows are a staple for network prime-time, but they are also popular entries on cable network schedules. MTV's *The Real World* has been one of the longest-running reality series. Its producer, Murray and Bunim Productions, was also behind the FOX series *The Simple Life* (starring Paris Hilton). As with many television genres, the community of successful producers is most often tapped to develop and produce new reality series. So, too, are the senior staff members who work on successful series. As a network executive works on-site during production, relationships grow. Notable work gets noticed. The networks constantly court new talent, new ideas. Senior producers get agents, and agents pitch new concepts.

As with other types of prime-time television, reality shows are usually (but not always) piloted. Some concepts are developed and go directly to air without a traditional pilot. This is often the situation with an idea that's especially hot, or one that will not make much sense until it is produced as a full series. Tests and presentations are made, but it's difficult to judge a reality series until the audience actually watches finished episodes.

## Production

Although reality shows are not scripted or cast in a traditional sense, they are well planned, and they are carefully orchestrated. Certain aspects of each episode are scripted in the traditional way: A host reads words written by a producer or a writer. Other aspects are shaped with the same care that once went into planning a complicated talk-show segment, or with the repeated run-throughs of game elements that game shows typically require prior to air—necessary to ensure smooth taping, especially during crucial competitive sequences.

In general, although the people who appear on reality shows are not professional performers (with the exception of the host), each series selects its cast with the same care associated with a drama or comedy. Thoughtful consideration is given to each participant, and to the likely chemistry between those who will appear on the air together. Casting a reality show requires a professional casting director, as well as input from the director and producers; as with a dramatic series, the final decision is with the executive producers and the network.

Reality shows often present unique production challenges. In general, the production situation must be safe and reasonably comfortable (or suitably rugged) for the amateur performers who appear on camera, but must also allow cameras and other equipment to maneuver in order to get the shots necessary to tell the story. Many reality shows require not only coverage of the main action, but coverage of secondary action as well as reaction shots and sideline interviews. When producing, for example, an audition episode of *American Idol*, the location can be selected and set up to ease production. Shooting actual customers in a real airport, as on *Airline*, requires an entirely different approach, perhaps made even more complicated by the strict security requirements now associated with a contemporary airport. Planning and shooting a series of *The Real World* episodes requires work in very close quarters, often with amateurs who may become quite emotional as relationships unfold and sometimes tatter. *Survivor*, which tends to shoot in faraway places with limited local resources, confronts the entire production staff and the performers with logistics issues quite unlike those that would be associated with, for example, the production of *Trading Spaces*, in which families paint and redecorate one another's bedrooms or family rooms. Often, reality shows involve some sort of secret or surprise, and this presents yet another practical challenge for the production staff and crew: how to be on location without complete control of the elements while maintaining and preparing an element that must be unknown to many of those with whom they share quarters.

The costs associated with reality shows vary widely. The budget for *Trading Spaces* or the similar *While You Were Out* involves a few cast members, some supplies and tools, a location crew, and housing for a few days. The costs associated with *Survivor: The Australian Outback* involve shipping a much larger crew halfway around the world to rig all sorts of special activities, and a higher level of complexity with regard to coverage and group competition (at the very least). The costs associated with an episode of *The Apprentice* are skewed by the line item for the series host; Donald Trump or Martha Stewart earn considerably more than the lesser-known hosts of most reality series. So how much does a reality show cost per episode? As little as $50,000 for a simple cable series. *Big Brother*, on CBS, reportedly costs just $300,000 per hour—about one-quarter the price of a drama—but the same network's *Survivor* costs about as much as a prime-time drama, over $1 million.

# CHAPTER 29
# NEWS PROGRAMMING

The evolution of television news provides yet another case study for the evolution of programming, marketing, and audience tastes.

On radio, regular news coverage came along relatively late in the game. In 1938, Edward R. Murrow initiated the first regularly scheduled evening news program for the CBS radio network. In 1948, Don Hewitt (later of *60 Minutes* fame) produced the first regularly scheduled weeknight television news. By 1951, Hewitt and fellow CBS innovator Fred Friendly had launched television's first news magazine, *See It Now*, hosted by Murrow (and based upon their radio show, *Hear It Now*). A year later, NBC introduced the *Today* show. These early developments established the framework for the next half-century.

Through the 1950s and 1960s, network affiliates developed and refined the local news format, airing twice or sometimes three times a day. The familiar format, which remains in use today, typically combined one or two newscasters reading brief reports, followed by a weather report and a sports report. In the 1970s, portable video replaced film, eliminating the time required for processing and allowing producers to schedule remotely produced news stories during both evening and late-night newscasts.

Cable news began with the 1980 introduction of Cable News Network, or CNN—an idea that the broadcast networks rebuffed, failing to understand the new business opportunities made possible by cable television and the changes in viewing patterns that would result. Even more unlikely was a channel filled with nothing but weather reports and forecasts. In today's technology-enabled home, life without The Weather Channel may seem unimaginable, and watching television news on one's cell phone is not so unlikely.

## BROADCAST NETWORK NEWS

ABC produces 36 hours of news per week, or more than one-quarter of the network's weekly feed to affiliates: *Good Morning America* (five days x 2 hours each), *World News Tonight* (seven days x 30 minutes each), *Nightline* (five days x 30 minutes each), *Prime Time Thursday* (1 hour), *20/20* (1 hour), *This Week*

(1 hour), and *World News Now* (five days x 3 hours each), plus regularly scheduled reports through the day, breaking news, and special event coverage. In addition, ABC News is responsible for www.abcnews.com, a large-scale Internet news site.

NBC starts its weekday schedule at 4:30 A.M. with *Early Today* (five days x 30 minutes each), and continues with three hours of *Today* (five days x 3 hours each, plus 2 additional hours on Sundays) and *NBC Nightly News* during the dinner hour (seven days x 30 minutes each). NBC also runs *Dateline NBC* twice weekly in prime time (two days x 1 hour each) and *Meet the Press* on Sunday mornings (1 hour). In addition, NBC News is associated with CNBC, a cable network filled with business news, and with MSNBC, a cable news network and news Web site. All told, NBC News produces about 30 hours of programming per week, plus the programming associated with its cable operations.

CBS News has long struggled with its morning show, now called *The Early Show* (six days x 2 hours each), but it has won consistently high praise for *Sunday Morning*, an arts and leisure magazine series (90 minutes). With two versions of *60 Minutes*, plus *48 Hours*, CBS News has been successful in its prime-time ventures (three days x 1 hour each). On Sunday mornings, CBS has long presented *Face the Nation* (30 minutes). *CBS Evening News* (seven days x 30 minutes each) rounds out the schedule, with CBS offering about two-thirds of the news programming associated with ABC News. The Web site, www.cbsnews.com, is somewhat popular, but www.cbssportsline.com is the more popular CBS information Web site.

The FOX network does not offer a daily news schedule to affiliates, but it does program *FOX News Sunday* to keep a major presence in Washington, DC. For FOX, nearly all of the action is in cable (see following page).

Neither UPN nor The WB maintain network news operations.

PBS is mainly known for *The NewsHour with Jim Lehrer*, which airs on weeknights during the dinner hour. The documentary series *Frontline* and various PBS specials and special event coverage provide public television viewers with additional news information. *Wall Street Week* also supplies regularly scheduled financial reporting.

Each network's signature news show is the evening news. The network feeds a live half-hour evening newscast to affiliates at 6:30 P.M. Eastern time, again at 7:00 P.M., and at least one more time for West Coast affiliates, either as a videotape of the original production or, if stories have changed, as a new production. These programs are often seen outside the U.S. as well. The networks' morning shows have also become signature pieces.

Special events are an important part of network news coverage. Some, like political conventions, are scheduled and planned in advance; others, like the outbreak of war or the death of a world figure, may preempt regularly scheduled programming. News executives have the option to preempt programming with breaking stories, but they must operate with considerable discretion. In theory, they consult closely with entertainment (or sports) executives. For shorter reports and updates, preempting several minutes of a program is generally preferable to preempting commercials.

Each of these networks employs approximately a thousand employees in its news division, mostly based in New York City. A Washington, DC, bureau concentrates on national news, and some other bureaus—London, for example—contribute regional stories. In the U.S., network affiliates contribute local stories, but major stories are often reported by network correspondents on location.

The maintenance of a worldwide news organization responsible for dozens of hours of original programming each week is an expensive affair, and the largest networks have substantially reduced their budgets and staffs related to international coverage.

In the past, network news divisions were cost centers that brought distinction to their corporate owners. In today's more cutthroat corporate world, the news divisions have found the combination of morning shows and prime-time programming to be profitable. Upscale audiences with higher-than-average cost per thousand viewers (CPMs) help to support the evening news programs.

## CABLE NEWS NETWORKS

When CNN launched in 1980, the formula was straightforward: 24 hours a day, seven days a week of news coverage. The standard formula, consisting of a news anchor at a desk and reporters filing stories from around the world, didn't do well in the ratings. Certainly, there have been days and weeks when America has been glued to CNN. These have been the exception.

For many years, CNN attempted to fill the more valuable day parts with more than just news coverage. Larry King's long-running prime-time talk show is one of many examples of programs that broke the CNN format. With the coming of MSNBC and FOX News Channel, CNN has changed. Now, it closely resembles its two competitors, with a blend of straight news coverage and personality-driven talk shows. On CNN, those personalities include Wolf Blitzer, Lou Dobbs (a money news host), Paula Zahn, and Anderson Cooper. On FOX News, the network's popular shows include *The O'Reilly Factor* and *Hannity & Colmes*. On MSNBC, it's radio personality Don Imus in the morning (simultaneous with the daily broadcast of his radio program) and an evening filled with shows like *Hardball with Chris Matthews*, *Scarborough Country*, and *Deborah Norville Tonight*. Each of these programs thrives upon controversy, generally programming with a strong leaning to the conservative side. On the whole, these networks have become more comfortable with commentators who get ratings than with the objective reporters of the old school.

CNN remains the world's largest news organization, with over 4,000 employees worldwide. CNN also produces hundreds of hours of weekly news programming, compared with two or three dozen hours a week by NBC, ABC, or CBS. For more traditional news coverage, CNN continues to offer *Headline News* (with short stories) and CNNI (CNN International), which relies upon the older CNN formula.

Launched in 1985, CNNI first served mainly American visitors to hotels abroad; now it is distributed to more than 100 million households outside the U.S. and operates 24 hours a day. There are six CNNI signals distributed to Asia, Europe, Latin America, and the U.S., accommodating differences in time zones. CNNI is also distributed in multiple languages, and dubbed in many countries (CNN Español operates as a stand-alone service). In addition, CNN Airport Network operates in U.S. airports, carrying mostly news but also coverage of some live sporting events.

During prime time, approximately one million people are watching CNN in the U.S. MSNBC gets about half as many viewers, while FOX News attracts roughly twice the number of viewers as CNN, driven by a combination of opinionated talk shows.

The revenues for a cable network are based upon advertising revenues and monthly fees from cable operators. CNN generates approximately $1 billion per year in revenues, most of it from a roughly equal mix of cable subscription fees and advertising. CNN receives about 35¢ per subscriber per month, well over twice the amount collected by its competitors, FOX News and MSNBC. Roughly one quarter of CNN's revenues pay for news coverage and other programming costs. Approximately the same amount is profits. The remainder are costs of operations, engineering, marketing, and development. By comparison, MSNBC's cost structure is considerably lower, as it benefits from NBC's news operation. So too, however, are MSNBC's revenues. Generally, the company's revenues and expenses are about one-third of those associated with CNN. FOX is larger than MSNBC, and in recent years has made significant improvements in programming and revenues.

## WEATHER

For weather information, The Weather Channel has long maintained a near monopoly (in 2005, NBC launched a competitive channel). The Weather Channel is owned by Landmark Communications, a comparatively small media entity (see page 153). In addition to its 24/7 coverage, The Weather Channel has been especially successful in expanding its value proposition to local cable operators, and to other platforms, including the Web. It has become one of the best-known brand names in the cable television business. Unlike most cable networks, The Weather Channel is watched at least once per week by nearly every cable television viewer.

As part of a private company, The Weather Channel does not report financial information.

## BUSINESS NEWS

For business news, there are two competitive networks: CNBC, owned by NBC, and Bloomberg Information Television, one of several business news services provided by Bloomberg (whose founder, Michael Bloomberg, became the mayor of New York City). Bloomberg also operates business news radio stations, a magazine publisher, a book publisher, a Web site, and a professional services data network used by financial professionals. All are concerned with business and financial news. However, CNBC is by far the larger and more powerful domestic business news network, with over 80 million cable households in the U.S. CNBC Asia is available in 36 million households, while CNBC Europe serves about 200 million households in Europe, Africa, and the Middle East (both CNBC Europe and Asia are joint ventures with Dow Jones). By comparison, Bloomberg is seen in about 30 million U.S. households and about 200 million households worldwide.

C-SPAN is a noncommercial network that mainly features live coverage of government proceedings. C-SPAN was formed in the 1970s, at a time when the cable system operators thought it would be wise to provide federal legislators with their own cable network. Although it is never a ratings leader, C-SPAN has helped to define cable television in the U.S.

## LOCAL NEWS

Nearly all of the CBS, NBC, and ABC affiliates produce their own daily newscasts, as do many of the FOX stations and some UPN and WB affiliates. In total, there are certainly over 1,000 local newscasts produced every morning, afternoon, evening, and night, and perhaps as many as 2,000. Well over 500 stations are employed in the practice of local news coverage, and it seems likely that more than 25,000 people work in local news today.

For most major-market local news departments, the programming day usually begins at 6:00 A.M. and, in the larger markets, as early as 5:00 A.M., with a half-hour or hour-long broadcast. A very short time later, the staff turns to brief local news, weather, sports, and commuter information cut-ins for the network morning program (*Good Morning America*, etc.).

A noon newscast has become common. At some stations, this newscast includes not only news, weather, and sports, but an interview or community outreach activities as well.

In most large markets, the evening newscast is at least an hour long. This newscast is the focus of the station's entire news operation, because it reaches the largest number of viewers. The most prestigious anchor appears on the 6:00 P.M.

program, along with the station's best reporters. Many stations also program a 5:00 P.M. newscast, which often features softer material such as interviews and community outreach.

Almost all ABC, CBS, and NBC network affiliates program an 11:00 P.M. newscast. Stories seen on the 6:00 P.M. newscast are reworked, updated, and usually shortened for a half-hour broadcast of the late news. In most large markets, a FOX, WB, or UPN affiliate broadcasts a 10:00 P.M. newscast as counterprogramming against network prime-time and to capture viewers who go to sleep early.

On some local stations, the news department also produces a weekend news program, news magazine, news/talk show, or public-affairs program.

## Operations

The success of a local news operation depends largely upon two factors: the quality/appeal of the "front four" (the 6:00 P.M. newscast's two coanchors, weather reporter, and sportscaster) and the creative and managerial abilities of the news director. Certainly, credit goes to producers, writers, reporters, and other contributors. Still, the solidly crafted newscast, hosted by well-liked, respected on-camera talent, is critical.

The news department is almost always the largest department at a local television station. In the biggest markets, such as New York, Los Angeles, or Chicago, the staff is likely to total about 200 people. In a midsized market, the staff may still be over 100; the average staff size for ABC, CBS, and NBC affiliates in Seattle (market number 12), for example, is approximately 125 people. Smaller market stations employ as many as 30 or 40 full-timers.

The *news director* oversees coverage, budget, community relations, and production, and is responsible for almost all aspects of staff selection and supervision. Major decisions, such as changing an anchor or major reporter, are made with the station's *general manager* (see page 7).

An *executive producer* is assigned to each news program. At a large major-market station, one EP might be assigned to the morning news and noon news, another to the 5:00 P.M., another to the 6:00 P.M., and yet another to the 11:00 P.M. At most stations, however, one or two EPs supervise all news programming. Early-morning and late-night newscasts may be broadcast without the executive producer actually present in the newsroom.

One step down from the executive producer is the *producer*, in charge of preparing the newscast and supervising the broadcast. Consulting with the news director, the producer decides which stories will air and in what order; which stories will be shortened or dropped because of breaking news or interviews that run longer than anticipated; and whether to pass late-breaking information to an on-camera newscaster via newly written pages or by speaking directing into the newscaster's IFB (a clear plastic earphone).

A *staff director*, typically a full-time employee who also directs some public affairs or local commercials, directs the newscasts.

Most of the *news staff* is concerned with newsgathering, writing, and preparing stories. Staff resources at most stations include five to twenty reporters, five to ten crews (usually two people per crew, though one-person crews are becoming more common), and five to ten videotape editors. In a large market, eight or ten assignment editors work the assignment desk. Most stations employ between five and twenty reporters.

The *assignment desk*—the heart of the newsgathering operation—keeps in close contact with the police and fire departments, the mayor's office, the municipal government, local politicians, and community groups. Some information arrives in a well-organized manner—the mayor's public relations staff arranges a press conference, a publicist furnishes news about a visiting celebrity and arranges a local interview, local activists announce a rally at a specific time and place. But most leads come from telephone tips, aggressive investigative research by the station's reporters, and police radio transmissions. In a sense, the assignment desk is a resource-management system, because a limited number of reporters, crews, and vans must cover only the most important stories. Since changes in assignment or location are common, everyone keeps in close touch either by cell phone or by private radio. In theory, the assignment desk makes objective choices. In practice, pressure from the station's management and from local political leaders may affect coverage.

Most national stories are provided in the network feed. Stations also subscribe to several news wire services, notably AP (Associated Press). Other specialized wires include Bloomberg, Reuters, PR Newswire, and SportsWire. CNN Newsource revolutionized the industry by sending a 24-hour feed of news stories rather than individual packages a few times per day. Station fees for these feeds vary depending upon market size, and are negotiable.

## News Anchors and Reporters

Most television stations have long-term contracts with anchors, who are often significant contributors to the station's local brand personality. Although local traditions vary, a certain amount of typecasting is common. The 6:00 P.M. newscast is anchored by one or two seasoned journalists; the 5:00 P.M. newscast may be hosted by one of these anchors, with a third anchor who is newer to the market or lesser known. That third anchor may also do the 11:00 P.M. or the noon newscast. The morning and weekend newscasts are frequently hosted by a reporter gaining anchor experience. In the largest markets, where weekend newscast slots are more meaningful in terms of advertising revenues, regular weekend anchors may be employed.

In a major market, the lead anchor usually earns $500,000 per year or more (New York City, Los Angeles, and Chicago have some million-dollar anchors), with the other anchors earning several hundred thousand dollars per year. There are local exceptions, both higher and lower. In truth, market size is the most significant factor: Anchors working in the smallest markets typically earn $50,000 to $75,000, sometimes less. Weekend anchors generally earn about half as much as weekday anchors; their contracts usually call for three days of general assignment reporting in addition to weekend work.

Reporters may be hired and assigned in several ways. Most stations hire general-assignment reporters, then assign several of them to specific beats (e.g., city government). Some will also hire a few specialty reporters (e.g., health and science), but these stories may be covered by general-assignment reporters. A top reporter at a major-market station can earn over $200,000 per year (once again, more in New York City and Los Angeles), but most reporters at major market stations earn between $75,000 and $150,000. Market size is again the primary factor; overall, reporter salaries are generally in the $35,000 to $50,000 range. A reporter with a specialty or a particular beat often earns a small premium.

## Weather

Weather reporting is a self-contained function at just about every television station, supervised by the news director but requiring little ongoing staff or administrative support. Weather is a principal reason why viewers tune to local news programs; women generally make this viewing choice, and the appeal of the weather reporter plays a major role in this decision. There are essentially two types of television weather reporters: those who are trained meteorologists and those who are not. Some stations insist upon trained scientists, but visual appeal and personality are generally more meaningful than technical knowledge.

The weatherman or -woman is generally supported by a fully equipped weather station. This setup includes not only the typical measurement instrumentation (thermometer, barometer, hygrometer, and so on) but also computer access to one or more national weather services. One service provider, AccuWeather, feeds both raw weather data and full-color video maps that can be used on the air for national, regional, or local forecasts. If the weather reporter is a trained meteorologist, he or she may use this information and construct a custom forecast. Some stations have also invested in sophisticated computer equipment that assists in forecasting, and in computer-graphics equipment to add color, movement, and other weather information to maps.

A television station with early-morning, noon, evening, and late-night weather reports typically employs either two or three weather reporters. In a top-10 market, the job pays up to and over $300,000; in a top-20 market, the scale is $75,000 to $150,000; in smaller markets, the job typically pays $25,000 to $50,000. Because of their training and their appeal to both male and female viewers, weathermen and -women usually earn more than sports anchors.

## Sports

At a major-market station, one sports reporter will appear on the evening and late-night newscasts, and a second will appear on weekends, filing field reports several days each week. In the largest markets, a third field reporter and a sports producer may complete the team; in medium-sized and small markets, the entire sports department usually consists of two reporters.

Sports reporting is largely dependent upon game footage, which is available from a number of sources. Networks and their affiliates generally provide feeds to one another at no charge as an accommodation. Major League Baseball and the NFL provide a daily feed during the season on a contract basis. CBS Newsfeed (see page 10) also includes sports footage; its services are provided—for a fee—on an exclusive basis to one station in each market.

A major-market sports anchor typically earns up to $250,000—sometimes more, if the person is especially well known (a former local sports hero, for example)—or if the contract includes game coverage or a weekend wrap-up show. Even in the top-10 markets, most sports reporters earn under $150,000, and in the top-20, under $75,000. Outside of the largest markets, salaries are more often in the $35,000 to $50,000 range.

## News Consultants

Since many local stations share the same needs and challenges, viable ideas are borrowed and adapted from one market to another.

To keep ahead of the competition, many stations employ a consulting firm. In theory, a news consultant represents the viewer's point of view, bringing the station a great deal of knowledge about the audience and about successes in other markets. Frank N. Magid Associates and ARD (Audience Research & Development) are among the largest news consulting firms. News consultants work on a confidential, exclusive basis with one station per market; contracts are annual.

Ideally, a news consulting firm analyzes audience response to a station's news programming, and presents information about trends that may be taking shape. The firm does research to demonstrate how viewing habits and lifestyles are changing, and suggests ways to shape the programs, their scheduling, their content, and their presentation accordingly. Typically, a news consulting firm will also work closely with newsroom personnel, offering specific suggestions to improve job performance, efficiency, and on-camera presentation. While this service can be critical, it may also be problematic: Since the consultants emphasize presentation over news content, their very presence may be an annoyance to the news staff. Still, their input can be useful, provided that it is taken as useful advice that may improve ratings, and not as gospel truth. The consulting firm usually visits each client station five or six times per year, staying two or three days each time.

## LOCAL AND REGIONAL CABLE NEWS NETWORKS

Roughly two dozen local and regional cable networks supply all-day, all-night news coverage. Most are in major markets. The largest operation is a connected group of News 12 channels from Cablevision, serving the Bronx, Long Island, and other regions within the New York metropolitan area. There are news channels in Phoenix, central Florida, Chicago, New England, one for the entire state of Ohio, another serving primarily Manhattan, and more. These channels are generally advertiser-supported basic cable services.

## NEWS MAGAZINES

For decades, ABC and NBC struggled to develop a news magazine series with the kind of audience appeal and ratings associated with CBS's *60 Minutes*. In today's marketplace, each of the networks fills several hours of prime time with news magazine programming. These programs usually cost less than other prime-time hours because some of their costs are associated with the general news budget, and are not necessarily allocated to a production budget for the individual program or series. Production is not elaborate: a crew on location for several days, one or several producers, and a reporter who handles interviews and voice-overs but rarely does the research or investigative work required for storytelling. These projects are efficient because they fit comfortably into a network news operation that is already set up to shoot stories with reporters on location and edit them for maximum audience appeal. The studio hosting a news magazine tends to be simple: one or two anchors speaking directly to the camera.

The key to a successful television magazine is a consistent flow of stories that the audience wants to watch, week after week, along with reporters who are both appealing and are skillful storytellers. Also, the mix of stories matters: some celebrity profiles, some hard-hitting exposes, a bit of human interest or humor, and so on. In the early months of 2005, for example, CBS's Sunday program *60 Minutes* aired stories about new Oscars host Chris Rock; the $20 million Gates project in New York's Central Park, by artist Christo; baseball player Jose Canseco and steroid injections; a nine-year-old piano prodigy; a 14-year-old soccer wiz; the president of Ukraine discussing his poisoning; dogs saving their owners' lives; a former tobacco whistleblower who is now an educator; and a Marine battalion in Iraq. Critically speaking, there is no investigative journalism here; nearly all of this is "soft news." As it turns out, "hard news" is mainly sensationalism, mostly reserved for sweeps periods on all of the network news magazines.

One variation on the prime-time news magazine format is the long-running *CBS News Sunday Morning*. Here, the content is strongly oriented toward art and cultural trends.

## DOCUMENTARIES

Several thousand television documentaries are produced each year in the U.S., typically with budgets in the range of $75,000 to $250,000. Many are produced by or for just a few cable networks, such as Discovery and its various digital channels or The History Channel. In many cases, these projects are coproductions with media companies in other countries, who share production costs and distribution revenues. PBS programs several regularly scheduled documentary series, notably *Frontline* and *American Experience*. From time to time, a Ken Burns documentary or documentary series appears on PBS, often to better-than-average ratings for the network. Local public television stations also produce documentaries about local issues, events, personalities, or history, but not on a regular basis.

The broadcast networks rarely program documentaries because they do not, as a rule, generate a large enough audience. Documentaries are not ratings champions: In today's world, viewers tune out just about any program showing black-and-white footage. The days of biographical documentaries have also faded (once the core of A&E's schedule, *Biography* seems to be completing its run). On occasion, a major network anchor will become involved in a particular issue, resulting in a prime-time documentary (which is often more like a single-topic news magazine), but again, these are exceptions. On the major commercial networks, news magazine programs have largely replaced documentaries, although some public television stations produce their own documentaries about local history and social issues.

### Program Development

Program development for documentary production more or less follows these steps. First, the producer develops the creative concept based on his or her personal interest, or on a programmer's interest in one or more shows about a particular subject (e.g., the environment). Other idea sources include popular books whose rights are available, or the work of an individual or institution that has attracted public notice. The producer then works out a budget, writes a proposal describing the project, and pitches it to programmers and other sources of financing—foundations, sponsors, endowment organizations, foreign broadcasters, and such. Although some documentaries are funded quickly, these are the exceptions; one to three years are usually needed to gather production funds. Production is typically small-scale-single-camera with plenty of editing—and the staff is minimal. The schedule, though, can run almost a year.

### The Business of Documentary Television

A distinguished, high-quality, hour-long documentary special costs over $500,000 to produce. Domestic cable ad revenues are not likely to total more than $200,000 (hence, the budget for a cable documentary in the $100,000-plus range). This leaves two markets to be mined: international and home video. Assume a home-video retail price of $19.95, and a return to the label of about $10 per unit. About $3 can be earmarked for recoupment of production costs, and in today's market, 50,000 unit sales is a reasonable domestic estimate for a title with name value, so that adds $150,000 to the pot. The gamble: at least $150,000 in international sales to cable, broadcast, and home video.

Not every documentary costs a half-million dollars. Most documentary series episodes cost considerably less than $200,000. This budget is possible on a series whose production systems encourage real savings. A&E's *Biography* is the best example of this approach.

Since documentaries are not widely regarded as big moneymakers, a producer can usually raise the necessary funds without selling off either ownership interests or creative control.

## CONTENT CONSIDERATIONS

News programming depends in large part upon stories about people, and many of these stories involve negative information. While the function of news programming is to tell stories accurately, fairly, and without bias, there are gray areas. Some news stories involve information of a sensitive nature. And in some situations, sources of information ask to remain private, for fear of damage to personal reputation or injury.

## News Sources

As a rule, television news, particularly on a local level, tries to be nonconfrontational. Facing the choice of digging deeply into a murky story or avoiding potential legal problems, most stations will try to convince reporters that the legal hassles are not worth the trouble. Still, there are instances in which stations do air controversial stories, and reporters must protect their sources. The rule of thumb here is corroboration: If the protected source's information can be verified by a second source, then the station will usually go with the story.

If a news source specifically asks to be protected, then it is generally accepted that the reporter has a moral responsibility to protect the source. Some stations will stand by their reporters' ethical judgment. The use of unnamed sources has dramatically increased over the past decade.

On the network level—where stories that have national impact more often require the protection of sources—each news department has guidelines regarding procedures. In general, the reporter must explain the situation to the news director, who generally involves the division's senior vice president or president in the decision to go with the story. Legal counsel is present at the meeting as well. Networks typically stand by their reporters, presenting a formidable united front to any parties that challenge the reporter's information or judgment.

In addition, every network news organization abides by internal rules, developed over decades, that are related to accuracy, fact-checking, sources, and fairness. Each network also maintains and frequently updates a set of standards and practices that apply to all programs and all marketing and advertising activities.

# CHAPTER 30
# SPORTS PROGRAMMING

Until the early 1970s, most televised sports programs were local (with the exception of NFL games, which have never appeared regularly on local television). Typically, a major-market broadcaster bought the rights to cover a local team and broadcast some or all of the season's games. If a game was not covered on television, fans turned to local radio as the alternative. National sporting events, from the Kentucky Derby to the World Series, have been covered by the broadcast networks since the 1950s.

The 1970s brought cable television and a growing recognition of the national audience for televised sports. In 1970, ABC brought football to prime time with *Monday Night Football*. Through the 1970s, the networks' weekend schedules were increasingly devoted to sports coverage, dramatically increasing the amount of coverage for college football and for sports that were previously featured only in anthology shows, like ABC's popular *Wide World of Sports*. The popularity of such programming laid the groundwork for the 1979 launch of ESPN, cable television's first network devoted entirely to sports coverage. When ESPN began, fewer than 20 percent of U.S. households subscribed to cable television. As a result, ESPN's clout with rights holders and advertisers was severely limited; the same was true of other cable networks covering sports. Regional sports networks were the first to make inroads, initially sharing relatively inexpensive rights previously held exclusively by local television broadcasters. In time, the regional sports networks dominated, often dismaying local fans who slowly learned to pay for games that they had previously seen for free.

Over the past decades, rights costs for the best sports packages have more than tripled. For example, ABC paid an average of $147 million per year for *Monday Night Football* games in 1987, 1988, and 1989; the cost per year in 2005 was $550 million.

In today's marketplace, cable television serves nearly as many households as does broadcast television (roughly 80 percent, in fact). Most local games are seen on regional sports cable networks. National cable networks now compete with broadcast networks for rights to major sports leagues and events. With both viewers and rights in place, advertisers are not at all reluctant to support cable coverage of television sports.

Broadcast television is, by and large, a single-revenue business. Advertising revenues fund the network's capital and operating costs, including the acquisition of sports rights (and their related production and promotion). Cable television networks sell advertising, but they also earn monthly subscriber revenues. ESPN, for example, charges cable operators about $2 per month in exchange for rights to carry the network. With over 80 million ESPN subscribers in the U.S., the network earns nearly $200 million per month—over $2 billion per year in subscription revenues that are simply not accessible to ESPN's broadcast—only competitors. An additional 80 million households can access ESPN outside the U.S.

## THE BUYERS

The primary deep-pocket buyers of sports rights in the United States are FOX (with its sister companies FX, FOX Sports Net, and various FOX regional networks), NBC, CBS, ABC (with its sister company, ESPN), and Turner Broadcasting (TNT and TBS). According to *Street & Smith's SportsBusiness Journal's By the Numbers 2004* (the source for many of the statistics in this chapter), here is how the four largest buyers have invested their money in 2005 and beyond.

NBC's biggest investment is in the Summer and Winter Olympic Games. One deal, worth $2.3 billion, secured 2004, 2006, and 2008 coverage; another, worth an additional $2 billion, added the 2010 and 2012 Games. NBC's National Football League deal, running six years, is worth $3.6 billion and provides a new weekly broadcast—the NFC prime-time package, which NBC decided to run on Sunday nights—plus two Super Bowls and championship games. In addition, NBC and Turner share a $2.4 billion, six-year NASCAR deal (as does FOX, whose contract runs eight years). NBC is also in a deal with the PGA (Professional Golfers' Association) for five events (the same deal provides fifteen events per year to CBS and fourteen to ABC). Most of the other NBC deals are exclusive. The network paid just over $50 million for five years of rights to the Triple Crown horse races, a deal which expired in 2005. A similar amount was paid for Wimbledon in a four-year deal. NBC also paid $45 million for the right to broadcast five years of Notre Dame college football—a somewhat unusual arrangement.

FOX's biggest investment has been the NFL's NFC Sunday afternoon football package. The current deal, in place from 2005 until 2011, is a $4.3 billion commitment for FOX and includes two Super Bowls plus various championship games. FOX's portion of the NASCAR deal was originally going to cost $2.4 billion for eight years concluding in 2008, but was changed to a six-year deal with FOX and with a combination of NBC and Turner—each paying Nascar $1.2 billion, for a total of $2.4 billion. Some of this programming was intended for FOX and some for the FOX-owned FX network. FOX also owns SPEED, which reaches about half of U.S. cable households with NASCAR and other motor sports, as well as other action-oriented sports programming. SPEED has its own deal for a NASCAR Craftsman Truck Series.

FOX is the only broadcast network in a deal with Major League Baseball. This six-year deal is worth $2.5 billion, an indication that baseball remains a major player, albeit one worth less than football. The other big baseball force is ESPN (see below).

With ESPN paying $1.8 billion for each of eight years, a 45 percent increase over the value of the previous ABC deal, ABC's longtime broadcast franchise *Monday Night Football* became a cable series in 2005. ABC's investment in football—still its biggest ($4.4 billion over eight years)—is slightly less than its $4.6 billion payment for six years of NBA rights, ending in 2007–2008. ABC also has deals with the PGA (see NBC above), the National Collegiate Athletic Association (NCAA) for college football's Bowl Championship Series ($400 million for four years, ending in 2006), and the U.S. Figure Skating Championships (worth considerably less than other sports, with a deal worth only $96 million for eight years). ABC also holds the rights to the IRL (Indy Racing League) events—such as the Indianapolis 500—for which it has paid over $60 million per year in a deal that ended in 2004.

In addition to the PGA deal detailed above, CBS has invested heavily in an exclusive $6 billion, 11-year deal (running from 2004 until 2015) for the NCAA Men's Basketball Tournament (promoted as "March Madness"). CBS also handles the USTA Tennis Open and the Masters golf events—one worth just over $150 million for a four-year deal that ended in 2004, and the other a more complicated deal because coverage runs without commercial interruption.

Among the cable players, ESPN is by far the largest and most powerful. With 24 hours a day, seven days a week to fill on at least two networks (ESPN and ESPN2, plus a news network and other properties), ESPN has investments in just about every sport, and not solely for big-league game coverage. For example, in baseball, ESPN's properties include *Baseball Tonight*, the Little League World Series, and more. ESPN has agreements to televise NFL, Major League Baseball, NBA, NHL, NCAA basketball and football, and a great many smaller sports, such as bowling and billiards—a total of about 65 sports in all.

TNT is also a significant participant in rights acquisition, generally with a more specific focus. Deals as of 2004 were with the NBA, NASCAR, and the PGA. TNT also has a rights deal to broadcast Atlanta Braves games nationally. The NBC/Turner deal for NASCAR is worth $1.2 billion over six years and ends in 2006.

USA Network concentrates on a smaller list of sports events, mainly PGA, and maintains a longtime relationship with the Westminster Kennel Club for a leading dog show. After a spell on Spike, *WWE Raw* has returned to USA.

FX, owned by News Corporation, holds rights to NASCAR. It's a $200 million-per-year deal serving both FX and its sister network, FOX.

HBO and Showtime have seen continued success with the promotion of specific boxing events. Some of these matches have even been popular as pay-per-view events—provided that the match-up is perceived by viewers as worth the money.

The College Sports Network is a smaller network that is emerging as a multi-platform brand for a wide range of college sports.

Team by team, most of the action is with regional sports networks. More than half of these networks are regional channels owned by FSN (often in a deal with Cablevision's Rainbow Media, which shares ownership and manages operations; see below). For teams in the NBA and NHL, dollars associated with these deals vary widely, as do the terms: Terms as long as ten years (some longer) are as common as three- or five-year deals. Furthermore, there is "shoulder programming" to be considered—pre-game and post-game shows that also generate revenues. Local baseball coverage is often shared, with some games going to a local broadcaster but most to a regional sports network. Once again, rights fees, terms, and other aspects of the deal are based upon local market conditions. In Chicago, for example, large cable operator Comcast Chicago, in partnership with the owners of the Cubs, the White Sox, the Bulls, and the Blackhawks, has created a new regional sports channel, eliminating the Rainbow-controlled FOX presence entirely.

FSN (FOX Sports Net), part of FOX television, is a network of 20 regional sports channels that collectively reach nearly 80 million homes in the U.S. Thirteen of these channels are owned by FSN, and the rest are affiliates. These regional outlets carry live NBA, NHL, and MLB games, plus college and high school games. FSN is the cable television home for 62 of the 82 domestic NBA, NHL, and MLB teams in the U.S. In addition, FOX operates National Sports Partners, a rep firm that sells advertising time for most regional networks and for nearly all Major League Baseball teams.

Many of the largest national rights deals have not proven profitable for the broadcast networks involved. While a certain part of cost can be attributed to network brand development and the undeniable power of sports to draw new viewers, the sheer reality is that the rights costs have not been justified by the available revenues. As a result, the spiraling rights costs may slow. Then again, the networks' interest in new revenue streams may provide even richer deals in the future, as the combination of analog and digital television, recorded media, video-on-demand, distribution to mobile devices, and other developments is likely to entice the networks to continue paying richly for the sports rights they now require in order to operate a viable network.

For cable networks, however, sports contracts tend to provoke two revenue streams: subscribers and advertisers. The combination is often profitable.

## THE SELLERS

With average regular season broadcast ratings in the range of a 10, and some higher, the NFL is television's most valuable sports programming. Week after week, ESPN's *Sunday Night Football* averages an 8 or higher in its universe, and ABC's *Monday Night Football* averages an 11 or higher. The NFL's season is shorter than most other sports, and teams play just once a week. Viewers and advertisers respond to the limited supply with greater demand. What's more, the once-per-year impact of the Super Bowl has become an advertising phenomenon—and a significant annual pop culture event. Boasting an industry-leading 40-plus rating, and almost never less than a 60 share, the Super Bowl has consistently increased the price of its average 30-second commercial. In 2005, for example, the cost was over $2.4 million per spot.

By comparison, NBA games average about a 2.5 rating during the regular season, and in a good year, a rating of 10 or more for the finals. The NBA playoffs are consistently among the highest rated of all cable programs.

Major League Baseball's regular season ratings are under 3 for network games, and well under 2 for cable games. The World Series generally delivers between a 12 and a 16, depending upon the season and the teams. The All-Star Game performs in a similar range. In general, World Series viewership has been declining—Nielsen reported a rating of 15.6 in 2004, compared with a 17.4 in 1996— but the number of countries showing the games on television has dramatically increased, from just 20 in the 1980s to well over 200 countries today (this phenomenon is true of many sports, but baseball has done especially well overseas). Interestingly, there is a market for Little League as well: The ABC telecast of the Little League World Championship game typically scores about a 5 rating.

The NHL is less popular, rarely scoring more than a 1 rating, even for All-Star games. Still, the Stanley Cup Finals do deliver significant viewers, in the range of a 3 in past years, but as low as a 2 for the 2003 finals. (By comparison, the Daytona 500 scores between a 10 and an 11.) ESPN put together a three-year deal worth a reported $200 million in 2004 for cable coverage, but the League's broadcast deal with NBC included no guaranteed-rights fee. The NHL then experienced serious internal problems, causing a major lapse in televised games.

Most NASCAR Winston Cup Series races do better: a 6 or 7 rating for the best races. NASCAR is a promising franchise; the sport has been consistently gaining popularity. The Indianapolis 500 rates slightly lower, and most IRL (Indy Racing League) events barely score a 1 rating. The same can be said for MLS (Major League Soccer) events during the regular season.

The Masters tournament does best among golf events, with a Sunday rating of 8 or 9 (the Saturday rating is typically lower). The PGA Championship varies from year to year—as low as a 4, as high as a 7—and the U.S. Open golf events do about as well. Tennis events score about half that. In 2003, Wimbledon got a 2.9 rating for the women's final and a 2.2 rating for the men's final. The Australian Open, French Open, and U.S. Open scored ratings in the 2 to 3 range.

When there's a Triple Crown winner in sight, the springtime Kentucky Derby, Preakness Stakes, and Belmont Stakes rate as high as a 10, but without a well-publicized contender the numbers drop to half that amount. The Tour de France runs on a smaller network, the Outdoor Life Network (the race is quite long, and demands a healthy number of hours on the air). Rating: about half a point.

The old WWF (World Wrestling Federation) became WWE (World Wrestling Entertainment) in 2002, and also bought WCW (World Championship Wrestling). WWE is a public company with about $300 million in annual revenues resulting from three primary sources: several hundred live events staged each year, television coverage of these events, and merchandising. Bear in mind that wrestling has been a television mainstay since the 1940s. WWE updates the formula with a combination of branded events and series for television audiences. Wrestling has been successful pay-per-view fare from the start, and in 2003, WWE programming was responsible for a remarkable 5.5 million buys (U.S. and international combined). The WWE manages two brands for its popular weekly television programming. *WWE Raw* is among the most popular brands on cable television, with *Monday Night Raw*, seen on USA, among cable's most successful overall programs. The other television brand, *SmackDown!*, provides a series for Spike, and another for UPN. Syndicated versions of both *Raw* and *SmackDown!* are also seen on local stations. A long list of television networks outside the U.S. have purchased rights to WWE programming. Books, magazines, videogames, Web sites, and branded merchandise complete the picture for a very successful "sports entertainment" business.

Boxing has also been a television staple since the medium's inception, but the industry never came together in anything like the commercial form associated with WWE. Instead, major boxing events seen on television are more often associated with individual promoters, who sell rights to individual championship bouts for as much cash as possible. HBO and Showtime have been the most frequent buyers of high-profile boxing events, but the most exciting match-ups are more often sold as pay-per-view events. FSN and ESPN2 also feature boxing.

The NCAA (National Collegiate Athletic Association) is an administrative and coordinating body for sports programs in over one-third of U.S. colleges and universities. The NCAA oversees the television aspects of nearly 90 sports championships, from swimming to volleyball to lacrosse to women's water polo. The best-known NCAA television deals are made for college football and basketball, because these appear on larger networks, but the smaller College Sports Television (CSTV) hosts a number of other events. FOX Sport Net has deals with Pac-10 (Pacific-Ten) and ACC (Atlantic Coast Conference) basketball, and with Pac-10 and Big 12 football. In fact, each network has its own conference deals, in addition to deals with individual colleges and universities. Some local stations also have similar deals with local institutions.

And then there are the Olympics. During prime time, the 2002 Salt Lake

City Games averaged a 19.2 rating with nearly 170 hours of network coverage. The previous Summer Games, in Sydney, Australia, averaged a 13.8, with closer to 160 hours of network coverage. As a rule, the Winter Games score a 10 percent higher rating than their summertime counterparts, but this is an oversimplification and does not take into account the many factors affecting ratings of a large series of events played over a period of multiple weeks. Location, for example, plays a role: Summer games played in the U.S. tend to get higher ratings (among U.S. viewers) than those staged abroad. Another factor: Many more events are presented to summer viewers—over 250, in comparison with 60 or 70 during the winter.

NBC has provided the U.S. with Olympic coverage since 2000. Rights to the 2000, 2004, 2008, and 2012 Summer games cost $715 million, $793 million, $894 million, and $1.18 billion, respectively. Rights to the Winter Games for 2002, 2006, and 2010 cost $555 million, $613 million, and $820 million.

## PRODUCTION AND OPERATIONS

The buying and selling of rights is only one aspect of television sports. In fact, rights agreements are typically negotiated by a small group of attorneys and senior executives (often joined by network executives and high-level corporate attorneys because of the amounts of money involved). Most people who work in sports television have nothing whatsoever to do with rights negotiations. More often, their role is the production and marketing of sports programming.

If a contract is a large one, then the project is treated much like any other television series. One or several executives provide leadership and management, and serve as high-level liaisons with the league and the teams. Producers are assigned to each telecast. A series producer (who may be called a "supervising producer") takes charge of packaging: the graphics package, the overall style, the music, and so on. A team of broadcasters (announcers) covers the games, but with a large number of games, two or more teams of announcers may be used. Then it's a contest of logistics, criss-crossing the country so that appropriate on-site preparation can be completed prior to game time. In each city, a freelance technical crew typically handles cameras, audio, and lighting, but a core technical staff may travel as part of the network supervisory group.

For smaller projects, the team is more likely to be composed entirely of freelancers, hired either due to past experience with the lead executive or simply because they are located in the appropriate city.

On the marketing side, advertising sales are typically handled by either a sports advertising group or by the network's regular ad sales force. Publicity and promotion are typically associated with the sports division. Often, television coverage is part of a broader sports marketing strategy supported by the league or the individual team.

## NICHE PLAYS

Mainstream sports coverage is the heart and soul of the sports television business, but there are other angles to play, sometimes quite profitably.

## CSTV

CSTV Networks runs college sports programs and coverage 24 hours a day on a cable and satellite network called College Sports TV. In addition, the company operates SIRIUS College Sports Radio. With more than 6,000 hours of original programming per year, a strong suit in women's coverage, an increasing group of rights, and savvy multi-platform brand building, the future for CSTV appears promising. In addition, the company operates over 200 broadband Web sites for university sports departments.

### High School Sports

Some cable television systems now regularly cover high school sports. If audience interest is high, sale of commercial time in these programs can more than pay for the cost of covering the game. Since there is rarely competition for rights—and because showing the game generally increases local interest in the team—rights payments are uncommon.

From time to time, an entrepreneur will attempt to organize a larger business around high school sports.

### Historical Sporting Events and Documentaries

Sports coverage loses value immediately after it is telecast. Still, many World Series and Super Bowl games have sold well on videocassette to collectors. ESPN Classic, a digital cable and satellite channel, features a combination of stories about legendary athletes and notable teams or matches, and coverage of games that resonate in fans' memories.

Some sports documentaries have succeeded in home video and, occasionally, on cable, but audiences generally prefer live coverage. Now and then, a sports documentary will find a mainstream audience. Original sports documentaries are uncommon, except when a network like ESPN decides to memorialize a large number of athletes or teams, as it did with its *Sports Century* series. Each sport has its own management system for historical material. Major League Baseball claims ownership of all games since the inception of television coverage. Older baseball footage may be hard to find, and rights are typically cleared by the library providing the footage. The NFL, the NHL, and the NBA operate in a similar fashion, though there may be some dealings with the individual teams as well. Golf and tennis footage is usually owned by the original production company, the network, or the association that granted the television rights. Use of college sports coverage must be cleared by either the appropriate conference that made the television deal or by the individual school (or sometimes by both).

Often, simply finding old sports footage is as difficult as determining who owns the rights and who can negotiate a deal. Many games were never recorded; if they were, the material may have been destroyed or lost. Most stock-footage houses archive sports footage, but their libraries tend to be spotty.

When rights are granted, they should include the right to show both the players and the game. As for the fans and anyone who was in or near the venue before, during, or after the game, releases may be necessary—particularly if the material will be used outside of its purely historical context.

## ADVERTISING

Although more women are watching sports than ever before, sports programs remain the best way to consistently reach large populations of male viewers. In 2003, GM spent $380 million on advertising during sports television, and Anheuser-Busch spent $233 million. Other large advertisers included Daimler-Chrysler, Pepsi-Cola, Sony, Miller Brewing Company, Time Warner, Yum! Brands (owner of Pizza Hut, among others), and Toyota. GM spent 30 percent of its advertising money on the NFL and 22 percent on college basketball; Major League Baseball got only 7 percent, and the NBA games got 11 percent. Anheuser-Busch also emphasized football buys, spending fully 48 percent of its funds on the NFL, with 10 percent for MLB and 10 percent for NBA games. These strategies were typical of the top advertisers.

The viewer's median age for all sports on broadcast television is 46 years. NHL and NBA games skew younger, with a median age of 37. So do NFL regular season games, with a median age of 40. Major League Baseball skews older, with a median age of 49 for both regular season games and the World Series. Golf's median age is 53, while figure skating and horse racing's Triple Crown skew even older with an average age of 56 years.

As a rule, women 18-plus comprise one-third of all sports viewers. They over-index on the Triple Crown races (46 percent), and under-index on NBA basketball's regular season with less than 30 percent. The sports events for which women viewers most outnumber men is the U.S. Figure Skating Championships; women comprise two-thirds of the viewers. Teenagers don't watch as much sports on television. As a rule, people age 12 to 17 account for between 3 and 7 percent of viewers. In fact, the only sport that breaks the 10 percent median for teenagers is the NBA regular season, with an 11 percent.

In terms of income, the wealthiest viewers tend to watch the Masters golf tournament, golf's U.S. Open, the NHL Cup finals, and the NCAA Bowl games (football). Baseball's World Series also does well with upscale viewers. Viewers with the lowest incomes tend to favor the NASCAR Busch circuit, the NASCAR Nextel Cup, and surprisingly, the U.S. Figure Skating Championships.

## SPORTS TELEVISION OUTSIDE THE U.S.

Although the U.S. has transformed sports into a marketing juggernaut, sports programming is—and always has been—a significant aspect of television in almost every country. The U.S. game called "football" doesn't mean much outside the U.S. and a handful of other countries, but the "real" football (called "soccer" in the U.S.) is the most important franchise in Europe and Latin America. FIFA (Fédération Internationale de Football Association), which licenses World Cup Soccer, sold the global rights for the 2002 and 2006 match-ups for $2.24 billion; the high price helped to bankrupt one lead buyer, Germany's Kirch Group. Throughout Europe, soccer matches are as ubiquitous as baseball or basketball in the U.S. During the season, on a satellite service, viewers may choose between a half-dozen or more simultaneous telecasts.

ESPN International started in 1988 and operates 16 networks outside the U.S., mostly in Asia and Latin America. France's Eurosport reaches over 95 million homes in 54 countries, and is the principal European source for football (soccer), tennis, motor sports, rugby, cycling, and more. Many of Eurosport's viewers can watch sports coverage in their native language. Among many other worldwide ventures, FOX Sports International owns Prime Deportiva, currently in 18 countries via a single feed. FOX Sports World is a player in the U.K.

Sportel, held in Monaco each October, has become a leading international marketplace for the sale of sports rights. Several additional Sportel marketplaces are also in operation.

# CHAPTER 31
# TALK SHOWS, VARIETY, MUSIC, AND MORE

For decades, television's prime-time dramas and comedies were the dominant force in programming. They were the programs that most interested viewers and advertisers. In the 1990s, with the proliferation of nonfiction programs on cable television, the pattern began to change. Reality series became popular, and have remained so (see page 215); many are more active, robust versions of game shows, whose original form has been nearly forgotten by television programmers. Most nonfiction formats remain stable because they continue to attract audiences.

## TALK SHOWS

Talk shows are presented in one of roughly six forms. These formats overlap, but it's useful to explore the genre by breaking it down into categories.

The first, currently represented by Tony Danza and Ellen DeGeneres, combines aspects of comedy, variety, and celebrity talk. Regis Philbin and Kelly Ripa work in this format as well. These shows are fun, friendly, generally succeed on the basis of the celebrity host, and provide good company for daytime audiences. Past hosts who have succeeded in this durable format include Rosie O'Donnell, Mike Douglas, and Dinah Shore. Many celebrity hosts have attempted this format, but few have succeeded for more than a season or two. There's a certain magic that must happen between host and audience, and when that magic is absent (regardless of the host's talent or dedication), the show does not achieve the necessary ratings.

The second, more or less originated by Phil Donahue in the 1970s, is an issues-oriented talk show featuring a small panel of either experts or ordinary people in extraordinary circumstances. Oprah Winfrey has been especially successful in transforming this format, in part by combining certain aspects of the celebrity-based variety talk show. Others have succeeded by sticking with this basic format, often featuring people in difficult situations. Jerry Springer developed a reputation for taking the low road here, while others have presented a broader variety of issues and people, notably Maury Povich and Montel Williams.

The third type of talk show is the one-on-one. This is the format pioneered by Edward R. Murrow. It has subsequently been developed, in various ways, by

Dick Cavett, David Frost, Ted Koppel, Charlie Rose, Larry King, and most recently, by CNBC's Donnie Deutsch. This format is not easy; it demands a host who is a good listener, one who can focus attention on a wide range of topics.

The fourth format has become a staple for cable prime-time: the political talk show featuring a host/anchor and a group of outspoken commentators and guests. Greta Van Susteren, Tucker Carlson, Bill O'Reilly, and Sean Hannity and Alan Colmes are among the talk-show hosts working in this format on various news-oriented cable networks.

The fifth and sixth types of shows are network staples. *Good Morning America* and *Today* are typical of the morning talk/news programs that have been produced for decades. The network late-night talk show is the sixth format. With minor variations, this is the desk-and-couch format made popular by Johnny Carson. Today's talk-show hosts working in this format include Jay Leno, David Letterman, and Conan O'Brien.

In general, talk shows are among television's least expensive formats. The host salary may be high (the entire show relies upon the success of the host), but the rest of the production is often very simple. In most cases, the program is televised from a relatively small studio, with a handful of cameras. Guests are not paid, although some receive AFTRA or SAG minimums. The production staff typically involves just a few producers and assistants. Remote production is usually minimal.

New network and cable talk shows are launched each year. As a rule, a few syndication slots open, and a few new celebrity- or issues-based shows are developed. There is far less change on network morning and late-night shows. New talk shows are typically produced either by a large syndicator (Universal is responsible for both Jerry Springer and Maury Povich) or by a cable network. Staff producers are often previous talk-show staffers with experience on similar shows.

## GAME SHOWS

Once a daytime and syndication staple, game shows now occupy up to an hour on local stations' schedules. By 2005, only *The Price Is Right* had survived as a network daytime game show, and only *Jeopardy!*, *Wheel of Fortune*, and *Hollywood Squares* appeared on major network affiliate schedules. *Family Feud* and *Pyramid* also appeared on smaller network affiliates, and *Who Wants to Be a Millionaire* was in daytime syndication. Otherwise, game shows appeared on only a small number of cable networks. Comedy Central, for example, usually runs one or two game shows, and MTV also schedules a game show from time to time. But for the most part, audiences and advertisers have lost interest in the format, despite the extraordinary popularity of the prime-time editions of *Who Wants to Be a Millionaire* only several years before. Even the Game Show Network was renamed GSN, mainly to separate itself from the traditional game-show genre.

A new game show requires experienced hands for development. In fact, game shows are quite complicated to develop properly. In short, the game itself must work, both as a competition among on-screen contestants and as passive entertainment for the viewer at home. Extensive play-testing is always required, along with several minds that can invent and modify game concepts. This is a somewhat specialized domain, and the sheer number of people who understand the intricacies is dwindling. Similarly, game-show production is somewhat specialized: a world of game boards and video displays, scoring units, prize displays, judges, and security of questions. After a game show is developed, however, it can usually be produced at a lower cost than most other types of television. Recording four or five complete episodes per day is not unusual for game-show production; in just two weeks, it's not unusual to record 30 or 40 half-hours.

Game shows remain popular outside the U.S. Many program formats, such as *Wheel of Fortune* and *The Price Is Right*, are produced in local versions in other countries. FremantleMedia is one of several companies that sell game-show rights in these countries, and also produce or coproduce locally.

## AWARDS SHOWS AND VARIETY SHOWS

When the term "variety show" is used, it's tough not to think in terms of Carol Burnett or Sonny & Cher. With the exception of a few unsuccessful attempts, star-based variety shows are no longer carried on the schedule, but variety remains alive in other forms. *America's Funniest Home Videos* and *Whose Line Is It Anyway?* are consistently popular contemporary variety shows. Relatively inexpensive productions, they have been repeated many times on both broadcast and cable television.

There is a long list of awards shows that also fit into the variety category, but not as series. In addition to the Grammy, Academy, Tony, Emmy, and Daytime Emmy Awards, there are the People's Choice, Country Music Association, American Music, Nickelodeon Kids' Choice, and SAG Awards, among others associated with movies, music, television, and more.

People watch awards shows mainly to see celebrities and to share in the glamour. There's a pop culture component, a gossip component, and a sense that what's happening is somehow important. Several awards shows have risen to the level of major annual event (the Academy Awards and the Grammy Awards, for example).

Most awards shows are well-established television properties. Launching a new awards show is difficult, but with the right network executive and the right sponsor, a talented and experienced producer can occasionally make it happen.

Rental of the hall, design and construction of the stage and scenery, acquisition of footage, booking the stars, rehearsing the performers—these are all standardized processes for the small number of production companies who specialize in such events. Celebrities require very special handling, of course. The level of complexity, and the sensitivity demanded of the production staff and crew, generally result in the same basic group of people moving from one show to the next. Newcomers rarely supervise these productions.

Most of the events are produced live; some are taped for airing shortly after the event. Available sponsorship dollars must pay for production and provide a reasonable profit. In a small number of special cases, the sale of international rights adds considerable revenue (the Academy Awards, for example, are seen throughout the world).

One special case is the Spanish-language *Sabado Gigante*, shown every Saturday night since August 1962 (according to the *Guinness Book of World Records*, it's the longest-running television variety show in the world). Seen by over 100 million viewers in 32 countries, the music, game, comedy, and variety series is produced in Miami and seen in the U.S. on the Univision network.

Another special case is *Saturday Night Live*, the longest-running weekly variety show in the history of American television. For three decades, the series has provided a combination of an opening monologue, humorous commentary on the week's news, comedy sketches, and a popular music act. The series has provided a foundation for the careers of many notable comedy actors, and the basis for more than a dozen popular motion pictures. Consistent with the traditions that date back to Sid Caesar's 1950s variety shows, there is a staff of writers working quickly to provide an ensemble of comedians with material to rehearse throughout the week. By Saturday, all of the material has been rehearsed, and final determinations are made. This is old show business, with actors racing about in odd costumes, quick scene changes, bits that are presented live (some work, some don't), lots of risk-taking, careers made through invented characters that take hold with audiences, career opportunities lost because the bit was cut at the last minute. Combining traditional show business with a rock 'n' roll attitude, *Saturday Night Live* has exhibited a consistency largely attributed to one gifted producer, Lorne Michaels. His success is a constant reminder that the show's the thing—and that corporate ownership and visionary executives simply cannot do what a successful show can. It can bring people back week after week, year after year, decade after decade.

## SPECIAL-INTEREST PROGRAMS

Although the press tends to cover the high-visibility comedies, dramas, talk shows, specials, and news magazines, a great many of the hours on cable networks are devoted to special-interest programming.

One of the most popular series on PBS is *Antiques Roadshow*, in which antiques dealers appraise individual items found in America's attics. Travel programming is sufficiently popular to occupy an entire channel (Travel Channel, owned by Discovery) and at least 5 percent of many public television stations' schedules. Cooking shows are another public television staple, now also featured on Food Network, along with other cuisine and lifestyle programming. HGTV's schedule is filled with design and lifestyle programs; TLC follows a similar strategy. The History Channel features endless documentaries, and narratives that utilize existing footage to tell stories about, for example, *Modern Marvels*. There's a channel for golf, another for tennis, another for racing (Speed), and yet another for outdoor sports programming (another public television staple in many parts of the country). Special-interest channels include Animal Planet, Court TV, DIY, Fine Living, Discovery Flight, Discovery Health, Bridges (American Muslim Television), and more on the way.

Initially, each of these networks either produced or repackaged low-cost programming: Food Network began with show after show in small kitchen setups; The History Channel began by repacking the old Hearst Movietone newsreels and similar product. As their audiences grew, mainly through carriage on more cable systems (and on satellite), cable networks developed relationships with advertisers. This provided more money for higher-quality original production, which, of course, attracted larger audiences and more advertising dollars. The cycle isn't always perfect, but the basic theory has worked for most cable networks.

Filling 24 hours each day, 7 days each week, for 52 weeks each year, is no easy task. Dozens of programs are required by each network, and there is a constant need for new programs to replace the ones that are underperforming. Network headquarters are located throughout the U.S., and so are their program suppliers. In some cases, programs are produced specifically for the network. In others, the producer of a special-interest program may license it to the network for a limited number of plays over a specified term. Then the producer may sell the property to another network. At the same time, the producer may offer the series via home video or, in the coming distribution environment, via a broadband Internet video service in association with advertising, or as part of a subscription deal. Some special-interest programs can be sold to Canada or the U.K.

As a rule, special-interest programming tends to cost far less than other program forms. A $50,000 budget for a quality half-hour is an industry standard, but it is possible to produce certain types of series (e.g., a sewing or quilting series) for far less.

## CONCERTS AND PERFORMANCES

Musical performances have been a television staple since the invention of the medium. Only a small number of regularly scheduled music programs have succeeded in the long-term. *Austin City Limits*, produced for public television stations, has featured more than 500 different artists in its three-decade run. *Grand*

*Ole Opry* has been seen for decades on various television outlets, the latest being the Great American Country network. Among showcases for contemporary music, A&E and MTV have been successful with regularly scheduled performance programs featuring contemporary artists, and HBO schedules the occasional blockbuster special with a major musical star. From time to time, one of the broadcast networks will air a one-hour special featuring a major country or popular music star.

Year after year, the most reliable provider of musical performance programming has been PBS. In the 2004–2005 season, the PBS *Great Performances* series featured Eric Clapton, Leonard Bernstein's *"Candide" in Concert*, Andrea Bocelli, Rod Stewart, the American Ballet Theater, Josh Groban, and more. *Evening at Pops*, featuring the Boston Pops Orchestra, has been shown on PBS for 35 years.

However, as a general rule, television audiences tend not to watch musical performance programming in large numbers. This, plus the complexity and cost of each production and of working with top performers, tends to limit the amount of musical performance programming seen on television. At this stage in television's development, musical performance programming is relatively scarce. Several attempts at cable networks devoted to jazz, classical, or other genres have resulted in a switch to general entertainment formats; Bravo and A&E are both rooted in early attempts that featured a healthy amount of musical performance programming. Still, there may well be untapped audience interest for the right network featuring the right music.

The production of a live performance need not require the rental of a large hall, nor the engagement of a large, highly sophisticated technical facility and crew. Many performances can be produced very simply and effectively within reasonable budget guidelines. What's more, digital audio production allows extraordinary fidelity to the real sounds of the music.

## Music Video

For many viewers of music on television, the right format is the music video. By mixing story, imagery, dance, special effects, and musical performance, music videos are produced to promote artists and to sell records. As a rule, music videos are funded by record labels; it is typical to spend about $100,000 for a video likely to air on MTV and other cable networks. Some videos have been produced for as little as $5,000 or $10,000, but others have cost well over $1 million. Artists who are early on in their career and anxious for record label attention may self-fund a music video on a modest budget.

When the record company finances a video, the label usually owns the copyright, and thus the right to exploit the video in all markets (nowadays, this means television, home video, and the Internet). The artist performs on the music video without receiving any additional fee, but may receive a small royalty from the sale of compilation videos (after the label recoups its investment in production).

The production company and other creative contributors do not benefit from these royalties, but may participate in royalties generated by the sale of home video compilations.

Producing a music video is a specialty. Each music video is, in essence, a commercial to promote record sales, but the creative team often envisions the project as something closer to a small film of very high quality. Sets are constructed, large crews are employed, and because major musical stars are often involved, music industry politics often become a factor.

While music video production companies tend to be based in New York, Los Angeles, Nashville, London, Tokyo, and other music centers, companies that specialize in music videos are located in many other cities as well.

A music video production company is typically an alliance between a producer and a director. In the best of circumstances, the producer and director collaborate to develop the initial creative concept, later refining it by working directly with the artist, the artist's management, and the record label (each may have a different degree of involvement). Then the producer attends to the usual details: hiring crew, securing locations, and managing the budget. The director works with the performers, the choreographer (if there is to be any dance or specialized movement), the art director, and the wardrobe designer or supervisor. Most music videos are conceived, produced, and edited in about two to four weeks, from start to finish.

Rates and fees are negotiable. Mainstream production companies usually take 15 percent of the production budget for general overhead, plus 5 percent of the budget as the producer's fee and 10 percent as the director's fee. A small, well-managed mainstream production company can produce between 15 and 20 music videos per year, with budgets approaching $100,000. A larger outfit may employ a significant number of producers and directors, and turn out dozens of videos each year. Many music video production companies also produce commercials.

# CHAPTER 32
# CHILDREN'S PROGRAMMING; ANIMATION

From the start, television programming for children has been closely aligned with the sales and marketing of children's toys, soft drinks, candies, and other merchandise. And, from the start, children's programming has been comprised of a combination of cartoons on the one hand and live action with comedy, music, and puppetry on the other.

After several years of early experimentation and tinkering at both the network and local levels, by around 1952 or so it became clear that Saturday morning was the best time for children's television, and that a combination of live actors, songs, puppets, the occasional cartoon, and a smattering of short action films was the formula for a successful series. This formula could certainly describe *Sesame Street*, which came nearly two decades later, but it was first successful with the likes of *Howdy Doody* (which starred puppets) and *Winky Dink and You* (which starred cartoon heroes and live performers). Old movie serials featuring cowboys and space patrols became television series with similar themes. By the early 1960s, these types of shows were eclipsed by a new format: the cartoon show.

While the broadcast networks concentrated their attention on Saturday mornings, independent local stations and some network affiliates offered afternoon and early evening blocks filled with cartoons, *The Three Stooges*, and *The Little Rascals*, often hosted by a clown, a cop, a ranger, or some other fantasy or comedy figure (sometimes trained in vaudeville). Networks and local stations also offered morning programming for children; *Captain Kangaroo* had an especially long run, from 1955 until 1985 (it is surpassed only by *Sesame Street* as the longest-running children's program in the United States).

On public television, *Mister Rogers' Neighborhood* and *Sesame Street* have been staples for more than one generation of children. No other PBS series have run so long, but several other PBS children's series have helped set the same high standard by combining education and entertainment.

Acknowledging a great many notable exceptions, cartoons have become the dominant force in children's television. They fill the network's Saturday morning schedules; they dominate the schedules and high-value advertising deals for

Nickelodeon and Cartoon Network; and they fuel an extremely powerful merchandising and licensing business. Live-action and shows with unconventional animation run a close second, and are often the source of a breakout hit series, be it *Pee Wee's Playhouse*, *Where in the World is Carmen Sandiego?*, *Barney and Friends*, or *Blues Clue's*. Many live-action series have been very successful both as television properties and as the basis for merchandise and other licensing activities.

## THE CHILDREN'S TELEVISION MARKETPLACE

Since the 1960s, the children's television marketplace has been dominated by cartoons, most often cartoons made for television or as shorts for motion picture theaters.

The current marketplace for animated children's product includes domestic and international broadcast and cable networks and, in many countries, home video. There are more children's programming outlets today than at any time in the past, but Cartoon Network and Nickelodeon combined typically deliver about 80 percent of children's viewing. Still, producers must look to more than one market for the financing of an animated series. For some series, merchandising and licensing revenues are meaningful, but for most series, these revenues are minimal. (The situation is complicated because of the number of brand extensions, series based upon older series or motion pictures, and so on.) Nonetheless, with outlets actively developing new properties, the marketplace for animation is a dynamic one.

The marketplace for live-action programming is more limited, and more traditional in terms of deals and financing. Nickelodeon typically runs one or more live-action series (*The Amanda Show*, for example), as well as the occasional off-network acquisition (*Sabrina, The Teenage Witch*). The Disney Channel has had some success with live-action series (*Lizzie McGuire*, *That's So Raven*), but only in the midst of a schedule dominated by cartoons. The marketplace has matured: The networks have a keen sense of what "works" and tend to follow one another's successes with similar projects. This often results in a combination of imaginative uses of the television format, kid-sized versions of adult shows (*Trading Spaces*), and traditional story fare.

The more specialized preschool television market, nurtured by *Captain Kangaroo*, *Mister Rogers' Neighborhood*, *Sesame Street*, and *Blue's Clues*, is now the province of Noggin (a Nickelodeon network) and Nick Jr. Other networks, such as Disney, PBS Kids, and TLC (with Ready Set Learn!), also offer preschool programming.

Several revenue streams are associated with this marketplace. The first is advertising. Children's television programs have long been the best place to advertise toys, games, candy, soda, and certain types of clothing. This has been true since the 1950s (and before, as the practice is a carryover from radio), and despite a smattering of rules over the years, the use of television as a marketing medium to reach children remains essentially unchanged. In the United States, annual advertising revenues associated with children's television are approximately $600 million to $700 million. The second revenue stream is associated with cable network fees: A dollar or two or three is collected monthly by every cable operator, then passed on to Nickelodeon, Disney Channel, Cartoon Network, and other cable networks (the situation is similar with regard to satellite channels). With nearly 75 million cable television households in the U.S., monthly revenues paid to children's cable networks amount to well over $100 million, and annual revenues exceed $1 billion. The third revenue stream is licensing and merchandising (detailed below), with a gross of several billion dollars per year. The fourth is the sale and licensing of programs and formats to television networks, distributors, and producers outside the U.S. In total, the children's television market in the U.S. is probably valued at $6 billion to $8 billion.

## Distribution: U.S. Broadcast and Cable Networks, and More

On the cable side, Nickelodeon is the dominant network force in the United States and several other countries, and a dominant programming force whose properties are seen in over 150 countries by over 500 million households throughout the world. Nickelodeon started in 1979 as a noncommercial network, an inducement for parents to subscribe to then-new cable television service. Owned by Viacom, Nickelodeon is a television network, but it is also an enormously successful brand in its own right. Among its brand extensions are a dozen Web sites; Nickelodeon movies; self-sustaining Nickelodeon cable or satellite networks in Australia, Japan, Scandinavia, Korea, the Philippines, Latin America, and the U.K.; and a variety of digital cable channels, which include Noggin (preschool, teens), Nickelodeon Games & Sports (GaS), Nicktoons, and Nick Too. The network's program assets include some of the highest-rated television series in the history of cable television; these include *Rugrats*, *SpongeBob SquarePants*, and *Blue's Clues*. Nickelodeon is among the most active networks in terms of new program development.

The other dominant force in children's cable is Cartoon Network, owned by Time Warner (which also owns Kids' WB!) and operated as part of the Turner Broadcasting System (which also owns Boomerang). Launched in 1992, Cartoon Network is also one of basic cable's highest-rated networks. Cartoon Network Europe is broadcast in multiple language feeds; Cartoon Network Latin America operates in a similar fashion. Cartoon Network Japan is a joint venture with ITOCHU (the world's eighteenth largest corporation). Cartoon Network was enabled, in part, through the acquisition and consolidation of large cartoon libraries—including the Hanna-Barbera, Warner Bros., and MGM libraries—but the network is now known for original properties (*Powerpuff Girls*, *Foster's Home for Imaginary Friends, Adult Swim*), select off-network or syndication hits (*Yu-Gi-Oh!, Family Guy*), and revitalized favorites (*What's New Scooby-Doo*).

The broadcast networks have ceded the responsibility for children's programming to corporate brethren. Disney operates ABC Kids, and many of the programs are also seen on the Disney Channel (*Kim Possible, That's So Raven*). The CBS schedule is programmed by its sister Viacom company, Nickelodeon, so it is dominated by Nickelodeon series. NBC's schedule is leased to Discovery, which is not a sister company. The NBC time slots are filled innovatively, with a game/reality show, a science-fiction drama, and several cartoons (one based in nature, the other in archeology). Generally, the NBC schedule skews slightly older than the CBS and ABC schedules. FOX BOX is leased to 4 Kids Entertainment, a public company that built its reputation with *Pokémon* and, subsequently, *Yu-Gi-Oh!*. On The WB, the Saturday block—called Kids' WB!—consists of cartoons from various sources, and trades shows with Cartoon Network.

The DIC Kid's Network is a relatively new (debuted 2003) approach to children's television distribution. The network provides a custom program block to a total of 450 FOX, UPN, and WB affiliates, while offering the entire package to major advertisers as a single "network." Each day, the DIC Kid's Network provides three individual distinct feeds, totaling six half-hour series, from its library—successfully satisfying FCC requirements for educational programming on local stations while simultaneously delivering high ratings to stations and advertisers. The network is the latest in a series of innovative programming decisions by a longtime producer and distributor of children's programming.

PBS Kids has built a successful umbrella brand with an impressive array of programs that appeal to kids but steer clear of violence and include at least some educational content. These days, PBS Kids is about cartoon series like *Arthur* (based on a children's book series), *Sagwa* (an Asian cat), *Clifford the Big Red Dog*, and *Dragon Tales*, with a periodic mix of new episodes from *ZOOM, Sesame Street, Reading Rainbow*, and other PBS staples. PBS Kids is a collection of nearly two dozen properties—some short-form, some seen only in a small number of markets, many national favorites. PBS Kids has established a niche with a distinctive group of properties that are sufficiently differentiated from commercial children's programming to be called their own. Like other children's, programmers, PBS Kids derives some revenues from licensing and merchandising, from international program sales, and from home video products. As part of PBS, the PBS Kids division does not accept advertising, but it does receive money from PBS, CPB, "Viewers Like You," and various foundations and corporate donors.

## DEVELOPMENT OF AN ANIMATED SERIES

Initiated by the tremendous success of *The Simpsons* on FOX and of the first three Nickelodeon cartoon series (*Ren & Stimpy, Doug*, and *Rugrats*), and encouraged by the persistent need for new programming on multiple cable networks and by the success of many animated feature films, the animation business has grown up. Companies in the United States, Asia, and Europe now employ hundreds of people for the immense daily effort required to produce hours and hours of original animation.

As in other forms of television, a small number of animation suppliers tend to dominate the schedules. Often, these suppliers benefit from long-term relationships based upon past successes. (The early Nickelodeon series were notable because they were produced by suppliers who were not well-established.) DIC is a dominant supplier with its own network (see above) and dozens of properties, including *Madeline* (children's books); *Inspector Gadget* and its newer edition, *Gadget Boy*, and *Gadget and the Gadgetinis*; and a library of programs based on Archie Comics, Stargate, and more. 4Kids Entertainment has the Nintendo properties (*Kirby*, *Pokémon*, etc.), *Teenage Mutant Ninja Turtles*, even the American Kennel Club. Nickelodeon and Cartoon Network produce their own cartoons through their own animation studios, and also buy from suppliers (such as Warner Animation). Cartoon Pizza is one of several smaller shops with major credentials: Jim Jinkins and David Campbell were the principals in Jumbo Pictures, responsible for *Doug*, on Nickelodeon and later on Disney. Klasky Csupo is the company behind *Rugrats*, *Wild Thornberrys*, and various animated commercials. Frederator Studios, which supplies Nickelodeon's *The Fairly Odd Parents* and various Cartoon Network series, is led by Fred Seibert, a former Hanna-Barbera Studios president whose roots go back to the earliest MTV and Nickelodeon marketing campaigns. Typically, these companies are based in the Los Angeles area or in New York City. Nelvana (*Franklin, Little Bear, Beyblade*) and Cookie Jar Entertainment (*Arthur, Caillou*) are based in Montreal; Nelvana is now part of Corus Entertainment, a large Canadian media company, and Cookie Jar (formerly Cinar) was acquired in 2004 by private investors.

Although production budgets vary, it's difficult to produce even a modest half-hour of television animation for less than $125,000. Prices may exceed $500,000 for the finest series. In general, the cost of each episode in a half-hour animated series is likely to be in the range of $300,000 or more. Unfortunately for producers, the networks rarely pay the cost of production; their license fees provide only a modest percentage (10 percent to 50 percent) of the necessary funding. Additional monies must be found through foreign presales (selling the series before it is complete, often at a lower price than it might fetch once complete) and merchandise licenses (for video games, toys, etc.). Often, the production company bears part of the expense, hoping to recoup and turn a profit if the series is successful. This is a principal reason the market is dominated by established companies who can put together financing based upon relationships and past success, rather than by newcomers without affiliations and history.

Sources for children's properties are extremely varied. Some come from children's books (*Arthur, Clifford the Big Red Dog*), and others are developed along with toys (Nintendo's *Kirby*) or trading cards (*Pokémon, Yu-Gi-Oh!*). Some are imported from Japan or from other countries (*The Smurfs* came from Belgium, also the source of *Tin Tin*). Some children's series are based upon successful animated motion pictures (*Timon & Pumbaa*) or comics. More often, though, the concepts are original, in part because there aren't enough established properties to support the business, and in part because merchandising and licensing revenues can be controlled and not shared with established creators or other owners.

Settling on the way the characters look is often the source of colorful conversations between the creative team and the network or distributor. In theory, this is easier when a new series is based upon existing characters from another medium, but in practice, it is every bit as complicated because the long-term value of a license is at stake. The choice of voice actors is not as controversial. A surprisingly small community of professional voice actors provide the majority of cartoon voices, and most of these performers carry zillions of different voices in their heads.

Once characters are developed, sample scripts are written and sample animations are produced and tested. Then characters are changed, combined, and deleted. New ones are added. Voice actors are changed to better suit the characters' personalities.

Production is routinely digital, handled through software, not through old-fashioned animation cels. After the key creative work is completed in New York or Los Angeles, animation studios in China, Taiwan, India, Korea, and Ireland handle the detail work—the same work, produced in the United States, would cost roughly twice as much.

## Lead Time for Animated Series

Because of the number of steps involved, and the sheer number of hours required to draw and animate a half-hour series, an animated series requires more lead time. Production of a pilot usually starts a year or more prior to the first airdate. Here's how the timing might work for a typical animated series:

**Month 1:** Producer develops general concept and preliminary character sketches.

**Month 2:** Producer revises concept and character sketches, then pitches first network, which makes suggestions and ultimately turns down the project.

**Month 3:** Producer pitches another network, which makes suggestions for changes in characters, style, voices, and story lines, but agrees to finance a pilot. Pilot goes into production.

**Month 4:** Contracts are negotiated, but not signed. Designers are hard at work on characters and background concepts. Writers are revising scripts. Arrangements are being made for off-shore production.

**Month 5:** Contracts are signed. Pilot is in full production.

**Month 6:** Pilot is in post-production.

**Month 7:** Pilot is tested and evaluated by program executives.

**Month 8:** Series begins production.

**Month 12:** First episode is delivered.

By comparison, a game show or sitcom would require approximately half as much time. (Of course, schedules vary, and many animated series have moved from concept sketch to broadcast series in record time.)

## LICENSING AND CHILDREN'S TELEVISION

Children like to play and they like to watch cartoons. Television provides the cartoons. Toymakers provide the play experience, frequently with toys that are closely aligned with television properties.

Consider, for example, the wide range of merchandise associated with *SpongeBob SquarePants*: an aquarium set, jumping jellyfish toys, an alarm clock, a telephone, a shower radio, a CD player with AM/FM radio, a treasure chest clock radio, a karaoke machine (cassette or CD), a remote control TV set, books, CDs, DVDs, boxer shorts, t-shirts, hooded sweatshirts, fitted caps, wristbands, finger cuffs, running pants, a skateboard, an art desk, a doodle desk, several styles of backpack, a cookie jar, storage tubs, animation cels (priced as high as $350), Christmas tree ornaments and stockings, Halloween costumes, a table and chairs, a sofa, a parafoil kite, an inflatable pool, a 26-piece backyard water park, a bounce around (like those you see at school fairs), a bath and wash set, tableware, throw pillows, a pillowcase, a comforter, a slumber bag, a wastepaper basket, a musical wastepaper basket, and three Barbie sets with a Barbie doll and a *SpongeBob SquarePants* character. Each of these products provides an ongoing royalty stream for the licensor—and this list does not include special promotional deals with fast food restaurants, car companies, and the like. Certainly, the number of licenses that achieve this level of success is small, but this kind of list has been associated with a number of properties, including several Nickelodeon hits, *Barney and Friends*, *Thomas the Tank Engine*, *Sesame Street*, and more. In the past, valuable licenses tended to fade after a just a few years. With cable television, successful properties tend to stay on the air for a longer period, so the merchandise associated with, say, *Rugrats* has been selling well for more than a decade.

When the network also controls the license, merchandising revenues may well play into the business of programming decisions.

There are three components in the licensing business. The licensor, which is the company that holds the master rights to the copyright, is most often a network or large production and distribution company. The licensee may be a toymaker, but is as often a maker of sleepwear or t-shirts. The third component is the licensing agent—the dealmaker whose broad-based industry experience helps to link each property with the best possible licensee. Some companies maintain their own licensing departments, but a smaller number actually possess the necessary expertise to identify the best possible licenses, manage and grow the license, and deal with the inevitable decline in the value of the license. This expertise is best acquired either by hiring a licensing director with a real-world track record, or by working with an experienced licensing agent for a series of projects before bringing the effort in-house. Smaller production companies are often wise to work with a licensing agent or to organize their company for growth in the licensing sector. Toymakers, in exchange for valuable licensing rights, will sometimes pay as much as 30 percent of production costs in a new cartoon or live-action series. They may own a part of the property as well.

## FCC RULES: EDUCATIONAL CONTENT ON COMMERCIAL STATIONS

After considerable haggling, the television industry and the FCC agreed to a compromise intended to increase the educational quality of children's television (see page 293). Beginning in 1997, stations were required to program at least three hours per week of educational programming for children. This mandate can be fulfilled with network, syndicated, or local programming. In the past, educational programming has virtually assured lower ratings, so local stations have tried every possible strategy to label commercially appealing programs, notably sitcoms and cartoons, as educational. This time, the FCC will be watching more closely. Affiliates of CBS, NBC, and ABC will most likely receive network programs to fill at least some of the mandated hours, but FOX, UPN, and WB affiliates will need syndicated series to fill the slots. Local programming, in general, is not an option—quality children's programs cost serious money, and no single station can afford to produce a competitive program with the limited advertising dollars available in a local market. For an expanded discussion of these regulations, see page 293.

The ruling does not affect cable networks.

## THE INTERNATIONAL MARKETPLACE

With cable and satellite now prevalent in most of the world's television markets, it is rare to find an operation without at least one network devoted exclusively to children's programming. Often, that network is associated with Nickelodeon,

Disney, FOX, or another media brand familiar in the United States. Many of the programs seen in the U.S. are also sold to other countries, and although the voices may change for local consumption, the costly animation video does not typically require further investment.

In Canada, children watch Teletoon, a cartoon network owned by Astral Media, Corus Entertainment (which also owns Nelvana, an animation house), and Cookie Jar Entertainment; Treehouse, a channel for younger children owned by Corus; and YTV, Canada's largest children's channel, a commercial enterprise also owned by Corus. Some 40 percent of annual Teletoon revenue is paid to Canadian animation companies, making Teletoon the largest supporter of the Canadian cartoon industry.

In the U.K., the choices for children are more limited. Disney Channel, Nickelodeon, FOX Kids, and Cartoon Network are dominant forces, each with a combination of U.S. and U.K. programming. CBBC is a stand-alone channel operated by the BBC, but some CBBC children's programs are also seen on BBC1 and BBC2. The ITV stations also present children's programming, on a service called CITV.

As a rule, most national broadcasters in other countries program several hours per day for children. Nickelodeon, Disney Channel, FOX Kids, and other branded services either operate stand-alone analog cable/satellite channels or new digital channels, or both. Further details about children's television around the world can be found in Part 11.

In addition, many of the larger broadcast networks program blocks for children. Typically, these blocks are filled with a combination of programming produced within the country and acquisitions from other countries, such as the United States.

For the producer, the price paid per half-hour of children's programming is the critical issue. For many large countries (France, Japan, Australia), budgets per half-hour are about $5,000 (U.S.), sometimes as high as $10,000, but just as often as low as $2,000. For some series, the price is tens of thousands of dollars (often with a requirement for partial ownership or profit participation), but most often, in most countries, the purchase price per half-hour is a few thousand dollars at best.

## COPRODUCTIONS

Coproductions are common. For a coproduction deal, the appeal of the principal characters must be universal—or they must at least appeal to audiences in the countries of those who are doing the deal. It is best if the character or license has been previously established, most often as a toy, book series, comic book series, or motion picture. This unique selling point, or "hook," is essential to the selling process. A production team with a previous hit series can also be the hook.

Rights negotiations are the next step, and they can be complicated, especially if the property is well established and the project is intended for international exploitation. Then comes the process of shopping the project around. Most coproducers are very selective, and make their decisions based on highly subjective criteria. Creative control is always an issue; partners who are active in children's television are best suited to coproduction, but they're often opinionated and focused on their own individual business needs (particularly when one partner is involved with an educational or public agenda). Most coproduction deals are made between just two companies: one a producer, and the other either a distributor/producer or a network/media company. If the deal looks as if it will close, the producer gets to work, investing in character design, story lines, and so forth. It is not unusual for the attorneys to work for months on finalizing the deal, even though production has already begun. Delivery dates, not contracts, determine production schedules. And yes, there is some risk for the producer in this approach—which is why partners are chosen with the utmost care.

# PART 8

# REGULATION OF PROGRAMMING

# CHAPTER 33

# FREE SPEECH AND THE FIRST AMENDMENT

## HISTORY OF FREE SPEECH IN THE U.S.

In the early history of the United States, the founders of our federal government shared a thorough understanding of the need for governmental power—and a healthy fear of the abuses to which such power is prone. Therefore, between 1789 and 1791—shortly after the adoption of the Constitution—the states ratified the Bill of Rights, a series of ten amendments to the Constitution. The purpose of these amendments was to limit the authority of the newly established central power. The First Amendment established three fundamental aspects of liberty: freedom of speech, freedom of religion, and access to government. It reads as follows:

> Congress shall make no law respecting an establishment of religion, or prohibiting the free exercise thereof, or abridging the freedom of speech, or of the press; or the right of the people peaceably to assemble, and to petition the Government for a redress of grievances.

Television has repeatedly been recognized as a medium that is subject to First Amendment protection.

At first, the limits on governmental power in the Bill of Rights applied only to Congress (that is, the federal government), although some states enacted similar measures in their own constitutions. After the Civil War, a series of additional constitutional amendments were adopted that did apply to the states. Perhaps chief among these was the Fourteenth Amendment:

> No State shall make or enforce any law which shall abridge the privileges or immunities of citizens of the United States; nor shall any State deprive any person of life, liberty, or property, without due process of law; nor deny to any person within its jurisdiction the equal protection of the law.

No specific reference was made in the Fourteenth Amendment to the Bill of Rights or to the First Amendment. In the first half of the twentieth century, however, a series of judicial decisions confirmed that the Fourteenth Amendment concepts of due process and equal protection "incorporated" most of the Bill of Rights' elements and made them applicable to the states. The applicability of the free speech and free press aspects of the First Amendment to state laws was recognized by the Supreme Court in decisions between 1925 and 1931.

The language of the First Amendment is extremely broad. Congress and, by incorporation, the states "shall make no law . . . abridging the freedom of speech, or of the press." If taken literally, this wording would seem to imply that speech, the press, and (by extension) television, are to be completely free of governmental regulation. Notwithstanding the plain language of the amendment, however, courts have always recognized exceptions and balanced the government's interest in various content restrictions against the free speech "interest" expressed in the First Amendment. The results of this process are rules that govern the content of television programming.

## RULES GOVERNING CONTENT

The content of television production is subject to a series of laws and restrictions—most of them imposed by our legal system, some of them imposed by the television industry on itself as a matter of self-regulation. Some of these rules, such as those governing obscenity, are enforced directly by the government with criminal penalties. More prevalent are the laws enabling private individuals and companies to control the use of creative properties, the expression of certain kinds of hurtful falsehoods, or the invasion of rights of privacy and publicity.

These rules and restrictions can be viewed negatively—as handcuffs on the activities of a program creator—because they conflict with the freedoms granted by the First Amendment. They can also be viewed positively, as rights that can be asserted to protect the economic and moral interests of individuals, businesses, and the community. However they are considered, these restrictions form the legal structure within which programming is created. Anyone participating in the production process will benefit from a working knowledge of them.

The following three chapters deal with these content rules. The level of detail in a general treatment such as this must be, by its very nature, somewhat superficial. In addition, many content issues are governed by state law, and there are likely to be variations in the law from state to state, even when the laws recognize the same underlying principles. When we do cite specific state laws, we have paid particular attention to the laws of California and New York, since so much of the television industry is concentrated in these states. In cases for which an exact knowledge of the applicable state or federal law is important, it is advisable to consult an attorney.

# CHAPTER 34

# INTELLECTUAL PROPERTY: COPYRIGHT

There is one restriction on television content that itself has a constitutional basis. Article 1, Section 8 of the Constitution reads: "Congress shall have power... to promote the progress of science and useful arts by securing for limited times to authors and inventors the exclusive right to their respective writings and discoveries . . . ."

Following this lead, Congress has created a series of copyright laws, starting in 1790. The most recent general revision was enacted in 1976. Works created before January 1, 1978, (when the 1976 Act took effect) were subject to the provisions of the 1909 Copyright Act. For events after December 31, 1977, these works are governed by the 1976 Act, modified by certain special provisions. All works created since January 1, 1978, are fully covered by the rules of the 1976 Act, which introduced several innovations discussed more fully below. The major developments in copyright law since 1976 have been the changes made necessary by the U.S. joining the Berne Convention, which became effective March 1, 1989, and the attempt made in the Digital Millennium Copyright Act of 1998 to shape the law to the challenges of the emerging electronic marketplace of ideas.

## SCOPE OF FEDERAL LAW

Under the 1909 Act, most unpublished works were subject to state law protection under theories of "common law copyright." With a few limited exceptions, such as stage plays, federal copyright extended only to published works. Under the 1976 Act, federal copyright was extended to cover all unpublished works as well, and the role of state law almost completely disappeared.

## RIGHTS AND PROTECTIONS UNDER COPYRIGHT LAW

### Material Protected by Copyright Law

Copyright law gives protection for "original works of authorship." Section 102 of the 1976 Act states:

(a) Copyright protection subsists, in accordance with this title, in original works of authorship fixed in any tangible medium of expression, now known or later developed, from which they can be perceived, reproduced, or otherwise communicated, either directly or with the aid of a machine or device. Works of authorship include the following categories: (1) literary works; (2) musical works, including any accompanying words; (3) dramatic works, including any accompanying music; (4) pantomimes and choreographic works; (5) pictorial, graphic, and sculptural works; (6) motion pictures and other audiovisual works; (7) sound recordings; and (8) architectural works.

(b) In no case does copyright protection for an original work of authorship extend to any idea, procedure, process, system, method of operation, concept, principle, or discovery, regardless of the form in which it is described, explained, illustrated, or embodied in such work.

Television programs receive protection as "motion pictures or other audiovisual works." Scripts are protected as "literary works" or "dramatic works"; designs, as "pictorial, graphic, and sculptural works." Indeed, any creative work that is "fixed in a tangible medium of expression" (and thus satisfies the constitutional requirement of a "writing") can potentially be covered by copyright protection—provided it is not simply an "idea," "concept," or "principle."

Courts have held that the expression of an idea is copyrightable, but that the underlying idea itself is not. Infringement occurs only if there is a "substantial similarity" between a protected element in the copyrighted work and some element of the new work. Of course, it is not always easy to tell where a raw idea leaves off and protectable expression begins. The point where an illegal rip-off occurs is a matter for judgment in each case, and a lawyer's advice may be helpful. There is also the "smell test": if the proposed use "stinks" to you, it probably will stink to a judge.

To prove an infringement of copyright, there must be evidence of copying. Proof of actual copying can be inferred from access, which indicates the opportunity to copy. If the similar work was a truly independent creation, no infringement has taken place. Although ideas are free from copyright protection, they can be subject to contractual protection (see page 276). Names of characters and names of shows, like ideas, are not subject to copyright protection. They can, however, receive protection under theories of unfair competition: if an association with the name is strongly established by another use, there could be public confusion over the new use (see page 287).

Length also matters to some degree—both in deciding if there has been copying and in the fair use context (see page 268). Even so, a few clever lines of fiction or a few bars of music can constitute protectable expression; for example, the short, popular song "Happy Birthday" is protected. Media formats, however, fall into a gray area. For instance, the idea of a game show that awards prizes for answering questions cannot be copyrighted, nor can such aspects of a game show as a board listing the questions, a pretty female costar, or a display that indicates the score. But a near clone of the total look and overall feel of a particular game show would probably be found to be a copyright violation.

Like ideas, facts in and of themselves are not copyrightable. Still, whether fact or fiction, a particular motion picture or video sequence, as shot and preserved on film or tape, is very likely to have enough expressive content for copyright protection, if only in the choices made in framing the shot. Therefore, one must be particularly careful in copying verbatim video clips or recorded audio segments. Courts have implied that video clips as short as seven or eight seconds can contain enough expression to merit protection, notwithstanding the doctrine of fair use.

## Rights Protected by Copyright Law

United States copyright law gives the copyright owner(s) a particular set of exclusive rights in a work in the United States. The general rules are set forth in Section 106 of the 1976 Act:

> Subject to sections 107 through 122, the owner of copyright under this title has the exclusive rights to do and to authorize any of the following:
>
> (1) to reproduce the copyrighted work in copies or phonorecords;
>
> (2) to prepare derivative works based upon the copyrighted work;
>
> (3) to distribute copies or phonorecords of the copyrighted work to the public by sale or other transfer of ownership, or by rental, lease, or lending;
>
> (4) in the case of literary, musical, dramatic, and choreographic works, pantomimes, and motion pictures and other audiovisual works, to perform the copyrighted work publicly;
>
> (5) in the case of literary, musical, dramatic, and choreographic works, pantomimes, and pictorial, graphic, or sculptural works, including the individual images of a motion picture or other audiovisual work, to display the copyrighted work publicly; and
>
> (6) in the case of sound recordings, to perform the copyrighted work publicly by means of a digital audio transmission.

The copyright owner controls the making and distribution of reproductions of the work, including prints, computer files, and DVDs. In most cases, however, once an authorized copy has been sold, further dispositions of that particular copy are free from control. This is sometimes called the "first sale doctrine." A special exception to this rule, however, prevents the rental of sound recordings and computer software. Rentals of authorized video copies are not restricted.

No one can create a derivative work without the owner's authorization. This includes the production and/or distribution of sequels, remakes, series, spin-offs, dubbed versions, novelizations, and any other work that embodies elements of protected expression from the original work.

The owner controls the public performance or display of a copyrighted work, but its private performance or display is not restricted. For example, a DVD or videocassette can legally be shown for free by its rightful owner in the home to family and normal guests. Charge admission, however, or change the venue to a public bar, and the showing probably becomes a public performance, subject to the control of the copyright holder.

## Authorship and Work for Hire

Under the 1976 Copyright Act, the author or authors of the work own the copyright, from the moment of the work's creation. Joint authors share the ownership of their copyrighted work. Unless they agree otherwise, each joint owner can authorize the nonexclusive use of the work, subject to a responsibility to account for the other author's share of any earnings. Exclusive licenses require the consent of all authors. To avoid confusion, it is often advisable for joint authors to enter into an agreement covering the licensing of their work.

The "author" is not always the living person who creates the product. Under the "work for hire" doctrine of the 1976 Act, an individual or company that employs the actual creator can be deemed the author. "Employment" generally means just that: showing up for work on a regular basis and having the necessary tax and social security payments drawn from one's paycheck (see page 414). These rules on actual employment are relaxed in the case of audiovisual works for film or television, where a consultant's or other independent contractor's work can be "for hire" if there is a signed written agreement expressly confirming this fact. Collective works, translations, compilations, tests, atlases, and instructional works can also be considered works for hire on this basis.

## OBTAINING COPYRIGHT PROTECTION

The formal requirements for obtaining copyright protection have been significantly loosened under the 1976 Act, and even further liberalized by the Berne Convention changes. Under the old (1909) act, publication with notice and registration were both necessary for federal protection, but copyright now attaches automatically at the moment of creation.

## Copyright Registration

Under the 1909 law and, to a lesser degree, the 1976 law prior to the Berne Convention's amendments, registration at publication was a requirement for any protection. Although copyright itself is no longer at stake, some of the protections awarded under copyright can be lost by the failure to take certain registration steps. For a work of U.S. origin, which cannot claim all the protections of the Berne Convention, registration is a prerequisite for bringing a copyright infringement case against a third party. Registration can be done at almost any time to make a suit possible, but should be done as soon as possible to avoid procedural delays. Early registration (within three months of publication) is also necessary in order to claim attorney's fees and the statutory damages provided under the 1976 Copyright Act for infringement of a published work (see page 272). The Berne Convention removes these incentives and penalties with respect to most foreign-source works.

Copyright registration forms as well as information about current fees and procedures can be obtained by writing to the Copyright Office, Library of Congress, Washington, DC, 20540, or through the Web site at www.copyright.gov.

## Copyright Notice

Until the Berne Convention took effect in the U.S. on March 1, 1989, giving notice of copyright in a conspicuous place on the work itself was required to preserve protection for a published work; even now it remains a good idea. The statutory notice combines three elements. The first element is a use of the word "copyright," the abbreviation "Copr.," or the symbol ©. For sound recordings, the symbol is also used to indicate a copyright notice. The next element is the year of first publication of the work; certain private circulations of a work do not constitute publication. The third element is the name of the entity—whether a real person or a business—that is claiming copyright ownership. By custom, notices have gone on or near the title page of a written work, or in the head credits or final credits of a film or television program. Publication of a copyrighted work prior to March 1, 1989, without this type of notice could result in a loss of copyright protection. Provisions for correcting errors in notice are also set out in the law.

Since March 1, 1989, the Berne Convention makes notice unnecessary for protection, even for U.S. authors. Notice is still necessary under the Uniform Copyright Convention, which continues in force for the U.S. and adds protection in a few additional countries, most notably the countries of the former U.S.S.R. Notice is also useful in deterring potential infringers, in establishing the chain of title on the work itself, and in negating an "innocent infringement" defense. As a rule of thumb, if displaying or distributing the work makes one think that claiming copyright protection might be necessary, then putting on the appropriate copyright notice is probably a good idea.

## Deposit of Copyrighted Works

In order to help build the collections of the Library of Congress, a prerequisite of registration was always the deposit of two complete copies of the best edition of the work. Even with the current voluntary registration, in order to keep the collection complete the law requires sending along two copies of the best edition of any published U.S. work to Library of Congress within three months of publication. If the work is a motion picture or television program, the deposit requirement is one complete copy of the unpublished or published work and a separate written description of its contents, such as a continuity, press book, or synopsis. For certain classes of works, where deposit of the whole is difficult or impractical, special exceptions can be made. For sculptures or certain qualifying motion pictures, for instance, a deposit of photographs or other identifying material may suffice. Care should be taken to follow the deposit requirements spelled out for the particular form of registration.

## Supplemental and Substitute Proofs of Copyright

In addition to the copyright law procedures, authors sometimes take additional steps to help prove their rights in the material they have written. For instance, the Writers Guild of America is a registry for television and film scripts, treatments, and other material, and online registration is now possible—see www.wga.org. Registration with the Guild does not provide any additional legal protection other than that normally provided by copyright, but it can serve as useful evidence that the author in question created the material. In fact, the registry is primarily used to establish that an idea or written material existed on a certain date. While registered works are rarely withdrawn as evidence for copyright or contractual disputes, written confirmation from the Writers Guild registry that a work was deposited on a given date is more frequently requested as evidence. This service cannot be used to establish credit for a given work, however, and registration does not imply credit for authorship. Registration is open to members and nonmembers of the WGA alike.

As a similar evidentiary matter, authors sometimes mail copies of their work to themselves in a sealed envelope, hoping that the postmark will provide some proof as to the date of creation and the original authorship of the writer. This measure is of dubious value, and of no value whatsoever if the envelope is opened prior to its formal presentation as evidence.

## Compulsory Licenses and Other Specific Exceptions

There are certain exceptions in the copyright law to the exclusive rights normally enjoyed by a copyright holder. For instance, various compulsory licenses are granted under the 1976 Copyright Act. Section 111 gives cable systems a compulsory license to retransmit any material going out over the air on a traditional U.S. television broadcast. For distant signals imported into the area, the cable system must make a required payment to the Copyright Office. The Copyright Royalty Tribunal then acts as a disbursing agent, distributing payments among the program copyright holders who file claim (see page 53). With the enactment of the Copyright Royalty and Distribution Reform Act of 2004, much of the oversight and application of this process will be in the hands of three full-time copyright royalty judges. Appeals from their determinations will be heard by the United States Court of Appeals for the District of Columbia Circuit.

Similar compulsory license provisions exist under Section 119, setting up a statutory license for certain satellite rebroadcasts of superstations and network stations in otherwise underserved areas (see page 50). This provision also seeks to encourage the setting of fees by voluntary negotiation.

The Copyright Royalty Tribunal and the Royalty Judges also have jurisdiction over the licensing rates that public broadcasters pay for certain published nondramatic musical works and published pictorial, graphic, and sculptural works (see Section 118 of the Copyright Act). This exception doesn't cover programming itself, just some elements that might be used in programming. Other television-related exceptions to the copyright holder's rights include the right of a transmitting organization, such as a station or cable company, to make "ephemeral" copies of the work for help in duly licensed transmissions (see Section 112 of the Act).

Section 110 permits the performance or display of copyrighted materials "in the course of face-to-face teaching activities of a nonprofit educational institution, in a classroom or similar place devoted to instruction"—provided, in the case of audiovisual works, that the copy being shown was lawfully made. Under Section 108, libraries and other archival institutions can also do limited copying to keep the items in their collection in good condition.

## Fair Use

The 1976 Copyright Act finally codified what used to be court-made law that the "fair use" of copyrighted material does not represent an infringement of copyright. Section 107 of the 1976 Act provides that "the fair use of a copyrighted work . . . for purposes such as criticism, comment, news reporting, teaching (including multiple copies for classroom use), scholarship or research, is not an infringement of copyright." The statute goes on to specify four factors that are to be taken into account, nonexclusively, in determining whether fair use has been made:

(1) the purpose and character of the use, including whether such use is of a commercial nature or is for nonprofit educational purposes;

(2) the nature of the copyrighted work;

(3) the amount and substantiality of the portion used in relation to the copyrighted work as a whole; and

(4) the effect of the use upon the potential market or value of the copyrighted work.

Fair use does not require the permission of the copyright holder. In the television context, fair use permits the use of short excerpts of films, television programs, and other copyrighted works for purposes such as news, information, reviewing, and teaching. Excerpts of a little over a minute or more from a feature film, however, have been held to be excessive and beyond the scope of fair use, and, as a practical matter, E&O insurers (explained on page 272) may balk at relying on fair use to justify copyrighted excerpts in excess of 30 seconds. Fair use is generally not permitted for material that has not been previously broadcast or otherwise published, although the statute makes it clear that this is not in itself a bar to fair use.

## The First Amendment and News Items

In limited cases, the First Amendment also provides a means, analogous to fair use, for reproducing copyrighted works without permission. This exception to copyright law pertains to cases in which the information in the copyrighted work—typically a film clip or still photograph—is so newsworthy in and of itself that, in the words of Nimmer on Copyright, "no amount of words describing the idea . . . could substitute for the public insight gained through the photographs." This rationale has been applied to photographs of the My Lai massacre in Vietnam and the Zapruder film of the Kennedy assassination, and probably applies to the Abu Ghraib prisoner abuse pictures as well.

## TERM OF COPYRIGHT

The 1909 Act provided for an initial copyright term of 28 years from the date of publication or, in the case of unpublished works, 28 years from the date of registration. That statute established a further renewal term, also of 28 years, available for the extension of the copyright. Prior to 1992, failure to renew pre-1978 copyrights put the work in the public domain; now, renewal is automatic through the operation of law. The renewal term was progressively extended until the 1976 Act set it at 47 years, giving a total of 75 years of protection to works that have been properly copyrighted and renewed under the 1909 Act.

In 1998, responding to strong lobbying from intellectual property owners and faced with Disney's particular concern that Mickey Mouse was due to go out of copyright, Congress added another 20 years, making the new term 95 years. Works that had already gone into the public domain didn't get re-protected, and thus any work published before January 1, 1923, is now in the public domain. Any pre-1978 copyright published since then, even if properly renewed, will eventually go into the public domain in the United States 95 years after its copyright date, provided that Congress doesn't buckle under yet again around 2018 and add more time to the term. The term of foreign copyright protection can vary, with some countries giving shorter protections, some the same, and others longer.

Thanks to the 1998 extensions, post-1978 works now have a copyright period lasting the life of the author plus 70 years. In the case of works with multiple authors, the time runs from the death of the author who is the last to die. Works made for hire and works published under pseudonyms now have a copyright term of a flat 95 years from the date of initial publication or 120 years from the date of creation, whichever expires first.

## Termination of Transfers

Copyright law permits authors (and once the authors are deceased certain specified individuals) to terminate outstanding licenses, assignments, and other transfers of copyright after a specified period has passed. These termination windows reflect the intention that certain aspects of the renewal copyright were meant to benefit authors and not assignees. Section 203 of the 1976 Copyright Act provides a right of termination for post-1978 transfers of rights. This allows the copyright holder—or, if he or she is dead, a designated family member—to terminate grants of copyright by notice to the grantee given within a five-year window that starts either (i) 35 years from the date of the grant, or (ii) in the case of grants covering rights to publish the work, 40 years from the grant or 35 years from publication, whichever is earlier. This termination will shut off new uses under the grant, but the continued use of derivative works prepared by the licensee prior to the termination is permitted. Thus, a television film made under a valid grant can still be shown after the termination. It may, however, have to face competition from a new version made under the grant of new rights.

There is also a provision allowing the termination of grants made prior to 1978. Under Section 304 of the Copyright Act, an author or designated family member can terminate prior grants within a five-year window starting either on January 1, 1978, or 56 years from the date the copyright was originally secured, whichever is later. This allows the author or his or her heirs to enjoy the benefits of the extended renewal term given by the 1976 Act and later extensions. There is also an exception permitting the continued use of previously created or derivative works.

In the case of each of these termination rights, no advance waiver will be effective. It should also be noted that in the case of a work for hire, the employer is actually considered the author, and so the paid creator would not have the benefit or these terminations.

There is one further termination right, which carries over from the 1909 Act. Under Section 304(a), the renewal procedures for pre-1978 copyrights still in their first term are preserved. Grant of the renewal term could be made by the author in advance. This grant, however, is not effective against the authorized family members, who could exercise the renewal right if the author died before he or she did. This gives an unlimited termination right to the family members in this narrow circumstance, although it can be waived in advance by the family members. The statute holds no exception for derivative works, and a Supreme Court case has established that there is no automatic right to continue to exploit already produced films or television programs based on such a terminated grant. Over time, the works for which this is a problem have naturally made their way through the system, and the problem is largely moot.

## Exclusive Licenses, Assignments, Mortgages

The copyright law requires that an exclusive assignment or license (including a mortgage or other security interest in the copyrighted work) be in a signed document in order to be effective between the parties. Indeed, in order to be effective against certain third parties, any such exclusive license or assignment should not only be executed as a signed agreement, but also be recorded with the Copyright Office. This gives legal notice to the world in general of the contents of the license or assignment.

## COPYRIGHT INFRINGEMENT

A copyright is infringed when someone exercises one of the exclusive rights granted by the 1976 Copyright Act without the consent of the copyright holder, without approval from a licensee of the copyright holder, or without the excuse of a compulsory license, fair use, or other exception. In order to win a lawsuit over an infringement, the plaintiff must prove several key elements. To begin with, it must be shown that there is a valid copyright in the material. The person suing must be either the copyright owner or the holder of an exclusive right that is being infringed. The exclusive-rights concept also applies to beneficial rights. For instance, an author who has assigned his or her original rights to someone else while retaining a royalty interest may still be able to sue as a beneficial-rights owner.

It must also be shown that a protected element of the original work has been used in some forbidden way. This involves establishing two points: first, that the infringing item or element is "substantially similar" to the protected work, and second, that the protected work was actually the basis for the infringing item or element. The former is determined by the judge or jury via straightforward comparison, without the testimony of experts. The latter can be proven directly or inferred so long as the plaintiff can prove that the alleged infringer had access to the original work. For instance, if the original author had kept the original work in a trunk and never showed it to anyone, there could be no infringement because access was impossible.

Generally, an outraged copyright owner can sue not only the original infringer, but also anyone along the chain of publication. Lack of knowledge that a protected work is being infringed is not a defense, although it may reduce damage liability. For instance, if a scriptwriter plagiarizes a protected book in a teleplay and then sells it to a producer as an original piece, the producer, network, and individual stations can all, in theory, be sued as infringers.

## Errors and Omissions (E&O) Insurance

This kind of exposure to liability makes Errors and Omissions (E&O) insurance a key part of any contract for distribution or telecasting. Most such contracts call for the producer to get and maintain E&O coverage for at least the first few years a program is shown; sometimes the required coverage period is linked to the three-year statute of limitations on copyright claims. E&O insurance also covers claims for libel, slander, privacy, and publicity; it does not usually cover contract disputes. Coverage limits of $3 million for all occurrences and $1 million per single claim are common. Most distribution agreements call for the naming of the distributor as an additional insured party on the policy.

E&O insurers generally require that certain clearance procedures be followed, and sometimes a list of steps to take is printed on their application form. In addition to setting out the insurance requirements, this list is also a useful reminder of good production practices. E&O insurers are by nature fairly conservative in the risks and uncertainties that they are willing to tolerate on a production. Any project that will rely on fair use or First Amendment arguments to justify using material or depicting an individual should consult with a lawyer experienced in dealing with E&O insurers.

## Remedies for Infringement

The winning plaintiff in an infringement lawsuit has several possible remedies available. The first is an injunction against any further infringing use. The court can also force a recall of copies still in the channels of distribution, or forbid further unauthorized showings.

In addition to putting a stop to the infringement, the aggrieved party can also recover damages and profits. The damages may be set to reflect actual harm suffered, such as lost sales; recovering profits involves compensating the plaintiff with the economic benefits of the infringement. Both approaches are inherently speculative and may be inadequate to right the wrong. For instance, if a money-losing TV show is based without permission on a copyrighted film that also lost money, an amount of real damages and improper profits may be hard to prove. It is for such a situation that copyright law has established *statutory damages*. This is a set amount that a court can levy as damages—an award based simply on the infringement itself, which does not require proof of a particular level of actual harm. For most infringements, the range of these damages is currently $750 to $30,000 for all infringements of a given copyright; for willful infringements, the statutory damages can be up to $150,000. Awards of legal fees may also be given, which in some cases may exceed actual damages.

## Criminal Penalties

In addition to the *civil* remedies discussed above, there are also *criminal* penalties for infringement done "willfully and for purposes of commercial advantage or private financial gain." Serious commercial piracy of motion pictures (including television programs) involves making, selling, or distributing more than ten copies, including distribution by electronic means. For criminal sales with a retail value of more than $2,500 within any six-month period, the penalty is a fine of up to $250,000 and up to five years in jail. Repeat offenses can be punished by up to ten years in jail. The use of counterfeit trademarks in such trafficking can result in even higher penalties and fines. Noncommercial piracy can receive jail terms of up to three years for a first offense and six years thereafter.

## Piracy: Taping, DVD, and File-Sharing

Before the advent of home video, DVDs, and computers, the unauthorized copying of an audiovisual program was expensive and difficult. Infringing uses of such copies were relatively easy to police. Home video machines started the change; now computers, DVD burners, file-sharing programs, and the Internet are vastly accelerating the potential for piracy by generating both a simple mechanism for creating copies and an international medium for their distribution, whether for sale or by gratis exchange.

*Time-shifting*, the practice of recording shows off a broadcast station, or a cable or satellite service for later viewing, is probably the most benign (and the hardest to police) of these activities. When VCRs first came into use, the production community brought suit against Sony in an attempt either to stop the sale of VCRs or to set up an extra charge on the sale of blank cassettes that would be deposited into a group fund. Producers would then collect a share of this fund, much as they do with compulsory cable license fees. This scheme was squashed when the U.S. Supreme Court held that home recording for the purposes of time-shifting constituted fair use, not copyright infringement. More recently, digital video recorders (DVRs) such as TiVo and ReplayTV have upped the ante by making time-shifting much easier. They are also making alliances with satellite broadcasters and other content providers, with an interesting mix of permissions and restrictions accompanying the links. The interaction of these recorders with the broadcast flag rules described below will produce its own set of challenges, although the approach on the table at this writing looks likely to be permissive within a single recording and playback machine. Overall, the DVR world is likely to offer more authorized options but be less freewheeling than the VCR days.

The Internet is shaping up as the real challenge to copyright holders in television. As bandwidth availability and digital compression advance, the slow transmission times that acted as a brake on video file-sharing are fading away. As television itself goes digital (see page 38), the possibilities are increasing, causing more and more concern among television copyright owners. The Digital Millennium Copyright Act of 1998 addressed some of the challenges new technology poses to the existing legal structures. For example, the 1998 Act exonerates from liability all online service providers who unwittingly provide a conduit for the transmission of illegal copies. In order for a service provider to qualify for the limits on liability, it cannot be complicit in the practices, and it must move to stop infringing activities that are called to its attention. Colleges and universities often provide Web access; where student file-sharing is a common practice, the institution may be forced to try to control these violations in order to fend off liability.

The shift to digital television is creating a new opportunity for appropriating programming and a new technological fix—the "broadcast flag"—in an attempt to counter it. In the past, taping or otherwise copying analog off-air content usually led to relatively poor replication, making it an inadequate source for sharing and selling unauthorized copies. The high-quality digital signals coming into the home now via digital broadcast, cable, and satellite are not so limited. At the instigation of the major film studios, in 2003 the FCC adopted technical rules permitting the addition of a broadcast flag to the signals. This digital tag will alert complying copying and playback equipment that the film or program in question is not meant to be copied in a way that it could be shared with others, and the technology will disable the attempt. Is this actually the wave of the future? In May, 2005, a three-judge panel of the Federal Court of Appeals for the DC Circuit overturned these rules, holding that the FCC had exceeded its authority in proposing them. Given the persistence of the players, an attempted appeal to the Supreme Court seems likely. The eventual shape of this or any similar approach is still to be determined.

Outright piracy—that is, the unauthorized copying and commercial sale of works not publicly disseminated by broadcast or cable, or the unauthorized copying of any program or film for commercial purposes—is punishable by the civil and criminal statutes of copyright law (see page 272). While at a practical level the practice of copying tapes, DVDs, or files for friends and family is unlikely to come to anyone's notice, the potential penalties are stiff. Commercial piracy is a major concern of the production and distribution communities; they expend considerable resources in the U.S. and in some other countries on finding and closing down pirates.

## INTERNATIONAL COPYRIGHT LAW

### International Implications of U.S. Copyright Law

The scope of U.S. copyright law is essentially domestic. Although unpublished works by foreign authors are fully protected, that protection will cease on publication unless (i) one or more of the authors is a national, domiciliary, or governmental authority of a country that has a copyright treaty with the U.S. or is a stateless person; (ii) the work is first published in the U.S. or in a country that is, at the time of publication, a treaty party; (iii) the work is a sound recording that was first fixed in a treaty party; (iv) the work is a physical work (pictorial, graphic, sculptural, or architectural) incorporated or embodied in a building in the U.S. or a treaty party; (v) the work is first published by the United Nations or the Organization of American States; or (vi) the country of origin is covered by a special presidential proclamation. The law of most foreign countries is similarly limited, and will not protect a U.S.-source work unless there are applicable international agreements in effect.

The U.S. was a relative latecomer in joining the conventions (most notably, the Berne Convention and the Universal Copyright Convention) that offer the major degree of international copyright protection. U.S. copyright law evolved with a variety of idiosyncrasies that did not meet the requirements of the conventions, and that the U.S. was reluctant to give up. Therefore, up until 1955— when the U.S. joined the Universal Copyright Convention (UCC)—protection of a U.S. work abroad depended upon either the existence of an individually negotiated treaty between the U.S. and the foreign country in question, or the simultaneous publication of the work in the U.S. and a country (frequently Canada) that was an adherent to one or more of the conventions. The UCC was, in fact, tailored to permit such elements of the 1909 Act as the notice requirements, which were not permitted under the Berne Convention. The UCC gave protection throughout much of the world, but there were still gaps, some of which could be closed by joining the Berne Convention. With the adoption of the 1976 Copyright Act, many of these inconsistencies were eliminated, and the U.S. began seriously to consider joining Berne as well.

The principal stumbling block to joining the Berne Convention was its requirement that moral rights (see page 286) be protected. Once it was determined that the U.S. gave enough protection to moral rights to qualify without changing existing law, Congress ratified the Berne Convention, which came into effect on March 1, 1989. Adherence to Berne did require some changes to U.S. law, however, particularly in the area of formalities (see page 266). Foreign works coming under Berne get even easier treatment on the registration point—copyright registration is not a prerequisite to bringing a lawsuit.

Under Berne, U.S. works receive the same protection in another Berne country as applies to works originally copyrighted in that country. In some cases, this can include a copyright term in excess of that granted in the U.S. Whenever a question of foreign copyrights is raised, it is wise to consult with a knowledgeable expert.

International copyright protection gained additional support in the 1990s through the activities of the World Trade Organization (WTO) and the World

Intellectual Property Organization (WIPO). As part of the most recent revisions of the General Agreement on Tariffs and Trade (GATT), a new side accord was ratified, called the "Agreement on Trade Related Aspects of Intellectual Property Rights, Including Trade in Counterfeit Goods," or, more usably, TRIPS. This agreement established certain minimum standards for intellectual property protection as a prerequisite for WTO membership. In large degree, it piggybacks on the Berne rules, but it does not require the moral rights protection that clashes with traditional U.S. free-market notions (see page 287). It does require some form of compensation for video rentals in countries where pirating is widespread; the WIPO copyright treaty has taken a similar approach. TRIPS also extends protection to computer programs and sound recordings.

## Approaches to Copyright-Related Laws in Other Countries

Measures such as Berne and TRIPS have led to some convergence in the copyright and related laws around the world. Nonetheless, some significant differences in approach remain and are worth noting. Most importantly, much of the world views the Anglo-American "copyright" approach as being excessively driven by economic considerations and insufficiently weighted toward creative and artistic concerns. Reflecting this difference, the doctrine of moral rights has been accepted in much of the developed world. American television producers are sometimes surprised by the limits that moral rights doctrines can place on certain kinds of exploitation, particularly anything that involves chopping up an existing work.

The country-by-country variations that may be involved are beyond the scope of this book—the summary of U.S. law set out above would need to be repeated over and over. Nonetheless, awareness of the potential for significant differences is critical. If international production or exploitation is an important element in the finance and use of a television project, the producers and distributors should identify the key target jurisdictions and take steps before production begins to address any peculiar needs that arise under their laws.

## PROTECTION OF IDEAS

Although it is not possible to copyright an idea, this does not mean that an idea is completely unprotectable. In most of the United States, it is possible to obtain at least some protection under contract theories for an idea disclosed to another when the two parties have made a deal requiring compensation for the idea. For instance, a signed contract to pay for disclosing an idea will normally be enforced. A studio or producer may request a well-known author to submit raw ideas for programming, and can agree to pay for the ideas. The most notorious example of such an arrangement was the subject of a lawsuit that found that Art Buchwald had supplied the idea behind the film *Coming to America.*

Buchwald had a signed contract with Paramount Pictures promising to pay him for ideas he supplied, with extra payments and net profits due if an idea were actually used as a basis for the film. Buchwald's victory over Paramount was not complete; after years of making money, no net profits have been generated by *Coming to America.*

Where there is a signed contract, the most frequently contested issue is whether or not the idea in question, or enough of it to be recognizable, was actually used. An idea, by its very nature, lacks those expressive elements that would give rise to copyright protection. Therefore, the standard of similarity necessary for an idea case is generally less stringent than that which would be required for a copyright infringement case. Frequently the contract will provide words such as "based on" to indicate the necessary relationship between the idea and the final product. In applying the "based on" concept, courts have used a variety of analyses, including a kind of mental paternity test. If it can be shown that the end product evolved naturally from the original idea, the final product will be held to be based on the idea, even if many changes have been made and the number of actual elements in common has become relatively sparse. Any defendant in such an action will try to show a different source for the end product.

Even in the absence of a signed, written agreement, courts will sometimes still give protection to the provider of an idea. For instance, if there is a verbal understanding or if it is the accepted expectation in the industry that a payment would be made if the idea was disclosed and used, then an implied contract will sometimes be found. Other theories for giving implied protection are "unjust enrichment," fraud, and the breach of a fiduciary relationship. For example, if an attorney (who has a fiduciary relationship to his client) uses for his own profit a television program idea disclosed by the client in confidence, it is likely that the client would be able to recover the fair value of the idea from the attorney.

In some states, such as New York, it must be shown that the idea was original and novel before any contract protection, whether express or implied, will be given. In such a state, an idea that was relatively obvious may not be given any legal protection.

## UNSOLICITED MATERIAL

The desire of authors to impose implied contracts on producers, on the one hand, and the desire of producers, on the other hand, to avoid them, has led to a variety of strategies in the submission of unsolicited material. Some producers refuse to review any unsolicited material, returning such submissions to the sender either unopened or unread and thereby protecting against future copyright infringement suits. Other producers will review such material, but only after sending a letter to the person who has submitted the material, seeking to counter any implication that a contract exists for its use (see sample letter in

Appendix 1.2) Some producers find these actions too time-consuming—they simply send rejections for material they don't wish to use and negotiate agreements for material that they do wish to use.

Writers, when submitting unsolicited material, will sometimes seek to imply that payment is to be made, even if non-copyrightable aspects of the material should be used. A writer may enclose with the material a letter that spells out, in some nonthreatening manner, that the writer expects to be compensated if the material is used by the producer. While the efficacy of these one-sided letters is open to question, they are probably better than nothing.

In the end, the writer's greatest protection probably comes from the fact that it is usually relatively inexpensive, in the overall scheme of a production, for an established producer to pay a rights fee of some kind to the persons actually supplying ideas for the program. Indeed, such a license with one person can provide, under the paternity-test theory, protection against claims brought by other potential originators of the idea. Before bringing charges of theft for aspects of a project that was casually submitted, the aggrieved writer should consider that similar ideas may have been suggested to active production companies on more than one occasion.

# CHAPTER 35
# PROTECTION OF PERSONAL RIGHTS

## LIBEL AND SLANDER

*Libel* and *slander* are twin actions frequently linked under the word "defamation." *Defamation* has been defined as the publication or broadcast of false information, not otherwise privileged, which exposes the person (or other entity) so described to hatred, contempt, or ridicule; which causes the person to be shunned or avoided; or which has the tendency to injure the person in his or her occupation. Liability attaches not only to the individual who writes or speaks the falsehood, but to any other entity "publishing" it as well. Dissemination by a broadcast or cable network, satellite, video device, Web cast, or local station will generally constitute such publishing, although a cable system or Internet provider, simply relaying a service that it does not control, may be free from challenge on the theory that it is a mere transmitter.

These are difficult and confused areas of the law. Indeed, one of the most respected legal treatises on the subject once declared:

> It must be confessed at the beginning that there is a great deal of the law of defamation which makes no sense. It contains anomalies and absurdities for which no legal writer has ever had a kind word, and it is a curious compound of a strict liability imposed upon innocent defendants, as rigid in extremes as anything found in the law, with a blind and almost perverse refusal to compensate the plaintiff for real and very serious harm (*Prosser and Keaton on the Law of Torts, 5th edition*, 1984).

Libel involves written defamation and slander involves spoken defamation—the distinction is one of the anomalies, mentioned above. In the case of slander, it is frequently necessary to prove actual specific damages, while in the case of libel such damages can often be presumed from the nature of the defamatory writing. Although it is still open to some dispute in a few states, any form of recorded television production will generally be treated under the laws of libel even though it is not in a written form. Purely live broadcast may instead constitute slander in some states.

## Requirements for Defamation

The first prerequisite for defamation is that the offensive statement must in fact describe the person complaining of the falsehood. The actual name need not be used for the claim to succeed, so long as a reasonable person would think that the person complaining is the one to whom the defamatory statement in fact refers. Defamation claims have been upheld even when not only the name has been changed, but also many of the personal characteristics, such as body shape, hair color, and age. If the claimant can show that there was sufficient identifying detail to lead reasonable people to believe that he or she was the one being talked about, then an action for defamation can be sustained.

Ironically, the very act of changing names and some character traits can give rise to the kind of falsehood that is actionable. Therefore, if fictionalization of a real character is to take place in a program, the writer, producer, and director are advised to go to great lengths to clearly distance the fictionalized character from its original model. Coy references to a real person, made under the veil of fiction, can be dangerous. Defamation applies only to living persons, though, so the reputation of a dead individual receives no protection from libel and slander.

The second requirement for defamation is that the statement in question must be false. Truth is, in and of itself, a complete defense against defamation. There is also a distinction between fact and opinion. The courts have held that an opinion in itself is not subject to being true or false; it merely represents the opinion of the speaker. The difference between opinion and fact, however, is not always possible or easy to discern. The statement "Joe is a liar" on the one hand constitutes an opinion as to Joe's veracity; on the other hand, it can be taken as a statement of fact that Joe lies about things. Even though "opinions" are not absolutely safe from challenge, in practice it is still generally helpful to couch controversial conclusions as matters of opinion. The talk-show host who begins every third sentence with "Well, in my opinion" is demonstrating the influence of somebody's legal department.

The third element of defamation is that the false statement must expose the person to some kind of harm to his or her reputation. Thus, the statement "Joe loves his country," even if false, would not generally be judged defamatory. False imputations of dishonesty, adultery, or venereal infections, however, are clearly within the danger zone.

## Defamation and the First Amendment

Overlying these traditional aspects of defamation are requirements imposed by the First Amendment of the Constitution. In order to encourage robust reporting and a free exercise of the creative arts, the Supreme Court held in 1964 in the famous case of *New York Times v. Sullivan* that the First Amendment prevents recovery for defamation against a public figure unless some kind of fault is demonstrated. In order to recover damages, a public official or other public figure who has been harmed must show that the author or publisher of a defamatory statement had "actual malice" in publishing the falsehood. Actual malice in this context does not mean hatred; rather, it has the technical meaning of either an actual knowledge that the statement in question was false, or a reckless disregard for the truth or falsehood of the statement. In the case of a private individual, the Supreme Court set the standard at negligence in checking out the information that is published or broadcast, requiring that greater care be taken by the producer or reporter.

As a practical matter, a finding by the courts of malice for statements made by the established media about a public person is rare. The author and publisher of the supposedly libelous material will probably have exercised at least some care in their research. This includes checking sources, seeking confirmation, and asking for a response from the affected person. The negligence standard as applied to non-public figures is somewhat more stringent; therefore, the author and broadcaster of material relating to private figures should exert themselves even more than normal to ensure a truthful program. The distinction between a public and private person is sometimes a tricky one, and is frequently linked to context. A person who saves the president's life will be a public person within the context of that event, but may still be a private person in the context of his or her home life. In either case, a court will very seldom impose liability on a journalist, writer, or producer who can demonstrate that he or she has acted within normal journalistic standards of professional responsibility.

## Prior Restraint and Damages

In enforcing the rules against libel and slander, a court will almost never prevent publication in advance. Such a limit is called a "prior restraint" and, as an absolute exercise in information control, is repugnant for First Amendment reasons. The more common remedy for a proven case of defamation is damages. As discussed above, in certain instances it may be necessary for a plaintiff to prove actual damages to reputation. In other cases, damages will be presumed from the statement itself. The chance of a plaintiff winning a suit and obtaining substantial damages is more likely for claims dealing with sexual matters or other general societal taboos than in the context of a political debate, where a certain level of robust charge and countercharge is expected and tolerated.

## Bad Behavior by News Reporters

The death of Princess Diana during a high-speed paparazzi chase in 1997 underscored a somewhat different question regarding the behavior of those involved in gathering news, as distinct from the information gathered. This was also a factor in the mid-1990s Food Lion case, when ABC News planted undercover workers in the meat department of the supermarket chain suspected of foul practices. ABC lost in the lower court because of the "fraud" involved in getting its reporters employed. Courts are not always able to disassociate the poor methods of news collection from the effects of legitimate news so collected. Keeping news-gathering behavior within the realm of legality is important.

## PRIVACY AND PUBLICITY

The related rights of privacy and publicity are relative newcomers to American law. They have evolved considerably over the last hundred years, and they are still evolving. The right of privacy was first discussed in a *Harvard Law Review* article written in 1890 by Samuel Warren and the eventual Supreme Court Justice Louis Brandeis. They suggested that a right to be left alone existed in the "common law"—that is, as a matter of judicial recognition, without ever having been enacted by a legislature. The first test of this approach came in a 1902 New York judicial decision, which held that no common-law right existed. This decision led to the passage by the New York state legislature of a statute creating a "right of privacy." The successor to this statute, New York Civil Rights Law, Section 50, now reads:

> A person, firm or corporation that uses for advertising purposes,
> or for the purposes of trade, the name, portrait or picture of any
> living person without having first obtained the written consent
> of such person, or if a minor of his or her parent or guardian,
> is guilty of a misdemeanor.

A companion provision, Section 51, provides a civil damage remedy for violations of this right. The items covered in this section are extended to include "name, portrait, picture or voice."

If the New York court was hesitant to create a new right based on a *Harvard Law Review* article, the courts in many other states were not. For instance, in 1905, the Georgia Supreme Court held that the right of privacy did exist even without a statute. California has also recognized a common-law privacy right. Over the years, most states have come down on one side of this choice or the other. Many states that did not recognize the right under common law subsequently adopted statutes frequently based on the New York model.

Another law review article—this time published in 1960 and written by famous legal commentator William Prosser—had a significant impact. Prosser suggested that the law of privacy had four parts: (1) a right against intrusion into a person's life and affairs, including by eavesdropping and spying; (2) a right against the public disclosure of embarrassing private facts; (3) a right against being put in a "false light"; and (4) a right against the appropriation of a person's identity by others, particularly for commercial purposes. The last of these four was an aspect of the right that is also covered by the New York statute and its imitators. Although Prosser was writing as a private citizen and not as a judge or legislator, his analysis was adopted as the basis of the law in many states, particularly in those where the right of privacy was held to exist in common law.

The right of publicity is similar to New York's statutory privacy right and Prosser's fourth right of privacy. The two major distinctions that have come to be most frequently recognized are (1) that the right of publicity will be strongest in cases where the person in question actually exploits his or her persona, and (2) that the right of publicity can survive the death of the person whose identity is being exploited. The privacy right, as with defamation, was generally viewed to terminate on the death of the person in question. Thus, in 1985, California adopted a pair of statutory publicity right provisions, supplementing its common-law and statutory rights of privacy. One, Civil Code §3344, covers living persons. The other, §3344.1, permits the heirs of a deceased celebrity to continue to exploit his or her identity in commercial products for a period of up to 70 years after the celebrity's death. Significant exceptions allow the use of the identity of a deceased celebrity in historical, non-promotional contexts.

By 2005, most states had adopted, either by statute or as a matter of common law, some form of the rights of privacy and publicity. Most states, at a minimum, protect living people against commercial appropriation of their names and likenesses. There is, however, tremendous diversity between the laws of the different states as to which further aspects of the rights they recognize. Given the confusion on these issues, it is important to know which state's rules will apply. In general, courts will apply the law of the domicile of the person seeking privacy or publicity protection. While this rule may help courts in reaching a decision, or a local programmer with only one or two states to worry about, it is less helpful to the producer or distributor of national programming.

Luckily, the free-speech provisions of the First Amendment of the United States Constitution supply an overall national standard, at least with respect to factual statements on matters of general public interest. The Supreme Court ruled on the problem in 1967, in the case of *Time Inc. v. Hill*. This case involved a New York privacy lawsuit by members of a family who had been the victims of a crime some years before. *Life* magazine, a Time, Inc. publication, had run an article that set scenes from a play based loosely on this crime in the family's old house. The article implied inaccurate details about the family and the crime. (Interestingly, Richard Nixon represented the family in its appeal.) The Supreme Court held that privacy claims by public figures (including, in this case, the family) would require a showing of the same element of "malice"—knowing falsehood or reckless disregard for truth—that had to be proved for a defamation claim.

Even without reference to the First Amendment, most privacy statutes and common-law formulations on the state level have been interpreted to hold that truthful biographical, informational, or news uses are "noncommercial" and therefore not a violation. This conclusion would apply even to a program broadcast on commercial television in a for-profit manner. An extension of this logic allows, without consent, the name and likeness of an individual who appears in the program to be used in advertisements for the program itself—and, provided that the name and likeness are linked to the program in some way, they can even be used in ads for the service that runs the program.

## REALITY PROGRAMS AND DOCUDRAMAS

The laws—and exceptions—governing the rights of defamation, privacy, and publicity display themselves vividly in the context of reality shows and docudramas, both of which involve the depiction of real people.

In the case of reality shows, potential problems are most frequently taken care of by requiring that people depicted must sign a release. A particularly comprehensive form is included at Appendix 1.3. In our age of wannabe celebrity, many people will agree up front to a startlingly complete waiver of all potential claims for defamation, privacy, publicity, and copyright. Provided that there was no fraud or misrepresentation in the inducement process, most courts will give effect to these kinds of waivers. The potential problems come from the more spontaneous formats, when not everyone who shows up on camera is cleared and contracted in advance. Some latitude is provided by the factual basis rules and the First Amendment; the particular circumstances should be reviewed before broadcast. Unless a written waiver is required by the particular state law (as it is in New York), sometimes an interviewer can ask for permission as the camera and sound roll. A "yes" answer is a record of the permission given.

In the case of docudramas, the application of the constitutional aspects of libel, slander, privacy, and publicity law must overcome an inherent contradiction. There is supposedly no First Amendment protection for a depiction that is knowingly false or deliberately fictionalized; as discussed above, this is the essence of the malice standard that applies to both defamation and privacy/publicity. Yet a docudrama is, of necessity, a fictionalized presentation of events based in truth. A print biographer can perhaps claim the goal of absolute accuracy, but a docudrama producer never can. To begin with, the words spoken—unless they come directly from court transcripts or other verbatim sources—will always be, at best, reconstructions of past events. The characters will be played by actors and not by the involved people themselves. The requirements of production will inevitably cause deletions and compressions of events and characters. Quite conscious fictionalization is a necessary part of the process, and the docudrama is a legally permissible art form.

The leading opinion as to the docudrama's blending of fact and fiction arose from the film *Missing*. In his opinion, Judge Milton Pollack stated:

> Self-evidently a docudrama partakes of author's license—it is a creative interpretation of reality—and if alterations of fact in scenes portrayed are not made with serious doubts of truth of the essence

of the telescoped composite, such scenes do not ground a charge of actual malice (*Davis v. Costa-Gavras,* 5, 654 F. Supp 653, 658 [S.D.N.Y. 1987]).

The *Missing* case and other docudrama cases suggest this simple guideline: A docudrama producer may use limited fictionalization, creating composite characters, incidents, and dialogue, provided that the end result, with respect to any material questions, is representationally true, and provided that such representational truth has been arrived at responsibly.

Docudrama producers should consider the following procedures in order to help keep their productions within legally permissible bounds:

- *Select a topic and characters of legitimate public interest.* The First Amendment protections will be much less helpful in the examination of private events in the lives of private people.

- *Depict dead people.* Death wipes out protection against defamation and the right of privacy (although not the right of publicity).

- *Get releases where possible.* If releases can be obtained, they provide the best line of defense. However, it may be better never to ask for a release than to ask and be refused.

- *Do voluminous research.* The backup work for a docudrama should be even more rigorous than the research for a hard news piece. Minor incidents and personality traits should also be noted. A wealth of accurate detail from numerous sources will give the scriptwriter the raw material from which to work, and will provide a higher level of protection. All research must be recorded and catalogued so that it can be easily referenced as the review process goes forward.

- *Maintain a factual basis for every aspect of the script.* Even with those scenes or characters that are fictionalized, there must be a factual basis for the truth they represent. Invented dialogue should reflect the opinions of the speaker. Although it is clear that excursions into representational truth are permitted, there is a point at which fictionalization goes too far. As a general matter, the more controversial or emotionally charged the item, the more literal the depiction should be; sex and nudity are particularly dicey. The film should also respect chronology, and should try not to use composite characters to portray major figures.

- *Require a legal review of the script and film.* A legal review will act as a useful check on the natural exuberance of producers and writers, and can prove helpful in demonstrating lack of negligence and malice.

- *Use disclaimers.* An appropriate disclaimer, alerting the audience to the presence of fictionalized elements, should be placed in the credits. The greater the prominence of the disclaimer, the greater the protection it offers.

## MORAL RIGHTS

The doctrine of moral rights developed in continental Europe. In addition to the "economic rights" Americans traditionally associate with copyright, European authors generally have a second set of "moral rights" in their work. In their classic form, these rights include (1) the right to control publication; (2) the right to withdraw the work; (3) the right to have authorship accurately attributed; and (4) the right to maintain the integrity of the work by preventing desecration and unauthorized changes. These rights are typically held to be inalienable: They are not subject to a general waiver. In most countries, the rights are transmitted after death to the author's family or to a designated representative; in some countries, such as France, the rights are said to be perpetual.

In the context of audiovisual productions, which are by their nature collaborative works, the European jurisdictions typically recognize at least the scriptwriter and director as the "creators" of the work, with the power to exercise these rights. Some countries add to this list the composer of the musical score and author of any underlying work. The existence of these moral rights can significantly restrict the exploitation of an audiovisual production. For instance, French filmmakers have effectively barred the colorization of their old black-and-white films for the French market, at least without specific consent. The re-editing of films for use on television, such as cutting for time purposes or inserting ad breaks, may also be restricted. In effect, the original version cannot be tampered with by the producers without the express approval of the designated creators.

In the U.S., there has been a general resistance to expressly recognizing the existence of any moral rights. Ironically, U.S. copyright law, by giving the author control over publication and over the preparation of derivative or otherwise infringing works, actually does accord the author the power to control all of the usual moral rights as a matter of contract. Other U.S. laws, such as privacy, libel, and unfair competition, cover some of the same territory as moral rights. When the U.S. joined the Berne Convention on copyright, which requires moral rights protection for authors, Congress pointed to these various existing roles to justify going forward without changing U.S. law. The big difference between U.S. law and the moral rights provisions adopted by many other Berne Convention signatories is that classic moral rights cannot be contracted away on a general basis—only in specific instances. By contrast, the equivalent U.S. copyright protections and other legal rights can be, and usually are, waived completely for all circumstances. The U.S. approach has proven acceptable under the Berne Convention, and TRIPS does not require moral rights.

The American freedom to waive moral rights is both a blessing and a curse. On the one hand, it permits a freer commerce in film and television programming than is possible in Europe. In the case of a commissioned product with high commercial value and low artistic pretense, such as *Frasier* or *SpongeBob*, waiving moral rights probably causes no loss to society. On the other hand, some people consider colorizing the best black-and-white films as deplorable as painting a mustache on the *Mona Lisa*.

There is, however, a critical difference between television product and a painting such as the *Mona Lisa*. The painting is a one-of-a-kind object, and a mustache on it would be an irreparable act. A television film or other program, by contrast, is quite freely reproducible, and changes such as colorization or editing can be made without in any way damaging the existing copies of the original work. Congress, in acting on the colorization issue, recognized this by setting up a mechanism for the preservation of certain designated film masterpieces in their original form. It also required that colorized versions of these films disclose prominently that the colorization was done without the participation of the original creative team, if that is the case. As a practical matter, these disclaimers have been broadly adopted for application to most colorized films, whether or not required by law.

In the final analysis, the arguments for an unwaivable moral rights law depend on a view of the creative processes that at heart belongs to the nineteenth-century. In this view, the author/artist is a special being, with the power to pierce the veil of ordinary existence and bring us all, through art, into contact with the sublime. Under such a view, the artist must retain control over each particular use of his or her work. For most areas of television production, it makes more sense for the producer to be free to obtain general waivers of these rights, particularly when the creative person has been commissioned and well compensated to exercise his or her craft.

## UNFAIR COMPETITION

The laws of unfair competition protect the names and reputations of individuals or companies from being falsely involved in connection with goods or services. (See page 99 for a more detailed discussion.) At the federal level, this law is embodied in the Lanham Act; there are also similar state principles. The laws of unfair competition can protect individuals and organizations against the use of their names or other indicia of identity in such a way as to falsely suggest the origin of a program. Thus, it would be actionable to use a well-known title or make some other statement implying that a program was authorized by—or originated with—someone who had not given his or her consent.

# CHAPTER 36
# PROTECTION OF SOCIETY

Most of the issues relevant to the content of television programming—such as copyright, privacy, and publicity—are private rights that are exercised or waived by the private entities involved. There are, however, certain restrictions that are imposed and enforced as a matter of criminal and civil law by our government, on the theory that they protect society at large. In keeping with the principles of the First Amendment, these rules are neither very numerous nor very broad in their applicability. Nonetheless, they can have quite powerful repercussions. Perennial concerns include sex, drugs, and violence. Societal jitters on these subjects lead to periodic attempts to increase the level of censorship. For instance, in the 1990s the V-chip (see page 296) combined program content ratings with a device that can screen out certain programming. The 2004 Super Bowl broadcast, with its prime-time bare breast and raunchy ads, helped fuel a more aggressive approach by the FCC to sexual matters, particularly on broadcast television.

## OBSCENITY
Notwithstanding the loosening of constraints over the past 30 years—or perhaps in reaction to this loosening—the taboos against sex in parts of U.S. society are very strong: so strong, indeed, that certain kinds of particularly graphic sexual speech or depiction are held to be simply outside the coverage of the First Amendment. Since material labeled "obscene" is not protected by the First Amendment, it is subject to outright banning and criminal prosecution by the federal and state governments. The key question, therefore, is what constitutes obscene material. The Supreme Court, as the final arbiter on this matter, has wrestled with a definition of obscenity over the years, and has produced a series of pronouncements. Perhaps the most forthright, if the least specific, was the statement by one Supreme Court justice that he knew pornography when he saw it.

The currently applicable test for obscenity was enunciated in the case of *Miller v. California* in 1973. Under this test, for material to be obscene, all three of the following factors must be proven: (1) the average person, applying contemporary community standards, would find that the work, taken as a whole, appeals to prurient interests; (2) the work, as measured by contemporary community standards, depicts or describes—in a patently offensive way—sexual conduct specifically defined by the applicable state law; and (3) the work taken as a whole lacks serious literary, artistic, political, or scientific value.

This standard, when reduced to its bare essence, is not too different from "I know it when I see it." In effect, if the material contains explicit sexual depictions that are likely to arouse and offend (in the opinion of the judge or jury) a sufficiently broad segment of the population, it will be deemed obscene—unless the work has some aspect of general merit that removes it from punishment. Because the strength of the sexual taboo has ebbed somewhat in many communities in the past 30 years, the community-standard aspect of this test has led to the permitting of fairly explicit sexual material, particularly in major urban centers.

The dissemination of overtly sexual material by television is generally limited to such media as home video, satellite delivery, or late-night, local cablecast; in each case, adults have a personal choice as to whether or not to view it. In fact, the Supreme Court has held that the private possession and perusal of obscene material in the home is not punishable. The consenting-adults argument, however, is no defense for transactions in obscene material: A private sale of an explicit videotape from one adult to another could still be illegal. From a practical standpoint, though, few people are likely to complain about truly private transactions unless they involve minors, violence, or some other aggravating factor, and such sales are relatively unlikely to be punished.

Most states have anti-pornography statutes of one kind or another on their books. Some carry very serious criminal penalties. The enforcement of these statutes—or lack of enforcement—reflects the level of community concern. In conservative areas, prosecutors and other enforcers of these laws may stand to gain more politically by bringing cases against supposedly obscene material than will prosecutors in more permissive places such as New York City and Los Angeles. There are also serious federal criminal laws forbidding the dissemination of obscene material. For instance, there are laws against shipping obscene material, including videos, in the mails or via interstate commerce. In 1996, Congress adopted the Communication Decency Act, a short-lived attempt to regulate indecent material on the Web. Widely viewed as an exercise in cynical overreacting by legislators eager to court "family values" credit at the expense of well-established First Amendment jurisprudence, these provisions were overturned by the Supreme Court in 1997.

## Obscenity and the FCC

There are federal laws and FCC regulations governing the appearance of obscene and indecent material on broadcast television, and of obscene matter on cable television. Ironically, in its original formulation in the Communications Act of 1934, the prohibition against the use of indecent language via radio was paired with a provision forbidding the FCC to exercise any censorship over the content of broadcasts. The prohibition has since been moved out of the Communications Act and into the title on Crimes and Criminal Procedure. It reads, at 18 U.S.C. § 1464:

> Whoever utters any obscene, indecent, or profane language by means of radio communication shall be fined under this title or imprisoned not more than two years, or both.

The distribution of obscene material via cable or subscription television is punishable under both Title 18 and the Cable Act. Title 18, § 1468, provides:

> (a) Whoever knowingly utters any obscene language or distributes any obscene matter by means of cable television or subscription services on television, shall be punished by imprisonment for not more than two years or by fine in accordance with this title, or both.

> (b) As used in this section, the term "distribute" means to send, transmit, retransmit, telecast, broadcast, or cable-cast, including by wire, microwave, or satellite, or to produce or provide material for such distribution.

> (c) Nothing in this chapter, or the Cable Communications Policy Act of 1984, or any other provision of Federal law, is intended to interfere with or preempt the power of the States, including political subdivisions thereof, to regulate the uttering of language that is obscene or otherwise unprotected by the Constitution or the distribution of matter that is obscene or otherwise unprotected by the Constitution, of any sort, by means of cable television or subscription services on television.

The Cable Act, in Section 639 [47 U.S.C. § 559], provides:

> Whoever transmits over any cable system any matter which is obscene or otherwise unprotected by the Constitution of the United States shall be fined under title 18 or imprisoned not more than 2 years, or both.

There have been differences between the FCC's approach to broadcast television and its approach to cable and satellite television. For some time, the broadcast rules have applied not only to "obscene" material, but also to material that is merely "indecent." Indecency includes the use of offensive words, even in contexts where no graphic sexual description is involved—thus the problem with George Carlin's famous seven words you can't use on the airwaves. Indecency also includes non-sexual nudity, such as Janet Jackson's Super Bowl halftime wardrobe malfunction. While 24-hour bans on broadcast TV indecency have been struck down, Congress in 1992 mandated a late-night "safe harbor" of midnight to 6:00 A.M. FCC rules implementing this were largely upheld in 1995, rolling the starting time back to

10:00 P.M. In the late 1990s, Congress and the FCC initiated a new approach to sexual content in broadcast television: ratings and the V-chip (see page 296).

The laws governing cable services, however, provide only for the prohibition of obscene material. So far, there has been a tradition of greater latitude in the cable area, although the conservative Congress and FCC of the Bush era have begun to suggest a more restrictive approach. The tradition of tolerance is partly due to the lesser legal control of cable in general—and also to the fact that the decision to receive cable is elective, and that in most cases, the more risqué channels can be switched off at the box in the home. Public-access services have been particularly active in showing non-obscene nudity, largely in a late-night time slot. Use of non-obscene sexual images and language is a matter for the programming policies of the cable system and network, exercised largely in light of commercial considerations. Satellite services, with their increased pay-per-view capacity, are also more open to non-obscene sexual content. Hardcore material would still fall afoul of the obscenity standard.

## NATIONAL SECURITY AND POLITICALLY MOTIVATED CONTROL

In limited circumstances, the government can censor material that would endanger national security. This authority has been quite narrowly defined, applying only when an immediate, specific threat from the publication or telecast of the material can be demonstrated. For instance, it has been held that the government could prevent the publication of the sailing dates of transports or the number and location of troops in time of war, or suppress a magazine article explaining in full detail how to build a hydrogen bomb. In the Pentagon Papers case, by contrast, the Supreme Court allowed the publication of a Department of Defense in-house study critical of the conduct of the Vietnam War; the government had simply not met the heavy burden of justification necessary to stop the information from flowing.

The 9/11 attacks and the considerably increased concerns over national security that have followed have led to the government's greater attention to controlling information and the population's greater acceptance of such control. The Patriot Act, for instance, allows the government unprecedented powers to keep its own workings secret and to spy on terrorism suspects. Follow-on laws may extend this trend.

The government and the military can sometimes limit the access of reporters, including television newspeople, to sensitive material and locations. To its credit, the U.S. military made particular efforts to include "embedded" reporters with frontline units in the Iraq war. As a *quid pro quo* for obtaining access to military areas and missions, however, reporters will sometimes agree to limit certain aspects of their stories. This self-censorship, encouraged by the government, can be quite effective. In the post-9/11 era, national security has also resulted in calls to suppress broadcasting tapes released by terrorist organizations. Government officials sometimes sign contracts agreeing to keep certain information secret, and these contracts can be enforced in the courts.

While the government has always sought to manage news—particularly news that may be potentially embarrassing—recent trends have carried this management to new heights, with techniques including the release of politically one-sided broadcast material masquerading as disinterested news footage, the use of dummy reporters and news conferences, and the heavy-handed condemnation of perceived "bias" whenever there is disagreement or criticism. While such efforts may not carry official legal sanctions—at least not yet—the chilling effect can be significant and is troubling to those who believe that a free press is one of the bulwarks of American liberty.

## PRE-TRIAL PUBLICITY

The First Amendment guarantees of free speech sometimes come into conflict with another constitutional guarantee: the right to a fair trial. It is sometimes claimed that pre-trial publicity of a particularly inflammatory nature can so prejudice public opinion about a criminal case that it becomes impossible for the defendant to receive a fair hearing by a jury. As a result, in certain very rare cases, there may be an injunction against publishing or televising a particular piece of information about the case. This remedy is granted only on proof that no other option, including moving the location of the trial to a city or town where the case is less well known, will protect the rights of the accused.

## "SON OF SAM" LAWS

In the 1980s, the federal government and many states adopted so-called "Son of Sam" laws. These laws are aimed at preventing a criminal from being able to profit from selling the rights to the story of his or her crimes to the media. In the late 1970s, New York City was the scene of a series of brutal attacks by a psychopathic killer who sent notes about his crimes signed with the name "Son of Sam." Enraged at the notion that this criminal might profit from selling the media rights to his crimes, New York state enacted a statute that confiscates any monies paid to the criminal (or to entities such as agents collecting on his behalf) for books, movies, magazine articles, or television shows in which the crime is reenacted or the criminal's "thoughts, feelings, opinions or emotions" about the crime are expressed. The funds so confiscated are given to a crime victims' compensation board, which then disburses them to victims of the crime. Similar laws were enacted by the federal government and by many states.

In 1991, many of the first generation "Son of Sam" laws ran afoul of the Constitution. The U.S. Supreme Court held that these laws could violate free speech. Since then, states have focused on broader laws permitting victims to attack criminals' assets more broadly, although even these laws may run into constitutional problems in the future.

## CHILDREN'S PROGRAMMING

Protecting children from "bad" programming and ensuring that "good" programming is available have long been popular social and political goals. After many years of false starts, canceled proceedings, and vetoed legislation, in 1990 Congress finally enacted a law regulating children's television. The Children's Television Act of 1990 restricts the amount of advertising that can run in children's programming on both broadcast and cable television to 10.5 minutes per hour on weekends and 12 minutes on weekdays (shorter periods are restricted proportionately). The Act also requires the FCC to regulate program-length commercials, and calls on broadcast stations to serve "the educational and information needs of children through the licensee's overall programming, including programming specifically designed to serve such needs." The degree to which a broadcast station has met this standard is considered in connection with license renewal.

This mandate has led the FCC to set a number of implementing rules. The FCC defines children's programming as that which is aimed at 12 years old and under. "Program-length commercials" are defined as "a program associated with a product, in which commercials for that product are aired." This continues to allow product-driven shows to air, but if direct sales pitches for the product are contained within the program or in adjacent spots, then the entire program counts against the commercial time limits. Furthermore, promotions for programming other than the "core" programs discussed below count against the advertising limits.

The FCC's approach to educational and informational programming distinguishes between programming that furthers the educational and informational needs of children age 16 and under, and "programming specifically designed to serve those educational and informational needs." This specifically designed programming (also called "core programming") must designate serving such needs "as a significant purpose"; must air between 7:00 A.M. and 10:00 P.M.; must be regularly scheduled weekly fare; must be at least 30 minutes in length; and must have its educational and informational objective and the target child audience specified in writing in the station's Children's Television Programming Report. Stations broadcasting at least three hours per week of such core programming are conclusively deemed to comply with the public-service requirement for this issue. Because the definition of "educational and informational needs" is left open and vague, there is still considerable leeway in the rules. There is also the possibility of showing that other forms of programming can meet the public-service requirement. Nonetheless, most stations are meeting the three-hour safe-harbor rule, and most networks are being more intentional about their offerings.

The advent of digital television, coupled with other new technologies, is adding some further wrinkles. The basic rules will apply to a digital broadcaster with a single programming stream. Channels that opt to run additional streams of free programming will need to add further core children's programming—an additional half hour for every 1 to 28 hours of additional free programming presented. The core requirement need not be part of every stream, but it must receive at least the level of broadcast quality as the programming that gave rise to the additional obligation.

The FCC has also taken notice of the commercial aspects of Web sites linked to programs. Rules adopted in 2004 allow Web links to be displayed on an unrestricted basis provided they lead to a site whose content is adequately noncommercial. The standards set include a requirement that the on-air characters not be used to help sell products or services. By mid-2005, the FCC had not prohibited interactive links from the program directly to commercial Internet sites, largely because such approaches are not widely in use, but it has suggested it will review such links as they emerge.

## VIOLENCE ON TELEVISION

The level of violence on U.S. television often surprises visitors from other developed countries; for whatever reason, violent acts are a staple of U.S. programming. After many failed efforts to mobilize legislative and regulatory controls, the 1996 Telecommunications Act gave the FCC the power to work with the television industry to develop a TV rating system to disclose violent, sexual, or indecent content. This system pairs so-called "V-chip" technology (discussed below) with content-based ratings keyed both generally and specifically to on-screen violence. Until the American public as a whole loses its taste for violence-laced fantasy, violent programming will remain a significant presence on television. Indeed, the availability of V-chip blocking may even lead to an increased level of violence in those shows willing to accept a higher violence rating.

## SELF-REGULATION BY THE TELEVISION INDUSTRY

The private side of the television business regulates itself for the protection of society. Industry-wide self-regulation has been held to impinge on the antitrust roles, so industry-wide controls have been hard to maintain without some government sponsorship. For instance, the National Association of Broadcasters code relating to program content was abandoned in 1982 as part of the settlement of an antitrust suit brought by the Justice Department, which saw the code as an example of impermissible coordination between supposedly competing businesses.

Where a government mandate exists, such as with the V-chip, cooperation is made easier. For instance, the authorization for the V-chip was passed by Congress in 1996 as part of the Telecommunications Act. It provides both for an exemption from antitrust rules for companies coming together to cooperate on a program ratings system and for regulations set by the FCC to code these standards in a form that can be "read" by a programmable device in a television set (the V-chip).

## Traditional Self-Regulation: Standards and Practices

Even before the ratings and the V-chip, considerable control was exercised at the individual company level. Each network maintains a standards and practices department, which reviews programming and advertisements in the light of company-wide standards. This department issues and administers in-house guidelines on a variety of issues. Many of its concerns reflect the need to conform to the FCC restrictions described in Chapter 6, the intellectual property rules described in Chapter 34, and the personal rights requirements described in Chapter 35. Other standards and practices recommendations reflect the twin goals of serving the good of society and preserving the image of the network (and, by association, of its advertisers). The areas of concern are predictable: alcohol, criminal activities, drugs, human relationships, obscenity, physical infirmities, race, religion, color, age, national origin, sex and sexuality, and violence. The list reads like a program guide for some of the more popular daytime talk shows, or an assignment board for a local news team during sweeps weeks; all of society's hot and tricky topics are there.

The stated requirements of the networks on these issues tend toward the general and platitudinous. One network, in setting guidelines for programming on "human relationships," declared: "The presentation of marriage, the family, interpersonal relationships, and other material dealing with sexuality shall not be treated exploitatively or irresponsibly, but with sensitivity." This pious injunction to "be nice about things" is at odds with the fact that *nice* is usually not as interesting to most of the audience as *nasty*, or at least mildly nasty. Applying standards that are worded this way is a matter of balancing the prospect of attracting a big audience with the consequences of offending some of its members. Where the balance comes out changes over time. Reflecting increases in societal acceptance of crudity, the word "ass" became acceptable on the broadcast networks in 1997. The outcry that followed the 2004 Super Bowl broadcast has pushed the pendulum back in the other direction.

Outside of broadcast networks, institutionalized hand-wringing over program content is much less common. Most cable and satellite services, for instance, are aimed at specific target groups; the broadcast networks still seek to reach a broad cross section of American society. The programming people at a cable or satellite network are generally in touch with what their audience wants to see, and if they get a little too aggressive, a memo from the advertising salespeople will usually correct the matter. There are few centralized "politeness brigades" to keep things within bounds.

Where they exist at networks, cable companies, or local stations, the standards and practices departments and their rules serve to institutionalize, on a private basis, the kind of community-standard approach that underlies the Supreme Court's rulings on obscenity. What is prohibited and what is permitted reflect general societal taboos. As usual, sex comes in for considerable regulation. Violence, which until recently has been subject to much less societal condemnation, is permitted to a far greater extent. Predictably, as the pressure to control some of this violence grows at a societal level, the violence level of television programming is coming under more and more scrutiny by both broadcast and cable companies.

## Content Ratings and the V-chip

In the 1990s, the combination of increasing concern over the content of television programming (particularly on-screen violence) and technological advancement produced a public/private initiative on the control of program content. The approach was not prohibition at the front end by banning certain kinds of content. Rather, the idea was to provide the consumer in the home both with sufficient information about the content of programs to make advance decisions and with a device to help enforce those decisions when the consumer's children are turning on the TV set.

As described above, the keys to the public side of this were provisions included in the 1996 Telecommunications Act, mandating the FCC to set disclosure conventions and technical standards for devices that can interpret codes included in the shows and then block shows with offending ratings. Compliance is voluntary, but including the V-chips themselves in U.S. television sets is mandatory. The Act also confirmed the antitrust exemption for companies in the private sector to cooperate in developing the ratings system. On the private side, after some high-profile arm-twisting by then-President Bill Clinton, most major television production and distribution companies have come together to assist in developing the ratings code and have agreed to put the code listings in programs.

Established in 1997, the ratings promulgated by the industry alliance in effect in 2005 are:

| | |
|---|---|
| **TV-Y:** | Appropriate for all children. |
| **TV-Y7:** | Appropriate for children 7 and older. |
| **TV-Y7-FV:** | Programs in the Y7 category with more intense or combative fantasy violence. |
| **TV-G:** | Appropriate for a general audience. |
| **TV-PG:** | Parental guidance suggested. |

**TV-14:** Parents strongly cautioned—probably not suitable for children under 14.

**TV-MA:** Mature audiences only.

The phrasing of these ratings reflects the influence of the MPAA ratings system "voluntarily" in effect for theatrical films.

Within these categories there is an additional tier of ratings, which indicates the specific content concerns behind the age ratings. These labels include:

**S:** Sexual content

**V:** Violence

**L:** Coarse language

**D:** Suggestive dialogue

In practice, the V-chip approach has been a disappointment. A combination of factors—including the continued presence of older sets in many homes, as well as parental ignorance, indifference, and technical incompetence—has prevented it from being widely used as a tool for keeping objectionable programming under limits.

## PUBLIC PRESSURE

In the end, decisions regarding the content of television programming in the U.S. are highly dependent on the desires of the public. Television production is so costly that unless there is an anticipated market for the resulting program, it will not be made. Furthermore, most programming depends upon commercial support, and few product manufacturers will want to antagonize public opinion by sponsoring programs that significant special-interest groups might protest as offensive. In fact, consumer campaigns can be quite effective in persuading sponsors and other program supporters to leave certain types of content without financial backing. The mass-distribution systems of broadcast television are much more susceptible to this type of boycott than is the essentially personal world of home video; cable and satellite transmission lie somewhere in between. In sum, the content of programming reflects what the audience wants: Society protects itself on the issues that truly arouse public opinion, and leaves the rest to find their markets.

# PART 9

# PRODUCTION

# CHAPTER 37

# A RAPIDLY CHANGING PRODUCTION ENVIRONMENT

For television's first 30 years, programs were produced by well-equipped, well-funded TV stations or by one of three networks or by motion picture studios. Television equipment was simply too costly, too large, and too demanding in terms of maintenance for general use. By the mid-1970s, portable video equipment emerged as an interesting alternative to studio production; since that time, the capabilities of this equipment have steadily increased while the weight, cost, and maintenance demands have steadily decreased. At the same time, many colleges and universities have developed successful undergraduate programs in television and media production. These factors, encouraged by a vastly expanded television distribution environment, have wholly altered the television business.

## MORE PRODUCERS, MORE DISTRIBUTION

In the 1960s, not many people knew a television producer. There were far fewer television programs on the air—arguably less than 5 percent of the number of shows produced today. Shows were smaller and simpler, so most shows employed just one producer—not a staff of producers as it is done today. The skills required to be a successful producer seemed to combine a rarefied comprehension of show business and the theatrical savvy of a top Broadway director. In time, audiences developed their own media literacy, and the role of producer seemed less exotic. Still, it was a role that intrigued many baby boomers, who enrolled in the few available media and communications courses, and learned how television worked. In the 1970s, there was a vague promise of more television channels, and sure enough, by 1980 or so, new cable networks needed young producers who could, for example, supervise a shift at CNN or manage the VJ segments that appeared between MTV's music videos. Generally, these projects were even simpler, and far less costly, than older programs. Producers trained in the 1980s learned how to do more with less. Many cable network executives understood the paradigm shift; television could be done on far smaller budgets than anyone thought possible.

In the 1990s, producers began to press for the use of the latest digital equipment, which permitted lower-cost production and post-production that could be accomplished on far smaller setups that producers could buy rather than rent by the hour. By 2000, the circle had completed itself. Producers are now provided with remarkably small budgets because the networks know that crews can be kept to a minimum, that equipment is often owned by the production company, that editing is done in-house on a small Avid system or, in some cases, on Final Cut Pro. Producers are kept away from television studios, which rent by the day and require large crews, and are instead encouraged to produce programs in the field, where costs are now modest. Television studios are still in use, of course, but mainly for news programs and talk shows. Soundstages are in use for situation comedies and dramatic programs. Gone are the game shows and variety shows that once filled television studios with large staffs and larger technical crews; instead, there are reality shows and news magazines produced, largely, in the field by a small staff.

For many years, ideas for new shows were pitched by an energetic producer with a written proposal. While this system is still in place, many program pitches now involve at least some video, produced on low-cost equipment and funded by the producer. If the concept shows promise, the producer may be asked to submit a brief videotape showing the concept or the talent, again funded by the producer (perhaps with a modest investment from the network). With large number of production companies offering similar capabilities (and probably more than a few with a similar idea), the marketplace now favors the buyer—except when big stars or major producers or writers are central to the concept.

## SMALLER CREWS

Prior to the current generation of digital video equipment, a field crew generally required a director, a videographer, a sound engineer, and an extra hand typically trained in lighting. In today's world, three jobs become one; the director and videographer are often the same person, and the sound work is usually monitored in the camera. An extra hand is still necessary sometimes, but for simpler projects, it is no longer essential.

As the veneer of show business has faded, the need for makeup, hair, or wardrobe has faded somewhat as well. So, too, the role of the writer, as on-camera talent is often a real person dealing with talking points rather than a full-scale script.

## PRODUCTION AND POST-PRODUCTION EQUIPMENT

Every few years, the equipment required for field production becomes smaller, less costly, and more capable. As of 2005, the standard for many productions was either Sony's DVCAM or Panasonic's DVPro format. Both are small digital video formats that allow for duplication without image degradation. One step down is the MiniDV format, camcorders that are smaller, lighter, and less costly, with only a modest sacrifice in image quality.

While it is possible that yet another small-scale video format will be introduced for professional use, there is little future value in videotape of any kind. Digital video is more efficiently stored as digital files, which are in turn more readily and more quickly ingested into digital video servers. These servers are rapidly becoming the playback system of choice for television studios, master control facilities, and post-production setups. In time, the archival videotape libraries found at many networks and local stations will vanish as well, replaced by video servers that allow instant access to any spot on any program in the library. What's more, libraries will be interconnected via a faster version of the broadband Internet, and accessible via wireless technology.

One of television's most labor-intensive processes is video editing. New digital systems support video tagging in the field, allowing acceptable segments to be automatically assembled before the video files reach the editing room. Video editing is now wholly nonlinear. In its previous iterations, video editing required one segment to be dubbed from the playback machine to the record machine; then the next segment was added, and so on down the line, until the production was complete. Nonlinear editing allows the producer to insert segments of any length at any point in a timeline. This timeline approach is now well over a decade old; in time it, too, will probably be updated. It is not uncommon for high school students to learn how to edit video on a home computer, just as they learn to do word processing. With progressively smarter software and this advanced level of video literacy among even the most junior editors, video editing will only become faster and less costly.

## CHANGES IN DISTRIBUTION

The changes in production are not limited to equipment. Independent producers whose only options in the past were community cable access or the entrepreneurial sale of their own duplicated videotapes now serve a global market via the Internet. Tapes have given way to DVDs, and DVDs are now giving way to a more efficient form of direct-to-consumer distribution via broadband Internet. Many IPTV (Internet Protocol TV) services are available, both from large enterprises and from the smallest of companies operated part-time out of a home office. In other words, it is now possible to operate a video-on-demand or fully scheduled television service from a video server in one's home or office, a service that reaches viewers, subscribers, or other customers anywhere in the world.

Just as cable made dozens of networks available, Internet distribution will make hundreds of channels available. Some channels are already serving very small audiences, highly targeted groups of particular interest to, for example, specialty advertisers. New Century Television, operated by one of this book's authors, currently offers hundreds of hours of television programming via the Internet. If a program is watched on a computer screen, is it a television program? There is no reason to even consider the question, as the two screens are gradually becoming one.

# CHAPTER 38
# DEVELOPMENT AND PRODUCTION PLANNING

One frequently asked question is, "How do I get a show on the air?" There is no single answer.

## CONCEPT DEVELOPMENT

In New York, Los Angeles, and several other U.S. metropolitan areas, there is a community of television producers, television program executives, and (in some situations) television packagers generally responsible for the programs seen on most of the networks. While this community is established, often with long-term connections between people, the opportunity for new members always exists. What's more, a steadily increasing number of television shows are now produced in places other than New York and Los Angeles, in part because networks are now based in so many places throughout the country.

Television programs are born in several different ways.

A creative person may concoct an idea, often the result of observing the current marketplace and adding or altering a key element. For example, *Medium* is a fairly traditional police procedural, but it adds the element of a psychic; *Monk* is another detective series, made unique with a lead character whose life is filled with phobia. Wholly original ideas are less common, but they do appear on network schedules at times. *Arrested Development*, for example, was an idea that went nowhere until a clever packager presented the series not as a typical family sitcom, but as a satire.

Television producers and programmers are notorious copycats. If a home makeover show or a biography series works for one network, it isn't long before similar shows appear on many networks. Sometimes, the new idea is an old one with a twist. Sometimes, the new show isn't a new idea at all, just a copy with a different title and a different cast.

The copycat notion is related to the cyclical nature of television program formats. Several years ago, when ABC succeeded in prime time with a game show (*Who Wants to Be a Millionaire*), more game shows appeared in the prime-time schedule for the first time in almost 40 years. Just a few years later, there are no prime-time game shows, nor are there likely to be in the foreseeable future.

Ideas sometimes do materialize independently around similar topics. One network decides upon a reality show about boxing, and suddenly there are two shows on other networks, plus a new interest in women's boxing prompted by a completely unrelated motion picture (*Million Dollar Baby*).

The more strategic approach is to fully understand an audience, and to develop programming based upon audience patterns. This is a tricky process that requires a thorough understanding and appreciation of market research, a skill set that is not a part of most television programmers' arsenal. While it is true that market research more often looks at the past and present than at the future, a great deal can be learned by studying lifestyle patterns and viewing trends. While this approach does not assure a hit series, it can be helpful when formulating entirely new strategies.

More often, though, programs are acquired and/or produced to support a specific brand identity. MTV, for example, no longer trades on its musical heritage, but instead builds on a unique sensibility that underlies the likes of *Cribs* and *Pimp My Ride*, and also allows the brand to expand to the MTV Movie Awards while maintaining credibility with its audience. A&E has been successful in reinventing its brand. The network started with arts programming, then moved to a schedule filled with off-network dramas, and when the audience began to age, moved again to reality series, including *Dog the Bounty Hunter*, *Airport*, and *Growing Up Gotti*. This, plus the success of *Law & Order* reruns, set the stage for A&E's large, and now very brand-centric, acquisition of *The Sopranos*.

## PACKAGING

Few television series are sold on the basis of the idea alone. Programmers generally require a *package*, a collection of key assets that differentiate one property from another. The concept for the project is, of course, paramount, but the key performers, the producer, and the story line are also closely related to the concept and how it will be executed. If a concept comes with a marketable performer, a producer with experience in the genre must be added, either by the show's creator or by the network. If the package comes without a performer, or without the "right" performer (as defined by the network buyer), then the project may be placed on hold until appropriate talent can be added to the package.

Every project is packaged; that is, every project is an assembly of various ideas and talented people. Network prime-time series are packaged in a more formal way. Many, if not most, of the comedies and dramas seen on prime-time network television are the result of packaging by a top talent agency, such as the William Morris Agency, that works to combine several clients (writers, producer, performers) into an appealing package that fits a particular network need (and provides the agency with an additional packaging commission). This proactive approach has been responsible for numerous successes for the William Morris Agency, including Showtime's *Queer as Folk*, ABC's *Who Wants to Be a Millioniare*, NBC's *The Weakest Link* and *The Cosby Show*, CBS's *Everybody Loves Raymond* and *The King of Queens*, and more.

Series packaging fees charged by the William Morris Agency are a standard 5 percent of the license fee paid by the network. Other agencies, such as ICM, CAA, and Endeavor, typically charge about 3 percent—and struggle to get any more from the networks. One of the more successful series packaged by the William Morris Agency, helping to justify their long-standing 5 percent charge, was *Who Wants to Be a Millionaire*, one of ABC's all-time biggest success stories. According to *Electronic Media* (now *Television Week*, an industry trade magazine), the William Morris packaging fee for the hit series *The Cosby Show* resulted in over $30 million in commission payments resulting from the series' eight years on NBC. The same magazine reported a 5 percent commission, shared between Morris and CAA, related to the CBS series *Everybody Loves Raymond*. This deal was worth $125,000 per episode (a comparatively small portion of the $5 million per episode that CBS pays to HBO Independent Productions and David Letterman's Worldwide Pants production company—a deal negotiated by Morris and by CAA).

Typically, the packaging fee is only part of the story. The agency receives between 5 and 10 percent of the syndication proceeds, plus a few additional points in profit participation. Performers and key producers/writers also share in adjusted net profits. These formulas are complicated, but they have become standard aspects of negotiation in the network community.

## PRODUCTION PLANNING AND BUDGETING

As a project is sold, a full-scale budget, schedule, and production plan must be prepared by the producer or production company. Hundreds of thousands of dollars are involved, and in many cases, budgets run in the millions. Careful budget planning is critical to assure that the project can be delivered without exceeding the available funds, and to assure that the producer earns a reasonable profit.

It's usually best to begin planning with a daily or weekly schedule. This schedule typically lists the key tasks that must be accomplished each week from the earliest stages through completion and delivery. Planning is often organized by weeks; shooting is often organized by days. This information is then used to work out the costs associated with the staff (weeks) and with the talent and crew (days).

Most television budgets are set up in a relatively standard cluster of categories. Often, the staff category is one of the largest. It includes a list of every producer, writer, manager, assistant, and so on, then lists the salary (and benefits) or fee for each person on the staff, multiplied by the number of weeks required from each individual staff person. The costs associated with these roles vary depending upon the project, but in major markets and/or cable series, an estimate of $50,000 to $75,000 per episode is reasonable for a working producer. On network prime-time series, the talent category often represents the largest dollar amount; on a weekly cable series, a host earns $5,000 to $10,000 or more, depending upon the importance of the show. The director and his/her staff may be included in the general staff category or may be carried as a separate category. Directors of cable series generally earn about $500 to $1,500 per day.

The costs associated with studio or location production are defined by the day of shooting and by the complexity of the production. One day in a fully-equipped three-camera studio with a crew of fifteen people costs $7,500 to $10,000. Typically, the crew complement includes a technical director who switches cameras and may supervise the technical crew; several camera operators; additional camera utility crew if a jib (an extended camera arm that allows high shots and sweeping shots from above) or a handheld camera is required; a video engineer; an audio engineer; a lighting director; one or more maintenance engineers; and various assistants. Every project has its own special requirements, so it's wise to budget for rentals of additional lights, microphones, monitors, or other equipment that may not be available in sufficient number for a particular project.

One day with a three-person field crew, on the other hand, costs $1,500 to $2,500. Typically, this crew is led by a videographer (who often owns the equipment), plus two people who handle lighting, stagecraft, audio, or similar tasks.

Stage settings can be rented. If sets are designed and built from scratch, then a production designer, set designer, or art director is required, at rates that vary from as little as $5,000 to as much as $25,000 or more. These rates vary depending upon the size and importance of the project, and the overall project budget. Similarly, the cost of building a set varies; a modest set can be built for a few thousand dollars, but it's not unusual for a major set to cost more than $50,000—the money goes to labor (construction, painting, etc.) and to materials. Back in the studio, the set must be put together, requiring a stage crew, and at the end of the project, the set must be struck. If the scenery is to be stored for later use, this, too, must be budgeted.

If the project is shot on location, then logistics must be arranged in advance. Often, this involves rental of local facilities and/or vehicles. The staff, performers, and crew must be housed, and the number of hotel nights must anticipate the time prior to the shoot for preparation of the location, and for restoring the location to its original condition after the shoot. Meals and per diem fees must be budgeted as well.

Some projects involve specialized wardrobe. Here, there are costs associated with meetings, time spent shopping (no small task if the producer or the performer is finicky), purchases (some clothing can be "traded-out"—provided free by a retailer or manufacturer in exchange for an on-screen credit), tailoring, replacements (a second tie that matches the first, for example), and, if necessary, the design and building of specific wardrobe or costume pieces. If the project requires multiple costume changes (this is not uncommon on a children's or a variety show), then a wardrobe staff must be in the studio or on location to care for the wardrobe and to help the performers into and out of costume.

Similarly, some projects involve special hair or makeup. Sometimes, these two roles are combined, and one person is hired to do both jobs. However, if multiple performers must be prepped and ready for shooting at the same scheduled time, then more than one hair and/or makeup person is required (the cost of an additional hair or makeup person is considerably lower than the cost of a crew and studio waiting around until a performer is ready to go). As with costumes, it is sometimes necessary for a hair or makeup person to prepare special or custom pieces (hairpieces, prosthetic devices), and both time and money must be allotted for things like shopping, preparation, fitting, coloring, and so on.

A television project also operates as a kind of small company. Costs are incurred, and bills must be paid. Rentals and leases must be arranged. The staff must be housed in a functional office, complete with phones, computers, desks, copy and fax machines, office supplies, Internet access, an overnight shipping account, and more. Property, liability, and other insurance are usually compulsory; accounting and legal services are often necessary budget items, too. There may be some travel required, and someone must be paid to make the necessary arrangements. Often, production people work late and, on shoot days, arrive early, requiring additional security. On shoot days, it's often more efficient to feed the staff and crew, especially if the shooting location does not provide easy access to lunch facilities. When the staff works late, food is usually provided (so that the staff may continue working). On larger shows, members of the staff may be required to work through lunch, prepping the afternoon. Performers, who require a break in order to relax prior to an afternoon's work, are best pampered with lunch; this saves time getting into and out of wardrobe and, perhaps, makeup.

The hiring of necessary staff and crew is done entirely by personal referrals. Typically, small groups of people on the staff have worked together before, or share acquaintances. Every major market has an assortment of technical crew people who have worked together for years, sometimes decades.

Once again, every type of project is unique. A prime-time reality series works within industry practices that are very different from a locally produced morning talk show. A producer who is experienced in the genre can budget, plan, and set up a project properly. A producer who lacks experience in the genre can call on friends for help, but there's no substitute for experience.

# CHAPTER 39

# PRODUCTION FINANCING AND DEAL-MAKING

Obtaining finance for a production is a critical and often difficult task, and the deals that get the money on the table are at the center of the television business. Since the earliest days of television, there has been a struggle by the companies and individuals who actually produce for television to retain ownership rights, and future income potential, for the material they create. On the other side of this struggle are the owners of distribution—the networks and independent distributors—who seek to use their control of production capital to ensure an outright purchase, taking the financial benefits of ownership away from the producing community. While the producing community has always had an uphill fight in this competition, recent trends in media concentration have made the outright purchase model more and more the norm in television. At the 2005 National Association of Television Program Executives (NATPE) convention, the ever-outspoken Ted Turner advised would-be producers to go into the restaurant business instead. This is an excessively pessimistic assessment; while the rules have shifted somewhat, those independents who can adapt to the new environment can still prosper.

The world of production financing can be broken down into six general categories: internal working capital, customers and clients, suppliers, outside and inside investors, banks and other lenders, and foreign partners.

## INTERNAL WORKING CAPITAL

The early stages of a program's development are usually funded internally. Many production companies—and nearly all television stations and cable networks—budget a certain amount of money per year to develop new projects. Once the program is developed, it will often be "pitched" or "shopped" to other potential participants, and one component part of the deal will be funding for further development of the project.

If the production organization is a distributor or network, then all of the project's development, and some or all of its production, may be financed with internal capital. Sometimes, money is approved only for each incremental step, and additional approval is needed to move the project to the next step. This approval is based on a growing sense that the project will come together as planned, and that it will reach a sufficiently large audience.

In some cases, internal funds are used to produce a demonstration video or a pilot, which then becomes a selling tool to attract additional investment from other companies.

Internal working capital can also be used to make up for the shortfalls that occur because of delays in receiving funds from outside sources. Unless advances from customers or distributors are paid on time—and unless all suppliers are patient and understanding of the cash-flow crises that typify the production process—the production schedule is likely to be affected until a certain check arrives and clears. A production company should have ready access to cash or a line of credit in order to smooth out the bumps in cash flow.

Internal capital is also used to close gaps in production funding. For example, if a project is 95 percent financed by other sources, the production company may decide to cover the remaining 5 percent from its own reserves in order to begin production. Sometimes, this is preferable to pre-selling rights to make up the difference—rights that might be more valuable once the program is made.

## CUSTOMERS AND CLIENTS

Customers and clients are the most common source of production financing, particularly for independent producers. Television is a business in which networks, cable companies, and video distributors pay sizable sums—either in advance, on delivery, or as a combination of the two—for the product they need. Customers and clients can take many forms, depending mainly on the type of distribution system. Increasingly, the customers buy all or part of the rights in the program as part of the deal, or have their license fee treated in whole or in part as an investment. Many programs are produced for private concerns: A corporation requiring a training video, for example, typically pays the entire cost of development and production and ends up as owner of the final product.

In some cases, a combination of two or more customers furnishes funding for a program. For instance, a commercial broadcaster could account for partial financing, and a syndicator's advance for the remainder. Or a cable network could provide some financing, with a European broadcaster making up the balance. Going to multiple sources makes deals more complex, but often allows the producer to remain the owner of the program. However, with the increasing focus by most U.S. media companies on property ownership, this kind of split arrangement has become less prevalent in the domestic context.

## SUPPLIERS

Suppliers of production-related goods and services, like television studios, mobile production facilities, and post-production facilities, may also provide a form of production financing. In exchange for profit participation or partial ownership in a property, these facilities may offer reduced rates or may defer billing until the project earns enough money to pay back both the initial amount and a premium. Supplier financing is most common for pilots, in which facilities and/or personnel may be traded for the promise of a production contract if the series is commissioned. If that occurs, the supplier will make back its money and then some.

Supplier financing is also common in the home video industry, particularly for independent producers who distribute their own product. In such a case, the DVD and tape duplicator may not only manufacture finished product on credit or without charge, but may also supply warehousing, shipping, and inventory control in exchange for profit participation or partial ownership.

## INVESTORS

Television and video are glamorous businesses that attract certain types of investors. Investors essentially come in two forms: those who are unaffiliated with the television and/or video industries (*outside investors*), and those who are involved in some aspect of the television business and who will buy into a project while acquiring certain distribution or telecasting rights (*inside investors*).

### Outside Investors

For the pure-equity investor with no other means of benefiting beyond a share of revenues, a television or video project is likely to be a difficult investment. There are at least two potential problem areas. First, television and video programs do not "earn out" in any predictable fashion. This can make any investor nervous, and an inexperienced one hard to handle. Second, if a producer is relying on outside investment money, he or she may be working outside the established production community, and may lack easy access to production or distribution resources that are essential to a reasonable return and a predictable budget. Nor is it only the investor who may have problems. On a project that is running late and perhaps over budget, with one or more investors anxious to recoup their investments more rapidly than the marketplace will allow, the possibility of all-out panic may cause the producer to question the wisdom of working with outsiders.

That said, there are many isolated instances when outside investment has proven successful, sometimes with enormous returns for both investor and producer. Wall Street investment firms, major insurance companies, and other traditional sources of investment capital generally invest in television through big production entities like studios, distributors, and networks.

### Inside Investors

Distributors and end users of programming often invest in production. Although the distinction between the distributor and purchaser-as-end-user can be blurry, there is an important difference between the two.

The distributor usually pays a production advance. This is deemed an investment (especially if it is not fully covered by pre-sales), since it depends on unpredictable market factors to generate a return. In exchange for taking the risk, the distributor usually gets a share of profits. Of course, by controlling at least some aspect of distribution and revenues, the distributor is able to influence the risk of an eventual return.

A purchaser/end user—for example, a network—is not trading an investment for a return. Instead, it is paying outright for particular rights or territories (in the form of license fees, for a network) and using the program in an active business of its own. Increasingly, however, purchasers want to be treated like investors; they want the recoupment and profit positions traditionally associated with true risk-taking investors. Most recently, the trend has been for a major end user to insist on becoming the rights owner of the completed production. If the end user is supplying essentially all of the production finance, this is at least a doable proposition, although it reduces the producer to a hired hand. If the end user is essentially seeking all of the rights but is not providing all of the money, then it is probably not worth wasting further time on the deal.

Historically, production companies got some help in dealing with this kind of end-user pressure. Because of the singular power they once wielded, the major broadcast networks could leverage the producers and distributors that supplied them with programming into selling all rights. This caused the FCC to institute the financial interest and syndication ("fin-syn") rules, which at one time forbade the networks from maintaining a financial interest in the independent productions that they carried on their prime-time schedules. With the increasing role of non-network television of all kinds, and after years of negotiations between the FCC and the networks, the FCC in 1995 abolished these rules (see page 45), contributing to the trend toward network ownership at the expense of producers.

## BANKS AND OTHER LENDERS

Banks and other lending institutions sometimes play a part in the production financing process, but only if a loan can be secured with property that can be readily valued and turned into cash. Unsold rights to specific program properties are difficult to present as collateral because of their inherently speculative nature. Besides, most lenders do not understand the intricacies of show-business accounting. Therefore, most lending activity is either large-scale—multimillion-dollar loans to studios, networks, syndicators, and technical facilities—or dependent upon the existence of a firm pre-sale.

For the independent producer or production company, a bank will make a loan only if there is a bona fide contract with a creditworthy distributor or end user that provides for set payments on a firm schedule. The bank is essentially covering cash flow—if there is a period in which the producer requires cash, but the distributor or end user will not provide the necessary amount until a later point in production, a bank may give a bridge loan. The risk of a failure to deliver is offset by a completion bond and other forms of insurance. These safeguards are standard practice in film production, and while they apply to made-for-TV movies, they are not often part of series production for which incremental adjustments can be made.

Loans for project development, or for independent production without pre-sales, are almost impossible to obtain on a commercial basis because of the risk involved.

In some cases, the contribution of an equity investor will take the form of a high-risk, nonrecourse loan, generally with a substantial "kicker," such as a large share of net revenues. While this is technically a loan, it is actually more accurately treated as an investment.

## FOREIGN PARTNERS

With the rise of globalization, companies outside the U.S. have sometimes become sources of production capital for American programs. Historically, foreign sales came after the fact, as part of the profit margin for either the independent producer or for the acquiring financier. More and more frequently, though, the foreign investment is arranged up front to minimize production deficits, again either by the producer or by an acquiring company laying off risk. Sometimes, foreign television companies maintain development offices in Los Angeles and New York City.

Foreign investment in U.S. production is generally linked to a license of rights. In its simplest form, the deal is basically a pre-sale, with the possibility of profit participation and sometimes partial ownership. More often, however, investment from foreign sources is part of a coproduction package. In a relationship that resembles a partnership (regardless of its strictly legal structure), the domestic producer and a foreign coproducer each provide certain elements of the production budget. The project may be shot overseas, for example, using facilities provided in whole or in part by the foreign coproducer. Coproduction often involves cash from the foreign partner as well, supplementing the cash available to the U.S. producer from licenses to a domestic broadcaster, distributor, satellite or cable network, or home video company. Partners usually share the distribution rights—each usually retains broadcast, satellite, and cable rights in its home country—and split the revenues according to a negotiated formula. These deals are complicated, however, by the domestic-content requirements that commonly apply to foreign broadcasters and by fluctuating foreign exchange rates.

## ADVERTISERS

Sometimes advertisers play a significant role in program development and production. Procter & Gamble, for example, owns a production company that supplies several long-running network soap operas. P&G has also coproduced *Sabrina, The Teenage Witch, Clueless*, and the syndicated *Real TV* with Paramount. Buena Vista and Kellogg's worked together on children's programming; *101 Dalmatians* and *The Mighty Ducks* animated series were part of a program block supported by Kellogg's advertising dollars. There are other isolated instances and the occasional joint venture, but in general, advertisers do not become involved in the details of program development or production. As a rule, an advertiser simply wants to place commercials in a program environment that delivers the right kind of viewers in sufficient numbers.

## SYNDICATION AND DISTRIBUTION: A CLASSIC MODEL AND A TIME OF CHANGE

The U.S. and global television markets have seen significant increases in ownership concentration in recent years. This, coupled with the emergence of the FOX, Warner Bros. (The WB), and Paramount (UPN) networks and the trend toward more in-house and fully commissioned production, has lessened the importance of the classic distribution routes for independent production. Symptomatic of these changes was the near collapse of the NATPE marketplace for syndication and distribution in 2002 and 2003. This centerpiece of competitive television marketing regained ground in 2004 and 2005 with the help of new management and an understanding that even in a changed industry, there is a place for an event that brings so many of the players together to meet, mingle, and wheel and deal.

Although they have declined in importance, the classic models of distribution are worth understanding. Not only do they persist in the industry, but they still provide a framework and a vocabulary within which other kinds of deals are structured.

### The Relationship between Producer and Distributor

In the classic model of television programming, the producer manufactures the product, and the distributor takes care of sales and marketing. A successful product combines competent work by the producer with effective sales and marketing clout from the distributor.

Most producers who remain truly independent license the rights to their product to experienced distribution companies. This is especially true in markets that are difficult to sell without a specialized sales force, as in syndication and foreign markets. In some cases, production companies have formed their own syndication companies or home video labels. Ideally, this allows the producer to retain more revenues and pay closer attention to individual product marketing.

## The Typical Distribution Deal

The independent producer often licenses a distributor to sell a program or series in a particular territory or group of territories for a specified period of time. The distributor then retains a negotiated percentage of revenues as a fee, frequently 30 percent to 35 percent (though this figure varies widely, depending upon the product, markets, and advances involved), plus reimbursement for certain distribution expenses (see page 320). The distributor will recoup any advance made to the producer, and may retain a certain amount as profit participation, particularly if the advance was sizable. The distribution deal's definitions and limitations are negotiable, based on bargaining strength, industry tradition, and company policy, and there are many variations on the theme. A checklist of issues in distribution deals appears in Appendix 2.1; a model distribution agreement is reproduced in Appendix 2.3.

## Revenue Streams: Recoupment

So far, the discussion in this chapter has centered on the spending side of deals. Of equal importance is the revenue side where, with luck and clear contract language, investments are recouped and profits are earned and shared. When a party finances a commercial venture, it is almost always with the intention of recouping the investment and realizing some profit. A television network recoups the investment in its programs by selling time to advertisers, usually earning a profit, too. A home video label recoups by selling DVDs to dealers and consumers. Even the sponsor of a public television program hopes to recoup its investment, either in cash (from the proceeds of additional sales) or through publicized goodwill.

A true investment in a production is generally not tied to a sale of particular rights; rather, a true investment is generally recoupable in some kind of priority position from all sources of income generated by the property. However, as end users press to be treated as investors, at least for a portion of the fee, the process of repaying investors can become quite complicated.

## Recoupment Priorities

Recoupment usually occurs "in the first position," or from gross revenues received, before any profits or other revenue deductions are allowed. However simple this may sound, there are many layers of activities and entities that are involved in the revenue stream of a television program. At each layer, deductions are made, and the net at one level is the gross at the next layer down; for example, the distributor's net is usually the producer's gross. The time when any particular investor's recoupment right "plugs in" may be hotly negotiated. In most cases, distribution costs are recouped at a higher level than production costs.

## Multiple Priorities

With only one party eligible to recoup its investment at any given level, the formula is a relatively simple one. The investment is one of a list of items that are deducted from revenues at that level prior to determining the net. The situation becomes more complicated when several parties are entitled to recoupment, particularly when their investment contributions are not equal to one another. Two related issues must be considered: the relative size of each investor's share and the order in which each investor may extract dollars.

The simplest formula is called *pari passu,* a Latin term meaning "by a like step." In *pari passu* recoupment, each party receives funds at the same time, but in proportion to its percentage investment at a particular point in time. The following example illustrates the *pari passu* formula: Party A has invested $2 million (50 percent) in a production; party B, $1.2 million (30 percent); and party C, $800,000 (20 percent). When the first $100 arrives from any and all revenue sources, the parties receive $50, $30, and $20 respectively, at the same time. *Pari passu* recoupment is a fair means of sharing both risk and reward.

Recoupment *by position* is the opposite of *pari passu* recoupment. The party in the first position receives some or all of its investment before anyone else, then the party in the second position recoups, then the party in the third position, and so on down the line. Take the same $100 income, the same investments as above, and an agreement for party A to recoup 100 percent of its $2 million investment in the first position. Party A would then receive the entire $100 and all additional dollars up to $2 million. Parties B and C would receive nothing until party A recouped, and then would take their recoupments in turn.

There are several variations on these formulas. In order to provide the other parties with some income, party A might agree to accept less than 100 percent of the income, or to open "windows" for the others at various positions before its own complete recoupment.

In another variation, one or more of the parties might be entitled to recoup more than 100 percent of the original investment. Some deals offer, for example, 200 percent recoupment but no future involvement in profits (or some lesser involvement in profits). From the perspective of the investor, a formula based on a multiple of the original investment is simple and easily managed. From the perspective of the producer, such a formula limits the long-term distribution of profits, and keeps the project's ultimate profitability unknown to the recoupment partners.

## Separating and Combining Revenue Streams

A successful television program or series is likely to generate revenues from a variety of domestic and foreign sources. Sometimes the streams are split apart and treated as different "pots" for recoupment purposes. For example, the producer of a made-for-television movie may get an advance from one distributor that will cover domestic syndication and cable sales, and another advance from a second distributor that will cover all foreign markets. Frequently, each of these two distributors will recoup its respective advance only from revenues from its own territories and markets. Given the fact that the distributor's efforts will help shape the success of the program in its own area, this is a reasonable arrangement. An outside investor, in contrast, will usually recoup from all revenue sources.

Revenue streams can also be tied together, with the proceeds from one market helping to cover the recoupment of costs or advances in another area. This technique is called *cross-collateralization*, from a banking term that refers to mortgaging separate properties to support a single loan. Separate programs are sometimes cross-collateralized to cover the costs that each one runs up on its own; in that case, the programs would have to break even on an aggregated basis before a net would be earned on any one of them.

## What Gets Recouped

The definition of what is recoupable is a critical point in negotiations. Since distribution costs, production costs, and advances are all subject to recoupment, these are prime areas for definitional license—here is where "Hollywood accounting" earns its reputation for legitimized theft. Every piece of overhead, interest, or other types of "indirect" costs that gets added by contractual agreement to the more truthfully labeled "direct" costs, means a shifting of money from the net participants to the recoupment participants. This issue leads directly to the next topic: net profits and other "back-end" participation.

## Profit Participation and Other Back-End Formulas

*Profit* is both a magical and a cursed word in television. Fortunes have been generated by the sale and resale of specials, series, and motion pictures to network, cable, satellite, syndication, home video, and foreign markets. Often, those fortunes are not shared by people with a "net-profit" share or some other formula for back-end participation. (A "back-end" payment refers to money that comes out of revenues, as opposed to a "front-end" fee, which comes out of the production budget.) There are two principal reasons behind this all too frequently accurate statement. The first is the convoluted and blatantly one-sided terms of participation agreements that are presented as take-it-or-leave-it propositions to back-end participants. The second is the "creative accounting" that shifts costs back and forth among various projects, with the most successful ones bearing the greatest burden of items allocated for recoupment. This section will examine both of these problems in detail, as well as several other obstacles to the profitability of any production.

### The Problem of Labels

In theory, being a gross participant is better than being a net participant. But in the end, labels mean very little—it is the details in the definition that truly matter.

*Gross revenues* should mean the total amount of money received, prior to any deductions. A network's gross, for example, should equal the total amount of money paid by the sponsors for advertising on the program. Even this simple explanation demands refinement, though; sponsors buy their commercial time through advertising agencies, which typically retain 15 percent of the sponsor's payment as a commission.

From the producer's perspective, gross might also be defined as the total monies received by the producer from the program's distributors (i.e., the "distributor's net").

A director or writer who negotiates to receive a percentage of the producer's gross is likely to have his or her own definition. This "gross" might well be offset by agency commissions, legal fees, or a stunning variety of incidentals—from the costs of shipping distribution materials to foreign countries for potential licensing, to a full recoupment of basic production costs. The gross is now an *adjusted gross.*

Although specific terms may vary, adjusted gross often functions as a synonym for what most people would call "net" or "net profits," though the adjusted gross will usually have fewer questionable deductions. The words "net," "profits," and "net profits" should be meaningful terms, but they have become so debased through misuse that they are often scorned, even as labels, by anyone with sufficient negotiating power. Other kinds of back-end payments involve flat fees or bonuses in place of, or in addition to, a percentage in a net or gross formula. "Points" are percentage points, and represent the percentage share of whatever is being divided ("net points," "gross points," and so on). Even the word "revenues" can be misleading. Many agreements only recognize revenue after it has come to rest in a particular account in a particular country, even though that may be months or even years after the check was cashed by the foreign subsidiary of the U.S.–based distributor.

In order to get to the root of a typical profit definition, one must ignore the customary meanings of certain terms and focus on the legalese of the profit-participation agreement itself. Hidden there will probably be many of the following issues concerning the recipient of the profit share ("Participant") and the payer of that share ("Company").

### Revenue Adjustments

On the revenue side, there are many ways in which the Company can defer acknowledging funds that have actually been deposited into its bank accounts. International companies have a particularly wide scope for this action. A common clause in profit definitions says that no funds shall count as being received until paid in dollars into the U.S. accounts of the Company. If the Company has foreign subsidiaries, they can collect foreign revenues in foreign currencies and leave them overseas indefinitely, as a kind of permanent loan from the Participants who are entitled to them. This can be avoided by insisting on a time frame for the repatriation of funds held by the Company or its affiliates.

A few countries, however, still present a "blocked currency" problem: restrictions on money leaving the country. This can be circumvented with an agreement allowing the Participant to set up his or her own account in the country and to take the appropriate share of blocked funds directly. The Participant may not be able to get the funds out of the country either, but at least they are available to spend there.

Another method the Company can use for delaying recognition of monies received is the use of reserves and the related concept of "earned." The theory is that advances made are not really earned until the product is delivered, since they could conceivably be rescinded if something went wrong with the program. Therefore, the logic goes, all advances must be held in reserve until it is clear that there will be no problems. This line of thinking has been stretched to the point of declaring that no license fee is earned until the contract has been completely performed. The license may run over several years—and even after the program has run several times with no problems, some, or even all, of the licensing fee may be held in reserve and deemed not yet earned.

These delay tactics can be compounded, quite literally, when they are combined with clauses allowing the Company to earn interest on unrecouped amounts. If income that is actually on hand can be considered nonexistent, then the Company will expect interest to be paid on these funds, piling on extra charges to be recouped (even on overhead costs and production fees). Another problem with interest is that the Company charges the prime rate plus some number, whereas it pays lenders several points less. All of these practices can be countered by limiting interest charges to amounts *actually* paid on amounts *actually* outstanding on expenses *actually* incurred.

Company delay can also be used to influence the exchange rate at which foreign receipts are converted into dollars. If the foreign distributor of the program is an affiliate of the Company, it will wait for the moment when the foreign currency is weak to report income, diminishing the dollar total. Similarly, any expenses or deductions will be converted and deducted when the foreign currency is strong. A fair contract will specify average exchange rates or key the rates to specific dates for evaluation.

## Fees

Revenues to Participants are also reduced with double charging of fees. The Company collects a fee for selling a program in a particular market, then turns around and sub-licenses it to another organization, which also deducts a percentage fee from its gross. It seems unfair that the Company keeps its full fee when someone else is being paid to do the work—especially when the "someone else" turns out to be an affiliate of the Company, or even a direct subsidiary. This kind of inside licensing for double fees, which is especially common with foreign sales and in other ancillary markets, can be prevented by capping the total amount of fees that can be charged by every party involved in selling into a particular market, and by forbidding the charging of additional fees for work done by an affiliate of the Company.

## Exaggerated Deductions

Having taken steps to delay and minimize the receipt of income, the Company may try to increase the number of deductions that it will take.

The first group of deductions consists of "adjustments" to the gross such as collection costs (legal actions for bad debts), agent fees, and applicable taxes. Tax deductions should cover taxes specifically withheld from the project's revenues, not the general income taxes of the Company. If there is a benefit to the Company from an offset or tax credit, the fair share of this should be added back against the taxes deducted or even, if possible, passed along to the Participant.

The next set of deductions is usually the recoupment of distribution and marketing costs. One might think that these expenses are the cost of doing business, and should be covered by the Company out of its distribution fee; this is sometimes the negotiated result. But in the film business, where the practices originated, these expenses are sometimes huge, given the prints and advertising necessary for a major release, and so they are recovered separately. The approach has been transferred over to television deals, even though the costs of distribution are generally much smaller.

Most Participants are willing to accept the deduction of direct, out-of-pocket costs of getting the programs on the air: tape stock, dubbing, shipping, customs, and so on. The trouble starts when these and other services are performed in-house and then charged against the program as a hefty fee. The Company may also tack an overhead allowance onto these charges, so the program's earnings are in effect being charged twice for expenses that the fee should cover. Add an interest factor while these charges remain unrecouped, and the meaning of "Hollywood accounting" becomes ever more clear.

Sales and marketing costs present additional opportunities for Company abuse. Television distribution may not involve massive media campaigns aimed at the general public, but there is quite extensive marketing targeted to potential end users: printing brochures, dubbing sales tapes, travel costs, phone expenses, attendance at conventions and sales markets (see page 325). In the classic model, armies of television executives have descended on markets in Cannes, New Orleans, and Las Vegas to wheel and deal, trying to outdo one another with expensive display booths and celebrity appearances. Though many Participants grumble at the lavishness of these efforts, they at least acknowledge that "you have to spend money to make money." The problem comes when the expenses are allocated among the various properties that the Company represented at such functions. If the Company went to Cannes with a list of 20 properties, it may return with lucrative sales for only five of them. It is useless to allocate the expenses to the failures (since these properties may never make enough money to repay them), so the successes are made to bear the burden of the costs. While the successes probably do occupy a disproportionate amount of the Company staff's attention, the Participant does not expect its own program to carry most of the Company's overhead, especially in addition to the fee that is deducted. Some unscrupulous companies even allocate the same costs to more than one program, and end up making money on every expense they incur.

Some of these problems can be thwarted with language in the agreement between Participant and Company that requires deductions to be "directly related" to the program and to be "actual, out-of-pocket" expenditures. Another approach is to simply impose a cap, either as a percentage or (less commonly) as an absolute amount, which deductions for such items cannot exceed.

"Double counting" is another deduction tactic. Residuals may turn up twice as deductibles, as may insurance and other program-related costs. Sometimes an expenditure is calculated as both a distribution cost and a production cost; even worse, overhead and interest expenditures are added to both occurrences, even though overhead on distribution expenses is relatively rare. If the intricate language of the contractual formula permits these practices, it is hard to call them fraud.

After distribution fees and expenses have been deducted, the revenue stream—or what is left of it—is applied to recouping the production costs or the distributor's advance. If the Company is recouping the full production costs, these, too, are often defined in a one-sided manner. For example, most produc-tion budgets include a general overhead factor, sometimes 20 percent or more. In theory, this factor is supposed to cover all of the small expenses of ongoing Company overhead that are attributable to the program but that do not appear in the official budget. In practice, though, many of the Company's profit calcu-lations already account for a wide array of overhead costs, including telephone bills and the cost of parking spaces at the Company's main office. The Participant should keep the overhead factor within reasonable bounds, and should question the addition of interest to overhead and overhead to interest.

The Company's boilerplate definition of "penalties" may allow it to recoup, for instance, 150 percent of the "normal" production cost if the program is over budget. While the argument goes that this is an incentive to the Participant to keep expenses under control, the Company may insist on penalties even when it has final approval on all artistic and business matters relating to the production.

## Percentages of Percentages

Once the Company has taken all its deductions, the issue is just what the "points" promised to Participants are percentages of. Are they 10 percent of the "producer's share" of net profits? Because there is a customary 50/50 or 60/40 split between investor and producer, 10 percent of the producer's share will be no more than 5 percent of the full 100 percent. In addition, if the promised percentage is 10 percent of the "producer's retained share" of net profits, any other grants that the producer has made will be taken off the top before the points are calculated, so the Participant's actual share shrinks even more.

### General Defenses Against Profit-Participation Abuses

In addition to the specific remedies described above, there are some more general measures to protect a Participant from a Company's creative accounting methods. First, the long, standard-form profit definition in the profit-participation agreement is usually drafted to protect the Company as much as possible; a relatively short statement, with language limiting overhead and other general allocations, can tilt the agreement back in the Participant's favor. Second, the Participant should insist on a most-favored-nation clause. This item is derived from the laws of custom duties, where a "most favored nation" must have the benefit of any concession granted to any other country. In the world of profits, this means that the Participant cannot get a worse deal than anyone else in an agreed-upon class. If the class includes other recipients with some bargaining power, the entire deal may improve some; and if the deal includes the Company or its key executives, the deal might get better still.

### Accounting Rights

One of the most effective means of monitoring a Company's questionable practices is the Participant's right to have an accounting done of the Company's financial books and records on a project. Most clauses will grant the Participant the right to audit the books within a certain time period after receiving the statement, or the right to have a "qualified representative" conduct the audit. The records will be made available at the Company's offices, during regular business hours. The right to audit may be limited to a single audit of any given period; any claims must be made shortly after the inspection. Sometimes the Company will hinder the right to an audit with so many restrictions and such short time intervals that the clauses become almost meaningless.

Auditors do turn up irregularities, even with a relatively honest Company; the problem is that such audits tend to be expensive, although a profit-participation agreement may provide for the Company to pick up the tab if serious shortfalls are discovered.

### The Alternative to Profit Participation: Fixed Payments

For those who are skeptical of profit participation and its many blind alleyways, there are alternatives. The easiest way is to structure a bonus or royalty arrangement keyed to reaching easily measurable targets—such as the number of programs actually produced. For example, every time a week of shows is made, the Participant could receive a flat dollar figure as a royalty or bonus: more shows, more money. If these shows air more than once, a further formula can be devised;

if these shows air outside the U.S., then each show that airs in a specified list of countries triggers a specific payment. If the series reaches the three- or four-year mark, making syndication possible, then a bigger bonus is triggered.

Some producers receive bonuses when a program reaches, or exceeds, a specific rating point. Some receive bonuses when a pilot triggers a series order, or when a second, third, or fourth year of programs is ordered. Bonuses may be used in combination with revenue-based profit participation. Bonuses may be paid "against" profit participation (that is, deducted from later earnings, if any) or they may be paid in addition to these monies.

In summary, there are no absolute rules regarding profit participation; every situation is different. For those few players with sufficient clout, the terms of profit participation are highly negotiable; for everyone else, "net" is a very flimsy concept.

## HOW DEALS GET DONE

How are deals actually made so that a production can be financed? The key to the process is experienced participants who know how to play the game, who can untangle complications and reconcile contradictions at least enough to have some type of deal letter signed. (Sometimes the deal letter is all that gets signed; it is not uncommon, with a series several years into production, for the various lawyers to be still wrangling over the terms of the long-form agreement.)

The following section describes some of the essential elements involved in making a deal for production financing.

### Who the Players Are

Certain television executives make programming decisions and have the power to make financial commitments to a producer. Most networks and distributors have a programming or acquisitions department, which is where much of the initial action takes place. Typically, this department employs creative executives and associates who evaluate and shape the artistic aspects of the program, and businesspeople who judge the program in terms of its cost and revenue potential. The inevitable tensions between creative vision and cost control play out daily between these factions; a successful project satisfies both parties.

On the selling side are the production companies, independent producers, directors, writers, and anyone else with a good idea. The trick is getting the project in front of the right person on the buyer's side. Many submitted projects get shunted to low-paid readers (who may not have much experience) for a review, and a reader's report that is bad can doom a worthy project to obscurity. The project must be seen by someone actually empowered to make a commitment. Personal relationships can be essential here. One of the keys to a successful production career is a PDA (or Rolodex) full of senior program executives who will take your call, have lunch with you, or even share a weekend on your boat.

For a newcomer, a well-connected agent, manager, or attorney can help open the doors—for a price.

Programming decisions are rarely made by one person. Typically, a network or distributor builds staff consensus prior to any commitment. Ultimately, the head of programming must make the final decision, but this decision is rarely made without consulting others in the program department. Sales and marketing personnel are often part of the process, especially if advertising or rights sales are an important part of the package.

In some instances, the project is developed in-house at a media company, and then contracted out to a dependable production company. In this context, getting the deal depends on a track record for bringing in high-quality production values on time and on budget rather than on the ability to give a sparkling pitch. The producer is more of a competent general contractor than a visionary architect.

## Where the Players Meet

The players get together in formal meetings scheduled at their offices, in restaurants, or at other business venues. There are also short-notice meetings and impromptu appointments at conferences, sales markets, and conventions, and in informal settings like skiing in Aspen, on the beach in the Hamptons, or sailing off the south of France. Even a haircut can give the barber the chance to make a pitch; hairdressers have risen to some of the most powerful positions in Hollywood.

### Formal Meetings

Although a written submission is often required in advance, and some work can be done over the phone and via the Web, if you are trying to pitch a project there is no substitute for a face-to-face meeting in a formal setting. A good part of the art of the deal is the ability of a seller to infect the buyer with enthusiasm for a program. Selling projects in any television market—whether local, national, or international—also requires spending time in the city or cities where the principal buyers are located, setting up the necessary rounds of meetings, and cultivating the connections and contacts that will put the person pitching the project into the system. With rare exceptions, this cannot be done effectively if the producer is not a regular part of the local scene.

### The Hubs

The premier deal-making location, both for national and international productions, is still the Los Angeles area; no place rivals L.A. for the concentration of television business people. The next most important center in the U.S. is New York City. Because of the companies located in other cities, some deals are also made in Chicago (Tribune), Washington, DC (PBS), Atlanta (Turner), Miami (the Latin entertainment industry), and Nashville (headquarters of the country music business). In Canada, Toronto dominates the television business, although

Vancouver and (to a lesser extent) Montreal are also important Canadian centers. Internationally, Tokyo, London, Paris, Munich, and Rome all have concentrations of power, with secondary hubs in São Paulo, Sydney, Mexico City, Madrid, and Barcelona.

Although the hubs are critical, they are not for everyone. They are often hard places to get a start. Before setting out to find fame and fortune in the big ponds of the television business, an aspiring producer should consider starting out locally. It is often easier to use the resources and opportunities of a local community to acquire basic experience, establish a reputation, and create a demonstration reel. Furthermore, "life in the fast lane" isn't for everyone. There are vibrant television communities all over the U.S. and in many locations around the world. It is possible to create a fulfilling, productive, and financially rewarding career in television without ever setting foot in southern California.

### Conventions, Markets, and Social Occasions

There is a series of annual conventions and markets in the U.S., Europe, and Asia, where relationships are built and nurtured, programs are bought and sold, and deals are made (or at least discussed). In the U.S., the remaining important meeting is the syndication market sponsored by NATPE. NATPE was created to allow syndicators to show their programs to a wide range of buyers from around the country, and these meetings have been central to the syndication sales business. As discussed above, with increasing centralization, such markets are not as important as they once were. Syndicators now sell mostly to station groups, not to individual stations, and deals are made throughout the year. After all, NATPE nearly disappeared in the early 2000s.

Still, there is not yet a replacement for getting the national television community together, and all kinds of business occurs at these conventions, from finding a new advertising sales company to arranging a corporate merger. Provided the executives can take the time from buying and selling current product, NATPE gives an opportunity to pitch, follow up on, and commit to new projects.

As the television business becomes more global, international program markets have become more important to U.S. producers and distributors. Internationally, the most important conventions are held in Cannes: MIPTV takes place in the spring, and focuses on sales to the traditional broadcast markets; MIPCOM is in the fall, and covers all aspects of the television and video business, including cable and satellite. Asia Television Forum, held in Singapore, represents a fast-growing cluster of television markets. Other events include the famous Cannes Film Festival (typically held in the late spring) and the less significant film and television festivals held throughout the world. At these gatherings, the production, finance, distribution, and end-user communities from around the world forge alliances, initiate coproductions, and generally discuss deals. While few of these transactions are finalized in the hotel bars by the slopes or on the chartered yachts by the pier, many deals are launched before the week of hectic meetings is finished.

Informal contacts in social situations are also a prime starting point for presenting and soliciting television projects. While it is often bad form to let discussions centered on business dominate interaction at a party, there is plenty of room for mentioning a possible project and setting up a formal meeting to talk further about it. This kind of networking may be difficult for an outsider; in time, as personal relationships are built, it becomes easier. Professional organizations, like the National Academy of Television Arts and Sciences, at both the national and regional level can provide opportunities to meet established players in a natural context. Remember, however, that relationships take time to build, and an overly aggressive business pitch in a collegial setting can backfire.

## Negotiating the Deal

Television is often a rough-and-tumble world, full of strong characters who have gotten ahead by imposing their wills on others and making deals on their own terms. These people are likely to be adroit at the manipulation, flattery, intimidation, and enticement that go into getting one's own way. Nowhere are these skills more evident than at the bargaining table. Countering these personalities is not always easy, especially when you're selling a product that will make or break your company, and you have little leverage. If you are in this position, it is hard to hide it: There are few secrets in the industry, and the other party is likely to know precisely who they are dealing with. Nonetheless, there are a few bits of preparation that can guide anyone through the negotiation process.

The first step is examining your own position, weighing its strengths and weaknesses. Identify your minimum requirements; if these are not met, it's best to walk away. The next step is to put yourself in the other side's shoes: What are their strengths, weaknesses, and minimum requirements? This exercise will help you determine just where—and how far—you can push. Do your homework about the deal as well. If you haven't read the fine print or don't know the industry custom on a particular point, you can be pushed around by someone who has and who does. Use your advisers—agents, managers, lawyers—wisely; don't defer all decision-making to them, but borrow their knowledge, experience, and skills in the manipulation game.

If the other side insists on yelling and screaming, preserve your dignity by leaving the table or hanging up the phone—if they really want the deal, they will come back to you in a more civilized fashion. Another technique that sometimes is successful is to ask the screamer if they are feeling okay, and whether aspirin or a drink of water would help. And remember, behavior during a negotiation is often a key indicator of behavior during production. (If the negotiation is hell, do you really want these people as partners?)

Once the basic deal is done, a letter agreement can confirm the key points. Since the monied party typically drafts the contract, the wording is likely to favor that party. Negotiation is expected, and several conversations about changes are acceptable. At a certain point, usually the third, fourth, or fifth discussion about changes, this becomes annoying busywork for the other party. So pick your shots, give in on some points, and push hard on others. If the other party becomes weary of your changes, note that this may be a tactic. It may also be a sign that you are driving the other party crazy.

Timing is also a factor. Insisting on the last drop of blood can draw out the deal process by weeks or months. Most deals have their ripe moment, when attentions are focused and the market is ready. Missing that moment can do far more harm than missing the last triumph in the negotiations or subsequent contract changes. In addition, the television community is small enough that a reputation for gouging at the negotiating table can come back to haunt you. Be firm, but leave something for the other side to take home; there is considerable value in being "a pleasure to do business with." There is also value in being "a tough negotiator." Striking a balance is the key.

# CHAPTER 40
# PRODUCTION COMPANIES

Television programs are produced by a wide range of entities, from individuals to small companies to large multinational corporations. The widespread availability of low-cost digital production and post-production equipment has substantially reduced the barrier to entry, but most of the television business continues to be dominated by industry professionals.

Many television projects are produced by company employees. A roughly equal number are produced by vendors and suppliers, whether independent producers or production companies. The former sometimes suggests a producer who works alone; the latter may be one or two people in an office with an Avid, or may be a division of Viacom with many employees.

## IN-HOUSE PRODUCTIONS

Television networks and local stations employ producers to control costs, to manage brand identity, and for logistical reasons. Staff producers typically earn less than freelance producers or employees of an outside production company. Producers who work directly for a company become involved in the company's unique culture, and are held responsible for shaping the company's brand identity. In some instances, this unique identity can be difficult to communicate to outsiders, especially if it is a work in progress. Logistics often dictate the need for in-house producers. Local television news operations and cable networks that supply a 24/7 studio feed require the producers to be a part of the minute-by-minute activities; this is difficult to do with an outside company.

Many corporations employ in-house producers for their own internal communications needs. For a corporation with large-scale training needs, or a company-wide television news network, a staff is essential. Outside production companies often handle video news releases (VNRs), other marketing communications projects, and, in some cases, the more labor-intensive training projects (which may require more time or specialized resources unavailable in-house).

# PRODUCTION COMPANY/CLIENT RELATIONSHIP

## Work-for-Hire

The most common relationship between a production company and a client is a work-for-hire relationship. That is, the client provides specifications for a particular project, the production company submits a bid and proposal, a price is set, and work begins. The production company serves the client and receives payments based upon a schedule of deliverables. There is no discussion of asset ownership or participation in any future revenues; the client simply owns everything.

This type of relationship is clean, simple, and extremely common. This is the type of relationship most common when the output is training materials, marketing communications, music videos, fund-raising videos, and other projects requiring short-term commitments. This relationship is also remarkably common with programs produced for cable networks.

The fee is typically paid one-third upon signing, one-third on the first day of principal photography, and one-third upon delivery of final materials. On larger projects, the production company may be paid weekly, biweekly, or monthly for the run of the production schedule. This is common when the production company consists of just one or two people operating more as "permalance" (permanent freelance) contractors—very nearly employee status.

## Work-for-Hire with Residuals or Royalties

In essence, this is a work-for-hire relationship. There is a difference, however: The production company is entitled to receive a percentage of revenues either before or after the client has recouped the production investment (and, sometimes, the marketing investment as well).

If the work is created by a member of the Writers Guild (see page 347), then there may be mandatory payments required by the collective bargaining agreement. In some cases, a member of the Directors Guild of America (DGA), Screen Actors Guild (SAG), or the American Federation of Television and Radio Artists (AFTRA) may also be entitled to such payments.

## Work-for-Hire with Profit Participation

This format is also common in both cable and network television. The production company receives a negotiated percentage of the project's profits based upon a complicated definition of net revenues. These definitions routinely favor the client, and, often, the production company sees an amount that is considerably less than expected, or no money at all. Every deal is different, but the general range of 5 to 10 percent of net revenues, after deductions, is a reasonable starting place for discussions.

Since this arrangement can be complicated, cumbersome, and the cause of ill feelings, many production companies instead opt for a combination of bonus payments and elevated fees based not upon revenues, but upon specific performance. If, for example, a program achieves a certain national rating, or is renewed for a third season, then the production company receives the additional money. This approach works for the client, who typically pays less money than it might if the net revenues mechanism worked properly; it also requires considerably less internal accounting and auditing. The approach also works for the production company, based upon the theory that a reliable cash payment is better than one that's theoretical and difficult to monitor.

## Joint Venture

A joint venture is not a partnership. Instead, it is the coming together of two independent organizations, typically for a specific project. Each side contributes assets, services (particularly production facilities and distribution), and/or cash, and each side receives a percentage of revenues after the deduction of specified costs. More often than not, a joint venture is a relationship between equals, each of whom possesses the resources to accurately account for incoming dollars, and to accurately audit one another's accounts. In a joint venture, it is not uncommon for the production company to either supply or arrange for some of the project's financing, and/or to provide in-kind services in lieu of a cash investment.

In the world of prime-time network production, joint ventures are common. Often, the joint venturers are the television division of a motion picture studio, a producer under contract to that studio, and a television network. The joint venture format allows the studio to maintain control of the property after the initial network run is complete. Each of the studios maintains a television syndication division for sale of programs to cable television and to broadcast and cable markets outside the U.S. In the past, home video releasing rights were also controlled by the studio. Today, the networks are more deeply involved in those rights.

## TYPES OF PRODUCTION COMPANIES

### Very Small Production Companies

Most production companies are very small. Often the "company" is really just one person who periodically hires specialists on a project basis. More than a few such companies operate in living rooms, dining rooms, and basements. Equipped with an Avid or Final Cut Pro editing system (small enough to fit into a bedroom corner), a digital camcorder or two, and some audio and lighting equipment, these production companies handle a remarkable amount of work throughout the industry. Many promos, commercials, demo tapes, video news releases, and other projects are produced by very small production companies.

## Small Production Companies

An equally large number of projects are handled by small production companies consisting of two, three, or a few more people. Often, one or two people concentrate on client relations and business development. Another supervises projects. Others provide specific creative services. Some of these companies are formally organized as partnerships or corporations, and operate in permanent offices. Others project that image, but in fact work as very small companies of freelance contributors. In order to support an office and a group of full-time employees, a regular project flow is essential. Despite the best of intentions, many such companies fail because they cannot sell enough projects to assure the necessary cash flow.

It may seem wise to approach the marketplace with a team in place, ready to handle any and every relevant project. In fact, it is wise to begin somewhat informally, sell a few projects, and grow organically, adding part-time or freelance people rather than full-time employees or partners. On the one hand, this approach can be tricky, but on the other hand, a staff will expect to be paid. As soon as a project comes in the door, partners and employees will expect to collect on their investment of time spent on the company. Few project budgets can support their own development.

As a rule, the best way to start a small production company is to work either alone or with just one partner. A small company run by three people, each with equal say, is often cumbersome; a small company with four or five people on equal footing is a real challenge, despite their range of contacts and talents. An additional person can be added on a project basis—so his or her income expectation is based upon project performance, not upon company performance.

In a production company owned by several partners, there will be questions about compensation. One approach is to compensate each person based upon company revenues: Every project's revenue goes into the same pot, and each person receives a salary based upon their status in the industry and what the company can afford to pay. Another approach, which often proves problematic, is to pay the partners based upon their roles in specific projects. This approach falls short for three reasons. First, it does not compensate partners for company roles unrelated to the actual production: creative development, sales of projects that do not materialize, negotiation, attendance at industry events, budgeting, relationship building, and so on. Second, the client may decide to exclude one of the partners from the project. Third, the compensation associated with specific roles may vary; a project may, for example, require six weeks of a producer's time, but only two days of a director's time.

There are no easy answers here, but anyone contemplating a partnership (or a corporation whose shareholders are the people running the company) should compare notes with other production companies before making commitments to one another.

## Midsized Production Companies

Cable networks have enabled several small production companies to grow to 100 employees or more. One example is the former Stone Stanley Productions, which produced *Legends of the Hidden Temple* for Nickelodeon, *Oblivious* and *Joe Schmo 2* for Spike, *The Man Show* for Comedy Central, and *The Mole* for ABC. Another is Philadelphia-based Banyan Productions (*Trading Spaces* for TLC, *Ambush Makeover* for the FOX stations, *A Baby Story* for TLC). Weller/Grossman (*Wolfgang Puck* for Food Network, *Simply Quilts* for HGTV, A&E's *Top Ten*, *History Alive* for History Channel) is managed by a team of six people: two partners who also serve as executive producers of many of the company's projects, another executive producer, a development executive, a production executive, and a chief financial officer. Weller/Grossman has produced over 3,500 episodes. Banyan produces approximately 500 hours of television each year. All of these companies were founded in the early 1990s, just as original productions for cable were becoming financially viable.

For cable network programmers, there is real security in working with companies like Stone Stanley, Banyan, and Weller/Grossman. Specializing in cable programming, they tend to offer an appealing combination of existing resources and the forward-thinking marketplace understanding that is essential for their survival. With over a decade's experience, each of these companies is well connected at many cable networks. Still, a midsized company is easily pigeonholed, and these companies have been successful, over time, in broadening from a base of specific expertise. For many years, Banyan was mainly associated with soft reality shows seen on TLC during the daytime, and Stone Stanley was mostly known for midlevel cable network game shows. Both companies have expanded their range, but neither in a truly significant way. (The key decision: Stick to what the company does best, or expand for the future?) By comparison, Weller/Grossman has always managed a variety of project types.

## Production Companies with Studio Deals

Jerry Bruckheimer, a successful movie producer who has made a very lucrative transition to television—his company produces *Cold Case*, the CSI franchise, and *Without a Trace*—works with "a multimillion-dollar annual overhead and development fund provided by Warner Bros.," according to the *Hollywood Reporter*. Although Bruckheimer's deal is particularly large, the arrangement is common practice. Wolf Films, responsible for the *Law & Order* shows, is housed at Universal Television. Stephen Bochco has long been associated with Twentieth Television. Glenn Gordon Caron's series *Medium* was developed and is produced in association with Paramount Television and actor Kelsey Grammar's production company.

The majority of comedies and dramas seen on network and cable television are produced within the auspices of a major motion picture studio's television operation. For a writer-producer, the setup is ideal. He or she is provided with an office with a staff, the power and authority of a major motion picture studio, and easy access to program staff and crew. This type of deal is generally reserved for established producers with a significant track record, but smaller deals are often negotiated for promising writers with more modest producing credentials.

These relationships provide the studios with a steady flow of projects. Warner Bros., Paramount, Universal, and similar companies offer studio and post-production facilities; wardrobe, set, and casting departments; and the marketing power needed to exploit the programs. Each studio also maintains a development staff, which maintains close ties to the network program buyers, and a business affairs department staffed with attorneys who know how to make network television deals. For the producers, and for the networks, the studios also serve as banks, providing deficit financing in exchange for distribution rights, and providing what amounts to bridge loans so that production may commence, continue, or complete without reliance on client payments. Studios also maintain relationships with other studios and distribution companies outside the U.S., which often allows for coproduction and cofinancing arrangements, and for additional distribution.

Reality shows, which do not generally require the same sorts of facilities, are sometimes produced in association with a network's own production company. They may also be developed and produced by a smaller independent production company, or by the U.S. division of a global company, such as Endemol or FremantleMedia.

Network television production companies traditionally operate on an annual cycle that results in new series debuting either in September, January, or during the summer. Pitches typically begin during the fall and end during the winter. Pilots are made in the springtime and tested with sample audiences and with advertising agencies a short time later. The networks announce their fall schedules in early summer; the first new episodes are completed by early August. In fact, new series are now introduced throughout the year, but the traditional schedule continues to guide the process.

## Production of Syndicated and Cable Series

More often than not, a new program for syndication is based upon the talents of a single individual—Tony Danza or Ellen DeGeneres, for example. Typically, a large television syndicator will negotiate a contract with the promising performer and then attach a producer to the project so that it can be developed. (Sometimes, the performer comes with his or her own producer.) The production is made within the auspices of the syndicator or its affiliated television production company. This annual cycle involves pitches to station groups and advertising agencies during the spring and summer. In the fall, the pilots are made, and the first carriage deals are announced with station groups. The National Association of Television Production Executives (NATPE) convention, held annually in January, often results in additional sales. If the project is acquired by stations representing a sufficient portion of the U.S., then production proceeds during the summer in anticipation of a September debut.

Cable networks receive pitches from a wide range of producers and production companies, from the largest studios to the smallest independents. New cable series debut throughout the year, but the sharp emphasis is on debuts in early summer (an early lead in a relatively uncluttered marketplace), September, and January. Cable advertising is now tied to the upfront buying season (see page 73), so all of the important new series are announced no later than June.

## Production of Public Television Programs

Throughout the country, there are production companies that specialize in programs for public television. In general, these companies are allied with a producing or presenting station, or with a leading distributor of programs to public television stations, notably NETA (National Educational Telecommunications Association), APT (American Public Television), or PBS.

Pilot Productions, well known for the *Globe Trekker* series, began production of *Adventure Golf* in 2004. The series, whose per-episode cost is $130,000, is distributed by APT. The company is based in London. A La Carte Productions has supplied public television stations with cooking and other types of programs for 15 years. Their many familiar projects include multiple series with *Julia Child*, *The Frugal Gourmet*, *Lidia's Italian-American Kitchen*, and *Martin Yan Quick & Easy*. Based in San Francisco, A La Carte Productions is currently in a distribution deal with APT.

Florentine Films has produced many of PBS's most popular documentary series, including *The Civil War* and *Baseball*, both featuring the work of filmmaker Ken Burns. Florentine Films is based in New Hampshire. For a more complete list of public television projects, producing stations, and distributors, visit www.current.org/pipeline.

Public television projects usually require some corporate or foundation funding, so the timetable for development is often extended until this funding is secure. Still, PBS tends to parallel the commercial networks by debuting, or at least announcing, upcoming series in September of each year. As a rule of thumb, projects take about two-and-a-half years from concept to air. The better part of the first year is spent in development and raising money; the second is spent working with the presenting member station, or with PBS (often a shorter period if working with APT or NETA). Production often begins at the end of the second year or the start of the third year.

## Production of Non-broadcast Projects

It is possible that the majority of hours produced on video are never seen on any television network or local station. Once again, the non-broadcast industry is comprised of companies of widely varying sizes (but no company with the size or revenues of, say, Twentieth Television).

A great many small projects are produced for corporate communications and for training. Many of these are produced by outside production companies. These projects may be viewed on an internal corporate video network, on a Web site, on CD-ROM or DVD, or projected on a large screen in a meeting. Some of these video projects are seen only one time; others are distributed to thousands of people in a sales force, and used for years as a primary sales tool. Some are distributed to the press, others directly to consumers through virtual marketing leading to a specific Web site. American Express, for example, has produced several projects featuring comedian Jerry Seinfeld and his pal Superman. BMW has also been successful with a series of Web-distributed films (the distinction between a film and video is blurring; sometimes, the terms are inaccurately used interchangeably).

Video projects sold directly to consumers have also become popular—and many of these are never seen on television. Texas-based Liliedahl Publications specializes in a single niche (art instruction), and handles its own marketing and distribution. Liliedahl is a small company with a library of art instruction videos; most sales are made directly via its Web site. *Lady of Shallott*, for example, is a detailed demonstration (nearly four hours long) of oil painting, resulting in a picture reminiscent of old masters. The video sells for $85. The cost of the disc and packaging is just a few dollars; a net of $80 or more goes to cover the investment in production cost, advertising, and of course, profit. The production itself is not elaborate, so recoupment occurs early in the sales cycle. A marketing deal with a leading oil paint manufacturer further encourages sales and helps to limit cash expenditures. The company offers several dozen such videotapes, and benefits from repeat customers.

New Jersey–based Cushman Bolton Productions specializes in high-end travel video used within the travel industry for promotion. Clients include leading hotels and resorts. The company sells its videos through various retail sources, generally for about $25 per half-hour program. By combining client and entrepreneurial video activities, the company has developed an impressive product line. Some of these programs have been seen on the U.K.'s Travel Channel, but Cushman Bolton intentionally limits distribution to maintain asset value in the library.

Philadelphia-based Medical Broadcasting Company, or MBC, specializes in health care communications for pharmaceutical companies. It's now part of the WPP Group, one of the world's largest marketing communications firms.

Every major metropolitan area supports several firms that specialize in video production for corporate clients. Many of these firms now offer digital design, Web services, and other marketing communications services. Some also develop and market their own products. These additions to video production attest to a changed marketplace. Video production is now offered among a list of services. Few companies (apart from those operated by one or two people) can survive on video production services alone.

# CHAPTER 41

# PRODUCERS, DIRECTORS, AND WRITERS

This chapter describes the roles of people who work "above the line." In general, these jobs are creative, managerial, or administrative, or involve performance. People who work "below the line" are typically involved in staging, engineering/technical, or logistics. The "above" and "below" designations may have originated in early Hollywood, where those below the line were associated with the fixed costs of the operation. In fact, there are many stories about these terms, but their actual origin is unclear.

## PRODUCERS

On a broadcast network prime-time series, the *executive producer* (or *EP*, now a common term) usually supervises all creative aspects of the program. On some projects, where the art of the deal is critical to arranging financing or distribution, the executive producer credit may be taken by the person who arranges for the money—and in extreme cases, this person may not know (or care) much about the small details of making a television program. For this type of executive producer, television is a business, not an art.

The title is more clearly defined in local television. At a local station, the executive producer in charge of news reports to the news director. For stations that continue to create and produce original programs, the executive producer for non-news programming supervises original productions and reports to the program director.

The duties of the executive producer often include hiring and supervision of staff members, approval of key performers, approval of script and/or format, arrangement of technical facilities, and general business affairs. Some executive producers become more directly involved in specific aspects of the project, such as casting, scripting, or deal-making. In theory, the executive producer's job is supervision and guidance, not execution. In practice, particularly in prime-time television, an executive producer may also be a writer or may work very closely with the director in the studio or on the soundstage. This is not always the case, though. Some (and after a few seasons, nearly all) executive producers hire a staff to do the work, and then move on to the next deal and to the development of the next project.

The *producer* of a television program is the person responsible for the various creative, logistic, budgetary, and technical aspects of a project or series. He or she reports to the executive producer, who effectively acts as the chairman of the board to the producer's president. While the executive producer is concerned with the grand scheme and client/customer contact, the producer is charged with day-to-day task and staff management. That said, some producers are concerned only with the creative aspects of production, and others are concerned only with logistics.

Most prime-time network series employ a handful of producers focusing on the development, production, and delivery of segments (for a news magazine) or episodes (for a comedy or dramatic series). Many producers of prime-time programs are also writers who shape the program's characters, story lines, and guide overall development through close supervision of other writers as well as direct involvement in casting decisions.

The title of *senior producer* is one of several that exist between the executive producer level and the producer level. Like a supervising producer, it's a means to elevate an individual to a somewhat higher level, while reserving the highest level (executive producer) for another person or for a later time.

A *line producer* is directly responsible for logistics, schedules, and budgets. Contributions to the creative effort are of secondary importance. It is not generally a creative role.

A *segment producer* is responsible for specific segments within a larger production.

*Associate producer (AP)* is another term that can be defined only within the context of a particular project or series. On a talk, game, or variety show, an associate producer may have duties as a writer, some or all of the time (and so by calling the person an AP, the production may avoid WGA jurisdiction; see page 347). On a talk show, an associate producer may be in charge of finding and scheduling ("booking") guests, and may supervise the resulting segments in the studio. On a magazine show, an AP may be a field producer— writing, directing, and editing stories. An associate producer on a network series is frequently in charge of post-production, but may also serve as the producer's point person for casting, working with writers, managing the budget and schedules, and so on. These duties are also common for APs on variety shows, music and comedy specials, and information programs (such as home video how-to programs). In its pure form, the job of associate producer entails assisting the producer, taking care of time-consuming details, and supervising the other staff members. Often, the associate producer is a liaison between senior and junior staff members, and between different departments (such as public relations and accounting).

The *production assistant (PA)* is a junior staff member. Newcomers understand that the PA job is the first rung above internship, but many PAs are more experienced, and may be in line for an associate producer job. A *production coordinator* usually occupies the gray area between PA and AP, and is often assigned tasks associated with an associate producer. *Control room production assistant* is a more specialized job that involves logging tapes and time cues. The control room PA duties may overlap with those of the associate director (see below), and so may be under the jurisdiction of the Directors Guild of America (DGA) in some situations.

## Producer Agreements

There are two key clusters of issues in every agreement for a producer or executive producer. The first is based on rendering services; the second is related to the creation of programs or program elements. Executive producer and producer agreements are typically two to ten pages long (more if a profit definition is involved) and tend to cover many details related to term of employment, fee structure, on-screen credit, job responsibilities, and termination. Many production companies hire staff without any written agreement at all, though a short memorandum is advisable detailing the key points of the business arrangement and addressing the transfer of rights.

The following items should be covered in all producer agreements. (For the sake of convenience, the word "producer" is used to include executive producer, producer, associate producer, and the other classifications listed above.)

- *The business relationship between the hiring entity and the producer.*
  This must be clearly defined. Is the producer an *employee* or an
  *independent contractor?* This distinction is important for purposes
  of tax liability, personal injury insurance, unemployment insurance,
  workman's compensation, vesting in pension plans, and ownership
  of the proceeds of creative work. An employee typically works on
  premises provided by the employer, under the employer's direct
  supervision or control. An independent contractor, on the other
  hand, works for himself or herself. Although he or she may work
  at an office or in a facility provided by the hiring company, this is
  usually a matter of convenience, not a condition of hiring. An independent contractor does not receive the typical employee benefits.

  The creative efforts of an employee are considered to be a *work for
  hire*, and their copyright passes to the employer. That is, the employer,
  and not the employee, is legally the author or creator of the work. In
  order for the creative work of an independent contractor to be considered a work for hire, it must be specifically described as such in a
  written work-for-hire agreement between the independent contractor
  and the hiring company.

The distinctions between employees and independent contractors are explained in greater detail in on page 414.

- *A description of the services to be rendered by the producer.* Such services may be stated in a general way, as in "the duties and obligations typically required of a producer of a major-market television news program." The description may also be a long list of specific responsibilities followed by a catch-all phrase like "and all of the other duties typically required of a producer of a major-market news program." The best agreements provide a detailed list of the prospective employee's day-to-day responsibilities, but allow flexibility for personal growth.

- *The degree of exclusivity.* May the producer serve in a similar capacity on projects that are unrelated to the employer's programs? And may the producer serve in other capacities—as writer or director, for example—on other programs?

- *Compensation—how much, and when it will be paid?* Employees are usually paid weekly, biweekly, or twice a month; independent contractors are often paid semi-monthly or monthly. One popular alternative is linking partial payments to the project's schedule: An independent contractor might receive one-quarter of the total payment upon signing the agreement, one-quarter on the first day of shooting, one-quarter on the start of editing, and one-quarter on delivery of the finished project. The formula varies, but the underlying philosophy is to pay the producer a reasonable wage while ensuring his or her involvement through the end of the project. While it is clearly to the producer's advantage to front-load the payments, most agreements reflect a reasonable compromise.

- *A description of the rights granted to the hiring company, with regard not only to the current project(s), but also to projects in development.* For example, if a producer begins development of a new project for a cable network while an employee of the network, the network will own all rights to the project unless some other arrangement is described in the agreement. In another example, if a segment producer working on a magazine show develops a story that the employer subsequently sells as a TV movie, the segment producer's involvement in the secondary property must be clear from several perspectives, notably possible employment on the movie project, financial compensation as a member of the movie production's staff, and any additional compensation from the movie's profits. (Whether the segment producer gets any of these benefits is entirely subject to negotiation, though in this instance, tradition does not favor the segment producer's negotiating position.) Some hiring companies will not make commitments regarding future work, in effect dissuading employees and independent contractors from discussing new concepts with their employers.

- *Who has the right of "final cut," or the right to declare a program complete?* In a few cases, a producer will have final artistic control; usually, though, the production company or network will retain this right. Related issues include control over marketing, distribution, and other business decisions.

- *The on-screen credit to be received by the producer.* This should be clearly described—not only the wording, but also the prominence and placement of the credit. Will it appear on every episode? In first position? Full-screen or shared? What happens to these promises if additional producers are hired?

- *Representations, warranties, and indemnities.* In the representations and warranties section of a producer agreement, the producer states that he or she is free to enter the agreement, and that there are no agreements presently in effect that would affect his or her ability to perform the services described in the new agreement. The producer also confirms that any ideas brought to the project will be either original or in the public domain, and that any such ideas will not violate the rights of any other person or institution. The notion of rights here relates to copyrights and property rights as well as to personal rights—the rights to privacy and to protection from defamation, slander, and libel (see Chapter 35).

  Too many agreements are one-sided: The producer makes representations and warranties, but the hiring company does not. Ideally, both parties should present a comprehensive list of what they represent and warrant to each other. (The concept of representations and warranties is discussed in greater detail on page 408.)

  The indemnities section that usually follows may include foreboding language; it provides both parties with clear financial remedies should any of the representations, warranties, or other terms of the agreement be breached or proven untrue. This section is often quite technical and requires a lawyer's reading. In essence, indemnification clauses detail who will pay the costs of defending against losses, and who will pay in the case of judgments that require damages. (For more about indemnities, see page 409.)

- *Credits.* Most agreements require the producer to allow the hiring company, and its licensees, to use the producer's name, biography, photograph, and so forth in the marketing of the program. In some instances, the producer may retain the right to remove his or her name from the program's credits and from any related advertising or promotional materials, typically to disassociate himself or herself from a product gone bad.

- *The right of the producer to reimbursal for travel and entertainment expenses within a reasonable amount of time.* Such expenses may be limited by a process of preapproval, by budget parameters, or by company policies (employees may not be permitted to entertain one another on the expense account, for example). Some companies will not reimburse items over $25 without a receipt. Reimbursement within 30 days of submission of the expense report is reasonable. It's usually best for individual employees to limit their credit card purchases on behalf of the production; a production account with assigned retail vendors (such as office supply stores and nearby restaurants for late-night meals) has become common practice.

## DIRECTORS

A television *director* provides three essential skills: ability to guide performers to their best work, taste and discretion to compose and select the optimum visual presentation, and technical know-how to supervise a crew of engineers and operators.

Although the specific responsibilities of the director's job vary depending upon the type of project, it is fair to say that most directors spend about half their time planning, and the other half rehearsing, shooting, and/or editing. The planning phase usually begins with a series of production meetings to determine technical requirements such as set and lighting design. The director will also interact with the cast and the performers.

On a situation comedy, the director typically works a five-day week. A typical week's schedule might run as follows: The first morning is devoted to a script reading with cast members. In the afternoon, the director plans camera angles, frequently with the help of an associate director, and screens the edited version of the previous week's show. He or she spends the second day on the set, working with the performers. The third day is a camera rehearsal where performances and camera angles are integrated (sitcoms are produced on videotape with multiple cameras). The fourth day brings more rehearsal, and the recording of two (sometimes three) takes of the show. At this point, the director spends most of his or her time in the control room, offering performance comments only when necessary. The fifth day is devoted to screening and working with the editor to select the best reading of each line in the script. Some directors are more involved with editing than others.

If a single director handles the entire series, or shares it with perhaps one other director, then a season-long contract is common. Most sitcoms work with several directors who are paid per episode and may be guaranteed a particular number of episodes per season. Directors of hour-long dramatic series follow a similar schedule. A director of soap operas follows a similar routine, though the amounts of time for rehearsal and shooting are compressed in order to produce five shows per week. Several directors may share duties on a single daytime drama series, shooting one or two days per week and prepping on the others. Since soaps run for years, principal directors are typically hired as staff.

On a news program, the director becomes active once tape pieces begin to arrive from the editing rooms, usually starting a few hours prior to air and continuing throughout the broadcast itself. The format of a news program is predetermined, but the director must review the entire script, screen as many of the edited videotape stories as possible (or at least their first and last few seconds), and prepare for any live interview segments. News directors are generally employed as full-time staff working for the station or network.

Talk shows are generally recorded, or broadcast live, one per day or, in a condensed schedule, perhaps two or even three per day. Rehearsal typically precedes the recording of each episode by an hour or so. A director is usually hired for the entire season, and paid a weekly salary as a freelancer.

Game shows are generally recorded in batches of three to five half hours per day, typically for several weeks in a row. Then the staff returns to the office for several weeks to prepare more game material (such as questions), book more contestants, and so forth. The director is paid per week of completed programs, on a freelance contract.

## Associate and Assistant Directors (ADs)

When a studio production involves more than three cameras and a small number of other cues (such as sound or lighting cues), the director is frequently assisted by an *associate director (AD)*. The AD is responsible for all communication with videotape recording and playback facilities, and with departments that do not require the director's explicit creative attention, such as audio- or videotape recorders and playback. The AD also times all segments, calls countdowns to time cues, prepares logs of all audiotape and videotape recordings plus playback material, and maintains schedules.

Associate directors work on videotaped and live shows. Sometimes, when there is a great deal of real-time coordination or when a production's tradition demands, the AD is assisted by a control room production assistant.

*Assistant director* is a film term that applies when a television program is shot on film. A film AD is in charge of the set; he or she issues call times for the cast and crew, prepares production reports (including actual time spent filming each scene, breaks, downtime due to equipment or personnel problems, and so on), and serves as the eyes of the production company on the set.

*Freelance directors* typically select their own freelance ADs. Staff directors work with the AD assigned to their program. Although ADs are paid considerably less than directors, they are employed on the same basis as directors on most productions.

## Directors Guild of America

The Directors Guild of America, or DGA, is a trade union for directors. The organization represents television, commercial, and motion picture directors, as well as associate and assistant directors, stage managers working in television studios, and some production assistants and associates. The DGA has negotiated collective bargaining agreements with the commercial networks and with production companies that supply the networks with programming, but the DGA's jurisdiction is limited. In television, the broadcast networks are signatories to DGA collective bargaining agreements, but many cable networks are not. A network or production company that is a signatory to a DGA agreement agrees to hire only DGA personnel (or a director who will subsequently join the DGA). The DGA also has contracts with some suppliers to the syndication and cable markets, but there is no DGA agreement covering syndication in general, or basic cable. Although many nonfiction programs seen on basic cable networks are directed by nonmembers, most fiction seen on U.S. television is directed by a DGA member.

A member of the DGA can only work for companies and networks that are DGA signatories. In other words, union members can work only in union shops, and cannot work in non-union shops. Although there are notable exceptions, cable networks that output a large amount of daily or weekly programming produced in a studio are non-union shops, and cable networks that produce a regular schedule of original film or fiction programs are union shops. Since the distinction can be cumbersome, from time to time the DGA issues waivers or negotiates project-based deals for its members. This practice allows union members to work for non-union shops, while also allowing the DGA to maintain its integrity and viability.

There are two basic agreements for television: the DGA Basic Agreement (BA), and the DGA Freelance Live and Tape Television Agreement (FLTTA, pronounced "flita"). Why are there two agreements? The BA, by and large, covers dramatic programming, and FLTTA covers nonfiction (see complete agreements on the DGA Web site at www.dga.org). The following should provide a general understanding of some of the key points in these agreements:

- Under the BA, a director of a network prime-time, hour-long dramatic program would receive a minimum of $32,874 for seven days of work, including preparation and shooting. Rates for sitcoms are comparable, but rates for studio series are considerably less. For a dramatic half-hour network prime-time show, the rate is $19,361 for prep and shooting. A onetime network variety hour-long special, covered by FLTTA, pays $26,098 for up to 18 days of work.

- *When directing a pilot for a series, the director is entitled to additional compensation if the series is ordered.* The director receives additional compensation for development services, for directing talent tests, for shooting underwater or in flight, and for other special situations. These are *economic rights,* and there are many such rights in both the BA and the FLTTA.

- *The director receives residuals for replays.* For a network prime-time program, the director receives 100 percent of the "network prime-time reuse fee"—a specific, negotiated fee for the replay of a program. For other types of programs, or other distribution, separately negotiate reuse fees may apply. For plays that fall outside of this fee, the first rerun pays 50 percent of the base for a network run (or 40 percent of the base if the program ran in syndication); the second rerun pays 40 percent of the base (30 percent for non-network); and the residual scale works its way down to 5 percent for the thirteenth and each subsequent run. These numbers are provided only as rough figures; a detailed explanation of the current rates can be found in the DGA agreement.

- *The production is required to pay fringe benefits on behalf of the director to a health plan managed by the DGA and the signatory companies.* The amounts are as follows: 5.5 percent of gross salary for pension, plus 8.5 percent of gross salary for health and welfare. In addition, the director contributes 2.5 percent of gross compensation for his or her own pension.

- *The duties of the director vary based upon the type of program and the production's requirements.* For a one-hour episodic program, for example, the DGA rule of "one program, one director" applies, but for a daytime drama, several directors may contribute to the work of making each episode (and the director who contributes the most to that episode is identified, credited, and paid as the show's director). Also in creative rights, the director is entitled to edit the program, subject to the producer's approval.

- *In general, "creative rights" in the agreements are organized in pre-production ("prep"), production, and post-production.* During prep, the director should participate in casting and key creative staff decisions. If there's a script, the director should receive it no less than 24 hours prior to the start of prep (and hopefully, well before that time). A director should be involved in every creative decision. Creative rights protect the integrity of the director and his or her work; a director should be informed of the transmission of electronic images or sounds from the set. After production, the director should be allowed to finish his or her work without interference. If additional scenes, retakes, or looping is required by the producer, then the director has right of first refusal to do this work. Also in creative rights, the director is entitled to edit the program, subject to the producer's approval.

The standard DGA agreements serve as the foundation, but individual directors may benefit from additional compensation as producers, or as profit participants beyond the terms of the DGA agreements.

## Producer-Director Hyphenates

A *producer-director* is one person who performs two jobs. From the perspective of the producer-director, the combination provides a high level of control, plus the flexibility to pursue the most enticing creative aspects of both jobs. The job title and the premium salary are also appealing. From the perspective of the hiring company, a producer-director combination is a way to save money on two significant line items. The total paid to one individual is almost always less than the total that would be paid to two; sometimes, the combination can be hired for a premium of only 30 or 40 percent.

The *field producer*, one type of producer-director hybrid, evolved with the use of portable video equipment. Single-camera production is more like simple filmmaking than traditional multi-camera television production—one person can produce, write, and direct a "field piece." In terms of hierarchy, a field producer is roughly equivalent to a segment producer, who in turn can be equal to or just above an associate producer.

## WRITERS

Most television programs require the services of at least one *writer*. When several writers are employed, a *head writer* often supervises the group.

The specific responsibilities of the television writer vary, depending upon the project and its requirements. A news writer may research a story, assemble and double-check the facts, and produce a work of journalistic substance; alternatively, a news writer may do little more than rewrite stories taken from wire services. Frequently, the job involves a little bit of both. A writer of children's programming takes an active part in developing program segments and character interaction, then scripts the sequences. Writing a daytime drama involves contributions to an ongoing story line; senior writers and producers determine the plot, and the writing staff then scripts individual episodes based on story outlines. A writer of prime-time comedy or drama usually submits a basic story outline, which is revised with notes from the story editor(s) and/or producer(s). This then becomes the basis for a first, second, and polished version of the script, which goes through similar revisions. Scripts are almost always changed after they've been read by performers; the amount of change depends upon the production schedule, the performer's degree of control, and the degree to which the script "works" as it moves from page to stage.

Some writers function as staff members or employees; others work on freelance contracts, which may be similar to working on assignment for a specified number of scripts per season. These creative works are acquired by the production company or network, and the writer surrenders all (or most) rights, at least for a period of time. Most writers also prepare their own original scripts in the hopes of getting hired, or selling their own series, and these are owned by the writer until sold.

## Writers Guild of America

In fact, there are two Writers Guilds of America (WGA): Writers Guild of America East (WGAE) and Writers Guild of America West (WGAW). Both negotiate and administer the same collective-bargaining agreements and share a pension and a health benefits plan. Combined, these organizations represent over 13,000 professional writers working in motion pictures, television, radio, and interactive media, but not commercial advertising. The WGA negotiates agreements with the networks, syndication companies, and other entities involved in hiring writers to create television programming. When a production company or network becomes a signatory to the WGA, it agrees to the terms of the Minimum Basic Agreement (MBA), which requires that all writers hired by the company are members of the WGA (or will become members, as described below). When a writer becomes a member of the WGA, he or she cannot write for a company that is not a signatory to the MBA. A production company can hire a writer who is not yet a WGA member; in these instances, the writer must join the WGA within 30 days of employment. Otherwise, the signatory company will be required by the WGA to terminate the writer's employment.

To become a signatory, a company contacts the WGA and requests an application. A new company may be required to provide financial assurances prior to employing any writers. When a writer is hired, payments are made directly to the writer, with a pension and health contribution paid to the Writers Guild Health Fund & Pension Plan on the writer's behalf. If a writer earns a sufficient amount per year, he or she can qualify for a year's health coverage at no cost.

To become a member of the WGA, a writer must have an agreement with a signatory for work. To verify the signatory status of a company, it's best to check with the WGA. Within 30 days of the start of employment, the writer must apply for membership and, if eligible, then join the WGA. The initiation fee for freelance writers in WGA East is $1,500, and in WGA West, $2,500. Members are required to pay $100 per year for dues, plus 1.5 percent of gross compensation related to WGA contracts (0.25 percent is also placed in a strike fund, so members may borrow interest-free in case of a strike).

The following are the key elements of the WGA agreement:

- *Minimum rates for the writing of a story, first draft teleplay, and final draft teleplay.* These rates are based on the length of the program and whether it airs in prime-time, daytime, or late-night. Additional rates are quoted for rewrite and polish; for plot outline, backup script, and narration; and for a show format (a complete explanation of the history and characters on a series). If the program is produced for pay TV or home video, and if it is in the style that normally airs in network prime time, then the network prime-time rates apply. Rates are higher for pilots than for series.

- *Rerun compensation.* Calculating these payments can be complicated, and readers are advised to refer to the WGA Basic Agreement or the Schedule of Minimums for a complete explanation and the latest information. Compensation for other types of programs is similar in approach, but different with regard to specifics: Check the current Basic Agreement for details. Residuals and reuse fees are also paid for replays on basic cable, for home video releases, and for foreign runs.

- *Compensation for writers hired on a weekly basis, who work as staff members.*

- *The minimum rate at which a production company, network, or distributor may purchase an existing work from a WGA member.* The minimum for options is 5 percent for the first 180 days, and 10 percent for each period of 180 days thereafter.

- *Additional compensation.* This applies for a writer if a remake is made, or if a sequel is created based on his or her work—or if a character that first appeared in his or her work becomes the central character in a spin-off series or appears in other episodes.

- *Payment rates.* Rates and a required number of writers, for variety shows. Rates for quiz and audience participation programs on both network and syndication; for daytime serials (soap operas); and for religious programs, documentaries, and news programs.

- *Benefits.* The requirement that the hiring company pay 6 percent of the writer's gross compensation to the WGA pension fund, plus

6.5 percent of the writer's gross compensation to the WGA health and welfare fund.

- *Rules regarding travel and rules regarding notice prior to termination.*

- *Rules regarding appropriate credits.* The MBA is very specific about the form and placement of credits: the terms "written by," "teleplay by," and "story by" have particular meanings. These terms may trigger specific residual payments, or lead to "separation of rights," whereby a writer who originates the project can hold back certain rights for himself or herself.

## Writer Hyphenates

Since the writer is so critical to the creative development of a television project, many writers follow a natural inclination toward greater involvement in the production. Many writers become producers or directors. Some become performers (and some writers performed before they became writers).

The *writer-producer* is common in the prime-time community, where capable writers are highly valued, and where they are frequently given the opportunity to stretch their creative muscles. In the best of circumstances, a writer-producer molds a series and its characters with special insight; in the worst, the writer-producer can be a difficult hindrance to efficient production—power placed in the wrong hands. Some writer-producers concentrate on writing (and rewriting the work of others), wielding the producer's power only when needed to win a creative point. Others concentrate on rewrites, or supervise performers or a writing staff without generating original scripts on their own. Every situation is different.

The *writer-director* is doing two discrete jobs. In the office and through the planning stages, he or she concentrates on writing; in the studio or on the soundstage, directing requires total attention, and the writing is either delayed or scheduled for off-hours. As with the producer-director, two fees are paid, based on DGA and WGA agreements; a writer-director hyphenate working on a non-union show is likely to be paid a fee that is less than a full writing fee and a full directing fee combined.

The *writer-performer* is frequently found in comedy. Many successful television comedians have worked on the writing staff of previous comedy programs, or they've been stand-up comedians. The transition from writer or performer to writer-performer often evolves naturally, though the process can be accelerated by an aggressive agent or manager. When a comedian is the central character on a network prime-time series, he or she is often an executive producer of the series.

# CHAPTER 42

# PERFORMERS

Most professional television performers are members of one or both performers' unions: AFTRA (American Federation of Television and Radio Artists) and SAG (Screen Actors Guild). AFTRA's jurisdiction has traditionally been videotape and live productions, as well as radio programs and commercials produced on videotape; SAG's jurisdiction has been television programs produced on film, film commercials, and theatrical motion pictures. AFTRA has local offices, or locals, in most of the 30 largest U.S. markets. SAG works out of about 20 regional branch offices, including New York City, Los Angeles, Chicago, Boston, and Miami.

The vast majority of performers with the skill and talent required for successful on-camera performance are members of AFTRA, SAG, or both. Therefore, most programs seen on network, major-market local, and national cable television feature performers working under an AFTRA or SAG agreement. Although producers are loath to admit it, the rules of these unions are not too burdensome. What producers do tend to dispute, however, is how the payment of residuals is becoming more complex and expensive as distribution markets continue to evolve.

## AFTRA AGREEMENT BASICS

The AFTRA Network Television Code was first negotiated in 1952, and it has been revised many times to reflect current trends in television programming, production, marketing, and distribution. Rates paid to artists vary depending upon the type of program. The current Code covers eight types of programs: non-dramatic (game shows, variety shows, reality); entertainment news; daytime dramas; network dramas seen on ABC, CBS, NBC, and FOX; FOX programs that started production prior to November 16, 2003; WB and UPN dramatic prime-time programs; non–prime-time dramas; and syndicated dramas (including UPN and WB shows that started production prior to July 1, 2004). At first, all of this seems complicated, but a patient reading of the agreement (available at www.aftra.com) helps to clarify.

Rates also vary depending on the category into which a performer falls. Covered under all of the AFTRA agreements, exhibits, rate cards, and so on are basically ten types of performers, each assigned a particular rate for hours, days, weeks, or whatever time period is appropriate. These performance categories are: principal performers, performers who speak five lines or less ("under fives"), and voice-over announcers (actually, this is two categories: one for those who speak more than ten lines, and one for those who speak less; narrators are considered to be principal performers). In addition, there are group dancers (soloists and duos are considered to be principals); chorus singers (again, two categories: groups of three to eight, and groups of nine or more); specialty acts; sportscasters; background actors; warm-ups (the person who "warms up" a studio audience but whose performance is not recorded); and stand-ins.

The third set of variables is related to the programs themselves. Rates are based upon program length, not upon the amount of time that a particular performer appears. If the program is produced for airing more than one day per week, then a weekly rate applies (this is a discounted day rate). A specific number of hours of rehearsal are included in each rate, along with the period during which these hours may be scheduled (additional rehearsal hours, and an extended period of rehearsal days, may be arranged based on additional payments).

How does all of this work in the real world? Here are several working examples.

Principal performers appearing in a prime-time series receive a minimum of about $700. A principal performer is any performer who speaks more than five lines, or otherwise occupies a principal role (there are definitions in the contract, but most anyone whom you would notice on camera as a performer receives principal performer status). Solo and duo singers receive about $50 more per day, and those in groups receive about $50 less. If the performer appears for an entire week, the rate is about $2,500, the equivalent of approximately three-and-a-half days of work.

Principal performers who appear in a major role on a half-hour television series receive a minimum fee of about $3,500 per episode; those appearing in an hour-long program receive about $6,000. Contract players on a series receive less per episode (about $2,400 per half-hour, or $2,900 per hour), but they do work more regularly.

An "under five" receives about $400 per day; as other rates, this varies depending upon the program length (the rate is about $150 for programs from 5 to 15 minutes long, and over $500 for programs longer than 90 minutes).

In addition, there are work rules. Each day's work involves a "minimum daily call": a minimum number of hours that the performer is expected to be available. A performer cannot work for more than six hours without a meal break (or a penalty fee must be paid by the producer). If a performer wears his or her own clothes or wig, they receive a fee ($10 for each outfit, $25 for formal wear). If a performer appears in a series, he or she may be entitled to vacation time and holiday pay. Additional compensation is paid if the performance or related conditions are considered hazardous. Performers are paid a specified per diem for work on location, plus meals, travel expenses, and hotels. In addition, they are paid $75 per day for non-work, non-travel days on location. Producers are also required to maintain a $200,000 insurance policy for performers working on location.

There must be a 12-hour break between the end of work on one day and the start of work on the next (a penalty is charged if the break is less than 12 hours). Meal breaks are just over an hour long (a half-hour for the second meal, if it's catered). A rest period of five minutes must be provided for each hour's work.

If a performer receives a fee that is higher than minimum scale (this is called an "overscale payment"), the producer may apply fees due for overtime, wardrobe, and travel against the overscale payments.

Performers who are required to add or remove hair on their face or head are paid $35 to do so. As for nudity, this is done at the performer's option, a decision made after the performer has read the script.

Principal performers receive screen credits; for other performers, it's useful to check the wording of the agreement.

Performers who appear in network prime-time reruns receive 100 percent of their original compensation, but only up to a "ceiling." After the fee reaches the ceiling, the producer may continue to run the program without additional payment to the performer. For other programs, after an initial 60-day period, replays are paid at 75 percent of gross compensation for the first replay, and 75 percent more for the second, then 50 percent for the third, fourth, and fifth replays. Then it's 10 percent for the sixth, and 5 percent for each additional replay. The scale for reality shows starts at 50 percent and declines more rapidly.

A producing company that is a signatory to the AFTRA agreement is required to contribute to AFTRA's Health & Retirement Funds. Depending upon the type of project, the contribution due is based upon a percentage (12.6 percent) of the performer's gross compensation. (*Gross* includes the amount actually paid to the performer before deductions, plus overtime payments, commissions paid to third parties such as agents, fees paid for the use of a performer's own wardrobe, and related subsidies.)

When work is completed, payment is due no later than the Thursday following the last working week. Specific rules apply for performers who are working for extended periods of time. Penalties apply for late payments.

Performers are not usually paid for interviews and auditions of reasonable length, but they are entitled to payment for excessive time (e.g., over one hour). If the audition is a more formal affair, then the performer receives half the program rate.

For an ongoing series, a specific number of weeks' notice must be given if a program is canceled.

AFTRA arbitrates conflicts with producing companies on behalf of its members.

# SAG AGREEMENT BASICS

As with AFTRA, there are several types of SAG agreements—for commercials, for network programs, for motion pictures, and so forth. Once again, readers are encouraged to carefully review an up-to-date version of the relevant agreement, since there is a wide range of work rules and rate structures involved. For more detailed information, and for the newer agreement, visit www.sag.org.

The 2001–2005 SAG Theatrical Motion Pictures and Television Agreement includes the following terms.

The minimum rate for day performers is $678 per day. Based upon previous years, this rate is likely to be about $700 to $750 per day in the next new agreement. There are many special types of performers, whose needs are specifically addressed in the agreement. For example, the day rate for all performers applies to stunt performers, but airplane pilots are paid a considerable premium. Singers receive a small premium, and a rate less than $678 if they appear as part of a group (and still less if they mouth the music without actually singing on the recording). There are rates for on- and off-camera singers, and similar rates for dancers.

Performers may also be hired by the week, generally for three to four times the day rate, or for three days, also at a discounted rate.

In general, performers are not paid for interviews or auditions, but the agreement does require the producer to pay a penalty if the performer is kept waiting for more than an hour (it's questionable how many producers actually pay this penalty). Performers are paid for makeup, hair, wardrobe, and fitting calls, typically with a one-hour minimum if the work is not done as part of a full workday. These rules vary depending upon the performer's term of employment. Performers are paid for certain types of travel time (typically when the transportation is provided by the producer). Performers receive a minimum meal allowance on location: $12 for breakfast, $18 for lunch, and $30 for dinner.

Performers are generally entitled to a rest period of 12 consecutive hours between performances, plus a rest period of 56 consecutive hours once per week. For each violation of a rest period, the producer must pay a fee of approximately one day's pay.

Similarly, there are rules for meal breaks. The first meal break must occur within six hours of the first call. There are some nuances here, so producers and performers should read contract terms carefully.

A workweek may begin any day of the week, and consists of any five of seven consecutive days. Premiums are paid when the performer works on a sixth or seventh day during a workweek. This situation becomes more complicated when the television project is a major special with a lot of rehearsal or pre-tapes, or when the project is on location with a variety of factors affecting production.

A workday consists of eight consecutive hours (plus meal breaks). Work during the ninth and tenth hours is paid at time-and-a-half. Work after the tenth hour is paid at double the standard rate.

Payments are due within five days after the work is rendered. If there is a delay, penalties apply.

Performers receive additional compensation for reruns, but arrangements vary depending upon the usage. For example, on pay television, ten plays or one year's use (whichever comes first) are permitted before the performer is entitled to receive a fair portion of 6 percent of the project's worldwide gross. On broadcast television, residuals for UPN and WB are lower than for other networks. For other markets, the rules are different. There are also payments due for foreign use.

In addition to payments for work, producers also make a mandatory contribution on behalf of the performer to SAG's pension and welfare fund. These payments are based upon 13.5 percent of gross compensation, with several notable exclusions.

There are special provisions with regard to safety, and others for working with minors.

One big concern for SAG is the proliferation of reality shows. In the period from 2003 to 2005, SAG's estimated job loss was over 9,000 union jobs.

## CASTING

There are several sources of performers for television productions.

### Talent Agencies

A talent agency is a company that specializes in representing performers, although many agencies represent producers, writers, directors, and other key creative people as well. Most successful performers working on the national scene are represented by a large agency; the William Morris Agency, ICM, and CAA are among the biggest. There are also smaller boutique agencies that either specialize in particular formats (game shows, daytime drama, sports, news) or offer a level of personal service that a larger agency rarely delivers to most of its clients.

Although the business arrangements vary with specific performers, an agency typically collects a 10 percent commission on gross earnings for every job within the entertainment industry—whether the agency arranges for the work or not. The performer's paycheck is sent to the agency, which deducts a commission and issues a new check to its client. If the job is not within the entertainment industry, and was not arranged by the agency—hosting a presentation at an automotive industry trade show, for example—the performer is normally paid directly, without agency involvement.

Contrary to the dreams of many performers, agencies do not usually seek out work for their clients. Instead, agencies are responsive to the needs of the marketplace. When producers, networks, or advertising agencies are casting for a program, they usually call the larger agencies, as a matter of course. The smaller agencies do their best to keep up with what's happening, and to stay on the active list of various casting entities.

Some well-known performers work without an agent, instead employing an attorney to negotiate fees on their behalf. In most cases, the attorney earns an hourly rate for services. Some high-powered Los Angeles attorneys take a commission of 5 percent or more in addition to, or in lieu of, an hourly fee. (A more detailed discussion of the roles of agents, lawyers, and business managers appears in Chapter 43.)

## Photographs, Résumés, Videotapes, Web Sites

A photograph is a kind of calling card for a performer. The standard format for a performer's photograph is a recent 8 x 10–inch glossy photo with name printed below the photo. On the back is a printed résumé or list of performance credits, union affiliations, and contact information (address and phone numbers for agency, home, and answering service).

Videotapes can be effective résumé tools—if the casting person takes the time to screen them. It is simply faster to scan a pile of photographs; performers whose photos are promising may be evaluated on videotape, but more often an in-person meeting or audition is the first step. Some types of productions (i.e., local news shows) make extensive use of videotapes for casting decisions.

For some types of performers—news reporters and anchors, for example—visibility via a Web site may be a useful career-building tool. With streaming video, it's easier for potential clients in larger markets to see the television journalist in action. This strategy is less effective for actors, for whom the in-person audition remains a blessing and a curse.

## Interviews and Auditions

As a prerequisite to getting a job, performers expect to be interviewed and auditioned, sometimes several times.

An interview generally runs under 30 minutes (often under 15 minutes), and offers the producer or casting director an opportunity to speak informally with the candidate. The session is useful in learning whether the candidate can ad-lib, how the candidate presents himself or herself, how he or she responds to others, and to a certain extent, the candidate's personal interests and motivations. Under the show business veneer, a casting interview is a job interview, and is subject to the same restrictions and standards that rule all employment proceedings. Questions about age, religious affiliation, marital status, race, and color should not be asked; to do so may bring about a complaint and an investigation of company hiring practices.

An audition may be held in addition to, or in place of, an interview. The audition typically requires the performer to read lines, or to ad-lib within a structured situation. For example, a news reporter may be required to read a report aloud (in an office, on videotape, or live on the air) or to prepare a sample story; a sportscaster might be recorded doing play-by-play at an event. Some auditions require the candidate to interact with other performers.

Often, the first round of auditions is casual, and does nothing more than eliminate the least likely candidates. It may be conducted by an associate producer, who reports the most promising candidates to the producer, executive producer, and network executive(s). A director may be actively involved in the first round or may join in as serious contenders are selected; this depends on the type of project and on the personal style of the producer, director, and others who have worked together before. A second round of auditions is usually more intensive, yielding between three and five finalists. A third round of auditions, now conducted with great attention to detail, allows the producer and others involved in the process to make a final decision. There may be more rounds or fewer, depending upon the situation. If a substantial amount of work is required during the auditions, AFTRA or SAG may require that the performer(s) be paid.

## NEGOTIATING A PERFORMANCE AGREEMENT

Producers must balance two key issues when hiring talent: working within budget limitations and attracting the best possible performers to the project. AFTRA and SAG prescribe minimum fees for performers working in productions within their jurisdictions. In non-union cases, market conditions unofficially dictate rates, subject to minimum-wage regulations. Many performers, particularly those with experience, want to be paid more than the minimum fee. In many such cases, the performer sets a day rate for his or her services; this rate is usually negotiable, particularly if employment is for an extended period.

Before the producer tests anyone or sits down to final auditions, it is important that a *pre-test option* is negotiated. A pre-test option fixes the basic terms of the agreement should the performer be successful in the audition. Without such an option, the network or distributor may "fall in love" with a particular performer and insist that the producer deliver that performer regardless of price. This situation can place the performer in control, and a savvy agent can drive the price very high. A pre-test option caps the performer's rate—an essential protection for the producer.

For well-known performers, or performers with strong agency or legal representation, the producer and the agent may spend hours, days, even weeks negotiating the fine points of daily vs. weekly vs. per-show salary, travel arrangements, profit participation, on-screen billing, use and appearance of the performer's name in advertising, and other such details.

A letter agreement is an appropriate form of contract for hiring the performer. This agreement should set forth the dates that the performer will be needed, the fees that will be paid, the arrangement regarding residuals, and so on. SAG and AFTRA have standard forms for certain kinds of hiring.

A more formal agreement may be prepared for high-paid performers, or for anyone working on a project where lengthy contracts make good business sense. Appendix 3.2 is a typical short-form agreement for services, adaptable to the performer context.

## NON-UNION EMPLOYMENT

Most established television performers are members of AFTRA and SAG, and most major producing organizations are union signatories as well. However, many smaller production companies, home video companies, business video companies, and cable networks are not signatories to agreements with the performance unions. The most common reason is the added cost of benefit payments and residuals. Some of these companies are poorly equipped, both financially and administratively, to pay ongoing residuals, while others simply want a more favorable arrangement. A non-union shop can hire anyone it pleases because it is not beholden to an agreement that says otherwise. A union performer, however, is in violation of his or her agreement when working for a nonsignatory within the union's jurisdiction, and may be subject to a penalty.

In certain situations, both AFTRA and SAG have negotiated "one-shot" short-term agreements covering particular projects, allowing a nonsignatory company to hire union performers. AFTRA and SAG have been among the most reasonable unions in television, but even their flexibility has its limits.

## WORKING WITH PERFORMERS

The performer is expected to do his or her job by following the instructions of the producer and director, who represent the production's management and owners regardless of whether this expectation is explicitly worded in a contract. Most performers recognize this authority, take instructions, add their own creativity, and work hard to please their employers. The ideal situation is a lively give-and-take, with each party respectful of the other's role, but with a certain challenge and spice thrown in so that each does the best possible work. Ultimately, the performer should be comfortable with the words, the style, and the presentation involved in the role.

Conversely, a strong performer matched with a needy director or production team can head off problems and present a polished product despite poor preparation, less-than-skillful direction, or troublesome production technique. To put this another way, experience counts for much in the television business, and a good performer can save a production.

Some performers, however, display a defiant attitude that can undermine the director's ability to complete the program or the producer's promises to a client. When there are problems, the performer can either (i) do the best he or she can under the circumstances; (ii) fight the director and do what he or she believes is right, regardless of consequences; (iii) complain to the powers-that-be; or (iv) leave. In rare instances, he or she may attempt to have the offending producer or director fired, or try to take over. Both of these actions are predicated on the belief that the audience strongly associates the performer with the program, and that producers, directors, and writers are dispensable. The performer may win these battles—particularly if the producer feels that he or she has no choice—but will, in the process, acquire a reputation for "trouble."

## Celebrities

Celebrities live by special rules—even though being famous and being a capable television performer are not always synonymous, and even though celebrity alone does not guarantee that a given performer is well suited for a particular role or project. Celebrities are typically paid considerably more than minimum union scale and, depending on the project, may receive profit participation as well. Many celebrities are accustomed to special treatment and perks as part of the deal.

With few exceptions, celebrities are represented by agents, lawyers, or managers, who negotiate on their clients' behalf. The negotiation usually begins with a producer's offer, typically countered by a statement of the performer's going rate. Once the basic price is set, the negotiation moves on to profit participation (if relevant), perks, and working conditions. First-class airfare is required in the union agreements, but many celebrities request additional tickets for family members or other traveling companions. Hotel accommodations and per diems may be subject to the same sorts of requests; these are generally honored if the expense is not too great.

In the best of circumstances, working with a celebrity brings the staff and crew to its professional best. The presence of a celebrity on the set also forces attentiveness to the schedule, since well-known performers are available only for brief time periods. Sometimes, working with a celebrity is a disappointment, especially when a huge ego is part of the package. In these cases, difficulties can be anticipated and minimized by speaking with other producers and directors who have worked with the performer in the past.

Often, celebrities who are not at the peak of their careers are available for reasonable prices. Those with a pop culture heritage often trade on their most famous role (Barbara Eden, for example, who played the lead role on a popular 1960s series *I Dream of Jeannie*), but some performers spend years trying to separate themselves from these signature roles. Others simply don't work as often as they once did. It's important to be sensitive to each individual performer's situation and not to make assumptions, regardless of the performer's reputation, past history, or—most importantly—the traits of the character that a performer may have portrayed years ago.

## Working with Children

Several key issues must be considered when hiring young performers. To start with, every state has its own child labor laws; these should be reviewed early in the planning of a production. The following are key provisions common to most child labor laws.

As a general matter, minors cannot be hired for any activity that may be hazardous or detrimental to the minor's moral development. This is an area open to interpretation; the state agency will not issue a work permit if it believes that there may be a problem.

If the work interferes with ongoing school education, then a teacher must be hired, and hours must be allotted to classroom work. This is not an issue for infrequent short-term hires; the parent or guardian simply decides whether to take the child out of school to work.

A parent or guardian must be present while the child is working. For instance, the California code requires that the parent or guardian be present within sight or sound for all minors under 16 years old. This is based upon the Coogan Law, named for child actor Jackie Coogan (later, Uncle Fester on *The Addams Family* television series) to protect the earnings of children. A similar law has been passed in New York.

For each age group, there is usually a maximum amount of time allowed at the workplace, a maximum number of working hours allowed, and a minimum number of rest, recreation, and education hours. Travel time may be considered part of the working day. In California, for instance, children age 2 to 6 are allowed up to six hours at the workplace, including up to three hours of working time and not less than three hours of rest, recreation, and education. Children age 9 to 16 can be at the workplace for up to nine hours, and can work up to five hours on school days or seven hours on days off, with three hours minimum of schooling and one hour minimum of rest and recreation.

Unless they are ratified by a court, most ongoing agreements for services are voidable by the minor at any time. In most (but not all) states, a parent or guardian can sign a sample release form (see following page) on behalf of a minor. Children are paid equal to what an adult would earn in comparable roles. Payments are made to a parent or guardian, who disburses monies to the benefit of the child. In some states, room and board can be deducted by the parent or guardian as well as professional expenses such as travel, clothing, and legal and accounting fees. Essentially, the parent or guardian becomes the trustee for the child, and is held to standards common for fiduciary relationships.

A production's work permit can be revoked if the commissioner or other supervising authority detects wrongdoing or abuse of rights or privileges. (Also see discussion of minors and contracts on page 408.)

## Working with Unpaid Performers

Many of the people who appear on television are unpaid; they are interviewed, they appear in the background in entertainment and news footage, or they are the subjects of news reports. But most people who appear on television do so because they want to. The majority of these unpaid performers are willing to cooperate with the television establishment, and will generally agree to sign whatever documents are necessary to ensure an appearance.

### The Release Form

A *release form* (see Appendix 4.3) is a type of contract; it deals with three types of rights, described briefly below and in detail in Chapter 35.

Any creative expression is usually the property of the creator—in this case, the person signing the release form. In essence, this is a matter of copyright (see Chapter 34). The rights of privacy and publicity are the rights to control the commercial use of a personal likeness or other identifying characteristics (see Chapter 35). If uses beyond the original program are contemplated, these rights should be specifically released.

The right against being libeled or slandered gives redress against someone making assertions that are untrue and harmful to the reputation of another person (see page 279). Under the U.S. Constitution, anyone is allowed to be wrong in such assertions, provided that he or she did not act with negligence with respect to a private person, or with malice or reckless disregard of the truth with respect to a public person.

A typical release form always contains an affirmative grant of rights. It may also contain representations and warranties as well as a preventative grant.

The *affirmative grant* says that in exchange for good and valuable consideration, the unpaid performer grants the right to record and exploit his or her image, and to exploit his or her name and persona. Typically, the right is granted in perpetuity, for all uses and all media anywhere in the world—not only in the production itself, but also in anything connected with advertising and publicity. With such a grant, the producer can exploit programs including the unpaid performer at his/her sole discretion.

The *representations and warranties* section, if present in the release form, includes a promise that nothing said by the unpaid performer will be libelous or will otherwise violate the rights of any third party, and that the statements are free of claims.

The *preventative grant* or *waiver* says that the person who signs the agreement will not make any claims against the producer on issues of copyright, privacy, publicity, defamation, or for any other cause.

Release forms are advisable whenever any unpaid performer speaks on a television production, particularly outside of a news show or other factual context of public interest. For those who appear but do not speak, discretion and circumstances serve as a guide. Members of a studio audience should be ticketed; the use of the ticket is a transaction that shows the intent to participate on the part of every audience member, and a statement to this effect may even be printed on the ticket. People who are part of a crowd observing a public event, or the staging of an event for a television show, may be used in context in cutaway shots. But if anyone will be appearing prominently, it is advisable to secure a signed release form.

# CHAPTER 43

# REPRESENTATION AND MANAGEMENT

A substantial industry has been built by agents, attorneys, accountants, and other specialists who advise and act on behalf of people working in television. Sometimes the notion is that creative people are often poor businesspeople, and that involving business professionals can help generate more money while untangling contractual problems. For all of us, however, professional advice and representation can be a significant help in getting projects and careers launched and tended.

## AGENTS

By definition, an *agent* is someone authorized to act on behalf of someone else, the *principal.* The law of agency is a law of delegation of power. In television, and in the entertainment business at large, an agent is a representative who negotiates deals on behalf of clients and, under the best of circumstances, helps find work for these clients as well.

Agents are extremely common in some areas of the television business, and virtually nonexistent in others. They are an important part of the commercial network production system, and they actively participate in most important talent agreements for network, syndicated, pay cable, and local television productions. Agents are not part of the corporate or business video industries, except when high-priced talent (such as a well-known director, composer, or writer) is involved. The situation in home video and basic cable is similar. Agents tend to specialize, so a performer who appears on daytime drama may have one agent for that activity, and another at the same agency for voice-over work. This is often the case for writers and directors as well.

The largest agencies have offices in Los Angeles and New York, and, frequently, smaller ones in Chicago, London, Nashville, and several other major cities around the world. The William Morris Agency, ICM, and CAA are among the most powerful agencies, representing performers of every description, as well as writers, directors, producers, scenic designers, and other creative personnel. Their domain is not limited to television—larger agencies maintain literary, motion picture, theatrical, sports, new media, and even corporate departments.

Smaller agencies may devote more attention to individual clients, particularly the lesser-knowns. Practicality in seeking representation is a virtue, and this type of agency may be better for those just starting out. Some agencies specialize in particular markets, such as news anchors and reporters, juvenile performers, or soap opera performers. Others offer full service, from book publishing to legitimate theater, usually with a concentration of power in one or two areas. Lists of agencies and opportunities for new talent to seek representation can be found on a number of Web sites.

Within the entertainment industry, the pecking order among the big three and such emerging powers as United Talent Agency (UTA) and the Endeavor Agency is always a matter for current gossip, jockeying, and fascination. Agents and clients shift back and forth intermittently, putting one company "on top" one year and another the next. Unless there is some particular piece of deal-making power in the hands of a particular agent, a wise client will find good representation with someone he or she trusts and avoid short-term fads and fashions.

Agencies and creative people can work together for specific periods of time or on a per-project basis. For newcomers, an agreement to work together on a single project can sometimes be arranged; if the project is a success, the agency expects the creative person to sign up as a long-term client. Contracts generally run one to three years, and may be limited to only one type of representation—for performance but not for writing, for example. The agency receives the client's paychecks; deducts a commission of 10 or 15 percent of all income, including fees, royalties, and profit participation; and pays its client the balance. If the client finds his or her own work, the agent is still entitled to the commission, under the terms of most agency agreements.

When an agency works closely with a producer—helping to sell the program to a distributor and supplying many of its own clients to the cast and staff—then the agency is said to be "packaging the project." For such packages, the agency receives 5 percent or more of the total project revenues, but typically does not deduct commissions from the client's individual income. A variation on such packaging has been the format deal, where program concepts first tried in one market are moved on to others. Programs such as *Who Wants to Be a Millionaire* have successfully moved from the United Kingdom to the U.S., making fortunes in the process.

An agency frequently negotiates all terms and conditions of every agreement, from fees and profit participation to screen credit. After the basic terms have been hammered out by the individual agent, the agency's attorneys or the talent's individual lawyer attend to the details.

## Regulation of Agents and Other Representatives

Many states regulate the activities of agencies, either as a part of the regulation of employment agencies in general or under rules specific to the entertainment business. Under such regulation, the agent must register and obtain a license. Failure to do so can lead to civil and even criminal penalties, including the cancellation of the agreements for representation and the refunding of fees previously taken. These laws also generally restrict the fees that the agent can charge to his or her client. Official talent agents are not the only ones to whom these regulations apply; a manager or other representative who performs agent-like functions may be under the jurisdiction of the agent rules as well. The Association of Talent Agents (ATA) is a good source for further details on regulatory issues; see the Web site at www.agentassociation.com/frontdoor/agency_licensing.cfm.

In New York, Article 11 of the General Business Law concerns licensing of all employment agencies, within which are special rules applicable to a "theatrical employment agency." A theatrical employment agency includes any person or company that procures, or attempts to procure, employment or engagements for motion pictures, radio, television, and other categories of the entertainment business. As for the manager-as-agent, the statute specifically excludes from its definition of a theatrical agency "the business of managing such entertainments, exhibitions or performances, or the artists or attractions constituting the same, where such business only incidentally involves the seeking of employment therefor." Although the words "only incidentally involves" are fairly restrictive, this provision at least recognizes that the activities of an agent and those of a manager inevitably overlap. New York's Department of Consumer Affairs, which oversees these laws, invites managers who wish to confirm their status to write and seek advice.

A New York theatrical agency must register with the state and file a great deal of information about itself, its personnel, and its business premises. It must post a $10,000 bond and file copies of its standard agreements. There is a limitation on the maximum fees that the agency can charge: 10 percent of the compensation payable to the talent (orchestra, concert, and opera fees can go up to 20 percent). Failure to comply is a misdemeanor punishable in some cases by up to a year in jail, and can lead to the return of fees. Further information on regulation and registration is available at home.nyc.gov/html/dca/html/034.html.

In California, Section 1700.4 of the Labor Code defines a "talent agent" as one who seeks "to procure employment or engagements for an artist or artists." "Artists" include performers, writers, directors, cinematographers, composers, lyricists, arrangers, and other professionals in the entertainment industry, including, specifically, the television business. The manager problem is addressed in three ways. First of all, the regulations do not cover the activity of procuring recording contracts. Second, a manager can help an agent do his job, at the agent's initiative. Third, there is a one-year limit on bringing claims that a manager has acted as an unlicensed agent.

Other California requirements follow the normal pattern of registration and oversight. The law requires that a fee schedule be filed with the state and conspicuously posted, but there are no set maximums. Form contracts must be filed and approved, and a $10,000 bond is required. Civil penalties are available, but an agency's failure to obtain a license is not subject to criminal punishment.

Even when they do not have problems under the specific talent-agency laws, managers, attorneys, and other artists' representatives generally owe fiduciary duties, similar to those owed by agents, in their relationships with their clients. Fiduciary duties require that the representative act with strict probity and avoid conflicts of interest. While the representative is allowed to earn an appropriate fee, it may not use its relationship with the client to obtain benefits for itself at the client's expense.

The various talent guilds, and performer unions such as AFTRA and SAG, usually have their own restrictions on the activities of agents, including caps on the fees that can be charged. There is frequently a specific form of agency contract that the union requires to be used.

## ATTORNEYS

Attorneys have two principal roles in television: to negotiate and document deals, and to "clean up messes."

Attorneys are usually paid by the hour, and most will be happy to allow the client to set the working parameters. Some clients are competent deal-makers, who consult the attorney as they plan the terms and remain in contact as problems crop up during the negotiation. The lawyer may then draft the agreement from a basic memorandum of terms written by the client, or the lawyer may draft the entire agreement from information gathered at a meeting or telephone conversation. Alternatively, the lawyer may be asked to review an agreement drafted by the other party in the deal. In each of these situations, the client controls the amount of work done by the lawyer, thereby limiting the number of hours and the resulting legal bill.

Clients may also choose to assign most of the deal-making job to the attorney, from structuring the deal through negotiation, drafting, and reviewing the agreement. The lawyer works on his or her own schedule, contacting the client to review the key points of the deal. This is a more costly technique, but it frees up the client to do what he or she does best. Such work may be clone on a flat-fee basis, but only under circumstances that suggest minimal risk for the attorney and the law firm.

The "messes" to which attorneys attend generally involve three areas: contracts, rights clearances, and finance. Contracts are not only made, they are sometimes bent and broken—an attorney can offer strategies for dealing with breached promises, and usually works with the other party (or its lawyers) to reach a compromise solution.

Rights matters are best dealt with before the fact. Typical rights problems concern the depiction of people and their stories without a release, or the use of portions of other people's creative work, such as film clips or music excerpts. If an attorney has the chance to review the script or the program in advance, he or she can point out those instances where clearance is necessary. Such an advance review is usually required by the E&O insurer (see page 272). Sometimes the attorney does do the follow-up work. Routine matters can be handled by the production staff or by rights clearance services specializing in particular areas, such as music or film clips. If items are missed before or during production and claims are made, the production company's attorney—together with the insurer—will assess the seriousness of the situation and take the lead in remedying it.

Finance problems are often more serious, and inevitably involve attorneys. Sometimes an agreed-upon payment schedule is not being followed by the financing entity, and the attorney is asked to cajole and threaten to obtain the money; perhaps the production company is at fault because it is running over budget or behind schedule. Asking for this type of legal help is expensive, and the attorney (since he or she is working for a client in financial distress) often asks for his or her fees up front.

Most large and medium-sized production companies have several attorneys on staff. A general counsel usually attends to corporate affairs, and may become involved in the most important deals. A business affairs department handles the work related to programming and production; most, if not all, of the dealmakers in the business affairs department are attorneys. A separate legal department drafts contacts and works to prevent and clean up messes.

In this litigious society, attorneys have become an integral part of the production operation. Lawyers should be consulted on any issues related to copyright, insurance, employment practices, government agencies, other producers or production companies, possible instances of libel or slander, music usage, the selection of a program title, and distribution agreements. In sum, almost any agreement signed by a network, station, production company, or individual should be reviewed by an attorney.

## BUSINESS MANAGERS AND PERSONAL MANAGERS

A *business manager* helps to oversee the day-to-day financial aspects of a client's business life. The business manager typically receives all incoming checks, keeps the checkbook, makes sure that taxes are paid correctly and on time, deals with the banks, negotiates car leases and other such details, pays the credit card bills, keeps track of receipts for tax preparation, and works with the accountant to prepare taxes. For such services, a business manager may charge a flat monthly fee or, at most, a commission of 5 percent of the client's income.

A *personal manager* is more difficult to define. In theory, an agent is supposed to get jobs, while a personal manager, who is not legally an agent, is supposed to build a career. In fact, personal-management contracts frequently insist that the manager is not qualified to act as agent, and that he or she will not help the client to find work. Instead, the personal manager offers advice and guidance.

In the real world, successful personal managers sell access to powerful decision-makers and provide personal attention. Whereas an agent is likely to represent 50 clients, a personal manager handles only five or ten. A personal manager helps the client to make career decisions—about the way he or she looks, the company he or she keeps, the roles that should be accepted and rejected. All the while, the personal manager introduces the client to people who can make a difference. As with all representatives, some personal managers are better than others.

The fee for a personal manager usually ranges from 15 percent to 25 percent of the client's entertainment income. Colonel Tom Parker, Elvis Presley's personal manager, reportedly charged 50 percent—and was probably worth every penny.

## ACCOUNTANTS

Accountants serve as record-keepers and advisors. The record-keeping function is required for management information and planning, for investors, for tax authorities, and in the case of public companies, for the SEC. Even a solo operator, such as a freelance associate producer, should have an ongoing relationship with an accountant or accounting firm. Billing is typically based on hours worked, though flat rates for special projects, such as tax preparation, may be negotiated on a case-by-case basis.

The advising function is equally important. Accountants are excellent sources of information relating to tax rules and government regulations on, for example, unemployment insurance. The financial implications of a new project should be reviewed by an accountant while it is still in the planning stages.

Accountants, bookkeepers, and auditors also play a role in production, either as full-time or freelance members of a production staff, or as outside contractors. Large productions require careful financial management and a regular (often daily) reckoning of expenditures. A production auditor provides detailed cost reports to a centralized production office on a regular basis, highlighting areas of potential difficulty. Some auditors play a broader role, keeping an eye on the entire production and reporting any problems or potential problems to a production supervisor.

When the project is completed, the production accountant or production auditor works with the production manager to confirm that all invoices have been paid, that all deposits have been returned, and that there are no outstanding bills or expense reports lost in the towering piles of paper and files typically found in a production office. Submission of a final cost report is frequently specified in a production agreement; a final payment to a producer or production company may depend upon it.

The situation is less complex with ongoing production or programming ventures, such as a series. Staff, freelance, or outside accountants prepare and/or review the books regularly—once a week or once a month, depending on the amount of work involved. They may also prepare the payroll or keep track of royalties. The role of the accountant is an important one; sloppy accounting practices can cause serious problems for independent production companies, and may cause considerable embarrassment for the personnel in charge of expenditure control.

# CHAPTER 44

# LOCATION AND STUDIO PRODUCTION

## SHOOTING ON LOCATION

Location production refers to a shoot done anywhere except at a studio. Common locations include business offices, homes, sporting venues, city streets, restaurants, and nightclubs.

## Permissions

For all types of production (with the exception of news coverage), it is necessary to secure permission from the owner of the location prior to setting up to shoot (see Appendix 5.2). This permission frequently requires negotiating a daily or hourly fee for use of the premises. An insurance policy may also be required; such a policy should cover the property owner for any liability due to personal injury in connection with the production, and should guarantee payment to the property owner in case of physical damage to the property. Failure to secure these arrangements in advance usually results in costly production delays as the producer or production manager negotiates on the spot—or else in rescheduling the shoot.

If the location is outdoors in a public area, or if the project involves any public areas for setup or vehicles, then the municipal or other local government should be contacted well in advance of the shoot. A municipal permit usually carries a fixed daily fee, and must be prominently posted on one of the vehicles during the production. In larger cities and for large-scale productions in less populated areas, the city or state film commission can help to make the necessary arrangements. When no such office is available, it is advisable to contact the mayor's office. Fees are generally fixed on the basis of the scale of production; under-the-table payments are uncommon.

If police protection is required, a flat fee is charged per man-hour or per man-day. It is considered poor style (and is also illegal) to tip officers, but it is generally acceptable to treat the officers as if they were members of the production team—to feed them while on location and provide comfortable rest areas during breaks. Friendly relations go a long way toward smooth, problem-free operations. On some productions, similar interaction with the local fire department is required as well.

## Location Crews

Most major cities support a small community of freelance television technicians, camera people, audio and video engineers, and so forth. Frequently trained in local television news and sports, these versatile crew members work either individually or in small companies that offer not just engineering capability, but everything from location planning to shooting, editing, and duplication of the finished tape.

Crews support themselves by working freelance for a variety of clients. Corporate work (training videos, video news releases, product demonstrations, point-of-purchase merchandising videos, etc.) usually accounts for the bulk of each individual crew member's regular client base. Local, syndicated, and network programs may also hire these crews when their own staffs are overextended, or when a situation arises that favors freelancers. An example of the latter is, say, a news story breaking in Boise, Idaho: a Seattle-based freelance crew might be able to reach the location faster than a network crew based in San Francisco.

Crews are hired in two different ways. For most projects, the easiest way to hire an entire crew is to contact a production company that specializes in single-camera work. The company quotes a daily or weekly package price, not only for the crew members but for all of the necessary equipment. Many of these crews offer résumé reels; it is also wise to check references with previous clients. One can also hire each crew member individually, and this may be the better choice if a particular videographer is a must or if the client company owns equipment. This method, however, is frequently more costly, because individual crew members may not own every piece of equipment needed for the job. The producer also accepts more technical responsibility, especially if the crew members are unaccustomed to working together.

The size of the crew depends upon the job, and is best determined by discussing the job in detail with the crew chief (usually the camera operator). For electronic news gathering (ENG) work, a two-person crew can move quickly and cover most stories: One person lights and operates the camera, the other is in charge of audio and video recording. With lightweight portable gear, one- or two-person crews can handle a remarkable range of jobs. For most productions, however, using a three- or four-person crew is preferable, and is more likely to result in flawless sound and picture quality. With this setup, the camera operator works with a lighting assistant, one engineer handles audio, and another engineer does video.

Most crew-hiring deals are made via telephone, followed up with a letter (or a fax) confirming the business arrangements: the dates, the number of working days, the rate (per-day, per-week, or flat rate), a promise to provide transportation and accommodations, confirmation of necessary insurance, and a payment schedule. A typical payment schedule is 50 percent upon hiring and 50 percent upon completion of the shoot. If the job includes editing, then 35 percent paid on hiring, 35 percent on completion of the shoot, and 30 percent on completion of editing is common. Many crews mark up the cost of tape stock, so for larger shoots, the producer can save money by buying stock ahead of time. If anything goes wrong with producer-supplied stock, the producer pays for the reshoot; if anything goes wrong with crew-supplied stock, then the crew will often reshoot at no charge or at a reduced rate.

## Multiple-Camera Crews and Truck Rentals

Single-camera coverage is ideal for news, interviews, magazine stories, and speeches. But additional cameras are necessary for most seminars, meetings, sporting events, and other productions where multiple performers or simultaneous visual images must be captured in real time.

Many small production companies own small vans equipped with modest control room facilities (usually not more than three cameras). These facilities are frequently modular, so they can be removed from the van and set up anywhere, provided that electrical power and shelter from weather are available.

Mobile facilities range from these minivans to full-scale control rooms on wheels that can handle a dozen or more cameras and seat just as many engineers and members of the production staff. Several of these "trucks" are available in most major cities, but the nature of the mobile video business is travel. It is not unusual to find a Pittsburgh-based truck accepting assignments throughout the East and Midwest; in fact, a good deal can probably be struck if the Pittsburgh-based truck is already in St. Louis and is needed for a shoot in Kansas City or Chicago. Trucks are mainly used for sports coverage and, to a lesser extent, for concerts and other special events.

A truck is usually rented with all of the necessary equipment and several key engineers and technicians. Additional crew members may be hired by the mobile video company—which is likely to be in contact with experienced personnel all over the country—or supplied by the producer. Payment terms for the truck are usually 50 percent on hiring and 50 percent on completion of the shoot; the crew is paid after the shoot. Once again, the deal is made by phone (usually to a distant city) and then confirmed in writing.

Specialized mobile facilities, for multiple-track audio recording or for the generation of on-site electrical power, are also available for rental.

## STUDIO PRODUCTION

Nearly all television broadcasting stations own and operate at least one studio on the premises, and many operate two or more. These studios are used for daily production of the news and for some public affairs programming. In addition, studios are rented for the production of local commercials and, on occasion, to other clients such as corporate video producers.

Each of the broadcast networks operates studios in New York City, Los Angeles, Washington, DC, and Chicago. In New York, these studios are used principally for news, morning programs, sports coverage, and daytime dramas. In Los Angeles, the studios are used mainly for situation comedies, game shows, daytime dramas, and variety shows. Network studios in Washington and Chicago are used for news and public affairs programs and some syndicated talk shows; ABC's *Nightline*, for example, is based in Washington, and so is NBC's *Meet the Press*. When a network and an O&O are housed in the same physical plant, studios, crews, and editing facilities are frequently shared by both organizations.

Many independent programs are not produced in television stations or network facilities, though. Los Angeles, New York, Chicago, and other cities support independently owned and operated television studios that are rented to producers. Manhattan's Chelsea Piers, formerly shipping warehouses, has been home to *Law & Order* and other series. Silvercup Studios, a former bread factory located just across the river in Queens, is another large facility; it has hosted *The Sopranos, Sex and the City*, the ABC sitcom *Hope & Faith*, and many motion pictures, including *Gangs of New York, Meet the Parents, Analyze That, When Harry Met Sally*, and more. Clients of Kaufman-Astoria, an old movie lot also located in Queens, have included *Sesame Street, The Cosby Show, Where in the World is Carmen Sandiego?*, and various motion pictures.

Many cable networks operate their own facilities; Food Network, for example, is located in a renovated building above a food market in downtown New York City. In Los Angeles, many old movie soundstages have been converted into television studios. Studios are available for rental in the Disney/MGM and Universal complexes in Orlando, Florida. In Chicago, Oprah Winfrey's Harpo Studios is home to her own talk show and to outside projects; there are other independent studios in Chicago as well. There are fine studios in some seemingly out-of-the-way places such as Nashville's Opryland, which includes one of the nation's largest studios and is the home of the Grand Ole Opry, a huge theater-style studio. Many producers also rent studio space in Canada, where production costs tend to be low; Toronto and Vancouver are production centers for both Canadian and (to a lesser extent) American programming. Fewer television programs are produced in television studios, however, so the need for such facilities—particularly large facilities—is a dubious investment (unless the facility is funded in large part by a long-term production client).

Studios rent their facilities by the day, usually with a half-day minimum. Short-term projects—home video productions, television specials, pilots, commercials, corporate video training tapes, and product demonstrations—usually pay higher day rates than long-term clients do. Since the rental of studio space is a perishable commodity, facilities are happy to package multiple days, weeks, or months at a deep discount.

A television studio is rented as a facility ready for production, complete with a control room, a lighting grid, power, a poured (flat) floor, and cable connections for lights, cameras, monitors, microphones, and other necessary equipment. Use of the control room, dressing rooms, makeup area, and limited office space is always part of the deal. Additional charges mount up quickly for essentials—extra cameras, extra lighting equipment, painting and repainting the floor or walls, purchase of colored lighting gels, additional personnel—to customize the studio for specific production activities. Some of these costs may be paid directly by the producer, but any costs not covered this way are subject to the studio's markup.

A film soundstage may be larger than a television studio. Many soundstages are used as television studios, with lights and other equipment added as needed. In this instance, the control room is often a mobile production van or a temporary setup in a nearby office area. These temporary control room facilities are called a "fly pack."

Studio rentals are always negotiable. The price of the studio should be highest on "full fax" (full facilities) days—days when the studio and all of its equipment are needed—and far lower, perhaps 75 to 80 percent less, on days when the studio is being used to set up or strike equipment and scenery. There is more flexibility with the costs of the studio, the equipment, and the facility's full-time personnel than there is with items that the studio must purchase on the client's behalf. It may be worth checking into the prices of those items purchased from outside, because the studio may not shop for the best possible prices on items it will buy for the client (since it passes the cost through), and the markup on these items—as well as on phone and copier usage—may be unacceptable to the production budget.

A studio deal can be complicated, so it is advisable to arrange at least one in-person meeting. This meeting should include the producer or production manager (who actually makes the deal), the director, and if the production is complicated, one or two key members of the technical staff. The facility's sales staff assesses the needs of the production, then submits a bid for the job. After soliciting bids from several studios, the producer or production manager starts negotiating. Upon agreement on key points, a one- or two-page letter agreement confirms the deal and the dates, listing the resources that will be provided by the studio, the price for the entire job (or the price of each day), plus the cost of overtime.

It is wise to leave some room for modification; most television productions change during pre-production, and a deal that is too tightly structured may cost the producer more money than anticipated. Hard negotiating is not recommended, because if there is a breakdown of mutual goodwill, studios can easily add costs for items not included in the original bid. The studio bills some items at its discretion, and if the facility is treated fairly, there are usually fewer surprises when the final bill arrives.

Payment arrangements vary. A common deal is 10 percent to hold the studio dates—refundable if the production is canceled within 48 hours of the shoot—with 45 percent due on the first shooting day and 45 percent on completion. If the client rents the facility regularly, the final payment can be made as late as 30 days after completion.

## TECHNICAL AND STAGING UNIONS

In the major U.S. markets, three technical and staging unions dominate the broadcast network television business: the International Alliance of Theatrical Stage Employees (IATSE), the National Association of Broadcast Employees and Technicians (NABET), and the International Brotherhood of Electrical Workers (IBEW). Each one negotiates rates and rules with employers on behalf of its members, assures fair working conditions, and operates a pension and welfare fund. The terms and conditions vary with each union's agreement, but there are some generally applicable rules. These concern the number of hours in a standard workday; the additional payment due for overtime hours; payment for work on weekends and holidays; notification of call times, changes, and cancellations; rest periods and turnarounds (the number of hours between working days); meal periods and penalties for missed meal periods; hazard pay; travel, food, and lodging; and the need for a payroll bond.

More than half of all television stations are unionized, most often by IATSE, IBEW, and NABET. The Teamsters represent employees at a few dozen stations, and the United Auto Workers at just one, in Flint, Michigan. (For a general discussion of the role of unions in the television business, see page 415.)

## IATSE

The International Alliance of Theatrical Stage Employees (often known as just IA) was founded in 1893, when all show business was onstage and electronic media was still decades off. Stage carpenters, propertymen, and electricians built this union; projectionists were added as film exhibition became a business enterprise. IA members are also hairstylists, makeup artists, story analysts, cartoonists, set designers, teachers (of working children), editors, and in some cases, sales or marketing personnel. IA members work in legitimate theater, motion picture production, motion picture exhibition (projectionists), and in network and local television production.

IATSE is represented by local chapters throughout the world, with over 800 in the U.S. and Canada. The organization of these local chapters, and the areas in which members may work, are guided by local traditions and by negotiated agreements. In San Francisco, for example, members of IATSE Local 16 are not involved in television production. In Los Angeles, 16 IATSE television and motion picture locals operate in a variety of production crafts and geographic regions; Local 44 (Affiliated Property Craftsmen) supplies propmasters in the area, while Local 695 (International Sound, Cinetechnicians and TV Engineers) supplies audio engineers. Local 706 is the chapter for makeup artists and hair-stylists working throughout the U.S., its territories, and Canada (with the exception of 13 eastern states). In New York, IATSE is the union for stagehands.

There are IATSE locals in more than 500 cities throughout the U.S. and Canada. The entire union has 60,000 members, more than one-third of the people working in television.

## NABET

The National Association of Broadcast Employees and Technicians succeeded the Association of Technical Employees (ATE), which was organized in 1933 to represent employees of NBC Radio. When the NBC Blue network was spun off to form ABC, jurisdiction expanded to the new network as well. As the broadcasting and cable television workers sector of the Communications Workers of America (CWA), NABET represents most of the technical crew members who work at network facilities, radio stations, and television stations owned by NBC and ABC; at many local radio and television stations not owned by NBC or ABC; and at some production companies. The word "Employees" in the union's name is appropriate: Half of the union's members are anchors, reporters, producers, directors, desk assistants, talent coordinators, graphic artists, and other nontechnical personnel. In addition, NABET covers makeup artists, hairdressers, stagehands, script supervisors, and some film crews—anyone employed in broadcasting. NABET competes with AFTRA, DGA, WGA, IATSE, and IBEW to represent employees.

There are roughly 38 NABET locals in approximately 36 cities, with over 10,000 members working in television. In New York and in Los Angeles, one local serves ABC, one serves NBC, and one serves film workers. In Washington, DC, and in Chicago, one local serves all members working for ABC and NBC. San Francisco has one local for ABC and independents. Locals also contract with independent stations and other television production companies.

Until 1974, NABET operated in Canada as well as the U.S. NABET Canada is now autonomous.

## IBEW

The International Brotherhood of Electrical Workers was formed in 1891 to represent telephone company employees. In 1931, IBEW started representing CBS radio engineers and technicians. Today, IBEW (sometimes called IB) represents approximately 10,000 workers at over 200 television and radio stations throughout the U.S. and Canada. The union has signed national contracts with CBS and FOX, and represents workers at every type of affiliated station including CBS, NBC, ABC, FOX, WB, UPN, and PBS as well as Spanish-language stations from Telemundo and Univision. IBEW also represents workers at the United Nations, HBO, Madison Square Garden, and Sony Music Studios.

## INSURANCE

Whether working on location or in a studio, the producer uses several types of insurance to limit the risks involved in creating television productions. It is important to work with a company that specializes in this type of insurance, since most insurance agents will be generally unfamiliar with the intricacies of this type of policy. Equally important, collecting on a claim will be far less problematic when working with experienced insurance professionals. One long-time industry leader is Albert Ruben, now a part of the larger insurance firm AON.

An *Errors & Omissions (E&O) policy*—also called a *producer's liability policy*—insures against claims based on violation of copyright, personal rights, or property rights, including infringement of privacy. Although the range of coverage may vary depending upon the type of production and the risk involved, an E&O policy should protect the producer against suits for libel, slander, and privacy/publicity violations (see Chapter 35). In addition, an E&O policy protects against claims on the creative concepts used in the production: the originality of the concept, the script, the characters, the music, the production design, and so forth. The E&O package for most productions is a routine matter, but it may take on special importance when the risk is higher. For example, with a magazine program, a celebrity might claim libel, slander, or defamation of character. Another example is a basic story line with a history of copyright problems and lawsuits.

There are several companies that supply E&O coverage (see also page 272). The so-called production package typically protects the producer against losses due to property damage or personal injury. It contains some or all of the following coverages, again depending upon the producer's level of risk and the costs involved:

- *Faulty Stock, Camera, and Processing Insurance* pays for reshooting and other losses due to problems with the set's physical equipment, the raw materials used, or the editing facility.

- *Negative Film Insurance* covers physical damage to the master videotape(s) or film negative.

- *Weather Insurance* covers delays due to inclement or unusual weather.

- *Aviation Accident Insurance*, *Marine Accident Insurance*, and *Animal Mortality Coverage* are examples of special coverages, and are self-explanatory.

- *Extra Expense Insurance* reimburses the producer for the costs of any delays due to failure or loss of any equipment, wardrobe, and so on.

- *Third Party Property Damage Insurance* covers property that is donated, loaned, or rented to the producer.

- *Cast Insurance* pays the producer for any costs from delays related to key cast members who become ill during the course of shooting and editing. If a cast member dies, and material must be reshot or re-edited with a new performer, Cast Insurance covers this situation as well.

- *Comprehensive General Liability* covers damage to vehicles loaned, rented, or donated to the production. Coverage is available for props, sets, and wardrobe, as well as for lighting, camera, and sound equipment.

- *Worker's Compensation and Employer's Liability* is not exclusively a type of production insurance; it also provides coverage against claims for workers who are injured or disabled on the job. The cost and coverage varies on a state-by-state basis—high in California, lower in New York. There are surprises in some states, so research is necessary.

As with any insurance policy, there are limitations on coverage. Faulty Stock, Camera, and Processing Insurance, for example, does not cover errors in judgment made by the camera operator, such as the use of the wrong film, improper loading, or incorrect or inappropriate use of the camera. Similar limitations apply to most of the types of insurance listed above.

Insurance can be expensive, so coverage should be selected with a thorough understanding of the risks involved, the costs of correcting problems without insurance coverage, and the likelihood of mishaps. An E&O policy and a basic production package are required in almost every contract for financing or distributing a program. Because the costs of coverage do vary, it is advisable to request bids from several companies that specialize in production insurance. Special Cast Insurance may be required if a key cast member is especially old or in poor health. Other types of specialty insurance may be required by contract if production conditions are unusual—if dangerous animals will be used, for instance, or if shooting will take place in a rough inner-city neighborhood.

One further note: deductibles are often high, so the producer should make some allowances for loss, damage, and theft in order to insure items valued in the hundreds or low thousands of dollars. This will cover the producer for small problems that do not warrant, or do not qualify for, a claim.

An accurate estimation of costs can be made only by an insurance agent. For budgeting purposes, it is normally safe to gauge insurance costs at roughly 3 to 5 percent of the below-the-line portion of the total production budget. However, if there are above-the-line elements subject to risk, then these should factor into the estimate. Factors may include risky shooting situations (i.e., underwater photography, scenes involving explosives), dicey rights issues, situations that may adversely affect property owned by others, and so on. If the project is relatively small, then that 3 to 5 percent should be increased. The cost of insuring a pilot will be proportionately far higher than the cost of insuring an entire series. Part of the reason may be minimum fees due regardless of the size and budget of the production. A blanket policy held by a larger company may help reduce costs; an independent producer or small production company will usually pay more for insurance than a larger company would.

## MUSIC

Music has always been a part of television production. Early studio shows routinely included a live band; the remnants of this creative approach are still seen on, for example, *The Late Show with David Letterman* (in an homage to tradition, the band is called the CBS Orchestra). In time, recordings replaced live musicians. Today, the entire package is often put together by just one musician working in a studio with sampled instruments and sophisticated software. The music is packaged for a series, often for a very low price.

When live musicians are seen on a television variety show, such as the Academy Awards or *The Tonight Show with Jay Leno*, they are working under a union agreement that prescribes rates, rules, and residuals. Sometimes these performers appear under an American Federation of Musicians (AFM) agreement, and sometimes they appear under an AFTRA agreement—the one that pays more is the one that is used.

Musicians who appear in music videos generally do so as part of a contract with their record label. These performances are considered to be promotion, not television programming. The studio musicians were paid for their work on the original sound recordings. If musicians appear, either playing or pretending to play, then they are paid a day rate for their work on the music video. This rate allows for unlimited plays on MTV and other cable networks. If the music video generates additional income—for example, as a for-sale item—then residuals and/or direct payments are due to the musicians.

When musicians arrange, orchestrate, conduct, or perform on a musical score for a network prime-time series or a high-profile cable series, the work is often done within AFM jurisdiction, and under a union contract. The composer's services are negotiated separately. Once again, this provides a negotiated rate structure, and also assures the musicians ongoing residual revenue should the project succeed in secondary markets, such as off-network cable reruns.

When working on a national show for a cable or broadcast network, a single musician working under an AFM Television/Film Agreement would receive $251.86 for three hours of work resulting in up to 15 minutes of recorded music.

If the musician plays a second instrument during the session, this is called "doubling," and the musician receives a 50 percent premium for the first instrument and 20 percent for each "double" thereafter. When music is composed, played, and produced by a small team or an individual using a desktop studio or similar, it is difficult for the AFM to manage or track. This type of music is often associated with reality shows, game shows, and such, particularly on programs produced for cable networks.

The AFM operates nationally in the U.S. and in Canada, and through the auspices of 250 local offices. A list of locals can be found at www.afm.org.

(For a more complete discussion of music in television, see Chapter 47.)

# CHAPTER 45

# POST-PRODUCTION, COMPLETION, AND DELIVERY

## POST-PRODUCTION

Post-production is an umbrella term that covers editing, the addition of special effects, sound mixing, and preparation of the completed master tape. There are several phases in the post-production process, and the complexity of each step is defined by the needs of the project. This process has been dramatically changed by the current generation of digital video and audio editing equipment, and will continue to change as videotape is replaced by more efficient digital storage systems.

Regardless of whether recordings are made to tape or to disc, they must be viewed, logged, and noted so that an editing plan can be devised. This plan is then implemented by loading the video into an editing system, selecting the best takes, and placing them into a timeline.

In some sequences, the logical progression of video images guides the structure of the timeline. In others, narration, dialogue, or a music track guides the placement of the video. Either way, the process is more or less the same: laying pieces into place, then adjusting the in and out points of each one, making corrections, and adding effects.

### Final Cut Pro, Avid, and Other Editing Systems

Until the 1990s, nearly all video editing was done in facilities that rented by the hour, or by a staff of dedicated editors who worked in dedicated rooms filled with complicated, largely inscrutable equipment. Nowadays, most producers and directors are also competent editors quite comfortable on an Apple computer running Final Cut Pro, or on a similar system. Some are even proficient on more advanced systems, such as those made by Avid Systems.

For shorter projects, or those involving nonfiction segments, desktop editing systems costing considerably less than $10,000 are very popular. For longer or more demanding projects, an Avid or similar system costing $100,000 or more is often more desirable; these projects often require a skillful editing professional.

In truth, a professional video editor will almost always do a better job than a producer-director who has some editing skills. An editor develops a practiced eye and tends to notice the slightest imperfections. More importantly, though, a professional editor is simply more likely to bring a fresh perspective, a wider range of options, a better sense of timing, a keener understanding of available special effects options, a superior sense of how best to use special effects, and so forth. Similarly, a professional sound mixer will offer a much higher level of quality with regard to music mixing, sound effects, use of narration, and such. In a world where the need for "faster" and "less expensive" provides constant budget pressure, the importance of these roles may be minimized. In short, professionals are almost always worth the extra expense.

## Editing Deals

When working with an editor or with an editing facility, the deal should be based on an hourly charge. Often, editing is a difficult budget item to estimate accurately. The time required is based upon the competence of the camera work and the director's coverage; the unpredictable direction that a project sometimes takes when it hits the editing room; the equally unpredictable comments from clients and network executives; and more. Even if a project is flat-rated, the flat rate should reflect a maximum number of hours.

Since post-production is the final step in the overall production process, editors and editing facilities are often the last to get paid. For new clients and for clients who have not established a reputation for paying bills on time, most editing houses have strict rules regarding the removal of tapes from their premises prior to payment of invoices. The best way to minimize problems is to estimate the cost of the job, pay a portion as a down payment (20 percent is common), and cut a check for the estimated balance, to be held in reserve until it is due. If the final total is more or less, adjustments can be made. If the project seems likely to exceed the budget estimate, incremental payments are frequently requested by the editing facility. Unpaid bills or portions of bills are an unfortunate fact of life in the post-production business.

A *lab letter* (see Appendix 6.2) is an agreement between the post-production facility or "lab" (a film term carried over to television), the producer, and a financier or distributor. It says that the lab has tapes and/or films and will not release the materials without permission of the authorized party (distributor or producer); that the distributor or producer may use the materials within the lab for duplication or further editing; and finally, that the lab will not put a lien on the materials or hold them unavailable if the party has unpaid debts to the lab. Each party is allowed access, provided that they have paid their own bills to the facility.

## USE OF EXISTING MATERIALS

Some television projects are put together in whole or in part by assembling existing materials, including photographs, illustrations, film, and videotape footage.

Strictly speaking, every piece of existing material that is protected by copyright should be cleared by the copyright holder for use—regardless of the amount of time that the sound or image is heard or seen, regardless of the size or character of the intended audience. This means that a producer must identify and contact the copyright holder for each item, then describe the production, how the material will be used within it, and where the program will be distributed. In many cases, the copyright holder will have already sold properties for use on television, so past experience may be the basis for either a fixed rate or negotiation. An agreement should be signed before the material is edited into the production. This agreement should detail the name of the program, its intended market and audience, the item to be used, limitations on its use, and the payments due.

In the real world, clearances are important, but in some cases a producer does not obtain them. If, for example, a production is to be seen internally by a small number of company employees, or if the production is a rough demo made to secure future funding, a producer sometimes takes a chance and proceeds without the necessary clearances—but this action is never without an element of risk. If the material is seen for only a very short time, or if it is distorted or manipulated to a point where recognition may be difficult, then once again the producer may choose to risk using the material without a clearance. The copyright holder is under no obligation to sell or license the material, of course, and many copyright holders routinely turn down requests for usage (whether for certain types of productions or for any production at all).

If the copyright holder is difficult to reach, and the producer has made a conscientious effort to contact the party, then the producer can take the risk of using the material—with the understanding that the copyright holder may see the production. Once the copyright holder is aware that the material is being used, the producer may negotiate a reasonable fee. But the copyright holder may have little motivation to negotiate in a reasonable fashion, and he or she may quote very high rates, demand that the material be removed from the program, or insist that the program be pulled from distribution as long as it contains the material. If the program has already aired with the material included, the copyright holder can stop the program from being shown or distributed until the material is removed, or can charge a very high licensing fee to retain the material.

Items that are in the public domain—material on which the copyright has not been renewed, for example—may be used without clearances. It is sometimes difficult to determine or to verify ownership; in these cases, the producer must make an honest, earnest effort to determine whether or not the item in question is in the public domain. Clearing music is especially tricky; a song or composition may be in the public domain, but the specific recorded performance may be protected by copyright, thus requiring clearance. Short excerpts, particularly on news or information programs, may fall into the category of "fair use," which does not require permission in some cases (see page 268). This is a limited exception, however, and should not be stretched beyond its proper bounds.

If a program is produced for distribution, the distributor must document all clearances. If something is not cleared, it is advisable for the producer to keep a history of contact (or attempted contact) with the copyright holder and advise the distributor of the potential for difficulties later on. (See Chapter 34 for more on copyright and the protection of creative properties.)

## SCREEN CREDITS

The completion of a television program frequently involves on-screen credits for people who worked on the production. The form and style of these credits largely depend upon tradition, negotiated agreements with individual staff and crew members, and rules set forth in union and guild agreements. On a network drama or situation comedy, for example, an individual full-frame credit (a credit that is the only one on-screen at a particular time) is shown at the start of the program for the producer(s), writer(s), and director, usually in that order; the other names appear at the end of the program. On most other programs, such as game, talk, news, magazine, and variety shows, all of the credits are shown at the end. These end credits begin with the producer(s), director, writer(s), production staff, and technical crew, then move on to music, design, business, and other departments. There is a trend against full-screen credits and long credits; viewers don't find credits interesting, so they're more likely to change channels.

The exact job titles and running order of credits are usually determined by the producer, who is guided by contractual requirements, union requirements, and personal judgment. Sometimes, for example, the executive producers appear first on the credits; sometimes they appear last. Networks frequently have their own conventions and policies on what credits are allowed.

The name of the program or its logo do not need to appear on the credits. Some producers prefer to see it; others do not. In fact, a television program may be produced without including credits of any kind. A copyright notice, however, must be included at some point in the program. It is most often shown either just before or just after the end credits. A proper form for the copyright notice is as follows:

Copyright © 2008, Nirkind Worldwide Media, Inc.

The title of the program need not be included in the copyright notice. Some producers include the words "All Rights Reserved" in addition to the copyright notice, but this is redundant. The notice should be large enough to be read clearly on any television set. For more on copyright notice and protection, and for instructions on the submission of a program to the copyright office, consult www.copyright.gov/.

## DELIVERABLES

When a program is complete, one of the staff members should arrange all of the important documents, neatly typed, in a production file or production book. Such materials are routinely required by distribution agreements in a section or schedule called "Delivery Requirements," but they should be assembled upon completion of every television production, regardless of its intended market, and kept in a file that is cross-referenced to the master videotape. The following "deliverables" are likely to be required—along with the master tape (and sometimes work tapes)—before an independent producer or production company can receive final payment:

- *Agreements.* All cast, staff, crew, music, set design, and other agreements. If the program is likely to have a commercial life beyond its initial showing, a memo outlining residuals should be included here as well.

- *Credit List.* The list of screen credits, as it appears on the final version of the program.

- *Release Forms.* Each form should be labeled to identify it with the person appearing in the program.

- *Final Budget Accounting.* On a larger production, a final accounting may not be possible until 60 or 90 days after completion because invoices may arrive late; still, the most accurate and up-to-date accounting possible should be included, sometimes accompanied by copies of all paid invoices.

- *Final Script.* A final script, if available, is especially useful if the production may be edited in the future. A show rundown, listing each program element and its duration in minutes and seconds, should be included as well.

- *Music Cue Sheet.* This details every piece of music, along with its composer, publisher, running time, and, preferably, time-code position in the program.

- *Insurance Forms.* A copy of the producer's E&O policy should be included in the file; for many productions, such as those done by a local television station, coverage will be part of a larger policy and need not be included.

# CHAPTER 46

# DESIGN

The design of images is an extremely important aspect of the television business, one whose impact is often assumed but rarely considered as a significant strategy. Several networks have forged unusually successful alliances between screen design and brand identity—that is, when you turn to a particular channel, you know which channel you are watching because of the way it looks. Certainly, Bloomberg's multi-windowed screen is distinctive: It reduces the moving video image to about half the screen, using the rest for news and data. The Weather Channel has developed its own distinctive look, as has QVC. Nickelodeon and MTV employed successful design concepts as their brands were becoming well known. Most networks make limited use of design, however, utilizing little more than a logo and the latest look in background graphics and typography. Some networks are easily recognized by distinctive logos: CBS's eye, NBC's simplified version of their traditional peacock, MTV's giant M, CNN's type treatment, Court TV's fingerprint, PBS's encircled head.

The distinctive look of a particular show may also be a contributor to its success. The look of *The Simpsons*, for example, is different from every other animated series. The public television series *Teletubbies* and several other children's series also benefit from a unique look. VH1 has been successful in developing a fun and differentiated look for its various pop culture documentary commentaries, such as *I Love the 90s*. In an environment with hundreds of channels, a unique visual look can cause viewers to stop and take notice. In other words, good design can be a competitive advantage.

## PROMOS

At many stations and networks, on-air promos are an afterthought, a necessary process but not one held in high esteem. This is foolish thinking. TV Land and Nickelodeon have both been very clever in utilizing their promos to help to establish brand identity, which has caused viewers to watch programs that they might otherwise bypass.

An on-air promotion department is typically a function of either the programming department or the marketing department. Ideally, promos are produced as on-air marketing campaigns, scheduled long in advance and developed with optimal resources. As a part of marketing, on-air campaigns are often well co-ordinated with events and off-air promotions and advertising. More often, however, promos are produced with insufficient notice and only the resources available at the time. The result is usually functional, but rarely as effective as an on-air promotional campaign might be. Measure this effectiveness against the revenues that could instead be captured as a result of selling the airtime to an advertiser, and the cost of a lost opportunity becomes clear. Strategic use of a promotion department is a smart investment. Rush jobs probably don't have much of an impact on viewing patterns.

## ANIMATION

In the 1990s, the animation business woke from a lengthy slumber. The success of *The Simpsons* on FOX; the triple-header success of *Ren & Stimpy*, *Doug*, and *Rugrats* on Nickelodeon; and several popular animated feature films from Disney brought about a renewed interest in new animation productions for television. Several new animation production houses opened, providing a steady stream of new television projects. Nickelodeon became a major producer of animation through an elaborate in-house production setup.

The industry's renewed interest in animation was prompted by a combination of new audiences and advertiser response, and new animation techniques made possible by more powerful computers and related software. As companies moved from the tedium and high cost of cel animation (where each frame must be drawn and painted by hand), animation facilities opened in Ireland and in Asia, where, the reduced cost of labor made new animated series possible within television budgets.

Every animation project begins with a combination of character and story line. Generally, the characters and their world drive the story line. The character must have a distinctive look and personality, and this usually begins the old-fashioned way—with an artist sketching (he or she may "sketch" on a computer, but most artists begin the process with a pencil and a whole lot of bad ideas on crumpled paper). Some story lines work with one central character (Nickelodeon's *Dora the Explorer*), but only if that character is surrounded by a supporting cast of regulars. A pair of characters is a very popular animation format, used for *The Flintstones* (Fred and Barney), *Ren & Stimpy*, *Angry Beavers*, and many others. One variation is a main character with a sidekick (*Dexter's Laboratory*) or a main character surrounded by a group (*Top Cat*, *Fat Albert & the Cosby Kids*, *Hey Arnold!*, *South Park*, *Pokémon*). A family is also a popular format, used for *Family Guy*, *King of the Hill*, *The Simpsons*, *Rugrats*, and more. So, too, is a team (*Fantastic Four*, *Aqua Teen Hungerforce*, *Powerpuff Girls*, *Justice League*).

Animations are often staged in a fantasy environment, a world that operates within its own rules (and with its own inside jokes). The classics in this genre include *The Flintstones* and *The Jetsons*; one especially successful example of this approach is the more recent *SpongeBob SquarePants*. *Dragonball* also takes place in its own fantasy world. Other series, like *Family Guy* and *The Simpsons*, redraw and skew the real world.

Animation is magic. No matter how much technology is applied, the key to successful animation is successful character development, script writing, and acting. This does not change even when a powerful computer is inserted into the process. The visual side of animation is typically led by a director, who works closely with animators and artists. The audio side is somewhat less complicated and labor intensive, requiring a fairly traditional soundtrack composed of voices, sound effects, and music.

One key component to winning animation is the choice of voice actors. Nancy Cartwright, the longtime voice of Bart Simpson, previously provided voices for *My Little Pony*, *Pound Puppies*, and several other cartoon series before landing the role as Bart; similarly, Dan Castellaneta worked his way up from Earthworm Jim to eventually become Homer Simpson. June Foray, who was the voice of Rocky the Squirrel, worked on a spectacular number of cartoons, from *Garfield* to *The Gummi Bears* and *The Smurfs*. Brad Garrett, well known for his live work on *Everybody Loves Raymond*, was also the voice of the Big Dog on *Two Stupid Dogs*. Billy West was Stimpy, then became both Ren and Stimpy. In Los Angeles and, to a somewhat lesser extent, New York, there are actors who specialize in voice work. Other traditional actors, some quite well known, also do voice work on a regular basis, where for once there is no need for makeup or hair or costumes or hot lights—just say your lines and move on, and have fun doing it! A long list of celebrities, from Rita Moreno and Phil Hartman to Jon Lovitz and Tim Curry, have provided character voices. One voice actor often provides multiple voices for the same program; it's quite remarkable to watch this type of voice actor at work. Harry Shearer, who provides so many different voices on *The Simpsons*, is a wonderful example of the voice actor's versatility. AFTRA and SAG rules ensure that an actor who provides multiple voices receives fair compensation.

The client approves several key stages of the production process: the storyboards, a rough version of the animation, and then the finished work. Since animation projects proceed over the course of weeks, incremental reviews by the client are common, especially on larger or more complicated projects. This process is essentially the same for both traditional film animation and for computer animation techniques. Normally, fees are paid in installments of percentage payments keyed to the production schedule.

## PRODUCTION DESIGN

Once an essential aspect of every television production, the need for scenic design and set construction has faded as fewer television programs are produced in television studios. The need for art direction continues, but on a somewhat smaller scale, often akin more to the decoration and propping of an existing location than to the creation of a wholly new visual environment. Some reality shows, however, involve a fair amount of production design, even when the show takes place on location.

For a traditional studio-based series, such as a news or talk show, or for a situation comedy or a drama, the production designer is brought into the process while the project is in its planning stages. He or she meets with the producer(s), writer(s) and director(s), and discusses the functional requirements. For the CBS series *Without a Trace*, for example, much of the action takes place in the modern, open bullpen office area where many of the characters have their desks, and where the timeline whiteboard is seen throughout each episode. In addition, lead investigator Jack Malone's office is a frequently used set. The settings for the long-running sitcom series *Seinfeld* were, primarily, certain rooms of Jerry's apartment and the hallway outside. Other sets were developed as needed: Elaine's apartment, Elaine's various offices, George's office at Yankee Stadium, various areas in Kramer's apartment, various restaurants, and so on. The game shows launched in the late 1990s, notably *Who Wants to Be a Millionaire*, made good use of powerful stage settings to establish mood. That series also demonstrated the impact of a combined scenic and lighting design.

For each of these projects, the process is more or less the same. The staff and the script dictate certain functional elements and a certain style. The designer returns to his or her office, does some preliminary sketches, then works one or two ideas up into a *rendering* (a drawing or computer illustration). This then becomes the basis for further discussion. Changes are made based upon functional concerns (e.g., a countertop might need to be made larger to accommodate multiple performers standing around it), budget concerns (the fancy materials need to be scaled back, or certain set pieces must be modified or eliminated), or aesthetics (the designer's ideas don't quite match what the show's creators had in mind). Modification is common. The second rendering is usually very close to the final version. A bit more alteration, often due to financial constraints or small changes in the show's direction ("Oh, sorry, we've eliminated that character..."), and the design is ready for planning and budget estimate by the scenic shop.

The scenic shop uses the designer's detailed plans to work out a firm budget based upon labor, materials, transportation (from shop to stage or studio), and installation (sets arrive in pieces). Often, additional painting or finishing is required once the set is in place. There is some back-and-forth about the items within the estimate, a few more changes, and a go-ahead. Then, in a matter of weeks, the scenery is built and delivered.

While this is going on, the director typically spends time with the production designer and the lighting designer or director. Every television setting is designed and installed in close cooperation with the lighting staff. This is necessary for reasons of logistics and scheduling (lights must be hung before the set goes up) and for aesthetic reasons.

At the same time, the production designer works closely with the wardrobe staff to fully integrate the look of the show. On a news magazine, this is less essential. On a science fiction or children's series, this type of coordination is a must.

Reality series operate in a somewhat different way. The production designer helps to select the location, and then designs specific set pieces to establish mood and/or to serve specific functions. For example, if huts or other lodgings need to be built and will be seen on camera, then they must be designed with a look that's consistent with the brand's imagery. When *American Idol* goes through its audition sequences in hotels, the look is casual, but it is carefully considered in terms of mood, camera positions, and, increasingly, places for appropriate product placements (see page 84). The performers arrive in their own choice of wardrobe, but the judging panel are dressed by wardrobe professionals.

Many programs have ongoing needs—more sets, special pieces, and so on. The original set designer, who has been paid a fee for the initial design, is often retained by the production; otherwise, an assistant on the designer's staff attends to the ongoing needs of the project. The original designer is available for larger projects, but day-to-day problems and projects are normally the domain of the more junior designer. Some projects have larger needs: *Saturday Night Live*, for example, has an ongoing need for new scenery.

## Design Agreements

Most designers routinely negotiate on their own behalf. Increasingly, though, top designers are working with agents or, in some cases, with attorneys.

Design agreements are sometimes verbal. This is because the entire job may take only a month, while the written agreement may take longer to draft, revise, redraft, and sign. Sometimes, the producer or designer requires a brief written agreement stating basic terms. Any agreement—written or verbal—with a scenic designer should cover the following elements:

- *A list of responsibilities,* including the conceptualization and rendering of a scenic design acceptable to the producer, with necessary revisions; supervision of construction and painting; on-site supervision of load-in and strike(s) (see page 391); availability for revisions and new scenic elements.

- *A payment schedule.* The designer is typically paid half of the fee on acceptance of preliminary designs and the rest when the set is physically in the studio (or when the program first airs). There may also be incremental payments pegged to acceptance of the completed design, but the short time that the designer works and the number of weeks from invoice to payment often make incremental payments unwieldy.

- *A negotiable weekly fee,* if the designer is working on a series in network or syndicated television. This fee may also involve a promise to maintain ("babysit") the production.

- *A credit for the designer,* usually Production Designer, Art Director, or Scenic Designer. The use of this credit is largely negotiable.

- *Ownership of the designs.* Sometimes, all rights in the designs are transferred to the production company; increasingly, however, designers are seeking to keep the copyright themselves (subject to limits on re-use) and to license rights to the producer only for the specific production.

## The Scenic Artists Union

One union for scenic artists is United Scenic Artists Local 829, part of the International Brotherhood of Painters and Allied Trades (IBPAT). It's an AFL-CIO affiliate representing over 140,000 people, mostly paperhangers, decorators, scenic artists, and professionals in related fields (many outside the entertainment fields). Technically, Local 829 has jurisdiction nationwide through three business offices in New York, Chicago, and Los Angeles; in practice, though, its jurisdiction over the television industry is primarily in New York. Los Angeles art directors and related personnel usually work under the jurisdiction of the Art Directors Guild Local 876, an IATSE affiliate. If a union designer wants to work for a company that is not a union signatory, a project-specific agreement can usually be arranged.

The locals set minimum rates for television productions, commercials, and motion pictures, and require a pension and welfare payment of 10.5 percent of gross earnings, with a cap. As with other unions, there are rules regarding minimum call, meal periods, rest periods, penalties, and notification of calls and changes. Many designers do not strictly adhere to these rules since they are trying to get the job done within limited studio hours and before rehearsals begin, but the spirit of the rules is certainly respected on most productions.

## Transportation, Setup, Strike, Reset

Television scenery is usually built to the designer's specifications by scenic construction shops. Other types of construction shops can do the work, but the results are generally better with a shop that specializes in television. Work is done on a contract basis between the shop and the producing company. The shop submits a bid with payment terms; once the bid has been negotiated and is acceptable to both parties, work begins in accordance with a delivery schedule.

The shop is supervised by the designer—who visits several times during the construction and painting—but the shop actually contracts with, and is paid by, the producing company.

The scenery on network television and on much of syndication and pay TV is built in union shops, where union workers stamp each piece of scenery with a union symbol (a "bug"). If the program is to be produced in a studio with union stagehands, it is important to coordinate the activities of the union members who construct, truck, and load the set into the studio. If all of these workers are members of IATSE, as is often the case in New York and Los Angeles, then the coordination is routine. If a variety of unions are involved or if one of the links in this chain is to be non-union, then arrangements must be made (and sometimes negotiated) in advance.

Television scenery is fragile, and should be moved only by companies and stagehands experienced in the trucking of scenery. The scenic construction shop usually makes arrangements for trucking.

*Load-in* is the process of removing scenery from the truck and assembling it in the studio. The trucking crew unloads, and stagehands hired for work in the studio set up. The crew chief follows the designer's floor plan for instructions as to placement, but the designer is available to answer questions. In some studios, under union rules, the designer is allowed to touch but not move scenery. (Some crews are more lenient than others, and some designers assume more responsibility than others do.)

*Striking a set* is the process of removing it from the studio or, in some cases, taking it apart and setting it aside to make room for another show. The potential for damage is increased when the set is struck and reset often; in such cases, a long-term maintenance deal with the designer may be wise. Several stagehands who work on the show generally earn extra pay for working on strikes and resets; since these activities often take place before or after regular production hours, overtime pay scales are frequently involved.

## INTELLECTUAL PROPERTY CONSIDERATIONS

Most artists work either as employees or as independent contractors on a work-for-hire basis (see Chapter 40). The proceeds of their work, therefore, belong to the employer or client who becomes the copyright holder. There are, however, two subtleties to be considered.

First, most artists—and most creative people, for that matter—are especially competent in certain styles and types of work. It is not unusual for an artist to rework an idea previously submitted to or prepared for another client. Since ideas are not subject to copyright protection (see Chapter 34), the new work need not infringe on the rights of the former client, unless a great level of restriction was specified in the first contract.

Second, a situation may arise in which the work of the artist is exploited beyond the parties' original intent. For example, an artist is hired to create an animated character for use in an industrial film, and that character proves to have value beyond its original use. Continuing ownership of the character (as opposed to its first appearance in the industrial film) may belong to the artist, or to the company that owns the industrial film, or to both parties. In the case of a true freelance arrangement, if the producing company intended to purchase rights to the character beyond its original use in the industrial film, the rights should have been clearly specified, or included in a grant of all character uses in all markets in perpetuity. If the work was made for hire, then the producing company, as a matter of law, owns the rights. Ideally, the contract should provide for continuing financial participation for the artist, even if the artist does not own part of the copyright. Even better (for the artist), the original contract should allocate only those rights that the producing company will actually exploit, reserving all other rights for the artist. Since situations like these are rarely simple, the reader may wish to consult an attorney who specializes in such matters.

A graphic design is subject to the same legal considerations as any other creative element in a production. Under copyright law, the use of a particular image requires the permission of the owner of that image. In addition, the work may not infringe on the rights of any third parties (see Chapter 34); any photographs or graphic works that are owned by third parties must be cleared for use within the context of the program. Companies that sell old photographs and other vintage graphics set rates based on the type of production, its distribution, and the number of times the program will be seen. These rates are flexible if the material will be seen by a very limited audience, or if the production leases multiple images. The producer should confirm that the rights fee covers all types of possible uses—otherwise, he or she will be held accountable for infringements. If a graphic element is owned by a third party who is not in the business of selling images, then the rate should be based on a fair market price. Signed agreements must be completed prior to inclusion of the image in the production.

There is a gray area with regard to the use of public images. The trade "dress" and trademarks of commercial products, such as packaged goods and their labels, are owned by their producers, and normally should not be used without permission. If the material itself is the subject of a legitimate public-interest program, however, the First Amendment will generally permit its use, provided that no false designation of origin is implied. Photos and video images of public figures can also be used in a news or public affairs context; otherwise, the trademark, privacy, and publicity roles can prevent use without permission (see Chapter 35). Images may, under certain circumstances, be used for satire or parody without permission of the rights holder. Art in museum collections can be especially troublesome. Because the museum may hold the only copy (or one of a limited number of copies) of a particular work of art, the institution's permission may be required in order to use that work, or some representation of that work, regardless of its age or origin.

There are no clear rules regarding the line of demarcation between truly original images and existing images that have been transformed to create new originals. The legal question is whether the new work is close enough to the old one to constitute a "derivative work." This is determined by a highly subjective test of "substantial similarity" (see page 263). As a practical matter, if the artist or the rights holder who owns the original image is likely to recognize the connection and demand money, deny permission to use the original image, or insist that the new work infringes on the work's copyright, then the new work is probably too similar to the original image to be used without permission. New images that satirize older ones are subject to greater latitude, since satire is a recognized exception to usual copyright protections.

# CHAPTER 47

# MUSIC

The music business is a highly evolved one in its own right. Music on television is a complicated subject, involving issues that range from ownership of compositions and recordings to the creation of original music. Readers wishing additional detail should consult the most recent edition of *This Business of Music*, by M. William Krasilovsky, Sidney Shemel, and John M. Gross.

## MUSIC AND COPYRIGHT LAW

Three aspects of copyright law apply specifically to the use of music in television: synchronization rights, performance rights, and master use rights.

### Synchronization Rights

The copyright holder of a musical composition controls its reproduction in fixed, or recorded, form. The right to reproduce music on a record, tape, or compact disc is called a *mechanical license* (the term is leftover from the days of player pianos and music boxes). A record company must acquire a mechanical license if a copyrighted composition is fixed or recorded in a way that can be read or replayed by a mechanical, electrical, electronic, or computer device.

A *synchronization right*, or *sync right*, is, in effect, a kind of mechanical license. The sync right permits the music to be fixed to an audiovisual recording. The grant of the sync right permits the producer and/or distributor of a film or television program to affix a particular piece of music to the film, tape, videodisc, computer file, or other audiovisual embodiment. This license has traditionally been obtained by the television producer, either through direct negotiation with the composer or via the music publisher. A synchronization license is not needed for a live show because the element of recording is absent; only a performance right is needed. If the live production is taped or filmed for later use, however, then a sync right is necessary to cover the incorporation of the music in this physical form.

### Performance Rights

The second aspect of copyright law that applies to television music comes into play when the program is shown to the public—the right to control public performances of the composition. When a television program, commercial, or other audiovisual form is disseminated publicly, whether by satellite, terrestrial broadcast, Internet streaming, or cable, this constitutes a public performance of the music contained in the program. The *performance right* must be licensed from the copyright holder; this license has traditionally been secured on a blanket basis (see below) by the local station or cable network, usually from a performing rights society.

If the music is only incidental to the dramatic content of live action—for example, a radio is playing a particular song in the background of a television program—then the right is called a "non-dramatic" or "small" performing right. If the music is an integral part of the drama of the program, as with a film musical or a televised opera, then the right is called a "dramatic" or "grand" performing right. The grand and small rights are generally administered in a very different fashion, as separate aspects of music publishing.

A private viewing of a DVD or videotape at home will generally not constitute a public performance requiring a license. However, if money is charged for the viewing, or if the viewing takes place in a commercial establishment (a bar, for example), then the viewing may be considered a public performance, and may require the acquisition of a performance license. Smaller bars and restaurants (less than 3,750 gross square feet) and small retail establishments of other types (less than 2,000 gross square feet) were given a statutory exemption in 1998. Larger establishments may also be exempt if they have a limited number of televisions and speakers.

## Master Use Rights

The synchronization and performance rights relate to the composition itself, but not to any specific embodiment of that music in a recording. Since sound recordings, as well as compositions, have been covered by U.S. copyright law for some years, it is probable that any production using preexisting musical performances will need permission to use the recording as well. This permission is called a *master use license* and is obtained from the copyright holder in the recording—typically the record company in question.

## MUSIC PUBLISHING

The administration of both the synchronization and performance rights falls under the general activity of music publishing. A composer and a music publisher enter into a business arrangement in which the publisher agrees to administer these and other rights on behalf of the composer, acting as a clearinghouse and collecting agent for producers and others seeking to license the musical compositions. Music publishers vary greatly in their size, their clout, and their ability to make money for their client composers. Even composers of considerable stature license their songs to music publishing companies, though some artists own their publishing companies, in whole or in part. Grand performing rights are sometimes withheld by the composer from an overall publishing arrangement and licensed through a different publishing company or agent.

A music publisher—like any other publisher—is responsible for the marketing of the property, the negotiation of licensing agreements, the collection of revenues, the issuing of royalty statements, and the payment of royalties.

The traditional split of performance and synchronization revenues between publisher and composer is 50/50. Sometimes, a publisher may yield to negotiating pressure and grant some of its usual share to the composer in what is called a *copublishing arrangement*. The publisher, in turn, may deduct an administrative fee and/or charge for out-of-pocket expenses before revenues are distributed. In some cases, the publisher has pressured the composer to grant a portion of his or her 50 percent, but few publishers are successful in this effort (see following page for discussion of performing rights organizations).

## OBTAINING A SYNCHRONIZATION LICENSE

The television producer typically negotiates for the synchronization license prior to including the music in the production; if the rights are too costly, he or she can then move on to another composition. These rights can be obtained either directly from the composer (and lyricist, if there is one), by arrangement with the music publisher, or with the help of some kind of clearance service. In the past, the Harry Fox Agency specialized in this activity, but it has now stopped acting in this field. The cost of the sync license can be substantial for a well-known work. Finding the right person to deal with has often been a major impediment to licensing existing works. Online resources for matching compositions with publishers can be found at the ASCAP (www.ascap.com), BMI (www.bmi.com), and National Music Publishers Association (www.nmpa.org) Web sites (see below for more information).

In many television productions, the producer commissions the music, keeping the cost of the sync license low as part of the overall deal for the composer's work. This is possible because the performance license fees for a commissioned work—which the producer typically does not pay—can be extremely lucrative for the composer and for whomever is serving as the music publisher. Many producers own music publishing companies specifically to cash in on a share of the music revenues. In an extreme case—such as a show with daily, weekly, or national exposure—the composer and publisher may absorb all of the recording costs just for the opportunity to collect their share of the performance license fees. These are collected from television stations on an annualized basis; complicated formulas determine how much stations pay and how much publishers and composers receive.

# PERFORMANCE LICENSES AND PERFORMING RIGHTS ORGANIZATIONS

Music publishers normally do not collect small rights revenues directly. Instead, monies are collected by performing rights organizations: ASCAP (American Society of Composers, Authors and Publishers), BMI (Broadcast Music, Inc.), and—for European works, and for a growing list including some religious and gospel music—SESAC (originally, Society of European Stage Authors and Composers). Similar organizations exist in most other developed countries.

Performance fees can also be negotiated and paid directly to the composer or publisher. This is called "source licensing," and remains a relatively uncommon practice. ASCAP and BMI grew out of a need for composers to band together to monitor the performance of music onstage, in live concerts, on radio, and later, on television. Neither the artist nor the publisher can possibly monitor every usage—a live band in North Dakota, a music video played on a local cable system in Oregon, a radio station in Florida, and so on. The performing rights organizations were formed to track usage, collect the appropriate license fees, and divide the income fairly among rights holders.

After the deduction of overhead, the income from these sources is allocated to particular compositions and divided between the composer (and lyricist, if there are lyrics) and the publisher on a 50/50 basis. If no publishing company is listed on the cue sheet (see below), and the performing rights organization is unable to find the proper publisher, then the publisher's share goes uncollected. If there is no individual composer associated with the work, his or her share goes uncollected.

## Blanket Licenses

Most performance rights licensing takes place at the level of the broadcast station or cable network. Rather than negotiating deals for each individual use, stations and networks use blanket licenses. A *blanket license* allows the licensee to use any item in the performing rights organization's catalog for a specified period of time, without the need to negotiate for the performance right of each individual composition. Cue sheets provide the basis of allocating blanket license fees to ASCAP and BMI members. Some cable networks work only with original or library music, and do not routinely work with ASCAP or BMI material.

## Tracking Usage

In theory, ASCAP and BMI attempt to track the use of every piece of music used on every television program airing on every national, regional, and local broadcast, cable, and satellite system. Indeed, when the stakes are high and the audiences are large—as on network television—tracking is extremely accurate. On local and other forms of television, though, the tracking may be somewhat less rigorous. The key to tracking is the music *cue sheet*. A cue sheet is a list of every piece of music used in a particular television program or film. The cue sheet lists the title and running time of each piece of music, as well as its composer, lyricist (if any), publisher, copyright owner, and performing arts institution (ASCAP, BMI). This list is generally delivered to the network or distributor along with the video master; copies should be provided to the exhibitor and, in turn, to the appropriate performing rights society every time the production is publicly shown. ASCAP provides a sample cue sheet at www.ascap.com/playback/2005/winter/cuesheets.html; see another sample at Appendix 4.7. The performing arts organization feeds all of this information into its computers, and works out a formula that is used to determine the performance license fees due to the composer and publisher.

## Grand Rights

In those special cases where a grand license is required, ASCAP and BMI are not involved; instead, the license is sought directly from the publisher or from the composer and lyricist.

## Performers

As noted above, the rights to the specific performance must also be cleared. If the producer is dealing with existing recordings, the copyright owner in the sound recording is the probable locus for all of the necessary rights. If the music is to be specifically recorded for the program, then an assignment of rights should be obtained from all performers. Information on dealing with union musicians can be found at page 378.

# PART 10

# LEGAL AND BUSINESS AFFAIRS

# CHAPTER 48
# CONTRACTS

Contract law is one of the great developments of Western mercantile culture. Under contract law, courts will grant the force of law to an arrangement agreed upon by private parties. But courts will not enforce every statement or promise— for instance, a gratuitous or frivolous offer may be nullified. What courts will enforce is a serious transaction between two or more parties in exchange for value on all sides. This value is sometimes called "consideration," and it is a necessity for a binding agreement. In some instances, however, consideration can be supplied by the known reliance of one party on the promise of the other, even if nothing of material value is being exchanged.

## VERBAL AND WRITTEN AGREEMENTS

Notwithstanding the old truism that an oral agreement isn't worth the paper it's written on, verbal deals were generally enforceable under common law until 1677. The change came with the adoption in England of the "statute of frauds," a measure intended to prevent the frauds that may occur whenever there is no signed, written agreement. Although the U.K. has since dropped its statute of frauds, most U.S. states have adopted some form of it. Typically, the following must all be in writing and signed in order to be enforced: sales agreements for goods over $500, contracts requiring performance over a significant amount of time (commonly a year), the sale or transfer of real estate, contracts for marriage, and contracts of guaranty and surety. In television, verbal agreements are often used for short-term employment, particularly if there are no rights in intellectual property or privacy being transferred. But whenever rights are being transferred, or whenever any future service or right is contemplated, a written agreement should be used.

The signed agreement need not be contained on a single piece of paper. If a distributor writes a signed letter offering to license a program to a station, and the station sends back a signed letter saying it accepts the deal, the requirements of the statute of frauds will be met. Informal documents such as job orders, booking sheets, and deal memos can also constitute a sufficient writing.

In most states, it is also necessary for one party to deliver the contract to the other party, or to the other party's representatives, for a contract to be formed. If you sign the deal but keep the signed copy to yourself, delivery has not occurred and the contract is not yet binding.

As discussed on page 271, federal copyright law requires that an exclusive assignment or license take the form of a signed document in order to be effective. Similarly, some privacy-law statutes require that any waiver of privacy rights be set in writing.

In the television business, sometimes a *deal memo* is sent; this confirms a deal without any provision for signature. On the other hand, sometimes correspondence and contract drafts may go back and forth for months without the necessary final agreement getting signed. In some cases, the money may be paid, the services may be provided, the program may be broadcast on national television— and still no signatures.

In cases in which a contract is not signed but performance has gone forward, the courts are at least aware that some kind of agreement existed between the parties: They have "performed" the agreement. The courts will seek to determine what the deal was governing the performance, and will enforce it even though the technical requirements of the statute of frauds have not been met. An even broader interpretation is the concept of reliance. If one party makes a verbal or written promise to another party, and knows that this other party relies on the promise, then the promise can often be enforced even in the absence of any signed contract.

Since the television industry is clearly somewhat casual about signing agreements before work begins on projects, sometimes term sheets, confirming letters, or deal memos—even if unsigned by the other side—are used to guide a court once performance has begun, particularly if these items go uncontroverted. The ultimate weapon, short of a signed contract, is the *reliance letter*. It gives notice to the other side that the party is actually relying on the submitted terms, even though there is nothing yet signed. Of course, the other side can send back a "don't rely" letter, or even a "don't rely but we are relying" letter. If performance continues and a dispute breaks out, the courts may have a hard time untangling the record.

## CONTRACT FORMATS

The signed document embodying a contract need not be in any particular form, but it must include adequate evidence of the necessary terms of the agreement, and must indicate the intent of the signatories to be bound by it.

In effect, anything that says, "This is a contract, these are the parties, and these are the terms," should do the job. Over time, a series of generally accepted forms have evolved. The oldest and most formal is the *indenture form*. The wording is derived from the forms used for contracts in the late Middle Ages and looks something like this:

AGREEMENT

This agreement made as of this 1st day of January, 2006, by and between the Smith Corporation, a Delaware corporation, and John Doe, an individual,

WITNESSETH

WHEREAS, the Smith Corporation wishes to undertake a transaction with Doe and Doe wishes to undertake a transaction with the Smith Corporation;

NOW, THEREFORE, the parties hereto agree as follows:

Buried within the arcane language of this form is a simple statement: The document is a contract between Smith Corporation and Doe; the reasons for the contract are that Doe and Smith Corporation want to do a deal; the deal is as follows. Such a contract might close:

IN WITNESS WHEREOF, the parties hereto have executed this Agreement as of the date first above written.

_____

John Doe

SMITH CORPORATION

By:_____

Lisa Smith, President

A more modern but equally enforceable form of contract is the letter agreement. The letter agreement begins by stating who the parties are, and that the letter is a contract. A typical starting clause might read:

John Doe
123 Main Street
Anytown, U.S. 12345

January 1, 2006

Smith Corporation
456 First Street
Anytown, U.S. 12345

Dear Ms. Smith:

When the enclosed copy of this letter is signed on behalf of the Smith Corporation and returned to me, this letter will set forth the terms of our agreement concerning the deal to be done between us on the following terms:

Such a contract might close with:

Please confirm that the foregoing accurately represents the agreement between us by executing the enclosed copy on the indicated line and returning it to me.

Yours sincerely,

John Doe

ACCEPTED AND AGREED:

SMITH CORPORATION

By:_____

Lisa Smith, President

Similarly, a memorandum form may be used to set forth an agreement:

From: Smith Corporation
To: John Doe
Re: Deal
Date: January 1, 2006

This memorandum will set forth the terms of our deal and, when signed on the indicated lines below, will constitute our binding agreement.

The memorandum form usually closes with some type of signature lines.

None of these forms has any special advantage as a matter of law, although particular industry segments may have their preferences or traditions. They are all equally binding as contracts. By and large, the indenture form is considered more formal than the letter agreement, and the letter more formal than the memo. As a matter of style, the formality of the agreement should match the complexity of the transaction. For instance, the memo form is fine for a deal that can be adequately described within a page or two. If the agreement requires several pages, the letter agreement is better; if dozens of pages are necessary, the indenture form may be the most appropriate format.

## E-mail and Other Digital Agreements

There is no inherent impediment to forming contracts via an exchange of e-mails, provided that they clearly spell out the classic elements of offer and acceptance, and contain a sufficiently clear statement of the agreed terms. The informality of e-mails may make attention to detail on matching up terms particularly important. While the process is not fully complete, many legal systems are recognizing that the intentional sending of an e-mail, particularly one with accurate indicia of origin, can supply the equivalent of a signature. In cases where verification is particularly important, digital signature protocols are being developed that will give relatively safe authentication procedures.

## Form Agreements

People in the television business frequently use preprinted form agreements, which can be real time-savers—with two provisos. First, the contract must fit the deal, and vice versa. Although using a form agreement helps save on legal costs, this can be a false economy if the form simply isn't the right one, or if the deal has a complication not covered by a standard form. Second, the forms must be fair enough for both parties to actually sign. Although when using a form agreement there is always the temptation to make it as favorable as possible to the drafter, the contract cannot be so one-sided that no one will sign it.

## Writing Style

As a matter of law, a contract does not require any particular style of writing; it need only state, in language that is specific and clear, the principal terms of the deal. A certain style of writing known as "legalese" has developed over the years, but to the extent that it confuses the untrained reader, legalese is not recommended. In certain instances, time-honored legal formulas may save space or provide shorthand for complicated concepts. In general, though, if the use of legalese might lead to a misunderstanding, the contract should be worded in plain language instead.


# CONTRACT VALIDITY

## Necessary Terms

To be enforceable, a contract must contain certain critical, basic terms. If the price, dates, or items to be sold or licensed are absent or are left to future negotiations, the entire contract will probably not be considered binding by a court. In such cases, there just isn't enough actually agreed upon to constitute a real deal. The common television industry practice of leaving terms for later good-faith negotiation runs the risk of rendering at least the provision—and perhaps even the entire agreement—unenforceable. To prevent this possibility, negotiation clauses should never be for basic terms, and when they are used, they should outline a detailed procedure with specific dates, parameters, and other objective criteria on how negotiations are to proceed.

## Order of Terms

The order in which terms of an agreement are set forth does not affect its binding nature; as a practical matter, however, a good agreement should read easily and logically. Thus, it is customary to begin with the terms of greatest importance and then proceed to the more minor details as the contract progresses. In drafting a contract, one should begin as if telling an uninitiated person about the contents of the deal. A program license agreement, for instance, might well start by saying that a license is being granted and then move on to describe the programs and the term or territories involved. The next topic might be the compensation for the license; further topics would include representations and warranties of the parties (see page 408); and the final provisions might cover choice of law (see page 407) and other technical matters.

## Signatures

Any signature that identifies the signing party and its intent to be bound is adequate for a contract. Thus, the use of a first name or initials, if effective on these points, can constitute a signature. Although it is the custom in this country that signatures should appear at the end of a document, there is no requirement for this in most states, provided the signatures appear at a place in the document where they demonstrate the necessary intent to be bound. The agreement is generally signed at an indicated space, frequently on a line over the printed or typed name of the person signing. This signature line should also specify the capacity in which the person is signing in order to make clear whether it is as an individual, as an officer of a corporation, or as a partner, agent, or trustee. Also, if the person is signing on behalf of another entity, the signature line should be preceded by the word "by" to designate that the person is signing on behalf of the entity, such as a corporation or partnership, and not on his or her own behalf.

## Witnesses, Notaries, and Seals

Corporate and personal seals are generally not a necessity for agreements. In most instances, the signatures on a contract do not have to be authenticated by witnesses, and the contract does not have to be signed in front of a notary public (although these steps can be useful as evidentiary matters should the signature ever be disputed). For land transactions and other circumstances in which the contract is to be filed as a matter of public record, witnesses or notarial authentication may be required, but this is seldom the case for a television contract. In some instances, a corporate seal may be used as an additional piece of formal evidence to authenticate that a corporate action was properly taken.

## Originals

Original signed contracts are clearly preferred by a court called upon to enforce an agreement. If an original signed version is not available, however, the best available copy will have to be presented to the court. A conformed copy, a photocopy, or even a faxed copy of the signed original is usually considered acceptable—as long as there is sufficient evidence establishing that the signed original existed and that the offered copy is a true copy of it.

## Initialing

Initials next to a change in the contract indicate that the parties were aware of that change at the time of signing and that it was not inserted after the fact by one of the parties. In the case of changes added, whether by hand or in print, to an otherwise clean agreement, it is advisable to initial the changes to minimize the potential for future disagreements. Likewise, initials at the bottom of a contract page indicate that it is one of the original pages and that substitute pages have not been inserted. Unless a conflict between the parties is likely, the level of trust is exceedingly low, or a high degree of formality is desired, the individual pages of an agreement do not have to be initialed—particularly if each party will have a fully signed copy.

## Signing Authority and Powers of Attorney

Real people can sign for themselves; business entities, being artificial creations, cannot. Therefore, people must sign on behalf of business entities. The ability to sign on behalf of an entity hinges on the person's having either general or specific authorization to do so. In the case of a corporation, one can generally presume that the chairman, the president, or a senior vice president is authorized to execute most customary business contracts for a company. For a contract involving large amounts of money, however, specific board approval may be required to grant the authority. The other party to such a deal may request to see a certified copy of this board action, together with certified specimens of the signatures of the officers who are signing. In the case of a partnership, any general partner can usually sign on behalf of the partnership and bind it. Contracts involving a limited liability company should be signed by a manager or, if no managers are designated, by a member. Again, it can be prudent to confirm the authority by examining the underlying documents.

A person acting under a power of attorney can also bind a business entity—or an individual—within the scope of the granted power. Talent agents will sometimes sign on behalf of their clients and, if properly authorized as agents, will have the power of an attorney-in-fact for entering contracts within the scope of the agent's authority. If this is not so, it may be grounds for the agent's client to disown the contract, particularly if it was not reasonable to think that the agent had the power to sign.

In the final analysis, the ability of a party to bind another entity is usually evaluated on the basis of apparent authority. If the entity in question has apparently authorized the agent to sign—and this authority is relied upon by a person who could not have possibly known that the agent actually had no such power—then the entity will be bound by the signature. For better or worse, in most television deals the parties rely on the apparent authority of an appropriate corporate officer to bind the corporation to the contract, without requiring the inspection of the corporate resolution granting the power.

## Dates

Every contract should have a date indicating when it was signed, when it is to be effective, or both. Certain widely understood codes apply in giving a date. For instance, if an agreement is to be effective on a date that is specified, but which is not necessarily the date of signature, this date should be expressed with the words "as of." A contract that reads, "This agreement, dated as of the 1st day of January, 2006," could actually have been signed weeks before or after January 1, 2006. By contrast, if the contract date is to indicate the date of actual signing, then "as of" should not be used. Instead, the words "This contract, made this 1st day of January, 2006" imply that the signatures were affixed on the date given—also the effective date.

Sometimes a date is put next to the signature line to indicate the date of signature. This practice can be used in conjunction with an "as of" date for the entire contract, showing both the effective date for the agreement *and* the actual dates of execution.

## Stationery and Letterhead

There is no magic to the use of stationery or letterhead in connection with an agreement, although in some situations there may be some evidentiary value in the use of original letterhead. If the letter agreement form is to be used, it is logical that it appear on the customary letterhead of the party that is writing the letter.

# MATTERS OF LAW

## Choice of Law

Contract law is basically state law, and there are inevitable variations between the states on specific points. The choice of which state's law will apply to the contract is too frequently neglected by contracting parties. Sometimes, the variations in contract law between different states can have significant implications.

Parties cannot simply choose any law, however, to govern their agreements. There must be some relation of a logical and substantial nature between the law that is chosen to govern the agreement and the subject matter of the agreement, the location of the parties in general, or the location of the parties at the time of signing. In the absence of an affirmative choice of law, the applicable state law will be chosen by the court seeking to enforce the contract. As a starting point, most courts will prefer their own local law. A court may consider other factors as well, such as the respective domiciles of the parties, the state in which the contract performance is to take place, and the state in which the contract was signed.

## Minors

Minors—children under the age at which they become independently responsible adults (in most states, at 18)—receive many protections under traditional common-law principles. At common law, most contracts with a minor can be voided by the minor at any time until he or she becomes an adult, and for a reasonable time thereafter. Some states, recognizing that such a blanket rule would not be appropriate for a contract that is not abusive, have made provision for a court to review such a contract; if the court approves it, the contract would be binding and not voidable.

In California, for instance, the Family Code gives a court the discretion to approve a wide range of entertainment industry agreements with minors, including contracts for acting services, management and agency agreements, and grants of rights in creative properties and life stories. No time limit is set on the duration of service contracts, beyond the seven-year limit generally applicable in California. Although traditionally a parent or guardian has overseen (and sometimes abused) the receipt and application of a minor's earnings, by California law a portion of the minor's gross earnings should go into a special "blocked account" that will only be released when the beneficiary reaches adulthood.

New York law is more limited on the scope of entertainment industry agreements with minors that the court can approve. Although the court can permit service contracts, management agreements, and agency agreements, these documents cannot have terms of greater than three years (although certain negative covenants [see page 413] and participation agreements may extend beyond the three-year limit). In addition, New York law does not empower courts to approve grants of rights in intellectual property, although the "work for hire" doctrine may take care of much of this at the copyright level. A New York court may also require an account set aside to hold a portion of the minor's earnings until maturity. Under the terms of the New York privacy law, a parent is specifically authorized to waive privacy rights without a court proceeding.

In New York, California, and many other states, there are labor law regulations, discussed more fully on page 359, that apply to the employment of minors generally and in the context of film and television production specifically.

## Representations and Warranties

Many contracts contain items called *representations and warranties*—fancy words for promises about statements of fact. Thus, if a party represents and warrants that the contract was signed on Tuesday, he or she is stating that it is a fact: Tuesday is the date when the contract was signed. If this fact turns out to be wrong and damages result, this is grounds for a suit by the other party for a breach of the contract. Representations and warranties are frequently linked in the television world to statements about rights clearances and the authority to enter into agreements. As a general matter, parties only make representations and warranties about matters with which they are personally acquainted or over which they have personal control. In some instances, a representation and warranty can be softened by the insertion of "to the best of the party's knowledge" or similar words. In this case, a breach will not occur if the statement proves wrong—but it will occur if the representing and warranting party knew before signing that the statement was wrong. Claims under a "to the best of knowledge" representation and warranty can bog down into arguments over what constitutes "knowledge."

## Indemnities

An *indemnity*, frequently paired with representations and warranties, is a promise by one party to pay specified costs and losses of another party. In the contract context, an indemnity clause generally says that if Party A suffers a loss because of Party B—for example, because one of the representations and warranties proves to be untrue—then Party B will make good on Party A's losses and will cover any expenses. An indemnity should be given only for matters to which the giver agreed, to which the giver has provided a representation and warranty, or which are otherwise within the indemnifying party's knowledge, control, and legitimate risk.

Indemnities can have important wrinkles. One is whether the indemnity covers only *breaches* (actual defaults) or whether it also covers *alleged breaches* (defaults which someone else asserts). With an alleged breach, if someone wrongfully sues Party B with the claim that certain rights were not cleared, and if that claim is then defeated in court, then Party A, as the indemnifier, would still have to reimburse Party B for the costs of the lawsuit. If it were an indemnity limited to actual breaches, the indemnifying party (Party A) would not be called upon to pay the costs of Party B. Unless specifically mentioned, indemnities may not include legal fees, and so a provision for reasonable attorney's fees is frequently inserted. Indemnities sometimes give the indemnifying party a right to be involved in directing any litigation for which he or she is financially responsible. Likewise, the indemnifying party sometimes has the right to approve any settlements for which it will have to reimburse the other party.

## Duration

Although in most instances the term or duration of an agreement is up to the parties to decide between themselves, there are some general limitations that can apply. Most courts will impose some time limit on service contracts, if only as a matter of public policy to prevent endless employment commitments. In New

York, factors such as the level of compensation and the customs of the industry are considered. In California, the legislature has set a statutory limit of seven years for any contract for personal services.

There are also limitations on the duration of certain grants of rights. Under the Copyright Act, there are reversions permitted of copyright transfers and licenses (see page 270). Options, including those for turnaround, may be subject to the arcane "rule against perpetuities." This rule prohibits property (including creative works) from being tied up with contingent rights for endless periods. As a rule of thumb, options that are open for more than 21 years may be subject to cancellation.

## Contrary to Law or Public Policy

A court will refuse to enforce individual terms—or indeed, whole contracts—which it deems to be contrary to public policy. For instance, contracts for murder or theft will not be enforced. Also, laws on certain points may take precedence over the agreement of the parties. California's limit of seven years for employment agreements is one example of this.

## Force Majeure

*Force majeure* describes a circumstance in which performance of the contract is rendered impossible or unreasonably difficult by the intervention of a force beyond the control of the affected party. In television productions, this might include earthquakes, labor disputes, fires, wars, or other natural and manmade disasters. In such a case, the contract can be suspended or even terminated with consequences less than for full breach of contract. Television contracts frequently describe in detail those events that constitute *force majeure*, as well as the consequences—including the suspension and termination of the contract.

## Incapacity

Television contracts, particularly those for talent services, frequently have clauses dealing with the incapacity of the talent due to illness or injury. In most cases, after a short waiting period, the producer can choose either to suspend the contract and start it up again when the talent recovers, or to terminate the contract without further obligation.

## Breaches

What happens when one or both parties to a contract fail to live up to the deal they have made? This failure, often called a *breach* or a *default*, can occur in several ways. One party can fail to carry out an affirmative obligation (making a payment or delivering a finished program), or can breach a negative obligation (by failing to adhere to an exclusivity provision). If a representation and warranty turns out to be false, this can also cause a default.

A default or breach may be grounds for action if it is "material." Technical lapses that have no real consequences for the aggrieved party are generally shrugged off as "nonmaterial" by a court brought in to settle the dispute. If seemingly trivial points are indeed of importance, a party can strengthen his or her hand by inserting provisions that full performance of them is "of the essence" (see page 412). Even then, if the default is truly trivial, a court may still disregard it.

Contracts will sometimes provide time periods for remedying certain kinds of lapses, generally running from when the failing party gets notice of its default. This allows accidental failures to be fixed without the whole contract going into default.

Sometimes a party declares that he or she is not going to be bound by the contract. Even though there may not yet be any actual failure to perform, such a statement can constitute an anticipatory breach, particularly if it is not disclaimed after a request for confirmation by the other side.

## Remedies

If a contract is in material breach, the injured party has a number of possible responses. As a starting point, there are certain measures of "self-help." For instance, the aggrieved party can suspend his or her own performance under the contract: If a producer has failed to make payments required by the contract, an actor may stop showing up at the set. If there is a dispute over who is in breach, however, suspension of performance can be a dangerous step. If money is due for a print, for a soundtrack, or for other production elements, the lab or sound mixer may be able to hold onto the material under a "mechanic's lien" until the debt is paid.

While a dispute is pending, the aggrieved party should seek to mitigate his or her damages, taking whatever steps are reasonably available to minimize the losses coming from the breach. Thus, if contracts with suppliers can be canceled, this should be done; if another purchaser for the project is waiting in the wings, he or she should be considered. A failure to mitigate can be held against the aggrieved party when it comes time for a court to make good his or her losses.

Beyond the self-help steps, the aggrieved party may have to go to court—or, if the contract so provides, to arbitration—to get satisfaction. If there has indeed been a breach, a court or arbitration panel normally awards damages—that is, payments that will rectify the losses incurred. In deciding how much to award, the first consideration is *restitution,* or reimbursing the aggrieved party for any out-of-pocket losses that the failure of the contract has caused. An additional consideration is *lost profits,* some or all of which a court may force the breaching party to pay. If the defaulting party made profits through breaking the deal ("unjust enrichment"), a court can force some or all of these profits to be turned over to the aggrieved party. There is also the possibility of an award of *punitive damages,* although this is unlikely in a contract case, absent some elements of especially willful misbehavior. If the case involves a copyright claim, the statutory damages provided by the Copyright Act may apply (see page 272).

In addition to damages, a court may grant *equitable remedies* (the term refers to the old-fashioned courts of equity in which these remedies evolved). Equitable remedies are given only when money damages are inadequate in some fashion. These remedies include *specific performance*, an order by the court that the contract be carried out. Specific performance is appropriate if the contract is for the sale of some existing tangible item, such as a motion picture negative; it is untenable in the case of a contract to perform some kind of skilled service, such as writing, acting, or directing.

*Rescision*, or the undoing of the entire contract, may be an appropriate remedy if there has been a sale of rights in a program for which no payment has ever been made. A third equitable remedy is *injunction*, a court order that forbids some act—for example, the telecast of a show for which the rights were improperly cleared.

Equitable remedies tend to be more powerful contractual medicine than simple damages; therefore, courts tend to use them only if it is shown that damages will not do the job of providing adequate recompense. In addition, the parties themselves may have agreed in the contract to waive equitable remedies. Producers and distributors particularly dread the possibility of an injunction on the entire program because of a payment dispute on a talent contract. This waiver often occurs when rights are being transferred or credits given.

## LAWYERS' TERMS IN EVERYDAY LANGUAGE

Contracts frequently use terms and expressions that have very specific legal meanings. However, these meanings may not be obvious to the layperson who reads them in a contract or, even worse, includes them without consulting a lawyer. This section addresses some of these words and phrases, and explains the perils and pitfalls they involve.

- *Time is of the essence.* This phrase means that the actions specified in the contract must be taken on or by a particular date. There is no extension, no grace period, no time to remedy. If the event does not happen on the date specified, there is potentially a serious breach of the agreement.

- *Best efforts.* More than just a good try. Some states will interpret this phrase to mean the very best effort of which the person is capable— including, if necessary, making a significant financial sacrifice or employing the utmost effort. A better formulation for giving something a good try is to "endeavor in good faith."

- *Consultation vs. approval.* *Consultation* on a matter means just that: the other party must consult you. It does not mean that they have to agree with you. After fair consultation, they may tell you, "I appreciate your ideas, but I don't want to use any of them." A *right of review* is similarly limited. A *right of approval,* by contrast, permits the party to say *no* and make it stick. A requirement for written approval is essentially an evidentiary matter, to avoid swearing matches between parties over what was only verbalized.

- *Reasonable vs. sole discretion.* There is an implied duty to act reasonably and in good faith under a contract. Nonetheless, it is frequently written in television contracts that certain actions can be taken only if they are "reasonable," or if there is a "reasonable basis," or if they are taken "reasonably." Such a provision is often linked to a circumstance in which one of the parties is empowered to take a discretionary action, such as exercising approval. If approval is "not to be unreasonably withheld," or "is to be given on a reasonable basis," this puts some limit on the discretion of the approving party. Should the approving party fail to approve something, the other party can claim that this failure is unreasonable and then proceed anyway, with some possibility of not being found in breach of the contract. By contrast, a phrase like "in the party's sole discretion," when linked to an approval right, makes it probable that a whim of the approving party will be enforceable— and that any action taken by the other party in disregard of that whim is risky.

- *Covenants.* "Covenant" is a fancy word for an agreement or promise. Covenants are sometimes divided between *affirmative covenants* (promises to actually do things) and *negative covenants* (promises to refrain from doing things). A contract will usually be binding without ever mentioning the word "covenant."

# CHAPTER 49

# WORK RELATIONSHIPS, UNIONS, LEGAL ENTITIES, AND TAX ISSUES

Several types of working relationships and business entities are commonplace in television program development and production, station and network ownership, and program distribution. These forms are also common to other industries.

## EMPLOYEES AND INDEPENDENT CONTRACTORS

An *employee* is an individual who works directly for a business entity. Typically, an employee works under the direction and supervision of an employer, usually in accordance with a fixed schedule, in facilities provided by the employer. The employer pays the employee a salary, with deductions taken for federal, state, and local taxes, and makes contributions to a worker's compensation fund and social security in the name of the employee. The employer may also provide health insurance and benefits such as a pension fund, profit-sharing, an expense account, and a company car. An employee does not hire other employees, except as a representative of the employer.

An *independent contractor (IC)* is an individual who is self-employed; an independent contractor may also be a company, partnership, or corporation. Unlike an employee, an IC works without direct supervision of the employer, sets his or her own hours, and frequently works at his or her own location rather than at company facilities. An IC is normally paid a gross fee for services rendered, and is responsible for the payment of all taxes, insurance, and other monies due to government agencies. An IC costs the hiring company less to maintain than an employee; with an IC, the employer does not have responsibility for all of the related costs discussed above. Rules regarding deductions for home-office and other business expenses are generally in favor of the IC (see page 426); employees have a tougher time justifying the use of a home when a traditional office is provided. An independent contractor may hire other independent contractors or even employees on his or her own account.

Sometimes an employer in effect hires an employee but seeks to save money (illegally) by calling the employee an "IC." In this scenario, the employer may avoid some liability in taxation, social security, unemployment insurance, and workman's compensation in the short term. But the penalties can be severe: The employer may be liable for taxes not paid by the employee and for additional penalties.

The employee/contractor distinction can be of considerable importance under copyright law when determining the owner of a work for hire. Unless alternate contractual arrangements are made, the courts will usually judge the creative results of employment as a work for hire, whereas the ownership of an independent contractor's creations must be specifically transferred by written agreement (see page 265).

# UNIONS

Most productions made for the mainstream television marketplace involve unions that represent on- or off-screen talent or crew. (Several of these unions are discussed in Chapter 44.) Unions and employers are regulated by federal law, particularly the National Labor Relations Act (NLRA); state law, once very active in this area, has been largely preempted by the federal rules.

## Voluntary Union Production

Because the television unions have attracted a substantial number of high-quality professionals, many broadcasters and production companies voluntarily choose to use union labor. In effect, using union labor is like buying brand-name goods: Although they cost more than no-name products, by and large one knows the quality one is getting. The union choice may also reflect a desire to avoid the difficulties that can plague a production if there should be a dispute over representation or jurisdiction.

If a company has decided to use union labor in one or more job categories, it can either hire members directly by becoming a union signatory or, as in most cases, it can arrange for a service company that is already a signatory to provide the workers. If the company will be the direct employer, then it contacts the appropriate union about signing a union agreement. This agreement establishes the minimum terms and conditions for employing union members. For small independent companies, bonds or personal guarantees by the owners may be required to ensure payment of wages and benefits in the case of a budget shortfall or other financial problems.

The union agreement typically requires the employer to use only union labor in the agreed-upon category, either on the project in question or in all the company's activities. The NLRA imposes limits on this kind of hiring agreement, however. The most a union contract can legally require is that any employee hired in a unionized job pay initiation fees and dues; the employee need not agree to other union membership provisions, such as exclusivity (that is, the role that he or she can work only for a union signatory). In "right-to-work" states, even this provision is dropped, and the union signatory can hire non-union workers, who must nonetheless be treated the same as union employees.

Even outside the right-to-work states, organizations can often use both union and non-union employees. The affiliation agreement with a union typically has the effect of moving downward on a chain of corporate subsidiaries, not upward. Therefore, the company should investigate having a subsidiary company become the union signatory. That way, while one branch of the corporate tree will be union-only in the specified job categories, other branches may be able to operate union-free. In addition, becoming a union signatory in one job area does not necessarily mean across-the-board affiliation; many companies are signatories with some of the television unions and not with others.

A union can sometimes compel an employer to recognize its role in bargaining. If enough employees (30 percent) in an appropriate bargaining unit (usually a particular job category) get together and request a union election, the employer must comply. If the election is in favor of the union, it will then have the right to negotiate a contract with management; if the union loses, it is barred from trying again for 12 months. Should any company find itself facing a union-organizing campaign, it should seek advice from professionals experienced in labor relations. A more detailed guide to the NLRA is available at www.nlrb.gov/nlrb/shared_files/brochures/basicguide.asp.

While most of the talent unions do not have overlapping jurisdictions (for example, the film/videotape split of SAG and AFTRA), some of the craft and technical areas are potentially represented by more than one union. This is sometimes an accident of history—who organized what union when. If a company without an established union tie is contemplating using union labor in a field where there are alternative choices, it is sometimes possible to pick in advance the more attractive union, based on rates, skills, work rules, and so on.

## Non-union Production

When the budget permits, union production is usually the easiest choice. Non-union personnel may be hired when the budget is tight; when some aspect of the union work rules or residual structures would be a burden on the production; or when the production is being done for a company whose tradition is non-union in certain categories. Sometimes the unions will cooperate with a producer on a limited budget, cutting special deals to reflect unusual circumstances. Some of the unions even have special codes for low-budget or noncommercial productions. It can be worth talking to the union if the hardship is real and the concessions sought are not too major. In other cases, the employer may have the money but may still opt for non-union personnel to avoid irksome restrictions, or simply to help the bottom line.

Using non-union labor can be a plus, particularly where there is a reservoir of solid independent talent from which to draw. Often, young people starting in the television business are not yet signed to a union, and will be willing to work for less money to get the experience and a credit. Even experienced workers may choose to remain non-union, enjoying the freedom to seek jobs on their own terms. However, especially when undercapitalized and independent operators are involved, there may recur old problems of exploitation and nonpayment that led to the founding of unions in the first place; employees should approach these jobs with their eyes open.

Using unionized labor for a company that is not a union signatory can be risky for all concerned, especially if it lasts for any significant length of time. Assumed names are sometimes used, rendering the credit largely useless for résumé purposes. If the union finds out, it can fine or even expel the offending members. Once hired, on the other hand, the union members can also turn around (particularly once they are found out by the union) and seek union representation for the entire production. This can put the producer in a bind because it is illegal under the NLRA to fire an employee for union activity. The last thing most producers need is a representation battle in the middle of production.

## Foreign Productions and Unions

The application of U.S. union jurisdiction to employment outside the U.S. has created some controversy. Under U.S. labor law, the jurisdiction of U.S. unions over foreign employment is limited. If the employer is U.S.–based, then union jurisdiction may apply, even to shooting abroad. But even if the employer is truly foreign-based, and the employment (typically shooting and post-production) takes place abroad, the unions sometimes try to assert authority if the deal was made in the U.S., or if the union member leaves the U.S. specifically to negotiate the agreement. The validity of this "location of the deal" approach is open to question, but some prospective employees—particularly those with savvy agents—have been known to just happen to run into a foreign producer while "coincidentally" traveling to Canada, Mexico, or St. Barts.

The ambiguity and evasion inherent in such an approach has led at least one entertainment talent union, SAG, to seek universal coverage as a matter of member solidarity. In 2002, SAG issued Global Rule One, an approach that took the traditional U.S.–based union contract exclusivity of its old Rule One and extended it as a worldwide principle. The inspiration for this rule was partly to give economic protection to SAG members and partly to combat the more general problem of "runaway" production, i.e., filming in foreign jurisdictions where production costs, including labor, may be significantly cheaper than in the U.S.

As mentioned above, the legal basis for exerting this kind of foreign jurisdiction is open to question. Nonetheless, the existence of the rule has strengthened the hand of SAG members to ask for full SAG treatment in foreign employments.

Given the attractiveness of U.S. talent for a worldwide audience, the measure has met with some success, particularly in the realm of feature films. Its impact on the world of television is less clear; SAG's film-based jurisdiction (see page 350) makes it less central for television in these days of production via electronic formats, and so far AFTRA and the below-the-line unions have sympathized but have not taken a similar step.

# BUSINESS ENTITIES

## Sole Proprietorship

The sole proprietorship is an individual doing business on his or her own behalf. In most states, a sole proprietor using a fictitious business name must be identified and registered by filing a "doing business as" (DBA) certificate with a designated authority (e.g., a county clerk or the secretary of state's office—check local law). A sole proprietor may hire employees but must personally comply with tax, social security, insurance, and other employee-related government requirements. A sole proprietor is also subject to unlimited personal liability for all debts, claims, and obligations of the business. A sole proprietor pays personal income tax on the profits from the business; for larger businesses, this can become rather complicated, and retaining the services of a good accountant throughout the year is recommended. Outsiders can make investments in the form of a loan, or by contractual arrangements that set a rate of return. If profits and losses are shared, however, the law may deem the entity to be a partnership.

## Partnership

Traditionally, there were been just two types of partnerships: general and limited. A general partnership is an association of two or more persons who jointly own and operate a business, typically sharing profits and losses. A *limited partnership* has two kinds of partners: general partners and limited partners. The *general partners* are responsible for the operation of the business and are liable for its financial obligations; the *limited partners*, who are not involved in the operation of the business, are passive investors liable only up to their stated capital contributions. More recently, the *limited liability partnership (LLP)* and the *limited liability limited partnership (LLLP)* have joined the list in many states. They run just like the general partnership and limited partnership, respectively, but will also give limited liability to the general partners if a necessary filing is made.

Partnerships do not pay federal taxes on their income. Instead, profits and losses are passed on to the partners, who pay taxes as individuals. Profits and losses from the partnership can be offset by the performance of other ventures, but limited partners and other passive investors face restrictions, which often limit the offset to other so-called passive investments. The partnership must file an information return with the IRS and with applicable state and city agencies. It may also be subject to sales, property, and other non-income taxes.

## General Partnerships

A *general partnership* is usually formed by negotiating and signing a partnership agreement that defines the duties and rights of the partners. In most states, the partners can be any recognizable independent entity: individuals, agencies, limited liability companies, corporations, trusts, even other partnerships. The agreement normally specifies the amount of capital or the kinds of services that each partner is to contribute to the partnership, and it specifies how profits and losses are to be allocated to the partners (profits may be treated differently than losses). The agreement may also detail how the partnership is to be operated: who is to work full-time, and in what capacity; whether unanimous agreement is required to admit new partners; how partnership decisions are to be made; and how and when the partnership is to be dissolved. If particular conditions are not specified, or no formal agreement has been signed, the relevant state law will apply and will usually provide answers to these and other questions. As to third parties, each general partner is individually liable for all of the debts, claims, and other obligations of the partnership, unless a filing has been made establishing it as an LLP.

In most states, a partnership using an assumed name must file an assumed name certificate with the county clerk or some other designated official. It must also comply with employment rules and other laws applicable to any business structure.

## Joint Ventures

Under U.S. law, a *joint venture* is a general partnership formed for a specific, limited purpose, such as the production of a particular television program or series. Joint ventures are governed by the agreements founding them and by normal partnership rules.

## Limited Partnerships

A *limited partnership (LP)* is similar to a general partnership except that it has two kinds of partners: general and limited. A limited partner is akin to a shareholder in a corporation—a passive investor who is not individually liable for the debts of the company. Traditionally, a limited partner could not, by law, participate in the day-to-day management of an LP without risking the loss of limited partner status, although this rule is being relaxed in a number of states. Because it resembles both a partnership and a corporation, the LP has often appealed to a partner who wants to supply capital but doesn't want to be involved in management. However, this role is diminishing in contemporary use with the rise of the limited liability company (more below).

Limited partnerships are governed by the rules similar to those that apply to general partnerships, with some key differences. For instance, statutes authorizing

LPs go to considerable length to ensure that third parties are not led to believe that the full credit of limited partners is standing behind the debts of the limited partnership.

In order to form an LP, the general partner(s) must file a certificate of limited partnership in the office of the appropriate state official (e.g., secretary of state, county clerk). This certificate generally states the name (which typically must include "LP" or "Limited Partnership"), address, and class of business of the partnership, as well as the name of each partner, his or her address, and his or her status as a general or limited partner. In some states, the certificate also details each limited partner's contribution to the partnership (in cash or property); to what extent any additional contribution may be required; and the right of each limited partner to compensation (a share of income, for example). The certificate must be amended whenever the information changes. A general or limited partner may be an individual, a general partnership, a limited partnership, or a corporation. Several states also require the publication of this information in a local newspaper.

If a limited partner's name is used in the name of the limited partnership, or if he or she takes part in the management of the business, then he or she may be considered a general partner, no matter what the agreements say. Still, a limited partner usually has the right to give general advice concerning the operation of the business, to inspect the books periodically, to receive a formal accounting on a regular basis, and to seek dissolution of the business by court order. A limited partner may also do business with the limited partnership; for example, a limited partner may loan money to the limited partnership.

The partnership agreement may authorize or restrict the admission of additional limited partners. The agreement may provide an order of priority among the limited partners with respect to profits or return of their contribution. In the absence of such an agreement, all limited partners are considered equal, usually on a *pari passu* basis (see page 316).

Typically, a limited partner may not withdraw his, her, or its money unless (i) the other partners consent; (ii) the certificate is canceled or amended to reflect the reduced capital of the partnership; or (iii) the assets of the partnership exceed its liabilities (excluding the liabilities of the partnership to the general and limited partners for their respective contributions). If the partnership is being dissolved, then procedures are detailed either by state guidelines or by the partnership agreement. If a limited partner withdraws, that partner still remains liable for the amount of money withdrawn (plus interest) if that money is needed to pay debts incurred before the withdrawal.

In the past, there were many tax advantages to investing through limited partnerships, which were frequently used for tax shelters. As with other partnerships, losses could be passed through directly to partners, including the limited partners, but profits were not subject to double taxation. Tax reform has severely limited the benefits by making limited partnership income and loss "passive." Passive losses can only be offset against passive income, which does not include wages and fees. This has put an end to most LP investments motivated by tax savings.

In keeping with the overall trend permitting more and more limitations on liability, some states now offer the option to create a *limited liability limited partnership* (*LLLP*) wherein, with the right kind of filing, the general partners can receive limited liability treatments as well.

### Limited Liability Companies

Over the past couple of decades, the world of business organizations has been significantly altered by the addition of a new hybrid form: the *limited liability company* (*LLC*). Previously, business owners who wanted to limit their personal liability for the debts of the business had to use either a corporation, which was not always as flexible as might be desired and which had significant tax complications (see below), or a limited partnership, which gave limited liability only to non-active participants. With the adoption of the LLC across the U.S. (and with the addition of the LLP and LLLP—see above), business owners can now gain the flexibility of a partnership along with the limited liability of a corporation.

In order to form an LLC, it is necessary to file "articles of organization," typically with the state's secretary of state. These articles usually set forth the name of the LLC (including the required words "Limited Liability Company," the abbreviation "LLC," or some other permitted variant); its registered address; its agent for service of process; the name and address of each organizer (who need not be one of the business principals); and any personal liability which the owners are assuming. It must also describe whether the LLC is to be managed by its members (i.e. owners) as a whole or by some designated group of "managers" who may or may not be members as well. Certain other principles of management may also be put in the articles, although these usually are part of the basic operating agreement between the members. Although the LLC statutes of most states provide backup "default rules" by which the LLC can be run, in most cases these rules can be superseded by the provisions of the operating agreement. In the hands of a skilled attorney, this gives the LLC tremendous flexibility.

From a tax standpoint, the LLC is a major beneficiary of the current "check the box" approach to classifying non-corporate business forms. The organizers of an LLC indicate to the IRS whether they want the LLC taxed as a partnership or as a corporation merely by checking the appropriate box on an election form. This further flexibility has helped to make the LLC very popular as a form for organizing new businesses in the U.S., and one that just about anyone setting up a new business should at least consider.

In many states, even the LLC is no longer the last word in hybrids; the LLP, mentioned above, is also an interesting form. This innovation initially came about to allow limited liability to be applied to law firms and accounting firms that could not, for certain licensing reasons, be LLCs. These LLPs have taken on a life of their own for some small businesses as well, particularly with the option of "check the box" tax treatment. It may be worth asking an attorney about the availability and advisability of using an LLP for a new business.

## Corporations

In Latin, the root word *corpus* means "body." As this suggests, the corporation is viewed in the eyes of the law as a separate legal entity, a body distinct from any other entities that may own interests in it. Most U.S. corporations are established under state laws by filing a *certificate of incorporation*, sometimes called "articles of incorporation," with the appropriate state official (usually the secretary of state). This certificate first states the name of the corporation, which must usually indicate corporate status by including the words "Incorporated," "Corporation," "Limited," or an abbreviation of any of these terms—specific terms vary from state to state. The certificate also indicates the business location; its purpose; the number, type, and stated value of shares, along with a description of the rights or restrictions applicable to any type of stock; and the duration of the corporation (usually perpetual). Amending the corporate certificate normally requires special majority approval of the stockholders, and there may be other requirements in addition. Further rules regarding the operation of the corporation (usually called the "bylaws") may be written and used, but they do not need to be filed. The bylaws provide specifics on how the company is to be operated; if neither the bylaws nor the certificate covers a particular matter, then standard rules under the governing state law apply.

Those who have invested in the corporation become stockholders, but the class of their shares, and the rights that go along with them, may vary. *Common shares* normally carry some form of unlimited profit participation and some form of voting power. *Preferred shares* normally carry a first right to profits (though frequently with a limit) and may entitle the shareholder to limited voting rights within the corporation.

Various hybrid types of shares may be created for specific purposes. Shares of stock are normally transferable; they can be bought or sold at any time, subject to certain state, SEC, and company restrictions. Profits are paid as dividends in accordance with the rules regarding types of shares, or are held for corporate expansion. Shareholders may inspect the books and records of the corporation, and if they believe that the directors or officers are behaving improperly, they may take legal action to stop the wrongdoing and seek damages.

Traditionally, the business of a corporation is overseen by a board of directors, which often consists of three members or more, elected yearly by the shareholders.

If there are fewer than three shareholders, then there usually can be fewer than three seats on the board of directors. The board is responsible for setting corporate policy, for approving significant corporate actions (like large expenditures), and for electing the principal corporate officers.

There is often flexibility in the type of officers elected, although some states require a president and a secretary, and treasurer and vice president are other common officers. Function-based titles are also common, either by themselves or coupled with the traditional set: *chief executive officer (CEO), chief operating officer (COO), chief financial officer (CFO)*, and *general manager (GM)* are all in frequent use. Further creativity with titles is possible, within the limits of the bylaws and the desires of the board of directors.

Since corporations are treated as separate legal entities, they file income tax returns and pay taxes on income. They do not have the "check the box" options enjoyed by LLCs and LLPs. Profits are taxed at the corporate level, and dividends to shareholders are taxed as individual income. The exception is the S corporation (described below).

Some corporations with few stockholders and actively engaged owner-managers elect treatment as "close corporations." Many states permit close corporations to be governed as if they were partnerships. With the advent of LLCs and LLPs, however, the need for this option has diminished.

## S Corporations

The *S corporation*, formed in accordance with Sub-Chapter S of the IRS Code, is a special type of corporation for tax purposes. (The regularly taxed corporation described above is technically called a *C corporation*, a term rarely used.) An S corporation has the same basic organizational structure as a regular corporation, but has some of the tax advantages of a partnership. S corporation status is obtained by filing an election within two-and-a-half months of formation or, with respect to succeeding years for established companies, within two-and-a-half months of the start of the year that precedes the year that the election is to take place.

An S corporation must file an information return with the IRS, but it pays no federal income tax. Instead, profits and losses are passed on to shareholders, and monies are treated as personal income. This helps to avoid double taxation on profits and allows losses to be deducted (up to the shareholder's investment in the S corporation). Excess losses may be carried over from previous years on personal returns—subject to limitations that are best described by an accountant familiar with current IRS regulations.

An S corporation may have up to 100 stockholders, none of whom can be nonresident aliens or commercial entities. In addition, an S corporation cannot be a subsidiary of another corporation. Other rules are equally stringent. Additional information can be found in the instructions to IRS Form 2553. Some states do not recognize S corporations as distinct from regular corporations for purposes of state income tax.

### Loan-Out Corporations

Individuals active in the entertainment business have often used *loan-out corporations* as a vehicle for providing their services. The theory of a loan-out corporation is simple enough. The individual forms a corporation that he or she controls. This corporation hires the individual who formed it, with the salary to be set from time to time to reflect the activity of the corporation and its other financial needs. Then the individual gets a job, either short-term (a writing, directing, or acting assignment) or long-term (becoming executive producer on a series). Instead of the individual being hired directly, the deal is made with the loan-out company, which in turn lends the services of its employee. In order to give the hiring company legal comfort that the individual will be committed to doing the work, the individual invariably signs an *inducement letter*, which confirms that he or she will do the work and will look only to the loan-out corporation for compensation.

The original reason why many people in the television business set up loan-out companies was to take advantage of favorable tax breaks that were available to corporations but not to self-employed individuals. In particular, there were considerable advantages in the amount of pension monies that could be saved on a pre-tax basis. Over the years, most of the benefits have been eroded by reforms to the tax laws; furthermore, the IRS has taken a dim view of loan-out arrangements, and has challenged their use in some cases. Nonetheless, many people with loan-out corporations have kept them in place, in part to preserve old benefits (such as existing pension plans, profit-sharing plans, or health-insurance relationships); in part because they provide some centralization to a fragmented set of employment relationships; and in part because certain kinds of deductions—such as those for a business car or a personal assistant—may be less scrutinized by the IRS if taken by a corporation rather than an individual.

Setting up and maintaining a loan-out corporation does involve some trouble and expense, so anyone who considers forming one should consult with a tax advisor over the potential costs and benefits.

## FOREIGN ENTITIES

With the increased globalization of television, video, and other media, many foreign entities are now doing business in the U.S. These entities will have their own names, roles, and forms, governed by the laws of the country in which they are established. As with U.S. business forms, the initials associated with a foreign company's name sometimes tell you about its origins and character. Some commonly used examples are:

- *AG (Aktiengesellschaft):* This translates to "stock corporation," and is used in Germany and other German-speaking countries. While this form often denotes a publicly traded company, not all AGs are publicly traded.

- *GmbH (Gesellschaft mit beschränkter Haftung):* Also a German term, meaning "company with limited liability." GmbH indicates that the company is incorporated but privately held.

- *NV (Naamloze Vennootschap):* A Dutch corporate designation, which includes, but isn't limited to, all publicly traded Dutch companies.

- *PLC (Public Limited Company):* A public company in the U.K., Ireland, and some other English-speaking countries.

- *SA (Société Anonyme):* This designation is applied to many limited liability corporate entities in France and several other countries.

- *Sarl (Société à responsabilité limitée):* A designation used in France and other French-speaking countries to denote a privately held company.

For an extensive listing, see www.corporateinformation.com/defext.asp.

Different countries also have different governance structures and different names commonly applied to important corporate officials. In the U.K., for instance, the role of director and CEO has often been combined in a person called the "managing director." In Germany, AG corporations have a double board: the Vorstand (usually made up of the CEO, CFO, and other top management) and the Aufsichtsrat (a "supervisory board" overseeing management and representing shareholders).

Any entity (a corporation or an individual) not normally resident in the U.S. that is judged to be "doing business" in the U.S. may be liable for U.S. income taxation and subject to state corporate qualification. If U.S. taxes apply, then the company must fill out a tax return covering all worldwide income allocable to the U.S., and must pay at the applicable standard rate (for example, personal or corporate). Cross-border coproduction deals can be deemed partnerships doing business in the U.S., and potential foreign-production partners should structure the arrangement to avoid U.S. tax involvement. A nonresident foreign entity that is not judged to be doing business in the U.S. may receive income earned from business dealings with U.S. companies or from passive investments in the U.S. without filing a U.S. return—although a withholding tax of up to 30 percent will often be deducted at the source of payment. This approach varies by tax treaty—these frequently exist between the countries in question. Individual entertainers and production workers may also be subject to withholding at a flat or treaty-determined rate. Further information is available from the IRS in

Publication 515, Withholding of Tax on Nonresident Aliens and Foreign Entities, and in Publication 519, U.S. Tax Guide for Aliens.

## TAX ISSUES FOR U.S. RESIDENTS AND COMPANIES

### Business Deductions

Many people in the television business are self-employed or work freelance, or are otherwise without a permanent business affiliation. For tax purposes, these people will need to deduct a variety of expenses related to their work. Unfortunately, the IRS has made the deduction of many of these expenses more and more difficult. For instance, freelancers often work out of their homes, and would like to deduct the expense of a home office. This is now possible only if the home office is fully dedicated (100 percent) to work purposes: A desk in the corner of what is otherwise a bedroom, living room, or family study will not qualify. In addition, home-office expenses can only be deducted from the income that the business conducted from that office actually produces. More information is available in IRS Publication 463, Travel, Entertainment, Gift, and Car Expenses; Publication 535, Business Expenses; and Publication 587, Business Use of Your Home (Including Use by Daycare Providers).

Home workers are often writers or artists. The IRS has required writers to hold off on deducting some kinds of writing expenses on projects until the project is completed. The IRS also generally forces a writer to treat advances as taxable income when the advances are actually received, as opposed to delaying until delivery of the finished work.

### Production Advances, Expenses, and Costs

The tax treatment of production advances, expenses, and costs can be a source of potential problems to a production company. On the expense side, a television project is a capital asset, and the expenses associated with its development and production should be capitalized by the producing entity until such time as the project is put into distribution, sold off, or abandoned. If it is sold or abandoned, all of the costs then become deductible. If the project is put into distribution, or the producer otherwise retains an ongoing participation, the costs are deductible over a period of time. This period is usually the anticipated economic life of the program as calculated using the "income forecast method," which ties the deductibility to the rate at which the anticipated revenues are received.

In most instances, however, the producer will have received advances over the course of the production to help finance the program. In a worst-case scenario, the IRS could characterize these advances as income that is taxable when received—yet not allow any deduction of the related expenses until the program is delivered or shown. If these two events—the receipt of the advance and the showing or delivery of the project—fall in different tax years, it is conceivable that there could be a distorted amount of income recognized. Most production companies avoid this by claiming that they are not in receipt of the advance until the program is delivered, and that until that point, the advance is really just a non-taxable loan. If this approach is taken, it is useful to be sure that the documentation is consistent. Producers also point out that if the advance is income, then the show has in effect gone into service already, so that they should deduct its expenses. Unfortunately, the theoretical underpinnings of these arguments may be open to question. Any production company that is likely to be receiving substantial production advances should consult with tax advisors to help structure ways to avoid unrealistic bulges in taxable income.

# PART 11

# TELEVISION
# OUTSIDE THE U.S.

# CHAPTER 50
# OVERVIEW OF INTERNATIONAL TELEVISION

In an increasingly global television marketplace, there are two key factors to consider. One is the growth and power of large media companies, and the other is rampant local tradition. In many nations, it is common to find a combination of the following television services.

One or more public television networks, such as Canada's CBC, Britain's BBC, or Japan's NHK, are traditionally distributed via broadcast technology (these are called "terrestrial" channels). These networks are typically funded through taxes on television sets, through other taxation, or by government subsidy. Many of these networks are a half-century old, and some have roots extending back into radio days, to the 1930s and, in some cases, the 1920s. Often large organizations that are woven into the social fabric of their nation, many of them operate multiple television networks, radio networks, publishing companies, and more. In today's world—in an environment with hundreds of channels available via satellite, and with program distribution via the Internet and wireless technologies also likely to alter the landscape—these organizations are being reconsidered in terms of their size and their purpose.

Two or more commercial television networks are also typically distributed as terrestrial channels at no charge to viewers. In some countries, privately owned television was a difficult idea to establishment, so growth came slowly. In others, commercial networks have been a part of television since the medium began. In many countries, the 1990s brought a wave of new channels, each owned (in whole or in part) by a significant media company and funded through the sale of commercial time.

Specialty channels, such as sports or children's channels, are typically distributed by a combination of cable and satellite television, and are routinely sold in multiple-channel packages. Additional offerings, typically movie channels, are also sold à la carte (similar to the way that HBO is sold in the U.S.). Some specialty channels are developed for use within one or several neighboring countries as well. Many are owned by large media companies, such as Viacom's MTV Networks or Scripps Networks, and are seen, with regional variations, in a number of countries. It is not unusual for a successful international network to be available in 150 countries (the U.S. Census Bureau lists 227 countries; each of the top 150 are home to over 1,000,000 people).

In addition, a small number of news networks are truly international. CNN is one, and BBC World is another. These networks are seen, in English, throughout the world.

Nearly all networks program either in the local language(s)—networks in the U.S. are almost entirely English or Spanish, for example. In some cases, programs are shown in their original language in a neighboring country: RAI One, an Italian network seen in France, retains the Italian language. Acknowledging exceptions such as this, it is fair to say that nearly every network seen in Japan is distributed in the Japanese language, and that the same is true for Brazil, Spain, Denmark, and most other countries. The only common exception is the motion picture; these are sometimes broadcast in their original language, almost always with local subtitles.

## INTERNATIONAL BRANDS AND NEW TECHNOLOGIES

For most of its history, television has been a medium associated with a particular region. To cover Canada, for example, individual analog transmitters are located in Vancouver, Toronto, Montreal, Halifax, and so on, so that any home with an antenna can receive these channels at no charge. With cable television, most people in and near cities and towns pay to receive a national feed, eliminating the need for local transmitters and for local television stations in the broadcast sense. With satellite television, there is no local wiring nor any local facility— only a national feed from the sky, which can be received by those who both pay a fee and possess the necessary equipment.

With the Internet and various wireless technologies, these models are changing. Broadband Internet allows television signals to be transmitted from a video server located anywhere in the world, to be received by individual computers located anywhere in the world. The notion of geography is not a factor, nor is much sense of a local brand serving a local community (or a national brand serving a national community). A wireless receiver further corrupts the idea of television, for the receiver may be any place at all—in a car, on a walking trail, in the office, in a hotel room. The notion of a television being in a single physical place simply disappears.

This sets the stage for worldwide television brands, along the lines of CNN or BBC. Look for more global media brands, with and without concessions to local traditions or languages, as the investment community and viewers continue to exchange local tradition for membership in an increasingly global community. Some television brand names are already well known in many areas of the world. Many of these are local versions of cable networks that started in the U.S., and then expanded distribution abroad. In Australia, for example, subscribers to the local satellite service can watch Animal Planet, Disney Channel,

MTV, ESPN, CNBC, CNN, Discovery Channel, Hallmark Channel, National Geographic Channel, Nickelodeon, Showtime, Turner Classics Movies, Cartoon Network, and The History Channel, along with a roughly equivalent number of channels based in Australia.

## INTERNATIONAL PROGRAM SALES

Twice each year, thousands of international program buyers and sellers converge upon Cannes, France, to participate in MIP conferences—the world's premier audiovisual market (MIPTV in April, and MIPCOM in October). On the buying side, there are network programmers and, increasingly, buyers for other platforms, such as handheld television devices. On the selling side, there are national television networks that control rights to individual programs in search of new revenue, as well as large media companies and producers who are either exploiting their existing properties or seeking out deals to produce new projects. In addition, there are agents and brokers who specialize in buying and/or selling properties for clients. For those seeking a broad understanding of the international program marketplace (particularly the European marketplace, which is one of the world's largest), a visit to either of these conferences is time well spent. (For more information, visit either www.mipcom.com or www.miptv.com.)

Most television programs are difficult to sell outside of their country of origin, but there are a number of notable exceptions. Italian schedules include, for example, *The Simpsons*; *Will & Grace*; *The Gilmore Girls*; *Walker, Texas Ranger*; *Malcolm in the Middle*; and *JAG*. A look through just about any nation's television guide will result in a similar collection of seemingly random selections from current and past television series from the U.S. An experienced international sales executive develops a nuanced understanding of which programs are most likely to sell to which broadcasters in which countries, but this occurs over a period of years. What's more, the process is often filled with surprises.

A look at the lists of top programs (December 2003–January 2004), published by World Screen's *TV Data* magazine (www.worldscreen.com/tvdata), found *CSI* among the most-watched programs in the Netherlands, along with the older BBC series *Keeping Up Appearances*. In France, none of the top series were imports. In South Africa, *The Weakest Link*, and in Venezuela, *Quien quiere ser millonario*, were among the most-watched series—both local versions based upon successful game show formats seen in many countries.

Among the top children's series in Venezuela, you'll find *Scooby Doo, Where Are You!*; *Los Simpsons*; *Tiny Toons Adventures*; and *Pinky elmyra and the brain*— all with Spanish-language voices. *Jimmy Neutron el niño genio*, *Las adventuras de los tiny toons*, and *Tom y Jerry* were popular in Mexico. Children in France continued to enjoy *Asterix*, which is locally made, but the list also included the Canadian series *Arthur*, the American series *Franklin* and *Kim Possible*, and *Dora l'exploratrice. Los Simpsons* was the top children's series in Spain, followed by *Rugrats*. In South Africa, the list included two *Dragonball* series, along with *The Little Mermaid, Cyberchase,* and *Franklin.*

## OVERVIEW OF WORLD TELEVISION MARKETS

Many U.S. companies see the world in two discrete halves: our country and the other countries. Since the individual markets outside the U.S. can be difficult to comprehend, the natural—although invalid—assumption is that each country's system is in some way based upon a U.S. model. Indeed, some systems were originally based upon a U.S. model, but they have since evolved. In some countries, the government or an agency owns and operates the television networks. Some countries permit private networks, but only in partnership with the government. And although it may be convenient to refer to "Japanese television" as if all of Japan's networks function as a single entity, NHK and Fuji are very different companies.

Canada is the largest market for programs produced in the U.S.; programs from the U.K. and Australia are seen about as often in Canada as they are in the U.S. Most French-language programs seen on Canadian television are produced domestically. In order to protect Canada's national identity, a quota system for domestic programs is in effect.

Germany, the U.K., France, Spain, and Italy are the most active buyers and sellers of television programming in Western Europe. The Scandinavian and Benelux countries are medium-sized markets. The importance of television in Eastern Europe is growing, and as the business climate stabilizes, investment is increasing and audiences are growing. Pan-European networks, generally specializing in a particular type of programming, are seen throughout the western part of the continent via DBS (direct broadcast satellite) and cable systems.

Japan and Australia are only slightly smaller than the largest European markets. Japanese companies occasionally coproduce with European broadcasters, and own, either jointly or wholly, worldwide entertainment companies. Australia supplies some English-language programming seen in the U.S., the U.K., and elsewhere. Taiwan, Hong Kong, the Philippines, Thailand, India, China, and South Korea are all considered to be smaller markets for Western-style programming, but this is changing, and many Western networks are now available to viewers in these countries via satellite. Language and cultural issues are beginning to melt away, as television exerts its considerable power on older cultures.

In Latin America, Mexico and Brazil are medium-sized markets dominated by large, powerful networks. Mexico is a leading supplier of Spanish-language programs seen in the U.S. and throughout Latin America; Venezuela is a vital player in South America. The smaller countries and the islands buy programming, but their populations are generally small, so license fees are low.

The Middle Eastern countries are minor markets, often with tough censorship rules. African nations are not considered vital television markets, but South Africa and Egypt are emerging as significant regional players. Slow growth of terrestrial television is no longer an issue; stations are easily received by any household with a TV and a satellite dish. As Africa slowly becomes more Westernized, cultural differences become less significant. Still, a general lack of involvement in the global business marketplace currently makes most African and Arab countries marginal players in terms of television.

Rapid changes in technology, politics, and economics are certain to alter the pecking order overseas. The importance of Asian countries is likely to grow, and some countries in Latin America and Africa are likely to mature into robust markets as new media develop and systems of distribution become more sophisticated, and as international television companies seek new markets to compensate for mature growth in their primary territories.

## Prices

If you visit www.worldscreen.com, you will find a Program Price Index that lists the ranges paid for various types of programs in various markets throughout the world. Using an hour-long dramatic series as an example, it's clear that the U.K. is the best market, paying $10,000 to $150,000 for each hour, and that Germany is also a strong market, paying $5,000 to $20,000. Canada pays $10,000 to $25,000 for most English-language hours, and $35,000 to $140,000 for the scarcer French hours; supply and demand drives this market, just as any other. In Latin America, Brazil and Mexico are among the best markets, paying roughly $5,000 to $10,000 per hour. In the Pacific area, Australia is a strong market at $15,000 to $40,000 per hour, and Japan typically pays a bit more. Most countries, such as Finland and the Netherlands, pay just a few thousand dollars per hour. In general, small or developing countries pay a few thousand an hour, and countries with more limited economies pay just a few hundred. Children's programs fetch $5,000 to $15,000 in the countries with the largest commercial television industries, but more often up to a few thousand dollars per episode. The best documentaries are sold to the U.K. or Germany for $15,000 to $25,000.

## TELEVISION STANDARDS

Through the second half of the twentieth century, three analog systems were used throughout the world to transmit, receive, record, and play television programs. In the U.S., Canada, and much of Asia, the standard has been known as NTSC (National Television System Committee). Developed in Germany, PAL has been the standard in the U.K., Western Europe (except France), and much of South America. SECAM, developed by the French, is the standard in France and throughout the Middle East. A modified version of SECAM is standard in Eastern Europe and many of the former Soviet bloc countries.

These standards remain in effect, but they are giving way to a new, more versatile digital standard that will allow considerably improved interchangeability of videotapes, discs, and files. In the meantime, a multi-standard television and related record/playback gear are common, as are format conversions by specialist firms. Basically, there are two digital television systems. Most countries use the DVB-T/COFDM standard, while the U.S. uses the ATSC/8-VSB standard.

# CHAPTER 51
# CANADA

Since its inception in the 1930s, broadcasting in Canada has been a mix of public and private endeavors. Adopting the most appealing aspects of the U.S. and the U.K. systems, Canada developed its own model, with one additional twist: Canada is home to two different cultures, each with its own language—there are both English-language and French-language channels.

Approximately 32 million people live in Canada. Most English-language specialty television channels count about 5 million to 7 million subscribers; most French-language channels count about half as many.

As the Lincoln Report (formally called *Our Cultural Sovereignty: The Second Century of Canadian Broadcasting*, and published by the Standing Committee on Cultural Heritage) explained, "English-speaking Canada shares a border, and a language, with the world's largest and most dominant producer of audio-visual programming. Canadians are constantly exposed to a mass media that endlessly promotes American shows and stars. American producers can sell programs at a price far below what it would cost to make similar shows in Canada. Canadian programmers argue that American hits provide the revenue that allows the networks to invest in Canadian programs."

On a typical Canadian cable system, some channels from the U.S. are intermingled with channels from Canada. On a large Montreal cable system, for example, the first 15 channel positions are occupied by Canadian channels some from Montreal, some from Toronto. Channels 16, 17, and 18 are occupied by the CBS, NBC, and ABC affiliates in Buffalo, New York. This cable system also carries BET, TBS, WNED (the Buffalo PBS affiliate), WTVS (a Detroit public television station), and various commercial and public stations from Seattle, Washington. It also carries WGN from Chicago, a U.S. superstation, and KTLA, a WB station from Los Angeles. (Viewers in Montreal are seemingly exposed to a wider range of American television than many viewers in the U.S.!)

When a U.S. program airs simultaneously airs in Canada on a Canadian network affiliate and also on a U.S. network affiliate, the U.S. commercials are replaced by Canadian commercials. This protects the revenue of the Canadian network, but it occasionally disappoints viewers. One oft-cited example is the

Super Bowl, in which the U.S. commercials are often more entertaining than the coverage of the sports event itself.

## CANADIAN CONTENT AND CANADIAN PRODUCTION

A Canadian network can acquire a newly produced U.S. dramatic prime-time production for as little as $100,000 per hour. This is possible because the U.S. series has already been funded by commercial revenues back home. Many of these series are heavily promoted, and so they attract large audiences and significant advertising dollars. Often, the low acquisition cost is accompanied by a high return for the Canadian network on advertising: Sales of over $300,000 are not uncommon.

When a Canadian network develops and produces an original production, the financial structure is wholly different—and ultimately, not nearly so profitable. Canadian production costs tend to be far lower than U.S. production costs, perhaps $1 million for an hour of prime-time television (in comparison with two or three times that number in the U.S.). However, distinctively Canadian, few of these series have substantial value outside of Canada. Unfortunately, this leaves the advertising value of such programs typically under $100,000. For a Canadian network to remain vital while still carrying a high percentage of Canadian programming, the solution has been a combination of tax incentives and government subsidies. This situation makes life as a Canadian producer difficult, since license fees paid by networks are often insufficient to cover the necessary production costs.

To determine which productions will receive these tax breaks and subsidies, Telefilm Canada and the Canadian Television Fund rely upon a scoring system that measures the details of Canadian content through the CAVCO (Canadian Audio-Visual Certification Office) code. Generally, creative control must rest in Canadian hands. Points are then assigned for key creative and technical people who are Canadian. The CAVCO scale also applies as one of several systems by which broadcasters are judged. CBC/SRC, the state-owned public broadcasters, are required to broadcast Canadian content for 75 percent of every broadcast day, and 80 percent during the peak viewing hours of 7:00 P.M. until 11:00 P.M. Private television broadcasters are not judged quite so harshly: a 60 percent requirement is applied to the entire year's schedule, with 50 percent from 6:00 P.M. until midnight. This is an advantage for the privately owned channels, as higher-rated U.S. programs can play in the heart of prime-time, and the less-viewed 11:00 P.M. slot can be used to satisfy requirements. The rules for cable and specialty television are more flexible, but they do exist for every channel.

Funding of Canadian programs is a constant challenge for Canadian producers. The combination of agencies, organizations, and funds can be daunting, and their requirements are sometimes in conflict. The need for access to the global market is very real, and very consistent with practices throughout the world. Several Canadian animation companies have been successful in this regard, but for mainstream story producers, Canadian content and world marketing are sometimes at odds with one another.

Canada's annual television advertising revenues are between $2.5 billion and $3 billion, roughly one-third of all Canadian advertising revenues but hardly sufficient to support an entire nation's television activities. According to the CFTPA (Canadian Film and Television Producer's Association), approximately $3.5 billion was spent on Canadian television production in 2004.

## Canadian Radio-Television and Telecommunications Commission (CRTC)

Canada's CRTC serves the traditional regulatory role concerning all forms of television, radio, telephone, and satellite communications, but it also serves a significant role in assuring the independence of Canada's media. From the earliest days of Canada's confederation, the country's long winters and fragmented population distribution have necessitated a sophisticated and unique national communication system. As the U.S. media industry has grown to become the world's largest, the CRTC's role has responded to protect, or at least to encourage the stability of, Canada's own broadcasters.

Governed by the Broadcasting Act of 1991 and the Telecommunications Act of 1993, the CRTC serves two distinct purposes. The Broadcasting Act ensures that Canadians have access to a wide variety of programming, including a great deal of programs produced by and for Canadians. The Telecommunications Act guides service suppliers to fair trade practices and reasonable pricing. The CRTC plays a role in determining and enforcing a specific ratio of Canadian to non-Canadian content within particular networks and schedules, and also by assuring Canadian ownership and control of Canada's broadcast system. The basic practice of regulation involves keeping tabs on over 3,300 broadcasters of various sorts (radio and television stations, satellite systems, etc.), as well as nearly 80 telecommunications carriers. The following can be found on the Commission's Web site (www.crtc.gc.ca): "Our mandate is to ensure that programming in the Canadian broadcasting system reflects Canadian creativity and talent, our linguistic duality, our multicultural diversity, the special place of aboriginal people within our society and our social values. At the same time, we must ensure Canadians have access to reasonably priced, high-quality, varied and innovative communications services that are competitive nationally as well as internationally."

Perhaps the most significant activities of the CRTC involve Canadian content. The Web site explains the concept simply: "It's about Canadian artists and Canadian stories having access to Canadian airwaves." This mission is taken very seriously, and is the reason why so many of Canada's specialty channels (those available via cable or satellite for an additional fee) are so distinctly Canadian. Typically, the requirement is 60 percent Canadian content in prime time. Without this regulation, Canadian media could, in theory, be overrun by content from the nearby U.S. media powerhouse.

The CRTC imposes many other restrictions and limitations on the use of the public airwaves. Hard liquor is one of several product categories that cannot be advertised on Canadian television (this type of restriction exists in most countries). In addition, scripts for food products are subject to approval. Abusive language is not permitted on the grounds that society must be protected from obscenity. The Commission issues and renews station licenses, and issues sanctions when a problem exists. Occasionally, it will attach conditions to a station's broadcast license or license renewal. For example, if better work in children's programming is desired (or demanded) by the public, this will be stipulated in the license grant. If complaints have come to the attention of the CRTC regarding cultural stereotyping, violence, or other objections, the CRTC may act on these matters as well. The CRTC's highest priority, though, is ensuring that broadcasters provide a substantial quantity of high-quality Canadian programming. If a broadcaster has been financially successful, the CRTC may increase the quota of Canadian content required, or the amount of money spent on Canadian productions. This is quite different from the way that the FCC and most other regulatory bodies operate. Still, the CRTC does not act as a censor. In fact, the CRTC does not intervene with regard to specific programs, only to general programming direction.

The new Broadcasting Act passed in 1991 granted the CRTC jurisdiction over cable television, satellite delivery, fiber optics, and other new technologies. The CRTC does not regulate home video.

## CANADIAN BROADCAST NETWORKS

### CBC

Founded in 1936 as Canada's version of the BBC, the government-owned Canadian Broadcasting Corporation operates radio and television networks and other services in English, French, and aboriginal languages. It is best to think of the CBC not as a television or radio operator, but as a cultural institution that has everything to do with enhancing Canada's arts, culture, storytelling, and heritage.

CBC's television operations are supported by tax revenues (in 2004, $873 million in parliamentary funding) and by commercial revenues (nearly $300 million from advertising and program sales, plus another $225,000 from other sources). Overall, the CBC spends about $500 million for English television service, plus nearly $300 million for French television service.

The CBC owns and operates television stations (English and French) in the provincial capitals and other large cities. In smaller cities and outlying regions, CBC programming is carried by privately owned affiliates. One of Canada's largest employers, the network employs over 8,000 people. It operates a pair of domestic radio networks as well as Radio Canada International, a world band service. The CBC's main headquarters are in Ottawa; the English-speaking networks are based in Toronto, and the French-speaking networks in Montreal.

The Lincoln Report comments, "Many commentators have viewed the CBC as an insurance policy. It is the last line of defence [sic] in a media system increasingly dominated by American programming and American values. It also plays a vital role in a system where there is increasing corporate concentration in the private section. The CBC ensures that other voices will be heard. In Quebec and in francophone communities across the country, Radio-Canada is seen as a buffer against the domination of English-language media." In accordance with CRTC rules, "the programming provided by the Corporation should . . . be predominantly and distinctively Canadian."

CBC Television, the English-language television network, is anchored by two key news programs: *Canada Now* each night at 6:00 P.M. and *The National* each night at 10:00 P.M. In the evening, there's a regular run of the U.K.'s popular *Coronation Street* at 7:00 P.M.; two nights a week, a movie (Canadian or otherwise) shows in prime time. There are various dramatic series (for example, *This Is Wonderland*, a law series set in Toronto), and some short-run series such as a four-hour, two-night report about global *Sex Traffic*. Mornings are filled with lots of quality children's programs, mostly Canadian, some from the U.S. Afternoons are devoted to special interests, such as *Antiques Roadshow* (Canadian edition); *Best of Fashion File*; a popular British soap called *Emmerdale*; a twisted news satire called *This Hour Has 22 Minutes*; a distinctly Canadian comedy series called *The Red Green Show*; and notably for a public broadcaster, a daily dose of *The Simpsons*, followed by the popular worldwide (75 countries) hit comedy/reality series, *Just For Laughs*. *Hockey Night in Canada* has been one of the CBC's most popular series since the beginning of the network.

CBC Newsworld is a 24-hour news channel from the CBC, but it's not all news, all day. Instead, news programs share the schedule with a prime-time run of *Canadian Antiques Roadshow*, *Rough Cuts* (a news magazine), and several other programs.

CBC Country Canada is a digital channel filled with programs about all regions of Canada.

## SRC

Canadian French-language television is parallel in structure to the English-language system; the CBC's French network is Société de Radio-Canada (SRC). Headquartered in Montreal, SRC owns and operates eight stations in Quebec City and in other French-speaking city centers, and completes its national network with five private affiliates. Canadian content fills 80 percent of SRC's prime-time schedule.

ARTV is a French-language art channel operated with SRC and several other Canadian media companies (see page 443).

## APTN

Launched in 1999, the Aboriginal Peoples Television Network offers a blend of news, children's programs, education, variety—in short, a full palette of programs for Canada's native peoples. Sixty percent of the programming is presented in English, 15 percent in French, and the remaining 25 percent in various aboriginal languages. At least 70 percent of the programming must be Canadian in content. Much of the programming comes from independent producers, many of aboriginal origin. Funding issues for this relatively new channel are still being sorted out.

## CPAC

Cable Public Affairs Channel is a nonprofit, commercial-free service covering government affairs, particularly House of Commons, Senate, and Supreme Court activities. It's owned by Rogers Cable, Shaw Cablesystems, and Vidéotron, three of Canada's largest cable system operators.

## VisionTV

VisionTV is a unique service that provides multicultural and multi-faith religious broadcasts. Licensed in 1987, half of the network's schedule is filled with cornerstone programming with broad appeal. The other half is a mosaic of programming provided by various religious groups, who pay for the airtime.

## TVO/TFO

TVOntario (TVO) and its French-language counterpart TFO operate as public television stations whose schedule and format somewhat resemble PBS in the U.S. Mornings consist of quality children's programming, and afternoons are filled with a combination of education and self-improvement programs. The evening schedule includes documentaries (such as National Geographic specials), mysteries, quality films, and documentaries. TVO also broadcasts programs related to its UTVO service, a partnership with 20 Ontario colleges and universities.

Organized as a Crown agency, TVOntario is available throughout the province, and also reaches 350,000 neighboring Quebec households via cable and satellite. Like PBS, it's a membership organization, but a very large one with over 89,000 members. And, like PBS, TVO is also concerned with GED, independent coursework, teacher and student resources, and more. In short, TVOntario is the educational broadcaster in Ontario, but over 30 years, it has become a model for public broadcasting throughout the world.

Knowledge TV in British Columbia and the Sasketchewan Communications Network are also provincial broadcasters with an educational schedule.

## FRENCH-LANGUAGE CHANNELS

As a rule, French-language broadcasters show a far higher percentage of Canadian-made programming than their English-language counterparts. Little is imported from France because the cultural differences are too pronounced; tolerance for dubbed or subtitled programming is also low. As a result, a vibrant French-language production community has grown up in and around Montreal, in the province of Quebec—including an animation industry that regularly supplies the U.S. with quality children's programming.

In recent years, most of the top-20 shows in Quebec are original Canadian productions. This was not always the case. In fact, in the mid-1980s, French-language broadcasters made several decisions to end the reliance upon American series. Suspecting that French-speaking viewers would prefer to watch original programming in their own language, producers and broadcasters intentionally built their own system of celebrities, original stories, and ultimately, the hits that were required to capture and maintain viewer attention.

Télévision Quatre Saisons (TQS), or Television Four Seasons, operates television stations in Quebec City, Montreal, and several other cities in the Quebec region. The network is a joint venture between COGECO and Bell Globemedia.

TVA, owned by Quebecor Media, also operates stations in Montreal and other cities in Quebec. It works six stations, and four more are affiliated with the network. In addition, it operates LCN, a news channel, and owns part of Channel Escape.

Tele-Quebec, primarily funded by Quebec's provincial government, is primarily an educational station (particularly in the daytime schedule). Secondary funding is received via sale of commercial time during specific dayparts. In prime time, Tele-Quebec competes with a select group of dramas, some original productions, some shows produced in France, and some independent productions. Canadian content accounts for 80 percent of total broadcast hours.

TV5 is a Quebec channel also available via satellite to more than 135 million households worldwide. TeleQuebec, Radio Canada, and TV Ontario provide programming for the network, as do French networks throughout the world.

Most specialty channels are English-language, but some have French equivalents, generally based in Montreal. RDI (Le Reseau de l'Information) is a 24-hour all-news channel. Le Canal View focuses on quality-of-life issues, health, and the outdoors, and takes the format of talk, documentary, service, and movies. Canadian content fills half the day. Musimax serves the same demographic with a 24-hour music video schedule; it is owned by Montreal's Radiomutuel and Toronto's CHUM.

# CANADIAN MEDIA COMPANIES

As in the U.S., the Canadian television industry is dominated by a small number of large corporations. However, in Canada the companies tend to be very Canadian in their focus—less international than in the U.S. or elsewhere.

## Alliance Atlantis

Alliance Atlantis was formed by a merger of two film and television production and distribution firms. In Canada, it's best known as the largest operator of specialty television channels (13 in all). In addition, the company coproduces and distributes television programming and owns about half of Motion Picture Distribution LP, the largest motion picture distributor in Canada. The broadcast group, which operates the channels, is roughly a $200 million (Canadian) business.

Alliance Atlantis holds majority ownership in BBC Canada; BBC Kids; Discovery Health Network; HGTV Canada; Life Network ("real life" television, from *Sexy Girl*, which releases a woman's "inner sexpot," to *Crash Test Mommy*, about moms changing places); and History Television (H&E), which is unrelated to the History Channel seen in the U.S. and elsewhere. In addition, Alliance operates, with lesser ownership, One: the Body, Mind & Spirit Channel; Scream (thrillers, suspense, terror); Showcase (movie channels and provocative series, such as Showtime U.S.'s *The L Word* and *Queer as Folk*), which also operates a few other movie channels; and Score (sports). Fine Living is a joint venture with Scripps, as is Food Network Canada.

## Astral Media

Formed in 1946, Astral operates radio stations, outdoor advertising, and television networks. In 2004, revenues were over $500 million (Canadian). The key name here is the Greenberg family, a longtime media dynasty in Canada. The Bronfmans, another well-known Canadian name, own nearly 20 percent of Astral.

Astral's French-language specialty television networks include Canal Vie, a channel for women; Canal Indigo, a pay-per-view channel operated by Viewer's Choice Canada (which is 50 percent owned by Astral); Teletoon (40 percent owned by Astral), with both an English and a French service; Super Écran, a set of four channels seen in eastern Canada, mainly focused on movies; Mpix, a classic movie channel with a sister time-shifted channel, Mpix2, again for eastern Canada; and Family, with much of its programming from Disney. In addition, Canal D is a specialty channel seen in Quebec with a varied format (celebrities, comedy, drama, science, movies); Ztélé, which skews somewhat younger, and is filled with magazine shows, documentaries, and science fiction; VRAK.TV serves a teen audience and is the top-rated network among teens and tweens; shows mainly traditional series but brands them as programs with strong emotional content (the tagline is "la télé des emotions"); and Historia is a French-language history channel. MusiquePlus, 50 percent owned by Astral, emphasizes live performance, music news, and pop culture; MusiMax leans more on music videos; both are seen in Quebec.

Astral Media Plus is an advertising rep firm that sells advertising sales for the specialty channels owned or operated not only by Astral, but by both Alliance Atlantis and Corus as well.

## Bell Globemedia (CTV)

Bell Globemedia is part of Bell Canada, the largest telephone company in Canada, a $20 billion concern. Bell Globemedia's two most significant assets are CTV, Canada's largest terrestrial commercial television network, and the *Globe and Mail*, Canada's leading daily newspaper.

Bell Globemedia owns 21 of its affiliates (three are owned by other companies), as well as 17 specialty channels. The most significant properties are CTV Newsnet, a 24-hour news channel; Le Réseau des sports (RDS, a French-language sports channel); and The Sports Network, Canada's leading sports service. In addition, it owns 100 percent of talktv, The Comedy Network, ROBTv (Report on Business Television, related to the *Globe and Mail*), and CTV Travel. Bell Globemedia owns a part of Outdoor Life, Discovery Channel, ARTV (a French-language arts channel jointly owned with Radio-Canada, Tele-Quebec, ARTE France, and Spectra, which stages the International Jazz Festival of Montreal and other festivals), Viewer's Choice Canada, and several other specialized channels.

## CanWest/Global Communications

CanWest is controlled by the Asper family, who made headlines in 2000 with the acquisition of metropolitan newspapers throughout Canada. The company now operates the Global Television Network in Canada, plus substantial percentage ownership in Australia's Network TEN, and various New Zealand and Ireland radio and television networks. CanWest also owns a large number of Canadian trade magazines and, through Network TEN, the second-largest outdoor advertising company in Australia, called Eye Corp.

The Global Television Network broadcasts throughout the country on 11 local stations, reaching nearly all of English-speaking Canada. Much of the programming comes from the U.S.

Among Canadian networks, Global Television Network owns about half of both Mystery and mentv, as well as interests in Prime TV (vintage sitcoms and dramas, many from the U.S.); CoolTV (jazz); DejaView (more old TV series); FOX Sports World Canada; Xtreme Sports (Thai kick boxing and other "high-voltage" programs from around the world); and Lonestar (vintage Westerns).

## CHUM

CHUM operates over 30 radio stations, a dozen local television stations, and over 20 specialty channels seen via cable and/or satellite in Canada. In addition,

CHUM is an active supplier to other channels throughout the world.

On a local level, Citytv in Toronto has long been a strong voice and an interesting creative force that is often held as a model for local broadcasters in the U.S. and elsewhere.

CHUM's many specialty channels include nine music channels (including MTV Canada); CLT (Canadian Learning Television); a regional news channel called CablePulse24 (CP24); and the Fashion Television Channel. In addition, Bravo is an arts channel that features *Inside the Actors Studio* and some music/arts programming that will be familiar to U.S. viewers of Bravo (not the same network, but their roots are related). The Canadian Bravo also features quality films and television series (*Law & Order*, for example). Star! is a celebrity news and feature channel. Drive-In Classics is a movie channel filled with exploitation cinema. Book Television features stories, many of which are tied back to books and literature (interpreted broadly: Alfred Hitchcock mysteries play here, and so do *Batman* episodes). Other channels include Space, Sextv, a Canadian version of CourtTV, and TV Land Canada.

Overall, CHUM has maintained a street-smart sense of fun, and this permeates nearly all of their channels. CHUM also operates a merchandising group and a store in downtown Toronto filled with snappy CHUM products.

Book Television, CLT, and Court TV Canada are in fact operated by Access Media, which is controlled by CHUM. Unrelated to television, Access also offers The Learning Annex and other commercial educational services, and operates an educational television station in Albert, Canada.

In fiscal year 2004, CHUM's revenues were over $560 million (Canadian).

## Corus Entertainment

Corus owns about 50 radio stations, as well as children's program producer Nelvana Limited and Canada's largest children's book publisher, Kids Can Press. Corus owns three over-the-air television stations, each affiliated with the CBC. In addition to interests in TELETOON, Food Network Canada, and Locomotion, Corus owns and operates several specialty channels distributed via cable and satellite. YTV is a popular children's television network, and Treehouse is a network for preschoolers that has evolved into a national brand promoting stage shows and other activities. W Network is a leading channel for female viewers. Country Music Television and Discovery Kids, each with a combination of U.S. and Canadian content, will be familiar to U.S. viewers. In addition, The Documentary Channel is a joint venture between Corus, the National Film Board of Canada, and several indpendent documentary producers. Scream is a joint venture with Alliance Atlantis.

Corus is majority-owned by Shaw (see below). In 2004, Corus Entertainment's revenues exceeded $650 million Canadian.

## Quebecor

In the U.S., Quebecor is known as one of North America's largest printing companies. With Quebecor's 2001 acquisition of the TVA Group, the company operates the largest French-language television network in North America, TVA. The TVA Group owns six of the network's ten affiliated stations, in addition to the news channel Le Canal Nouvelles (LCN), and has interests in mentv and in Mystery, plus some home shopping ventures. TVA is also the largest magazine publisher in Canada. TVA's Vidéotron is one of the world's bigger cable television operators, covering 80 percent of the large province of Quebec; Vidéotron has consistently been one of cable television's most innovative operators. In addition, Quebecor owns a sizable newspaper group, Internet ventures, a large music retail chain, and the largest chain of video stores in Quebec.

Quebecor's total revenues for 2003 exceeded $11 billion Canadian, making it considerably larger than most other Canadian media companies. Vidéotron contributed about $800 million (Canadian), and the TVA Group contributed about $350 million. Most of the company's revenues—more than $9 billion—came from Quebecor World, the printing operation.

## Rogers

Rogers is controlled by Edward S. Rogers, son of the founder. With revenues of over $5 billion (Canadian), Rogers is Canada's principal wireless voice and data communications firm, and its largest cable operator. Rogers Broadcasting owns nearly 50 radio stations across Canada, and Rogers Publishing owns and operates many of the country's most successful magazines, including *Maclean's* and *L'actualité*. In addition, the company owns baseball's Toronto Blue Jays, two Toronto television stations, and nearly 300 video stores.

Rogers controls and operates Rogers Sportsnet and The Shopping Channel. In addition, Rogers has a minority position in many specialty channels, including Viewer's Choice (pay-per-view), The Biography Channel, G4TechTV Canada, Outdoor Life Network, and more.

## Shaw

Shaw Communications is another leading cable multiple-station owner. Shaw's Star Choice also provides direct-to-consumer satellite services and maintains minority ownership in several specialty channels: MSNBC, Biography, and TechTV.

This $2 billion (Canadian) company is another family dynasty, held through various members of the J. R. Shaw family.

## CANADIAN INDEPENDENT PRODUCTION COMPANIES

Canada's cultural policies encourage its creative community and assure the growth of Canadian independent production companies. *Playback*, an industry trade magazine, lists the largest as Fireworks Entertainment (roughly $110 million [Canadian]); Lions Gate Films ($100 million); Corus Entertainment ($60 million); Pebblehut Too ($60 million); Zone3 ($50 million); Temple Street ($40 million); DECODE Entertainment ($37 million); Remstar Production ($31 million); and Peace Arch Entertainment ($29 million).

According to the CRTC, more than $1.5 billion is spent on Canadian independent productions each year.

## CANADIAN TALENT IN AMERICA

With the promise of higher salaries and greater opportunity (and perhaps fame), many of Canada's talented creative people choose to live and work in the U.S. Some do this from time to time, but many relocate. The list of Canadians who have made a name for themselves in U.S. television is a very long one that, for various reasons, tends more toward comedy than drama: among them, Dan Aykroyd, Raymond Burr (*Perry Mason*), Jim Carrey, James Doohan (*Star Trek*), Michael J. Fox, Lorne Greene, Phil Hartman, Jill Hennessy (*Law & Order, Crossing Jordan*), Lorne Michaels, Mike Myers, Colin Mochrie (*Whose Line Is It Anyway?*), Rick Moranis, Jason Priestly, and William Shatner.

# CHAPTER 52
# EUROPE

Europe is the world's most active television marketplace. There are more television households, more television networks, and more programs produced, bought, and sold here than anywhere in the world. With a wide range of languages and cultures, Europe is also one of the world's more complicated international marketplaces.

## UNITED KINGDOM

The U.K. is the second-largest English-language market in the world, and the second-largest television market in Europe (Germany is first). A total of 60 million citizens watch television in 24 million households—roughly one-fourth the size of the U.S. audience.

Broadcasting began in the United Kingdom in 1922 as a private collaboration of radio manufacturers operating their own stations. Five years later, the British Broadcasting Corporation (BBC) was established by Royal Charter. In 1954, Parliament passed a bill authorizing a second government-owned broadcasting corporation, the Independent Television Authority, later renamed the Independent Broadcasting Authority (IBA). In 1991, the IBA was succeeded by the Independent Television Commission (ITC), which regulated privately operated broadcast and cable companies. In 2003, Ofcom (Office of Communications) replaced the ITC and combined several other regulators, including the Broadcasting Standards Commission (BSC), Oftel, the Radio Authority, and the Radiocommunications Agency.

### Regulation of British Television

Ofcom is straightforward about the rules governing U.K. broadcasting, many of which can be found on the agency's Web site (www.ofcom.org.uk). The Programme Code, for example, provides boundaries for programs likely to be seen by children; monitors the portrayal of violence and sexuality; regulates charitable appeals and religious broadcasters; and so on. There are specific rules regarding program sponsorship and the amount and use of advertising on the commercial networks (the BBC is noncommercial; see below). In general, these rules set reasonable expectations for a civilized society, and are easily understood by any television executive or television viewer. (It is interesting to compare these clear, concise, reasonable rules to those impacting U.S. television, which are difficult to find and equally difficult to decipher.)

# BBC

The BBC is a massive organization that has been in existence since 1927 and broadcasting television since 1936. The former BBC Television Service held a monopoly on U.K. broadcasting until 1955, when the commercial ITV network was licensed amidst considerable concern for the future of television and society. Today's BBC employs well over 20,000 people, making it one of the world's larger media organizations. The BBC is generally funded through a mandatory television license; in 2004, each color television set was subject to an annual fee of £121 (over $200 U.S.), resulting in the collection of roughly £2.7 billion (about $5 billion). Other sources of BBC income were far smaller: just under £150 million from BBC Commercial Holdings, Ltd., and just under £225 million from grants related to the BBC World Service (these grants were provided by the U.K.'s own Foreign and Commonwealth Office). An additional £23 million was earned through subscriptions and other sources. The BBC's annual budget has been approximately £5 billion, rivaling that of NASA. The process of revamping the BBC began in 2005; the result will be a somewhat smaller organization.

The BBC operates a wide range of services, including two terrestrial television networks, local stations throughout the U.K., a range of digital television channels, and an enormous online operation (www.bbc.co.uk, with more than two million Web pages). The BBC also operates major activities in radio (roughly a dozen O&O radio stations, plus other radio stations throughout the U.K.), the music industry, and book and magazine publishing.

## BBC One

BBC One shares the top ratings spot in the U.K. with ITV (see page 452), generally reaching about 20 percent of the total available audience. It's here that many of the classic programs known throughout the world were regularly broadcast: *Doctor Who*, *Monty Python's Flying Circus*, *EastEnders*, *Antiques Roadshow*, and more. Many of the popular series shown on BBC One have been shown for decades: *Top of the Pops* (music), *The Sky at Night* (astronomy), *Question Time* (political debate), and *Blue Peter* (children's).

In March 2005, BBC One occupied half of BARB's (Broadcast Audience Research Board) top 75 network programs. The broadcast day begins with a morning show, *Breakfast*, followed by several soap operas (*City Hospital*, *Neighbors*, *Doctors*), and light reality shows (*Weighing In*, a weight-loss show, and *Bargain Hunt*, a competition). Late afternoon is given over to a branded Children's BBC

(CBBC) children's block that includes *Woody Woodpecker*, *What's New Scooby-Doo?*, *50/50* (a competition among schools), and *Blue Peter* (a kids' reality, activity, and magazine show). Children's programs tend to vary day to day, and are also seen on Saturday mornings.

By dinner time, BBC One is showing various news programs, followed by a reality half-hour and then, at 7:30 P.M., *EastEnders*, the highest-rated show on the schedule. There are two prime-time hours: This particular week in 2005, the slots were filled with a half-hour retrospective of *The Two Ronnies*, a vintage BBC comedy series; *Have I Got News For You*, a regularly scheduled topical news quiz; *Holby City*, a dramatic series that has been on for several years; *Hustle*, a popular series about con artists; and *Casualty*, another drama. (Each of the programs seen on the BBC has its own extensive Web site on the master BBC Web site, where one can become hopelessly involved for hours.) From time to time, a film fills prime time; during this week, *Raiders of the Lost Ark* played on Sunday night.

Prime time ends at 10:00 P.M., which is the traditional time for *BBC News* (there is also a BBC newscast at noon each day). Various talk, sports, lottery, and other informational programs then fill the time until about 11:00 P.M.

BBC One receives approximately one-third of the license fees collected by the BBC. The network is among the best-funded in the world.

### BBC Two

BBC Two receives about half as much money per year as BBC One, or about one-sixth of $5 billion (U.S.). This places BBC Two's spending beyond just about all of the U.S. networks.

What's on? Generally programs with a somewhat broader appeal, perhaps more youthful, more fun, lighter than the typical BBC One fare. You'll find the U.K. version of *The Apprentice* here, along with popular cooking game *Ready Steady Cook*, the game show *The Weakest Link*, and sports programs such as *World Snooker*. In general, BBC Two reaches about half the audience of BBC One, roughly 10 percent of viewers. The most popular series are *Gardeners' World*, *Fred Dibnah's Made in Britain*, *The Weakest Link*, *Around the World in 80 Treasures*, *University Challenge*, and other cooking, game, and travel series. The longtime game series *Mastermind*, in which a contestant sits in a black chair fielding difficult questions, is also a BBC Two staple.

### BBC's Digital Channels

The BBC operates a range of digital channels, available only via digital cable or digital satellite systems.

BBC News 24 is, as the name suggests, a 24-hour news service. Most of the day's schedule is filled with news anchors and reporting, but the schedule also includes several special features: *Sportsday*, *Business Today*, *HARDtalk*, and a pick-up of the U.S. news series *World News Tonight* from ABC.

BBC Parliament is similar to the U.S. cable television network, C-SPAN.

CBBC (Children's BBC) runs children's programs with generally positive messages through the morning, late afternoon, and evening. Daytime hours are filled with Class TV, with coursework such as *Primary Geography* introducing students to, for example, life in Bangladesh. There are some lighter cartoons, such as *Looney Tunes*, as well. CBeebies is another children's channel, this one for preschoolers.

BBC Three's target audience is younger adults. They are served by a mix of news, current affairs, music, arts, science, and educational programs, but the most popular are comedies, dramas, and pure entertainment programs. One of the young network's biggest hits has been *Little Britain*, which began on BBC Radio 4.

The more serious BBC Four is intended to provide "greater depth and range," generally offering programs that are intellectually stimulating and/or culturally enriching. As with BBC Three, BBC Four operates on a modest budget and reaches a modest audience. What's on? Documentaries about Winston Churchill, Charles Dickens, and the Islam nation; animated shorts under the title *Animation Nation*; favorite British musician Georgie Fame in concert; a magazine series that truly covers world affairs; the story of a notable British advertising agency; travelogues that combine architecture and history; and a concert from American singer Emmylou Harris.

## BBC Around the World

BBC America, familiar to American viewers as the original home of the well-received series *The Office* and *So Graham Norton*, is distributed by Discovery Networks. The two organizations are also connected in the distribution of the Animal Planet network in various countries throughout the world. The joint venture also distributes People+Arts, a Spanish and Portuguese channel filled with drama and reality programs.

BBC Canada is a joint venture with Canada's Alliance Atlantis Communications, a leading producer and operator of cable networks in Canada. The same joint venture operates BBC Kids in Canada.

BBC Prime is an international entertainment channel seen in over 100 countries via cable and satellite. BBC World is a 24-hour news and information channel that competes directly with CNN throughout the world. Both are commercial channels operated by the BBC.

## UKTV

UKTV is a joint venture between the BBC and Flextech, a division of large U.K. cable operator Telewest. These are commercial channels available to cable and satellite subscribers. The two key channels are UKTV Gold and UKTV G2, which make good use of the existing BBC comedy library. Similarly, UKTV Drama mines the BBC drama library, and UKTV History does the same for the historical documentary. Other UKTV channels include Food, Style, Bright Ideas (with an emphasis on health, beauty, and travel), Documentaries, and People.

UKTV Australia is a "best of BBC" cable/satellite channel from FOXTEL, Fremantle Media, and the BBC.

## Commercial Broadcasting

Despite a substantial faction of British lawmakers who were originally opposed to the idea of commercially supported broadcasting (Lord Reith of the House of Lords likened it to the bubonic plague), advertiser-supported programming began in 1955 with the licensing of ITV.

### ITV

Regional commercial television stations now operate throughout the U.K., generally as part of the ITV network. In the early 1990s, many of these regional licenses changed hands. Thames Television, for example, lost its weekday license for London broadcasting to Carlton; London Weekend Television (LWT) maintained its license to work weekends on the same channel (this is an unusual arrangement—most licenses are granted to single broadcasters).

ITV plc is one of the U.K.'s largest media companies. Its principal asset is the ownership of the regional commercial licenses for Channel 3 throughout England and Wales. The company is also among the largest television production companies in Europe. Formed in 2004 by a merger of two former ITV operators, Granada and Carlton, the operating budget is approximately £1 billion (roughly $2 billion U.S.)

ITV owns 12 of its 15 regional affiliates, and fills more than a quarter of its terrestrial ITV1 schedule with programs from independent producers. The concept here is to represent all of Britain, not just the London-centric perspective.

### ITV1

ITV1 is home to Britain's most popular television series, *Coronation Street*, and perhaps its second most popular series, *Emmerdale*—both are prime-time soap operas. It's here that *Who Wants to Be a Millionaire?* originated, and still airs. Among the other typical series are *Love Doctors*, in which romance problems are solved; a reality cooking series called *Hell's Kitchen*; *The People's Court*, followed each morning by a celebrity-oriented talk show called *This Morning*; *Rugrats* and *My Parents Are Aliens* in the afternoon children's block; and a fast-paced game show each afternoon called *Perseverance*. For the late afternoon, there's a daily talker, *The Paul O'Grady Show*.

### Other ITV Channels

ITV2 is a popular digital channel that sometimes expands upon the programs seen on ITV1 with shows such as *Hell's Kitchen: Extra Portions*, which features "gossip and backstage antics" from the original series, and *Emmerdale Secrets*, for those who can't get enough of the popular soap. *American Idol* runs here, as do *Married...with Children, Judge Judy, Late Night with David Letterman,* and *Quincy, M.E.* The satire *Footballers' Wives* is one of ITV2's more original offerings.

ITV3 is the newest of the channels, emphasizing detective dramas, films, updates, and reruns of old ITV favorites.

As with other cable news services, ITV News Channel features a combination of 24-hour coverage and talk shows.

## Channel 4

In 1982, when Channel 4 was launched, founder Sir Jeremy Isaacs promised programs "for everybody some of the time." With grand intentions to offer a true programming alternative and a nursery for new forms and new methods of presenting ideas, Channel 4 has delivered distinctive programming, although often for limited audiences. In fact, 75 percent of British viewers find something interesting to watch on Channel 4 at least once each week.

Channel 4 is a government-owned corporation without shareholders, without license fees, and without profits. Money earned through advertising is used to pay for programming (and promotion and operations). Until 1992, Channel 4's advertising was sold by ITV, but this is no longer the case. Still, C4 does not create its own programming; instead, it finances or cofinances productions, and also purchases completed work. Its market share is just under 10 percent. The network is entirely advertiser-supported. Channel 4 considers itself a "publisher-broadcaster"—all of its programs are acquired or commissioned from independent producers, and the network does not produce any of its own programs. Roughly half of the schedule is programming from the U.S. Also known as a source of film financing, Channel 4 completely financed *Trainspotting* and was involved with *Four Weddings and a Funeral, East is East, Touching the Void,* and others.

Channel 4's strength is in the desirable 16 to 34 age demographic: Roughly 30 percent of its March 2005 profile was in this category, compared with 23 percent for BBC1 and 21 percent for Five (see following page). Channel 4 also appeals to the smallest number of viewers over 55 years old; it's the only terrestrial network with fewer than 40 percent of its viewers in this zone. Like the somewhat more youth-oriented BBC Two, C4's audience has held fairly steady at about a 10 percent share over the past 20 years. (During the same period, ITV and BBC One have lost about half of their viewers, mostly to new channels.)

On the March 2005 list of most popular programs, C4's highest rated program was the imported U.S. series *Desperate Housewives*, and its second biggest hit was *10 Years Younger*, in which a dozen participants are given a makeover ("Anything from chemical peels and nose surgery to new teeth, new clothes and new hair," says the Web site).

A day on Channel 4 begins with some children's programs and music videos, followed by episodes of the U.S. series *Friends, Everybody Loves Raymond, Will & Grace, Third Watch*, and *Without a Trace*. In between and through the afternoon, there's a local travel series called *Coach Trip*, a half-hour of news, *The Great Garden Challenge*, and a celebrity interview show called *Richard & Judy*. This way, Channel 4 begins with less expensive programs imported from the U.S., then progresses through original programs that provide the network with brand identity. The evening starts with a run of *The Simpsons*, some news, and then a variety of comedy, drama, and reality: *Supernanny, Inside Elton's World* (an insider's view of Sir Elton John's life), and the occasional motion picture (*Anaconda*, for example).

### E4 and FilmFour

Like other networks, Channel 4 operates spin-off networks for digital and cable subscribers. E4 is a general entertainment service that skews young. It runs, American reality television (*Big Brother 6, Average Joe: Adam Returns, The Simple Life, Wife Swap*) as well as movies and reruns of U.S. series such as *Friends, Sex and the City*, and *Smallville*. Original productions include a fast-paced music charts show called *hit40uk* and a reality series called *Fool Around....*

FilmFour is a movie channel that runs toward higher quality (or at least more interesting) popular films: *Japanese Story*, the *Korean Save the Green Planet*, the emotional drama *The Principles of Lust*, the offbeat *Irma Vep*, and some older titles, such as *Only Angels Have Wings*, starring Cary Grant.

### Five

C5 (now simply Five), scheduled to launch in 1994, did not launch until the spring of 1997. Delivered as one of Britain's five terrestrial channels, this commercial network has a target audience of younger mainstream viewers, roughly 16 years old to 34 years old. In 2004, Five averaged approximately a 6.6 percent audience share. The network's most popular presentation was *Terminator 3*, and the most popular series was *CSI*, averaging a 16 share.

Five was initially owned by Pearson, CLT, and United News and Media. With various buying and selling over time, the network's ownership has now passed to the RTL Group, which owns the former CLT, among many other assets (see page 458).

Five spends roughly £175 million per year on programming, about one-fifth of the money spent by BBC One, but it has been successful in a great many genres. This new network is still struggling to find its voice for nightly news, but current affairs programs with a youthful edge have gained in both audience and respect. Arts coverage is considerably more wide-ranging and contemporary than typical coverage; programs based on particular art exhibitions have been popular, and in 2004, the channel sponsored Big Art Challenge, a national arts competition, also gained attention. *The Big Question* won a big audience by interviewing and detailing the ideas of scientists Richard Dawkins and Stephen Hawking, among others. *Ultimate Machines, Demolition Squad, Megastructures*, and *The Gadget Show* made science fun. *Extraordinary People*, a powerful human interest series, proved one of the network's biggest hits to date. In addition, there were programs about history, home decorating, a reality series called *The Farm*, and the popular automotive series *Fifth Gear*. And there are children's programs—*Milkshake* became a bona fide hit and a real showplace for animators who produce the likes of *Peppa Pig, Funky Valley*, and *Ebb and Flo*—plus some drama, history, and comedy. The programming is consistently imaginative, often edgy, and wholly unique. Here and there, you'll find an American import (*CSI, Joey*, or a random movie like *Judge Dredd*), but for the most part, Five is finding its own way with an audience whose size increases annually.

## More Digital and Cable Channels

Some digital and cable channels are available only to subscribers to one particular satellite service, such as Sky TV, but most are available throughout Britain.

Some of the names will be familiar, but the programs are often a blend of U.S. and U.K. offerings. From A to Z, among the well-established networks can be found Animal Planet, Cartoon Network, Discovery (with its various digital channels such as Discovery Wings), E!, FX, The Golf Channel, Hallmark Channel, The History Channel, MTV (with its various smaller digital channels), National Geographic Channel, Nickelodeon, QVC, and VH1.

In addition, there are some channels that may not be familiar to U.S. viewers, such as two channels from Paramount, the U.S. studio. In truth, this list goes on to include hundreds of television channels, most of which are watched by remarkably small numbers of households at any given time. Eurosport, a pan-European channel, is also popular (see page 462).

Flextech, which undertakes joint ventures with BBC on the various UKTV channels, also operates some of its own. These include LivingTV, which appeals mostly to women with *Extreme Makeover, Melrose Place*, and *The Swan 2*; Challenge, a very active game channel filled with poker and cult shows like *Takeshi's Castle* (a crazy Japanese stunt competition); Bravo, a men's channel unrelated to the U.S. channel of the same name, and featuring fighting, football (soccer), *Street Crime U.K.*, and reruns of *Knight Rider* and *CHiPs*; Trouble, a teen channel that's more popular than MTV; and Full On Entertainment, or Ftn, a general entertainment channel.

## Sky

Sky provides a range of popular movie and sports channels only to its own satellite subscribers (roughly 7.5 million of them at the end of 2004). Sky is provided by British Sky Broadcasting, or BskyB, which is one-third owned and generally controlled by a subsidiary of News Corp.; other investors are mostly financial institutions. Sky One is a popular channel in its own right, regularly beating out BBC Two in Sky households. This is accomplished through U.S. imports, high-visibility specials such as (in 2003) a Michael Jackson interview and a David Blaine magic show, high-impact sports, *Fear Factor*, *Britain's Hardest*, *Brainiac*, and more. Similarly, Sky News has become a popular news source—so popular, in fact, that it now provides Five's news coverage. Sky Sports channels (there are four) are now the place to watch the most important sporting events in the U.K., and Sky Movies shows 450 movies per week on its 11 movie channels.

## GERMANY

Germany is home to over 82 million people, making it the key market in continental Europe. Prices are highest, coproductions are the most flexible, and business is conducted in a way that makes sense throughout the world. There are nearly 35 million television households, and although the average German television household receives nearly 40 free channels, about 95 percent of them pay for television through either satellite or cable hookups.

Audiences are measured by GfK, a large market research company that is generally regarded as among the world's best. Germany is the world's second largest advertising market, with nearly €20 billion (approximately $25 billion).

Programming on Germany's public radio and television channels is funded, in large part, by license fees paid by owners of radio and TV receivers—just over €15 per month, with about one-third of the fee financing programs on ARD, ZDF, and their related channels.

## ARD

In an effort to limit the power of a centralized German government after World War II, the Allies placed the development of cultural matters (broadcasting included) in the hands of individual states (*Länder*). In some cases, the *Länder* combined resources; the result was a total of nine regional broadcasters in the 11 states comprising the former West Germany (each owned by its regional government), plus two more owned by the federal government. All of these are part of a network cooperative known as ARD, short for Arbeitsgemeinschaft der Offentlich-rechtlichen Rundfunkstalten der Bundesrepublik Deutschland (rough translation: the Federation of Public Broadcasting Corporations of the Federal Republic of Germany). ARD is more commonly called Das Erste ("First Channel").

ARD is a large state organization with an annual budget of approximately $6 billion and about 23,000 employees. It broadcasts from early morning until late night, showing a mix of sports, news, drama, and cultural programming with highbrow appeal. Regional member WDR (Westdeutscher Rundfunk), located in Cologne, serves the West; NDR (Norddeutscher Rundfunk), in

Hamburg, serves the North; and BR (Bayerischer Rundfunk), in Munich, serves the Southeast. Together, these three entities provide more than half of ARD's network programming.

ARD programs as one network for most of the day; the regional stations then program from the early evening onward. All ARD members are active locally, and all contribute at least some programming. ARD members work with independent production companies, acquire completed programs, and produce some of their own programming (such as local sports).

## ZDF

Zweites Deutsches Fersehen (ZDF), or "Second German Television," debuted in 1963 as a national public network, but not without a fight from the Länder, which believed that they alone had the right to establish broadcast stations. ZDF is owned by the 11 *Länder*, but operates one national service with decision-making centralized in the head office in Mainz, Germany. Still, ZDF mantans a bureau in all of the Länder capital cities and employs more than 3,500 people. In 2004, revenues from license fees equaled €1.5 billion, and advertising revenues added €118 million. With other revenues, ZDF's total 2004 revenues totaled €1.8 billion.

As with ARD, the programming is sophisticated; but unlike ARD, ZDF is a national service without local affiliates or local producing entities. Of the two, ZDF is more aggressive, both in ratings competition at home and in international ventures. Fully half of ZDF's program schedule is filled with current affairs, news, and factual or documentary programs; the other half is dominated by films and drama, plus a mix of sports, children's, and other formats. ZDF's market share is roughly 14 percent—comparable to the ARD share, and also equal to the share achieved by the top commercial broadcaster, RTL. Among the most popular ZDF programs is *Derrick*, a detective series and a very popular export.

### KI.KA (Kinderkanal) and Phoenix

KI.KA and Phoenix are joint ventures between the two public broadcasters, ARD and ZDF. The KI.KA network offers quality children's programming to Germany's children. Free of violence, it's a safe place for young viewers. Phoenix is a public affairs channel offering live coverage of political and governmental activities.

## ARTE

As the name suggests, ARTE is an arts and culture channel. Global film programming is a core attribute, as are themed evenings in which programs are related in some conceptual way. In addition, there are high-quality dramas; lots of documentaries; a wide range of live performances in music, opera, variety, dance, and more; and generally high-quality afternoon programs for children.

Seen in both Germany and France, ARTE is a joint venture between French and German broadcasters. ARTE France holds 50 percent of the venture; of that,

France Télévision owns 45 percent, the state owns 25 percent, Radio France owns 15 percent, and INA owns 15 percent. ARTE Deutschland GmbH owns the other half of the venture, which is equally shared between ZDF and ARD. In addition, the BBC and SVT (Sverges Television in Sweden) are coproduction partners, and the network is seen, in whole or in part, in Belgium, Switzerland, Spain, Austria, the Netherlands, Poland, and various Eastern European countries. This carriage is sometimes via broadcast, but more often via cable or satellite.

ARTE's annual budget for 2004 was €350 million, about two-thirds of it spent on programming.

## 3sat

3sat is a three-way venture between the public broadcasters of Germany (ZDF and ARD), Austria (ORF), and Switzerland (SRG). 3sat is seen throughout Europe via several satellites. Half of the program's schedule is ballet, opera, classical, and other types of music, but there are also documentaries, satire, news and cultural magazines, and even a cultural game show. During prime time, each of the national networks provides its best program from its own schedule. Accordingly, ZDF and ARD provide approximately one-third of 3sat's programming.

## Local Independent Channels

In addition to ARD and ZDF, the broadcast organizations in the *Länder* operate independent channels. Two of the biggest of these independents, WDR3 and BR3, are available on cable throughout most of Germany (and via cable and satellite throughout Europe). Private regional broadcasters include Berlin's 1A and FAB, Hamburg 1, and TV München (in Munich).

## RTL

RTL Group is now 90 percent owned by the large German media company Bertelsmann (the result of a merger between CLT-Ufa, and Pearson Television, now called Fremantle Media). RTL has ownership in over 20 television channels in Europe, plus more than two dozen radio stations. Bertelsmann owns one of Europe's largest printers, as well as Random House, half of the world's largest record company (Sony BMG Music Entertainment); and three-quarters of the magazine publisher Gruner + Jahr. RTL owns five networks in the U.K., plus M6 in France and RTL Television—Germany's most popular television channel.

Based in Cologne, RTL Television is seen throughout Germany on terrestrial, cable, and satellite TV. For more than a decade, RTL has been Germany's top network for the 18- to 49-year-old audience, with a share of about 17 percent. Key program formats include Formula One auto racing, *Wer wird Millionär?* (*Who Wants to Be a Millionaire?*), the action series *Alarm für Cobra 11*, *Doppelter Einsatz*, and the family series *Mein Leben & ich.*

RTLII launched in 1993, and gained success through a combination of top series (*Big Brother* was a big hit for the network), movies, news, documentaries, music, and children's programs. One popular nonfiction series is *Welt Der Wunder* (*World of Miracles*). Audience share in the key 14 to 49 age demographic is about 7 percent.

SuperRTL is a children's channel that typically gets 20 percent or more of the children's audience with programs like *Bob der Baumeister* (*Bob the Builder*) and *SpongeBob Schwammkopf*, plus an intriguing combination of games, sports, and other shows somewhat similar to Nickelodeon's offerings. SuperRTL is a joint venture with Disney.

VOX is a general interest network that makes good use of U.S. series (CSI, for example) and movies in key time slots, then fills in the schedule with lifestyle, cooking, and automotive series. A magazine series based upon the popular German magazine *Die Spiegel* is also a signature program. Average audience share is approximately 5 percent.

n-TV is Germany's leading 24-hour news channel. It has been on the air since 1992.

## ProSieben Group

ProSiebenSat.1 Media AG operates a wide range of media activities in television, advertising, and interactive media, including four wholly owned television channels. ProSeibenSat.1 Media AG is owned by two entities: Axel Springer AG and German Media Partners, LP, which includes some of the world's top media investment firms (Quadrangle Group, Thomas H. Lee Partners, Bain Capital, Quadrangle Group, and more). Overall, the group is a forward-thinking media company with considerable competence in new media activities. The group has over 2,500 employees and generally achieves nearly $2 billion per year.

Sat.1 is a very popular channel for the 18 to 49 demographic. It is also seen in local versions for nearby Austria and Switzerland. Most of the original programming is in German: comedies, telenovellas, movies, and dramatic series fill the schedule. Annual revenues for 2004 were roughly $775 million.

ProSieben appeals to somewhat younger viewers, mainly focused on the 14–39 demographic, with popular films and television series, notably *Desperate Housewives*, *Lost*, and other hit series. Movies for 2005 included *Monsters, Inc.*, *Star Wars: Episode II*, and other popular American favorites. ProSieben's comedies tend toward original German product. ProSieben also does well with sensationalist documentaries: One featured the murder of an ancient iceman. Annual revenues for 2004 were nearly identical to Sat.1.

Kabel 1 runs classic films, modern dramas (including *Without a Trace* and *Cold Case* from the U.S.), various nature documentaries, themed evenings, and special events. Kabel 1, a cable- and satellite-only service, is considerably smaller than the other two networks, with under €200 million in revenues for the year (the others are delivered as terrestrial channels in addition to cable and satellite).

N24 is a 24-hour cable and satellite news channel that benefits from a co-operative arrangement with CNBC's worldwide business news operation. It features prime-time documentaries, late-night talk shows, and news magazine programs. Revenues for 2004 were about €75 million.

The ProSieben group has output deals with many of the world's movie studios, as well as with Kirch Media (over 2,000 films plus 128 series), and shows 13 live games per season from the UEFA Champions League (soccer).

## Other Channels

Various commercial stations are licensed to operate in specific cities, but can generally be seen throughout Germany via cable or satellite. Viva, for example, is licensed in Nordrhein-Westfalen but is perceived as a music and pop culture channel for the entire country. Terra Nova, a nature channel, is also licensed in Nordrhein-Westfalen. MTV Deutschland operates this way as well, with home license in Bayern, while Bloomberg TV operates out of Hessen. There are many more such channels.

In addition, there are dozens of channels seen via cable television and/or satellite. These include 20 movie, sports, and other premium entertainment channels from the large entertainment company Premiere; various Discovery channels; The History Channel; MGM; Toon Disney; QVC Deutschland; and many more. The pan-European sports channel Eurosport broadcasts two German channels, and there is a version of the U.K.'s TV Shop channel as well.

## Regulation of German Television

Each of the 16 (post-reunification) *Länder* has its own rules and regulations for broadcasting and cablecasting, as well as its own media authority; these are based upon a national standard. The Federal Office of Post and Communications (Deutsche Bundespost) controls the technical side of television broadcasting and cablecasting for all of Germany.

Commercial broadcasters may air commercials any time of the day or night, provided that the total commercial time does not exceed 15 percent of the day's total airtime, or 20 percent of the airtime in any given hour. Neither prescription drugs nor tobacco may be advertised on commercial television.

Public broadcasters may not show any commercials on Sundays and national holidays; the only period that commercials can be shown on public stations is between 5:00 P.M. and 8:00 P.M. on regular Mondays through Saturdays. Advertisements are limited to just 20 minutes of total time per working day.

# FRANCE

Sixty million people live in France. They are served by several public service broadcasters and several private broadcasters, each with terrestrial licenses, plus great many additional channels available via cable or satellite. This situation has become increasingly common throughout Europe and the world. The remnants of France's television history are occasionally apparent, but the contemporary market's integration of many different companies and assets makes these roots difficult to discern.

## France Télévisions

The two public networks in France, formerly called Antenna-2 (A2) and France Regions 3 (FR3), are now part of a single organization called France Télévisions. The same organization operates several cable and/or satellite channels: France 4 and France 5, plus four special-interest channels. The overall budget is over €2 billion; two-thirds of that total comes from taxes, and the other third comes mainly from advertising sales.

France 2, the nation's second most popular network, emphasizes world-class news and documentary programs, and popular programming with a quality veneer. Popular children's series include *Tintin* and *Asterix*, both longtime favorites in French households. Sports, notably car racing and soccer, are staples. It is not unusual to see series from other countries on France 2, particularly comedies and dramatic series from the U.S., the U.K., and Germany. The 2005 schedule, for example, included *JAG*, *Boston Public*, *Friends*, and *Six Feet Under*.

France 3's mission is more youth-oriented, with *Scooby-Doo* and *Astro Boy* sharing the children's television spotlight with French series such as *Titeuf* and *Les Gnoufs*. *Thalassa* is a popular magazine series. Cinema fills out the schedule, along with documentaries, talk shows, cooking and special-interest programs, and more.

France 4 emphasizes the spectacular: Cirque du Soleil, concerts, high-profile specials, mini-series, sports, and movies.

France 5 (F5) is an educational and learning channel founded in 1994. Its mission is broad, but its budget, at about €163 million, is typical for a smaller channel. The channel employs just over 200 people, again typical for this type of operation.

France Télévisions jointly operates ARTE (see page 457), an arts and culture channel also seen in Germany.

## Commercial Channels

Three channels are licensed for commercial terrestrial broadcast in France: TF1, M6, and Canal+.

### TF1 (Television Francais 1)

Top-rated Television Francais 1 was a government-owned network until it was sold to Bouygues, a large French construction firm, and Maxwell, the British communications conglomerate. Bouygues is the controlling entity with a 41.5 percent stake.

TF1 is a general-interest channel with a wide range of program offerings: news, drama, comedy, sports, children's programs, news and magazine programs, and more. In 2004, TF1 dominated the ratings: 89 of the top 100 programs were seen on this network.

TF1 also owns all or some of eight additional channels. LCI, or La Chaîne Info, is a news channel, wholly owned by TF1, that offers bulletins on the half-hour and other news and talk programming throughout the day. TF1 competes with F5 and M6 on the children's ratings charts; TF1 favorites are imported programs *Dora l'exploratrice*, *Jimmy Neutron: un garcon genial*, and *La legende de Tarzan*. TF1 competes with F3 on reality and magazine shows, but dominates in dramatic series, mainly with detective and crime series, which include *Hors d'atteinte* and *Julie Lescaut*. TF1 also does well with reality entertainment series such as *Star Academy* (an international format).

Eurosport has been 100 percent–owned by TF1 since 2001. It is a pan-European channel customized for viewing in various countries outside France. To be more specific, Eurosport is seen in 90 million households in 54 countries with over 200 million viewers—it broadcasts in 19 different languages. This is an enormous operation, responsible for more than 4,000 new hours of television per year. Coverage includes soccer, tennis, cycling (including the Tour de France), motor sports, Olympic coverage, and much more. Eurosport News, launched in 2000, is seen in 70 countries. Eurosport 2 appeals to a younger audience; it launched in 2005. Eurosport also owns about half of Sportitalia, which launched in Italy in 2005.

Odyssée started in 1995 and is now one of France's most popular documentary channels. It is completely owned by TF1. Programming features nature, travel, history, science, and other topics.

TFOU is a children's channel that premiered in 2003, showing programs from 6:30 A.M. until 8:00 P.M. Favorite programs include *Pancho Show*, a talk show hosted by a popular puppet. Programming is changed every six weeks to keep children interested and intrigued.

TF6 is a joint venture between M6 (see below) and TF1. This channel programs general-interest product for a younger demographic (ages 15 to 34) and has proven remarkably popular. TF1 also acquired half of the Série Club channel from M6 in 2001. The schedule is mostly filled with comedies and dramas acquired from the U.S. and elsewhere.

TF1 is also involved with satellite channels offered by TPS (Télévision Par Satellite), including movie, sports, and children's channels.

## M6

RTL owns just under half of M6, which consistently scores an 18 market share for the "housewives under 50" category. The daily situation comedy series *Caméra Café* is one reason why. Two popular magazine shows, *Culture Pub* and

*Zone Interdite* are also consistent winners. Among reality shows, *Bachelor* also performs well.

M6 is also a media player in its own right, with interests in more than a dozen digital channels. Téva is among M6's most successful digital channels, known as "television d'émotions" and showing a schedule tailored for adults in their 20s and 30s (more females than males). *Ally McBeal* reruns play well here, as do programs about cooking and cuisine, design, reality programs such as *Nouvelle Star* (a reality series along the lines of *American Idol*), and imported dramas that skew young. The company's shopping channel, M6 Boutique La Chaîne, originally aired in 1998 as Club Téléchat. The music and movies channel W9 debuted in 2005 as M6 Music; like MTV, it also shows series television for a young audience. This arm of the company also operates a rock channel and a black music channel. In 2004, M6 acquired all of Paris Première, a fashion, culture, and special events channel.

TF6 and Série Club are joint ventures with TF1 (see above). M6 is also involved in publishing, music, and film distribution.

## Canal+

Canal+ (or Canal Plus) began as a broadcast pay channel in 1984. Its scheme differs from the U.S. model in that customers pay Canal+ directly; there is no cable operator between the pay network and its subscribers. Much of the programming follows the standard pay—TV formula: recent movies, sports, and major entertainment events. Owned by Vivendi Universal, Canal+ is a major player in French and European media. Group revenues for 2003 were just over €3.5 billion.

In France, Canal+ is best known as a general-interest television channel that shows more than 400 movies each year, plus a considerable amount of high-profile sports coverage. Just under half of the programming seen on Canal+ is motion pictures. In accordance with French rules regarding its operation, fully 60 percent of these films are European in origin, and 40 percent come from France. On the sports side, Canal+ airs League 1 football (soccer), the NFL's full season (including the Superbowl), and the America's Cup, plus plenty of rugby, soccer, sports magazine shows, and more. Sports programming fills approximately 12 percent of Canal+'s schedule. Other key strengths are investigative journalism (especially news magazines) and comedy.

Canal+ Le Bouquet is the organization's digital channel package featuring more movie channels and sports.

Canal+ Groupe also owns two-thirds of a series of theme channels. These include the 24-hour news channel TELE; six movie channels under the Cine Cinema brand (wholly owned by Canal+ Groupe); Jimmy, which runs *NYPD Blue, Friends, Six Feet Under, Dallas*, and other series from the U.S., the U.K., and elsewhere; Seasons, a documentary channel; Comédie!; and four channels under the Planete brand: Planete Thalassa, Planete Choc ("Shock"), Planete, and Ma Planete.

Outside of France, CanalSatellite is known as an operator of superior movie and sports channels, mainly distributed via cable and satellite. In addition, Canal+ has long been a producer and coproducer of theatrical motion pictures.

## Other Channels

Several dozen local television stations operate in France, some broadcast in local regions and others seen via satellite. One example is Clermont Première, which broadcasts how-to shows, weather, news, sports, documentaries, and other programs of regional interest on local channel 64 and on a local cable network.

Many more channels are seen on cable and via satellite. PinkTV, for example, is a channel for "gay and gay-friendly" interests, seen on every major cable and satellite system in France as well as Belgium. Shareholders include Canal+, TF1, Lagardère, M6, and Connection, not to mention monies from the head of Gucci and the founder of Yves Saint-Laurent. Mezzo is a music channel focused on jazz, classical music, opera, and dance, owned by a combination of Lagardère, Canal+, and France Télévisions. Equida operates several channels related to horses and horse racing; it's a joint venture between PMU, France Galop, Cheval Francais, and FFE—all companies involved in horse racing.

Lagardère, a major book and magazine publisher, operates theme channels including La Chaîne Météo (France's weather channel), Canal J (a children's channel), various MCM music channels, and more. Lagardère also operates MatchTV, which builds on its strong *Paris Match* magazine brand.

Among the many channels developed in the U.S. and now available in local versions in France are MTV France, Disney Channel France, Toon Disney France, Cartoon Network France, and Discovery Channel France.

## Regulation of French Television

The Conseil superieur de l'audiovisuel (CSA), or National Audiovisual Communications Council, is charged with the allocation of radio and television frequencies, as well as the assignment of transponders and the awarding of cable franchises. The CSA supervises program practices (limits on sex and violence, and the quota system described below) and appoints the heads of French public television companies.

CSA regulations prohibit commercial interruptions on the public channels, France 2 and France 3. The private networks, notably TF1, are restricted to 12 minutes of advertising per hour; TF1 is allowed one six-minute break during movie presentations (for La Cinq and La Sept, the breaks may be slightly longer).

French broadcasters are held to a quota of 60 percent European programming, of which 40 percent must be French. This naturally limits the amount of U.S. programming, although major U.S. series are still regularly seen in France.

Original French programming has its difficulties in the international marketplace, where English-language soundtracks are essential. These soundtracks add an average of 20 percent to the cost of the production. Still, international monies are often needed to complete a large production, so the extra costs can be worthwhile.

## ITALY

Over 58 million people live in Italy, but there are only about 19 million television households.

Two organizations dominate Italian television: Radiotelevisione Italiana (RAI), owned by a corporation that is in turn owned by the government, and Fininvest, a large private media concern owned by Italy's Prime Minister, Silvio Berlusconi. Because of this arrangement, Italian television is frequently called a "duopoly."

The RAI organization began in the 1920s with EIAR radio; RAI television began in 1954. RAI has long been linked with Italian politics, and this has been the cause of many problems—for example, Italy did not receive color TV until 1977, long after the rest of Europe. The RAI monopoly began losing ground in 1971, when a small, privately operated cable system started up in a northern Italian town. After three years of fighting, Tele Biella won the legal right to serve its region, paving the way for other local cable companies and local broadcasters. The courts continue to uphold the RAI monopoly for national broadcasting, but unofficial networks—called "soft networks" or "para-networks"—evolved as independent local stations throughout Italy. There are, in fact, 21 regional networks, most of which rely upon studios in Rome for most of their programming, adding only local news. Eight of these networks are owned by Berlusconi.

## RAI

RAI operates three networks: RAI-1, RAI-2, and RAI-3. Each network is managed independently, but all three share the same chairman. RAI-1 is Italy's highest-rated network; light entertainment (situation comedies, big-name variety shows, major series from the U.S. and elsewhere) is the strong suit. RAI-2 does not compete as aggressively, either as a counterprogrammer to the commercial networks or within the international programming marketplace. RAI-3, emphasizing news and culture, is the more traditional public channel, and often the most innovative; it relies heavily on nonfiction and factual programs, presents serious music, and has a distinctly Italian flavor. RAI-1's market share is in the low 20s, RAI-2's is in the mid-teens, and RAI-3's is about 10 percent. RAI also operates RAI Canale Sportivo, a live channel that specializes in soccer, cycling, and tennis.

RAI is Italy's leader in news and sports broadcasting. Approximately 75 percent of RAI's programming is live—a practice that differs from most of the world's public networks. Traditionally, news programming on the RAI networks has been party-controlled: RAI-1 by the Christian Democrats, RAI-2 by the AN or National Alliance, and RAI-3 by the various parties on the left. These factions are involved in the details of news operations—including the selection of staff and talent. Political change is a way of life in Italy, so the status of these affiliations does change from time to time.

RAI is supported by a combination of advertising, which is limited to four minutes per hour, and license fees. Tobacco and alcohol cannot be advertised on RAI. RAI Trade (formerly SACIS) is a commercial RAI subsidiary that buys and sells programmming for all three networks in the international marketplace, and also controls advertising for these networks. SIPRA sells advertising time for the RAI channels.

## Mediaset (Reteitalia)

Mediaset is a €3.5 billion company with holdings in Italy and in Spain (Tele5; see below).

In Italy, Mediaset owns the top-rated, advertiser-supported Canale-5 and the more specialist Rete4 (also known as Retequattro). Together with Mediaset's Italia1, which appeals to young men, the Mediaset networks command nearly half of the commercial audience in Italian television, according to Auditel (Italy's audience research firm). Mediaset's Reteitalia channels were built by scheduling U.S. imports, such as game shows (one hit series was *Routa della Fortuna*, known in the U.S. as *Wheel of Fortune*).

Canale-5's success is largely due to long-term hit shows—including *Paperissima*, *La Corrida*, and *Striscia la notizia*—and more recent programs such as *C'é posta per te*, the most popular Saturday night variety show. Canale-5 is also a major producer of drama; its series on saints and on civil hearings have performed especially well.

Italia1 is all about music, sports, and pop culture. Reality shows work well here, notably *La fattoria*, which places celebrities on a nineteenth-century farm without modern conveniences, and *Campioni*, about a popular football (soccer) team.

Retequattro broadcasts a wide range of sports, science, news magazine, and U.S. dramatic series (e.g., *Law & Order*, *24*).

Mediaset also operates a children's channel for digital subscribers.

## Other Channels

Odeon TV, owned by Pathe and other investors, is a private television network that reaches two-thirds of Italian households. Other national networks include RETE A and La7. Hundreds of regional stations are also in operation. Sky TV also operates in Italy as Sky Italia.

Cable television has not yet materialized in Italy, mostly due to the widespread dominance of Berlusconi and RAI. Stream—a new venture from Stet, one of the world's top ten telecommunications companies—has attempted to cable Italy's cities with digital technology. The success of this venture, and its potential to transform the entire Italian television industry, depends upon politics. Developments in satellite and Internet distribution are also likely to alter the landscape, allowing more competitors as the marketplace evolves.

## Regulation of Italian Television

Italy's Ministry of Post and Telecommunications provides RAI with its operating authority, but the Ministry of Finance controls and regulates RAI's expenditures, collecting the license fees that fund a large percentage of its operation (the equivalent of about $100 [U.S.]—among Europe's lowest set fees). Regulation of commercial television in Italy is limited.

# SPAIN

The reach of Spanish broadcasting extends throughout Europe and Latin America. Although only 40 million people live in Spain, the country's 12 million television households are only a fraction of the global Spanish-speaking audience (which includes, for example, over 100 million people in Mexico alone).

## RTVE

Spanish television has historically been dominated by a government broadcaster, the RTVE (Radio Television Española), which replaced SNR (Spanish National Radio, or RNE [Radio Nacional de Espana]) in 1973. According to industry magazine *Variety*, RTVE "rivals the Mexican media group Televisa, the largest Spanish-language consortium in the world."

There is no set license fee or tax in Spain; the RTVE networks support themselves through advertising and, to a lesser extent, through program sales to other markets. Although it is government-owned, RTVE essentially operates like a private company. Advertising is restricted to no more than eight minutes per hour, and further restricted throughout the day to an overall average of no more than six minutes per hour).

TVE 1, which debuted in 1955, is Spain's light entertainment network. TVE La 2 began airing in 1964, and emphasizes news, information and cultural shows, and programs of regional interest. Local TVE affiliates throughout Spain also offer their own programs during the TVE La2 schedule. TVE Internacional reaches 10 million subscribers in Europe and an additional 7 million in Latin America.

TVE 1 and TVE La 2 networks follow a long tradition of in-house production, though about one-third of their programming is currently acquired or jointly produced. They've historically been very aggressive regarding rights, mainly because they are so powerful. As the only large networks in Spain, these networks' audience share had historically been enormous. As new channels settled in, however, RTVE's market share settled into a range that is common for national public broadcasters: around 30 percent.

RTVE also operates several digital channels. Canal Nostalgia mines the RTVE library and repackages old programs and footage, with a strong emphasis on older pop music. Canal Grandes Documentales is a documentary-only channel that covers a wide range of topics, including nature, travel, geography, ecology, arts, science, technology, and more. Canal Clásico is a music channel devoted to the more classical forms of Spanish music: traditional concerts, operas, jazz, flamenco, dance, and more. Canal 24 Horas is a news channel. TeleDeporte provides 18 hours a day of major sports coverage and historical sports documentaries.

## Autonomas

Spain's regional channels, called *autonomas*, are publicly owned and funded largely by local governments. Advertising has proven to be a productive form of financing as well; Televisio de Catalunya (TV3), the largest *autonoma*, is funded exclusively through advertising revenues. Based in Barcelona, TV3 reaches roughly one-sixth of the Spanish population. Canal 33, a sister station owned by the same company, shares TV3's programming department. In the Basque region, ETB1 and ETB2 broadcast in the Basque language and in Castilian respectively. Televisio de Galaicia (TVG), Televisión de Andalucia (Tele-Sur), Televisión de Valencia, and Televisión Autonoma de Madrid (Telemadrid) are regional channels that reach small portions of the overall population. Telemadrid (RTVM) serves a young, affluent, urban audience, and because of its sophisticated programming needs, it is becoming an increasingly significant player in the world marketplace.

Many *autonomas* went on the air in the mid-1980s or later; all of them are affiliated as members of the Federation of Autonomous Channels, and may eventually form a network. These channels do work together in some acquisitions and coproductions with companies outside Spain.

## Private Channels

Private channels did not appear on the Spanish television scene until the early 1990s. Socialist Premier Felipe Gonzalez took the better part of a decade to pass a private television bill and to assign network franchises. The apparent reason: 80 percent of the Spanish public depends upon television as its primary source of information, so Gonzalez was reluctant to weaken the government's power to control information.

### Terrestial Channels

Three television channels operate with analog terrestrial licenses in the commercial sector. The most popular are Antena 3 and Telecinco (or Tele5). Antena 3 is 17 percent owned by RTL, with Rest and Kort Geding also owning 33 percent each. It's a popular network with rights to popular movies, *Los Simpsons*, *South Park*, and a wide range of hit Spanish programs. Antena 3 competes directly with

Telecinco, owned by Italy's Mediaset. Telecinco is strong in sports, movies, and popular series as well.

Canal+ España also operates as a commercial terrestrial channel in Spain.

## Sogecable

Many of Spain's specialty cable and satellite channels are supplied or controlled by Sogecable, a leading media company owned 24 percent by Spain's Prisa, 24 percent by Group Telefónica (Spain's large telephone company), 12 percent by Vivendi Universal, and about 30 percent by public shareholders. Sogecable operates a variety of specialty cable channels, but is also involved in film production, film distribution, theatrical distribution (much of this in association with Warner), and so forth.

Cinemanía and Documanía were the company's first theme channels, followed by an outdoor channel called Caza y Pesca ("Hunting and Fishing," but it covers more). The Cinemanía brand now encompasses four channels, including a classic film channel (Cinemanía Clásico). DCine Español, launched in 2003, is filled with motion pictures produced in Spain. Sportmanía is Spain's most popular sports channel, showing NBA basketball, NFL football, Major League Baseball, NASCAR, and sports events from Europe and the Pacific. Golf+ is Europe's leading golf channel. Viajar is Sogecable's travel channel. There is also a 50/50 joint venture with CNN, called CNN+, and a channel that carries FOX Kids. And there's a range of music channels under the 40TV brand: 50TV covers English- and Spanish-language music, while a sister channel, 40 LATINO, is devoted exclusively to Latino music.

As a result of a merger with Vía Digital, cable operator Sogecable now controls most pay sports and movie programming in Spain, both through its own brands and through Canal+ operations in Spain.

Media Park is a Catalan operator of seven themed channels, including Super Ñ (a children's channel), Buzz (music, animation, and extreme sports), Natura (nature documentaries), 18 (action and adventure films), and MGM (a movie channel).

## Regulation of Spanish Television

There is no single regulatory agency for television in Spain. Instead, duties are shared by Comisión del Mercado de las Telecomunicaciones (Telecommunications Market Commission) and by Ministerio de Ciencia y Tecnología (Ministry for Science and Technology).

Spain's private networks are generally owned by multiple partners. Government regulations stipulate that a broadcasting company is allowed only 25 percent non-Spanish ownership. Also, no single entity can own a percentage of more than one channel.

Spanish content regulations are also restrictive. Nearly half of the programs seen on Spanish television must be of Spanish origin. Also, 15 percent of programming must be original, produced by the license-holder.

## OTHER EUROPEAN COUNTRIES

The following European countries are medium-sized television markets.

### The Netherlands

There are 16 million people living in the Netherlands, comprising 6 million television households. The regulatory agency is called Commissariaat voor de Media.

Broadcasting in the Netherlands is quite complicated. The government owns individual networks, each of which are programmed by multiple companies, with each company representing a special-interest group. The special-interest organizations include many dues-paying members, who pay for subscription magazines with program listings. Each company has a social, political, or religious outlook that is, at least in theory, reflected in its programming. The result is a series of channels that are programmed, at various times, by different groups. (The Netherlands also supports a great many smaller local television stations.)

NOS (Nederlandse Omroep Stichting), the public broadcast network service, offers three channels. Netherlands 1 carries shows from a variety of religious and social groups, notably the Catholic KRO and EO. Netherlands 2 is programmed by NPB and by AVRO. Netherlands 3 is programmed by NPS, VARA, VPRO, and KRO. Programs from each of these groups are scattered throughout each network schedule; this helps to explain why each of these broadcasters publishes its own weekly program guide.

Other commercial stations include SBS6 (promoted as a reality-based programmer); TV 10 (owned mostly by Saban, showing many children's cartoons bolstered by some old subtitled U.S. series and some original game shows); and Music Factory (music videos). Another niche channel, launched in 1996 by several large Dutch media companies (Endemol, Philips, the Dutch phone company, and other partners), is Sport 7, whose schedule is 25 percent soccer. KinderNet is a nonviolent children's network with a good amount of U.S. product dubbed into Dutch. There is also a pay TV network called Filmnet.

RTL4 is a popular commercial television channel broadcasting to the Netherlands from Luxembourg. It is majority-owned by CLT (Compagnie Luxembourgeoise de Telediffusion), now part of RTL Group; 38 percent of the company belongs to VNU, and just over 1 percent to Philips. RTL4 built its base with children's programming, and then moved into family fare.

SBS 6 appeals to young viewers, often with provocative programming and a steady stream of programs from outside of the Netherlands,while NET 5 appeals to upscale, modern female viewers. Veronica, specializing in Dutch action films and television series appealing largely to younger male viewers, shares a channel with the children's channel Jetix. Each of these networks is owned or controlled by SBS Broadcasting.

Canal+ operates several cable and satellite channels in the Netherlands. Club is a risqué channel for women that deals frankly with sexual issues; it is seen in 20 countries throughout Europe, including the Netherlands.

## Belgium

Most of Belgium's 10 million citizens speak either French or Flemish (a language similar to Dutch). The result is two distinct television industries. (In fact, a third language, German, is spoken by a minority; Belgian public television channel RTBD serves this group.) Belgium is unique in another way: The country has 95 percent cable penetration due to the combination of small country geography and aggressive business practices. There is little interest in satellite reception in Belgium.

The Belgian regulatory agency is Vlaams Commissariaat voor de Media.

### French-Language Channels

RTBF Belgian Television operates two channels for French-speaking viewers: RTBF 1 (called La Une, or La 1) and RTBF 2 (La Deux, or La 2). La Une is a popular channel that combines French drama and comedy with some U.S. imports (for example, *Monk* from the U.S., and *Derrick* from Germany). There's also sports, comedy, news programs, and a daily block for children. La Deux is more highbrow, with music, culture, and documentary, but it's also a popular channel for sports. Though it is a government-owned broadcaster, RTBF has accepted commercial advertising since 1989. RTBF makes an honest effort in developing news magazine programs to emphasize Belgian issues and culture, but many of its programs are imported and dubbed into French.

On the commercial terrestrial side, CLT, part of the large media company RTL, broadcasts into Belgium from nearby Luxembourg. RTL1 is the top French-language station in the commercial realm, with *Star Academy Made in Belgium, Qui Sera Millionaire?*, and the popular news series *Le Journal*. Club RTL serves two audiences: children (mainly with cartoons) and during other day parts, men (with sports and movies). Plug TV, launched in 2004, is entertainment for tweens and teens.

Cable companies import a substantial number of channels from France, so there are fewer French-language specialty channels than Flemish-language specialty channels in Belgium (see below).

### Flemish-Language Channels

Flemish viewers are served by both public and private channels. Belgium's VRT operates three of the former, including broad-based entertainment and news channel één. Another is Canvas, formerly TV2, which focuses on news, documentaries, and programming for children (KETNET, a children's service, is part of Canvas). Also government-owned, and operated by Belgische Radio en Televisia, BRTN TV1 and BRTN TV2 feature mostly local programming, and neither service accepts advertising.

Commercial Belgian stations are also subtitled. Vlaamse TV Maatschappi (VTM) achieves a high market share, mostly with imported programs. VTM is advertiser-supported, and has been granted a monopoly for terrestrial commercial broadcasting in Belgium. VTM also operates the cable channel Jim TV, a music- and youth-oriented pop culture channel. VT4 has also been very successful with youthful audiences, attracting some of VTM's advertising revenues. VT4 generally builds its program schedule based on acquisitions.

Canal+ operates a variety of movie and entertainment channels in Belgium as well, and Sporza is a popular Belgian radio and television network. Kanaal Z, owned by the Roularta Media Group, is a 24-hour news channel. VIJF is a women's channel that airs imported programs including *Dr. Phil* and *Oprah*; Vitaya is a lifestyle channel, also aimed mainly at women. Yorin, from RTL, is a general-interest channel with a younger edge; its imported programs include *CSI: NY* and *The Nanny*.

## Sweden

Sweden is the most populous of the Scandinavian countries, with just under 10 million people (Denmark has just over half as many). Each of the Scandinavian countries maintains a distinct television and radio service, but some channels are seen in all of them, adjusted for language as necessary.

There are five terrestrial channels: two owned by the state, three by commercial enterprises. Swedish public television is financed entirely by receiver taxes; television advertising is not permitted. This is the practice in Norway and Denmark as well.

Stockholm-based SVT1 has a national emphasis and is Sweden's most popular channel. SVT2 has more of a regional focus; programming is general-interest, with the Swedish Educational Broadcasting Company supplying much of the daytime schedule. These two networks account for roughly half of Sweden's viewership.

Viasat's TV3 is a satellite channel seen throughout Scandinavia. Its schedule is built mostly from acquisitions, though some lower-priced productions, like game shows and news programs, are made by or for the network.

TV4 is a commercial terrestrial channel, and a popular one at that (nearly one-third of the market); it's home to the top-rated contemporary drama *Three Crowns*. Commercials are permitted, but only between programs; nothing related to tobacco, liquor, or products aimed at children may be advertised. In fact, a percentage of advertising profits must be assigned to finance children's programming.

Channel 5, owned by the Scandinavian Broadcasting System, broadcasts via satellite and cable, reaching between 40 and 60 percent of Swedish television viewers.

Among digital channels, SVT operates 24, a news channel; Kunskapskanelen, a learning channel in a joint venture with UVT; and Barnkanalen, a children's channel. SVT is funded principally by receiver fees.

# CHAPTER 53

# AUSTRALIA AND ASIA

Over the past decade, the Pacific television marketplace has grown rapidly. With a great many networks—and a very strong presence from FOX, NBC, and other multinational companies—many channels are available in just about every nation in Asia and, of course, in Australia and New Zealand. Australia has long been a source of programming for other English-language countries, besides being a solid filmmaker. Increasingly, Asia is becoming a supplier of programming for the international marketplace as well.

## AUSTRALIA

As in the U.K., the Australian television system is a combination of public and private networks. It is a country with more than 20 million people and 6 million television households.

The structure of the television industry was initially based upon the structure of the radio industry, with two types of operations: privately owned stations that carried advertising, and government-owned stations that were funded through taxes. The first licenses were granted in 1955 to commercial broadcasters in Sydney and Melbourne. By 1960, noncommercial stations were operating in all of Australia's largest cities as part of the Australian Broadcasting Commission, now the Australian Broadcasting Corporation or the ABC.

### Public Networks

#### ABC

With nearly 100 broadcast stations (from 600 transmitters), the ABC covers almost all of Australia. Programming is generally upscale, with a strong news and information focus. The ABC boasts the largest news-gathering organization in Australia—several hundred journalists on the continent and elsewhere. *The 7:30 Report* is a prime-time news and current-affairs analysis program that appears nightly; *Four Corners* is another respected current-affairs program. *Foreign Correspondent*, another prime-time series, features the ABC's worldwide news-gathering force in a nightly magazine. *Landline* provides rural news, and *Lateline* is a news wrap-up that airs nightly at 10:30 P.M.

Other programming on the ABC includes *Kath & Kim*, an earthy mother-and-daughter comedy that has been the network's top-rated series—a bona fide television hit complete with merchandise. *Sunday Afternoon* is a three-hour magazine-style program devoted to the arts. *Play School* is the longtime preschool children's television standard in Australia. Children (and many adults) also know B1 and B2, the stars of the series *Bananas in Pajamas*, which played for several years in the U.S. as well.

In terms of sheer number of broadcast hours, half of the ABC's programs are produced in Australia and half are imported. Children's programming is a very strong category, heavily reliant upon imports, occupying fully 20 percent of the ABC's schedule. Movies account for about 12 percent of programming; nearly all are imported. Entertainment programs also account for about 12 percent, but nearly all of these are locally produced in Australia. News and current affairs programs are popular, filling about 14 percent of the schedule (all produced in Australia). Local sports coverage gets a comparatively small share of hours (less than 3 percent), but scores high ratings. The ABC's share is typically about 14 percent, and this percentage has held steady for years.

The ABC is just short of a $1 billion (Australian) organization, with three-quarters of revenues coming from government appropriations and the remaining revenue mainly from overseas program sales. Just over half of the budget is devoted to domestic television. Approximately 4,000 people are employed by the ABC.

## SBS

Special Broadcasting Service, established as a public broadcaster in the early 1980s on UHF stations, serves Australia's ethnic minorities with a unique agenda. Programs are broadcast in more than 50 languages, with a different language heard every hour (over 60 languages are spoken on SBS's sister radio service). The objective is clear: to provide Australia's multicultural populations with their own broadcast voice.

Again in terms of sheer hours broadcast, SBS relies more heavily upon imported programs (75 percent), including about 17 percent of the schedule devoted to movies from outside Australia. A number of news and current affairs programs, which occupy over 40 percent of the schedule, are also imported (35 percent, in fact). SBS typically scores under a 5 percent audience share, but this has been steadily increasing since the early 1980s. A great deal of soccer is shown on SBS, which claims, "It is the world's most popular sport, and the sport most favoured by migrant and non-English speaking (sic) communities in Australia." SBS also covers cycling, motorcycling, gymnastics, and other sports that generally appeal to smaller populations, leaving Australian football, rugby, cricket, and tennis to other networks whose mission is to serve Australia's mass market.

The top programs on SBS are generally watched by about a half-million Australians. These are most often documentaries. In the 2003 season, for example, these included *In Search of Ancient Alexandria*, *Death of the Iceman*, *Empires of Stone*, and *Johnny Cash: The Anthology*. In 2004, popular programs included coverage of the *Danish Royal Wedding* (with over 800,000 viewers—a very large audience for SBS—because an Australian married the Crown Prince), *The First World War in Colour*, the *Eurovision Song Contest Final*, *D-Day: The Shortest Day*, and *The Food Lovers' Guide to Australia*. One cult hit on SBS is *Pizza*, a satire of multiculturalism presented via a streetwise sitcom.

Ninety percent of SBS funding comes from the government. The remaining 10 percent comes from advertising and sponsorship; unlike the ABC, which is not allowed to sell advertising, SBS may sell up to five minutes per hour. The annual budget is just under $200 million (Austrailian). About 900 people work at SBS; some are part-time employees.

## Commercial Networks

Three networks are licensed to operate as commercial broadcasters throughout Australia. As a rule, Nine Network has been the most successful, with an annual audience share that has exceeded 30 percent every year, for decades. Its closest competitor is Seven, which typically scores just under a 30 (and sometimes closer to a 25). The steady third place competitor, with a share of about 22, is Network Ten.

### Nine Network

PBL, or Publishing and Broadcasting Limited, is one of Australia's largest companies. With annual revenues of over $3 billion Australian, PBL owns assets in television, magazines, gaming, and entertainment. The company is more than 70 years old. It began as a magazine publisher, Australian Consolidated Press (ACP), whose successful titles include Australia's oldest magazine, *The Bulletin*, as well as *The Australian Women's Weekly* and *Woman's Day*.

In 1956, the company acquired a broadcasting license for Sydney and became the country's first television broadcaster. Fast forward to 1994, when various assets related to what became Nine Network Australia were merged with the ACP to form a new publishing company, PBL. In 1999, Crown Limited was added to the fold; its business is gaming, bars, and restaurants. Today, PBL owns Nine Network; a large resort casino in Perth; 25 percent of FOXTEL (Australia's leading subscription business); and 50 percent of Premier Media Group, which operates FOX Sports 1 and 2, the HOW TO Channel, and Fuel TV. PBL also owns a third of Sky News Australia. In addition, PBL is in a joint venture with MSN for ninemsn, the country's leading internet portal. PBL also owns Ticketek, the country's largest ticket broker.

In the 2003 season, Nine's most successful project was *The Block: The Auction* with over 3 million viewers, along with the always-popular *National Nine News*

*Sunday* with 2.4 million. The network also does well with its version of 60 Minutes and with other series and specials, such as *Test Australia: The National Driving Test*, *The TV Week Logies Red Carpet Arrivals* (a pre-awards show program); the holiday special *Carols by Candlelight*, and *Who Wants to Be a Millionaire*. *The Cricket World Cup* (Australia vs. India) was also a top choice. The season's biggest hit was *Dancing with the Stars*, a celebrity dance competition. In daytime, it's soap operas (*Days of Our Lives*, *The Young and the Restless*), and in prime time, it's often sitcoms (*The King of Queens*, *Malcolm in the Middle*), reality (*Survivor: Vanuatu*), or drama (*CSI*, *Third Watch*, *Joan of Arcadia*).

### Seven Network

Seven Network reaches only about three-quarters of Australian households. In 2003, Seven's most popular presentation, the 2003 Rugby World Cup Final (Australia vs. England), reached over 4 million people—a very large number for any Australian television show. The network's second-highest-rated entry in that season was another sporting event, the 2003 Melbourne Cup Carnival, with about 2.5 million viewers on race day. In terms of regularly scheduled programming, *Room for Improvement* often reached about 2 million people. In the 2005 season, *Seven News* was generally the number one commercial newscaster. The tabloid magazine series *A Current Affair* remains one of the network's more popular formats (seen in the U.S. on FOX). Other imported hit series include *Desperate Housewives*, *Lost*, and *The Amazing Race*; local hits include *Dancing with the Stars*, *My Restaurant Rules*, and *Home and Away*. Overall, the core demographic is the under-40 audience.

Aside from operating one of Australia's top television networks, as well as the popular 7 Sport network, Seven Network is also one of Australia's top magazine publishers. In fact, formed through an acquisition of Murdoch Magazines, Pacific Publishing publishes one out of every four magazines sold in Australia, including many titles familiar to U.S. readers (*Men's Health*, *Better Homes and Gardens*, and *Marie Claire*). Close links with the Australian Football League (AFL) allow the creation and management of large events, such as the Rugby World Cup. Seven also has naming rights and various marketing relationships with the large Telstra Dome stadium in Melbourne. Company revenues for 2004 were just over $1 billion (Australian). Television activities provided approximately 80 percent of these revenues.

### Network Ten (The Ten Group)

Network Ten is 15 percent owned by Canada's CanWest Global communications, and this has been a cause for concern for many Australians and for the Australian Broadcasting Authority (see below), which has investigated the impact of foreign control over domestic television networks. Approximately 1,000 people work for Network Ten.

The network's target audience is viewers under age 40. Ten's most successful programs in 2003 were *Australian Idol: Final Verdict* (the familiar reality/talent show format), the AFL Finals (Collingwood vs. Brisbane), and *Big Brother: Final Eviction* (reality). Many of the programs on Ten will be familiar to U.S. viewers: *The O.C.*, the *Law & Order* shows, *Medium*, *The Simpsons*, *Everybody Loves Raymond*, *Battlestar Galactica*, and *The Bold and the Beautiful*. Australian originals include *ROVE LIVE*, *Neighbours*, *Totally Wild*, and *Good Morning Australia*. As the principal AFL broadcaster, Ten is also a sports leader.

### Smaller and Regional Broadcasters

Southern Cross operates one metropolitan license plus seven regional licenses, so it reaches 42 percent of Australian households. It is also a radio broadcaster, and the operator of Sky Radio and other holdings. Prime Television, controlled by Paul Ramsay Holdings Pty Ltd., reaches 25 percent of Australia with eight regional television licenses. The WIN Corporation Pty Ltd. controls one metropolitan license and nine regional licenses, and reaches 26 percent of Australia's households.

## Regulation of Australian Television

The Australian Broadcasting Authority (ABA) was created by the Broadcasting Services Act of 1992. The new agency took over the licensing, regulation of programming ownership, and various control functions previously performed by the Australian Broadcasting Tribunal (ABT). In addition, the new ABA assumed responsibilities for planning the broadcasting spectrum (previously done by the Federal Minister for Transport and Communications and the Minister's Department, which is now reorganized under the Minister for Communications, the Information Economy and the Arts).

In 2005, the ABA merged with the Australian Communications Authority to create a new media and communications regulator, the Australian Communications and Media Authority (ACMA). This change, which occurs in parallel with changes in other nations, reflects the increased level of convergence of television, radio, telephones, computers, the Internet, and other technologies.

The agency is empowered to grant, renew, and cancel station licenses (as in other countries, licenses are cancelled very infrequently). Commercial television broadcasting licenses are subject to renewal every five years. The license is an agreement to honor restrictions regarding content, behavior of owners, and responsibilities to children.

### Australian Content and Advertising Requirements

A quota system related to Australian content assures a high percentage of the programs seen on Australian television will be domestic in origin. Australian identity, character, and cultural diversity are the assets to be protected and promoted. In 1996, ABA's Australian Content Standard (ACS) required commercial broadcasters to include 50 percent Australian programming between 6:00 A.M. and midnight. In addition, commercial broadcasters must schedule minimum amounts of original Australian drama, documentary, and children's programs. Preschool programming must be Australian-made.

The Broadcasting Services (Australian Content) Standard, revised in 2003, updates previous rules and subjects programs to "creative elements tests" to determine whether they can be applied to the required minimums for Australian programming on the broadcast networks. The overall annual minimum level is 55 percent of all programs shown between 6:00 A.M. and midnight. In 2003, requirements were raised for at least 20 hours of first-release Australian documentaries, and at least 25 hours of first-release Australian children's drama. On pay-TV movie services, at least 10 percent of the program budget must be spent on Australian dramas. Many of these rules also encompass programs made by and for New Zealand. For more about these rules, visit the Australian Broadcasting Society's Web site at www.aba.gov.au.

The Australian Content in Advertising Standard requires at least 80 percent of advertising time broadcast each year between 6:00 A.M. and midnight to be sold to Australian advertisers.

## FOXTEL, AUSTAR, and Joint Venture Subscription Networks

FOXTEL, the leading cable operator in Australia, is available to nearly three-quarters of Australian homes. Owned by News Corporation, the Packer group, and Telstra, FOXTEL directly operates cable services and also provides program packages to Optus, another leading cable MSO. FOXTEL employs over 1,800 people, plus nearly the same number of contractors and freelancers.

The FOXTEL package includes the combination of local and international channels now common throughout the world (except, perhaps, in the U.S.). In addition, FOX Sports operates eight digital sports channels (more than half are "footy" channels devoted entirely to AFL games). The BBC joint venture UKTV plays here as well. The Comedy Channel is a blend of original Australian comedy and series from the U.S. and elsewhere (*South Park* and *Whose Line Is It Anyway* are two examples). Showtime provides several movie channels (HBO does not), and FOXTEL packages several of its own. Similarly, MTV, VH1, and CMT are here, but so is another music channel, Channel [V]. Two sports channels, FOX Sports 1 and FOX Sports 2, are joint ventures between News Limited and PBL; the same relationship exists for Fuel.

AUSTAR is also a leading subscription television provider. AUSTAR's programming asset is called XYZ Networks, which either owns or distributes 11 channels in a joint venture with FOXTEL. These channels include [V] (along with its sister network, Club [V]), Arena, LifeStyle Channel, LifeStyle Food, and MAX. Optus is also involved in several joint ventures, including Adults Only, which is one-third each owned by FOXTEL, Austar, and Optus.

## JAPAN

Japan's 127 million people and 42 million television households are served by seven terrestrial networks. NHK General TV and NHK Educational TV are public networks owned and funded by the Japanese government. Fuji TV, Tokyo Broadcasting System (TBS), Nippon Television (NTV), TV Asahi, and TV Tokyo are commercial networks.

Programming is, by and large, original. Japanese people tend to prefer their own programming to Western-style productions. When representatives of Japan's networks attend international program marketplaces, they go mainly to sell, not to buy. Japanese series consistently perform better in Japan than U.S. or European programs, regardless of the success of these properties elsewhere.

### Public Networks

NHK (Nippon Hoso Kyokai, or Japanese Broadcasting Corporation) was originally based on the BBC model. It was set up in the radio era as a public-service system financed by license fees. These voluntary payments, called "receiving fees," come from thousands of fee collectors who appeal to the Japanese sense of honor and civic duty as they go door-to-door throughout Japan. NHK sets its own fees, subject to government approval; presently, the monthly fee is 1,395 yen (less than $15) per household for one or more color TV sets (less if paid six months or a year in advance, and slightly discounted if paid by bank transfer or through a postal money order). A household with a satellite pays nearly twice as much: 2,340 yen. Nearly all of NHK's revenue comes from either government subsidies or set license fees: Annual operating income for fiscal year 2005 was over 675 billion yen, with 96.5 percent of this money coming from receiving fees. Fully three-quarters of this money is spent on program production and transmission.

Like many state broadcasters, NHK is an enormous enterprise, comprising several dozen organizations, including the NHK Symphony Orchestra, for example.

NHK General's program mix is dominated by news, commentary, cultural shows, and educational programming. For many years, NHK was Japan's ratings leader, but because of increased competition from the commercial stations, NHK has dropped from first to last place in the ratings.

NHK Education is a second channel distributed via broadcast television. True to its mission, NHK Education provides lessons every day in conversational English, Spanish, French, and German, as well as programming for Japan's youth, from preschool through high school. These programs fill most of the hours; the other slots are filled with the occasional arts or sports program.

NHK also operates three satellite channels.

### Commercial Networks

Japan's five commercial networks grew from local stations operating in the Tokyo area. In theory, commercial networks are not permitted to operate in Japan. In practice, the more powerful Tokyo stations began transmitting their programs to affiliated stations elsewhere in Japan. Because the Tokyo stations were owned by newspapers with nationwide advertising capabilities, it wasn't long before the newspapers were selling national advertising for their television operations as well.

## NTV

Nippon Television (NTV), Japan's largest private network, went on the air in 1953. The network is supported by advertising. NTV's programming strengths include sports (especially Yomiuri Giants baseball games), talk shows, and the popular period dramas depicting old Japan. NTV also operates a record label (VAP), owns the Tokyo Verdy soccer league club, and runs the e-commerce site Nandaro Net. The company's total revenues for 2004 were over 300 billion yen. NTV's average market share is about 15 percent of viewers, making it Japan's highest rated network. NTV is also involved in cable and satellite channels: sports channel G+ (with extensive coverage of Yomiuri Giants), NNN24 (a news channel), Eco Music TV (music for relaxation), Music Japan TV Plus (pop music), and several other channels.

## TBS

The Tokyo Broadcasting System, which started in 1955, is a light-entertainment network. TBS's 2003 revenues for its television operations were approximately 250 billion yen. Popular programs included the 9th IAAF World Championships in Athletics in Paris, France; a drama entitled *Our Memories of the Sugarcane Field*; and a documentary, *What is The Man?*. Among regularly scheduled programs, the dramatic series *Say Hello to Black Jack* (based upon a comic book story) was a hit, as was *Drop-out Teacher Returns to School* (which dealt with truancy). The variety series *Tokyo Friendly Park II* was a highly rated series, as was *Nakai Masahiro's SMAP Friday*. TBS also operates a 24-hour news channel, Japan News Network (JNN).

## Fuji

Fuji TV is a general-interest network that features game shows, sitcoms, and variety shows. In terms of income, Fuji has long been Japan's top broadcaster. Programming tends to skew young, with strong appeal to female viewers. Fuji Television Network, Inc., employs nearly 1,500 people. Fuji Television is part of the Fujisankei Communications Group, which comprises almost 100 companies in television, newspaper publishing, magazine publishing, music, direct marketing, real estate, radio, and museum management. The newspaper group's *Sankei Shimbun* and the magazine's group's *ESSE*, a woman's magazine, are among the company's key assets. On television, Fuji's long-term hits include *Tokyo Love Story*, *Long Vacation*, and *HERO*. The recent hit *GTO*, about an unconventional school teacher, consistently achieves ratings near 30 percent—a very high rating for Japan. The suspense series *A Sleeping Forest* has been very successful as well, along with the comedy series *How Cool We Are!*. On the variety side, music is the key to the success of *Hey! Hey! Hey! Music Champ* and *SMAP x SMAP* (featuring the "super idol music group" SMAP). Sports coverage is also central to Fuji Television's schedule and strategy; successes include Formula Nippon auto racing, the World Judo Championships, the Japan Grand Prix, and K-1 (which combines karate, kickboxing, kung fu, and Thai boxing techniques). Fuji is also the largest shareholder in WOWOW (see following page).

## TV Asahi

TV Asahi also began in 1959 and has been especially successful with its news and talk shows. For at least 18 years, the network's 10:00 P.M. flagship news show has scored an average 14 percent share. Recent hits include *The Millionaire Detective*, a mystery and humor series; *Hitoshi Tadano: the Extraordinary Undercover Detective*; a relationship variety show called *London Hearts*; and *Apron of Love*, a cooking variety series. Revenues for 2005 were over 215 million yen (about $2 million).

## TV Tokyo

Operated by Japan's Nikkei Newspaper Group, the network (called TXN) reaches about 70 percent of Japanese households, and achieves a market share of approximately 8 percent during "golden time" (7:00 P.M. to 10:00 P.M.), and just over 7 percent during prime time (7:00 P.M. to 11:00 P.M.). Net sales for the company were just short of 110 million yen for fiscal year 2004. TV Tokyo does well with news and business programs, such as *News Morning Satellite* and the late-night *World Business Satellite* (WBS). TV Tokyo is also a leader in anime; the spectacularly successful *Pokémon* and *Yu-Gi-Oh!* franchises began here and are managed by TV Tokyo's rights management group. Other animation successes include *Hamtaro*, *NARUTO*, and *The Prince of Tennis*.

## SKY PerfecTV!

SKYPerfecTV! is a leading pay-satellite service owned by Sony, Fuji, Itochu, JSAT, Tokyo Broadcaster, and a handful of other companies. Annual revenues are approximately 70 billion yen. The company was one of several satellite subscription start-ups but has now taken a leadership role due to the closing competitors DIRECTV Japan and PlatOne; the result is over three million subscribers.

Many of the 145 channels seen on SKYPerfecTV! are Japanese in origin or are versions of U.S. channels altered for Japanese viewers. Channels are available individually or in various groupings. Purely Japanese channels include Space Shower TV, Music Japan TV, the Home Drama Channel, JNN Newsbird, Pioneer Karaoke TV, Yoshimoto Fandango TV, and more. Channels based upon familiar U.S. brands include Nikkei CNBC, CNNj, QVC, Cartoon Network, MTV,

Sports-i ESPN, and Bloomberg Television. Premium networks include the usual mix of movie and sports channels.

## WOWOW

WOWOW offers movies, music, drama, sports, theater, drama, and animation to 2.5 million pay satellite subscribers on analog channel Bs5 and digital channels 191, 192, and 193. In truth, 70 percent of the schedule is filled with movies. The company's annual revenues are typically over 60 billion yen per year.

## Regulation of Japanese Television

Japan's regulatory agency is the Ministry of Post and Telecommunications. Although Japan is one of the few large countries in which tobacco and alcohol can be advertised on television, the following businesses cannot buy commercial time on Japanese television: companies that arrange marriages, funeral parlors, hostess bars, and Pachinko parlors. The National Association of Commercial Broadcasters also has a regulatory code, but compliance is voluntary.

## INDIA

Founded in 1959, Doordarshan is India's public broadcaster and one of world's largest terrestrial networks. With 1,314 transmitters, Doordarshan reaches 90 percent of India's one billion people. The network operates more than 50 studio centers and concentrates on three main program formats: news and current affairs, education, and entertainment. Two popular educational programs are *Turning Point*, a science magazine, and *Tera Quiz*, about the environment. Doordarshan is set up for service at the national, regional, and local levels with two network feeds known as DD1 and DD2. Doordarshan also operates DD Sports, seen in more than 30 countries and featuring a combination of sports from India and around the world. DD Bharati is a distinctively Indian lifestyle channel, with programs on music, dance, heritage, health, yoga, meditation, and health care, as well as a leading children's channel. The Gyandarshan Channel is a joint venture of Indian governmental, educational, and cultural institutions in India; the channel is filled with career and curriculum programming.

The popular Zee brand launched with a single television channel in 1992; it's heavy on pop culture and light entertainment for a younger, sophisticated audience. Zee also operates India's largest cable MSO, known as Siticable, with a reach of over six million households. Zee employs over 1,400 people, with annual revenues of over $315 million U.S. Zee's brand portfolio includes: Zee TV; Zee Cinema (India's top movie channel); Zee News (the top news channel, in the Hindi language); Zee Music; Zee Café (English-language programming for urban and younger audiences); Zee Studio (movies, including the MGM library); Zee Gold (South Asian movies); Zee Marathi, Zee Punjabi, Zee Bangla, and Zee

Gujarat (channels for specific ethnic groups); Zee Trendz (fashion and style); KidZee (preschool programs seen in over 100 cities in India, the Middle East, Singapore, and Indonesia); Zee Smile (comedy); Zee Select (English-language action films); and Zee Classics (old movies). In addition, Zee owns ZedCA, an animation studio.

STAR pioneered pay-satellite service in Asia, currently broadcasts in over 50 countries, and is watched by over 100 million people per day. A wholly owned subsidiary of News Corp., *Star* offers more than 50 different satellite channels, including movie channels, sports channels, and light entertainment in a variety of local languages. In India, *Star* also offers National Geographic Channel, ESPN, The History Channel, adventure channel A1, and music channel [V].

Many other channels are available to viewers in India via satellite. Sony Entertainment Television provides Hindi family entertainment, including movies and television series. ETC Networks (half-owned by Zee Telefilms) operates two channels: one featuring Indian Music for the Hindi audience, and the other for Punjabi viewers. Sun Networks operates 13 television channels for four ethnic groups: Telugu, Kannada, Malayalam, and Tamil. The Tamil channels, for example, include a news channel, a music channel, and two general entertainment channels.

## CHINA

Chinese television is dominated by CCTV (Central Committee Television), the government-owned and -operated suite of a dozen channels. CCTV News is a 24/7 news service whose content is shaped by the Communist regime. CCTV Music, which debuted in 2004, features traditional Chinese music, and is filled with music appreciation and music lessons. CCTV Children premiered in 2003 and encourages respect, health, and other aspects of happy life as a Chinese citizen. The channel also features some animation and other programs, including *Famous Teacher, Famous School, With Everywhere Blue Sky,* and *The Social Ethics Moves.* CCTV E&F ("Español and Français") is filled with Chinese television programming in alternating four-hour French- and Spanish-language blocks.

CCTV1 airs quite a bit of news programming, plus positive programs about Chinese culture, such as *Great Soldier Approximately, Contemporary Worker,* and *Performance Sports Arena.* CCTV1 also broadcasts some Chinese soap operas and documentaries covering China's ancient legends and state leaders, but is perhaps best known for the *Spring Festival Gala.*

CCTV2 is a business and public-service channel with programs about economics, the law, personal service, family health, and investment, and for leisure time, *Lucky 52* and *Happy Dictionary.*

CCTV 3 is devoted to music, opera, theater, and literature. Programs include *Dance World, Foreign Literary Arts,* and *Vainly Hopes for the Theater.*

CCTV 4's focus is Chinese people in Hong Kong, Macao, and Taiwan. The channel began broadcasting in 1992, and is available via satellite in Australia and elsewhere.

CCTV 5 is the sports channel featuring soccer, racing, gymnastics, chess, sports education, the Olympics, and more. It broadcasts more than 1,000 live programs each year and is watched by over 300 million viewers in China. As such, CCTV 5 is the world's largest sports channel.

CCTV 6 is a movie channel, mainly focusing on Chinese cinema, that shows about eight movies each day. It is CCTV's second-most popular channel (CCTV 1 is first).

CCTV 7's schedule is shared by several formats. Each morning is filled with programs for preschool students; throughout the day, older students are served as well. Each week, the channel is used for 23 hours of military programs, including *The Military Report*, *The Chinese Armed Police*, and *Military Compound Culture*. The remaining hours serve Chinese farmers (often peasants) with *Becomes Rich After*, and *Today Village*.

CCTV 8 is half-filled with Chinese soap operas; the remaining time is filled with drama, education, and news programs. Roughly half of the programs are produced outside China.

Broadcast in English, CCTV 9 is filled with Asian and Chinese news, and with information about the Chinese economy and culture. It is broadcast via six satellites and throughout Asia and to Europe and the U.S.

CCTV 10 teaches viewers about modern science and technology, but also pursues "moral character, the scientific quality, cultural personal status" associated with learning.

Chinese drama and other cultural programming are the basis of CCTV 11. In this case, drama includes dance and other aspects of arts and theater.

On 12, CCTV provides programs about Chinese law, government, and society.

In addition, Beijing Television, known as BTV, operates ten channels. With a mix of general entertainment and news, these are among China's most popular.

Other channels are generally distributed via satellite, sometimes to Chinese audiences in China, sometimes to international audiences and Chinese abroad. Dragon TV, from Shanghai, is seen in China, Japan, Australia, and Macao. Guangdong Southern TV, known as TVS, features Cantonese programs. Fujian Southeast TV (SETV) is a satellite channel with entertainment and news. Hunan Satellite TV (HTV) serves a younger audience with an entertainment format. China Yellow River TV (CYRTV) serves the college and university community. Phoenix Info News Channel broadcasts general and financial news in Mandarin, 24 hours a day.

There are many more channels in China's provinces and cities. In general, they provide news and Chinese entertainment programs.

Subscribers to the Star satellite service can watch ESPN Asia, Star Sports, Star Movies, and Star World (which features many U.S. sitcom reruns, plus fresh episodes of *American Idol*). In addition, there's the BBC World service, Cartoon Network Asia, AXN (Asian action adventure), Bloomberg, and other channels seen throughout Asia.

## OTHER ASIAN COUNTRIES

The key name in the Philippines is ABC-CBN, the country's leading channel and the basis for The Filipino Channel, now seen in millions of U.S. households. ABC-CBN also operates Kids Central, Knowledge Channel, and the leading Filipino satellite service.

Indonesia has become a kind of manufacturing center for Asian dramatic series, known here as "sinetrons." Thousands of sinetrons are produced annually, activity that keeps hundreds of production companies active. Domestically, RCTI (Rajawali Citra Televisi Indonesia) is the leading commercial television network, and SCTV (Surya Citra Televisi Indonesia) is consistently in second place. The noncommercial government station is TRI (Televisi Republika Indonesia).

Hong Kong is the world's third-largest film producer—a major center for Asian television activity. Many international television firms have their Asian headquarters in Hong Kong. Locally, ATV operates two channels: Home, which broadcasts in Chinese, and World, which broadcasts in English. ATV is also one of the largest Cantonese program suppliers in the world. TVB is the other terrestrial broadcaster. It operates two channels that each maintain a remarkably high audience share: a Cantonese channel (Jade, with 81 percent) and a principally English channel (Pearl, with 74 percent). TVB produces more Chinese-language programming than any other company, and employs over 5,000 people. On both ATV and TVB, programming is mostly original, with some acquisitions from the U.K., U.S., Australia, Europe, and Asia. RTHK (Radio Television Hong Kong) is a public broadcaster that exhibits its programming on these commercial stations. RHTK programming is curriculum-based and cultural in orientation, but some programs have become popular.

With 16 million households, Korea is becoming a presence as both a buyer and a seller of programs in the world marketplace. At home, KBS, the public broadcaster, operates four channels: two terrestrial and two satellite. TV1 is a news, culture, and current-affairs channel, and TV2 is a family channel. The commercial-free KBS 1 is funded by subscription fees that are automatically added to the household's electrical bill. KBS 2 is a cultural channel, heavy on drama and variety shows. Another public channel, and Korea's most popular channel overall, MBC (Munhwa Broadcasting Corporation) emphasizes dramas, the most popular genre in Korea, with over 300 hours per year. Commercial broadcasters include SBS (Seoul Broadcasting System) and iTV (Kyung-in Broadcasting Limited), both with 100 percent original Korean programming.

# CHAPTER 54
# LATIN AMERICA

As a television marketplace, Latin America is typically defined as Mexico, Central America, and South America, but not the Caribbean Islands. Apart from Portuguese-speaking Brazil, the entire region is Spanish-speaking. Mexico and Brazil are the most significant markets, but well-established local media companies dominate, and so they have not evolved as major program buyers. Venezuela, a comparatively small country in terms of population, is a significant producer of genre programming. A combination of economic issues and comparatively small populations has kept other Latin American countries on the sidelines of the world television marketplace.

One especially popular format associated with Latin American television is the *telenovela*. A *telenovela* is similar in style to the U.S. soap opera, but it runs for a finite number of episodes. A typical *telenovela* runs between 120 and 200 installments—up to about a year's supply of hour-long episodes—and when it's over, it's replaced by a new one. Over 12,000 *telenovela* hours are produced each year, about 20 percent of them in Mexico and about 15 percent in Brazil—two of the largest producers. It is a $2 billion production business.

## MEXICO

Mexico is the fourth-largest television market in the hemisphere, behind the U.S., Brazil, and Canada. With 21 million television households, it's the second-largest Latin American market.

Mexican television consists of one group of broadcast channels operated by the government and a second operated under government concession by Televisa, which takes in about two-thirds of Mexico's advertising revenues, and by the newer TV Azteca, which collects the remaining one-third. Both commercial networks are major exporters of Spanish-language programs to the world marketplace. This duopoly controls Mexican television. To do business in Mexico means doing business with Televisa and/or TV Azteca.

## Public Networks

Channel 11 is operated by the Instituto Politecnico Nacional (National Polytechnic Institute) and shows movies and cultural programs, more than half of them imported. It was Mexico's first public television station, in operation since 1958.

Imevision, or more formally, Instituto Mexicano de Televisión, began in 1972 with the founding of a rural television network and now operates three channels: 7, 13, and 22.

## Private Networks

Salvador Novo, who chaired the Television Committee that investigated possible industry models in the 1950s, later called radio "spiritual tequila" and defined television as "the monstrous daughter of the hidden intercourse between radio and cinema."

### Grupo Televisa

Grupo Televisa is Mexico's largest media company and top-rated television broadcaster. Headquartered in Mexico City, Televisa operates four commercial networks. Of the 260 local broadcast affiliates that carry it, 225 are either wholly or partially owned by Televisa. The company is also a 51 percent shareholder in Cablevisión, a large cable operator, and a 60 percent shareholder in Innova, which operates the SKY home satellite service (in fact, Televisa itself also owns 30 percent of SKY in Mexico). Televisa owns a smaller stake in the U.S. Spanish-language network Univision, and on the radio side is a 50 percent owner of 17 stations in Mexico. Televisa is also active in sports, with three soccer teams, and its own soccer stadium. Editorial Televisa is one of the largest publishers of Spanish-language magazines in the world. Televisa's 2003 net sales were equal to $2.3 billion U.S.

Grupo Televisa is controlled by its chairman and CEO, Emilio Azcárraga Jean, whose trust owns 49 percent of the company. This family empire began with 13 radio stations in regions close to the United States and maintained strong connections with American company RCA, which dominated American broadcasting at the time. Televisa was formed in 1973 as a result of a merger between Telesistema Mexicano and Television Independiente de Mexico.

Televisa is an enormous operation—certainly the largest in the Spanish-speaking world—with over 20,000 employees. It produces over 10,000 hours of new programming each year. This library has proven valuable; in 1995, for example, 50,000 hours of Televisa programs were sold to networks all around the world. Many of these hours were telenovelas.

In Mexico, Televisa operates Channel 2, a general-interest channel with many original programs produced in Televisa's large production complex. Popular series include *telenovelas*, game shows, news programs, sports coverage, and more.

During the month of January 2005, Channel 2's comedies occupied nine of the top ten ratings positions. Channel 4 relies upon movies, sports, and imported series, such as situation comedies from the U.S. Channel 5 airs cartoon series that completely dominate the children's ratings—mainly with imports, including *CatDog, Jimmy Neutron, Tiny Toons,* and *Bob esponja*—and also does well with movies. Channel 9, which debuted in 1994, also relies upon movies and imports for much of its schedule. In addition, Televisa's border stations are FOX affiliates.

Outside Mexico, Televisa operates Univision in the U.S.

### Grupo Salinas

For more than two decades, Televisa operated a near monopoly: It was the only viable commercial television network in Mexico. A 1994 change in government policy resulted in the privatization of two television channels (7 and 13) and a chain of motion picture theaters. In theory, the new private company was to be operated only by an experienced broadcaster. In practice, the winning bid came from an executive with experience in electronics and furniture. (This story is a convoluted lesson in Mexican politics.)

Ricardo Salinas, who won the bid, has built a substantial ($3.7 billion) media company around the initial assets. Groupo Salinas now includes two television networks operated by TV Azteca; two large cell phone suppliers (Unefon and Movil@ccess); the successful consumer electronics retailer Grupo Elektra (Salina's original company); a bank with nearly 1,000 branches (grown from the loan business at Grupo Elektra); and several Internet operations.

TV Azteca operates two national networks in Mexico: Azteca 13 is the general-interest channel, and Azteca 7 is a youth-oriented channel. In addition, TV Azteca operates two networks for Spanish-speakers outside Mexico: Azteca International is seen in many countries in Central and South America, and Azteca America is a popular program format for LPTV (low-power television stations), particularly in the western states. The Azteca America network is also seen via satellite and on some cable systems in the U.S., as well as on some LPTV channels in the U.S.

TV Azteca is a major producer of Spanish-language programs, particularly general entertainment and novellas, which are now seen in over 90 countries. *La Academia*, a talent "starmaker" series, is one of the company's biggest hits.

## Regulation of Mexican Television

The basis of television regulation in Mexico is found in Article 42 of the Mexican Constitution, which establishes state ownership of the airwaves, and in Article 7 of the older 1857 Constitution, which deals with freedom of the press. The current guiding laws were passed in 1960 as the Federal Law of Radio and Television.

The Mexican government maintains close control over broadcasting through the Communication and Transportation Ministry, which handles frequency allocations and other technical matters, and the Interior Ministry, which supervises program and operational practices. Even private stations must provide the government with 30 minutes per day for "social advertising"—promoting good health, for example. Network facilities must be made available to the president on his request, and emergencies must be broadcast. To avoid surrendering a percentage of company ownership to the federal government, commercial operators developed the concept of *fiscal time*; the government uses 12.5 percent of each commercial network's daily schedule for its cultural and educational programming.

## BRAZIL

Roughly 160 million people live in Brazil: about 18 million in the São Paulo metropolitan area, another 11 million in the Rio de Janiero metro, about 5 million in the Belo Horizonte area, 3 million in and near Salvador, and roughly the same number in and around Fortaleza. Many Brazilians live in smaller cities, towns, and rural areas. In a country where cable television is something of a luxury, broadcast television dominates.

On the public side, there are two dominant channels, São Paulo 's TV Cultura and Rio de Janiero's TV Educativa.

On the private side, the dominant force has always been TV Globo, but SBT (Sistema Brasileiro de Televisão) and several other channels are also popular. TV Cultura has been the bright light, with award-winning programs and high ratings (generally, it's number three after Globo and SBT).

The Brazilian government operates regional stations, but does not run a network as such. Funteve is the controlling body for many, but not all, of these stations. The private networks operate as government concessions, and are extremely careful about breaching their relationship by airing politically or morally sensitive programming.

### Rede Globo

TV Globo, part of the Brazilian media conglomerate Rede Globo, is the country's most successful private network—and one of the world's largest broadcast entities. A private company controlled by the Marinho family, Globo began in 1965 with a local Rio de Janiero television license, then acquired TV Paulista to expand into São Paulo, and continued this path until it covered just about all of Brazil's 5,000-plus municipal districts with over 100 owned or affiliated terrestrial television stations. Some affiliates use the TV Globo brand name, others do not.

Rede Globo takes in 75 percent of Brazil's television advertising dollars with astonishing (and remarkably consistent) audience shares: 74 in prime time, 59 in the afternoon, and almost never less than 50. *Telenovelas* are one reason why: *O Rei do Gado* gets a 50 share; some score even higher. These soap operas appear in prime time, generally three different series running each night, with stories told over the course of about 200 episodes. A sitcom called *Sai de Baixo* is one of Globo's most popular series. All of Brazil's top-ten series are Globo series, generally with audience shares in the high 30s. Nearly every hour seen on Globo is produced by the company in its own studios. The network employs 8,000 full-timers plus another 4,000 regular freelancers. Globo is the world's largest television producer, responsible for over 4,000 original hours annually. Globo produces more than eight hours per day of original programming—plus news programming.

TV Globo consistently achieves 65 percent audience share with original productions, but selected U.S. series have also done well, notably *Lois & Clark* and *ER*. Globo also supplies Globo News (24 hours a day on cable), Canal Rural (agricultural news and information), and Telecine 2 (a multi-channel pay movie service). In addition, Globo is involved in a music channel, a 50/50 venture with FOX Sports, and other typical ventures.

## Other Commercial Terrestrial Networks

SBT is Brazil's second biggest private network. Started up in 1981, it is led by popular TV host and politician Silvio Santos, who hosts one of the network's highest-rated series, a Sunday night variety show. SBT buys more U.S. series than Globo; their range of purchases includes sitcoms, dramas, and movies. SBT also imports *telenovelas* from Mexico's Televisa. Overall, the appeal is somewhat downscale.

Beating Globo is nearly impossible, so the smaller networks program against SBT instead. Bandeirantes and Manchete, which debuted in 1967 and 1983, respectively, vie for third place and get 5 percent to 10 percent of the audience. Other broadcast networks in Brazil include TV Gazeta and Rede Record (a commercial network owned by a wealthy Protestant church called Igreja Universal).

In Brazil, pay TV is a battle of media titans: Globo from the TV industry vs. the giant publisher Grupo Abril. TVA is an MSO owned by Abril and a partner in the DIRECTV Latin America venture expected to blanket Spanish- and Portuguese-speaking viewers with a 50-channel digital satellite system. Globo's NET Brasil is currently the largest cable MSO with nearly one million subscribers in about 50 systems; also on Globo's side are Mexico's Grupo Televisa and the U.S.'s TCI. Soccer is a primary driver of pay TV viewership; the Club of 13 (13 of Brazil's 16 most popular teams) negotiates as a block; the current deal, involving both free and pay TV, is worth $250 million over three years (1997–1999).

## Cable and Satellite Television

Cable television is a luxury for most Brazilians, in a country where most programs are still watched over the air. One interesting variation on the usual cable television distribution scheme is the nonexclusive nature of cable television within municipalities. Various cable companies compete for each household, and it is not unusual to find a single household subscribing to multiple cable systems.

In time, cable operator Horizon is likely to consolidate the many companies into a more powerful single operator.

Satellite television is supplied by DIRECTV and SKY television.

As in other Latin American countries, the available channels are primarily sourced from the U.S.-based cable television network operations. Here, they are presented with Portuguese soundtracks. SporTV is operated by Globo, but ESPN and FOX Sports also operate Latin American channels seen in Brazil.

## Independent Producers

There is a considerable movement toward independent production in Brazil. This is due, in part, to an incentive system related to very high taxes that must be paid in relation to the employment of full-time workers. Independent producers work with independent contractors, thus entirely avoiding the notion of employment (and the related taxes). This system allows independent producers to package programs at a considerably lower rate than the networks themselves.

## Regulation of Brazilian Television

Private networks and television stations in Brazil must be owned by Brazilian nationals, so international involvement in Brazilian television is limited to coproductions. Also, all foreign films must be dubbed into Portuguese before they are shown on the air. The regulatory agency is Anatel.

# VENEZUELA

Venezuela's major media player is the Cisneros Group, or more formally, Organización Diego Cisneros (ODC). The company owns Venevisión and is a major investor in the U.S. Spanish-language networks, Univision and Telefutura, and in DIRECTV Latin America. Cisneros is also a majority stockholder in Caracol, the leading Colombian network, and in Chilevisión. Other investments include AOL Latin America; Cerveceria Regional, the second largest brewery and beer distributor in Venezuela; another large Peruvian brewery; and one of the largest supermarket chains in Puerto Rico. In addition, Cisneros is the Venezuela franchisee for Pizza Hut and operates other consumer retail businesses. Cisneros also owns mining and natural resource companies, a large maker of plastic crates (for beer and beverage distribution), and more.

Venevisión Continental is seen throughout Latin America via satellite and cable television. Its programming consists of the best of Univision, Venevisión, Caracol, and Chilevisión.

Locally in Venezuela, the two primary commercial networks are RCTV (Radio Caracas TV) and Venevisión. It's a close race for viewer attention: RCTV averages roughly a 49 percent market share, but Venevisión is the market leader with 51 percent. Often, the ratings race is won or lost on the success of *tele-*

*novelas*, such as *Angel Rebelde* and *Camila* on Venevisión, or *¡Qué buena se puso Lola!* or *Mi Gorda Bella* on RCTV. Venevisión's capacity permits the production of between six and ten of the Spanish-language soap operas at any given time.

Venezuela's public channels are Canal 5 and CVTV.

## CABLE AND SATELLITE CHANNELS

Although over-the-air broadcasts in many Latin American countries are more limited than elsewhere, there is an abundance of Spanish-language channels available with a paid subscription to either a cable or satellite television service. Many of the channels seen on these services are based upon U.S. brands. Familiar names include: Warner Channel, Sony Este (east), Sony Oeste (west), Universal Channel, E! Entertainment, MTV, Cartoon Network, Disney Channel, CNN Español, CNN International, Nickeloden, Hallmark, TNT, MGM, Playboy TV, HBO Family and a suite of HBO and Cinemax channels, FOX Sports, ESPN, National Geographic, Bloomberg, various Discovery channels, The History Channel, and more. From Canada, there's Much Music (from the CHUM group); Fashion TV; and Locomotion, an action-oriented channel previously co-owned by Cisneros company Claxon Interactive and still co-owned by Hearst. From Sony Pictures Television International, there's the global AXN channel, which shows action and adventure film and television series. Jetix is a global children's channel from FOX that makes use of programs from FOX and from ABC cable networks. HTV is a Latin music channel seen in many countries throughout the region.

# APPENDICES

## USER'S GUIDE TO THE CONTRACT FORMS

These Appendices are devoted to contract forms and related materials, and are also available at www.thisbusinessoftelevision.com, where the forms can be downloaded. The forms cover many of the kinds of deals that an independent producer, actor, director, writer, or other television professional will have to make. For the most part, we have not included contracts relating to station, cable system, or DBS operations, on the theory that such entities are more likely to have the benefit of regular legal counsel to help educate them and initiate any drafting. We have also left out most long-form or otherwise complicated contracts, for similar reasons. Standard-form union and guild contracts can generally be obtained directly from the organization in question—Web contact information is located throughout the text at the appropriate section.

To highlight the important issues and customary terms of the deals, each section of the Appendices begins with an issue checklist to be used as a reminder when negotiating or drafting. The checklist includes issues that may not have been addressed in the short-form agreements that we have included. The contracts themselves are meant more as educational tools than as specific models to be copied verbatim.

Should the reader wish to use the contract forms as the basis for actual agreements, we urge you to proceed with caution. The match between the form in the book and your actual circumstance may be less than perfect. Most of the agreements we have included are relatively short and somewhat simplified. While this makes them more accessible, there are, by necessity, possible concerns that have not been addressed. Variations in applicable law may also require changes to the basic form. We recommend that the reader consult with an attorney about any specific application.

## APPENDIX 1.1:
# RIGHTS ACQUISITION (ISSUE CHECKLIST)

1. What rights are being granted?

- Rights in a preexisting property?

- Rights in a life story?

- Rights in a newly created work, such as a script?

- Rights of privacy and publicity?

- Rights to use name, likeness, and biography in advertising?

- Rights in a title?

- Rights to change, alter, and edit?

- Rights in any successor work?

- Is the grant exclusive?

- Is the grant irrevocable?

- Is there any obligation to use the material?

2. Are there any reserved rights?

- Live stage rights?

- Publication rights?

- Internet rights?

- Any holdbacks?

3. What markets and media are covered?

- All television, film, and related rights?

- Broadcast television?

- Standard cable?

- Pay cable?

- Multipoint service?

- Open video system and video dial tone?

- Home video?

- Business and educational video?

- Direct broadcast satellite?

- Multimedia?

- Internet streaming?

- Internet downloading?

- Other new technologies?

- Theatrical film?

- Book publishing?

- Merchandising?

4. What territories are covered?

- The whole universe?

- The U.S. and its territories and possessions?

- North America?

- English-speaking countries?

- Europe?

- Japan?

- China?

- India?

- Other specific territories?

5. Is the deal an option?

- How long is the option?

- Can it be extended?

- Will *force majeure* extend it?

- Are there successive dependent options?

- How is the option exercised?

6. Is it a firm deal?

- Are there any preconditions?

- Is it pay-or-play?

7. What payments must be made for the rights?

- Is there an option payment?

- Is there an option extension payment?

- Do the option payments apply against the purchase price?

- What is the purchase price?

- When is payment due?

- What uses does the purchase price cover?

- Will additional payments be due for additional uses or subsequent productions?

- Is a profit share or other back-end participation being granted?

- Are there any expenses to reimburse?

8. What representations and warranties should be given?

- Is the work original or in the public domain?

- Does the grantor own the rights and have the right to grant them?

- Does the work contain any libelous or slanderous material?

- Does the work violate any rights of privacy or publicity?

- Does either the work or its intended use violate any rights of any third parties?

9. Is either party giving an indemnity?

- Does the indemnity cover alleged breaches or only actual breaches?

- Does the indemnity cover attorneys' fees and costs?

- Who controls the defense and settlement of any claim?

10. Are the agreement and the rights granted assignable?

- If so, does the original purchaser remain liable?

11. Does the grantor get a credit?

- Is it in the lead or tail credits?

- Is it on a single card or is it shared?

- Is it a verbal credit?

- Is there any credit obligation in advertising and promotion?

- Are the consequences of a failure to give credit limited in the customary way?

12. Are there limitations on the grantor's remedies?

   - Are injunctions prohibited?

   - Is rescision prohibited?

13. Is there any union or guild involved?

   - If so, what impact does it have?

## SUBMISSION RELEASE LETTER

[Producer Letterhead]
[Date]
[Name and Address]

Dear _____,

As you know, _____ ("Producer") is engaged in the production of television programs for exploitation in any and all entertainment media. In this context, Producer reviews various source ideas, stories, and suggestions. Such material may relate to format, theme, characters, treatments, and/or means of exploiting a production once completed. In order to avoid misunderstandings, Producer will not review or discuss ideas, scripts, treatments, formats, or the like submitted to it on an unsolicited basis by persons not in its employ without first obtaining the agreement of the person submitting the material to the provisions of this letter.

By signing the enclosed copy of this letter and returning it to us, you hereby acknowledge and agree as follows:

1. You are submitting to Producer the following material for its review:

2. You warrant that you are the sole owner and author of the above described material and that you have the full right and authorization to submit it to Producer, free of any obligation to any third party.

3. You agree that any part of the submitted material which is not novel or original and not legally protected may be used by Producer without any liability on its part to you and that nothing herein shall place Producer in any different position with respect to such non-novel or original material by reason hereof.

4. Producer shall not be under any obligation to you with respect to the submitted material except as may later be set forth in a fully executed written agreement between you and Producer.

5. You realize that Producer has had and will have access to and/or may independently create or have created ideas identical to the theme, plot, idea, format or other element of the material now being submitted by you and you agree that you will not be entitled to any compensation by reason of the use by Producer of such similar or identical material.

Very truly yours,
[Producer]

By:
AGREED TO AND ACCEPTED:
By:
Date:

## APPENDIX 1.3:
## PERSONAL RELEASE

1. BASIC INFORMATION
   Program:
   Production Company:
   Its Address:
   Individual Giving Release:
   His/Her Address:
   His/Her Age (check one): Over 18___    Under 18___

2. RELEASE
   The undersigned individual hereby grants to the above named Production Company, and its successors, licensees and assigns, the perpetual and irrevocable right to use the undersigned's name, likeness, voice, biography and history, factually or otherwise, and under a real or a fictitious name, in connection with the production, distribution and exploitation of the Program, and of any elements of the Program and any remakes or sequels based on the Program. Such grant includes use in advertising in connection with the foregoing, and use in any and all media, whether now existing or hereafter devised, throughout the universe. It also includes the right to make such changes, fictionalizations and creative choices as the Production Company may decide in its sole discretion.

   The undersigned individual: (i) agrees not to bring any action or claim against the Production Company, or its successors, licensees and assigns, or to allow others to bring such an action or claim, based on the Program or the depiction of the undersigned in the Program or the use of material relating to the undersigned in the Program or as otherwise described above, and (ii) releases the Production Company, its successors, licensees and assigns, from any and all such actions or claims that the undersigned may have now or in the future.

   The undersigned acknowledges the receipt of good and valuable consideration for the release and other grants and agreements made herein, and understands that the Production Company is relying on them in proceeding with the production and exploitation of the Program and elements thereof as authorized above. The undersigned warrants that the use of the rights granted hereunder and of any material supplied by the undersigned will not violate the rights of any third party.

3. SIGNATURE AND DATE
   Signature:
   Date:

## APPENDIX 1.4:
# SHORT-FORM RIGHTS OPTION AGREEMENT

Dear [Author]:

This letter, when signed by you, will confirm our agreement for an _____ option for us to acquire the exclusive television, film and allied rights in the work written by you (the 'Work'), and described in the attached Exhibit A, on the following terms:

1. In return for $_____, you are giving us the exclusive option for ___ months from the date of this letter to acquire the exclusive television, video, film, electronic streaming and downloading, multimedia and allied rights for the Work, in perpetuity, for exploitation worldwide in all media.

2. Should we exercise our option, we will give you notice and pay you a fee of $_____, less the amount described in Paragraph 1 above.

3. If we exercise our option, we will have the right to produce or co-produce one or more projects based on the Work, adapted as we feel necessary, or to license the production to any other producer, broadcaster, etc. We will have the right to use your name and likeness in publicizing any such production.

4. You do not grant us any literary publishing rights in the Work, other than the right to use customary excerpts and synopses in connection with productions. You warrant that the grant of rights you are making, and our exploitation of those rights as provided herein, will not infringe on the rights of any third party.

5. It is our intention to enter into a longer agreement containing these and other terms customary in the entertainment industry, but unless and until such a longer agreement is fully signed by both you and us, this letter will be the complete agreement between us.

Yours sincerely,
[Production Company]


By:
[Producer]


AGREED TO AND ACCEPTED:
[Author]


[Note: Attach Exhibit A describing the Work]

## DEVELOPMENT, DISTRIBUTION, AND FINANCE AGREEMENTS (ISSUE CHECKLIST)

1. What media are covered?

- All television, film, and related rights?

- Broadcast television?

- Standard cable?

- Pay cable?

- Multipoint services?

- Open video and video dial tone?

- Home video?

- Business and educational video?

- Direct broadcast satellite?

- Multimedia?

- Internet streaming?

- Internet downloading?

- Other new technologies?

- Theatrical film?

- Book publishing?

- Merchandising?

2. What territories are covered?

- The whole universe?

- The U.S. and its territories and possessions?

- North America?

- English-speaking countries?

- Europe?

- Japan?

- China?

- India?

- Other specific territories?

3. Are there any holdbacks or restrictions on rights, or territories not granted?

4. What is the term of the distribution contract?

- Is it for a term of years?

- Is it for the life of the copyright?

- Can it be canceled if the distributor defaults?

5. Is the distributor providing production finance?

- If so, what is the schedule of funding?

- Will the distributor have a financial representative on the set?

- Will the distributor take a security interest in the program and all related rights?

- Will the distributor require a completion bond?

- Will the distributor have the right to take over the production if the producer goes over budget?

- How will the investment be recouped?

- What share of profits or other back-end participation will be paid for this finance?

- Is a bankable pick-up guaranty being provided instead of cash advances?

6. What input will the distributor have into the production process? (In general, the more finance being provided, the more the input.)

- What production elements (writer, script, director, cast, designers, director of photography, music) are subject to distributor approval?

- What business elements (locations, facilities, labs) are subject to approval?

- Is the budget subject to approval?

- Are any individual agreements subject to approval?

- Are the producer's fees and overheads subject to approval?

- Is there a distributor overhead factor or production fee?

- Will the distributor bring the production in-house?

7. What are the required delivery items?

  - What are the technical items, tape masters, etc.?

  - Is a lab letter needed?

  - What are the nontechnical items, such as script, publicity materials, cue sheets, cast lists, credit lists, residual schedules, E&O insurance certificate?

8. What input does the producer have into the distribution process?

  - Will there be consultation or approval over publicity?

  - Does the producer approve the deals?

  - Are there minimum targets?

  - Does the producer approve any sub-distributors?

  - Is there any obligation to distribute, or termination for inactivity?

9. When does revenue start to be counted?

  - On actual receipt in the U.S.?

  - On receipt by a subsidiary or affiliate?

  - How are blocked funds in foreign countries handled?

  - Are there any deductions for taxes or other charges off the top?

10. What is the distributor's fee?

  - Is it the customary percentage of gross revenues?

  - Does it vary by territory and medium?

  - Is it inclusive of the fees of any sub-distributors, particularly affiliates?

11. What expenses can the distributor deduct?

  - Are there any caps?

  - Are the costs of physical distribution covered (tapes, satellite time, etc.)?

  - Are the costs of publicity and marketing covered?

  - Are there any limits on conference, sales market, and other travel and entertainment costs?

- Can the distributor deduct for interest, taxes, and a distribution overhead?

- Does the distributor pay and recover residuals, reuse fees, and music performance license costs?

- Who pays for initial and ongoing E&O insurance coverage?

- Who pays any litigation and collection costs?

12. How does the distributor recoup any advances and share in profits?

- Does the distributor recoup in the first position or does it share, *pari passu* or by some other formula, with other financing sources?

- Is any interest charged on outstanding amounts?

- How are profits determined?

- Does the distributor, producer, or any other party share in revenues on a different basis (gross, adjusted gross, etc.)?

13. What kinds of reports and accountings are given?

- How frequently?

- How detailed?

- What are the rights to audit these statements and the distributor's books and records?

- When do statements become unchallengeable?

14. What representations and warranties should be given?

- Is the program original and protected by copyright?

- Have all the necessary rights and clearances, including music rights, been obtained?

- Does the producer own the rights that are being granted free and clear, and does he/she have the right to grant them?

- Does the program contain any defamatory material?

- Does the program violate any rights of privacy or publicity?

- Does the program or its intended distribution violate any other rights of any third parties?

15. Is either party giving an indemnity?

- Does the indemnity cover alleged breaches, or only actual breaches?

- Does the indemnity cover attorneys' fees and costs?

- Who controls the defense and settlement of any claim?

16. Are the agreement and the rights granted assignable?

- If so, does the original distributor remain liable?

- Are sub-distributors permitted?

17. Are there limitations on the producer's remedies?

- Are injunctions prohibited?

- Can the rights revert on termination, or is rescision prohibited?

18. Are there any rights with respect to further projects, such as sequels, remakes, series, spin-offs, etc.?

# APPENDIX 2.2:
## SHORT-FORM DEVELOPMENT DEAL

This agreement between _____ ("Purchaser") and _____
("Producer") sets forth the terms of the agreement between them concerning
the development and production of the television project tentatively entitled
(the "Program"):

1. *The Program:* The Program as currently envisioned consists of:

2. *Development Steps:* Upon the authorization of Purchaser as indicated for each
   successive step, Producer will take the following development steps:

   (a) Step 1:
   Action [indicate step or steps to be taken, e.g., treatment, budget, script,
   rewrite, etc.].

   Completion Dates.

   Approval Dates [date for Purchaser to approve and commission next
   step, require a rewrite (if applicable), or cancel; date typically tied to
   completion date of step].

   Personnel [i.e., a named writer or production person or person to be
   designated by one or both parties at the time].

   Fees and Expenses Paid by Purchaser [can be a fixed amount, all
   approved costs, a mixture of the two, or some other approach; list
   payment schedule].

   Other Agreed Points.

   (b) Step 2:
   [Same list. Repeat as necessary for additional steps.]

3. *Production Commitment:* Upon the completion and approval of the final step
   set forth above, or at any other time during the development process mutually
   agreed between Purchaser and Producer, Purchaser shall have the exclusive
   right to commission the production of the Program by Producer, in accordance
   with the terms and conditions set out in the Agreement attached as Exhibit A.
   All major business and creative elements, including, without limitation, the
   budget, production schedule, facilities and locations, cast, production manager,
   director, writer and heads of technical departments, will be subject to the
   mutual approval of Purchaser and Producer. Such approvals may be given at
   any time in the development process. Should Purchaser and Producer fail to
   agree on any such points within a reasonable time after good-faith negotiation,
   then such failure to agree shall constitute a cancellation of development.

4. *Cancellation and Turnaround:* Should development be canceled, either by a failure by Purchaser to approve and commit to the next step under Paragraph 2 within the required time or by a failure by Purchaser to agree on a major business or creative element under Paragraph 3, then all rights in the program will revert to Producer, subject only to the right of the Purchaser to receive the following amounts should there be a production of the Program or of any other project substantially based on, or directly derived from, the Program:

   (a) from the production budget, upon the first day of taping, shooting or principal photography, Purchaser shall be reimbursed for all fees and expenses paid by Purchaser to Producer under this agreement, together with interest at the rate of ___ % per year on the balance of such fees and expenses outstanding from time to time (such interest not to exceed, in the aggregate, 100% of such fees and expenses); and

   (b) the following interest in the net profits, adjusted gross or other "back-end" formula from the revenues of the project, calculated and paid on a favored-nations basis with all other recipients of such a revenue interest, including the Producer and financing entity of the project, expressed as a percent of one-hundred percent of such revenue interest:

   > if Step 1 is completed, ___ %;
   > if Step 2 is completed, ___ %;
   > [etc.].

5. *Development Process:* During the development process (i.e., for so long as Purchaser has continuing rights under Paragraph 2), Purchaser may approach any third parties concerning finance, transmission or any other aspect of distribution of the Program. If any of such approach leads to a "pitch" or other formal presentation of the Program, Purchaser will involve Producer directly, and Producer will provide all reasonable assistance. Purchaser will pay the reasonable expenses of a representative of Producer attending a formal presentation, which occurs outside of the metropolitan area. During the development process, neither party will make any third-party commitment on any matter relating to the Program requiring mutual approval without the agreement of the other.

6. *Representations and Warranties:* Producer represents and warrants that (i) it is free to enter into and to perform this agreement; and (ii) the Program and any material to be included in the Program (other than material provided by Purchaser) is and will be either owned by Producer, or in the public domain, or fully cleared with respect to all applicable rights, and their use and exploitation as contemplated hereunder will not violate the rights of any third party. Purchaser represents and warrants that (i) it is free to enter into

and to perform this agreement; and (ii) any material provided by it to be included in the Program is and will be either owned by Purchaser, in the public domain, or fully cleared with respect to all applicable rights, and their use and exploitation as contemplated hereunder will not violate the rights of any third party.

7. *Miscellaneous:*

(a) The addresses, including phone and fax, of each of the parties are as follows:

    Purchaser:
    Producer:

(b) Notices and other communications hereunder may be sent by certified mail, personal delivery, courier service, e-mail, or fax, to the address specified above or such other address as may be specified by notice and will be effective upon delivery at such address or upon return, if undeliverable at such address.

(c) This agreement will be subject to the laws of the State of _____ applicable to contracts signed and to be performed solely within such state. It sets forth the full and complete agreement of the parties relating to the Program. It may not be modified except by a writing signed by the party against which the change is asserted.

(d) All payment to Producer hereunder will be sent to:

IN WITNESS WHEREOF, the parties have executed this agreement as of the date set forth below.

DATE:

[Purchaser]              [Producer]
By:                        By:
Title:                   Title:

[Note: Exhibit A should consist of the applicable form of production finance/distribution agreement or license. The form in Appendix 2.3, which follows and is part of this agreement, may be used.]

## TELEVISION DISTRIBUTION/FINANCE AGREEMENT

## Term Sheet

1. PARTIES:

   Distributor:  (hereinafter "Distributor")

   Producer:  (hereinafter "Producer")

2. ADDRESSES (with phone, fax, and e-mail):

   Distributor:

   Producer:

3. PROGRAM(S):

   (hereinafter the "Program(s)")

4. MEDIA (strike out anything non-applicable): (a) all television (including video); (b) theatrical; (c) Internet streaming and downloading; (d) multimedia; (e) book publishing; (f) and all other media, now existing or hereafter invented; (g) licensing and merchandising; and (h) except for:

5. TERRITORY:

   The whole universe except for:

6. TERM: _____, thereafter terminable per the Standard Terms.

7. PRODUCTION FINANCE/ADVANCE (if any):

8. PRODUCTION PROCEDURES (attach additional sheet(s), if necessary):

   Distributor Approvals:

   Approved Elements:

   Credits:

   Schedule:

   Budget:

   Overheads:

   Music Rights:

   Production Insurance:

   Completion Bond:

   Other Requirements:

9. REPORTING PERIODS:

10. DELIVERY ITEMS AND DATES (attach additional sheet(s), if necessary):

11. STANDARD TERMS:

    The attached Standard Terms are hereby incorporated by reference into this Agreement, subject only to any express modifications or additions set forth in this Term Sheet, including the following (attach additional sheet(s) if necessary):

12. COMPLETE AGREEMENT:

This Term Sheet, together with the attached Standard Terms and any Exhibits, constitutes the sole and complete agreement between the parties concerning the Program(s).

13. APPLICABLE LAW:

This agreement shall be construed according to the laws of the following State applicable to contracts made and wholly to be performed therein:

14. SIGNATURES:

Distributor:     Producer:

By:        By:

Name:       Name:

Title:       Title:

## Standard Terms

1. GRANT OF RIGHTS

Producer hereby grants to Distributor the exclusive right to distribute, license, market and exploit the Programs and all elements thereof in the Media and in the Territory. These rights include the rights to dub the Programs into foreign languages, and to make cuts and edits to meet standards and practices, censorship and time segment requirements, provided that Distributor shall not delete the credits or copyright notice as they may appear in the Programs.

2. MEDIA

The licensed media (the "Media") shall be those set forth in the Term Sheet. The grant of television rights shall permit Distributor to exploit the Programs and all elements thereof in all forms of television now or hereafter known, including but not limited to free television, cable television, pay cable television, pay-per-view television, subscription television, over-the-air pay television, open video system television, television via telephone and/or the Internet, video dial tone, closed circuit television, master antenna television, multipoint service television, direct broadcast satellite television, armed forces, in-flight use, video cassettes and video discs for home use, and non-theatrical educational sales (collectively "Television Rights").

3. LICENSED TERRITORY

The territory described in paragraph 5 of the Term Sheet shall constitute the "Licensed Territory."

## 4. TERM

The initial term of this Agreement is as set forth in paragraph 6 of the Term Sheet. The Agreement shall thereafter renew itself automatically for further periods of one (1) year, which renewal periods shall be subject to the right of termination by either party, at the end thereof, by the giving at least of ninety (90) days written notice to the other party.

## 5. DISTRIBUTION

Distributor shall seek in good faith, subject to Distributor's reasonable business judgment, to maximize the exploitation of the rights granted hereunder. Notwithstanding the foregoing, Distributor shall have the sole control over all distribution activities, and may at any time suspend or resume active distribution of the Programs, as it deems fit, without any penalty.

## 6. DELIVERY

Producer shall deliver to Distributor the delivery items described in paragraph 10 or in the Term Sheet and any other elements of each of the Programs that may be reasonably necessary for Distributor to perform Distributor's services hereunder. Except as preapproved in the Term Sheet, the Programs as delivered shall be subject to Distributor's sole approval for acceptance.

## 7. DISTRIBUTION FEES

(a) In consideration for the services Distributor is rendering to Producer hereunder, Distributor shall retain as its sole and exclusive property from all exploitation of the Programs the distribution fees described on Exhibit A attached hereto.

(b) In calculating such fees, "gross sales" shall be defined to mean all revenue (without any deductions), generated by the exploitation of the Programs by Distributor, including the gross amounts received by any of its subsidiaries or affiliates acting as sub-distributors, sub-licensees and agents. The commissions indicated above are maximum commissions for Distributor and any such subsidiaries or affiliates. If Distributor uses unaffiliated sub-distributors, sub-licensees, agents, etc., however, the fees of such entities shall not be subject to any limitation, but shall be deducted prior to calculating gross sales. Distributor and its subsidiaries and affiliates may take fees for additional services undertaken by them connected with the distribution of the Program, including fees for placing advertising in connection with syndication, provided that such fees shall not exceed those customary in the industry and shall not be subject to the limitations set forth above and shall be deducted before calculating gross sales.

(c) To the extent that Distributor may grant licenses longer than the term of this Agreement or, if this Agreement shall be terminated early for any reason, Distributor shall be entitled to receive commissions due to it in respect of all agreements, and extensions and renewals thereof, for exploitation of the Program in the Licensed Territory, and made by or on behalf of the Producer between the dates of the commencement and termination of the rights granted to Distributor hereunder.

## 8. DISTRIBUTION COSTS AND EXPENSES

After deduction of the fees described in paragraph 7 above, Distributor shall recoup from gross sales of the Programs all distribution costs and expenses that have been advanced or incurred by Distributor in connection with the distribution of the Programs hereunder.

The foregoing distribution costs and expenses shall include, without limitation, a pro rata share of festival and market expenses, costs incurred in connection with promotional cassettes, sales and withholding taxes, shipping of promotional material, the manufacture of prints and video-tapes, music and effects tracks, script duplication, publicity material, bank transfer charges, dubbing and production of foreign language tracks, advertising expenses and legal and agent fees.

Producer shall bear the cost of all rerun, reuse, residual and other similar payments required by any applicable union or guild agreement relative to persons performing services in the production of the Programs. Producer shall supply distributor with an accurate list of all recipients and rates of residuals and other similar payments. Distributor shall supply Producer with all necessary reports and information required to calculate and make such payments.

## 9. RECOUPMENT OF ADVANCES

After the deduction of the amounts set forth in paragraphs 7 and 8 above, Distributor shall recoup from the remaining proceeds to it from the Programs the Production Advance, together with interest thereon, as specified in paragraph 13 hereof.

## 10. REPORTS, PAYMENTS AND ACCOUNTINGS

(a) Distributor shall report and account to Producer in writing within forty-five (45) days after the end of each reporting period as set forth in the Term Sheet. A separate report will be issued for each of the Programs, although a series may be reported as a single unit. The reports shall contain reasonable detail and shall conform to customary industry practice.

(b) After retaining Distributor's fees and recouping the distribution costs and production finance as provided in paragraphs 7, 8, 9 and 13 hereof, Distributor shall attach to the report(s) a check payable to Producer in the appropriate amount for the balance of gross sales received during the period covered by the report(s). With respect to blocked or restricted funds, Distributor will report such funds to Producer and, to the extent permitted by applicable law, Producer will have the right to require Distributor to deposit Producer's share of such funds in a bank account established by Producer in the country where such funds are blocked or restricted.

(c) Distributor shall keep true, complete and accurate books of account and records pertaining to all financial transactions in connection with the performance of Distributor's obligations under this Agreement. Such books and records shall be available for inspection by Producer or its representatives at Distributor's place of business during normal business hours at a time or times mutually acceptable. No more than one such inspection shall occur within any twelve (12) month period, no statement shall be open to challenge later than two years after its receipt by the Producer, and no inspection shall be made as to any given statement more than once. Producer or its representatives shall have the right to make copies of the pertinent parts of all such books and records that directly relate to such financial transactions.

## 11. COPYRIGHT AND COPIES

(a) Producer shall ensure that its copyright in each of the Programs is properly protected and registered, if required, in any market in which the Programs are distributed.

(b) Distributor will not duplicate or otherwise reproduce the Programs in any manner, nor permit any of its sub-licensees to do so, except specifically in connection with the distribution of the Programs as permitted hereunder. Distributor will provide in all license agreements that its licensees will return any prints or tapes distributed by Distributor, or submit an affidavit of erasure or destruction, promptly after the expiration of the period of use permitted to any of such licensees. Distributor will use its reasonable efforts to obtain the return of such items or the submission of such affidavit.

## 12. WARRANTY AND INSURANCE

(a) Producer warrants that it has the right to enter into this agreement and that it has the right to grant Distributor the rights granted herein and that Distributor's exercise of those rights will not infringe or violate the rights of any third party.

(b) Producer warrants that it has obtained the necessary music synchro-nization and performance licenses for the exploitation of the Programs as contemplated herein other than those customarily licensed through a performing rights society; and that all musical compositions in the Programs are controlled by ASCAP, BMI or another performing rights society having jurisdiction, or are in the public domain, or are con-trolled by Producer (in which case performance licenses therefor are hereby granted at no cost to Distributor).

(c) Producer will maintain a standard Errors and Omissions insurance policy for the Programs during the term hereof having limits of not less than One Million Dollars ($1,000,000) for any single occurrence and of not less than Three Million Dollars ($3,000,000) for all occurrences taking place in any one year. Such insurance shall provide for coverage of Distributor, its affiliated companies and the officers, directors, agents and employees of the same.

(d) Distributor warrants that it has the right to enter into this Agreement.

13. PRODUCTION FINANCE
(a) As used herein, "Production Advance" shall refer to all sums advanced or paid by Distributor in connection with the production of the Programs, including (but not limited to) all amounts advanced to Producer under the Term Sheet and any residuals, royalties and/or clearance costs, insurance premiums, attorneys' fees and/or any other production related costs paid or advanced by Distributor in its sole discretion.

(b) Interest shall accrue on the Production Advance from time to time outstanding until repaid or recouped at a rate equal to the Prime Rate declared by Distributor's principal bank from time to time plus two percent (2%).

(c) Producer shall deliver the Programs as set forth in the Term Sheet. Producer shall be solely responsible for any costs relating to the Programs that exceed the amount of the Production Advance agreed to in the Term Sheet for the Programs.

(d) In the event Producer fails to deliver any of the Programs as provided in this agreement or is otherwise in material breach of this Agreement, then without limiting any other right or remedy of Distributor, Distributor shall be entitled to demand, and Producer shall immedi-ately thereupon pay to Distributor, the then outstanding amount of the Production Advance on any Program not yet delivered at the time of such demand, together with interest thereon as set forth above.

(e) To secure Producer's full and complete performance hereunder and any and all amounts owing to Distributor hereunder, Producer hereby grants Distributor a first priority lien and security interest in all right, title and interest in and to the Programs and each Program, and all elements, properties and proceeds thereof, whether now in existence or hereafter coming into being, and wherever located, including (but not limited to):

(i) the copyright in and to each Program;

(ii) all print, sound and/or videotape copies and/or elements of or relating to the Programs whether now or hereafter in existence and wherever located;

(iii) all literary property rights and ancillary rights as specified herein in relation to the Programs including, without limitation, all right, title and interest of Producer in the teleplays of the Programs;

(iv) all right, title and interest of Producer in the music used in the Programs to the extent of Producer's rights therein;

(v) all contract rights of Producer relating to the Programs in any and all media throughout the world as set forth herein;

(vi) all proceeds of the Programs and of any of the elements of the Programs referred to in (i) through (v) above, including without limitation all income and receipts derived and to be derived from the marketing, distribution, exhibition, exploitation and sale of the Programs and of said elements thereof, and all proceeds of insurance relating to the Programs and said elements thereof.

Producer agrees to execute such financing statements and/or other instruments as Distributor deems necessary or appropriate to perfect such security interest, and irrevocably appoints Distributor its attorney-in-fact to execute any such instruments in Producer's name should Producer fail or refuse to do so promptly on Producer's request.

(f) In the event Producer is in material default of this Agreement or materially breaches any of its obligations hereunder, then without limiting any other right or remedy of Distributor, Distributor shall have the right, but not the obligation, to take over and manage production of any or all of the Programs, without any obligation to Distributor as to the results of its efforts.

14. INDEMNIFICATION
   (a) Producer shall indemnify and hold Distributor harmless from and against any demand, claim, action, liability and expense (including rea-

sonable attorneys' fees) arising out of Producer's breach of any of the representations, warranties or provisions contained in this Agreement; provided that Distributor shall promptly notify Producer of any such demand, claim, etc., and that Producer shall have the right to control the defense and to approve any settlement thereof.

(b) Distributor shall defend, indemnify and hold Producer harmless from and against any demand, claim, action, liability and expense (including reasonable attorneys' fees) arising out of Distributor's breach of any of the representations, warranties or provisions contained in this Agreement; provided that Producer shall promptly notify Distributor of any such demand, claim, etc., defense and to approve any settlement thereof.

## 15. PRODUCER REMEDIES

The rights granted to Distributor hereunder are irrevocable, and the sole remedy of Producer in the case of a default by Distributor shall be an action for monetary damages.

## 16. NOTICES

Any notice required to be given hereunder shall be given by receipted fax, confirmed e-mail or certified mail to the parties at their respective addresses set forth in the Term Sheet or at such other address as either party may hereafter notify the other. Any notice sent by e-mail or by fax shall be deemed given on the day such notice is faxed or e-mailed. Any notice sent by certified mail shall be deemed given three business days after such notice is mailed.

## 17. NO PARTNERSHIP

This agreement shall not be construed so as to constitute a partnership or a joint venture between the parties hereto, and no party is deemed to be the representative or the agent of the other except as herein otherwise provided.

## 18. LAB LETTER

Producer shall supply Distributor with a lab access letter covering all material relating to the Program. Such letter shall be in form acceptable to Distributor in its reasonable discretion.

## EXHIBIT A: SCHEDULE OF DISTRIBUTION FEES

1. All Television Rights Except 2 and 3 Below:

(a) for sales in the United States:

(i) ____ % of gross sales for a national sale.

(ii) ____ % of gross sales for a syndicated sale.

(b) for sales in Australia, Canada and/or the United Kingdom:

    (i) ___ % gross sales for a national sale.

    (ii) ___ % of gross sales for a syndicated sale.

(c) for sales in all other countries: ___ % of gross sales.

2. For armed forces, in-flight and any other ancillary television use: ___ % of gross sales.

3. For videocassettes and videodiscs and other devices for home use and non-theatrical educational uses: ___ % of gross sales, provided that if Distributor or its subsidiary or affiliate actually manufactures and distributes the cassettes and/or discs, gross sales shall be deemed to equal 20% of actual retail sales, subject to Distributor's customary adjustments.

4. For theatrical release: ___ % of gross sales.

5. For licensing and merchandising: ___ % of gross sales.

## APPENDIX 2.4:
## SHORT-FORM HOME VIDEO LICENSE
## [WITHOUT INTERNET DOWNLOAD]

This agreement, when executed by the parties identified below as the Licensor and the Licensee, will set forth the terms of the agreement between them concerning the license of home video rights in the Program(s) described below.

1. Licensor Name, Address, E-mail, Phone and Fax:

2. Licensee Name, Address, E-mail, Phone and Fax:

3. Title and Description of the Program(s):

4. Distribution, Licensed Media; Territory; Term: The Licensor hereby grants to the Licensee the exclusive right to distribute the Program(s) in all aspects of home video, including tape, disc, chip and any other similar tangible medium capable of being played by an individual consumer on a home viewing device without transmission from a remote point:

   (a) in the following territories:

   (b) and for the following term:

   (c) subject to the following exclusions (if any):

   Except as expressly provided in paragraph 9, Licensee will have sole control over the exercise of its home video rights hereunder, provided, however, that if Licensee ceases to actively distribute the Program(s) hereunder, and fails to recommence active distribution within three months of a written request to do so from the Licensor, then the rights granted hereunder to Licensee shall terminate and revert to Licensor.

5. Advance and Royalties: The Licensee will pay to the Licensor the following consideration for the license granted hereunder:

   (a) An advance in the amount of $_____, payable upon delivery of the items specified in Exhibit A hereto.

   (b) A royalty at the rate of ___ %, to be calculated and paid in accordance with the procedures specified in Exhibit B hereto.

6. Publicity and Advertising: During the term hereof, Licensee will have the right to use the names, likeness and other attributes of personality of the performers appearing in the Program(s) and of the producer, director, writer and other principal off-screen contributors to the program in connection with advertising and publicity, for the distribution of the Program(s)

hereunder. Licensee agrees not to alter the titles and credits contained in the Program(s) (other than to add its own credit as video distributor at the very beginning and/or end of the Program(s)), and will abide by (and will require, as a matter of contract, all sub-distributors and other entities in the chain of distribution to abide by) all of the credit requirements specified in Item 2 of Exhibit A. No inadvertent or third-party failure to abide by such credit requirements will be a breach of this agreement provided that Licensee takes all reasonable steps to correct any such failure upon learning of it.

7. Warranties: The Licensor warrants that (i) it is free to enter into and to perform this agreement; and (ii) the Program(s) and any material contained in the Program(s) is either owned by Licensor, or in the public domain, or fully cleared with respect to all applicable rights, and their use and exploitation as contemplated hereunder will not violate the rights of any third party. In this regard, the Licensor agrees to pay any and all residuals, reuse, music or other similar rights fees or costs related to the exploitation and distribution of the Program(s) hereunder, except as may be expressly provided in Paragraph 9. The Licensee warrants that it is free to enter into and to perform this agreement.

8. Limits on Remedies: Except as otherwise expressly provided in this agreement, all grants of rights hereunder are irrevocable during the Term, and Licensor waives all rights to any equitable relief in connection with any breach or termination of this agreement. The foregoing shall not apply in the case of a breach of this agreement by the Licensee, not subject to unresolved litigation or dispute in good faith, which continues uncured for a period of one month following written notice of such breach to Licensee from Licensor.

9. Additional Provisions: The following additional provisions shall apply (include any agreements on approvals of the distribution process, designs, rights payments, and any other further agreements; if none, write "none"):

10. Miscellaneous: This agreement will be subject to the laws of the State of applicable to contracts signed and to be performed solely within such state. It sets forth the full and complete agreement of the parties relating to the license described herein. It may not be modified except by a writing signed by the party against which the change is asserted.

Dated:

LICENSOR  
By:  
Title:

LICENSEE  
By:  
Title:

EXHIBIT A
[Insert delivery requirements here]

EXHIBIT B
ROYALTIES:

Royalties will be calculated and paid in accordance with the following provisions:

1. Retail Price and Sale Date. Subject to the adjustments set forth below, the royalty will be calculated based on the suggested retail price of the Program(s) sold. In the case of a direct retail sale by Licensee or its affiliates, the retail price will be that actually received. A sale will be deemed to have occurred and a royalty will be payable, upon receipt by the Licensee or an affiliate of the purchase price for the item sold (or upon the accrual of any offset or other non-cash consideration), but reasonable amounts may be held in a good faith reserve for returns, if permitted, for a period not to exceed six months.

2. Adjustments. The retail price will be adjusted in the case of sales made at discount, remainder or other bona fide exceptions to Licensee's normal practices. In such a case, the retail price will be deemed to be twice the amounts actually received by Licensee or its affiliates from such a sale at wholesale, or, if Licensee or an affiliate makes the retail sale in such a circumstance, the retail price will be the amount actually received.

3. Payments and Reports. Licensee will provide written reports of sales, income and the royalty payable at the following intervals:

   All accrued royalties will fast be applied to the recoupment of any advance paid on the Program(s), and then will be paid by check included with the applicable statement.

4. Accountings. Licensee will keep complete and accurate records of the financial transactions relating to the Program(s), and shall not destroy such records for at least five years. Licensor will have the right to conduct an inspection of such books and records of the Licensee to verify the accuracy of the reports at Licensee's normal business premises during normal business hours, once within any twelve-month period. No report can be challenged any later than two years after it has been received by Licensor.

# SALES REPRESENTATIVE LETTER AGREEMENT

[Producer Letterhead]
[Representative Name and Address]

Dear _____,

This letter, when signed by you, will set forth the agreement between us concerning your acting as a sales representative for us in connection with the Programs described below, on the following terms:

1. Programs Covered. This agreement covers the following programs (the "Programs"):

2. Markets and Media Covered. This agreement covers sales and licenses of the Programs in the following markets (the "Markets') and media (the "Media") (describe the degree of exclusivity, if any, for each):

3. Term. The term of this agreement is as follows:

4. Sales Duties. You agree to use your best efforts to seek potential buyers and licensees (collectively "Buyers") for the Programs in the Markets and Media. Once you have identified a prospective Buyer, you will inform us of its identity and degree of interest. Although you will assist us in pursuing the possible sale or license, you will have no authority to finalize or enter into any agreement with the Buyer on our behalf, except as we may expressly grant by a separate written authorization.

5. Compensation. If we close a sale or license, either during the Term or within months of the end of the Term, of any of the Programs with a Buyer introduced to us by you hereunder for any of the Media and Markets, we will pay you a fee of ___ % of the amounts actually received by us during the Term and any time thereafter from such sale or license. We will pay you this fee within    days of our receipt of good funds on the payment to which it relates. Such fee shall be calculated and paid net of (describe any deductions which come off the top or from the sales representative's share):

6. Limits on Sales Representative. Nothing in this agreement will constitute you our agent or attorney in fact. You will not hold yourself out as having any greater authority with respect to the Programs and our business generally than has been expressly granted to you by us in this agreement.

7. Further Provisions. This agreement is subject to the following additional provisions [include any agreements on such topics as expenses, excluded contracts or other matters]:

8. Miscellaneous. This agreement will be subject to the laws of the State of _____ applicable to contracts signed and to be performed solely within such state. It sets forth the complete understanding of the parties relating to the sales representation described above. It may not be modified except by a writing signed by the party against which the change is asserted.

Please confirm that the foregoing accurately reflects our understanding on this matter by signing the enclosed copy of this letter and returning it to me.

Yours sincerely,
[Producer]

Accepted and Agreed:
[Sales Representative]

# TALENT AND SERVICE AGREEMENTS (ISSUE CHECKLIST)

1. What services are to be performed?

- Is the contract for acting, writing, directing, or some other creative service?

- Is it for producing, finance-raising, or some other business service?

- Is it for a mixture of services?

- Is the service being provided as an employee or as an independent contractor (see #2)?

- Are the services exclusive to the producer or the production?

2. How are the services to be performed?

- Are they subject to the producer's direction and control?

- Are they at locations designated by producer?

- Does the service provider retain any approvals or controls over the project as a whole, over his/her work process, or over the product?

- Are special facilities, accommodations, transport, or other amenities being provided?

3. What are the dates for the services?

- Are there dates for the delivery of certain items?

- Are the dates tied to the production process?

- Are they set to particular calendar dates?

- Can they be extended or altered?

- Will a talent provider be available for post-production services, such as dubbing or looping?

- What is the effect of *force majeure* or the disability of the service provider?

- What are the arrangements for rehearsals, wardrobe, travel, post-production publicity, and other additional services?

4. What rights are being granted?

- Rights in newly created product, like a script, direction, acting, etc.?

- Rights to use name, likeness, and biography in exploitation of the project, including advertising?
- Rights to change, alter, and edit?
- Is the product a work for hire?
- Is the grant exclusive?
- Is the grant irrevocable?

5. Are there any reserved rights?

6. What markets and media are covered?
    - All television, film, Internet, multimedia, and related rights?
    - Are there any restrictions?
    - Are merchandising and print publishing included?

7. What territories are covered?
    - The whole universe?
    - Any specific territories included or excluded?

8. Is the deal contingent or pay-or-play?
    - What are the contingencies or option aspects?
    - How long is the option?
    - Can it be extended?
    - Will *force majeure* extend the option?
    - Are there successive dependent options?
    - How is the option exercised?
    - Is it a firm, pay-or-play deal?
    - Are there any preconditions?
    - Is the pay-or-play commitment for the full amount?
    - Is there any obligation to use the services?

9. What is the compensation for the services?
    - Is there an option payment or holding fee?
    - Is there an option extension payment?

- What is the basic fee?

- Is it set to any union or guild rate?

- When is it paid?

- What is the fee for any overtime or work beyond the basic dates? (The producer should set this in advance.)

- Are additional payments, such as residuals or other agreed-upon amounts due for additional uses or subsequent productions?

- Are there any expenses to reimburse?

- Is there a profit or other back-end participation?

- What is the definition of such a participation?

- Is there most-favored-nation protection on the definition?

10. What representations and warranties should be given?

- Is any creative work either original and subject to copyright, or in the public domain?

- Does the service provider have the right to enter into the contract?

- Does the work product of the service provider contain any libelous or slanderous material?

- Does the work product violate any rights of privacy or publicity?

- Does either the work product or its intended use violate any other rights of any third parties?

11. Is either party giving an indemnity?

- Does the indemnity cover alleged breaches, or only actual breaches?

- Does the indemnity cover attorney's fees and costs?

- Who controls the defense and settlement of any claim?

12. Are the agreement and the rights granted assignable?

- If so, does the original producer remain liable?

13. Does the service provider get a credit?

- Is it in the lead or tail credits?

- Is it on a single card or is it shared?

- Is it a verbal credit?

- Is there any credit obligation in advertising and promotion?

- Are the consequences of a failure to give credit limited in the customary way?

- Are there any union or guild requirements?

14. Are there limitations on the service provider's remedies?

- Are injunctions prohibited?

- Is rescision prohibited?

15. Is there a union or guild involved?

- If so, what impact does it have?

- Have its minimums been met?

- Does the producer retain the maximum benefits available to it?

## APPENDIX 3.2:
# SHORT-FORM SERVICES AGREEMENT

This agreement, when executed by the parties identified below as the Employer and the Employee, will set forth the terms of the employment agreement between them.

1. *Employer Name, Address and Tax Identification Number:*

2. *Employee Name, Address and Social Security Number:*

3. *Duties and Services of Employee; Term:* The Employee will have the following duties and will perform the following services:

   All of the Employee's services and duties will be performed subject to the direction and control of the Employer and at such times and places as the Employer may designate. The regular term of the employment will be as follows [can be day-to-day or for a set period]:

   Employee will also perform any required services outside the regular term at mutually convenient times.

   The Employer will not be obliged to actually use any of Employee's services or work product, but the failure to use such services or work product will not in itself relieve Employer of the obligation to pay the compensation set forth herein.

4. *Compensation:* The Employer will pay the Employee the following compensation [include any bonus, overtime, benefits, or other agreed provisions]:

   The Employer will also reimburse the out-of-pocket expenses of the Employee relating to his/her employment, provided they are approved in advance by the Employer and customary documentation is presented.

5. *Warranties:* The Employee warrants that (i) she/he is free to enter into and to perform this agreement; and (ii) any material that she/he creates or adds to any project or production during the course of her/his employment will be either original or in the public domain and its use and exploitation will not violate the rights of any third party. The Employer warrants that it is free to enter into and to perform this agreement.

6. *Legal Requirements:* The Employee will abide by all applicable laws and regulations, including those under Section 507 of the Communications Act of 1934 prohibiting the undisclosed acceptance of consideration for the inclusion of material in a television program.

7. *Grant of Rights; No Equitable Relief for Employee:* The Employee grants all rights of every kind in the fruits and proceeds of his/her employment hereunder to the Employer and its licensees, successors and assigns. Any copyrightable material created by Employee hereunder will be treated as a work for hire, and the Employer will be the author thereof the Employee also grants to Employer and its licensees, successors and assigns, the right to use his/her name, likeness, voice and biography in connection with the exploitation of any project or program with which the Employee has been involved or associated through his/her services hereunder. All grants of rights hereunder are irrevocable and perpetual, and Employee waives all rights to any equitable relief in connection with any breach or termination of this agreement.

8. *Additional Provisions:* The following additional provisions shall apply [include any agreements on credits, any applicable unions and guilds, any locally-required provisions and any other further agreements; if none, write 'none']:

9. *Miscellaneous:* This agreement will be subject to the laws of the State of _____ applicable to contracts signed and to be performed solely within such state. It sets forth the full and complete agreement of the parties relating to the employment described herein. It may not be modified except by a writing signed by the party against which the change is asserted.

Dated:

EMPLOYER                  EMPLOYEE

By:                        Signature:

Title:                    Name:

## APPENDIX 3.3:
# SERVICE DESCRIPTION CLAUSES

The following clauses describe typical services required of a variety of production employees, and may be used in conjunction with the agreement in Appendix 3.2. Other service descriptions may be drafted following the same general model.

*Producer:*
Employee will provide all of the services customarily provided by the producer of a television program, including, without limitation, overseeing the business aspects such as budgets, finance and banking, the production aspects such as facilities, equipment and creative and technical staff, the rights acquisitions and the creative aspects such as scripts, director and casting. Employee recognizes that all such matters will be subject to the ultimate approval of the Employer.

*Director:*
Employee will provide all of the services customarily provided by the director of a television program, including, and without limitation, involvement in the pre-production aspects such as script development, casting, rehearsals and the selection of designers and music; directing the filming, taping or other production steps; and overseeing the editing and other post-production steps. Employee recognizes that except to the extent expressly otherwise agreed hereunder or as may be provided by applicable union agreement, all such matters will be subject to the ultimate approval of the Employer.

*Writer:*
Employee will provide the following services customarily provided by a writer in the television industry: [specify what is to be written, what editing, re-write or other general services are to be provided, and any applicable deadlines]. Employee recognizes that all such matters will be subject to the ultimate approval of the Employer.

*Actor:*
Employee will provide all of the services customarily provided by an actor in a television production, including rehearsals, makeup, wardrobe, and on-camera appearance, and at mutually convenient times and places subsequent to production, dubbing, looping, retakes and publicity support. Employee will play the role of

## APPENDIX 3.4:
# PERFORMER CONTRACT: DEAL MEMO

TO:  [Performer] and [Agent]
FROM:  [Producer]
DATE:

The following has been agreed between the parties listed above for the services of the Performer to perform as an actor in production company's television production entitled "_____".  Performer grants Producer all rights in his/her performance for exploitation throughout the universe in all media in perpetuity.

Role:

Start Date:

Compensation:

[Total]

[Pro rata per week]

Guaranteed Term:

Other matters (if not applicable, put "NA"):

Expenses:

Travel:

Lodging:

Union/Guild:

Other Arrangements:

Billing/Credit:

Location:

Estimated Schedule:

Personal Information:

Address:

Telephone:

E-mail:

SS #:

Agent Information:

    Address:

    Telephone:

    E-mail:

    SS/Taxpayer I.D. #:

Producer Information:

    Address:

    Telephone:

    E-mail:

    SS/Taxpayer I.D. #:

Signatures:

    Performer _____    Producer _____

# APPENDIX 3.5:
## PERFORMER CONTRACT: PRE-TEST OPTION AND SERIES OPTION CLAUSES

These clauses may be inserted at the appropriate place in an otherwise usual performer service agreement.

Pre-test option clause:

This letter will confirm that _____ ("Artist") has agreed to test for the role of (the "Role") in (the "Series"), a one-hour dramatic weekly series to be produced in _____ and such other locations as Producer may designate, by _____ (the "Producer"). The time and place for the test will be determined by mutual agreement. On the basis of this test, the Producer shall have the exclusive and irrevocable option to cast Artist in the Role by giving written notice to that effect to Artist's or Artists' agent on or before _____ , 20___. Should Producer exercise this option, Artist agrees to render his/her acting services to the Series, and the following terms shall govern Artist's employment in the Series.

Series option clause:

Date, Number of Options. If Producer exercises the initial option granted to it herein, Producer shall have five further consecutive, exclusive and irrevocable options, in each case exercisable no later than _____ , to obtain Artist's acting services hereunder in episodes to be produced in the immediately following production year. The base commitment to Artist for each production year for which any option is exercised is for _____ (___) episodes. In each production year, including the initial year, Producer shall have the further option, exercisable no later than [December 1] in such year, to employ Artist's services in connection with no fewer than (___) or more than (___) additional episodes for such production year, the number to be designated by Producer at time of exercise. Each production year hereunder will run from [June 15 to June 14], with the initial production year beginning June 15, 20___.

## APPENDIX 4.1:
# MUSIC (ISSUE CHECKLIST)

[See the issue checklists for Rights Acquisition (Appendix 1.1) and Talent and Service Agreements (Appendix 4.1) for general considerations applicable to music-related rights and services.]

1. What compositions and recordings are covered?

- Preexisting music?

- Prerecorded music?

- Specially commissioned music?

- Specially recorded music?

2. What rights are being granted?

- Synchronization rights?

- Small or grand performance rights?

- Master use rights in the recording?

- Rights to use name, likeness, and biography in advertising?

- Rights in a title?

- Rights to change, alter, and edit?

- Do the rights include the right to use the music in advertising and publicity?

- Are publishing rights being granted?

- Is the composition a work for hire?

- Is the grant exclusive?

- Is the grant irrevocable?

3. What media are covered?

- All television, film, Internet, multimedia, and related rights?

- Music only, such as a soundtrack album?

- Are there any specifically included or excluded media?

4. What territories are covered?

- The whole universe?

- Are there any specifically included or excluded territories?

5. Does the producer participate in the music publishing?

   - Who is the publisher?

   - What is the split—traditional 50/50 or some form of copublishing?

   - Are there any administrative, overhead, or expense deductions?

   - How are decisions on other uses and administrative matters made?

6. Are composing services being supplied?

   - What music is to be supplied?

   - What is the approval process?

   - What are the delivery dates?

   - Is parts-copying and arranging included?

7. Are recording services being supplied?

   - What music is being recorded?

   - Who handles and pays for booking the facilities and hiring the musicians?

   - Are union players being used?

   - Are real players or a synthesizer being used?

   - What kind of finished product is being delivered and in what technical format?

8. Are mixing and post-production services being supplied?

9. What payments must be made for the rights and services?

   - What is the composing fee?

   - What are the recording fee and expense payment?

   - When are they paid?

   - What uses do these prices cover?

   - Are additional payments due for additional uses in subsequent productions or a series?

   - Are there any expenses to reimburse?

10. What representations, warranties, and indemnities should be given?

11. What credit does the composer get?

12. Are there limitations on the composer's remedies?

13. Is there a union or guild involved? If so, what impact does it have?

# COMPOSER DEAL LETTER

[Producer's Letterhead]
[Date]
[Composer Name and Address]

Re: [Name of Program]

Dear _____,

This letter, when executed by you (the "Composer"), will set forth the agreement between the Composer and _____ (the "Producer") relating to the original music and recordings thereof (the "Music") for Producer's television series currently entitled _____ (the "Series") and a pilot for the Series (the "Pilot").

1. *Ownership of Copyright.* Producer and Composer will own jointly the copyright in the Music composed by Composer and all rights, title and interest therein (the "Rights") throughout the universe in perpetuity. In particular, producer will own fifty percent (50%) of the copyright in the Music and Rights and Composer will own fifty percent (50%) of the copyright in the Music and Rights.

2. *Use of Music.* Producer will use the Music in the Series unless the network or other primary licensee objects to the use thereof. Composer will provide the copy of appropriate masters of the Music to Producer. Composer will provide additional masters to Producer on a cost basis if and when required by Producer. Producer and Composer hereby irrevocably license such use.

3. *Compensation.* For all rights to use the Music in the Pilot and, if produced, the Series, Producer will pay the following compensation to Composer:

    (a) The sum of $_____ payable upon the signing of the agreement for the direct, out-of-pocket recording costs of the master tape for the Pilot.

    (b) The sum of $_____ if the Series is produced and the Music is used therein.

    (c) The sum of $_____ if the Series is produced and the Music is not used therein pursuant to Paragraph 2 hereof.

    Composer shall be solely liable for any third-party talent payments due at any time with respect to any use of the Music or the Rights hereunder.

4. *Small Performance Rights.* Customary small performance royalties will be shared as and when received through performance rights organizations. Producer, or a company designated by Producer, will act as publisher for this purpose and Producer and Composer will each take fifty percent (50%)

respectively of the Publisher's share and the Composer will receive one hundred percent (100%) of the writer's share.

5. *Credit.* Composer will receive on-screen credit in the closing titles of each program of the Series in substantially the following form:

Music By

No inadvertent or accidental failure to provide such credit shall constitute a breach.

6. *Decisions.* Administrative decisions, licensing arrangements and other business decisions relating to the Music and the Rights and not otherwise discussed herein will be resolved by the mutual consent of Composer and Producer.

7. *Representations and Warranties.* Composer hereby represents and warrants that:

(a) Composer is free to enter into this Agreement and is able to comply with the obligations and agreements hereunder. Composer has not made, and will not make, any commitment or agreement which could or might materially interfere with the full and complete performance of Composer's obligations and agreements hereunder or which could or might in any way diminish the value of Producer's full enjoyment of the rights or privileges of Producer hereunder.

(b) All material which Composer may write, prepare, compose and/or submit in connection with the Music (except any such material in the public domain) shall be wholly original with Composer, and no such material shall be copied in whole or in part from any other work or shall infringe upon or violate any right of privacy of, constitute a libel against or violate any right of any entity.

Please indicate your acceptance of these terms by signing the enclosed counterpart copy on the indicated lines below and returning it to the undersigned. While we will, in all likelihood, enter into a more detailed agreement containing additional provisions customary in the entertainment industry, unless and until such agreement is executed by us, this letter shall constitute the binding agreement between us relating to the Music in the Series and Pilot.

Yours sincerely,
[Producer]

By:
Title:
AGREED TO AND ACCEPTED:
[Composer]

# APPENDIX 4.3:
# PERFORMER RELEASE

[Producer Letterhead]

The undersigned Performer hereby releases the above specified Producer and its successors, licensees and assigns from any and all claims, actions and damages relating to or arising out of the use in any context and in any form by Producer, its successors, licensees and assigns, of the musical compositions described below and any recorded performances thereof in which Performer may have participated.

Performer irrevocably assigns to Producer any and all rights which he/she may have to such compositions and performances, and agrees that any matter subject to copyright which he/she may have created in connection therewith will be a work for hire, with Producer deemed to be the author. Producer, and its successors, licensees and assigns, may change or edit any aspect of such compositions and performances as it sees fit, and may exploit them throughout the universe in any medium now known or hereafter discovered in perpetuity.

Performer acknowledges that she/he has received good and valuable consideration for the agreements set out above, and that Producer is relying on these agreements in connection with its exploitation of the compositions and performances.

Signed:

Performer's Name, Address,
and Social Security Number:

Dated:

Compositions:

## APPENDIX 4.4:
# VIDEO SYNCHRONIZATION AND DISTRIBUTION LICENSE

[Adapted by permission from *This Business of Music*, by M. William Krasilovsky, Sidney Shemel, and John M. Gross.]

THIS AGREEMENT made and entered into this _____ day of 20___ by and between _____ ("Publisher") and _____ ("Licensee").

WHEREAS Publisher owns or controls the musical composition ("Composition") entitled _____ , written by _____; and

WHEREAS Licensee desires to utilize the Composition in that certain production entitled _____ ("Production"), and to reproduce the Production and Composition in videocassettes videodiscs and other media used in playing filmed and recorded programming (all such devices being referred to herein as "Videograms");

NOW THEREFORE the parties hereto do hereby mutually agree as follows:

1. In consideration of the royalties to be paid hereunder by Licensee to Publisher and the other covenants herein on the part of the Licensee, the Publisher hereby grants to Licensee the nonexclusive fight and license to reproduce and make copies of the Composition in Videogram copies of the Production and to distribute the Videograms to the public by sale or other transfer of ownership.

2. No right to rent Videograms is hereby granted to Licensee. If Licensee wishes to utilize Videograms via rental, Licensee shall advise Publisher in writing and the parties hereto shall negotiate in good faith the compensation or other participation to be paid to Publisher in respect of rental receipts.

   [NOTE: If there is a one-time payment for the Videogram license, then the foregoing license should be modified as follows: the first line of Paragraph 1 should be changed to read, "In consideration of the sum of $_____ to be paid by Licensee to Publisher upon execution hereof and the"; paragraphs 5, 6 and 7 are to be deleted; and paragraphs 8, 9 and 10 are to be renumbered 5, 6 and 7, respectively.

3. This license and grant is for a term of _____ years only, commencing on the date of this agreement. At the expiration or earlier termination of such period, all rights and licenses granted hereunder shall cease and terminate.

4. The rights granted hereunder are limited solely to the territory of (the "licensed territory").

5. As compensation to the Publisher, Licensor agrees to pay to the Publisher the following royalties:

a) As to each copy of a videodisc sold in the licensed territory and paid for and not returned, _____ and

b) As to each copy of a videocassette or other medium sold in the licensed territory and paid for and not returned, _____.

6. Accountings shall be rendered by Licensee to Publisher within sixty (60) days after the close of each calendar quarter, showing in detail the royalties earned, and any deductions taken in computing royalties. Publisher shall be responsible for paying royalties to writers and any third party by reason of the grant and license hereunder. No statement shall be due for a period in which Videograms are not sold. All royalty statements shall be binding upon Publisher and is subject to any objection by publisher for any reason unless specific objection in writing, stating the basis thereof, is given to Licensee within one (1) year from the date rendered.

7. Publisher shall have the right to inspect and make abstracts of the books and records of Licensee, insofar as said books and records pertain to the performance of Licensee's obligations hereunder; such inspection to be made on at least ten (10) days written notice, during normal business hours of normal business days but not more frequently than once annually in each year.

8. The rights and license granted hereunder may not be assigned or transferred, either affirmatively or by operation of law, without Publisher's written consent.

9. Publisher warrants and represents that it has full right, power and authority to enter into and to perform this agreement.

10. This agreement shall be deemed made in and shall be construed in accordance with the laws of the State of _____. The agreement may not be modified orally and shall not be binding or effective unless and until it is signed by both parties hereto.

IN WITNESS WHEREOF the parties have entered into this agreement the day and year first above written.

Publisher By:     Licensee By:

# TELEVISION FILM SYNCHRONIZATION LICENSE

[Adapted by permission from *This Business of Music*, by M. William Krasilovsky, Sidney Shemel, and John M. Gross.]

To:
From:
TV Lic. #
Date:
Composition:

1. In consideration of the sum of $_____ payable upon the execution hereof, we grant you the nonexclusive right to record on film or videotape the above identified musical composition(s) in synchronization or timed relation with a single episode or individual program entitled for television use only, subject to all of the terms and conditions herein provided.

2. (a) The type of use is to be:

   (b) On or before the first telecast of the said film, you or your assigns agree to furnish to us a copy of the Cue Sheet prepared and distributed in connection therewith.

3. The territory covered by this license is the world.

4. (a) This license is for a period of _____ from the date hereof.

   (b) Upon the expiration of this license all rights herein granted shall cease and terminate and the right to make or authorize any further use or distribution of any recordings made hereunder shall also cease and terminate.

5. This is a license to record only and does not authorize any use of the aforesaid musical composition(s) not expressly set forth herein. By way of illustration but not limitation, this license does not include the right to change or adapt the words or to alter the fundamental character of the music of said musical composition(s) or to use the title(s) thereof as the title or sub-title of said film.

6. Performance of the said musical composition(s) in the exhibition of said film is subject to the condition that each television station over which the aforesaid musical composition(s) is (are) to be so performed shall have a performance license issued by us or from a person, firm, corporation, society, association or other entity having the legal right to issue such performance license.

7. No sound records produced pursuant to this license are to be manufactured, sold and/or used separately or independently of said film.

8. The film shall be for television use only, including cable, satellite, Internet and home devices, and may not be televised into theaters or other places where admission is charged.

9. All rights not herein specifically granted are reserved by us.

10. We warrant only that we have the legal right to grant this license and this license is given and accepted without other warranty or recourse. If said warranty shall be breached in whole or in part with respect to (any of) said musical composition(s), our total liability shall be limited either to repaying to you the consideration theretofore paid under this license, with respect to such musical composition to the extent of such breach or to holding you harmless to the extent of the consideration theretofore paid under this license with respect to such musical composition to the extent of said breach.

11. This license shall run to you, your successors and assigns, provided you shall remain liable for the performance of all of the terms and conditions of this license on your part to be performed and provided further that any disposition of said film or any prints thereof shall be subject to all the terms hereof, and you agree that all persons, firms or corporations acquiring from you any right, title, interest in or possession of said film or any prints thereof shall be notified of the terms and conditions of this license and shall agree to be bound thereby.

(Licensor)
By

# PERFORMANCE LICENSE

1. BASIC INFORMATION.
   Program:
   Producer:
   Composition:
   Type of Use:
   Duration of Use:
   Composer: Lyricist:
   Publisher:
   Medium of Use:
   Territory of Use:
   Dates of Use:
   Number of Repeats:
   Consideration:
   License Grantor:

2. GRANT OF LICENSE.
   All capitalized terms used in this license refer to those items specified in the Basic Information set forth above. Provided that the Consideration is paid in full upon signing hereof, the undersigned License Grantor hereby grants Producer, and its licensees and assigns, the right to perform the Composition publicly through television in connection with the exhibition of the Program through the Medium of Use and throughout the Territory of Use. This license shall only cover the Type of Use and Duration of Use specified above, and shall only apply during the Dates of Use and only for the specified Number of Repeats. Producer represents and warrants that it has received a valid synchronization licensee for this use.

   The License Grantor represents and warrants that the License Grantor has the power to grant this performance license, and that the performance of the Composition in accordance with this license will not violate the fights of any third party. This license is subject to the receipt by the License Grantor from the Producer, on or about the first performance authorized hereunder, of a copy of the complete musical cue sheet for the Program.

3. SIGNATURES AND DATE.
   License Grantor:
   Signature:
   Name and Title:
   Date:
   Producer:
   Signature:
   Name and Title:
   Date:

## APPENDIX 4.7:
# SAMPLE MOTION PICTURE OR TELEVISION FILM CUE SHEET

[Adapted by permission from *This Business of Music*, by M. William Krasilovsky, Sidney Shemel, and John M. Gross.]

[Production Company Name]
[Program Title]
[Date]

| No. | Selection | Composer | Publisher | Extent | How Used | Time |
|-----|-----------|----------|-----------|--------|----------|------|
| **REELS 1 & 2** | | | | | | |
| 1. | Medley consisting of: | | | | | |
| | (a) Signature | Jane Doe | XYZ | Entire | Bkg. Inst. | 0.07 |
| | (b) Juniper | Jane Doe | XYZ | Entire | Vis. Voc. | 5.37 |
| 2. | Cowboys | Mike Roe | ABC | Partial | Bkg. Inst. | 0.34 |
| 3. | Medley consisting of: | | | | | |
| | (a) Juniper | Jane Doe | XYZ | Partial | Bkg. Inst. | 0.09 |
| | (b) Cowboys | Mike Roe | ABC | Entire | Bkg. Inst. | 0.45 |
| | (c) Juniper | Jane Doe | FGH | Partial | Bkg. Inst. | 0.38 |
| | (d) The Boys | Irv Grow | XYZ | Partial | Bkg. Inst. | 0.47 |
| 4 | The Girls | May Joe | ABC | Entire | Byg. Inst. | 0.05 |
| 5. | The Birds | May Joe | ABC | Entire | Vis. Voc. | 2.45 |
| **REELS 3 & 4** | | | | | | |
| 6. | Kermits | May Loe | ABC | Entire | Vis. Voc. | 2.09 |
| 7. | Kermits | May Loe | XYZ | Partial | Bkg. Inst. | 0.23 |
| 8. | Medley consisting of: | | | | | |
| | (a) Juniper | Jane Doe | XYZ | Partial | Bkg. Inst. | 1.40 |
| | (b) Cleo | Bob Smith | ABC | Entire | Vis. Voc. | 1.50 |
| | (c) Kermac | May Loe | ABC | Entire | Bkg. Inst. | 1.30 |
| 9. | Kermac | May Loe | ABC | Entire | Vis. Voc. | 1.25 |
| 10. | Medley consisting of: | | | | | |
| | (a) Juniper | Jane Doe | ABC | Partial | Bkg. Inst. | 0.24 |
| | (b) Cowboys | Mike Roe | ABC | Partial | Bkg. Inst. | 0.24 |
| | (c) Juniper | Jane Doe | XYZ | Partial | Bkg. Inst. | 0.12 |
| | (d) Cowboys | Mike Roe | ABC | Partial | Bkg. Inst. | 0.14 |
| | (e) Juniper | Jane Doe | XYZ | Partial | Bkg. Inst. | 0.30 |
| | (f) Cowboys | Mike Roe | ABC | Entire | Bkg. Inst. | 0.45 |

## APPENDIX 5.1:
## DESIGN/LOCATION (ISSUE CHECKLIST)

[Note: See the checklists for Rights Acquisition (Appendix 1.1) and Talent and Service Agreements (Appendix 4.1) for general considerations applicable to design and location agreements.]

1. How are the design services being handled?

- What is to be designed?

- What is the approval process?

- Who arranges for and oversees construction and fabrication?

- What are the delivery dates?

- What are the ongoing responsibilities of the designer?

- What is the initial compensation to the designer?

- What is the ongoing compensation to the designer?

- Are there residuals or reuse fees?

- Who owns the designs?

- Is there an applicable union or guild?

2. How is the location being arranged?

- Is a location manager or outside location service being used?

- Are you dealing with an owner or leaseholder who has the power to grant both the right of access and any necessary media rights?

- What are the times of access?

- Who is responsible for damages?

- Who is responsible for carrying insurance; what types and how much?

- Are changes and construction permitted?

- What maintenance staff is required, and who pays for it?

- What compensation is payable for the location use and any media rights?

# APPENDIX 5.2:
## LOCATION RELEASE

Owner/Tenant:
Producer:
Premises:
Program:

The undersigned Owner/Tenant hereby agrees to permit the Producer to use the Premises, both exterior and interior, for the purpose of filming, photographing and/or otherwise recording scenes for the Program. Producer and its licensees and assigns shall have the right to use the film, photographs and/or other recording made on and showing the Premises in any manner throughout the world in perpetuity without any limitations or restrictions.

Producer will have the right to film, photograph and/or otherwise record in and around the Premises for _____ days, commencing _____ (subject to change due to adverse weather conditions).

Producer will leave the Premises in the same condition as existed prior to its use, normal ware and tear excepted, and Producer will indemnify and hold the Owner/Tenant harmless from all claims for damages occurring during its use of the Premises, which arose out of its activities.

Owner/Tenant acknowledges that it has received good and valuable consideration for this grant and warrants that it has the authority to grant the rights granted herein with respect to the Premises.

PRODUCER
By:
Title:

OWNER/TENANT
By:
Title:

## APPENDIX 6.1:
## PRODUCTION FACILITIES AND EQUIPMENT (ISSUE CHECKLIST)

1. What production facilities will be used?

   - Which studio?

   - Which location(s)?

   - Which mobile unit (truck)?

   - Does the facility offer sufficient technical and staging resources for the production?

   - Can rentals fill in the gaps?

2. Does the facility provide adequate nontechnical support?

   - Are dressing rooms, makeup and hair, and wardrobe provided, or must facilities be rented?

   - Is an audience holding area needed? Is it available on the premises, or must other rental arrangements be made?

   - Is office space available for the production staff, or must it be rented? What is the cost of renting it from the facility? Is this a fair price?

   - Is parking available, or must arrangements be made?

   - Are dining facilities available nearby, or must catering be arranged?

3. On what basis will the facilities be rented?

   - Hourly?

   - Daily?

   - Weekly?

   - Monthly?

   - On a bulk rate, based on multiple uses?

4. What equipment and other facilities will be included in the studio or soundstage rental package?

   - Will lighting equipment be provided? How many instruments? What types? What are the capabilities of the lighting board?

   - Does the facility have adequate power and air conditioning to service the production?

- How many cameras will be provided? How many handhelds? How many pedestal cameras? How many with special mounts (such as cranes)?

- Will audio be handled by the house, or by an outside contractor?

- How many microphones will be provided? What types? Any special mountings? Are there any special charges or special technical issues related to the use of RF wireless microphones? What are the limitations of the house PA system?

- What type of equipment will be used to record and to mix the program?

- What audio playback facilities come with the package?

- How many videotape machines will be provided? What are the formats? What is the cost of additional machines?

- What is the make and model of the video switcher? Does it offer the flexibility needed for the production?

- What type of computer graphics devices (including character generator, DVE, still-store) are available?

- What are the capabilities and limitations of the communications system? Cell phone reception? WiFi connection?

- Is the facility available after hours for the scenic crew?

- What is the overall quality of the technical facility? Is the equipment relatively new and properly maintained? Does the facility offer the flexibility needed for the production?

5. Technical Crew:

- Who will hire the crew?

- Will the crew work under union rules? Which union?

- What are the hourly or daily rates for each individual crew member? What are the overtime charges?

- Are there any special work rules for crew members, such as guaranteed meal breaks or rest periods? Are there penalties associated with breaking these rules?

- Who will the key crew members be? Can the director approve these crew members? Can the director replace them?

6. Stage Crew:

- Who will hire the stagehands?

- Do they belong to a union?

- What are the rates and work rules?

- How many people will be needed to set up, run, and strike the production?

7. Financial Arrangements:

- Is a payment required to reserve the facility? Is it refundable? Under what circumstances?

- On what basis will the facility be billed?

- How often will the studio bill (for a series)?

- Will outside rentals and freelance personnel be billed through the facility (at a markup), or hired directly by the producer?

- Does the facility carry adequate insurance?

- What is the cost of using the facility's phones, copier, Internet access, and fax machine? For a big project, can the production install its own phone system?

- If the program is a pilot, is there any further responsibility to the facility regarding the series?

# APPENDIX 6.2:
# LAB LETTER

[Date]
[Name and Address of Laboratory]

Gentlemen:

The undersigned, ("Producer") has entered into an agreement (the "Agreement") with _____ ("Distributor") under which Agreement Distributor has been granted certain distribution rights in and to the television programs entitled _____ (the "Programs").

For good and valuable consideration, receipt of which is hereby acknowledged, it is hereby agreed, for the express benefit of Distributor, as follows:

1. You now have in your possession in the name of Producer the materials ("Materials") listed in Exhibit A attached hereto for said Programs; you certify that all materials are ready and suitable for the making of commercially acceptable release copies and duplicating material, including visual elements and soundtracks.

2. You will retain possession of all Materials at your laboratory located at _____ and you will not deliver any of said Materials to anyone without the written consent of Producer and Distributor.

3. Distributor and its designees shall at all times have access to said Materials.

4. You will at all times perform all laboratory services requested by Distributor or its designers relating to the Programs, which laboratory services will be performed by you at prevailing rates at Distributor's sole expense.

5. Neither Distributor nor Producer shall have any liability for any indebtedness to you incurred by the other.

6. You presently have no claim or lien against the Programs or the Materials, nor, insofar as Distributor is concerned, will you assert any claim or lien against the Programs or the Materials except for your charges for services rendered for and materials furnished to Distributor.

7. This Agreement is irrevocable and may not be altered or modified except by a written instrument executed by Distributor and Producer.

Please signify your agreement to the foregoing by signing where indicated below.

Very truly yours,
[Producer]

By:
AGREED TO:
[Name of Laboratory]

By:
CONSENTED TO:
[Distributor]

By:
EXHIBIT A

[For Videotape Productions]

(a) the fully edited, titled and assembled electronic master of each Program on SMPTE 1-inch Type C format videotape with fully synchronized sound;

(b) all videotape footage shot or created in connection with each Program including all title and credit sequences;

(c) all separate dialog tracks, sound effects tracks and music tracks recorded on magnetic media; and

(d) any scripts, notes and logs relating to the editing of the Programs.

# APPENDIX 7.1:
# BUSINESS ENTITIES AND TAX (ISSUE CHECKLIST)

1. What kind of business entity is appropriate?
    - Is the economy and simplicity of a sole proprietorship important?

    - Will there be more than one owner, requiring a partnership or a limited liability company or corporation?

    - Is the flexibility of a partnership or a limited liability company important?

    - If the business is for a limited purpose, would a joint venture partnership or a specific-purpose limited liability company be appropriate?

    - Is the limited liability of a corporation, a limited liability partnership, or a limited liability company important?

    - Would a limited partnership, if available, provide enough limited liability?

    - Are the tax benefits of a partnership or a limited liability company important?

    - Would a Subchapter S corporation provide enough tax benefits?

    - Is Subchapter S treatment available?

    - Is the corporate form or a limited liability company too expensive to set up and maintain?

2. What is the most advantageous state in which to establish the business?

    - The state where the headquarters of the business will be located?

    - Some other state where there will be a significant business presence?

    - A state with flexible and attractive corporate, limited liability company, or partnership laws and taxes, such as Delaware or Nevada?

3. If a sole proprietorship, partnership, or joint venture, have the usual filings been made?

    - The "doing business as" or "fictitious name" certificate?

    - The federal taxpayer identification number?

    - The employment-related filings at the state and federal level?

    - If a limited partnership, has the limited partnership certificate been filed and has any publishing requirement been met?

4. If a corporation, have the usual filings been made?

- The certificate or articles of incorporation?

- The federal tax identification number?

- The employment-related filings at the state and federal level?

- The federal and any state Subchapter S filing, if applicable?

5. If a limited liability company, have the usual filings been made?

- The certificate or articles of organization?

- The election of federal tax treatment as a partnership or corporation?

- The federal tax identification number?

- The employment-related filings at the state and federal level?

6. Have matters of governance and management been decided?

- Who are the officers, managers, or managing partners?

- Who are the directors?

- How are officers, directors, managers, and managing partners elected?

- How are day-to-day and major decisions made?

- Who has banking authority?

- Who decides to admit new partners or new members or sell more stock?

- Who approves mergers, sales of the business, major loans, and other significant business events?

- Who designates the lawyers, accountants, and other major service providers?

7. Have matters of finance been determined?

- Who is contributing to capital?

- In cash?

- In services, if permitted?

- In kind—equipment, rights etc.?

- Who is loaning money or other property?

- What is the return on these investments?

- Is there a priority return through contract recoupment, debt, or preferred stock?

- Has a budget estimate showing working capital needs been prepared?

8. How have management and financial matters been established?

- By default, as a matter of applicable law?

- If a joint venture, partnership, or limited liability company, in a written agreement?

- If a corporation, in the certificate of incorporation, in the by-laws, or in a shareholders agreement?

- Through a loan agreement and notes?

9. Have a lawyer and an accountant been consulted?

# INDEX